The Best Beaches

Good beaches with soul-warming sun, crystal-clear waters, and fragrant sea air can be found on virtually every island of the Caribbean:

- **Palm Beach (Aruba):** This superb strip of white sand is what put Aruba on the tourist map in the first place. Several publications have hailed it as one of the 12 best beaches in the world. It's likely to be crowded in winter, but for swimming, sailing, or fishing, it's idyllic. See Chapter 11.

- **The Gold Coast (Barbados):** Some of the finest beaches in the Caribbean lie along the so-called Gold Coast of Barbados, site of some of the swankiest deluxe hotels in the northern hemisphere. See Chapter 15.

- **Cane Garden Bay (Tortola, British Virgin Islands):** One of the Caribbean's most spectacular stretches of beach, Cane Garden Bay has 1½ miles of white sand and is a jogger's favorite. See Chapter 19.

- **Seven Mile Beach (Grand Cayman, Cayman Islands):** It's really about 5½ miles long, but who's counting? Lined with condos and plush resorts, this beach is known for its array of water sports and its translucent aquamarine waters. Australian pines dot the background, and the average winter temperature of the water is a perfect 80 degrees. See Chapter 23.

- **Luquillo Beach (Puerto Rico):** This crescent-shaped public beach, 30 miles east of San Juan, is the local favorite. Much photographed because of its white sands and coconut palms, it also has tent sites and picnic facilities. The often-fierce waters of the Atlantic are subdued by the coral reefs protecting the crystal-clear lagoon. See Chapter 31.

- **Trunk Bay (St. John, U.S. Virgin Islands):** Protected by the U.S. National Park Service, this beach is one of the Caribbean's most popular. A favorite with cruise-ship passengers, it's known for its underwater snorkeling trail, where markers guide you along the reef just off the white sands; you're sure to see a gorgeous rainbow of tropical fish. See Chapter 35.

For Dummies: Bestselling Book Series for Beginners

The Best Family Vacations

In addition to the choices listed here, be sure to see the Kid Friendly icon throughout this book, which indicates the best place to take your children.

- ✔ **Hyatt Regency Aruba** (Aruba; ☎ 800-233-1234 or 297-86-1234): Designed like a luxurious hacienda, with award-winning gardens, this resort is the most upscale on Aruba. Supervised activities for children ages 3 to 12 include games and contests such as crab races and hula-hoop competitions. See Chapter 9.

- ✔ **Hyatt Regency Grand Cayman Resort and Villas** (Grand Cayman Island; ☎ 800-55-HYATT or 345-949-1234): Safe and serene, Grand Cayman Island, with its 7-mile sandy beach, seems designed for families with children. No one coddles children as much as the Hyatt people, who offer not only baby-sitting but also Camp Hyatt, with an activity-filled agenda, for children ages 3 to 12. See Chapter 20.

- ✔ **Negril Cabins Resort** (Negril, Jamaica; ☎ 800-382-3444 or 876-957-5350): Rising on stilts, these wooden cottages with private decks add a sense of adventure to a beach vacation. Surrounded by tropical vegetation, families are only steps from the beach. Features for kids include a playground, computer games, arts-and-crafts lessons, and even storytelling sessions. Children under age 12 stay free if they share a room with their parents. See Chapter 24.

- ✔ **Hyatt Regency Cerromar Beach** (Puerto Rico; ☎ 800-233-1234 or 787-796-1234): This is the best place for kids in all of Puerto Rico. The big attraction is a water playground that contains the world's longest freshwater swimming pool: It's a 1,776-foot fantasy pool with 5 different depths, 5 interconnected free-form pools, and 14 waterfalls with tropical landscaping. As if that weren't enough, Hyatt also offers Camp Hyatt, a day camp for kids ages 3 to 12. See Chapter 28.

- ✔ **Wyndham El Conquistador** (Puerto Rico; ☎ 800-WYNDHAM or 787-863-1000): Children aren't forgotten amid the glamour and hoopla of this fabulous resort. Camp Coquí provides day care daily from 9 a.m. to 3 p.m. for children ages 3 to 12, at a price of $40 per child per day. Activities include fishing, sailing, arts and crafts, and nature treks. Baby-sitting services are available, and children ages 15 and under stay free in a room with their parents. See Chapter 28.

- ✔ **The Buccaneer** (St. Croix, U.S. Virgin Islands; ☎ 800-255-3881 or 340-773-2100): Posh, upscale, and offering extremely good service, this hotel is a longtime favorite that occupies a 240-acre former sugar estate. Its kids' programs (for ages 2 to 12) include a half-day sailing excursion to Buck Island Reef and guided nature walks that let kids touch, smell, and taste tropical fruit. See Chapter 32.

For Dummies: Bestselling Book Series for Beginners

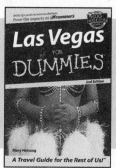

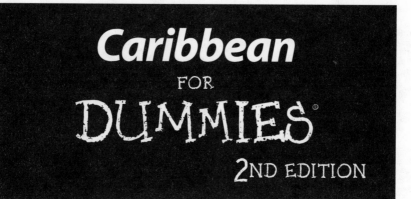

Caribbean
FOR
DUMMIES®
2ND EDITION

**by Darwin Porter & Danforth Prince
and Echo & Kevin Garrett**

Wiley Publishing, Inc.

Caribbean For Dummies®, 2nd Edition

Published by
Wiley Publishing, Inc.
909 Third Avenue
New York, NY 10022
www.wiley.com

About the Authors

Darwin Porter and Danforth Prince: A native of North Carolina, Darwin Porter was a bureau chief for the *Miami Herald* when he was 21, and later worked in television advertising. A veteran travel writer, he is the author of numerous best-selling Frommer's guides, including those to the Bahamas and Bermuda. He is assisted by Danforth Prince, formerly of the Paris Bureau of the *New York Times*. They have been frequent travelers to the Caribbean for years and are intimately familiar with what's good there and what isn't. They have also written *Frommer's Caribbean from $70 a Day*, the most candid and up-to-date guide to budget vacations on the market.

Echo and Kevin Garrett: Kevin's articles have appeared in *Affordable Caribbean, Atlanta Homes and Lifestyles, The Atlanta Journal-Constitution, BizTravel.com, Bridal Guide, Chicago Magazine, Coastal Living, Elegant Bride, Executive Getaways, Fantastic Flyer, Great Outdoor Recreational Pages, Investor's Business Daily, Islands, Modern Bride, Second Home,* and *The Self-Employed Professional.* He and Echo updated/wrote chapters on Aruba, Bonaire and Curaçao for *Rum & Reggae's Caribbean 2000.* An international award-winning photographer and member of the American Society of Media Photographers, Kevin's images (www.kevingarrett.com) have run in several of the preceding publications as well as *Voyages: The Romance of Cruising, Hemispheres, Los Angeles, Management Review, Sky, Smart Money, Southern Accents, Travel Holiday, Travel & Leisure, Weight Watchers,* and *World Trade.*

Echo worked as an editor at *McCall's,* then *Venture,* before going freelance in 1988, racking up credits in more than 50 national publications from *The New York Times* to *Money,* where she became a contributing writer covering travel. She was a founding editor for an award-winning Web site *BizTravel.com,* responsible for *Executive Getaways;* a contributing writer for "News For You," the best-read, front-page column in *Investor's Business Daily;* and a contributing writer covering hospitality and restaurants for *The Atlanta Business Chronicle.*

Publisher's Acknowledgments

We're proud of this book; please send us your comments through our Online Registration Form located at www.dummies.com.

Some of the people who helped bring this book to market include the following:

Editorial

Editors: Elizabeth Kuball and Amy Lyons

Cartographer: John Decamillis

Editorial Supervisor: Michelle Hacker

Editorial Assistant: Carol Strickland

Senior Photo Editor: Richard Fox

Cover Photos: Glenn McLaughlin/Corbis-Stock Market; Back: Mark Lewis/Getty Images

Production

Project Coordinator: Jennifer Bingham

Layout and Graphics: Sean Decker, Carrie Foster, Joyce Haughey, Barry Offringa, and Heather Pope

Proofreaders: David Faust, John Greenough, Charles Spencer, and TECHBOOKS Production Services

Indexer: TECHBOOKS Production Services

Publishing and Editorial for Consumer Dummies

Diane Graves Steele, Vice President and Publisher, Consumer Dummies

Joyce Pepple, Acquisitions Director, Consumer Dummies

Kristin A. Cocks, Product Development Director, Consumer Dummies

Michael Spring, Vice President and Publisher, Travel

Brice Gosnell, Publishing Director, Travel

Suzanne Jannetta, Editorial Director, Travel

Publishing for Technology Dummies

Andy Cummings, Vice President and Publisher, Dummies Technology/General User

Composition Services

Gerry Fahey, Vice President of Production Services

Debbie Stailey, Director of Composition Services

Contents at a Glance

Maps at a Glance

Table of Contents

Introduction

*W*e know that you've been looking for *Caribbean For Dummies,* 2nd Edition. About two minutes after we introduce ourselves to new acquaintances and tell them that we specialize in writing about the Caribbean, we inevitably get the question: Where should I go on my anniversary/honeymoon/birthday/vacation?

Of course, the shelves are groaning with guidebooks on the Caribbean, but this one is different. In *Caribbean For Dummies,* 2nd Edition, we guide you through choosing the right island for you and yours and take you on a romp that hits the high points of each. We don't try to give you an exhaustive guide to the Caribbean. Lots of other books do that (and often leave you more confused than when you started).

Indeed, we've left out a whole bunch of islands, sticking to those that are the most popular with tourists. And on the islands we do cover, we keep information pared to the basics: what you'll encounter when you land, where to stay, where to eat, and where to go to have fun while you're there.

How to Use This Book

You can use this book in three ways:

- ✔ **As a trip planner.** If you're trying to decide between two or more islands, we steer you in the right direction. Then you can skip straight to the chapters on your particular destination to plan every aspect of your trip, from packing the right stuff to getting the best deal on your resort.

- ✔ **As an island guide.** Bring this book with you to your island destination because we let you know what to expect and tell you our favorite places to go — from the best beaches to the coolest bars to the most romantic restaurants.

- ✔ **As a fun overview.** If you want to get a good feel for the Caribbean as a whole, read this book straight through, because we hit all the high points.

Please be advised that travel information is subject to change at any time — and this is especially true of prices. Therefore, we suggest that you call, fax, or e-mail ahead for confirmation when making your travel plans to the islands. The mail service to the Caribbean is extremely unreliable, so don't try that form of communication. Make sure you get a confirmation faxed or e-mailed back to you, and bring a copy with you on your trip.

The authors, editors, and publisher cannot be held responsible for the experiences of readers while traveling. Your safety is important to us, however, so we encourage you to stay alert and be aware of your surroundings. Keep a close eye on cameras, purses, and wallets — all favorite targets of thieves and pickpockets.

Conventions Used in This Book

In this book, we've listed our favorite hotels and restaurants, as well as information about special attractions on each island. As we describe each, we often include abbreviations for commonly accepted credit cards. The following list explains each abbreviation:

AE: American Express

DC: Diners Club

DISC: Discover

MC: MasterCard

V: Visa

We also include some general pricing information to help you decide where to unpack your bags or dine on the local cuisine. We've used a system of dollar signs to show a range of costs for one night in a hotel or a meal at a restaurant. Unless we say otherwise, the lodging rates are for a standard double room during high season. (Chapter 3 explains what high season is.) For restaurants, we give the price range for main courses. Check out the following table to decipher the dollar signs.

Cost	Hotel	Restaurant
$	Less than $100 per night	Less than $10
$$	$100–$150	$11–$15
$$$	$150–$225	$15–$20
$$$$	$225–$300 or so	$21–$25
$$$$$	More than $300 per night	$26 and up

Foolish Assumptions

As we wrote this book, we made some assumptions about you and what your needs may be as a traveler. Here's what we assumed:

- ✔ You may be an inexperienced traveler looking for guidance about whether to take a trip to the Caribbean and how to plan a trip to specific islands.

- ✔ You may be an experienced traveler, but you don't have a lot of time to devote to trip planning or you don't have a lot of time to spend in the Caribbean after you get there. You want expert advice on how to maximize your time and enjoy a hassle-free trip.

- ✔ You're not looking for a book that provides every bit of information available about the Caribbean or that lists every hotel, restaurant, or attraction you could experience. Instead, you're looking for a book that focuses on the places that will give you the best or most unique experience in the Caribbean.

If you fit any of these criteria, then *Caribbean For Dummies,* 2nd Edition, gives you the information you're looking for.

How This Book Is Organized

Caribbean For Dummies is divided into ten parts. The chapters within each part cover specific topic areas in detail. Feel free to skip around; you don't have to read this book in order. It's kind of like a cafeteria: You can pick and choose what you like.

Part 1: Getting Started on Your Caribbean Getaway

In this part, we tell you which islands you'll find in the Caribbean and give you comparisons and contrasts between the popular islands we cover in the book. Each Caribbean island is extremely different from the others, so you need to carefully consider which one sounds like the best fit for you. We also explain in detail the various "seasons" that are used to describe more– and less-popular times of year for people to travel to the Caribbean. We discuss what kind of prices and weather you can expect during each season. We talk about the dreaded H-word *(hurricane)* and discuss how much you should take hurricanes into consideration in your planning — if at all. We thoroughly explain the different accommodations you'll find in the Caribbean along with all the different meal plans and what *all-inclusive* means. Finally, we give resources and tips for families, seniors, travelers with disabilities, and gay and lesbian travelers planning a Caribbean trip.

Part II: Tying Up the Loose Ends

Here we wrap up all the critical information you need in order to decide whether to use a travel agent, a packager, or the Internet when planning your trip. We give you details about which airlines will get you where and what connections you can make to get to some of the more remote areas. You'll also find a chapter that helps you create a trip budget and answers all your questions about money in the Caribbean, from the currency used on each island to what size tips you should give. We wrap up this part by addressing safety concerns, discussing whether you should rent a car, explaining travel insurance, and covering other odds and ends.

Parts III–IX: The Islands

Now we get down to the fun stuff. For each island or island group — Aruba, Barbados, the British Virgin Islands, Grand Cayman, Jamaica, Puerto Rico, and the U.S. Virgin Islands — we give you the scoop on the hotel scene, what you can expect when you actually land on the island (from the airport to taxi drivers), what restaurants you should consider, and, finally, where to go and what to do to squeeze the most fun possible out of your Caribbean vacation.

Part X: The Part of Tens

Every *For Dummies* book has a Part of Tens. Here we tell you what we consider the best Caribbean souvenirs and where to get them, and we ruminate over the best local meals we've enjoyed in our island travels.

At the back of the book, we've also included a bunch of worksheets to make your travel planning easier. Among other things, you can determine your vacation budget, create specific itineraries, and keep a log of your favorite restaurants so you can hit them again next time you're in the islands. You can find these worksheets easily because they're printed on yellow paper.

Icons Used in This Book

Throughout this book, you'll find icons in the margins, which draw your attention to particular bits of information you may find especially helpful. Here's an explanation of what each icon means:

Attention, bargain hunters: If you're looking to save money, check out our bargain icons, sprinkled throughout the text.

This icon indicates that a specific place or activity has a special dash of local charm.

Watch for this icon to identify annoying or potentially dangerous situations, such as tourist traps, unsafe neighborhoods, rip-offs, and other things to avoid.

We sparingly give resorts, restaurants, and attractions the Kid Friendly icon, which indicates a place or event that children will enjoy.

This icon signals the most romantic restaurants, hotels, and attractions in the Caribbean.

The Tip icon alerts you to useful advice on how to plan and implement your trip in order to make the best use of your time and money.

Where to Go from Here

Whether you've been to the Caribbean a dozen times or have never set foot outside your hometown, we know that you'll find what you're looking for in *Caribbean For Dummies,* 2nd Edition. So sit back, relax, and enjoy your trip planning. After all, the planning part lasts a lot longer than the trip itself — why not make it part of the fun?

Part I
Getting Started on Your Caribbean Getaway

The 5th Wave   By Rich Tennant

THE ISLAND EXPERIENCE

Your glass of water...

In this part . . .

*P*lanning a trip to a place that you know only as a dot on the map? You need to get a sense of where you're going before you commit to the destination. In Part I, we help you point your compass in the right direction.

First, the basics: What is each island like, and which one will mesh with your island fantasy? Next come the details — like when you want to go and what kind of hotel is likely to fit your preferences. Finally, we offer valuable traveling tips, so your trip can fulfill your requirements as well as your dreams.

Chapter 1

Discovering the Caribbean

By Echo and Kevin Garrett

• •

In This Chapter

▶ Checking out favorite Caribbean destinations

▶ Examining the pros and cons of visiting more than one island

▶ Picking the right island for you — the fun way

• •

*W*e certainly needed a book like this before we embarked on our first Caribbean trip, which was on our honeymoon in 1982 — a gift from Dad. At our wedding reception, just before the stroke of midnight, Dad's secretary handed us three pages of single-spaced, typewritten notes listing the items that we'd need for our trip. Our vague fantasy of the Caribbean featured a sandy beach dotted with palms and high-rise hotels equipped with discos, glitzy casinos, and piña coladas. Like most people, we just sort of lumped all islands south of Florida into this formless mass and called it the Caribbean.

After scanning the list, which advised us to bring toilet paper, peanut butter, and insect repellent, we quickly figured out that where we were going and what we'd been expecting were completely different animals. We'd packed for our Caribbean fantasy, but our surprise destination was Green Turtle Cay, a tiny island in the Bahamas with one car and a population of 400 who rarely saw tourists.

We wound up having a wonderful time, but our travel experience could have been even better if we had been prepared. The lesson? If you choose the Caribbean for your vacation, you still have decisions to make. After all, we're talking about a whole different world. So slow down, get in the island groove, and smile. The Caribbean has stolen our hearts. We bet its magic will charm yours, too.

In this book, we give you an insider's view of some of our favorite islands. In this chapter, we hit the highlights on a whirlwind tour, leaving the wonderful history and culture of this fascinating part of the world for you to discover on your own . . . or not.

Finding the Island (s) That Are Right for You

If you're not sure which island you want to visit, you're in good company. Even the Caribbean's first tourist was overwhelmed by the choices. "I saw so many islands that I could hardly decide which to visit first," Christopher Columbus wrote to Spain's Queen Isabella. We know just how he felt.

Knowing that we've specialized in the Caribbean for the past decade, our friends are always asking us where they should go. That's a little like being asked which of your children you like best — each one has something special to offer.

That sweep of aquamarine blue-on-blue sea called the Caribbean stretches nearly 2,000 miles from Cuba to South America and encompasses more than 30 different nations and a mind-boggling 7,000 islands — give or take a few. Technically, the Bahamas and the Turks and Caicos islands aren't even in the Caribbean. As for the islanders themselves, they, too, are a diverse group, representing 100 different cultures. On most Caribbean islands, the majority of the population are descendants of African slaves.

Which island is right for you depends on what you enjoy and what kind of vacation you want. For example, our best friends love shopping, glittering nightlife, the beach, and golf, so we'd send them to Aruba, Puerto Rico, Jamaica, or St. Thomas.

Suffice it to say that we've never been bored anywhere we've traveled in the Caribbean. Whether you're the independent type who likes adventure and discovery, or you prefer to be pampered and veg out on the beach, there's a Caribbean island to suit you.

In this section, we list the Caribbean's top destinations, with the low-down on the ins and outs of each. A quiz at the end of this chapter pulls all this information together, helping you set your sights on the island that's right for you.

Introducing Aruba

Sugar-white beaches. Splashy casinos. A stark, other-worldly, cactus-dotted landscape known as the *cunucu,* where *divi-divi* (watapana) trees have been bowed to a 45-degree angle by the constantly blowing trade winds. Think Arizona with a beach, and you've got Aruba, an independent country within the Kingdom of the Netherlands.

Located a scant 15 miles north of Venezuela, this Dutch treat has a diverse heritage. In fact, the lyrical local language, Papiamento, is laced with Spanish, Dutch, and Portuguese, as well as African, French, and Arawak Indian dialects.

Aruba is surprisingly small — popular with the package-tour crowd and cruise ships, as well as honeymooners and families — but this island welcomed more than 1 million visitors in 2001. It is famed for its wide, 7-mile stretch of white-sand beach, where most of its 30 hotels are tightly packed. Aruba's tiny capital, Oranjestad, with its pastel, stucco walls topped by wedding-cake cupolas and terra-cotta roofs, makes for a nice afternoon stroll.

With more than 40 distinct nationalities represented in its population of 94,000, Aruba has some of the Caribbean's best and most varied dining options. You can look forward to an array of over 100 restaurants from which to choose.

If you want a hassle-free, relaxing introduction to the Caribbean, Aruba should be high on your list. The hotels offer great packages, and even though Aruba is one of the more far-flung islands, you can get a direct flight from several major cities in the U.S. and Europe. What we like about Aruba is that it's easy to navigate, and the people are hospitable. Even though the island heavily relies on tourism, you can feel the locals' genuine happiness to have you — they exude a small-town friendliness. Plus, thanks to a heavy Latin influence, the nightlife can't be beat.

However, sophisticated travelers will find little appeal on Aruba. We were disappointed to see the bland buildup along its stunning beaches. A moratorium now restricts new construction, but to our minds, the island had long ago reached the saturation point anyway. Although we had lots of fun on this island, Aruba is far from our definition of a tropical getaway.

Visiting Aruba, Bonaire, and Curaçao: As easy as ABC

We usually don't recommend trying to visit more than one island during your trip, but the ABC islands — as Aruba, Bonaire, and Curaçao are known — offer a golden opportunity. Both Bonaire and Curaçao rank among our favorites, though for different reasons. If you're a diver or nature lover, Bonaire (☎ 800-BONAIRE; Internet: www.infobonaire.com) should be a don't-miss on your itinerary. History buffs and culture hounds adore Curaçao (☎ 800-328-7222 or 305-792-7129; Fax: 212-683-9337; Internet: www.curacao-tourism.com). Thanks to Willemstad, its Dutch colonial capital, Curaçao has joined such sites as the Great Wall of China and the Pyramids as a UNESCO World Heritage Site.

As long as you've come this far, reserve a few days to visit Aruba's next-door neighbors: Bonaire, which offers the Caribbean's best diving and snorkeling, and Curaçao, which boasts a postcard-perfect Dutch Colonial city that looks like a mini-Amsterdam. Each island is just a brief plane or boat ride away.

If you want guaranteed sun, great food, plenty of activity, and a vibrant nightlife, Aruba is a good bet.

Top aspects of a vacation in Aruba include:

✔ **Lots of variety.** From gambling to windsurfing to horseback riding along the beach, Aruba delivers the fun factor.

✔ **Lively nightlife.** You won't feel overdressed in your designer duds on Aruba. You can try your luck at a dozen casinos, reserve a stage-side table for the productions at one of the showrooms, or dance the night away at hot spots.

✔ **Consistently perfect weather.** Aruba lies outside the hurricane belt. Trade winds and low humidity keep its average year-round temperature of 82 degrees from feeling uncomfortably hot. The island gets only 17 inches of rainfall annually.

✔ **Good vibes.** Cosmopolitan Arubans are friendly, and just about everyone speaks English.

But also consider the following:

✔ **It's built up.** High-rise hotels with little island flair crowd the prime beaches.

✔ **Tourism reigns supreme.** Forget your Robinson Crusoe fantasy.

✔ **The scenery is desertlike, not lush.** This dry, cactus-dotted countryside may clash with your vision of a tropical paradise.

Befriending Barbados

Steeped in English tradition and more straitlaced than some of its neighbors, Barbados has been giving the wealthy and famous the royal treatment for centuries. The easternmost of the Caribbean's Lesser Antilles chain, Barbados juts out into the Atlantic Ocean and used to serve as a gateway to the West Indies for ships coming to and from Europe and South America. As a result, its islanders got first pick of the bounty flowing into the Caribbean. The island's prosperity remains in evidence today, especially in the bustling shopping district (which we didn't find to be overly impressive or a bargain).

Known for its posh resorts from Sandy Lane to Royal Pavilion (think *Lifestyles of the Rich and Famous,* and you've got the picture), Barbados offers a range of accommodations, whether you're seeking idyllic days at an intimate guesthouse or the frenetic activity of a sprawling resort. During our first afternoon, high tea by the pool seemed an oddity, but by the second day, we slipped into the spirit and joined the other guests in this tradition. We felt like we'd been ushered into some special club. Coming from the land of biggie cups and super-sized fries, choosing exactly what kind of tea to steep and savor while daintily snacking on cucumber sandwiches was amusing and endearing. We used the time to socialize with the largely older British crowd who migrate to this island year after year. Barbados naturally would feel like a second home to them, considering that it was the only Caribbean island continually under British rule for three centuries, until 1966.

Another tradition to be aware of is dressing up for dinner; it's a must on Barbados. We quickly learned firsthand why Barbados has garnered international acclaim for its restaurants.

Barbados is also known for its gardens — again, the British influence. We came expecting the lush, junglelike beauty of St. Lucia or Barbados's wild cousin, Jamaica. Barbados is green, but years of use by planters have left its countryside restrained and managed.

The mood on Barbados is unmistakably civilized — so much so that we felt a little stifled and hamstrung by all the tradition. We were relieved to come upon surfers hanging out near **Bathsheba.** With their hip attitudes, they definitely clashed with the island's character, but they actually made us feel more at home. Barbados residents, called Bajans (pronounced bay-johns), cut loose only when it comes to rum. Bajans are extremely proud of the locally made rums, and several little dives around the island serve rum at all hours.

If your idea of paradise is the feel of an English outpost in the tropics, Barbados will be your cup of tea.

Top aspects of a vacation in Barbados include:

- ✔ **The dining scene.** Chefs on Barbados, unlike those on some Caribbean islands, are experimental, sophisticated, and eager to meet the challenge of demanding palates.

- ✔ **The scenery.** In the countryside you'll find some gorgeous vistas.

- ✔ **Snap-to service.** You won't want for attention; you'll have help at your beck and call.

But also consider the following:

- ✔ **You'll need to mind your manners.** The "have it your way" philosophy doesn't belong here — it's the Queen's rules all the way. Better polish up on which fork to use with which course.

- ✔ **You can find deals, deals, deals . . . not!** Rates are out-of-sight unless you're willing to look hard. Prices are high on everything from food to hotel rooms to greens fees.

- ✔ **You'll encounter claustrophobia-inducing roads and traffic jams around Bridgetown and the popular coasts.** Oddly, you're likely to find busy, narrow roads right next to your room at many hotels.

Breezing into the British Virgin Islands

Even if you've never been on a boat in your life, the British Virgin Islands (BVIs) will make you want to hoist a sail and swill some grog. Brace yourself for the moment when you finally glimpse Jimmy Buffett's idea of paradise. These sleepy little islands — like a giant's stepping-stones scattered across the sea — are a sailor's and water-lover's delight. You're never out of sight of the next island as you tool around on your choice of watercraft.

We're hesitant to write about how much we love the BVIs because we don't want them to change. Simply put, these exquisite, emerald-green islands will take your breath away.

Okay, okay, so getting here is a royal pain, but the extra effort is worth it. And because getting to the BVIs is neither easy nor cheap, you may feel like you have the islands all to yourself at times. You can fly into Tortola, but you'll probably need to ply the sapphire-blue Caribbean waters by water taxi or ferry to reach your hotel, villa, or guesthouse. Thankfully, you won't find any monolithic, high-rise hotels straddling the beaches here. You also won't find any rah-rah all-inclusive resorts.

Still a British colony, the BVIs — actually more than 50 islands are in the chain, though only a handful are inhabited — are remarkably undeveloped and sparsely populated, with only 18,000 inhabitants. Tourism began here in the mid-1960s when Laurance Rockefeller opened Little Dix Bay on Virgin Gorda. Like nearby St. John, much of the BVIs' land is preserved in national park areas.

If you must have your MTV, shopping, golf, or a happening casino, skip the BVIs. But if you want to chill out and spend your afternoons doing nothing more stressful than napping in a hammock by the sea, the BVIs are a perfect choice.

Although we noted a touch of British formality, the vibe here is casual and fun. When you're at the beach bar, you'll be sitting alongside captains of industry, rock stars, famous actors, and colorful local characters, all gathered to sip Painkillers — a rum concoction — with their new best friends.

About the only place where you'll see much evidence of tourism is at the most famous spot on Virgin Gorda, called **The Baths.** There, grand granite boulders frame the most perfect blue Caribbean you could desire. Cruise ships are allowed to dock on that island, but the number of passengers they can bring each day is tightly controlled.

The BVIs we cover in this book are:

- **Tortola:** The largest of the BVIs, Tortola is only 21 miles long. Its name means "turtledove" in Spanish. The BVI capital, Road Town, is here, as well as a huge marina filled with hundreds of yachts that account for half of the BVIs' "tourist beds."

- **Virgin Gorda:** Home to some of the most spectacular resorts in the BVIs, Virgin Gorda packs a world of beauty into a mere 8½ miles. It has two national parks, both great for hiking. (Gorda Peak reaches 1,500 feet.)

- **Anegada:** Although this stretch of land is within sight of the other islands, you can easily overlook the flat, sandy island that looks like a giant beach and feels like the ends of the earth.

Picnics on deserted beaches, sunset sails in a tiny boat, and morning walks where you don't run into another soul make the British Virgin Islands one of our favorites.

Top aspects of a vacation in the British Virgin Islands include:

- **Sailing, sailing, sailing.** Free spirits love just drifting from one isle to the next through Sir Francis Drake Channel.

- **An eye-popping, gorgeous setting.** The Caribbean doesn't get any better than this. You can truly find that island getaway and snag your own private strand of beach.

- **Unexpected fun.** When you're at Foxy's or Bomba's beach bar, you may encounter Jimmy Buffett plucking out his latest ode to sailing or the Beach Boys jamming the night away. Honestly.

But also consider the following:

- **No posh nightlife.** You'll need to whip up your own entertainment.

- **Transportation hassles.** Getting around can be expensive and time-consuming unless you rely on the regularly scheduled ferries.

- **Limited dining choices.** If you don't happen to like the chef at your hotel, you're cooked.

Greeting Grand Cayman

We have to be honest up front: Unless you're a diver or a serious snorkeler, go elsewhere. You can find more island flavor in other places for a much cheaper price. The Cayman Islands, the birthplace of the Caribbean's recreational diving, rely on a good reputation for their relatively healthy reefs and dramatic wall dives with almost 200 dive sites and visibility up to 100 feet. Of the trio that makes up the Cayman Islands — Grand Cayman, Cayman Brac, and Little Cayman, just south of Cuba — Grand Cayman is the primary draw with its famed 5½-mile-long **Seven Mile Beach.**

So why is Grand Cayman one of the top tourist destinations in the Caribbean? Diving aside, Grand Cayman is easy to reach and easy to navigate when you're there. It's safe and sanitized in every way. It's the kind of place where you can go to sleep in your beach chair, wake up, and still have all your stuff intact. English is spoken, U.S. dollars are accepted, and, most importantly, you are made to feel welcome.

Grand Cayman's top-drawer restaurants, cool attractions like Stingray City, tidy beaches, and a plethora of water sports make it a popular choice with families, honeymooners, and divers who are traveling with nondivers. Grand Cayman is also one of the main stops for the many cruise ships in the Caribbean.

If you crave glittery nightlife, Grand Cayman has gotten a little hipper over the last year or two, but we'd still send you to Puerto Rico or Aruba instead. Even though the banking industry has made this island wealthy, gambling it away at casinos isn't the thing here either. Expect to be in the company of the old-money crowd, whose idea of fun is watching the sun set from a lantern-festooned deck while celebrating happy hour at a British-style pub.

You'll find friendly, laid-back islanders who speak with a lilting brogue echoing their Scotch/Irish/Welsh heritage. They also probably have a bigger bank account than you do. About the only time a party atmosphere sets in is during **Pirates Week;** parades, street dances, and fireworks break out everywhere during this national event in October.

If you're the active type who loves water sports, gourmet food, and a dash of history, Grand Cayman is a winner.

Top aspects of a vacation in Grand Cayman include:

- ✔ **Divers' heaven.** The Cayman Islands are renowned for some of the Caribbean's best diving.

- ✔ **Great dining.** Gourmet restaurants offer truly inventive island cuisine.

✔ **Classy, but casual.** The Cayman Islands are sophisticated and upscale islands without attitude.

✔ **Untrammeled isles.** Peaceful Cayman Brac and Little Cayman lie within easy reach.

But also consider the following:

✔ **Your wallet will get hit.** The Cayman Islands are expensive, especially when it comes to food — although the island has taken the bite out of prices with discounts during the off-season in recent years.

✔ **Nightlife? What nightlife?** Diver tuck in early.

✔ **Day-trippers are everywhere.** The famed beach and popular dive sites get overrun — especially when cruise ships are in port.

Jamming on Jamaica

Quintessential ladies' man Errol Flynn called Jamaica "more beautiful than any woman I've ever seen." Nobody ever comes back from Jamaica and labels the island just "nice." Jamaica stands out from the other Caribbean islands as an in-your-face kind of place. It's an assault on the senses: the continual throbbing of reggae and rock-steady music that reverberates in taxis and on the streets; lush places with improbable names like Fern Gully and Bamboo Alley; the fiery taste of jerk chicken; and the plucky salesmanship of self-taught artists eking out a living in the craft markets.

Does your island fantasy include rafting a river and swimming in a blue lagoon? How about racing to the top of a waterfall, or sitting on a verandah sipping your morning coffee while overlooking the bushes from which the coffee beans were plucked? Choose your favorite sunny spot from Jamaica's 200 miles of beaches. Hike the 7,400-foot summits of the Blue Mountains. Cuddle under a heated duvet to ward off the cool mountain air at night.

Jamaica owes part of its success to the prevalence of all-inclusive resorts, which were first popularized here and have spread to several other Caribbean islands. However, these compounds have proven both a blessing and a curse. Many tourists like them because they take a lot of the guesswork out of their trip, letting them control the costs up front. Unfortunately, the self-contained attractions also make it highly unlikely that you'll venture from the cushy confines of your resort and experience the real Jamaica. In turn, the lack of tourists willing to actually visit the island and not just an all-inclusive resort has hit restaurants and attractions hard, making Jamaicans even more desperate for your business.

We have a love/hate relationship with the island. We adore the less-touristy parts and the way people quickly warm up if you're kind to them and show interest in their country. We abhor the brazen approaches of the shady characters peddling drugs and the prostitutes that you're likely to encounter on the beaches and outside the resorts' gates. Although the government has tried in recent years to educate the local population about how important tourists are to the economy, the message has had little effect on aggressive vendors and sometimes surly service people. On the other hand, if you're looking for local color and you're genuinely interested in this beautiful country, you can make friends for life here.

The island has four main resort areas — and some up-and-coming spots — each tempting in a different way, with tennis, golf, horseback riding, and water sports:

- **Montego Bay:** Here in Mo Bay (as it's called by locals), green hills cup the blue harbor of Jamaica's number-one tourist destination (some may say "trap"). One of the livelier Caribbean destinations, it offers everything from duty-free shopping to craft markets to legends of witchcraft at Rose Hall, an 18th-century plantation *Great House* (the plantation houses from the days when sugar cane covered the island) said to be haunted.

  On the plus side, you'll find a decent selection of restaurants and nightclubs in Mo Bay, which has brought in the college spring-break crowd. But Mo Bay is big, poor, and crowded, and it lacks the fine architecture that gives St. Thomas's Charlotte Amalie its allure. If you spend your entire vacation here, you're probably going to leave feeling a little let down.

- **Negril:** A hedonistic pulse courses through this resort area at Jamaica's western tip. Known as a counterculture escape in the 1970s (when it didn't even have electricity), this sleepy little haven had been discovered by tourists when the 1980s rolled around.

  Negril has retained its funky edge and is still celebrated for its sunsets and 7 miles of beach as soft as talc, but it has definitely been embraced by the masses, some coming for the clothing-optional sections of beach. The all-inclusive resorts occupy much of the fabulous beach with smaller properties tucked in between. Sunseekers looking for a little less frenzy can find it on Negril's **West End,** where boutique resorts hug the cliffs above a honeycomb network of caves. For a taste of what Negril used to be like, head to the southwest coach where **Treasure Beach,** a tiny fishing village, has been adopted by trendy, beautiful people as a hangout.

- **Ocho Rios:** Cruise ships regularly disgorge passengers in Ochi (the local name, pronounced oh-chee). The tourists stampede for the shopping and then make the obligatory climb up **Dunn's River Falls,** where a natural stone staircase leads to the top of the 600-foot cascading water. After that trek, tourists then run the gauntlet past vendors hawking "I survived the Falls" T-shirts. Unfortunately, that experience has led many to dismiss Ochi as a kitschy town for tourists. Actually, you don't have to venture far off the well-beaten path here to see Ochi's Eden-like nature — we love the **Coyaba Gardens** tucked away above the city. Ocho Rios boasts some of the country's more exquisite resorts, as well as our absolute favorite all-inclusive resort, Grand Lido San Souci.

✔ **Port Antonio.** Those who know and love Jamaica often pick lush and mountainous Port Antonio as the most romantic region of the country. Indeed, Port Antonio, on the northeast coast and in the foothills of the Blue Mountains, fueled Errol Flynn's passion and remains removed from the primary flurry of tourism. Rafting by torchlight on the gentle Rio Grande is the main to-do here. Although Port Antonio doesn't have the high profile of the other resort areas, stars like Johnny Depp, Glenn Close, and Robin Williams have fallen for it.

We're willing to overlook Jamaica's rough edges, because, overall, its rugged beauty delivers the quintessential Caribbean experience.

Top aspects of a vacation in Jamaica include:

✔ **Choice of destinations.** Whether your pace is languid or action-packed, you can easily find a resort area to match your vacationing style.

✔ **Cool digs.** Accommodations range from hyperactive all-inclusive resorts, to Old World villas where butlers serve tea on silver trays, to funky cottages by the beach.

✔ **The breadth of natural beauty.** The variations of Jamaica's terrain are unparalleled — expansive beaches; lush jungles punctuated with waterfalls; the cool, misty Blue Mountains; and savannas that echo the African plains.

✔ **All-inclusive resorts.** You'll know how much your vacation will cost before you even leave home. And you won't have to think of a thing when you're there.

✔ **The vibrant culture.** Reggae by the late Bob Marley still rules the airwaves from Houston to Copenhagen. In tiny crafts stores and grand galleries, you'll find earthy, made-in-Jamaica items, such as wood carvings and handmade pottery.

But also consider the following:

✔ **The most aggressive vendors in the Caribbean.** Travelers need to be cautious. Think New York City on a beach. Vendors on the beach and in the markets can be maddeningly persistent.

✔ **Traffic accidents.** The roadways here are in disrepair, and the island has the dubious ranking as one of the top spots for car wrecks in the world.

✔ **Grinding poverty.** Besides Haiti, Jamaica has the lowest standard of living in the Caribbean, and some visitors find it hard to enjoy themselves when the islanders are so obviously struggling.

✔ **Litter.** The natural beauty of the island is marred by trash.

✔ **Crime.** Unless you're a Bob Marley fanatic and want to make a pilgrimage to his house, now a museum, steer clear of Kingston, where much of Jamaica's crime occurs.

Partying on Puerto Rico

We admit it. We thought those winning commercials with stunning images of Puerto Rico challenging you to "Guess where?" were too good to be true. For many years, we went to Puerto Rico just because it was the main jumping-off point for the Caribbean, but we never spent any time there. Today, just thinking about this visual feast of an island makes our hearts beat faster. Puerto Rico scores high on our list of favorite Caribbean islands for more reasons than native son Ricky Martin can shake his "bon-bon" at.

This stunner of a destination dishes out everything that your heart could desire in an island vacation — all with a steamy Latin beat. The colonial city of Old San Juan, with its well-preserved forts and narrow stone streets overhung with balconies brimming with flowers, has managed to avoid the T-shirt tackiness that mars so many of this hemisphere's port cities. Yet with its chic art galleries and incredible restaurant scene, it has gracefully bridged the gap between old and new.

Those who want high-rise hotels, a happening beach scene, high-energy discos, and frenetic casinos can find it on Condado and Isla Verde in San Juan. That's our least favorite part of the island, because it's touristy with all the things we dislike: vendors hawking tacky trinkets and little island charm.

Puerto Rico has enough natural wonders to keep you more than occupied, including one of the world's largest river caves for spelunking, extensive rain forests for hiking, bioluminescent bays and good corals for diving, and 272 miles of Atlantic and Caribbean coastline for horseback riding, swimming, surfing, and walking hand-in-hand. The island also rates well with people who love golf and deep-sea fishing. Escape artists find a more laid-back scene in Vieques and Rincon. Think of San Juan like Miami. Vieques is considered the Spanish Virgin Island.

As for accommodations, Puerto Rico arguably has the broadest range of choices in the Caribbean, from a hotel converted from a 500-year-old convent to mega-resorts with all the bells and whistles. It also yields gems called *paradores* — clean, comfortable, and reasonably priced bed-and-breakfasts (B&Bs) that must pass government inspection.

Of course, because Puerto Rico is a U.S. territory, you'll never have a problem finding English speakers — although Spanish is the dominant language of the people. To make your life as a traveler even easier, you can take the cash you're most accustomed to; the U.S. dollar is the currency in Puerto Rico.

Puerto Rico runs the gamut. It packs sizzle to spare with a sexy nightlife scene, but eco-hounds and sports nuts will be in paradise, as will those souls who are content to sit on the beach sipping margaritas.

Top aspects of a vacation in Puerto Rico include:

- **A convenient location.** You won't have a problem getting to Puerto Rico. Almost all the airlines that service the Caribbean fly through this airport.

- **No passport, no problema.** You get the intoxicating mix of both worlds here: the exotic Latin flavor blended with the comforting familiarity of home. But if you're from the United States, you don't have to worry about a passport or changing money.

- **Living la vida loca.** Put on your designer duds and tango until the sun comes up. Puerto Ricans love the nightlife.

- **Culture club.** The art scene and intriguing history meld to bring a level of sophistication to Puerto Rico that you don't find on most of the other Caribbean islands.

But also consider the following:

- **The secret's out.** Puerto Rico is a popular stop for cruise ships, and its more-famous beaches (all are public) get crowded and dirty.

- **Hurricanes are regular visitors.** During the hurricane season, Puerto Rico regularly goes on alert.

- **Spring break and holiday crowds abound.** During the time that most people think about coming to the Caribbean, finding room at the inn can be almost impossible. Unlike other places, travel traffic doesn't slow down in April either, thanks to spring break and Easter celebrations.

Venturing onto the U.S. Virgin Islands

Blessed with about 300 sunny days a year, the U.S. Virgin Islands (USVIs) have deservedly been dubbed America's Paradise. The island group encompasses St. Thomas, St. John, and St. Croix, plus another 50 islets and cays, most of them uninhabited.

As an American territory, the USVIs are a breeze for U.S. citizens to visit. English is spoken everywhere, the currency is the dollar, and you don't need a passport. The other cool thing is that you can easily and conveniently visit more than one of these beautiful islands, awash in flowers ranging from brilliantly colored bougainvillea to fragrant jasmine to the cheekily named "jump-up-and-kiss-me," which has ruby-red blossoms. And you'll want to visit more than one, because they each have such distinctive personalities. In fact, we'd highly recommend arranging your trip with all three islands on the agenda. If you only have a week, though, pick two and save the third for next time.

The most populous of these islands, St. Thomas, is also one of the busier cruise ports in the Caribbean. Shoppers surge through its capital, Charlotte Amalie (pronounced ah-*mahl*-ya), scooping up jewelry, perfume, clothes, and trinkets. Eco-lovers flock to St. John, where two-thirds of the island is preserved as a national park and visitors who are in the know reserve tents in its popular campgrounds at least eight months in advance. The largest of the three, St. Croix, sometimes gets overlooked, but it's our favorite. St. Croix gives you the best of the other two. It has the beautiful architecture of Charlotte Amalie in its two towns, with a nice selection of shops and good restaurants. You can walk the streets and get a sense of history without being distracted by commercialism. St. Croix's natural beauty hasn't been swallowed up by development, either. In fact, its agricultural roots are still much in evidence.

St. Thomas. Celebrated for its duty-free shopping, gourmet restaurants, busy nightlife, golf courses, and lovely beaches, St. Thomas is by far the most cosmopolitan of the trio — and the most touristy. Frenetic energy courses through busy and historic Charlotte Amalie, where jungle-thatched hills and red-tile roofed houses surround a sapphire-blue harbor punctuated with every kind of craft from sailboats to gargantuan cruise ships.

The main shopping area is limited to a few congested waterfront streets, but it's great fun for strolling. A mind-boggling number of jewelry shops clamor for your attention, giving away cheap gems to lure you in.

If you're the type who simply must feel a strong U.S. connection, no matter where you are, St. Thomas will satisfy that need. Like any heavily populated U.S. city, Charlotte Amalie battles crime and grime, but common sense precautions will suffice.

St. Thomas boasts one of the Caribbean's more famous beaches: **Magens Bay,** a broad, U-shaped inlet edged by a mile of sugar-white sand. Whether you crave the reliable luxury of the Ritz-Carlton or want to cook your own meals in a bare-bones condo, you can find something to suit your wallet.

St. John. Although it's a mere 15-minute ferry ride away from St. Thomas, St. John feels like another world when you step onto the dock at Cruz Bay. Nature reigns supreme on lush St. John, which was largely transformed into a national park in 1956 and boasts challenging hills ideal for hiking and turquoise waters perfect for snorkeling. On the island's north coast, the necklace of pearl-white beaches rank among the world's best, including Hawksnest, Trunk Bay (whose coral reefs have been trammeled by too many tourists of late), and Cinnamon Bay.

Although neighboring St. Thomas wins the prize for the most shops, St. John gets our vote for the most intriguing — especially those at **Mongoose Junction.** Almost 200 of the island's 5,000 residents put "artist" on their tax returns. You can find some real treasures here. And for such a small island, its restaurant scene is surprisingly happening with some terrific new entries. Its nightlife has a collegial feel to it.

St. John is renowned for its eco-tents, but its selection of villas is dazzling, too. Its two traditional luxury resorts — the venerable, old-money Caneel Bay and newcomer Westin St. John — have plenty of fans as well. Count us among them. In other words, no matter where you stay on St. John, you'd have to be a grouch not to have fun.

St. Croix. Forty miles and a 20-minute plane hop to the south of St. Thomas, St. Croix presents a dazzling montage of scenery: powdery, white-sand beaches; cactus-dotted plains; mangrove swamps; stands of mahogany trees; and rain forests. Christiansted, the capital, remains virtually unchanged from 200 years ago when it was the centerpiece of the Danish West Indies, with waterfront arcades and an imposing ochre yellow fort at its heart. Rent a car for at least a day or two and just explore. You'll find exquisite botanical gardens, abandoned sugar mills all over the island, an artist who uses naturally fallen trees to carve island-style furniture, and Great Houses in various stages of restoration. Another good way to see the island is by horseback or by bicycle.

Not as popular with the cruise ships, St. Croix yields more opportunities for finding your own little private strand of sand. Two miles off the northeast shore, you can rest assured of claiming uncrowded territory. Have a champagne picnic for two on the beach of uninhabited **Buck Island,** a wooded nature preserve administered by the U.S. National Park Service. Nearby is a coral reef that President Kennedy had declared the nation's first underwater national park.

In the U.S. Virgin Islands, you don't have the sheer number of islands of the neighboring British Virgin Islands, but you'll find plenty to love.

Top aspects of a vacation in the USVIs include:

✔ **Spectacular beaches.** All three islands have glorious ones, especially St. John. Both diving and snorkeling are generally excellent.

✔ **Amazing, duty-free shopping.** The islands — St. Thomas is king of the hill — are known for bargains on liquor, crystal, china, linens, and perfumes. The duty-free allowance is $1,200 a person, twice that of other Caribbean islands.

✔ **American comfort.** If you're coming from the United States, you'll get an easy introduction to the Caribbean.

✔ **Top-notch water sports and sailing.** Consistent trade winds, deep cruising waters, and dozens of safe anchorages make the USVIs and neighboring BVIs a pleasure to sail or fish.

But also consider the following:

✔ **The (sometimes) madding crowds.** The shopping area in Charlotte Amalie is claustrophobic when the cruise ships disgorge.

✔ **The need to be on guard.** Travelers should use caution — and taxis — around Charlotte Amalie and Christiansted at night.

✔ **Too much like home.** If seeing all-too-familiar fast-food joints clashes with your dream of the tropics, St. Thomas probably isn't for you. Pockets of St. Croix are industrial as well.

✔ **Hurricanes.** Within two weeks of each other in September 1995, hurricanes Luis and Marilyn swept through the region, causing extensive damage to St. Thomas and St. John (both of which have completely rebounded). St. Croix was spared and subsequently discovered by the cruise lines that normally frequented St. Thomas. In the last few years, the USVIs haven't suffered a major hurricane.

Deciding How Many Islands to Visit on Your Trip

If you've never been to the Caribbean before, the thought of visiting more than one island is probably overwhelming. But island-hopping can be surprisingly easy, depending on where you decide to go. American Airlines and Air Jamaica have generous programs that make hitting more than one island surprisingly reasonable (see Chapter 5). Or you can catch a small regional carrier for less than $100, usually.

If you know that you're going to a particular island but you're interested in checking out what's nearby, see the "Having Fun On and Off the Beach" chapter for each destination. At the end of this chapter, we highlight easily accessible islands that you may want to visit. For more details, check the appropriate chapter, but this brief summary will get you started.

Both the British Virgin Islands and the U.S. Virgin Islands lend themselves beautifully to island-hopping. Indeed, in the BVIs you won't be able to help yourself. With the USVIs, it's a toss-up, but we recommend visiting at least two of the three. For that matter, as long as you have your passport, you can go back and forth between the BVIs and USVIs by boat or plane.

As we noted earlier in this chapter, two other Dutch islands are a short ride in a puddle-jumper away from Aruba. You can either visit Bonaire or Curaçao, but we wouldn't recommend trying to cram all three into your schedule.

Both Puerto Rico and Jamaica are so large that you'll be too busy to go anywhere else. However, we must mention one foray that has enormous appeal to U.S. visitors due to the forbidden-fruit appeal — a trip to neighboring Cuba from Jamaica. It's simple to arrange, but we've never tried it ourselves.

Hard-core divers may be lured from Grand Cayman to one of its smaller, laid-back sister islands, Little Cayman or Cayman Brac.

Visitors to Barbados should consider spending a few days on St. Lucia, which is a quick flight away but a whole different experience and one of our favorite islands for romance.

Narrowing Your Island Choices

Now that you have a thumbnail sketch of the differences among the Caribbean islands, it's time to figure out which one you'd most like to visit. This quiz will help you determine which islands are best suited to your vacation style and interests. Here's how you do it.

Step #1: Get to know your "Rate the Islands" scorecard

Your scorecard, which you'll find at the end of this chapter, has a column for each island and a row for each category in our island-rating system. Use this scorecard to compile a rating for each of the islands based on the special-interest categories that follow. The top five islands in each category will get a predetermined 1 to 5 points, based on how suited it is to the interest or activity in that category. Five points is the highest rating, one is the lowest. If an island isn't listed, assume that it scores a 0 in that particular category.

Step #2: Score the islands based on your interests and needs

Go through each category. Stop only at those categories that interest you. For example, if you're not a golfer, skip over the golf category entirely; don't plug in points for any of the islands in the "Golf" row of the scorecard. If you're into nightlife, stop at "If you want to party the night away. . . ." Insert each island's score into your scorecard.

Move on to the next category that interests you, and insert the scores into the appropriate row in your scorecard. Keep going until you've reviewed all the categories and given each island a score for each category that matters to you.

1) If you want to be in the lap of luxury . . .

Rating	Island	Why?
5 points	**Barbados**	White-glove treatment all the way at resorts fit for a king or queen.
4 points	**Jamaica**	A taste of the old Jamaica can be had — for a price — at resorts where you'll have a maid, gardener, butler, and cook to fulfill your every whim.
3 points	**Puerto Rico**	Dramatic and grand, the upscale resorts here consistently appear on lists of travelers' favorites.
2 points	**St. Thomas**	The Ritz Carlton, anyone? Need we say more?
1 point	**The BVIs**	Small, luxurious resorts with entire islands all to themselves.

2) If you want to party the night away . . .

Rating	Island	Why?
5 points	**Puerto Rico**	Live Latin music, sizzling dancing, great food, and gambling combine for a continual fiesta.
4 points	**Jamaica**	Almost every night, you can find live bands playing reggae, dance hall, and the latest sounds in Negril, Mo Bay, and Ocho Rios.

3 points	**Aruba**	Most resorts tag and Casino onto their names. Plus, good discos with a heavy Latin influence and Las Vegas–style stage shows.
2 points	**Barbados**	Rum shops, discos, and late-night dining make this scene sizzle.
1 point	**St. Thomas**	The cruise ships have brought gambling, nightclubs, and discos.

3) If you want to eat really well . . .

Rating	Island	Why?
5 points	**Puerto Rico**	Experimental, talented chefs — especially in Old San Juan — have made nouvelle Puerto Rican, New World, and fusion cuisine hot, hot, hot.
4 points	**Barbados**	European chefs flock to this eastern outpost of the Caribbean.
3 points	**Grand Cayman**	This wealthy, upscale island is one of the few in the Caribbean to have developed its own recognizable cuisine based around fresh seafood.
2 points	**Jamaica**	Whether you're paying top dollar for an elegant Jamaican dinner or eating jerk chicken from a roadside vendor, Jamaica offers mouth-watering variety.
1 point	**Aruba**	Its many nationalities, strong Dutch ties, and proximity to Central and South America make Aruba's dining scene one of the more memorable and varied in the Caribbean.

4) If you're looking for the Caribbean's most romantic beaches . . .

Rating	Island	Why?
5 points	**The BVIs**	Because much of the BVIs are accessible only by boat, you can find secluded beaches on islands that you'll be sharing with only iguanas and lizards.
4 points	**St. John**	Here you'll find those powdery-white, palm-lined, near-perfect beaches you've been dreaming of — and you're likely to have them virtually to yourself.
3 points	**Puerto Rico**	You can have your own private fiesta on (almost) virgin strands on Puerto Rico's Virgin Islands.

2 points	**Jamaica**	You may have to look a little harder for privacy, but this setting's hard to beat. Long Bay Beach is a stunner.
1 point	**St. Croix**	This gem boasts virtually untouched stretches of sand.

5) If you're watching your wallet, but still want to stay on the sand . . .

Rating	Island	Why?
5 points	**Jamaica**	Many bargain hotels compete for your business here.
4 points	**Puerto Rico**	Paradores (B&Bs) keep costs down.
3 points	**St. Thomas**	Three words: competition, competition, competition.
2 points	**St. Croix**	Eager to grab some attention from its better known sibling islands, this one offers deals, deals, deals.
1 point	**Aruba**	So many hotels crowd the beach that prices are slashed in the summer.

6) If you want to experience the real Caribbean vibe . . .

Rating	Island	Why?
5 points	**Jamaica**	Funky reggae, strong national pride, and native arts and crafts rule.
4 points	**The BVIs**	A Jimmy Buffett song come to life.
3 points	**Barbados**	Local rum shops, colorful chattel houses.
2 points	**Puerto Rico**	The Caribbean with a Latin beat.
1 point	**St. Croix**	A rural island with a funky edginess.

7) If you want Caribbean history and culture . . .

Rating	Island	Why?
5 points	**Puerto Rico**	The most beautiful colonial city in the Caribbean, combined with a hot art scene.
4 points	**Barbados**	Three centuries as an English outpost left a strong legacy.
3 points	**St. Thomas**	Charlotte Amalie's colonial buildings.
2 points	**St. Croix**	Two Colonial Dutch cities and sugar mill ruins bring the island's past to life.

| 1 point | Jamaica | A fantastic history as a haven for pirates and coveted prize among the colonial superpowers. |

8) If you want to tee off . . .

Rating	*Island*	*Why?*
5 points	Jamaica	Known for tricky winds, Jamaica is still tops after all these years — with courses like Half Moon and Tryall.
4 points	Puerto Rico	A range of choices, with two in the shadow of El Yunque rain forest.
3 points	Barbados	The Robert Trent Jones–designed Royal Westmoreland is a standout.
2 points	St. Croix	Guests on neighboring St. John and St. Thomas often fly over just for the golf at The Buccaneer (situated by the sea) and Carambola.
1 point	St. Thomas	President Clinton favored Mahogany Run when he was on the island.

9) If you're not getting older, just getting better . . .

Rating	*Island*	*Why?*
5 points	Puerto Rico	Easy access plus the Disabilities Act make Puerto Rico a piece of cake to visit.
4 points	Aruba	A is for: Always sunny, always flat, always safe, always beautiful.
3 points	Grand Cayman	Upscale and ultra-safe, with a world-renowned beach, diving, and golf.
2 points	St. Thomas	Accessible for cruise ship passengers with disabilities, plus cool historical sights and great shopping.
1 point	Barbados	A well-manicured, easily accessible Caribbean experience with good golf, good food, good shopping, and lots of history.

10) If you love hiking . . .

Rating	*Island*	*Why?*
5 points	St. John	Two-thirds of the island is designated as a national park, with more trails than you can shake a walking stick at.

4 points	**Jamaica**	The Blue Mountains, coffee country, and wildflowers.
3 points	**Puerto Rico**	The rain forests and jungles.
2 points	**The BVIs**	Ups and downs on Sage Mountain provide amazing views.
1 point	**Aruba**	Its national park.

11) If you're a nature lover . . .

Rating	*Island*	*Why?*
5 points	**The BVIs**	Unpopulated and well-preserved.
4 points	**St. John**	Preservation was at work here long before it was hip.
3 points	**Puerto Rico**	El Yunque, a magnificent lush rain forest.
2 points	**Jamaica**	Known for bird watching, the Blue Mountains, and the crocodiles in the mangroves of the Black River.
1 point	**St. Croix**	Rural, with a diverse landscape worth exploring.

12) If you want to check out music festivals . . .

Rating	*Island*	*Why?*
5 points	**Jamaica**	The reggae of native son Bob Marley is celebrated rollickingly with Reggae Sum Fest, plus Air Jamaica's Jazz and Blues Festival and Ocho Rios Jazz Festival.
4 points	**Barbados**	Barbados's jazz festival — Paint-It-Jazz — is worth the trip.
3 points	**Puerto Rico**	The Pablo Casals festival honors the great classical cellist.
2 points	**St. Croix**	Dig the Blues Heritage Festival here.
1 point	**Aruba**	Music all through its rollicking Carnival.

13) If you want to sightsee . . .

Rating	*Island*	*Why?*
5 points	**Puerto Rico**	Old San Juan.
4 points	**Jamaica**	Great Houses, waterfalls, mountains.
3 points	**Barbados**	Gardens, rock formations at Bathsheba.

| 2 points | **St. Thomas** | Historic Charlotte Amalie and grand vistas. |
| 1 point | **The BVIs** | The Sir Francis Drake Channel is the week-end pirate's playground. |

14) If you want to go diving or snorkeling . . .

Rating	*Island*	*Why?*
5 points	**Grand Cayman**	200 marked dive sites and visibility to 100 feet.
4 points	**The BVIs**	Wreck dives. So many islands, so little time.
3 points	**St. John**	Thank you, Mr. Rockefeller, for donating much of the land for this fabulous national park.
2 points	**Puerto Rico**	Night dives in bioluminescent bay.
1 point	**St. Croix**	Underwater National Marine Park and wall diving at Cane Bay.

15) If you want an array of water sports . . .

Rating	*Island*	*Why?*
5 points	**Aruba**	A world-class destination for windsurfing.
4 points	**The BVIs**	A sailor's paradise, plus surfing along Tortola.
3 points	**Puerto Rico**	From surfing to water-skiing to snorkeling, this island teems with water activities.
2 points	**St. Thomas**	Sailing capital of the Caribbean, plus snorkeling, parasailing, and deep-sea fishing.
1 point	**Grand Cayman**	In addition to diving, fishing, sailing, parasailing, jet-skiing, and a whole host of water sports await.

16) If you're craving peace and quiet . . .

Rating	*Island*	*Why?*
5 points	**The BVIs**	You can get lost here.
4 points	**St. John**	Villas tucked away high on the hills overlooking the sea.
3 points	**Puerto Rico**	The hills are restful.
2 points	**St. Croix**	Much of the island is still rural.
1 point	**Jamaica**	It's big enough that you can get away . . . if you really want to.

17) If you're traveling with children . . .

Rating	Island	Why?
5 points	**Puerto Rico**	Easy to get to, and Hyatt's top-notch kids programs after you're there.
4 points	**Jamaica**	Several kid-friendly all-inclusives with wonderful staffs.
3 points	**St. Croix**	Islanders love children and children love this island.
2 points	**Aruba**	Deep discounts in the summer on family packages.
1 point	**St. Thomas**	Familiarity with great water sports and plenty of activities.

18) If you want to get there quickly . . .

Rating	Island	Why?
5 points	**Puerto Rico**	The hub of American Airlines.
4 points	**Jamaica**	Air Jamaica's hub.
3 points	**St. Thomas**	The dropping-off point for all three U.S. Virgin Islands.
2 points	**Barbados**	Many direct flights from New York and London.
1 point	**Aruba**	Lots of direct air service and an easy 15-minute drive to any of its hotels.

Step #3: Tallying the scores to determine your final destination(s)

After you've reviewed the categories and plugged ratings into your scorecard, tally each island's score.

The winner — the island with the highest total score — should be your primary destination. If a second island scores high, consider splitting your time between the two islands. If a third island scores high and you have a good amount of time to spare, you may want to visit three islands. Scores really close? Flip a coin and vow to hit the one that comes in second on your next vacation.

"Rate the Islands" Scorecard

POINTS FOR:	Aruba	Barbados	British Virgin Is.	Grand Cayman	Jamaica	Puerto Rico	St. Croix	St. John	St. Thomas
1) Luxury									
2) Nightlife									
3) Great food									
4) Beaches									
5) Bargain rates									
6) Local color									
7) Caribbean culture									
8) Golf									
9) Senior appeal									
10) Hiking									
11) Natural beauty									
12) Music festivals									
13) Sightseeing									
14) Diving/snorkeling									
15) Water sports									
16) Peace and quiet									
17) Family friendly									
18) Easy access									
TOTAL SCORE:									

Chapter 2

Deciding When to Go

By Echo and Kevin Garrett

- -

In This Chapter

▶ Evaluating the seasons

▶ Forecasting the weather, island by island

▶ Planning your trip around festivals and carnivals

- -

*W*hen most people think of the Caribbean, they think of a place where they can escape winter's chill. The truth is, the Caribbean makes a magnificent vacation destination pretty much year-round. In fact, summer is one of our favorite times to visit. We enjoy the quick shower bursts followed by beautiful skies, rainbows, and gorgeous sunsets. In the broadest terms, the weather in this part of the world is tropical, warm, humid, and sometimes rainy.

In this chapter, we demystify the hotel lingo about seasons and explain the connection between the timing of your trip and the related expenses that you can expect to pay. We also give you an honest assessment of the dreaded *h* word — *hurricane* — and what it means for your Caribbean getaway. Finally, we tell you about the climates of the different islands and about the timing of various festivals and carnivals.

Translating the Seasons

When you plan a trip to the Caribbean, you can expect to encounter lots of talk about seasons: The Season, high season, holiday season, low season, shoulder season, rainy season, and hurricane season. For a place where the leaves don't change and the temperature rarely budges more than a few degrees either direction from around 80 degrees, you'll hear the word *season* tossed about an awful lot.

TIP

The reason seasons matter in the Caribbean has virtually nothing to do with the weather and everything to do with your room rate. For example, published room rates for a resort may include as many as a half-dozen different prices listed for the exact same accommodations. What you'll pay all depends on exactly when you visit; timing is everything when it comes to a Caribbean vacation.

Generally, seasonal differences break down something like this, but keep in mind that there are lots of variations:

- ✓ **Holiday season (also known as The Season):** December 15 to January 3

- ✓ **High season:** January 4 to April 14

- ✓ **Shoulder season:** April 15 to May 30 and September 1 to December 14

- ✓ **Low season:** May 30 to August 31

- ✓ **Hurricane season (overlaps with shoulder and low seasons):** June 1 to November 30

Holiday season and high season

The Caribbean's high season heats up right before Christmas and lasts through mid-April. During the holiday season, referred to on the upscale islands as simply The Season, longtime guests often snatch up reservations for the best lodgings years in advance. At Christmastime, Jamaica's exclusive Round Hill even turned away James Bond — er, Pierce Brosnan, who plays the character originally conceived by author Ian Fleming at his home on Jamaica.

So if you're going to a resort on Jamaica, Barbados, or the British Virgin Islands around the holidays (where being there during The Season means that you've achieved a certain station in life), be prepared to make your plans well in advance.

 The nicer hotels often have minimum-stay requirements in effect during the holiday season and stringent cancellation policies. If you plan a trip during the holidays, make your reservations as early as possible, expect crowds, and plan to pay top dollar for everything.

The last two weeks of January sometimes provide a slight lull in tourism, but high season shifts back into high gear in February and March, the busiest months in the Caribbean.

The forecast: If you're craving an escape and don't mind planning ahead and shelling out the bucks — rates reach their peak the last two weeks of December — this blast of sunshine is sure to cure your midwinter blues.

Shoulder season

In the shoulder seasons — late spring and the fall — prices are sometimes slightly reduced. Shoulder season is great if you want to go at a quiet time, because children are in school and few families are on the islands.

There is an exception to this rule, however: Between the Easter holidays and spring break, April is an extremely tough and expensive time to book a vacation on Puerto Rico. You may also have difficulties booking in Aruba, Montego Bay and Negril (Jamaica), and St. Thomas (U.S. Virgin Islands) at this time.

Some smaller resorts and restaurants close for repairs and maintenance in July, August, September, or October. So before you take an expensive taxi ride over to a top restaurant, call first to make sure it's open. You'll still need to make reservations for the most popular places anyway.

We've never found more than a few places shuttered, and lots of other options have always been available. The islands where closures could be a problem are the smaller ones like Nevis and Anguilla (neither is covered in this guide). We ran into a newlywed couple who had left The Four Seasons on Nevis to come to The Ritz-Carlton, St. Thomas, because they were so limited in their dining choices on tiny Nevis. "Everything was closed, and there wasn't anything to do," the young bride told us.

Rate reductions of 10 to 20% beat holiday season charges, but they're not as economical as in low season. In April and May, the weather barely differs from the bright sunshine of winter months, but in the early fall — especially September — you have to consider the possibility of hurricanes and tropical storms (unless you've decided on Aruba, which is below the hurricane belt).

Low season

If you come during the low season (or, as we call it, the slow season), rates drop like an anchor. Rates decrease as much as 60% in June, July, and August, making even some of the more exclusive resorts affordable. Travelers often make the assumption that because the Caribbean is so deliciously warm in the winter, it must be searingly hot in the summer. (That's not the case, but more on that in a minute.)

Because school is out and bargains for families abound, you'll see lots of kids during low season — especially from Europe. On some islands, several hotels and resorts band together with the tourist boards during the summer months to offer amazing deals for families as well as honeymooners.

In the last few years, the Caribbean has finally begun convincing people that it's a year-round destination. Despite that self-promotion, finding a hotel room in the low season is pretty easy. Booking your flight may not be as simple. Many nationals go home to visit during the summer — flights to Jamaica are especially full. And Europeans, who have much longer vacations than Americans, frequent the Caribbean in summer months. Reserve your flight as soon as you pick your destination.

If you have your heart set on a particular restaurant, call or e-mail ahead so you aren't disappointed. Chefs often take their vacations in the summer months (especially August).

Tropical storms can kick up quickly in Caribbean summers, but they usually pass just as fast, leaving brilliant blue skies in their wake.

You can get fantastic deals on rooms — how does as much as 60% off sound? — but you'll have to plan ahead for your flight (and fight to be seated with your family and friends). Don't expect everything to be open, either.

Hurricane season

Part of the Caribbean's low season dovetails with the hurricane season, which officially runs from June 1 through November 30, with September being the peak time for a hurricane to hit. Of course, the rainy season also mirrors hurricane season, though it doesn't last as long on some islands. (See Table 2-1 later in this chapter for the exact duration of the rainy season on each island.) Fortunately, in the tropics, rainstorms typically pass over rapidly.

We travel to the Caribbean all the time during hurricane season, because that's when we find great bargains. In all these years, we've only been evacuated once, and it turned out to be for nothing (luckily for St. Croix). Of course, that's no guarantee, and our good fortune certainly won't make you feel better if you're the one being sent packing by the storm.

Some Caribbean islands are better bets than others during hurricane season. Here's the rundown:

- ✔ Aruba lies outside the hurricane belt.

- ✔ Grand Cayman and its two sister islands were hit by Hurricane Michelle in 2001, but they have largely recovered from the hit.

- ✔ Jamaica's last big hurricane was in 1987 (resulting in Echo's parents being stuck in Negril for several days).

- ✔ The British Virgin Islands, St. Thomas, and St. John were struck hard by Hurricane Marilyn in 1995. In 1999 Hurricane Lenny struck the BVIs hard, but the USVIs weren't affected much.

Hurricane lingo

Because we'd never lived where hurricanes were much of a factor — Echo is from Tennessee, and Kevin hails from South Georgia — we had to take some time to catch on to all the hurricane lingo tossed around on CNN's Weather Channel (www.weather.com). Here's a rundown of what we've picked up from paying attention to the weather experts.

Hurricanes are rated by the following categories:

✔ **Category 5** is the most dangerous, packing winds of more than 155 mph (134 knots), which produce storm tides of more than 18 feet. That's strong enough to drive a palm frond through a coconut tree.

✔ **Category 4** has winds of 130 to 155 mph with a storm surge of 13 to 18 feet.

✔ **Category 3** has winds between 110 and 130 mph and storm surge of 9 to 12 feet.

✔ **Category 2** has winds from 96 to 110 mph with a storm surge of 6 to 8 feet.

✔ **Category 1** has winds of 74 to 95 mph with a storm surge of 4 to 5 feet.

When the weather forecasters talk about *tropical storms,* they mean a distinct circulation with winds exceeding 74 mph. Tropical storms can quickly turn into hurricanes and vice versa. As a hurricane loses strength, weathercasters define its intensity as a tropical storm.

✔ St. Croix, just 40 miles away from St. Thomas, was unscathed by the most recent round of hurricanes and Hurricane Marilyn. Its last major hit was Hurricane Hugo in 1989.

✔ Parts of Puerto Rico have suffered damage in recent years.

We don't want you to be naïve about how powerful and devastating hurricanes can be. Modern tracking systems, however, allow early warnings. So, unlike the old days when islanders were caught completely unaware, guests and residents alike can have at least four or five days' notice to get ready and decide what course of action to take. Other good news: Buildings have been reconstructed with more hurricane-resistant materials, enabling resorts in recent years to bounce back more quickly when they do get hit.

If a hurricane does threaten when you're in the Caribbean, hoteliers will provide as much information as possible so you can make an informed choice as to whether to stay or go. If you decide to leave, ask your concierge to call the airport as soon as possible to get a flight out. Do not try to get a few more hours in at the pool, because flights fill up quickly.

The best source for detailed and up-to-date information is the **National Hurricane Center** Web site at www.nhc.noaa.gov. If you want to see what hurricane seasons have been like most recently, check the site at

http://USAtoday.com/weather/basemaps/foreign/carib. Good
advice on what to do as well as predictions and current reports can be
found at www.fema.go/fema/trop.htm. Finally, a great place to see
what the weather experts are predicting is at http://typhoon.atmos.
colostate.edu/forecasts.

Here are some other good Web sites for weather information:

- ✔ **WeatherNet's Tropical Weather** is the largest collection of tropical
  weather Web site links. Find it at http://cirrus.sprl.umich.
  edu/wxnet/tropical.html.

- ✔ **Caribbean Weather Man** is based on Tortola in the BVIs and gives
  good information about that region, particularly for sailors. Check
  out www.caribwx.ccom/cyclone.html.

- ✔ **Caribbean Hurricane Updates** has chat rooms and local corre-
  spondents on the islands where you can get the real scoop. Check
  out www.gobeach.com/hurr.htm. A similar site with excellent
  background on the region's hurricanes is www.stormcarib.com.

When you're setting up a trip months in advance, there's no way to
predict the weather. However, you can take some precautions to make
sure that you're not hung out to dry. If you're traveling to an island
where hurricanes sometimes hit, ask the hotel to fax you its hurricane
policy in writing — just in case. Larger, more affluent properties are
much more likely to give credits toward future travel.

SuperClubs (☎ 877-GO-SUPER; Internet: www.superclubs.com),
which operates properties in Jamaica, St. Lucia, The Bahamas, St.
Kitts, and Brazil, introduced a No Hurricane Guarantee, which gives
guests full reimbursement for the total value of disrupted nights and
issues a voucher for a future stay for the same number of nights to be
used during the same month the following year. Meanwhile, **Sandals's**
(☎ 888-SANDALS or 305-284-1300; Internet: www.sandals.com) Blue
Chip Hurricane Guarantee provides guests with a replacement vacation if a hurricane directly hits a property and the all-inclusive activities are disrupted. You can take the replacement vacation at the
Sandals or Beaches resort of your choice, and you also get free
round-trip airfare.

Smaller properties often won't give refunds, no matter what. We strongly
urge you to consider buying trip interruption/cancellation insurance,
which covers everything from hurricanes to missed connections due to
snowstorms snarling air traffic Stateside. (See Chapter 7 for more on
purchasing insurance.)

If you hear that a storm has struck the Caribbean, and your island
vacation is on the horizon, don't panic. Remember that the region
takes up 1 million square miles. Fretting over a hurricane in St. Thomas
when you're going to Aruba is like someone in Chicago freaking out

over a tornado in Texas. Unfortunately, U.S. weather reports are often vague and inflammatory and talk about the Caribbean as one big mass.

If you're truly concerned, put in a quick call directly to your hotel — not the reservation toll-free number, which is usually in the U.S. Don't ask a general question about hurricane damage to the island. Ask specifics like:

✔ Do you have any water damage?

✔ How's your beach? (Sometimes an island does not have to suffer a direct hit from a hurricane to have damage to its beaches.)

✔ Are all your facilities open? (Restaurants, bars, and water-sports facilities near the beach are often likely to suffer damage.)

✔ If the property has been damaged, when will everything be back in order?

The forecast: As long as a hurricane doesn't blow in and you don't arrive in the middle of a week of rain, this season is a great time to snag terrific deals.

Weathering an Endless Summer

Aruba is the hottest Caribbean island and the one where you'll find sunshine practically guaranteed. St. Croix is the runner-up in terms of least rainfall. Aruba gets a mere 17 inches of rain a year, while Jamaica gets 78 inches. Table 2-1 shows what you can expect weather-wise in nine island locations.

Even on the greener islands like the Virgin Islands and Jamaica, rain showers tend to be brief. We've never once found ourselves stuck inside for an entire day because of rain. **SuperClubs** (☎ **877-GO-SUPER**; Internet: www.superclubs.com) has a "Jamaica Sunshine Guarantee," which means that for any day the sun doesn't show its face, guests are issued a credit voucher for that day's value (good for one year) toward another SuperClubs vacation.

The trade winds are always blowing in the Caribbean, keeping the temperatures pleasant. In fact, you may feel slightly cool walking on the beach at night, exploring a rain forest, hiking in the mountains, or dining in an overly air-conditioned restaurant.

The year-round average water temperature in the Caribbean is a warm 78 degrees F (25 degrees C) and reaches a bathlike 84 degrees F (29 degrees C) or so in summer. Surf conditions are localized, so if the waves or undertow are threatening on your beach, you can usually find sheltered calmer waters by taking a short walk. Ask hotel staff for recommendations.

Table 2-1   **Weather Averages**

Island	Summer Temperature	Winter Temperature	Annual Rainfall	Rainiest Months	Summer Water Temperature	Winter Water Temperature
Aruba	85°F (29°C)	81°F (27°C)	17 in (43 cm)	Oct–Dec	82°F (28°C)	82°F (28°C)
Barbados	82°F (28°C)	79°F (26°C)	47 in (119 cm)	June–Nov	83°F (28°C)	79°F (26°C)
BVIs	86°F (30°C)	80°F (27°C)	60 in (152 cm)	May–Nov	83°F (28°C)	78°F (26°C)
Grand Cayman	85°F (29°C)	75°F (24°C)	60 in (152 cm)	May–Oct	84°F (29°C)	79°F (26°C)
Jamaica	85°F (29°C)	80°F (27°C)	78 in (198 cm)	May–Oct	83°F (28°C)	79°F (26°C)
Puerto Rico	83°F (28°C)	77°F (25°C)	62 in (157 cm)	May–Nov	83°F (28°C)	79°F (26°C)
St. Croix	84°F (29°C)	79°F (26°C)	40 in (102 cm)	Aug–Oct	83°F (28°C)	79°F (26°C)
St. John	82°F (28°C)	77°F (25°C)	54 in (137 cm)	Aug–Oct	83°F (28°C)	79°F (26°C)
St. Thomas	85°F (29°C)	79°F (26°C)	44 in (112 cm)	Aug–Oct	83°F (28°C)	79°F (26°C)

Calendar of Special Events

As you consider when to go to the Caribbean, take a look at a calendar of ever-popular festivals — from jazz to reggae to Carnival — which can complicate the business of booking flights and hotel rooms. Because these dates change and more festivals seem to crop up each year, check with the tourist board of the island you intend to visit to make sure that you won't unexpectedly run into throngs of festival-goers — or to make sure you don't miss out on the fun.

Jamaica's Jazz Festival and Sum Fest rank among the most popular events, while every Tuesday evening Aruba celebrates the Bonbini Festival at Fort Zoutman with traditional dancing and music.

January

In mid-January, the Barbados **"Paint-It-Jazz" Festival** is one of the Caribbean's premier jazz events. It's a weekend jammed with performances by international artists, jazz legends, and local talent. For tickets, e-mail bdosjazz@caribsurf.com.

February

Colorful **Carnival** events whirl through Aruba's streets — kicked off by a children's parade — during a two-week period. Carnival usually occurs in February, but the dates vary from year to year. For the schedule of events, check the Web site at www.aruba.com or call ☎ 800-862-7822.

The week-long **Holetown Festival** is held at the fairgrounds in Holetown to commemorate the date in 1627 when the first European settlers arrived in Barbados. Food, carnival rides, the Royal Barbados Police Force Band, and mounted troops add to the enjoyment. For further information, call ☎ 246-435-6264.

Three weeks of opera, concerts, and theatrical performances are presented in Barbados during **Holder's Opera Season.** The open-air theater at Holder's House, St. James, seats 600, and the program has won acclaim for its productions, which have included headliner Luciano Pavarotti. For information, call ☎ 246-432-6385 or fax 246-432-6461.

April

Dubbed the "World's Greatest Street Party," Barbados's **De Congaline Carnival** is a festive celebration of music, dance, and local arts and crafts. Held at the end of April, the highlight is the Caribbean's longest conga line. For information, contact the Barbados Tourism Authority (☎ 246-427-2623; Fax: 246-424-0909; E-mail: NCF@caribsurf.com; Internet: www.barbados.org).

The British Virgin Islands' **Spring Regatta** is a sailor's dream with three days of sailboat races. It attracts boating enthusiasts from around the world (☎ 284-494-3286; Fax: 284-494-6117; E-mail: bviyc@surfbvi.com; Internet: www.bvispringregatta.org).

During the Grand Cayman's colorful **Batabano Carnival,** in the middle of April, revelers dress up as dancing flowers and swimming stingrays. Call ☎ 345-945-5982.

May

Gospelfest in Barbados features performances by Gospel headliners from around the world. For information, contact the Barbados Tourism Authority (☎ 246-426-5940; Fax: 246-228-8723; E-mail: info@barbados gospelfest.com; Internet: www.barbados.org).

June

If you want to see an utterly British parade spiced with island-style panache, check out the **Queen's Birthday Bash** on Grand Cayman. At the sportfishing competitions in **Million Dollar Month,** huge cash prizes are awarded, including one for a quarter of a million dollars that's given to the angler who breaks the existing Blue Marlin record. Contact the Department of Tourism for more information (☎ 345-949-0623; Fax: 345-949-4053; Internet: www.caymanislands.ky).

For world-class windsurfing, check out the **Hi-Winds World Challenge at Hadakurari.** Contact the Aruba Tourism Authority at ☎ 800-862-7822 or visit www.aruba.com.

July

Dating back to the 19th century, the **Crop Over Festival** in Barbados, a month-long event beginning in early July, marks the end of the sugar cane harvest with competitions, music and dancing, Bajan food, and arts and crafts. The grand finale of Crop Over is a huge carnival parade on Kadoonment Day, the first Monday in August, a national holiday and the biggest party day of the year; visitors are welcome to participate. Contact the Barbados Tourism Authority (☎ **246-427-2623;** Internet: www.barbados.org).

The British Virgin Islands' two-week **Emancipation Festival** starts at the end of July and goes into August. It also has the HIHO Festival, a windsurfing and sailing competition. Contact the tourist board at ☎ **800-835-8530** or 284-494-3134 or visit www.bviwelcome.com.

August

Jamaica's **Sum Fest** is a reggae party that draws top names, including the late Bob Marley's children. For information contact the Jamaican Tourist Board (☎ **800-233-4JTB** or ☎ 876-929-9200; E-mail: jamaica trv@aol.com; Internet: www.jamaicatravel.com).

October

The end of October in Grand Cayman sees the carnival-like atmosphere of **Pirates Week** (which really lasts ten days and includes a mock invasion of Hog Sty Bay by a mock Blackbeard and company). Visitors and locals dress up like pirates and wenches; music, fireworks, and a variety of competitions take place island-wide. Kids participate, too. Contact the tourism department (☎ **345-949-0623;** Fax: 345-949-4053; Internet: www.caymanislands.ky).

December

The best local *fungi* (Caribbean folk music performed with homemade instruments) bands compete at the **Scratch/Fungi Band Fiesta** on Tortola, BVI. Contact the tourist board at ☎ **800-835-8530** or ☎284-494-3134 or visit the Web site at www.bviwelcome.com.

Chapter 3

Pillow Talk: The Caribbean's Accommodations

By Echo and Kevin Garrett

• •

In This Chapter

▶ Understanding your lodging options

▶ Choosing the best facility for you

▶ Booking the best room in the house

• •

*I*n this section, we introduce you to the Caribbean's accommodation possibilities. We give you honest descriptions and try to make sure that you don't suffer a serious mismatch between your island fantasy and the reality awaiting you on the other side of your hotel door. That way, you can return home crowing about your wonderful experience rather than the resident, not-so-pleasant surprises.

Deciding Which Kind of Accommodation Works for You

The Caribbean runs the gamut in terms of places to stay. High-end accommodations are so fancy that they include a maid, gardener, cook, laundress, and butler, all in starched uniforms, standing ready to antici-pate your every whim. At the lower end of the scale, you can live your desert island fantasy in a beach hut (don't expect air-conditioning!) or in a small guesthouse for less than $75 a night. Our tastes lie some-where in the middle of these two extremes.

Travelers to the Caribbean typically have the following options:

- ✔ Hotels and resorts
- ✔ All-inclusive resorts
- ✔ Villas
- ✔ Condominiums and timeshares
- ✔ Guesthouses

Expectations and reality often clash for first-time travelers in the tropics. Life moves languidly in the Caribbean. Change comes slowly and in small increments — radically different from the instantaneous responses we expect from our point-and-click world. We feel cheated in the United States if our hotel room doesn't have at least two dataport lines, voice-mail that we can personalize, and HBO on the tube. In the Caribbean, concerns are different. In recent years, enormous battles have been waged at some of the region's finer resorts over whether to install phones and air-conditioning in the rooms at all. However, many hoteliers have capitulated and are adding direct-dial phones with dataports. Some small resorts now offer free places to check your e-mail, too, but others will charge you for the service.

Although all our recommended choices in the individual island accommodations chapters are located on the beach and have air-conditioning (unless otherwise noted), understand that some of the sexiest resorts in this region have no air-conditioning, no phone, no television, no alarm clock — not even *USA Today* or CNN.

Hotels and resorts: A variety of options

No matter what you're looking for, you can probably find something that suits your fancy. You'll find a tremendous range of hotel and resort accommodations, from small-budget places that provide a basic room with a bed and a bathroom all the way up to exclusive resorts owned and managed by some of the world's finer chains. The latest trend among Caribbean hotels is the addition of spa services and upgraded workout facilities.

On most islands, building ordinances require that structures be no taller than the tallest coconut tree. On Puerto Rico, St. Thomas, Jamaica, and Aruba, however, you can see high-rise hotels like those on Miami Beach. Chains operate the best properties on Aruba (Marriott, Hyatt, Sonesta, and Radisson), Grand Cayman (Westin, Hyatt, and soon The Ritz-Carlton), and St. Thomas (Marriott and The Ritz-Carlton). But many of the hotels listed in this book have fewer than 100 rooms, and several are considered boutique hotels, stylized and unique in character. We tend to favor these kinds of places.

Hotels and resorts often include meal plans and the use of facilities in their rates. (Chapter 6 discusses the different meal plans.) Even if a hotel or resort doesn't offer all-inclusive packages (explained in the next section), you can usually count on full use of the pool and non-motorized water sports. However, you may have to pay for use of a lounge chair on the beach and snorkeling or other equipment.

We recommend hotels and resorts for

✔ Honeymooners or couples who want to focus on each other.

✔ Families who want programs and sitters close at hand.

✔ Sports lovers who want all the facilities.

✔ First-time visitors to the Caribbean.

✔ Travelers with disabilities, because these places are much more likely to have appropriate facilities.

But staying at a hotel or resort also has its drawbacks:

✔ Many resorts and hotels lack island atmosphere.

✔ You may feel obliged to spend your time on the property, because you've paid so much to be there.

✔ Extra expenses for meals, drinks, and water sports add up quickly, and you're likely to get a shock at checkout if you've been charging everything to your room.

All-inclusive resorts: Simplifying your vacation

The all-inclusive concept, where you shell out the dough for your vacation in advance (with no tipping allowed after you get on the island), is essentially a one-price-buys-all package that includes your hotel room, meals, drinks, and activities. All-inclusive resorts have found their niche because travelers want to simplify their lives. The Caribbean's version of the concept started on Jamaica and now dominates the accommodation scene on that island. You'll run into the all-inclusive concept on Barbados, St. Thomas, and Aruba, and in a smattering of places across most of the other islands, too.

Recently, the top-tier all-inclusive resorts have been duking it out by adding more and more extras. For instance, stung by criticism in the early days that they were cheapskates when it came to food and drink, the big players all now serve premium brand alcohol and have been hiring better and better chefs for their restaurants. Now you may find yourself with half a dozen or so restaurants from which to choose — without ever leaving your resort.

Tipping tips

Many guests at all-inclusive resorts are under the mistaken impression that they do not need to tip baggage handlers at the airport and drivers who get you to and from your resort. That is not the case, and this misunderstanding has unfortunately created tension on both sides. Unless the person helping you is an employee of the resort, assume that you *do* need to tip.

The new battleground, however, appears to be in the spa arena. The words *and Spa* after the name of the all-inclusive resort are becoming almost as ubiquitous as the words *and Casino* after the name of almost every hotel on Aruba. Guests at many spa resorts get one spa treatment (full-body massages and facials are the most popular) per day included in their all-inclusive package.

We like all-inclusive resorts and have included our favorites in this book, along with several smaller boutique hotels and resorts that don't have the big advertising budgets.

The main operators of all-inclusive resorts in the Caribbean are:

- **Sandals** (☎ 800-SANDALS or 305-284-1300; Fax: 305-667-8996; Internet: www.sandals.com), which operates several couples-only properties

- **SuperClubs** (☎ 800-GO-SUPER or 954-925-0925; Fax: 954-925-0334; Internet: www.superclubs.com), which owns numerous properties in Jamaica and a few on other islands

- **Beaches** (☎ 888-232-2437; Internet: www.beaches.com), which has several family-oriented properties on Jamaica with one upscale property geared to adults and older children

- **Divi Resorts** (☎ 800-367-2484; Internet: www.diviresorts.com), which operates nine resorts on six Caribbean islands, including Aruba and Grand Cayman

- **Club Med** (☎ 800-CLUBMED; Internet: www.clubmed.com), which has a few "villages" in the Caribbean

Each company offers packages that allow you to get married for free when you book a honeymoon with them.

One of our favorite features of Sandals and SuperClubs is a cool program that lets you split your time between resorts within each company's range of accommodations. To us, that's the resort equivalent of ordering the fisherman's platter. You get to sample the best of everything. For example, SuperClubs allows you to book a stay at the slightly less expensive Grand Lido Sans Souci and then spend a few days of your minimum six-night stay at the more expensive Grand Lido Negril.

What you get at an all-inclusive resort varies dramatically, and the differences can be confusing. A Web site that rates all-inclusive resorts is www.all-inclusive.com/rate.html. It operates similarly to AAA Diamond Awards, using a ten-star rating, assigning point values to all the services and amenities. Sandals, which obviously has a vested interest, is a partner in the undertaking.

Good candidates for all-inclusive resorts are

- ✔ Honeymooners
- ✔ Families
- ✔ Inexperienced travelers
- ✔ The budget-conscious
- ✔ The super-stressed

The drawbacks to staying at an all-inclusive resort?

- ✔ **In order to feel that you've squeezed every last penny out of your vacation, you may feel obligated to spend all your time on the property, because you've paid so much to be there.** Every island is exactly the same when viewed from the cushy confines of an all-inclusive. You miss what makes the island special after you've traveled so far to get there.
- ✔ **Rah-rah activity instructors can wear on your nerves.**

Villas: Vacationing with the comforts of home

Villa is a broad word in the Caribbean. Basically, it means a rental property. Properties ranging from princely digs to modest bungalows fall into this category.

A villa promises two luxuries: space and good kitchen facilities. Villas usually offer more privacy than hotels and resorts and are tucked away on gated lots with either sea or mountain views. If you like the comforts of home, a villa is the way to go. Villas are particularly popular in the Virgin Islands, Jamaica, and Puerto Rico.

Villas rent for anywhere from less than $1,000 a week all the way up to thousands of dollars a day. Three couples traveling together can easily rent a villa for a week for less than $1,000 per person. We've been amazed at how reasonably priced some drop-dead gorgeous villas are, particularly on St. John. You can also find some good deals in Jamaica. Many villas must be booked for a minimum of a week.

We recommend booking a villa through a professional management company that's responsible for renting out and maintaining the house when the owner isn't on the island. (See our recommendation in the next paragraph or look at the back of the ad sections in *Caribbean Travel & Life* or *Islands* magazines.) Renting a villa from an individual can be a little iffy, because the Caribbean has a way of taking a toll on even the finest resorts. Unless an owner is extremely diligent about upkeep, a place can quickly slip below par. You also run the risk of renting a place where the decor looks like leftovers from a yard sale. In this book, we include only villas that we've inspected personally and recently.

For the preeminent source on villas, try **Unusual Villas** (409F North Hamilton Street, Richmond, VA 23221; ☎ **800-846-7280** or 804-288-2823; Fax: 804-342-9016; E-mail: johng@unusualvillarentals.com; Internet: www.unusualvillarentals.com). Owner John Greer, who has been specializing in villas since 1992, has an award-winning Web site with more than 1,500 pages dedicated to villas. He has more than 100 villas for rent on Barbados and Jamaica. On St. Thomas, he handles rentals for about 50 villas, and he deals with rentals on a total of 30 Caribbean islands.

Two other good sources for villas are: **WIMCO** (☎ **800-449-1553** or 401-849-8012; Fax: 401-847-6290; Internet: www.wimco.com), which represents villas on Barbados, Grand Cayman, the Virgin Islands, and several other Caribbean isles; and **Island Destinations** (☎ **888-454-4422** or 914-833-3300; Fax: 914-833-3318; Internet: www.islanddestinations.com), which represents villas on Jamaica, Puerto Rico, and the Virgin Islands as well as a few other Caribbean islands, and offers wedding and honeymoon coordinators.

So that you don't waste time and money on duplicate supplies, check with the management company about what the villa will have on hand for your use. Depending on the unit, you may be treated to a welcome platter of fresh fruit and a bottle of wine. You may find that you get access to a vehicle as part of the rental as well.

We recommend villas for

- ✔ Families
- ✔ A group of friends (You'd better be close, though, or you run the risk of fights over the master bedroom, which invariably has some cool feature that everyone covets.)
- ✔ Honeymooners or couples craving privacy
- ✔ Independent travelers who want to connect with the island

But staying at a home-away-from-home can also have a downside:

- ✔ You don't get the extensive dining facilities and other amenities of a resort.

- ✔ A villa may not offer daily maid service and other niceties (like a pool or Jacuzzi) that you consider vital to your relaxation.

- ✔ Few are located right on the beach; resorts usually snag the prime real estate.

- ✔ You definitely won't get (or be subjected to, depending on your point of view) the nightly entertainment that almost every Caribbean hotel trumpets.

- ✔ The good news is you're isolated. The bad news is you're isolated, so you'd better really like your traveling companion.

- ✔ Of all the travel options, villas are least likely to live up to their brochure promises.

Condos and timeshares: Apartment-style living

Condos and timeshares are popular options on Aruba, Grand Cayman, and the U.S. Virgin Islands (mainly St. Thomas). With these properties, you get apartment-style accommodations in a hotel setting. The amenities range greatly. At busy La Cabana on Aruba, for example, the experience isn't much different from staying at a large resort. (See Chapter 8 for a full review of the property.) The Ritz-Carlton on St. Thomas, the Westin St. John, and the Aruba Marriott have all entered the timeshare business in recent years with units that are on the same property as their respective resorts. Prices are comparable to what you'd pay at a hotel, but you almost always have kitchen facilities.

We recommend condos and timeshares for

- ✔ **Families.** You can feed your kids what you want and not have to suffer disapproving looks from the honeymooners at the next table when Junior flips his soggy cereal on the floor.

- ✔ **A group of friends.** Try to choose friends that you are familiar traveling with or with whom you feel comfortable discussing some ground rules before you go, however.

- ✔ **Older couples looking for quiet.**

- ✔ **Long-term vacationers.** Cooking your own meals is a great money-saving tactic for an extended stay on an island.

- ✔ **Independent travelers who want to connect with the island and its people.**

What are some drawbacks of staying at a condo or timeshare?

✔ You have all the comforts of home, *plus* all the work.

✔ The amenities are limited.

✔ You're trusting your tropical dream to someone else's decorating taste.

✔ When dinnertime comes, you're the staff as well as the diner.

Guesthouses: Living like a local

If you want lodging that resembles a bed-and-breakfast, guesthouses are the Caribbean's answer. In a guesthouse, only a few rooms are rented out, and the owner/manager lives on the property.

Guesthouses work well for bargain-hunters and those who like being under someone else's roof. You may get a light breakfast as part of your rate, which is usually $100 or less per night. If you plan to explore a great deal, this option may be good for you, too — you'll have a place to come home to after you satisfy your wanderlust.

We recommend guesthouses for

✔ Older couples who like the bed-and-breakfast concept

✔ Long-term vacationers on tight budgets

✔ The independent traveler who needs a home base

Here are some of the drawbacks of staying at a guesthouse:

✔ You may be far from the beach, without a pool.

✔ The digs may not be glamorous.

✔ You may not get along with your host.

✔ Housekeeping standards vary widely.

✔ If there's a problem, you're stuck dealing one-on-one with the house owner.

Getting a Great Room

Somebody has to get the best room in the house; it may as well be you. This is where the reservations agent in the hotel comes in handy: He will actually know which rooms are the best. Let the person know of any special event you're celebrating or any concerns you have. Ask how long the walk is from your room to the beach — you may find out that it's across the road, like most of the rooms at Hyatt Regency Grand Cayman. Ask the reservations agent which room he would want to book for a special occasion. If you have small children, ask which room is nearest to the kids' program.

Be clear about what's important to you. For example, some of the larger rooms at Caneel Bay, an exclusive resort on St. John, are less pricey because they aren't as close to the beach. If we were traveling with our boys, we'd gladly walk the few extra steps in return for more space for the four of us.

Specify what size bed you want, or you may find yourself with two twins — especially on British islands like Barbados.

Also check to see if the hotel is in the midst of renovation; if it is, request a room away from the work site. Ask if the rooms have been refurbished recently. The salt-water air, sun, and sand wreak havoc with bedspreads and other furnishings. You want something as fresh as possible, so ask for the most recently redone rooms.

If your resort isn't air-conditioned and relies on trade winds and ceiling fans for cooling, try to get a room as close to the sea as possible. You'll get more of a breeze if you're on the second floor or higher. Corner rooms with more windows give you that much more breeze coming through. At The Ritz-Carlton in St. Thomas, for example, the suites occupy the far-end corner of the building overhanging the bluff with a view of the harbor. Although the suites are air-conditioned, you can also open the windows out to the sea, as well as the doors onto the private wraparound decks.

Many hotels now offer nonsmoking rooms; by all means ask for one if smoke bothers you. Inquire, too, about your room's proximity to any of the hotel's open-air restaurants, beach bars with steel-pan bands, family pools with screaming kids, and discos blaring reggae — all sources of irritating noise that can be torture if you're a light sleeper.

If you aren't happy with your room when you arrive, talk to the front desk manager. For instance, we recently stayed at a resort where we were given a lovely room right on the beach. However, when we walked out the front door of our room, the trash receptacle for the hotel was behind a nearby wall and the smell was overpowering. If the wind hadn't shifted, we would have been in the manager's office. In a case like that, speak up. If the hotel has another room, you'll be accommodated, within reason.

For tips on saving money on your accommodations, see our list of pointers in Chapter 6.

Chapter 4

Planning Ahead for Special Travel Needs

By Echo and Kevin Garrett

● ●

In This Chapter

▶ Planning a family trip

▶ Taking the plunge (and we don't mean snorkeling)

▶ Enjoying an island honeymoon

▶ Searching for senior discounts

▶ Selecting the best sites for travelers with disabilities

▶ Locating gay– and lesbian-friendly businesses

● ●

Caribbean travel planning seems to inspire some common questions: How family-friendly are the islands? Where can couples honeymoon or even tie the knot? What discounts and privileges are available for seniors? Which islands have the best facilities for travelers with disabilities? And which put out the welcome mat for gay and lesbian travelers? If you're among those who have special needs or concerns about your Caribbean visit, read on — our discoveries can help you prepare for a delightful, rather than disappointing, getaway.

Ensuring a Fun, Safe Family Vacation

These days we're part of a growing number of families spending their summer and holiday vacations in the Caribbean. Eager to take advantage of this trend, hotels and resorts are scrambling to add facilities and services appealing to pint-sized customers. And that's not a tough task: Between the pool and the warm Caribbean Sea, the kids are already enthralled. Add in games like limbo, crab races, and reggae dance contests, and they're over the moon. And relatively new programs offering cultural and ecological exploration impress parents and children alike. For instance, your child could spend the morning learning from a marine biologist how to protect coral reefs or with an archeologist digging for Indian artifacts.

The last few summers we've spent our family vacations on Aruba and Jamaica, but all the islands mentioned in this book have family-friendly resorts, restaurants, and activities. Look for the Kid Friendly icon, which indicates our top choices.

Flying with kids

For us, probably the toughest part of traveling with our kids is that time-worn question, "Are we there yet?" Getting there with kids in tow is definitely not half the fun, but for most island destinations, the trip really isn't that bad. To us, it sure beats a long car trip.

Don't forget that when traveling internationally, children — babies, too — must have either a certified copy of a birth certificate (with a raised seal) or an official passport (see Chapter 7). Here are some other things to keep in mind when traveling with young children:

✔ Children's airfares are typically discounted 50%, but during peak season, the reduction may be as little as 33%.

✔ You can't expect many empty seats on Caribbean flights, so don't gamble on being able to seat your infant (under age 2) beside you. If you both want to be comfortable, buy a seat for your child. Ask about special children's fares.

✔ Order a kid's meal when you reserve your flight and ask about the airline's rules regarding carseats.

✔ Because Caribbean flights are so full, and because of the stringent new rules, you'll probably have to check your child's stroller. Make sure that you label the stroller with your name and where you'll be staying on the island.

✔ Make sure that you're seated together on the plane. Double check with your travel agent or with the airline directly. If you don't have boarding passes, get to the airport extra early to ensure that you get seats together. Caribbean flights are usually packed, and we've seen families separated by several rows.

✔ The bulkhead, which has extra space, is in high demand, but you may get lucky if you request it early.

✔ Pack four times the amount of favorite snacks you think you'll need. Delays can be lengthy these days and airport food prices are sky-high. Baby wipes (even if your children are older) come in handy, too. Also bring a large bottle of water for each child — especially if you're changing planes. For babies and toddlers, bring a large supply of diapers onboard with you, too.

✔ Let your child bring some small favorite toys. But don't bring expensive electronic ones that are likely to get misplaced or stolen. (Yes, we learned that the hard way.) On islands with high poverty levels, like Jamaica, we like to bring boxes of crayons and small items that we can leave behind for island children.

✔ To relieve painful pressure on eardrums, bring chewing gum for older children. Nurse or give babies a bottle on takeoff and landing to keep their ears from hurting.

✔ If you rent a car, request a carseat in advance. If a hotel is arranging transportation for you, ask if the vehicle being sent will have seat belts. We've found that even family-friendly resorts often send vans and cars with nary a seat belt in sight.

✔ For the return trip, ask at the hotel what food is served at the airport. If it doesn't sound like something your child would eat, request a packed lunch for the plane from the resort, which is often happy to accommodate you. Even if you have to pay a small fee, it's worth it, because food service is often pretty skimpy at island airports. Recently, we were stuck for eight hours in the departure lounge in Barbados along with several other families. The lone restaurant ran out of food.

Choosing a family-friendly resort

We've learned over the years that although most major resorts claim to have children's programs, the offerings differ greatly. Take a tour of the facilities before dropping off your kids. Some of the ritzier resorts accept children only at certain times of year, and then the staff's attitude may be one of tolerance rather than enthusiasm. A children's program in such a place may consist of a bored sitter stuck in a small room with several kids. We actually got a press release from one place trumpeting its kids' "program," which consisted of setting out cookies and milk for children each evening.

Always check before you book to make sure that you're getting what you think you're getting. Here are some good questions to ask:

✔ What is the ratio of teachers to children?

✔ How are the ages divided?

✔ How much beach or pool time do they get (with expert supervision, of course)?

✔ Where and what do the children eat?

Be sure to alert the workers to any food allergies your child has and double-check to make sure they really understand.

Some programs won't accept children who are not potty-trained. Others have skimpy or nonexistent offerings for teens. If you travel during a slow period, you may find that the kids' program hours have been cut or even eliminated entirely in response to diminished numbers of participants. If you've made special reservations for an evening out, double check the day before with the kids' program to be sure it will be operating. Baby-sitting services often require 24-hour notice, so you don't want to be caught scrambling at the last minute.

Make sure to let the children's program workers know where to find you in case of an emergency. If your children sunburn easily, slather on waterproof sunscreen first thing in the morning (it takes about a half hour before it starts working), because the child-care workers probably won't have time to apply it as painstakingly as you do.

Overall, rest assured that West Indians love children. So even if your resort doesn't have a formal children's program, you can find a reliable baby-sitter through your concierge or hotel manager if you want an evening out. Always give at least 24 hours notice and expect to pay $8 to $10 per hour for one or two children. Ask how the sitter will get home, too. We always give extra money for cab or bus fare if we're out late.

If your kids are older, almost all the islands have enough adventure activities to entice even the most stubborn teen or 'tween. Of course, the water sports are terrific everywhere in the Caribbean. We especially recommend the ATV riding and hiking on Jamaica; hiking and sailing in the Virgin Islands; spelunking and surfing on Puerto Rico; and *SNUBA* (a combination of snorkeling and diving where participants breathe through an airline that is connected to a boat on the surface; certification is not necessary and children can partake in the activity as well), windsurfing, and horseback riding in Aruba. Teens who are into scuba diving will enjoy Grand Cayman, but we've heard complaints of boredom from those who don't go for water sports. We think Barbados would be too buttoned up for teens as well.

You may want to warn teens that drug offenses are taken extremely seriously on the islands, and that if they get into trouble, they're considered guilty until proven innocent.

At family-friendly resorts, kids 12 and under usually stay and eat for free, although you may have to pay a daily fee for using the children's program. (Check when you reserve; it's usually about $30 to $80 per day.) During the summer low season (approximately mid-April through early December), off-season rates drop anywhere from 15 to 60%. Islands that offer excellent summer specials for families include Aruba, Barbados, Grand Cayman, St. Croix, and St. Thomas. Look for the Kid Friendly icon throughout the hotel chapters to find them.

Unfortunately, the typical kids' menu in the Caribbean is the greasy diet you find in the U.S.: burgers, fries, chicken fingers, and pizza. Fresh fruit is cheap and plentiful on most islands and makes a great snack. Just be sure to wash or peel it before your kids eat it.

For more information on traveling with kids, pick up Paris Permenter and John Bigley's book *Caribbean with Kids*.

Saying "I Do" in the Caribbean

According to *Brides* magazine, more and more couples are choosing to get hitched abroad. With the exception of Aruba, the Caribbean offers great options.

Almost all the larger hotels we mention in this book have on-site wedding planners, as do many of the smaller ones. Even better, basic weddings at most of the all-inclusive resorts are free. A company called **Weddings on the Move, Inc.** (☎ **800-444-6967** or 262-629-4499; Fax: 262-629-1740; E-mail: weddings@idoweddings.com; Internet: www.idoweddings.com) specializes in planning island weddings. If you prefer to handle everything yourself long distance, check out The Knot (www.theknot.com), where you can find free listings of wedding vendors, plus advice on good wedding locations and tips on how to choose vendors.

On St. Thomas, which has many, many weddings each year, Debra Williams, founder of **Fantasia's Island Romance** (168 Crow Bay, St. Thomas, USVI 00802; ☎ **866-ROMANCE**; Fax: 340-774-8009; E-mail: fantasia@islands.vi; Internet: www.fantasiaweddings.com or http://romancingtheislands.com), has been coordinating wedding services from the simplest ceremonies to lavish affairs on yachts since 1990.

For the basic legalities of a Caribbean wedding, contact the **Caribbean Tourism Organization** (☎ **212-635-9530**; E-mail: get2cto@dorsai.org; Internet: www.doitcaribbean.com) to request its "Weddings Requirement Chart," which tells you everything you need to know at a glance. Because the rules of a foreign wedding can change suddenly, though, call the tourist board about two months ahead of time for any last-minute updates. Generally speaking, the waiting period — if there is one — is only a day or two. The license fees range from $20 and the price of a stamp in Puerto Rico to $156.50 in the Cayman Islands.

Table 4-1 gives you the scoop on island-to-island requirements for nuptials in each location.

Table 4-1			Wedding Requirements	
Country	*Fee*	*Blood Test*	*Waiting Period*	*What You Need*
Aruba	No	No	14 days	Passports or original birth certificates and photo IDs, proof (original copy) of divorce or death certificate of former spouse (if applicable). Contact the tourist board for additional information.
Barbados	$75	No	None	Passports, proof of divorce or death certificate of former spouse (if applicable), letter from the authorized officiate performing service.
BVIs	$110	No	3 days	Passports or original birth certificates and photo IDs, proof (original copy) of divorce or death certificate of former spouse (if applicable).
Cayman Islands	$156.50	No	None	Passports or birth certificates and photo IDs, original or certified copies of divorce decree or former spouse's death certificate (if applicable), return or ongoing ticket, proofs of entry (Cayman Islands International Immigration Department pink slips or cruise ship boarding passes), letter from authorized officiating marriage officer.

Country	Fee	Blood Test	Waiting Period	What You Need
Jamaica	$6	No	3 days (varies with programs at different hotels and resorts)	Certified copies of birth certificates that include father's name, proof of divorce or death certificate of former spouse (if applicable).
Puerto Rico	$20	Yes (a blood test must be taken in Puerto Rico within 10 days of the wedding)	For the license send a request in writing 2 months in advance to Department of Health, Demographic Registry Office, Box 11854 Fernandez Juncos Station, Santurce, PR 00910 (☎787-728-7980).	U.S. driver's license or passport for non-U.S. citizens; proof of divorce or death certificate of former spouse (if applicable); letter accompanying Application for Marriage stating date of visit, length of stay, preference of date if having ceremony performed by a judge
USVIs	$50	No	8 days from the receipt of the notarized application; couples need not be on the islands when the application arrives.	Proof of divorce or death certificate of former spouse; $200 to be married by judge (if applicable); letter accompanying Application for Marriage stating date of visit, length of stay, preference of date if having ceremony performed by a judge.

Planning the Perfect Honeymoon

The Caribbean is a paradise for couples in search of romance. Honeymoon packages at most resorts are generous, even creative. Some all-inclusive resorts — on Jamaica in particular — are devoted exclusively to couples. The downside is that you'll be just two faces in a flock of lovebirds. In other words, don't expect anyone to go to great lengths and deliver beyond what's promised in your honeymoon package. Often, the honeymoon package is good enough, though, because you can be assured that you won't encounter conventioneers, family reunions, or young children.

If you have any special requests, fax them to the concierge about a month before your arrival; you want to give your hotel or resort plenty of time to make your dreams come true. Don't worry, they're up to the challenge. One concierge told us of a groom who requested different colored satin sheets and matching rose petals for each night of his honeymoon. The staff had to call all over the place to find king-size satin sheets in a rainbow of colors, but they did it.

Cashing In on Senior Discounts

Older people are treated with great respect in Caribbean cultures. However, you usually won't get special privileges or discounts for being over a certain age. Your best bet at getting discounts is on the front end by making reservations through a travel club for seniors.

If you're over 50, join **AARP,** formerly the American Association of Retired Persons (601 E St. NW, Washington, DC 20049; ☎ **800-424-3410** or 202-434-AARP; Internet: www.aarp.org). Always mention your AARP membership (which costs $12.50 a year) when you make reservations. You'll get discounts ranging from 5 to 20% on car rentals with Avis, Hertz, and National, as well as with cruises, hotels, and airlines.

Some car-rental agencies have maximum age limits; if you're over 65, you may not be able to rent with some agencies in the Caribbean.

Many airlines, including American, United, Continental, US Airways, and TWA, offer discount programs for senior travelers (ages 62 and above), but restrictions often apply on popular Caribbean routes. Rate reductions are worth asking about whenever you book a flight.

In some Caribbean cities, people over the age of 60 receive a slightly reduced admission at theaters, museums, and other attractions, and they can often get discount fares on public transportation. Carry iden-tification with proof of age, just in case.

Here are some more good resources for senior travelers:

✔ *The Mature Traveler,* a monthly 12-page newsletter on senior citi-zen travel, is a valuable resource. It is available by subscription ($29.95 plus $2 shipping for a year) from GEM Publishing Group, Box 50400, Reno, NV 89513-0400. GEM also publishes *The Book of Deals,* a collection of more than 1,000 senior discounts on airlines, lodging, tours, and attractions around the country; it's available for $9.95 by calling ☎ **800-460-6676** or e-mailing maturetrav@ aol.com.

✔ Another helpful publication is *101 Tips for the Mature Trav-eler,* available from Grand Circle Travel (347 Congress St., Suite 3A, Boston, MA 02210; ☎ **800-221-2610** or 617-350-7500;

Fax: 617-350-6206; Internet: www.gct.com), a travel agency specializing in vacations for seniors, including Caribbean cruises.
Traveling companions must be age 13 or older.

✔ **SAGA International Holidays** (222 Berkeley St., Boston, MA
02116; ☎ **877-265-6862;** E-mail: sales_info@sagaholidays.com;
Internet: www.sagaholidays.com) offers cruises in the Caribbean
for those 50 and older.

Ensuring Access for Travelers with Disabilities

Generally speaking, most of the islands in this book offer some options
for travelers with disabilities. Of course, public spaces in Puerto Rico
and the U.S. Virgin Islands are required by law to be wheelchair accessible, but at this writing, San Juan, St. Thomas, and St. Croix were the
only Caribbean destinations serviced by wheelchair-accessible van
companies.

Aruba, Barbados, Jamaica, and Grand Cayman have some wheelchair-
accessible hotel and restaurant facilities, but for the most part,
wheelchair-bound travelers will find accessibility still at third-world
standards in the Caribbean — with the exception of San Juan, St.
Thomas, and St. Croix. The mountainous British Virgin Islands present
very challenging travel and lack easy access. Traveling on those
islands requires going up and down lots of steps and getting on and off
a variety of modes of transportation. You won't find sidewalks there,
and many roads are unpaved.

The cruise industry is recognizing slowly that the needs of travelers
with disabilities have been overlooked in the Caribbean. By 2001, more
than 1,200 wheelchair-accessible staterooms (twice as many as in
2000) will be available on Caribbean cruise ships each week. New
cruise ships typically have a larger number of wheelchair-accessible
cabins than in the past. However, many of the Caribbean's ports still
remain inaccessible.

Howard McCoy, R.N., is a tour operator and planner who runs
Accessible Journeys (35 West Sellers Ave., Ridley Park, PA 19078;
☎ **800-846-4537** or 610-521-0339; Fax: 610-521-6959; E-mail: sales@
disabilitytravel.com; Internet: www.disabilitytravel.com).
The agency focuses primarily on travelers with mobility challenges
and is now the largest cruise wholesaler for wheelchair vacations in
the world. The company sponsors five to eight Caribbean cruise
groups with guaranteed space and guaranteed departure annually.

Travelers with disabilities may want to use a travel agent who specializes in special-needs trips. One of the better outfits that books

Caribbean cruises is **Flying Wheels Travel** (143 West Bridge or P.O. Box 382, Owatonna, MN 55060; ☎ **507-451-5005;** Fax: 507-451-1685; E-mail: thq@ll.net; Internet: www.flyingwheelstravel.com).

A World of Options, a 658-page book of resources for travelers with disabilities, covers everything from biking trips to scuba outfitters. It costs $35 and is available from Mobility International USA (P.O. Box 10767, Eugene, OR 97440; ☎ **541-343-1284,** voice and TTY; Fax: 503-343-6812; Internet: www.miusa.org). For information by phone, call the **Travel Information Service** at ☎ **215-456-9603** (voice) or 215-456-9602 (TTY).

The **Oxygen Traveler** (☎ **937-433-6007;** Fax: 937-848-7949; E-mail: oxygen0202@aol.com; Internet: www.access-able.com/tips/oxy.html) is not a travel agency but helps travelers who require oxygen and durable medical equipment for international and cruise travel. The company makes arrangements for transporting equipment to ships, airports, or hotels by working with travel agencies, health-care providers, and the cruise line industry. Right now, the company has contacts in Aruba, Barbados, Jamaica, Puerto Rico, and the U.S. Virgin Islands. The Oxygen Traveler may also be able to make arrangements on Tortola in the British Virgin Islands. Currently, it does not have any contacts in the Cayman Islands.

Vision-impaired travelers can contact the **American Foundation for the Blind** (11 Penn Plaza, Suite 300, New York, NY 10001; ☎ **800-232-5463;** Internet: www.asb.org) for information on traveling with seeing-eye dogs.

Traveling to Gay- and Lesbian-Friendly Destinations

The Caribbean should not be confused with New York, London, or any other metropolis where gays and lesbians enjoy relatively open lifestyles. In much of the Caribbean, homophobic attitudes are common. Most islands, like some U.S. states, have anti-gay laws on the books. The former British colonies in particular (like Jamaica and the Cayman Islands) frown on gay and lesbian relationships.

But this is not to say that gays and lesbians cannot vacation comfortably in the Caribbean. Shortly after the Grand Cayman flap (a cruise ship carrying a gay and lesbian group was denied landing rights), community members from St. John welcomed with love beads a small cruise ship carrying lesbian travelers. In general, the discreet can travel virtually anywhere in the Caribbean without fear of hassle. Most hotels are indifferent to the issue. Prominent exceptions are the Sandals and SuperClubs chains and a few other all-inclusive outfits.

They call themselves "couples-only" resorts, defined in strictly male/female terms.

Puerto Rico is home to the region's most visible gay scene and features a robust nightlife in San Juan. The U.S. and British Virgin Islands are other places covered in this guide where gays and lesbians will feel most comfortable.

A handful of Caribbean lodgings, although not necessarily gay-owned, have classified themselves as gay-friendly.

In San Juan, Puerto Rico:

- ✔ **Atlantic Beach Hotel** (☎ **888-611-6900;** Fax: 787-721-6917; Internet: www.atlanticbeachhotel.net)

- ✔ **Hosteria Del Mar** (☎ **8787-727-3302** or 787-727-3302; Fax: 787-268-0772; Internet: www.prhta@smallhotels.com)

- ✔ **L'Habitation Beach** (☎ **787-727-2499;** Fax: 787-727-2599; E-mail: habitationbeach@msn.com; Internet: www.habitationbeach.com)

- ✔ **Numero Uno** (☎ **866-726-5010** or 787-726-5010)

In the U.S. Virgin Islands:

- ✔ **Cormorant Beach Club Hotel,** St. Croix (☎ **800-548-4460** or 340-778-8920; E-mail: vacations@cormorant-stcroix.com; Internet: www.cormorant-stcroix.com)

- ✔ **Inn at Blackbeard's Castle,** St. Thomas (☎ **800-344-5771** or 340-776-1234; Internet: www.blackbeard.com)

- ✔ **Maho Bay and its sister properties,** St. John (☎ **800-392-9004** or 212-472-9453; E-mail: mahobay@maho.org; Internet: www.maho.org)

- ✔ **Sandcastle on the Beach,** St. Croix (☎ **800-524-2018** or 340-772-1205; Internet: www.sandcastleonthebeach.com)

In the British Virgin Islands:

- ✔ **Fort Recovery Estates** (☎ **800-367-8455** or 284-495-4354; Internet: www.fortrecovery.com)

- ✔ **Cooper Island Beach Club** (☎ **800-542-4624** or 413-863-3162; E-mail: info@cooper-island.com; Internet: www.cooper-island.com)

In Jamaica:

- ✔ **Hotel Mocking Bird Hill** (☎876-993-7267; Fax: 876-993-1133; Internet: www.hotelmockingbirdhill.com)

Part II
Tying Up the
Loose Ends

The 5th Wave   By Rich Tennant

"I asked for a seat near the steel drum,
but I don't see any steel drum."

In this part . . .

So you've decided which islands you want to visit and what time of year to go. Now what? In this part, we give you advice for booking the trip of your dreams — either through a travel agent or on your own. We help you determine the fastest and most economic ways to travel to your destination.

We also show you how to estimate the cost of your trip and keep it within your budget. Finally, we walk you through the details you need to know in order to have a smooth travel experience, from securing the necessary paperwork to packing like a pro.

Chapter 5

Making Your Travel Arrangements

By Echo and Kevin Garrett

● ●

In This Chapter

▶ Finding a knowledgeable travel agent

▶ Researching and booking online

▶ Grabbing a great deal on a flight

▶ Locating the right airline for your destination

▶ Deciding if package tours are right for you

▶ Cruising to the Caribbean

● ●

*T*raveling to your dream destination in the cheapest, most comfortable, and fastest way possible is a chief concern when you start to plan a trip. You may save a bundle if you read this chapter before making reservations the old-fashioned way.

In this chapter, we tell you whether you're wiser to do it yourself when booking your trip or work with a travel agent. We give you the latest tips on getting the best airfare and tell you which airlines fly to which destinations. We explain package tours, including what they mean for your wallet and what impact they have on your Caribbean experience. And, for those of you who think you'd rather float than fly, we offer some information on cruises, too.

Tapping the Talents of a Travel Agent

In recent years, the Web has made booking trips incredibly easy, so much so that you may start to wonder if you need a travel agent at all. The answer depends on you. During our travels, we've met many people who have booked their Caribbean vacations online. Armed with this book and a do-it-yourself attitude, you should have no problem going it alone. However, if you aren't Web savvy, if you like to talk over your choices with an expert, or if your trip is at all complicated (for example, you're island-hopping or making several airline connections), the safest bet is to go through a travel agent.

Getting the most for your money

Airlines and resorts have slashed travel agent commissions or eliminated them altogether, throwing travel agencies into turmoil. As a result, some travel agents now charge customers fees, such as $10 for an airline booking or up to $100 for planning a trip. More-complex trip planning may be based on an hourly fee — or you may not have to pay a penny, depending on the agency's business policy.

The agent's fee may be a small price to pay, because a savvy travel agent can save you hundreds — even thousands — of dollars as well as save you some headaches in the rapidly changing world of travel that we're all encountering. Travel agents are often aware of discounts, specials, and other promotions involving air travel, car rentals, and hotel accommodations. A knowledgeable agent can snag you a well-priced rental car with an upgrade and steer you to a better hotel room for about the same price as you plan to spend on an inferior place. A top-flight travel agent will also go the extra mile by finding a cheaper flight that doesn't require you to change planes several times en route. Or if the airline suddenly changes a schedule at the last minute — which is happening a lot in the Caribbean right now — messing up your carefully planned dream trip, a good agent can quickly untangle the mess.

Unfortunately, you may have a hard time finding that top-flight, knowledgeable travel agent who can plan your dream vacation for much less money than you'd imagined. Many travel agents have little practical experience with the Caribbean; in fact, after you read this book, you'll know far more than most! And if your travel agent has only glimpsed the Caribbean through Web surfing and brochures, you take a gamble if you rely on his or her choices. (Believe us, we've seen Caribbean resorts use every trick in their promotional materials to make their pools look gargantuan, their landscaping impossibly lush, and their location prime seafront.) If your friends can't recommend a knowledgeable travel agent, take a look at our list of Caribbean specialists in the next section.

We hate to be cynical, but most travel agents never even see some of the best resorts. Plus, many of these agents get incentives to steer clients to certain resorts. We've encountered people who've been told to skip some of the best resorts in the Caribbean in favor of large resorts that we know divvy out such rewards to loyal agents. The way the average travel agent explores an island is to take a trip sponsored by a big resort operator such as Sandals, for example. Sandals frequently brings a large group of agents in for what's called a *familiarization trip,* or *fam* for short.

Can you guess which resort has been named tops among travel agents worldwide for six years running? Surprise! It's Sandals.

To get the most benefit from your travel agent, do a little homework on your destination. We've already done much of the legwork for you by eliminating the peripheral attractions, substandard hotels, and blah restaurants that other guidebooks dutifully catalog. If you have Internet access, check prices on the Web before you meet with a travel agent, so that you'll be able to gauge how plugged in the travel agent is to the Caribbean scene. (See "Booking Your Trip Online" later in this chapter for more information.) Travel agents have little incentive to spend a great deal of time researching the best schedule and fare for you now that airlines have slashed their commissions. Arming yourself with some idea of what you want and the available fares will make your meeting or session with your travel agent far more productive.

Locating Caribbean specialists

The **Caribbean Tourism Organization** provides names of its recommended travel agents at ☎ **212-635-9530** or on the Web at www. doitcaribbean.com. Another source is **The Agency Coalition for Caribbean Tourism** (☎ **800-931-ACCT**), which will match you with the Caribbean travel agent nearest you. You can go online to find travel agents specializing in the Caribbean at the **Association of Retail Travel Agents** (www.artaonline.com) or the **American Society of Travel Agents** (www.astanet.com).

TourScan (☎ **800-962-2080** or 203-655-8091; Internet: www.tourscan. com) has specialized in the Caribbean since 1987. Twice a year it compiles information on all the different packages offered by tour operators, who often have prices that vary by hundreds of dollars for the exact same resort. Then it factors in the rack rates of upscale Caribbean hotels, smaller boutique hotels, guesthouses, and inns often not known by travel agents or carried by tour operators. The company also inputs information on bulk package airfares. Through its computerized system, the agency can then scan for the absolute best bargain package and come up with customized packages including airfare — even for unique and upscale places that normally don't offer any packages. All of this information makes bargain hunting a breeze. This agency offers the lowdown on 2,000 properties on 57 islands in the Caribbean, the Bahamas, and Bermuda. The information is available by catalog or on its Web site, which answers common questions. Trust us, TourScan can smooth the way.

Some agencies have narrower specialties, focusing on a particular island or type of vacation. For example, **Caribbean Connection Plus Limited** (☎ **800-893-1100** or 203-261-8603; Fax: 203-261-8295) is an especially good travel agency well-versed in assembling island-hopping packages. The agency covers 47 islands in the Caribbean as well as

Bermuda and the Bahamas. The no-nonsense owner knows her stuff and has been traveling to the Caribbean since 1967.

If you can get up and go at the drop of a straw hat, try **Changes in L'Attitudes** (3080 East Bay Dr., Largo, FL 33771; ☎ **800-330-8272** or 727-573-3536; Fax: 727-573-2497; Internet: www.changes.com). This agency, which has specialized in the Caribbean since 1985, has a terrific Web site that connects you to tons of resorts. It also lists specials and promotions with a heavy concentration on Jamaica with offerings on Aruba, the Cayman Islands, the U.S. Virgin Islands, and Barbados. Honeymooners and sailors will find some good deals here. If you register your e-mail address, the agency frequently sends out notices of deeply discounted, last-minute trips if you're able to travel within 21, 14, or 7 days.

If you think that you want to stay at an all-inclusive resort, **All-Inclusive Vacations** (21999 Van Buren St., Suite 4, Grand Terrace, CA 92313; ☎ **800-944-3862** or 909-824-8825; E-mail: jamaica@all-inclusive.com; Internet: www.no-problem.com) has specialized in discounted all-inclusive packages since 1991 and handles Sandals, Beaches, and Club Med. Its excellent Web site answers many common questions about all-inclusives.

Exploring Package Tours

Package tours are not the same thing as escorted tours, so if you're picturing something like "12 islands in 14 days" and being herded around in a group on a bus, don't worry. That's not the way anybody tours the Caribbean. (If you want that sort of trip, the closest thing would be a cruise ship that stopped at three or four ports.)

Defining our terms

Package tours are simply a way of buying your airfare and accommodations (and sometimes your car rental) at the same time, at a discounted rate. For popular destinations like the Caribbean, packages are a smart way to go if you don't want to deal with a travel agent. They save you a ton of money, and they're an easy introduction to the islands.

In many cases, a package that includes airfare, hotel, and transportation to and from the airport will cost you less than you'd pay for the hotel alone if you booked it yourself. That's because packages are sold in bulk to tour operators, who resell them to the public.

Packages vary as much as the islands themselves. Some packages offer a better class of hotels than others. Some offer the same hotels for lower prices. Some offer flights on scheduled airlines, while others book charters. In some packages, your choices of accommodations and travel days may be limited. Some packages will allow you to add on just a few excursions or escorted day trips (at prices lower than you'd pay if you booked them yourself).

Finding the best deal

Each destination usually has one or two packagers that are better than the rest because they buy in even bigger bulk. The time you spend shopping around will be well rewarded.

A good place to start looking is the travel section of your local Sunday newspaper. Also check the ads in the back of national travel magazines like *Caribbean Travel & Life, Islands, Travel & Leisure, National Geographic Traveler,* and *Condé Nast Traveler.*

If you don't want to research packages on your own, **Liberty Travel** will do it for you (☎ **888-271-1586,** or check local listings for a location near you; Internet: www.libertytravel.com). Liberty, with more than 50 years in the business, is the sixth-largest travel agency in the United States and usually boasts a full-page ad in Sunday papers. You won't get much in the way of service, but Liberty offers a quick way to find out about several Caribbean tour packages. Liberty books the bulk of its Caribbean packages with American Airlines.

Here are some packagers we like:

- ✓ **West Indies Management Company** (P.O. Box 1461, Newport, RI 02840; ☎ **800-932-3222** or 401-849-8012; Fax: 401-847-6290; E-mail: info@wimco.com; Internet: www.wimco.com), a Caribbean and Bermuda villa and hotel expert for 20 years, represents 1,100 villas and 100 hotels in the region. Most of the properties are on Barbados, The Cayman Islands, and the Virgin Islands. Its Web site was recently honored as the best vacation rental sites on the Web by Forbes.com.

- ✓ **Caribbean Inns, Ltd.** (P.O. Box 7411, Hilton Head Island, SC 29938; ☎ **800-633-7411** or 843-689-7411; E-mail: INNS4CARIB@aol.com; Internet: www.caribbeaninns.com), which has been in business since 1987, puts together Caribbean cruise packages and terrific honeymoon packages if you're interested in a small, intimate inn in the three– to five-star range or in villas.

- ✓ **Island Destinations** (☎ **888-454-4422** or 914-833-3300; Fax: 914-833-3318; Internet: www.islanddestinations.com) is a tour operator for upscale travelers that represents some of the more exclusive properties on 15 Caribbean islands, including 30 hotels and three groups of villas. This agency sends representatives to each property annually, so that they can match clients to the best place.

✔ If you want to stay at a villa, try booking through **Unusual Villas** (409F North Hamilton St., Richmond, VA 23221; ☎ **800-846-7280** or 804-288-2823; Fax: 804-342-9016; E-mail: johng@unusualvillarentals.com; Internet: www.unusualvillarentals.com). This company has more than 100 villas for rent on Barbados and Jamaica, and about 50 on St. Thomas, with a total of 2,500 represented throughout the Caribbean.

✔ For dive, leisure, and soft adventure packages (like kayaking), try **Maduro Dive Fanta-Seas** (4500 Biscayne Blvd., Suite 320, Miami, FL 33137; ☎ **800-327-6709** or 305-438-4222; Fax: 305-438-4220; E-mail: info@maduro.com; Internet: www.maduro.com). The company has offerings in Barbados, the Cayman Islands, and Puerto Rico, as well as on Bonaire, Curaçao, Tobago, Tortola, Saba, St. Lucia, and Dominica.

✔ **Caribbean Dive Tours** (732 Johnson Ferry Road, Marietta, GA 30068; ☎ **800-404-3483** or 770-578-8028) arranges dive trips to Aruba, Puerto Rico, the Cayman Islands, and other Caribbean islands.

✔ One of the leading Caribbean packagers for Canadian travelers is **Signature Vacations** (160 Bloor St. E., Suite 400, Toronto, Ontario, Canada M4W 1B9; ☎ **866-324-2883** or 416-967-1510; Fax: 416-967-1510; E-mail: asksignature@signaturevacations.com; Internet: www.signature.ca).

Other good resources are the airlines themselves, which package their flights together with accommodations. Your options include

✔ **Air Canada Vacations** (☎ **888-247-2262**; Internet: www.aircanadavacations.ca)

✔ **Air Jamaica Vacations** (☎ **800-LOVE-BIRD**; Internet: www.airjamaicavacations.com)

✔ **American Airlines Vacations** (☎ **800-321-2121**; Internet: www.aavacations.com)

✔ **Continental Airlines Vacations** (☎ **800-634-5555**; Internet: www.coolvacations.com)

✔ **Delta Dream Vacations** (☎ **800-755-4224**, 800-872-7786, or 888-346-3619; Internet: www.deltavacations.com)

✔ **Northwest Airlines World Vacations** (☎ **800-727-1111** or 612-470-1111; Internet: www.nwaworldvacations.com)

✔ **United Vacations** (☎ **800-328-6877**; Internet: www.unitedvacations.com)

✔ **US Airways Vacations** (☎ **800-455-0123**; Internet: www.usairwaysvacations.com)

Putting a Trip Together on Your Own

We know you're out there. The contrarian, the entrepreneur, the maverick who likes to be in control and do everything alone. After all, that's one of the main reasons you bought this book, so you could become an instant expert and make your own decisions. Well, read on. These next few sections give you all the essentials you need to blaze your own trail to the Caribbean.

Booking your flight

Getting to the Caribbean from the United States and Canada is relatively easy. With improved connections from the West Coast, many islands are seeing more visitors from that area who want to experience something other than Hawaii. With that said, you should do a few things to make sure that your flight goes smoothly.

Reserve early

Flights to the Caribbean tend to be extremely full. During the summer months, islanders who live in the United States go home to visit, and during the winter months tourists are flocking to the warm weather, so seats go quickly year-round. If you're trying to use frequent-flier miles to the Caribbean, you'll have to work way ahead. Only a small number of seats on flights are devoted to frequent fliers, and they get snapped up quickly.

Your quickest route and best price to the Caribbean may be on an airline you don't normally fly or on an airline you've never even heard of before. For example, Air Jamaica often has both of those important points covered, but many travelers have no idea that it's an option. Others are too intimidated to book a foreign carrier like Cayman Airways or Dutch-owned Martinair. Because you're getting into a whole new groove in the Caribbean, maybe you should try another airline.

From your part of the country, your best bet may be to get a cheap flight to Miami or San Juan, and change to another carrier from there. Our point is that it pays to be flexible.

The best way to get to where you want to go may be via another island. For example, visitors going to the British Virgin Islands may want to fly into St. Thomas in the USVIs and then take a ferry over to the BVIs, which are extremely close.

When your time to fly approaches, check back and make sure the airline hasn't changed its schedule. Lately we've heard of some situations where flights were cancelled or schedules changed significantly, but the passengers had no clue until they showed up at the airport. Don't assume the airline will notify you.

Stick together

When you book your tickets, make sure to request seats together for everyone in your party. If you travel with friends, or if your family members don't all have the same last name, ticketing agents definitely won't try to keep you together unless you request it. Arrive early at the airport to get boarding passes to secure your seats. We've been amazed at the number of couples (even honeymooners) and families who spend flights separated by several rows.

If you have any connecting flights, make sure you allow ample time to make your connection. For example, at press time, many American Airlines flights connecting to American Eagle flights in Puerto Rico allowed travelers only 55 minutes to make it. That's too narrow a margin for error with all the additional security checks and delays that travelers now have to deal with. We experienced a similar problem when we were returning from a trip to Peter Island in the BVIs, connecting via St. Thomas to Atlanta. When we looked at the tickets for the small inter-island carrier (called a *puddle jumper* on the islands) that was to take us on the 15-minute flight to St. Thomas, we realized the travel agent had only allowed an hour for the transfer. A year ago that may have worked, but we knew that with passing through customs and security there was no way we'd make it. Luckily we changed to an earlier flight. Sure enough, when we got to St. Thomas, it took about an hour and a half just to negotiate all the hoops to make our next flight.

Get a head start

We've found that booking the earliest flight out prevents us from getting caught in the frequent air traffic jams — especially if we have to make connections in Miami or Puerto Rico, which are always congested.

Figuring out who flies where

For many years, American Airlines and American Eagle, which fly to more than 40 destinations in the Caribbean, dominated from their Puerto Rico and Miami hubs. However, two factors have combined to give travelers more options: Air Jamaica has made Montego Bay its hub (previously, almost everything was funneled through Puerto Rico), and in 1998, American cut back on many of its nonstop flights out of the Northeast as well as on service from its San Juan hub to the Caribbean. Other carriers like Air Jamaica, Delta, US Airways, and Continental Airlines quickly scrambled to fill the void. The bottom line is better connections and improved access.

We really like flying Air Jamaica, which has brand-new jets, friendly flight attendants, and free champagne and wine throughout the flight. The food is consistently a cut above most airline fare, too. Air Jamaica, has been named "Best Caribbean Airline" for several years running at the annual World Travel awards.

Our least favorite airline is **Dutch Caribbean Express,** formerly called Air ALM. Passengers used to joke that ALM stood for "All Luggage Missing." The airline, which filed bankruptcy but seems to have changed in name only, also has a terrible reputation in terms of keeping to its published schedule. Stay away from this airline, unless you like hanging out in airports. We'd only fly Dutch Caribbean Express as a last resort.

Following is a list of the airlines that currently service the Caribbean and where each of them flies. Please note that air service is always subject to change.

- ✔ **Air Canada** (☎ 888-247-2262; Internet: www.aircanada.ca) flies direct from Toronto to Barbados and to Montego Bay and Kingston in Jamaica. It also serves Antigua, Aruba, Barbados, Grand Cayman, Guadaloupe, Jamaica, Punta Cana (Dominican Republic), San Juan, and St. Lucia from several Canadian cities.

- ✔ **Air Jamaica** (☎ 800-523-5585; Internet: www.airjamaica.com) has more than 350 flights a week with direct service from Atlanta, Baltimore, Boston, Chicago, Fort Lauderdale, Houston, London (two flights daily), Los Angeles (daily service with ten weekly flights), Manchester (England), Miami, Newark, New York's JFK, Orlando, and Philadelphia, to Montego Bay and Kingston airports. You can make connections to Antigua, Barbados, Bonaire, Grand Cayman, St. Lucia, Grenada, and Curaçao. Air Jamaica Express goes to Santo Domingo, Dominican Republic. In addition, a business arrangement with Delta Airlines and joint-fare arrangements and compatible schedules with United help extend access to more than 150 cities in the United States. After seven flights, the eighth one is free.

- ✔ **American Airlines** (☎ 800-433-7300; Internet: www.aa.com) and **American Eagle** (☎ 800-981-4757) service almost every destination in the Caribbean from several U.S. cities. For nonstop flights, American Airlines often can't be beat for U.S. travelers. Most trips to the Caribbean on this carrier now require a transfer at its San Juan hub connecting to American Eagle, which has 200 daily flights to and from 21 Caribbean destinations.

- ✔ **British Airways** (☎ 800-247-9297, or 0845 77 333 77 in the U.K.; Internet: www.britishairways.com) flies from London to Grand Cayman as well as Kingston and Montego Bay in Jamaica.

- ✔ **BWIA West Indies Airways** (☎ 800-538-2942 or 718-520-8100; Internet: www.bwee.com) has daily nonstop service to Barbados from New York's JFK and Miami. It also offers service to Barbados from Washington, D.C.'s Dulles on Tuesday, Friday, and Sunday and from Toronto on Tuesday and Saturday. After you land on Barbados, you can make a same-day connection to St. Lucia.

✓ **Cayman Airways** (☎ 800-422-9626 or 305-266-6760; Internet: www.caymanairways.com) has service from Houston, Miami, and Tampa to Grand Cayman, and connecting inter-island flights to Cayman Brac and Kingston, Jamaica.

✓ **Continental Airlines** (☎ 800-525-0280; Internet: www.continental.com) flies nonstop daily from Newark, New Jersey, to Aruba, San Juan, Grand Cayman, St. Maarten, and St. Thomas, and from Houston to San Juan, with seasonal service to Aruba.

✓ **Delta Airlines** (☎ 800-221-1212; Internet: www.delta-air.com) has daily nonstop flights from Atlanta to Aruba, Grand Cayman, San Juan, and St. Thomas. There's a seasonal flight from Cincinnati to San Juan. Via a business arrangement with Air Jamaica, Delta has flights from JFK to Montego Bay and Kingston, Jamaica.

✓ **Dutch Caribbean Express, formerly called Air ALM** (☎ 800-327-7230 or 305-592-7646) offers daily flights from Miami to St. Maarten and Curaçao and one nonstop from Miami to Bonaire on Saturday. At press time, its fate was up in the air and it was still using Air ALM's toll-free number, so exercise caution when booking with Dutch Caribbean Express.

✓ **Northwest Airlines** (☎ 800-727-1111 or 612-470-1111; Internet: www.nwa.com) has daily service from Minneapolis and Detroit — connecting through Memphis, Tennessee — to Jamaica. From December through April, Northwest offers daily service to Grand Cayman and the Dominican Republic, but those flights are only available during high season.

✓ **United Airlines** (☎ 800-241-6522; Internet: www.ual.com) flies direct daily from Chicago's O'Hare from both airports in Washington, D.C., to San Juan.

✓ **US Airways** (☎ 800-428-4322; Internet: www.usairways.com) has service from Baltimore to Grand Cayman, San Juan, St. Croix, and St. Thomas; from Charlotte to Grand Cayman, Montego Bay, San Juan, and St. Thomas; and from Philadelphia to Grand Cayman, San Juan, and St. Thomas. It has greatly expanded service to the Caribbean in recent years and now flies to Aruba, Antigua, Barbados, Dominican Republic, Grand Cayman, Jamaica, St. Lucia, St. Maarten, St. Thomas, and St. Croix.

✓ **Virgin Atlantic Airways** (☎ 800-862-8621, or 01293 747 747 from the U.K.; Internet: www.virginatlantic.com) flies to Antigua, Barbados, and St. Lucia from London.

Hopping island to island

Island-hopping in the Caribbean is easy via the numerous small carriers servicing the islands. You can often find alternative routes to get where you want to go even if an airline says a certain itinerary is booked.

Air Jamaica (☎ **800-523-5585** or 718-830-0622; Internet: www.airjamaica.com), **BWIA** (☎ **800-538-2942** or 718-520-8100; Internet: www.bwee.com), and **LIAT** (☎ **268-462-0700**; Internet: www.liatairline.com) all offer bargain fares that make visiting more than one island extremely affordable. For example, with Air Jamaica's "Island Hopping" package you can visit two islands for the price of your ticket to the farthest destination. With Air Jamaica/Air Jamaica Express's "Caribbean Hopper" for $399, you can visit three or more islands on one trip.

Here are other airlines to call if you plan to hip-hop in the Caribbean:

- ✔ **Air St. Thomas** (☎ **800-522-3084** or 340-776-2722; Internet: www.airstthomas.com) has service from St. Thomas to San Juan and Fajardo, and from San Juan and St. Thomas to Virgin Gorda.

- ✔ **Cape Air** (☎ **800-352-0714**; Fax: 340-774-3595; Internet: www.capeair.com), based in St. Thomas, services San Juan and Ponce, Puerto Rico; Tortola, BVI; and St. Thomas and St. Croix, USVI.

Hunting for the best airfare

Good airfares to this part of the world can disappear in the time it takes the ice in your drink to melt in the Caribbean sun. If you find a fare that sounds good, book it immediately. Generally speaking, you're most likely to find discounted fares to the Caribbean from May through December 15, which is the low season.

Consolidators, also known as bucket shops, are a good place to find low fares. Consolidators buy seats in bulk from the airlines and then sell them back to the public at prices usually below even the airlines' discounted rates. Their small ads usually run in Sunday newspaper travel sections.

Before you pay, request a confirmation number from the consolidator and then call the airline to confirm your seat. Be aware that bucket shop tickets are usually nonrefundable or rigged with stiff cancellation penalties, often as high as 50 to 75% of the ticket price. Protect yourself by paying with a credit card rather than cash. Keep in mind that if there's an airline sale going on, or if it's high season, you can often get the same or better rates by contacting the airlines directly, so do some comparison shopping before you buy. Also check out the name of the airline; you may not want to fly on some obscure third-world airline, even if you're saving $10. And check whether you're flying on a charter or a scheduled airline; the latter is more expensive but more reliable.

Council Travel (☎ 800-226-8624; Internet: www.counciltravel.com) and **STA Travel** (☎ 800-781-4040; Internet: www.sta.travel.com)

cater especially to young travelers, but their bargain-basement prices are available to people of all ages. **The TravelHub** (☎ 888-AIR-FARE; Internet: www.travelhub.com) represents nearly 1,000 travel agencies, many of whom offer consolidator and discount fares. Other reliable consolidators include **1-800-FLY-CHEAP** (☎ 800-FLY CHEAP; Internet: www.1800flycheap.com); **1-800-FLY-4-LESS** (☎ 800-359-4537); **TFI Tours International** (☎ 800-745-8000 or 212-736-1140; Internet: www.lowestprice.com), which serves as a clearinghouse for unused seats; or *rebators* such as **Travel Avenue** (☎ 800-333-3335; Internet: www.travelavenue.com) and the **Smart Traveller** (☎ 800-448-3338 in the U.S. or 305-448-3338), which rebate part of their commissions to you.

You may want to book a seat on a *charter flight.* Lots of the most popular Caribbean destinations have charter flights, though discounted fares have clipped the wings of some. However, they still can be found. Most charter operators advertise and sell their seats through travel agents, so check with the pro you've selected with our help.

Before deciding to take a charter flight, check the ticket restrictions: You may be asked to purchase a tour package, to pay in advance, to be amenable if the day of departure is changed, to pay a service charge, to fly on an airline you're not familiar with (this usually is not the case), and to pay harsh penalties if you cancel — but be understanding if the charter doesn't fill up and is canceled up to ten days before departure. Summer charters fill up more quickly than others and are almost sure to fly, but if you decide on a charter flight, seriously consider buying cancellation and baggage insurance. Also be prepared for late departure hours and long airport delays, because charters usually do not have priority.

Join a travel club such as **Moment's Notice** (☎ 718-234-6295; Internet: www.moments-notice.com) or **Sears Discount Travel Club** (☎ 800-433-9383, or 800-255-1487 to join; Internet: www.travelersadvantage.com), which supply unsold tickets at discounted prices. You pay an annual membership fee to get the club's hot-line number. Of course, you're limited to what's available, so you have to be flexible.

Join frequent-flier clubs. Airlines often give bonus miles on Caribbean routes, so you can rack up the mileage on your way to and from fun in the sun. Accruing miles on one program is best — that way you can rack up free flights and achieve elite status faster. But opening as many accounts as possible makes sense, no matter how seldom you fly a particular airline. Keep in mind that some of the airlines have partnerships with major air carriers, so you can get miles that way, too. It's free, and with frequent-flier status you get the best choice of seats, faster response to phone inquiries, and prompter service if your luggage is stolen, if your flight is canceled or delayed, or if you want to change your seat.

As for using your frequent-flier miles on Caribbean routes, good luck! We've never been able to use our miles for Caribbean forays. "Those seats are already taken," we're always told. Our advice: Call way in advance if you want to try to apply your miles on this route. If you've been saving up your miles, you may want to go ahead and use them all on a dream Caribbean vacation (presuming you can snag one of these precious seats). We're hearing rumblings that the airline industry is looking to severely curtail what these programs will do for you.

If you can travel on a Tuesday, Wednesday, or Thursday, you may find cheaper flights to your destination. When you inquire about airfares, ask if you can get a cheaper rate by flying on a different day.

The best time to book your ticket is just after midnight in the middle of the week. That's when the airlines download low-priced airfares to their computers. You also have a chance to purchase cheap seats that were booked but never ticketed. Obviously, you may have trouble finding a travel agent awake at that time to help you out. To access these midnight specials, call the toll-free reservation number for the airline or research and book your flight on the Internet. The next section walks you through the steps for making travel arrangements online.

Booking Your Trip Online

Researching and booking your trip online can save time and money. Then again, it may not. It's simply not true that you always get the best deal online. Most booking engines do not include schedules and prices for budget airlines, and from time to time you'll get a better last-minute price by calling the airline directly, so it's best to call the airline to see if you can do better before booking online.

On the plus side, Internet users today can tap into the same travel-planning databases that were once accessible only to travel agents — and do it at the same speed. Sites such as **Frommers.com, Travelocity. com, Expedia.com,** and **Orbitz.com** allow consumers to comparison shop for airfares, access special bargains, book flights, and reserve hotel rooms and rental cars.

But don't fire your travel agent just yet. Although online booking sites offer tips and hard data to help you bargain shop, they cannot endow you with the hard-earned experience that makes a seasoned, reliable travel agent an invaluable resource, even in the Internet age. And for consumers with a complex itinerary, a trusty travel agent is still the best way to arrange the most direct flights to and from the best airports.

Still, there's no denying the Internet's emergence as a powerful tool in researching and plotting travel time. The benefits of researching your trip online can be well worth the effort.

Last-minute specials, such as weekend deals or Internet-only fares, are offered by airlines to fill empty seats. Most of these are announced on Tuesday or Wednesday and must be purchased online. They are only valid for travel that weekend, but some can be booked weeks or months in advance. Sign up for weekly e-mail alerts at airline Web sites or check mega-sites that compile comprehensive lists of last-minute specials, such as **Smarter Living** (`http://smarterliving.com`) or **WebFlyer** (`www.webflyer.com`).

Some sites, such as **Expedia.com,** will send you e-mail notification when a cheap fare to your favorite destination becomes available. Some will also tell you when fares to a particular destination are lowest.

Travel planning and booking sites

Keep in mind that because several airlines are no longer willing to pay commissions on tickets sold by online travel agencies, these agencies may either add a $10 surcharge to your bill if you book on that carrier, or neglect to offer those carriers' schedules.

The following list of sites is selective, not comprehensive. Some sites will have evolved or disappeared by the time you read this:

- ✔ **Travelocity** (`www.travelocity.com` or `www.frommers.travelocity.com`) and **Expedia** (`www.expedia.com`) are among the most popular sites, each offering an excellent range of options. You can search by destination, dates, and cost.

- ✔ **Orbitz** (`www.orbitz.com`) is a popular site launched by United, Delta, Northwest, American, and Continental airlines. (Stay tuned: At press time, travel-agency associations were waging an antitrust battle against this site.)

- ✔ **Qixo** (`www.qixo.com`) is another powerful search engine that allows you to search for flights and accommodations from some 20 airline and travel-planning sites (such as Travelocity) at once. Qixo sorts results by price.

- ✔ **Priceline** (`www.priceline.com`) lets you "name your price" for airline tickets, hotel rooms, and rental cars. For airline tickets, you can't say what time you want to fly — you have to accept any flight between 6 a.m. and 10 p.m. on the dates you've selected — and you may have to make one or more stopovers. Tickets are nonrefundable, and no frequent-flier miles are awarded.

Smart e-shopping

The savvy traveler is armed with insider information. Here are a few tips to help you navigate the Internet successfully and safely:

✔ **Know when sales start.** Last-minute deals may vanish in minutes. If you have a favorite booking site or airline, find out when last-minute deals are released to the public. (For example, Southwest's specials are posted every Tuesday at 12:01 a.m. central time.)

✔ **Shop around.** If you're looking for bargains, compare prices on different sites and airlines — and against a travel agent's best fare. Try a range of times and alternative airports before you make a purchase.

✔ **Stay secure.** Book only through secure sites (some airline sites are not secure). Look for a key icon (Netscape) or a padlock (Internet Explorer) at the bottom of your web browser before you enter credit card information or other personal data.

✔ **Avoid online auctions.** Sites that auction airline tickets and frequent-flier miles are the number-one perpetrators of Internet fraud, according to the National Consumers League.

✔ **Maintain a paper trail.** If you book an E-ticket, print out a confirmation, or write down your confirmation number, and keep it safe and accessible — or your trip could be a virtual one!

Longing to talk to a real person

Although online agencies have come a long way, they don't always yield the best price. And if you think that you have even the slightest chance of needing follow-up services, such as itinerary changes, a travel agent who is easily reachable is still your safest bet. Though some of the online agencies employ agents who are available by phone, these sites are geared primarily for self-service. We've run into snafus trying to contact a live body when we had a problem. Let's just say customer service is still a work in progress.

Not all these sites are programmed to alert you to the big money you can save if you fly a day earlier or a day later than you initially plan. On the other hand, if you're looking for a bargain fare, you may find something online that an agent wouldn't take the time to dig up.

If you're truly afraid of typing in your credit card number, find a flight online and then book it by calling a toll-free reservation number or contacting your travel agent. But remember that cheap fares to the Caribbean can evaporate quickly, so don't waffle.

Being Aware of New Air-Travel Security Measures

In the wake of the terrorist attacks of September 11, 2001, the airline industry began implementing sweeping security measures in airports.

All about E-ticketing

Only yesterday *electronic tickets* (E-tickets) were the fast and easy ticket-free alternative to paper tickets. E-tickets allowed passengers to avoid long lines at airport check-in, all the while saving the airlines money on postage and labor. With the increased security measures in airports, however, an E-ticket no longer guarantees an accelerated check-in. You often can't go straight to the boarding gate, even if you have no bags to check. You'll probably need to show your printed E-ticket receipt or confirmation of purchase, as well as a photo ID, and sometimes even the credit card with which you purchased your E-ticket. Besides that, for Caribbean travel, we've found that E-tickets are not necessarily the ticket for smooth travel. Wise travelers still insist on the old paper version for Caribbean travel, especially if they're changing airlines en route or are planning on island hopping. Computer systems on the islands are sometimes slow or down, so paper tickets are easier. Plus, having that paper trail can become critical if you run into cancellations or delays; you may need to have a gate agent endorse your ticket or receipt so that you can hop the next flight on another airline.

Expect a lengthy check-in process and extensive delays. Although regulations vary from airline to airline, you can expedite the process by taking the following steps:

- ✔ **Arrive early.** Arrive at the airport at least two hours before your flight if you're heading to Puerto Rico or the USVIs, because they are considered domestic. Be there three hours ahead for other Caribbean destinations. Don't even think about cutting it close, because Caribbean flights are often once-a-day affairs. It's not like you can just catch the next one.

- ✔ **Try not to drive your car to the airport.** Parking and curbside access to the terminal may be limited. Call ahead and check.

- ✔ **Don't count on curbside check-in.** Some airlines and airports have stopped curbside check-in altogether, whereas others offer it on a limited basis. You can only use curbside if you're going to Puerto Rico or the USVIs. For up-to-date information on specific regulations and implementations, check with the individual airline.

- ✔ **Be sure to carry plenty of documentation.** A government-issued photo ID (federal, state, or local) or valid passport is now required. You may need to show this at various checkpoints. With an E-ticket, you may be required to have with you printed confirmation of purchase, and perhaps even the credit card with which you bought your ticket (see the "All about E-ticketing" sidebar, later in this chapter). This varies from airline to airline, so call ahead to make sure you have the proper documentation. And be sure that your ID is up-to-date. An expired driver's license, for example, may keep you from boarding the plane altogether. Keep close tabs on your ID, too. We check several times en route to be sure we have everything together.

✔ **Know what you can carry on — and what you can't.** The Transportation Security Administration (TSA), the government agency that now handles all aspects of airport security, has devised new restrictions for carry-on baggage, not only to expedite the screening process but to prevent potential weapons from passing through airport security. Passengers are now limited to bringing just one carry-on bag and one personal item onto the aircraft (previous regulations allowed two carry-on bags and one personal item, like a briefcase or a purse). For more information, go to the TSA's Web site, www.tsa.gov. The agency has released an updated list of items passengers are not allowed to carry onto an aircraft. Not permitted are knives and box cutters, corkscrews, straight razors, metal scissors, golf clubs, baseball bats, pool cues, hockey sticks, ski poles, and ice picks. Permitted items include nail clippers, nail files, tweezers, eyelash curlers, safety razors (including disposable razors), syringes (with documented proof of medical need), walking canes and umbrellas (though they must be inspected first). The airline you fly may have additional restrictions on items you can and cannot carry on board. Call ahead to avoid problems.

✔ **Prepare to be searched.** Expect spot-checks. Electronic items, such as laptops or cellphones, should be readied for additional screening. Limit the metal items you wear on your person.

✔ **Take every question seriously.** When a check-in agent asks if someone other than you packed your bag, don't decide that this is the time to be funny. The agents will not hesitate to call an alarm.

✔ **If you have no ticket, you have no gate access.** Only ticketed passengers will be allowed beyond the screener checkpoints, except for those people with specific medical or parental needs.

Cruising the Islands

A great way to see more than one island is on a cruise. Request a Q&A booklet from **Cruise Lines International Association** (☎ 212-921-0066; Internet: www.cruising.org). Some lines that sail in the Caribbean include the following:

✔ **American Canadian Caribbean Line** (☎ 800-556-7450; Internet: www.accl-smallships.com)

✔ **Carnival** (☎ 800-438-6744; Internet: www.carnival.com)

✔ **Club Med Cruises** (☎ 800-CLUB MED; Internet: www.clubmed.com)

- ✔ **Disney** (☎ **800-939-2784;** Internet: `http://disneycruise.` `disney.go.com/disneycruiseline/index`)

- ✔ **Windstar** (☎ **800-258-7245;** Internet: `www.windstarcruises.` `com`)

- ✔ **Seabourn Cruise Line** (☎ **800-929-9595;** Internet: `www.` `seabourn.com`)

- ✔ **Royal Caribbean** (☎ **800-327-6700;** Internet: `www.` `royalcaribbean.com`)

- ✔ **Windjammer Barefoot Cruises** (☎ **800-327-2601;** Internet: `www.windjammer.com`)

Because so many new cruise ships have come online in the last several years, you can easily find cruises at a deep discount — especially if you can wait till the last minute to make your plans. Check out the regular prices on the cruise line Web pages and then compare with the following discounters:

- ✔ **Cruises Only** (☎ **800-683-SHIP**) and **The Cruise Line, Inc.** (☎ **800-777-0707**) are sister companies whose specials can be booked online at `www.mytravelco.com`.

- ✔ **Spur-of-the-Moment Cruises** (☎ **800-343-1991;** Internet: `www.spurof.com`).

Because we could fill a large barge with information on cruising — and we have somewhat less space in this book — we suggest you check out *Cruise Vacations For Dummies,* by Fran Golden (published by Wiley), for more help in this area.

Chapter 6

Money Matters

By Echo and Kevin Garrett

• •

In This Chapter

▶ Deciding on which form of money to bring

▶ Estimating the cost of your trip

▶ Keeping a lid on the hidden expenses

▶ Cutting costs — without sacrificing fun

• •

*W*e know that money can be a delicate subject, so we've tried to make this chapter as painless as possible. We think that you'll be pleasantly surprised to know how *un*complicated money issues are when vacationing in the Caribbean. Making purchases is really no more difficult than when vacationing in, say, Las Vegas.

In this chapter, we work through the basic elements of planning a budget for your vacation by unveiling the hidden costs that could trip you up. We also show you how to cut costs without trimming your fun.

ATMs, Credit Cards, Traveler's Checks, or Cash?

Because we like to keep the hassle-factor as low as possible, we rarely change any money into local currency. U.S. dollars are readily accepted throughout the Caribbean. The only time we make the exchange is when we're planning to use public transportation; buses sometimes accept only exact change in the local currency. With that in mind, here are our tips for making the financial end of your vacation as worry-free as possible.

Turning plastic into cash

If you do decide to exchange money, you can easily find ATMs tied to U.S. banks through the Cirrus and PLUS networks throughout the islands — these give you the best exchange rates. For more details on ATM availability, you can call a staff specialist at the **PLUS system** (☎ 800-336-8472) who will give you a list of bank chains that honor PLUS ATM cards or Visa cards at their branch ATM machines. Or check out **Visa ATM Locator** (www.visa.com) on the Web. You can access prerecorded information regarding the **CIRRUS** network at ☎ 800-4CIRRUS or online at **MasterCard ATM Locator** (www.mastercard.com), for locations of Cirrus ATMs worldwide.

Be aware that if you use an ATM on an island where the official currency is not your own, you'll likely receive cash in the local currency.

In addition to using your ATM card, you can also go to a local bank branch in the Caribbean and request a cash advance on your credit card. Don't forget your personal identification number (PIN) if you plan on doing so.

Giving yourself some credit

MasterCard and Visa are the most widely accepted credit cards in the Caribbean, followed by American Express. Some places accept Discover, but many resorts and restaurants do not. Diners Club isn't widely accepted. We usually each carry a different credit card in our wallets. If you travel solo, carry two just in case you hit a snag with one. We like paying with credit cards, because then we have a paper trail to look at for budgeting purposes. We also have purchase protection, too, if one of our island treasures doesn't pan out.

You can also use a credit card to get local currency from an ATM. The exchange rate for a cash advance on a credit card is better than you receive when exchanging currency in the banks. On the downside, interest rates for cash advances are often significantly higher than rates for credit card purchases. Also, you start paying interest on the advance the moment you receive the cash. On an airline-affiliated credit card, a cash advance does not earn frequent-flier miles.

We've never had anything stolen on any of the islands. But if the unthinkable happens, almost every credit card company has a toll-free number you can call to get help. The credit card companies may be able to wire you a cash advance off your credit card immediately, and in many places, they can deliver an emergency credit card in a day or two. If your **Visa** card is lost or stolen, call ☎ 800-1518 (no, the number's not missing any digits) in Aruba, and ☎ 800-847-2911 in Barbados, the BVIs, the Cayman Islands, Jamaica, Puerto Rico, and the USVIs. If your MasterCard is lost or stolen, call ☎ 800-1561 in Aruba, and ☎ 800-307-7309 in Barbados, the BVIs, the Cayman Islands, Jamaica, Puerto Rico, and the USVIs. **American Express** cardholders and traveler's check holders should call ☎ 800-221-7282 for all money emergencies.

Your hotel's guest services or concierge can help you quickly take the appropriate steps as well. Cancel your credit cards immediately, after you've explained the problem to your hotel. Although you're unlikely to recover your lost purse or wallet, file a police report if you plan to make any claim on your home insurance policy or trip insurance policy for your losses. The companies often require a police report before they will honor any claims.

Steering clear of traveler's checks

We don't take traveler's checks to the Caribbean, because we feel they're more trouble than they're worth on the islands. Traveler's checks are such an anachronism these days that we've even seen people on the islands have difficulties getting them cashed.

If you do opt to carry traveler's checks, be sure to keep a record of their serial numbers (separately from the checks, of course) so you can be ensured a refund in case of theft. Also hang on to the name and toll-free number of the issuer — just in case your checks travel, as in away from your safekeeping.

Rolling in the green

Good news: If you bring U.S. dollars on your trip, you don't need to exchange them. They're accepted throughout the Caribbean. In fact, U.S. dollars are the official currency in the Virgin Islands — even the British ones — and Puerto Rico. We describe the local currencies and the exchange rate at press time in the "Settling into" chapter for each island.

We like to bring at least $100 in small denominations to have handy for tips and another $200 cash for shopping in craft markets and paying the airport departure tax at the end of the trip. (Only cash is accepted for this tax.) Locals on poorer islands such as Jamaica prefer U.S. dollars, and you get a slight edge in craft markets if you pay in U.S. dollars. Tips in U.S. currency are often better received, too.

European and Canadian currencies are not accepted at Caribbean establishments, but you can readily exchange them into the local money at banks, currency exchange offices, or at your hotel. The rate of exchange fluctuates daily according to international monetary markets. For the most recent exchange rates on a variety of currencies, check out www. xe.net/ucc.

When cashing or exchanging traveler's checks or exchanging currency, the bigger the bank the better. Beware of commercial money-changers or facilities in airports; you can pay 10% or more in fees for each transaction.

Calculating the Cost of Your Trip

We know that thinking about how much all of this Caribbean fun is going to cost is probably the last thing you want to do. We don't want to throw a wet beach blanket on your exotic dreams, but we actually think you'll be relieved after you work through the numbers.

Budgeting for your Caribbean vacation isn't difficult, but keeping a close eye on costs is another matter. Using the worksheets at the end of the book can help you come up with an idea of your trip's approximate cost. A good way to get a handle on all costs is to start the tally from the moment you leave home. Walk yourself mentally through the trip. Begin with transportation to your nearest airport and then add the flight cost, the price of getting from the airport to your hotel, the hotel rate per day, meals (exclude these if they're included in the hotel rate), and activities, shopping, and nightlife. After you've done all that, add on another 15 to 20% for good measure.

Adding up lodging expenses

In the Caribbean, accommodation expenses are going to take the largest bite from your budget. Keep in mind that, when you look at the price of an all-inclusive resort versus the price of a hotel, the all-inclusive rate appears inflated. Make sure to compare mangos to mangos, and take into account that you'll be shelling out extra for meals, drinks (many all-inclusives include premium alcohol in their rates), and activities if you're at a hotel or resort where the price covers only your room. (For more on the different types of accommodations, see Chapter 3.)

In each of the island accommodation chapters later in the book, you'll see dollar signs that indicate the price categories for lodging options. See the introduction for an explanation of those rate ranges.

Picking a rate range

Many Caribbean properties have up to a half dozen different rates during the year according to the season. Rates frequently plunge as much as 60% in the summer (low season), though the norm is more in the 20 to 40% range. The luxury resorts typically offer the biggest discounts, because their stratospheric rates have farther to come down. In this book, we let you know if a property is known for having special package deals worth asking about. (In particular, see the section on package deals in Chapter 5.)

You won't find many entries in the "dirt cheap" category in this book, because most of the places that are that cheap in the Caribbean we wouldn't feel comfortable sending anyone to. (Exceptions that spring to mind are Jake's on Jamaica and Hilty House on St Croix.) Low-end properties exist, but you're likely to be sharing a bathroom with strangers, and the cleanliness and service issue will be a big question mark. And, you're almost guaranteed not to get air-conditioning.

Many accommodations fall in the middle (still reasonable) price range, and if we mention a particular feature in the review, take that as an indication that the property had something noteworthy in that area. For example, if we mention the balconies, terraces, or nice sea views, those features are somehow a little or a lot better than similar properties on the island. (Many hotels have sea views, for example, but those views differ significantly from place to place.)

In the high-end categories, you can expect all the extras you'd get at a four– or five-star hotel anywhere in the world. We've had gargantuan Jacuzzis in our room, fruit trays and champagne on arrival, private butler service where our suitcases were unpacked for us, and all kinds of other extravagances. The expensive hotels often throw in the full use of all workout and non-motorized water-sport facilities (even including lessons for snorkeling and windsurfing sometimes). You'll often find CD players and dataport phones in the room. Several hotels and resorts have added extensive business facilities and free Internet kiosks, so that their guests can stay connected easily.

People often wonder whether they should shell out a lot of extra money for a sea view or a big room. That decision depends on the property and your own agenda. If you'll almost never be in the room anyway, why add that cost? But at some facilities, a sea view is vital to the experience. In our individual property reviews, we mention the places where the views and suites are really worth the additional expense.

Beating the rack rate

The *rack rate* is the official published rate that a hotel charges for a room. It's the rate you'd get if you walked in off the street and asked for a room for the night.

In all but the smallest accommodations, the rate you pay for a room depends on many factors, not the least of which is how you make your reservation. A travel agent may be able to negotiate a better price with certain hotels than you could get on your own (see Chapter 5 for details). That's because the hotel gives the agent a discount in exchange for steering business toward that hotel. Airlines frequently team up with hotels to give package deals, too, which can also mean more lopped off that rack rate.

Of course, hotels are happy to charge you the rack rate, but with minimal effort and planning you can easily do better. Reserving a room through the hotel's toll-free number may sometimes result in a lower rate than if you called the hotel directly. However, we've found that when it comes to the Caribbean, the people manning the central reservations number sometimes don't know about the latest special packages or deals on the island. In fact, the reservations agent is usually sitting at a desk in Florida or New Jersey and has never set foot on the island.

We strongly recommend that you make initial comparisons using the toll-free hotel reservation numbers or Web sites; narrowing your choices down to three properties. Then contact each resort directly via e-mail, phone, or fax to check the rates again. (Faxes or e-mails work best with islands like Puerto Rico and Jamaica, where the unfamiliarly accented English may be difficult to follow on the phone.) Make sure to ask about last-minute specials, and double-check to be certain that you're not missing some fantastic package that the U.S.-based reservation service hasn't been told about yet — that happens all the time. Many Caribbean resorts are now offering Internet-only specials, too, so don't forget to check for those deals. (The "Sweet Dreams: Choosing Your Hotel" worksheet at the back of the book is a handy form for keeping track of prices.)

When you agree on a rate, make sure to get a confirmation either by fax or e-mail that outlines in entirety the agreed-upon rate along with what's included — and what's not. Be sure the room category is what you asked for, too. Hoteliers are often loath to promise a particular room assignment, but if you're able to extract such a promise, get it in writing. Bring with you on your trip the confirmation of the deal you've worked out, to avoid any nasty surprises at checkout time.

Outsmarting the seasons

Room rates also change with the season and as occupancy rates rise and fall. (See Chapter 2 for a full discussion of how time of year affects hotel rates.) If a hotel is almost full, it's not likely to extend discount rates. If it's empty, it may be willing to negotiate. With many Caribbean hotels, you probably need to call nine months or more in advance to get a room during the popular winter months. In summer, you can almost always snag a deal.

Although you may feel a little like an ambulance chaser, if you're willing to put up with some hassle, you can try to book a trip to an island soon after a hurricane has hit. Resorts and airlines are left scrambling for customers. Hotels are often back on track quickly, but because of the media-induced panic, guests don't come back for weeks or even months. The palm trees will be tattered and you may have to put up with the sound of hammers, but the sun still shines.

If you travel with a group, consider staying in a villa. With three couples, you can easily rent a villa for under $1,000 per person for a week. **Unusual Villas** (409F North Hamilton St., Richmond, VA 23221; ☎ **800-846-7280** or 804-288-2823; Fax: 804-342-9016; E-mail: johng@unusual

villarentals.com; Internet: www.unusualvillarentals.com) represents a large number of properties in the Caribbean.

Tallying transportation costs

Most of the time, aside from your airfare to the Caribbean (see Chapter
5 for tips on how to decrease this particular expense), your transportation costs should be relatively low during your Caribbean stay. This is
especially true if you passed on the rental car or received a couple of
free days of car rental as part of your package deal.

Many package tours include transfers from the airport to your resort
or hotel. Several fine restaurants arrange free transportation, too; be
sure to inquire when you make a reservation. In either case, you still
need to tip the driver. See Chapter 5 for more details on booking a
package trip.

Taxi fares add up quickly, even on a less expensive island like Puerto
Rico, because attractions are often spread out. If you want to cover a
lot of ground for the best price, you're usually better off lumping most
of your touring into a single day and hiring a driver for the entire day at
a rate ranging from $60 to $100 (not including tip).

Don't plan on taking public transportation, except on Aruba and
Barbados where the bus service between the beach resort areas and
the main towns are quick, reliable, easy, and cheap. The public ferries
are the most reasonably priced way to get from one island to the next
in the British Virgin Islands and between the BVIs and St. Thomas or
St. John.

As much as possible, take advantage of the free transportation offered
by your hotel. If you pay attention to schedules, you can often find a
free shuttle to the nearest place for shopping or a special beach.

Figuring dining dollars

In each of the dining chapters, we include reviews of our favorite
restaurants, ranging from the pick of the high-end resort choices to
local finds with rock-bottom prices. Each has dollar-sign symbols to
indicate its price category; see the Introduction for an explanation of
those categories.

Where, when, and what you eat in the Caribbean makes a big difference
in your final vacation tab. To save money, we generally suggest signing
up for some sort of dining plan at your resort. Choose whatever plan
makes the most sense for you and your tastes. For example, if breakfast is the most important meal of the day to you, don't sign on for a
plan that only serves a continental spread.

Investing in a dine-around plan

If you visit Aruba, Barbados, Jamaica, Puerto Rico, or St. Thomas, you probably want to try some of the good local restaurants that each island is known for. But you also want to keep costs in check, so ask if your hotel offers a *dine-around plan*. That way you won't get stuck in a culinary rut or shell out tons of money for food. Even some of the all-inclusives — like Aruba's Allegro — now offer dine-around plans, recognizing that travelers crave variety.

Dine-around plans are not all identical, but the way they usually work is that you pay a flat fee for a certain number of gourmet meals (say three to five for the week). You then get to use your dine-around credits with the hotels or restaurants that are part of the program.

Dining at your resort

Most hotels offer a *European Plan* (EP), which means that no meals are included. If you see a *Continental Plan* (CP) listed, that means you get only a continental breakfast — juice, coffee, and some kind of bread. A *Breakfast Plan* (BP) signifies a full American-style breakfast. Another popular option, which leaves couples to figure out only the evening meal on their own, is the *Modified American Plan* (MAP), which provides two full meals daily. With the three daily meals of the *Full American Plan* (FAP), that's exactly what you'll be — full. Finally, *all-inclusive* means that you get three all-you-can-eat meals a day and (often) all the alcohol you can guzzle — sometimes including premium liquors and great wines.

Dining options have greatly improved at all-inclusive resorts in the last few years because travelers have become so much more sophisticated. Now most all-inclusive dining packages feature local dishes at least one night a week, and often you can find several local specialties amidst more familiar fare.

If you have special dietary restrictions and are staying at an all-inclusive or at a resort where you've signed on for an extensive meal plan, ask the reservation agent for the executive chef's name and send an e-mail or fax with your special requests about a month before you arrive. Most chefs consider pleasing their guests a point of pride, and they bend over backwards to accommodate you. However, because ordering special items on the islands can take time, you need to give chefs advance notice.

If you go for the popular à la carte breakfast buffet, expect to pay a staggering $20 or more per person, including coffee and juice. That's before tipping. And unless your cash flow is extremely good, don't even think about ordering room service. For one thing, the wait is often interminable, but you also have to add a tip on top of an already pricey way to dine.

Entertaining meals outside your resort

Outside the resorts, your dining choices generally fall into two categories: expensive and cheap. Dinner entrees at nicer restaurants routinely start at around $18, and a three-course meal for two with cocktails can easily soar past the $100 mark — before the tip. Why so much? Many products must be brought from outside the island, and the high costs of importing are passed along to you. On some islands, even the seafood is frozen and shipped in; we've had Maine lobster served to us in the Caribbean more than once. If that fact bothers you, be sure to ask your server about the origin and freshness of the fish before you order.

Also, keep in mind that the European connection is strong on these islands, and many of them attract some of the world's finest chefs, who consider spending time in the tropics a career perk. Although we may pay the same amount we'd pay at the best restaurants in Atlanta (and on pricey-to-dine islands like Aruba, Barbados, and Grand Cayman, our dinner tab may be closer to New York prices), we're legitimately getting a gourmet meal. Plus, we get the kind of killer view that is in short supply at home.

Happily, on the other end of the payment scale, eating cheaply in the Caribbean doesn't mean risking your health the way it sometimes does in Mexico. You rarely have to be concerned about the safety of the food and water in the Caribbean. If you're willing to eat where the locals do, you can find some terrific meals for around $10.

In terms of cheap joints, you can follow our recommendations or, if you're feeling adventurous, ask a local where to go. Don't expect much in the way of surroundings; you may sit on a plastic chair at a wobbly plastic table enlivened with plastic flowers. But you'll get to bask in the friendly Caribbean atmosphere, *limin'* (island slang for "hanging out") with the locals, and enjoying treats like jerk chicken with *bammy* (a fried Jamaican bread) or a bowl of *sopa de pollo con arroz* (Puerto Rico's answer to grandmother's chicken soup). For more authentic recommendations, see Chapter 37.

Going for do-it-yourself meals

If you plan to stay in a villa, condo, or guesthouse, you can cut costs by cooking your own meals. Some islands, like St. Thomas, now have low-price superstores where you can pick up supplies relatively cheap.

Before you lug things like salt and pepper with you, ask management to send you a list of what's already stocked in the kitchen. Remember that spices are cheaper on some islands, such as lush Jamaica.

Tapping more cost-cutting tips

Here are a few more ways to trim your dining costs:

✔ **Fill up at the breakfast buffet at your hotel.** If you eat late and eat well, you'll eliminate the need for a big lunch, especially if all you're going to be doing is lazing on the beach.

✔ **Share.** Portions are often pretty hefty, and if you eat everything on your plate, you may get that way, too. At least try splitting appetizers and desserts.

✔ **Take advantage of happy hours and the manager's welcoming cocktail party.** There are usually free nibbles, too.

✔ **Forget about the lobster; it's the most pricey item on the menu.** The freshly caught local fish is less expensive and often just as good or better.

✔ **Avoid your minibar, or use it to stash the less expensive drinks and snacks that you buy outside your resort.**

Toasting top prices for drinks

Unless you're at an all-inclusive where drinks are part of your up-front tab or you're content to drink water, another big expense will be drinks. Paying $2.50 for a soda isn't uncommon, and you won't get refills without paying again. If you have a minibar or fridge in your room, ascertain whether the drinks are complimentary before swigging them down. Some places put bottled water in your room, but then they expect you to pony up a pretty penny for every sip you take. If you're not sure, call the front desk.

On many islands, import duties raise the prices of wines and imported beers sky-high. We've found that wines are often barely drinkable because they're improperly stored en route (sitting in the broiling tropical sun on a dock somewhere) or, after they arrive, the bottles are not kept cool enough. Save money and your taste buds by drinking local. The Caribbean is noted for its rums and beers.

If your kids don't react well to too much sugar, beware of ordering juice on the islands. Often "juices" are actually fruit drinks, made up largely of corn-syrup sweeteners rather than pure juice.

Spending wisely on activities

Of course, the two main activities in the Caribbean — swimming in that beautiful, impossibly blue sea and basking on those sandy beaches — are absolutely free. However, if you're interested in activities like scuba diving, snorkeling, windsurfing, and waterskiing, they usually cost extra.

In recent years, more and more of the all-inclusives have started offering terrific freebies like scuba and windsurfing lessons, free water-skiing, and free snorkeling gear for the week. Some even toss in a free round of golf.

Water sports

Although the charges vary slightly from island to island, we've generally found a two-tank boat dive to run around $45 to $60. Snorkeling trips vary widely in cost, but if you're going out on a boat, you'll pay at least $30; just renting snorkeling equipment at a beach usually costs about $15. Windsurfing lessons and gear will cost close to $50 an hour, and water-skiing also goes for about $50 an hour. You also need to factor in the cost of a tip if you're receiving instruction.

Many variables are involved in calculating the costs of deep-sea fishing, but assuming that you don't mind mingling your lines with people you haven't met before, you'll probably pay at least $100 per person, including bait, fishing license, and ice to preserve your catch.

Golf

For golf in the Caribbean, greens fees run from about $80 at Jamaica's Sandals Golf and Country Club to about $130 at Aruba's Tierra Del Sol and Jamaica's Half Moon Bay. You also pay at least $15 for club rentals and a minimum of $15 for a manual golf cart. In Jamaica, you also have the quirky rule that you must have a caddy, who will of course need to be tipped. (The show makes the cost worthwhile: Your caddy carries your golf bag by balancing it sideways on his head.)

Sightseeing tours

You'll probably want to spend at least one day touring the island, even if you're on one like Grand Cayman where you won't find many interesting attractions. Sightseeing tours vary according to destination, duration, and extras like meals and snacks. But here's a rough estimate of cost: Expect to spend a minimum of $50 (including tip) for a half-day island tour of Aruba or Grand Cayman. For a full-day, guided tour including lunch and a stop for snacks on bigger islands with more to see like Barbados, Jamaica, and Puerto Rico (where there's *lots* to see), you're looking at about $80 minimum, including tip.

Stocking up on souvenirs

Shopping is the wild card. You can easily get away with buying a few inexpensive souvenirs at the craft markets, where you may pick up a handwoven straw hat for about $15 or a small basket of spices for $7. But at the other end of the spectrum, artwork by notable Caribbean artists can go for thousands of dollars. Don't miss the fantastic art galleries in Old San Juan; the duty-free scene in Charlotte Amalie on St. Thomas; the funky boutique shops on St. John; or the hip art galleries in Jamaica. (See Chapter 36 for our favorite local souvenirs.)

If you're eager to load up on luxury items from china to perfume, duty-free shops dot the islands. However, if you intend to shop for major items like jewelry, we urge you to do some comparative pricing at home first. You may have a very hard time determining which items are truly bargains in the duty-free shops; don't be fooled by signs trumpeting terrific deals.

Tasting the nightlife

Even the smallest resorts usually roll out a reggae or steel-pan band sometime during the week. Nightlife in the Caribbean runs the gamut from resort-sponsored theme nights (available on every island) to glitzy casinos (in Puerto Rico and Aruba). You can find high-class nightclubs where merengue and salsa rule (Puerto Rico and Aruba) and reggae rocks (St. Thomas), and you can enjoy Jamaica's street parties where locals mingle with visitors to the thumping beat of rock-steady, reggae, and *soca* (reggae dance music).

The action on Barbados is in the rum shops, and the funky beach bars in the British Virgin Islands are renowned for their rollicking impromptu parties. The best part is that the beach and street parties are free, and you'll usually only have a small cover charge ($5 to $10 per person) to gain entry into clubs. As for casinos, well, that all depends on whether you're feeling lucky.

Keeping a Lid on Hidden Expenses

A lot of visitors forget that a government tax, which ranges from 6% on Aruba to Jamaica's whopping 23%, applies to their final hotel bill. When you ask for lodging rates, clarify whether the tax is included in the quote; obviously that can make a big difference. We strongly urge you to ask the hotel for a written outline of everything that's included in the rate — faxed, if possible. We've run into people who were extremely annoyed because they thought they had a set rate, and the government tax came as a nasty surprise. The rates quoted in this book do not include government tax and service charges.

Tipping tips

For the most part, tipping is much the same in the Caribbean as in the rest of the world. Plan to tip 15% of the bill in a restaurant, $1 per bag to a bellhop, and $2 per night for a maid in a resort. (If your hotel is not very expensive, leave $1 a night on your pillow; leave it each day because the maids often rotate out.) Taxi drivers and tour guides get a 10 to 15% tip.

Tips are often automatically included in a bill (in European fashion). If you're in doubt, ask before you accidentally overtip. Bring along lots of small-denomination bills; otherwise, you're likely to end up giving a much larger tip than the situation calls for — or, worse, stiffing someone.

Telephone traps

Making long distance calls from the Caribbean is extremely expensive. Don't ever dial direct from your hotel room, unless forking over $50 or so for a five-minute call is no big whoop to you. Also, be aware that many Caribbean hotels charge even for attempted calls, and toll-free numbers are not free in the Caribbean. (We learned that the hard way, once winding up with a $30 phone bill for making a few calls to check on our brokerage account.)

In your room, you'll usually find long-distance instructions that give you some options, but you're best off using your calling card. However, we've had problems on some islands connecting to the appropriate operator, so call the front desk at the first sign of trouble and ask the hotel operator to guide you through their particular system. Unless a call is urgent, we've found faxing much less expensive. That way, neither party has to worry about the other person's availability to answer. Sometimes hotels have free Internet kiosks for their guests in the lobby area. If you do bring your laptop, remember that it'll cost you a mint to connect, so e-mail addicts beware. We heard one fellow laughing at his own stupidity. He'd downloaded a bunch of e-mails using the dataport in his room and got slapped with a $120 charge. Most U.S. cell phones and services don't work in the Caribbean, but you can rent them on the island if you're desperate. Buying a phone card locally can reduce your long-distance costs significantly, too. Ask your concierge for the best place to purchase one.

Trimming Your Costs

The Caribbean delivers plenty of thrills if you get a rush out of being a savvy consumer. Following are our best money-saving tips:

- ✔ **Go off-season.** If you can travel at nonpeak times (generally May through November), you'll find hotel prices that are as much as 60% off from high-season rates. But keep in mind that some resorts lower their rates more than others. Generally speaking, bargain hunters do best in Aruba, Jamaica, Puerto Rico, and the USVIs.

- ✔ **Travel on off days of the week.** If you can travel on a Tuesday, Wednesday, or Thursday, you may find cheaper flights to your destination. When you inquire about airfares, ask if flying on a different day will make your fare cheaper.

✔ **Try a package tour.** For many destinations, you can book airfare, hotel, ground transportation, and even a sightseeing tour just by making one call to a travel agent or packager, for a lot less than if you tried to cobble the trip together yourself. (See Chapter 5 for specifics.)

✔ **Reserve accommodations with a kitchen and do your own cooking.** If you can stomach having to wash dishes on your vacation, you can save a lot of money by not eating in restaurants three times a day. Even if you only make breakfast and an occasional bag lunch, you still save in the long run. One couple we know blew $90 on a basic dinner early in their stay on Grand Cayman. Subsequently, they bought about $100 worth of groceries and ate well for the rest of the week at their condo.

✔ **Always ask for discount rates.** Membership in AAA, frequent-flier plans, trade unions, AARP, or other groups may qualify you for discounted rates on plane tickets, hotel rooms, and rental cars.

✔ **Find out if your kids can stay in your room with you.** A room with two double beds doesn't cost any more than one with a queen-size bed. And many hotels won't charge you extra if the additional person is pint-sized and related to you. Even if you have to pay $10 or $15 for a rollaway bed, you save big bucks by not taking two rooms. Many resorts are now offering programs that let kids stay and eat free. Aruba has an island-wide program in the summer months that gives families big discounts and a bundle of freebies.

✔ **Try expensive restaurants at lunch instead of dinner.** Lunch tabs are usually a fraction of what dinner costs at most top restaurants, and the menu often includes many of the same specialties.

✔ **Cut down on the souvenirs.** Does your cousin really need another T-shirt? Oddly, we've found tacky items to be fairly pricey, especially in comparison to genuine island keepsakes.

✔ **Substitute less expensive activities for pricier ones.** Waverunners can be fun, but they cost a lot to rent, and the ride doesn't last that long. You may be better off spending a few hours snorkeling instead.

✔ **At your hotel, you should never make a direct-dial long-distance call from your room, send out your laundry, use items from the minibar, or exchange money.** (Many hotels consider money-changing a profit center.)

Chapter 7

Taking Care of Details

By Echo and Kevin Garrett

- -

In This Chapter

▶ Getting your ID papers in order

▶ Going through customs

▶ Buying travel and medical insurance

▶ Deciding whether to rent a car

▶ Packing wisely (and lightly)

- -

*A*lthough we can't cover everything from *ackee* (a Jamaican fruit) to *zouk* (an African-influenced Caribbean music) in this book, we can address a few of the more important must-knows. In this chapter, we help you make sure that your passport is in order and that you have the insurance coverage you need before traveling to the Caribbean. We also help you decide whether to rent a car on the islands, and we share some tips for packing what you need without bringing along pounds of unnecessary luggage.

Embarking on the Great Paper Chase: Passports, Please

Do you need a passport to go to the Caribbean? Sounds like a simple enough question, but the answer is more complicated than you may think. If you're a U.S. or Canadian citizen, you don't need a passport to visit the U.S. Virgin Islands or Puerto Rico, because they are U.S. territories. Aruba, Barbados, the British Virgin Islands, the Cayman Islands, and Jamaica all say that they accept alternative identification for U.S. and Canadian citizens (for example, a hospital-issued birth certificate with a raised seal, plus a valid driver's license with a photo ID), but the rules differ slightly from island to island and are subject to change. And in the wake of September 11, to simplify your life, we strongly urge both you and your children to get passports no matter where you're from and where you're going.

With security much tighter, we think avoiding any unnecessary hassles is wise. Please note that entry requirements are subject to change, and U.S. Customs has cracked down lately regarding what's acceptable identification when you're reentering the United States.

If you're from the United States or Canada and you don't have an up-to-date passport, you must have the following papers with you, unless you're headed only to Puerto Rico or the United States Virgin Islands:

- ✔ Either an official certified copy of your birth certificate (if it doesn't have a raised seal, it doesn't count), or an expired passport (which can't be more than one to four years old, depending on the island)

- ✔ An official photo identification, such as a valid driver's license

- ✔ A return round-trip plane ticket

Citizens from the U.K. must have passports and return-trip tickets to visit Aruba, Barbados, the British Virgin Islands, Jamaica, Puerto Rico, and the U.S. Virgin Islands. To visit the Cayman Islands, British citizens need a passport or a birth certificate and current photo ID.

U.S., U.K., and Canadian visitors don't need any special visas to enter the islands that we describe in this book. Citizens of other countries should call the tourist board of the country they want to visit to find out what documents they need to have in hand when they travel to the Caribbean.

Identifying requirements for kids

Children from the U.S. who are under 18 need to present a passport or an official birth certificate and an official photo identification. We recommend bringing a passport photo of babies and preschool children or a current school photograph of older children and teens. If you're traveling with kids, be sure to start the process to get the passport or birth certificate at least three months ahead, to avoid expediting fees and nail biting over whether that passport or birth certificate will arrive in time. If a child is traveling with only one parent or with grandparents, we also suggest bringing a notarized permission letter (with the child's photo attached) from the other parent or parents as a precaution. Be sure to authorize the person who has charge of the children to seek medical attention if the need arises. We've heard of one grandmother being turned away at the airport because she didn't have a notarized permission letter authorizing her to take her two grandsons out of the country. That situation may be rare in the Caribbean, but we're erring on the side of caution here.

Minor children from other counties, including Canada, are allowed to travel on their parent's passport. That's the most efficient way to handle the issue. However, if you're planning to bring children to the

Caribbean, we suggest that you call the tourist board of the island you plan to visit and confirm any special documentation you will need for anyone under 18.

Getting a passport

Obtaining a passport in the United States, Canada, the United Kingdom, Ireland, Australia, or New Zealand carries its own respective requirements, as covered in the following sections.

U.S. citizens

If you apply for a first-time passport, you need to do so in person at one of the following locations:

- ✔ A passport office (there are 13 in the United States)
- ✔ A federal, state, or probate court
- ✔ A major post office (*Note:* Not all post offices accept passport applications; later in this section, we provide a number to call to find the ones that do.)

When you apply, you need to present a certified birth certificate as proof of citizenship, and you're wise to bring along your driver's license, state or military ID, and social security card as well. If you're a newlywed with a name change, bring a copy of your marriage certificate. You also need two identical passport-sized photos (2 x 2 inch), which you can have taken at any corner photo shop. (You cannot use strip photos taken from a photo vending machine, however.)

For people over 15, a passport is valid for ten years and costs $60 ($45 plus a $15 handling fee). For those 15 and under, the passport is valid for five years and costs $40. If you're over 15 and have a valid passport that was issued within the past 12 years, you can renew it by mail and bypass the $15 handling fee. Allow plenty of time to renew your passport; processing normally takes three weeks but can take longer during busy periods (especially spring). If you're even remotely cutting it close,

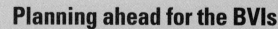

Planning ahead for the BVIs

If you're a U.S. citizen visiting the U.S. Virgin Islands, bring your passport if you want to make the popular jaunt over to the neighboring British Virgin Islands. That thought holds true even if you're arriving by boat. Many visitors have been turned away disappointed because they forgot the required identification. You can't set foot on the BVIs — not even from a privately chartered yacht — without that all-important passport.

we recommend paying an extra $35 plus the express-mail service fee to have your application expedited, which means that you can expect your passport to arrive within seven to ten working days.

To find your regional passport office, either check the U.S. State Department Web site (http://travel.state.gov) or call the **National Passport Information Center** (☎ 900-225-5674); the fee is 35¢ per minute for automated information and $1.05 per minute for operator-assisted calls.

Go to the Web site of the **U.S. State Department** (http://travel.state.gov), and click on Passport Services; you can get passport information there and download an application. Applications are also available at many post offices and travel agencies.

If you suddenly realize that you don't have the proper documentation, and you're leaving on your trip in two days, all is not lost. Though not a government agency, **Passport Express** (☎ 800-362-8196 or 401-272-4612; E-mail: info@passportexpress.com; Internet: www.passport express.com) expedites U.S. passports in as little as 24 hours after it has received your supporting materials. You can also download U.S. passport applications and instructions from the Passport Express site.

To use Passport Express, your departure date must be within three weeks. If your departure date is more than a week away, the fee is $100 plus $95 in government fees; less than a week away from your departure, the fee jumps to $150 plus $95 for government fees. The company's representatives walk your application through the guaranteed process and then send your passport back to you (via Federal Express) within 24 hours. Based on some of our own panic-inducing experiences, we'd use this service in a heartbeat if we found ourselves cutting it close again.

American Passport Express (☎ 800-841-6778; Internet: www.american passport.com) will process your passport for you in a week for $50, plus the cost of the passport itself ($75 for a renewal; $95 for a first-time or lost passport). If you need the passport in three to four days, the cost is $100, and for $150 you can receive your passport in 24 hours.

Canadian citizens

Canadian passports are valid for five years and cost $60. Children under 16 may be included on a parent's passport but need their own to travel unaccompanied by the parent. Applications, which must be accompanied by two identical passport-sized photographs and proof of Canadian citizenship, are available at passport offices throughout Canada, at post offices, or from the central **Passport Office,** Department of Foreign Affairs and International Trade, Ottawa, Ont. K1A 0G3 (☎ 800-567-6868; Internet: www.dfait-maeci.gc.ca/passport). Processing takes five to ten days if you apply in person, or about three weeks by mail.

Residents of the United Kingdom

To pick up an application for a regular ten-year passport (the Visitor's Passport has been abolished), visit your nearest passport office, major post office, or travel agency. You can also contact the **United Kingdom Passport Service** at ☎ **0870-571-0410** or search its Web site at www.uk pa.gov.uk. Passports are £30 for adults and £16 for children under 16.

Residents of Ireland

You can apply for a ten-year passport, costing 57 at the **Passport Office,** Setanta Centre, Molesworth Street, Dublin 2 (☎ **01-671-1633;** Internet: www.irlgov.ie/iveagh). Those under age 18 and over 65 must apply for a three-year passport, costing 12 . You can also apply at 1A South Mall, Cork (☎ **021-272-525**) or over the counter at most main post offices.

Residents of Australia

Apply at your local post office or passport office or search the government Web site at www.passports.gov.au. Passports cost A$136 for adults and A$68 for those under 18. The **Australia State Passport Office** can be reached at ☎ **131232;** travelers must schedule an interview to submit their passport application materials.

Residents of New Zealand

You can pick up a passport application at any travel agency or Link Centre. For more info, contact the **Passport Office,** Department of Internal Affairs, P.O. Box 10-526, Wellington (☎ **0800-225-050;** Internet: www.passports.govt.nz). Passports are NZ$80 for adults and NZ$40 for those under 16.

Dealing with Customs and Duties

If you tote expensive camera or computer gear or expensive jewelry, don't forget to register these items with customs before you leave the country. Otherwise, upon your return, you may wind up being charged a duty for them.

Unless Puerto Rico is your vacation spot, you have to go through U.S. Customs. (If you go to Puerto Rico, you can skip U.S. Customs and bring back as much stuff as you want, except plants, fruits, and vegetables that may not be allowed on the U.S. mainland.)

What's cool about Aruba and the USVIs is that you pass through U.S. Customs via the islands' airports. From all other points, you have to go through stateside, which means that if you bought more than $400 worth of merchandise on your trip, you must fill out a simple form stating how much you spent on the goods you're bringing back. Save receipts from duty-free stores, just in case. Each family member can bring a whopping $1,200 worth of goods back from the U.S. Virgin Islands — double the allowable amount from the other islands.

For more information, contact the **U.S. Customs Service,** 1300 Pennsylvania Ave., NW, Washington, DC 20229 (☎ **877-287-8867**) and request the free pamphlet "Know Before You Go." It's also available on the Web at `www.customs.gov`. (Click on "Traveler Information," then "Know Before You Go Brochure.")

Dressing for acceptance

Don't dress sloppily when you go to the Cayman Islands. If the customs officers think you don't look like you've got the money to bankroll your visit, they'll question you and may even demand proof that you have the bucks to lavish on your island getaway. Kevin forgot this quirky little rule on our last visit — plus, he had long hair at the time. Sure enough, he got stopped for questioning. (He was allowed in.)

Remember that until you pass through U.S. Customs, you technically do not enjoy the same rights as you do on U.S. soil. Customs officials are allowed to pull anyone out of line and even order a strip search without having any reason beyond how you look. Kevin recently cut his hair and shaved his beard, because, each time we came back into the country, we were faced with more and more questions from U.S. Customs officials. Maybe having a copy of this book with us next trip will help prove that we aren't just party animals looking for a good time in the islands.

Leaving keepsakes (and trouble) behind

Although the Caribbean has a reputation for being a laid-back region as far as drug use goes, in reality, marijuana (ganja), cocaine, and other illicit substances are just as illegal here as they are in the states. The islands have drug informants who turn people in to the authorities all the time, and the drug dogs in the airport are highly skilled at finding illegal drugs and other contraband. We've seen many people pulled out of line.

Using drugs or trying to smuggle them back are serious infractions, and in other countries you have no rights as a U.S. citizen. In fact, your hometown lawyer can't even represent you unless he or she is licensed to practice in the Caribbean. Penalties are severe, prison conditions are downright nasty, and you won't get bail.

Jamaica's reputation as a freewheeling place causes some people to think that they can get away with drug use on this island. In fact, that's where we've seen the strictest controls: two checkpoints with drug dogs before you get on a plane, and then another when you land. Once, while traveling, we met a woman from Texas who was on her way to visit her 19-year-old daughter in a Jamaican jail. She told us that her daughter had been caught with a small amount of marijuana at the airport and was serving an 18-month sentence.

No matter what a local tells you, you'll also get in trouble with U.S. Customs (and have your purchases confiscated) if you try to bring back any live souvenirs. Coral, sea-turtle shells, and even shells from the beach are contraband.

Securing Your Investment and Safety

Basically, when it comes to having a hassle-free sojourn, you need to keep three potential problem areas in mind: trip interruption, medical emergencies, and lost luggage. Here we spell out what insurance need, and what you can skip.

Trip cancellation/interruption insurance

If you plan an expensive Caribbean vacation or a cruise that requires you to pay most costs up front, we strongly advise you to spring for trip cancellation/interruption insurance. Good trip cancellation/interruption insurance covers you in a variety of scenarios. Policies typically reimburse you for the nonrefundable components of your trip if you have to cancel — for example, if a family member gets seriously ill or your hotel is damaged by a hurricane. Refunds can also be made on the unused portion of your trip and reimbursements made on your airfare home if your trip is cut short for covered reasons. Optional add-ons for these types of policies include medical and dental expenses, tour-operator bankruptcy, and bad weather. (Weather problems don't just include hurricanes — missed connections due to winter snowstorms in the U.S. may be covered as well.)

If you plan a trip to a small boutique hotel during hurricane season, trip cancellation/interruption insurance is vital. Most small places don't give refunds even if the hotel is severely damaged by a hurricane. Even if you're vacationing with SuperClubs or Sandals, both of which offer generous guarantees against having your trip ruined by a hurricane (see Chapter 2), we still recommend trip interruption/cancellation insurance because so many other things can cause problems.

Insurance policies offered through cruise lines and tour operators tend to be skimpy. Compare prices and policies with one of the companies listed here and get advice from your travel agent.

Trip cancellation insurance costs average between 6 and 8% of the total value of your vacation. If you travel with more than one person, split the cost so that your names all appear on the policy. This way everyone is eligible for medical evacuation insurance (explained in the following section), in case one of you has an accident or emergency.

The cost of travel insurance varies widely, depending on the cost and length of your trip, your age and overall health, and the type of trip you're taking. Insurance for extreme sports or adventure travel, for example, will cost more than coverage for a cruise. Some insurers provide packages for specialty vacations, such as skiing or backpacking. More-dangerous activities may be excluded from basic policies.

For information, contact one of the following popular insurers:

- ✔ **Access America** (☎ **800-284-8300**; Internet:www.access america.com)
- ✔ **Travel Guard International** (☎ **800-826-1300**; Internet: www.travelguard.com)
- ✔ **Travel Insured International** (☎ **800-243-3174**; Internet: www.travelinsured.com)
- ✔ **Travelex Insurance Services** (☎ **800-228-9792**; Internet: www.travelex-insurance.com)

Medical insurance

Check to see if your existing health insurance covers you in the Caribbean. If you belong to an HMO, make sure that you're fully covered when away from home. If you worry that your existing policy won't be sufficient, purchase travel medical insurance (see the list of reputable issuers of travel insurance in the preceding section).

If you have any serious health problems, if you're adventurous, or if you're a diver, make sure you have coverage that will pay for medical evacuation in case of an emergency, in addition to your regular insurance. **Divers Alert Network** (6 W. Colony Place, Durham, NC 27705; ☎ **800-446-2671** or 919-684-2948; E-mail: dan@diversalertnetwork. com; Internet: www.diversalertnetwork.org) has an excellent policy for divers that costs $35 a year plus the annual $29 membership fee. For $10 more you can cover the whole family. For emergencies worldwide, members can call collect at ☎ **800-684-8111** or 919-684-4326.

Another excellent resource for medical evacuation coverage is **International SOS Assistance** (P.O. Box 11568, Philadelphia, PA 19116; ☎ **800-523-8930** or 215-244-1500; Internet: www.internationalsos.com). This agency provides evacuation to the closest medical care facility that would be equivalent to what you'd get in the U.S. For $55 per person for up to 14 days ($96 per couple or $151 per family), you're covered for air evacuation and all travel-related expenses. This insurance does not cover hospitalization or other charges related to medical care.

If you require additional insurance, try one of the following companies:

- ✔ **MEDEX International**, 9515 Deereco Rd., Timonium, MD 21093-5375 (☎ **888-MEDEX-00** or 410-453-6300; Fax: 410-453-6301; Internet: www.medexassist.com).

- ✔ **Travel Assistance International**, 9200 Keystone Crossing, Suite 300, Indianapolis, IN 46240 (☎ **800-821-2828**; Internet: www.travelassistance.com). For general information on services, call the company's **Worldwide Assistance Services, Inc.**, at ☎ **800-777-8710.**

Lost-luggage insurance

Forget about taking out extra insurance on your baggage. This type of insurance is expensive and difficult to collect. We urge you not to carry anything with you that is very pricey anyway. (See the section on what to pack later in this chapter.) Although our luggage has never been lost in the Caribbean, we've met plenty of fellow travelers who've been in that unenviable position. Your homeowner's insurance should cover lost or stolen luggage as part of your off-premises theft protection; check with your agent for confirmation. U.S. airlines are responsible for up to $2,500 if they lose your luggage, but on international flights (including U.S. portions of international trips), baggage is limited to approximately $9.07 per pound, up to approximately $635 per checked bag. If you plan to check items more valuable than the standard liability, you may purchase excess-valuation coverage from the airline, up to $5,000. But when you read the fine print on your ticket, so many items are excluded — like electronics and computers — that you may have trouble collecting on the full amount. If you must carry something valuable on your trip, keep it in your carry-on bag.

If you arrive at a destination without your bags, ask the airline to forward them to your hotel or to your next destination; they will usually comply. If your bag is delayed or lost, the airline may reimburse you for reasonable expenses, such as a toothbrush or a set of clothes, but the airline is under no legal obligation to do so.

Lost luggage may also be covered by your homeowner's or renter's policy. Many platinum and gold credit cards cover you as well. Some credit cards (such as American Express and certain gold and platinum Visas and MasterCards) offer automatic flight insurance against death or dismemberment in case of an airplane crash, but only if you use that card to pay for your tickets.

Playing It Safe

The Caribbean is generally considered an easy place to travel. You don't have to get special shots to go to the islands that we recommend, and you don't need to worry about consuming the food and water. If you have any concerns about these issues, you can check the State Department's Web page for travel warnings at `http://travel.state.gov` or you can check with the **Centers for Disease Control** at its Web site (`www.cdc.gov/travel`).

One of our Jamaican vacations is particularly memorable, but not because of its pleasant and relaxing properties. The first morning, weekend warrior Kevin injured his back taking advantage of water-skiing at dawn. Next, our youngest son had an allergic reaction to the corn syrup sweeteners used in many of the tropical fruit drinks. A few days later, our older son began to shake uncontrollably and had to go to the clinic. He eventually was diagnosed as being extremely dehydrated — a common problem for children at play in the cool breezes of the tropics. Next, Kevin got an ear infection after he went diving.

The last straw came on our final morning, before we had to leave for the airport. Kevin was taking a farewell dip in the waist-deep end of the pool when he stepped on a metal bristle from the pool brush, imbedding the splinter in his foot. The bartender had to pull it out. Of course, we couldn't remember when he'd last had a tetanus shot, so we took yet another trip to the clinic. We were greeted there by name. Not one of our better trips.

Staying healthy

Clearly, vacations are not always smooth sailing when it comes to your health. Bring all your medications with you, but keep them in their original bottles so you don't run into problems with customs. Carry a prescription for more if you worry that you'll run out.

If you suffer from motion sickness, bring a remedy like Dramamine, even if you're not planning to be on a boat. You may suddenly decide that a sunset sail is irresistible. Plus, we've often found that the combination of heat and winding roads can cause problems even if we're not on the water.

If you have health insurance, bring your carrier identification card in your wallet. If you suffer from a chronic illness, talk to your doctor before taking the trip. For concerns such as allergies to medication, epilepsy, diabetes, or a heart condition, wear a Medic Alert identification tag, which will immediately alert any doctor to your condition and give him access to your medical records through Medic Alert's 24-hour hotline. To enroll with Medic Alert, you pay $35, which gets you a stainless steel bracelet or necklace engraved with information about your specific medical information. This effort is an especially good idea if you plan to dive or jog and likely won't have any other form of identification on you. Medic Alert charges a $15 annual fee, which is waived the first year. Contact the **Medic Alert Foundation,** 2323 Colorado Ave., Turlock, CA 95381-1009 (☎ **800-825-3785;** Internet: `www.medicalert.org`).

If you do get sick, ask the concierge at your hotel to recommend a local doctor. You'll get a better recommendation from a concierge than from any national consortium of doctors available through a toll-free number. If you can't get a doctor to help you right away, try the emergency room at the local hospital.

Island creatures great and small

Be prepared to see lots of lizards, geckos, and iguanas. You may even find the first two in your room, but they're harmless. They eat bugs, which is good, because you'll see those also. We've rarely had any problem with mosquitoes, except on the southwest coast of Jamaica in the summertime. The stiff trade winds seem to keep them at bay. But if you're one of those unlucky people who is a mosquito magnet, bring repellent or Avon's Skin So Soft, which seems to do the trick. What we almost always find on any fresh flowers or fruit trays in our room are tiny little ants, which are harmless.

Expect to see stray animals strolling in and out of even the nicer restaurants on the islands. As tempting as it is to pet and feed them, keep a safe distance from the many dogs and cats that you'll see on the islands — some heartbreakingly thin. Teach your children to do the same. We've seen youngsters get scratched and bitten when they disregarded the rules that apply back home. Rabies is rare in the Caribbean, but it does exist.

In the water, the best policy is to look but not touch. Some marine life inhabiting these waters can inflict nasty stings. Don water shoes so that you don't step on something painful. Coral inflicts cuts that almost always become raw and infected, and you can easily damage this living organism with just the slightest touch. If you step on a sea urchin — the ocean's answer to a porcupine — its spines will deliver a painful prick. Apply vinegar to the places where the spines go in, which look like giant splinters. The vinegar neutralizes the poison and helps draw out the spines. Jellyfish stings are infrequent but can also be painful. If you see what looks like a plastic baggie with tentacles floating on the water surface, move away immediately. If you get stung, don't rub the wound. Gently put baking soda on it (vinegar for a Portuguese man-of-war, which is more severe), and then remove any tentacles clinging to the spot. Barracuda and shark attacks are extremely rare. We have often seen barracudas and sharks on our dives, but we've never felt threatened. Avoid wearing shiny jewelry in the water, which can attract them.

Water, water everywhere, but is it safe to drink?

We like to bring bottled water with us on the plane to keep hydrated en route to the Caribbean, especially if we have a long ride to our hotel after we arrive on the island.

After you arrive at your destination, follow these tips to help prevent any illnesses from drinking contaminated water:

- ✔ **Drink bottled water if you're on an island after a major storm.** Tap water is safe to drink in the Caribbean, but sewage can sometimes seep into the water supplies during major storms.

- ✔ **Never drink from a freshwater stream, no matter how tempting it looks, because the water can contain dangerous parasites.** We've been with local guides that told us the water was fine, but we knew that cool water had potential problems.

Some of the ritzier island resorts provide you with bottled water at no charge if you request it, while others charge for bottled water. Before you swig those bottles in the minibar or the ice bucket, be crystal clear on whether the resort intended the bottled stuff as a freebie or not. We once wound up paying about $70 for a week's worth of bottled Evian and Perrier that we mistook as complimentary.

Protecting you and your valuables

In all our travels to the islands, we've never once had anything stolen or been the victim of any crime. We lived in New York City for 12 years, so we're fairly street-savvy. Our danger antennae did go up in Jamaica's craft markets (where vendors are overly aggressive), in Jamaica's airports (where drug dealers lurk), and on the beach in Negril (where drugs and sex are openly peddled). Of all the islands, we're most guarded on Jamaica, where poverty is an extreme problem. We're also on guard in the more densely populated areas of St. Thomas, Puerto Rico, and St. Croix — in descending order of concern.

What we mean by "guarded" is that we wouldn't walk about freely at night without first checking with our hotel to see if we should avoid any specific areas. We're also wary while browsing in the markets. At the same time, we like to buy on the islands, because we know that the vendors in the markets are desperately poor. Understand that bargaining is the norm in island markets, so don't be rattled at the back-and-forth. On the other hand, don't be bullied into buying something. If you aren't interested, politely and firmly say "no," and move on.

That said, even on Jamaica we never just ensconce ourselves behind the guarded gates of an all-inclusive hotel or resort and refuse to venture out. In fact, we highly recommend getting out to see the country and experience the culture. Just be smart. Don't take a stranger up on an offer to "guide" you around. Stick with guides known to your hotel.

On the islands we haven't mentioned in this section, we feel as safe as we do at home in Marietta, Georgia. But no matter which island we're on, we always exercise caution — just as we do when visiting an unfamiliar city in the U.S. Use your room or hotel safe to store any valuables. Never leave valuables lying on the beach or in a beach chair. We know that sounds obvious, but you wouldn't believe how many folks tuck their wallets in their towels and go for a stroll on the beach. Don't flash expensive baubles, cash, or credit cards.

Before you travel, make two copies of the key information pages of your passports, as well as your airline tickets and credit cards. On the same sheets, jot down international help line numbers to report lost or stolen cards. Leave one copy with a relative or friend back home. Keep the other copy with you — in a safe spot separate from your actual passport. Also bring two extra passport photos. If you do lose your passport or it gets stolen, the copy will help speed the replacement process. If you've brought traveler's checks, record the serial numbers and keep a copy in a safe place separate from the checks so that you can be ensured a refund in case of theft.

Scuba divers should keep a list of all equipment and their serial numbers. If your gear gets lost or stolen, file a police report immediately. Both that list and a copy of the report will be needed to collect on your insurance after you return home.

Deciding Whether to Rent a Car

When you live in a car-crazed society, you can have a hard time imagining a place where you don't necessarily need wheels. But just as you wouldn't rent a car in New York City (unless you were training to become a cabdriver), you may not want to rent a car on certain Caribbean islands either.

However, renting a car is a good idea on Barbados, Puerto Rico, and St. Thomas. Puerto Rico and St. Thomas are large enough that you need your own wheels if you want to get a full flavor of the island. You'll be dealing with the big U.S.-based chains in those locations. Barbados also begs for motorized exploration, and you can rent from local companies on that island.

Rent a car for a day or so to take a tour if it's part of a package, if you're a scuba diver, or if you're staying in a villa or condo on Aruba, Grand Cayman, or St. Croix.

You don't need a car on the British Virgin Islands or St. John. Renting a car in the BVIs is really more trouble than it's worth. The main mode of transportation between the various BVIs is via boat. If you stay in a villa on St. John, you may want to rent a Jeep, but that island is small, and you can get a taxi easily.

Rent at your own risk on Jamaica. If you're the adventurous type, renting a car on Jamaica can be fun. The driving style is supposedly British, but it's best described as third-world craziness. The country has the third-highest accident rate in the world, the roads are often in disrepair or under construction, and the police stop drivers frequently for infractions both real and imagined. See Chapter 25 for additional details.

If you determine that you want to rent a car, do so well in advance of your trip and make sure that the reservation agent faxes or mails you a confirmation, including the specifications on the car you were promised. Rental cars can be snapped up quickly during high season or during a festival or other event, so that piece of paper could become important. On more than one occasion, we've seen tired, angry people at car rental desks arguing with clerks that they had indeed reserved a car with the company. But because they had nothing to back up their claim, well, let's just say we don't think they got anywhere fast.

Because import taxes on vehicles are usually outrageous in the Caribbean, be assured that your rental car choices are going to be fairly limited. You'll probably be issued a Toyota Corolla or some other similarly small car. On many of the islands, though, Jeeps and small trucks are becoming increasingly popular with tourists. If you have dive gear or lots of water-sports toys to haul around, paying a few extra dollars for a Jeep or truck probably makes sense.

Don't forget your driver's license if you're going to rent a car. Seniors and students should bring proof of age and status, though discounts are limited in the Caribbean.

Getting a good rental rate

Car-rental rates vary widely in the Caribbean, from a modest $30 a day to $80 or even more. The price depends on many things, including (but not limited to) the following:

- Which island you're on
- The size of the car

> ✔ Whether the car has such niceties as four-wheel-drive (a good idea on mountainous islands like Jamaica and St. John) and air-conditioning
>
> ✔ The length of time you keep it
>
> ✔ Where and when you pick it up and drop it off
>
> ✔ Where you take it

On most islands, we rent the smallest car without air-conditioning and other expensive add-ons. (We often get upgrades, but even if you don't, a smaller car is easier to navigate on the narrow roads.) However, we do pay the extra few dollars to have an automatic transmission rather than a standard. The steering wheel may be on the opposite side from what you're used to, and you drive on the left side of the street on all Caribbean islands except Puerto Rico. We figure we have enough strange factors thrown into the mix without having to think about shifting gears, too.

If you need a carseat, be sure to ask if one is available when you reserve the car; request that it be put on reserve as well. However, if you have young children, we strongly recommend that you bring your own carseat for the highest level of safety.

Generally, you don't have to worry about drop-off charges in the Caribbean. In fact, most companies are so eager for your business that they offer complimentary delivery and pickup to and from your resort. Mileage is usually unlimited. (We guess the companies figure, "How far can they go? We're surrounded by an ocean!")

Some companies offer refueling packages, which require you to pay for an entire tank of gas up front. The price is usually fairly competitive with local gas prices, which are much higher than what you find in the U.S. However, you don't get credit for any gas remaining in the tank when you return the car. If you reject this option, you pay only for the gas you use, but you have to return the vehicle with a full tank or else face charges of $3 to $4 per gallon for any shortfall. If, like us, you like to squeeze in every last second on the beach or at the pool, finding a gas station on the way to the airport and messing with lines and paying the clerk may make you miss your plane. We'd rather take advantage of the fuel-purchase option.

When you ask about package deals to the Caribbean, find out if a few days' car rental is included; this perk is common, especially during the summer months. The car-rental value-added feature is a really good deal, because most of the islands are small enough that you can easily see everything worth seeing in that time frame.

If you can forego air-conditioning, you can save money on your rental. Asking a few key questions could save you a mint. For example, weekend rates may be lower than weekday rates. Ask if the rate is the same for pickup Friday morning as it is Thursday night. If you're keeping the car five or more days, a weekly rate may be cheaper than the daily rate.

Don't forget to mention membership in AAA, AARP, frequent-flier programs, and trade unions. Most car rentals are worth at least 500 miles on your frequent-flier account. Club or association memberships usually entitle you to discounts ranging from 5 to 30%. Ask your travel agent to check these rates.

Internet resources make comparison shopping easier. Check with your favorite travel site. Enter the size car you want, the city where you want to rent, and the pickup and return dates. The server returns a price. We find it somewhat difficult to get Internet resources to allow us to compare prices by changing the extras on the car, but at least you can get a general idea of the cost to expect.

You may also have to pay a nominal fee for a temporary local license. To find out more about car rentals, see the individual "Settling into . . ." chapter for the island you're considering.

Demystifying car renter's insurance

On top of the standard rental prices, other optional charges apply to most car rentals. The Collision Damage Waiver (CDW), which requires you to pay for damage to the car in a collision, is covered by many credit card companies. Check with your credit card company to see if you're covered before you go, so you can avoid paying this hefty fee of $10 a day and up.

When you ask your credit card company if it covers the CDW, make sure to explain where you're going, because coverage is not extended to all islands. For example, American Express has suspended coverage of car rentals on Jamaica. Many credit card companies exclude four-wheel-drive vehicles and trucks from coverage as well. Get details in writing from the credit card company that you think will cover your rental. Don't rely on a verbal guarantee from some operator on a toll-free information line.

The car rental companies offer additional insurance for liability (if you harm others in an accident), personal accident (if you harm yourself or your passengers), and personal effects (if your luggage is stolen from your car). If you have insurance on your car at home, you're probably covered for most of these unlikely events. A quick phone call to your insurance agent to make sure that you're covered internationally is a smart move. If your own auto insurance or credit card coverage doesn't cover you for rentals, or if you don't have auto insurance, buy the additional coverage.

Packing Like a Pro

Pros at traveling in the Caribbean try to limit themselves to carry-on baggage only, because the Miami and Puerto Rico airports have acquired a reputation for losing or misdirecting luggage. However, with rules tightening all the time about what you can carry on and Caribbean flights being full almost all the time, this advice isn't really practical anymore unless you're an expert packer or only going for four days or less.

For international travel, most airlines are now limiting passengers to one carry-on item, excluding purses. You won't be able to bypass this rule. If you buy anything large on the islands, don't count on being able to carry it back with you on the plane. You'll either need to check your purchase (by packing it in a piece of luggage that you brought, empty, on the way to the islands) or have it shipped home. Most shops will gladly pack and ship your purchases.

Turn to Chapter 7 to find out what is allowed and what is prohibited on an airplane.

Carrying on essential items

So what should you bring in that all-important single carry-on? Remember that it must fit in the overhead compartment or under the seat in front of you. Here are our suggestions:

- Books and magazines you may want in-flight
- Prescriptions
- Sunglasses for when you arrive
- Any breakable items you don't want to put in your suitcase
- A personal headphone stereo
- A snack in case you don't like the airline food — or there isn't anything to like
- Any vital documents that you don't want to lose in your luggage (like your return tickets and passport)
- The sweater or jacket that you may need on-board (We often find the airplanes overly cool and airline-issued blankets in short supply.)

Also you may want to put your bathing suit in your carryon; that way if you arrive at your resort and your luggage hasn't made it yet or your room isn't ready (a frequent occurrence at large resorts during high season), you can at least relax in your suit by the pool.

Remember that children are also entitled to carryons. You can let older children tote backpacks and some of their own gear. If you have young children, be sure to carry diapers (also pack plenty of diapers in your suitcase, because they're expensive on the islands). Bring the light-weight umbrella stroller for toddlers and babies. Most strollers fit in the overhead compartment; larger ones may have to be checked.

Stocking your suitcase

Don't bring your nicest luggage. We recommend something sturdy and hard-sided with wheels — you won't find many people-movers and moving sidewalks in the islands. Use a luggage strap that locks, which discourages pilfering and also will somewhat keep your belongings intact in case your suitcase pops open en route.

On the way to the Caribbean, put a temporary tag on your luggage listing your island hotel and phone number. Inside your luggage, tuck in your business card or tape a sheet of paper with your name and address.

When packing, start with the biggest, hardest items like shoes, then fit smaller items in and around them. Put things that could leak, like shampoo and suntan lotion, in resealable bags, away from anything that could be ruined if something seeps out.

When you pack for the Caribbean, put everything in a big pile and then automatically eliminate half. We're serious — whatever you bring, it'll be too much. Most islands are extremely casual, and you'll scarcely need much beyond your sunglasses, swimsuits, casual clothes (shorts and sundresses), sandals, and sturdy water shoes. (Pieces of coral and shells can wreak havoc on bare feet.)

Toting your diving gear

Don't forget your certification card (C-Card) and a logbook recording your recent dives. Good operators will want to see it before they allow you to make a boat dive or even get scuba tanks filled with air. And if you don't have a logbook, you'll likely have to take a check-out dive before you're allowed to proceed.

If you have your own fins, booties, mask, and snorkel, bring them. If you own a regulator, a buoyancy control device (an inflatable vest), a dive computer, or a wet suit or dive skin, bring those, too. You may think that you don't need the latter in the warm waters of the Caribbean, but when you get down 30 feet or so, you cool off quickly.

Bring decongestants and antihistamines with you to be sure that your nasal passages stay clear. These items are often scarce or pricey on the islands.

Don't forget your camera and film. The latter often sells out in the hotel gift shops. And if you can find it, the sky-high price will make you swoon. We learned the hard way.

Sun survival kit

Remember to bring plenty of extra sunscreen; it's a good idea to slather it on lavishly whenever you're outside. We recommend using a water-proof one with an SPF of 15 or more. For kids, we especially like the new lotions that come in fun colors. The colors fade an hour or so after they're applied, but initially they allow you to see exactly where you need more lotion.

If you're going to an arid island like Aruba, you may want to pack a water bottle and a small, portable, zip-up cooler to keep drinks cool while you tour around the island.

Women should bring a large hat or plan to buy one. (If you go to windy Aruba, you need to be able to tie it under your chin, or you'll be chasing it all over the island.) Men should bring a baseball cap or plan to buy a straw hat.

Clothing choices

Women may want to bring one or two nice dresses for evenings out or for visiting some historic churches and synagogues that don't allow shorts. Men should bring one dress shirt and one pair of long pants, which are requested at some casinos and restaurants. Jackets are required at only a handful of places on British-influenced isles like Jamaica and Barbados. Even the exclusive Jamaica Inn, which has been known for decades as a place where gentlemen were expected to wear a jacket and tie for dinner, has loosened up a little and done away with the tie requirement.

Humidity can leave you drenched in sweat, so bring natural fabrics. The Caribbean is one place where we have to nix basic black by day, because it's too hot. And ditch the cowboy boots (sweltering) and expensive jew-elry (which screams "Rich tourist — rob me!"). Yes, we've seen both faux pas (same couple).

Don't worry about ironing things. Nobody cares if you have a few wrinkles. And in the places where they do, irons are provided. The nights are generally warm and sultry, but some casinos, clubs, and restaurants — particularly on Aruba and Puerto Rico, where the Latin influence has everyone scrambling for designer duds — overdo the air-conditioning, so tuck in a light jacket or sweater. Don't bring dry-clean-only items, unless they can wait until you're back in your own neighborhood.

Bring sturdy walking shoes; Kevin has river-rafting shoes that are lightweight but give great traction for rain-forest treks. Also pack lightweight rain gear if you're going in the rainy season. High heels don't work on the cobblestone streets of Old San Juan or Charlotte Amalie.

Bring a few gallon-sized resealable plastic bags to pop wet swimsuits in if, like us, you like to hang by the pool until the last possible moment. Those plastic bags also come in handy when you're dealing with wet, sandy shoes.

Part III
Aruba

The 5th Wave   By Rich Tennant

In this part . . .

*I*f you're thinking about basking in Aruba's warm hospitality, we share our recommendations for the best accommodations on the island. We give you the ins and outs of traveling to Aruba and exploring the sights after you arrive.

Aruban cuisine is as delicious as it is diverse, and we guide you toward the most appealing restaurants on the island. Finally, we share lots of ideas for ways to spend those lazy, sunny days — both in and out of the water.

Chapter 8

The Lowdown on Aruba's Hotel Scene

By Echo and Kevin Garrett

● ●

In This Chapter

▶ Sizing up hotel locations

▶ Focusing on top hotel picks

● ●

Aruba's best asset is its people, the friendliest in the Caribbean. Not only do they deal with the teeming masses, but they also handle visitors with aplomb and a smile. Their hospitality is even more refreshing when juxtaposed against the concrete and plastic world of Aruba's hotel district, which sprouted in the 1980s along the island's best beaches.

Virtually none of the lodging properties on Aruba capitalizes on the island's surreal natural beauty. Familiar U.S.-based chains, condos, and timeshares, and a few small, individually owned hotels are congregated on the southwest edge of the island. The landscape looks like most of the architects watched too many reruns of the opening minutes of the old TV show *Hawaii Five-O*. Book 'em, Danno.

Aruba hosts a big share of U.S. travelers looking for an easy sun-and-sand vacation package in the Caribbean. A sprinkling of European tourists come as well, but most Europeans opt for neighboring Curaçao, which has far more architectural charm and is almost unknown to most U.S. tourists. Wealthy South Americans like Aruba for its proximity — it's only a few miles north of Venezuela — as well as its dizzying nightlife and casinos. Safe and clean, Aruba is also a consistent choice for the cruise ship lines because it lies outside the hurricane belt. Most of the large resorts have attached the words *and Casino* to their names in the past several years. The latest race is to grab the growing spa market. The **Marriott,** the **Hyatt,** the **Renaissance,** and **Playa Linda Beach Resort** all offer full-service spas, and **The Intermezzo Day Spa,** which specializes in garden-fresh Aruban aloe in its wraps and the exfoliating marine salt body scrub, is now at **La Cabana, The Mill, Allegro,** and

Holiday Inn. For families or budget travelers who prefer to save money by preparing their own meals, Aruba offers several timeshares, condos, and guesthouses.

Figuring Out Where You Want to Stay

Although Aruba doesn't have the range of accommodation choices you'll find on islands like Puerto Rico and Jamaica — no secluded little hideaways or unique inns — it makes up for this lack with good service and guaranteed sun. Almost all of Aruba's hotels (with more than 7,000 hotel rooms) are jammed adjacent to the wide, white-sand beaches on the island's calm southwest coast. Abutting a string of high-rise resorts is Aruba's most famous and aptly named beach: Palm Beach, which is popular with North and South Americans.

Low-rise hotels (as they're called by the locals) hug Eagle and Manchebo beaches, a quieter area that appeals more to Europeans. The most tranquil and widest point of Eagle Beach is in front of one of our favorite hotels, Bucuti Beach Resort. Because the hotel doesn't encourage families as vacation visitors and the resort is popular with Europeans, this part of the beach is the one spot where you may see a few topless sunbathers. (However, the practice is officially frowned upon in conservative Aruba.)

You can find some timeshares and hotels slightly inland from the beach, but we don't feature any of them in this book. We figure that if you go to Aruba, you go for the beach. The savings are so negligible if you stay at an inland location that we don't think it's worth having to walk five minutes to get there. The one exception is the Renaissance, which is downtown, adjacent to the waterfront. The Renaissance has its own small island for guests, with a plethora of watersports and good facilities.

Aruba's "One Cool Honeymoon," "One Cool Family," and "One Cool Summer" packages are extremely generous programs — the most comprehensive we've seen on the islands — that give participants more than two dozen freebies and deep discounts, including better room rates at several participating hotels. The honeymoon deal is now offered year-round, but the package for families and summer specials, which give goodies like free breakfast, free stays, and free snorkeling and sailing for kids, is valid only from June 1 through September 30. Newlyweds, families, and summer visitors just need to ask about the programs when they make reservations and remind the hotel (almost all participate) upon check-in that they want to participate in the package. You'll be given a card that you then show participating merchants on Aruba.

Aruba's Best Accommodations

All of our choices are air-conditioned (gotta have that luxury on one of the Caribbean's hottest islands) and all, except the Renaissance, are on Palm, Eagle, or Manchebo beaches.

The rack rates that appear for each accommodation are in U.S. dollars, and they represent the price range for a standard double room during high season (mid-December through mid-April), unless otherwise noted. Much lower rates are available during the off-season and shoulder season (see Chapter 2 for information on travel seasons). **Travel Unlimited** (☎ **800-228-1502;** Internet: www.travelunlimited.com) and **Aruba4you.com** (www.aruba4you.com) both specialize in packages that can get you good discounts.

Good Web sites for trip reports and a mother lode of information about resorts on Aruba include the following:

- ✔ **Aruba Bound!** (www.arubabound.com): This site offers an impressive, noncommercial collection of hard facts, informed opinions, and numerous links compiled by Aruba aficionados.

- ✔ **Visit Aruba** (www.visitaruba.com): Here you can find practical information, news items, and a snappy gossip column with the up-to-date scoop on what's happening on the island.

- ✔ **Aruba Bulletin Board** (www.aruba-bb.com): Go to this site for a lively exchange of information and opinion, where you can post questions to seasoned Aruba-vacation veterans and search for great timeshare-rental deals.

Cruise ship passengers may also want to log on to www.cruisearuba.com, sponsored by the **Cruise Tourism Authority Aruba.**

Allegro Resort Aruba
$$$$$ Palm Beach

Well-positioned on a lushly landscaped spot on Palm Beach next to the Hyatt, this nine-story all-inclusive underwent a $25 million renovation in 1998 when it was purchased by Occidental Hotels and Resorts. The upbeat mood is punctuated by the hubbub — water aerobics, volleyball, and scuba clinics — in and around the gigantic free-form pool enhanced with a swim-up bar, cascading waterfalls, and two nearby bubbling hot tubs. However, the popular pool area — studded with palm trees — gets crowded and loud during high season, with chairs and lounges on the beach and pool tough to snag. Iguanas roam the property freely, looking for handouts. Of the all-inclusives, though, this one is top-notch, and it's a favorite of young honeymooners. Entertainment six nights a week in the

Jardins Brasilien nightclub and the on-site casino's action win raves (free bingo twice a night and friendly dealers at the blackjack tables). The small, carpeted bedrooms have light rattan furniture, comfortable beds, small white tiled baths (in need of an update) along with combo tub/showers, and tiny balconies overlooking the beach. Upgrades to the higher floors yield only slightly better views, but they aren't worth the extra cost. The food (house wine served with dinner and all alcohol included) are a cut above what you find at most all-inclusives, and you'll get attentive service with a smile — which is definitely not always the case at all-inclusives. The resort gets kudos from us for recently adding a Dine Around Program with the Aruba Gastronomic Association, so guests get discounts and vouchers for 35 local restaurants. That effectively eliminates one of our main beefs with all-inclusives on Aruba: being cuffed to a resort's restaurants when so many on the island are worthy of a visit.

L. G. Smith Blvd. 83, Oranjestad. ☎ 800-858-2258 in the U.S., or 297-86-4500. Fax: 297-86-3191. Internet: www.allegroresorts.com. 417 units. Rack rates: Winter $2,880–$3,660 double per week; off-season $2,240–$3,178 double per week. Rates are all-inclusive with taxes and gratuities rolled in. AE, MC, V.

Aruba Marriott Resort and Stellaris Casino

$$$$–$$$$$ Palm Beach

The name Marriott doesn't usually register on our romance meter, but this eight-story stunner is an exception. This high-rise resort with 413 guest rooms, including 20 suites, occupies the most far flung spot at the end of the high-rise hotel district on Palm Beach. The biggest plus here is the oversized, sun-drenched guest rooms — newly renovated to the tune of $4.2 million as of July 2001 — at 500 square feet apiece with roomy 100-square-foot balconies that give you views of the island's best waters for windsurfing and Aruban fishing boats bobbing in the impossibly teal sea. (Request a room on the higher floors for a more dramatic vista; some have views all the way to the California Lighthouse.) The rooms have big bathrooms with dual sinks, deep tubs with showers, and full-length mirrors. They also have large walk-in closets. The Marriott and its adjacent timeshare property, Ocean Club, form a U-shape around the well-landscaped (though not lush like the Hyatt or Radisson) pool area. Also next to the pool are an iguana habitat, Red Sail Sports Water Sports/Retail Shop, workout facilities, and a small children's playground and center. However, the kid's program still comes across as an afterthought here, rather than a focus. The fact that the children's playground is in the broiling sun highlights the lack of thought. Families should look elsewhere, unless you have older kids who mainly want to windsurf. Some complain about the rockiness of the beach at this end, but we're too busy having fun windsurfing to focus on that. Wear water shoes, and you're fine.

L.G. Smith Blvd. 101, Palm Beach. ☎ 800-223-6388 or 297-86-9000. Fax: 297-86-0649. Internet: www.offshoreresorts.com. Rack rates: $235–$395 double. AE, MC, V.

Aruba Accommodations

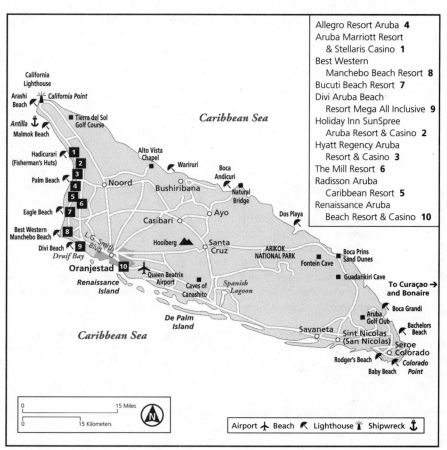

Allegro Resort Aruba **4**
Aruba Marriott Resort
& Stellaris Casino **1**
Best Western
Manchebo Beach Resort **8**
Bucuti Beach Resort **7**
Divi Aruba Beach
Resort Mega All Inclusive **9**
Holiday Inn SunSpree
Aruba Resort & Casino **2**
Hyatt Regency Aruba
Resort & Casino **3**
The Mill Resort **6**
Radisson Aruba
Caribbean Resort **5**
Renaissance Aruba
Beach Resort & Casino **10**

Airport ✈ Beach ↖ Lighthouse ☀ Shipwreck ⚓

Best Western Manchebo Beach Resort
$$$ Eagle Beach

If you can't afford the Bucuti, Manchebo, set amidst 10 acres of palms and brightly blooming bouganvillea, is your best bet with access to that same wide, quiet Eagle Beach. Also popular with Europeans, who have a knack for finding bargains, this sprawling low-rise — one of Aruba's first resort projects started in 1966 — appeals to divers and those looking for a low-key beach vacation. PADI Gold 5-star Mermaid Divers is on-site, offering scuba from custom-made dive boats and beginners' courses, as well as snorkeling excursions. This resort has comfortable, guest rooms (some open onto the beach) that were recently freshened with tropical brights. The staff gives friendly, personal attention in a relaxed atmosphere, and the resort offers live entertainment. It has a small, freshwater pool and dive shop. The beachfront chapel/pavilion is popular for weddings. Alhambra Casino and shopping complex is adjacent.

J.E. Irausquin Blvd. 55. ☎ *800-223-1109 or 297-82-3444. Fax: 297-83-2446. E-mail:* reserve@manchebobeach.com. *Internet:* www.manchebo.com. *Rack rates: $199–$215 double. Children under 12 stay free. Extra person charge $15 a night. AE, D, DC, MC, V.*

Bucuti Beach Resort
$$$$ Eagle Beach

If you don't feel like shelling out for one of the top-drawer hotels, this graciously European-style managed place is a great lower-priced alternative. It's also one of the few resorts that's geared to couples (children are discouraged entirely) and has a perfect location on the widest section of pristine Eagle Beach, far from the madding crowds. Constructed in a low-slung, hacienda style, Bucuti has big, sunny rooms, all stylishly decorated in bright Caribbean colors, with handmade furnishings custom-designed for the resort. Its guest rooms meld contemporary luxury with tropical chic and come with ceiling fans, microwave ovens, minibars, refrigerators, and coffeemakers. All have either queen– or king-size beds. There's an on-site grocery store, a place to do laundry, and a well-equipped workout area shaded under a huge palapa beach hut. The open-air, beachfront Pirate's Nest serves good food with generous portions (see Chapter 10 for more detail).

L.G. Smith Blvd. 55B (P.O. Box 1299, Eagle Beach). ☎ *297-83-1100. Fax: 297-82-8161. E-mail:* bucuti@setarnet.aw. *Internet:* www.bucuti.com. *Rack rates: $240–$270 double; for MAP (two meals daily), add $43 per person daily. AE, DC, DISC, MC, V.*

Divi Aruba Beach Resort Mega All Inclusive
$$$ Druif Beach

You can't miss this Mediterranean-style, low-rise resort with its new multi-colored exterior. Divi has made quite a comeback with its recently completed six-month refurbishment of its new open-air lobby with Jerusalem stone tiles and greenheart hardwoods, topping off an extensive redo of its restaurants, snack bar, and pool area. Dark wood Balinese panels and benches add to the look. In 2000, the oceanfront lanais got new king– and queen-sized beds, televisions, spreads, and curtains. Kept spic and span, the rooms — our picks are in the Vista II building — aren't luxurious, but they are mere feet from the exquisite, wide, white-sand beach. This busy, busy all-inclusive had lost its luster, but it's quickly found its audience again, primarily with young honeymooners and families looking to cap their costs. Most evenings a live DJ spins tunes out by the pool with dancing on the pool deck. Oranjestad is a five-minute drive. Also included in the package is complete use of the **Tamarijn Aruba Beach Resort Mega All Inclusive** next door, as well as nightly entertainment, theme nights, tickets to the Bon Bini Festival, and *Funbook!* coupons for the adjacent **Alhambra Casino.** One caveat: Guests hoard the skimpy supply of free floats and snorkels and save the grass huts overnight, even though it's against policy.

L. G. Smith Blvd. 93, Manchebo Beach. ☎ *800-554-2008 in the U.S., or 297-82-3300. Fax: 297-83-4002. Internet:* www.diviaruba.com. *Rack rates: $220–$255 double. All-inclusive includes all tax and service charges except airport transfers Children (maximum 2 per room with parents) up to age 17 stay and eat free (except Dec 1– Dec 31 when age is 11 and under). AE, D, DC, MC, V.*

Holiday Inn SunSpree Aruba Beach Resort and Casino
$$$ Palm Beach

This sprawling resort — which had a three-year-long $13 million facelift along with a redo of its Excelsior Casino — now boasts more than 600 guest rooms, and you need a map to figure out where everything is. This Holiday Inn is a busy place, right on a quarter-mile of the island's most popular beach, but it's great for families thanks to an excellent kids program — complimentary and with longer hours than others — and the fact that children 17 and under stay and eat free. Kids have their own center and a big, shady playground, too, adjacent to a special kids pool and the beach. A new game room has been added for teens. The friendly staff is eager to please, and the spartan guest rooms are unusually large and come with direct-dial phones with dataports, hair dryers, coffeemakers, irons, and ironing boards. Altogether, this Holiday Inn boasts three restaurants and five bars. However, management apparently thinks quantity makes up for quality. Even the solicitous waitstaff can't bridge the gap between the good presentation and what the food actually tastes like. Gourmands should dismiss the all-inclusive option and consider the dine-around program (see Chapter 10). Several meal plans are available. A car rental and tour desk, concierge, and shopping arcade are all on site.

J.E. Irausquin Blvd. 230. ☎ *800-HOLIDAY or 297-86-3600. Fax: 297-86-5165 (reservations); 297-86-3478 (guest). E-mail:* holidayinn@setarnet.aw. *Internet:* www.holidayinn-aruba.com. *Rack rates: $229–$269 double. Ages 17 and under eat and stay free in parent's room. AE, DC, MC, V.*

Hyatt Regency Aruba Resort and Casino
$$$–$$$$$ Palm Beach

Set on 12 acres fronting one of the more action-packed stretches of Palm Beach, this $57 million Mediterranean-style tropical oasis attracts families and couples. Built in 1990, it's centered around a $2.5 million, three-level, lushly landscaped pool water park. It gets our vote as one of the top ten most luscious pools in the Caribbean. Black swans, flamingos, and scarlet macaws inhabit its 5,000-square-foot lagoon, and the tri-level pool boasts cascading waterfalls, two secluded hot tubs, and a two-story waterslide. (One caution: The stone around the pool gets too hot for bare feet.) Families love this beautiful place, and romantics do, too. If you're active types who love options but hate the frantic, circus-like atmosphere that sometimes plagues resorts that pedal numerous activities, this excellently managed place is sure to sate your restlessness without sacrificing privacy. You rarely feel overrun by other guests — except during high season when you're trying to get a shade hut on the beach. Service overall is excellent, with our only less-stellar encounters happening at the front desk. Guests in the 29 Regency Club rooms get a private concierge, upgraded linens, and other bells and whistles. The resort has five terrific restaurants and four bars; a beautiful pool area, a lively casino; on-site shops; the full-service Stillwater Spa with sauna, steam, and massage; and Red Sail Sports — in case you want to scuba dive, jet ski, or windsurf.

J.E. Irausquin Blvd. 85. ☎ *800-233-1234 or 297-86-1234. Fax: 297-86-1682. Internet:* www.hyatt.com. *Rack rates: $400–$500 double. AE, DISC, MC, V.*

The Mill Resort
$$$ Palm Beach

In December 2002, this resort completed a full renovation of its lobby (now with waterfalls), front desk, pool deck, and all the rooms. This complex of two-story concrete buildings with red roofs is set in an arid, dusty location inland from famed Palm Beach, near the Wyndham and the start of the high-rise hotel section. The resort, popular with the gay community (though its bar, which was a gay hangout, has been redone and lost its following), is adjacent to a large, modern re-creation of a Dutch windmill, a kitschy Aruban landmark. Units surround a free-form, freshwater pool and wading pool for kids. The sliver of beach used by Mill guests lies across the busy highway, a five-minute walk away, with its own beach facillities with towel hut, chaise lounges, and beach attendant. The room decor is bright tropicals, with white rattan furniture and white floor tiles; studio units have king-size beds and sofabeds, full kitchens, and dining corners. The royal suites have king beds, whirlpool tubs, and balconies, as well as mini-fridges and coffeemakers. Junior suites offer two double beds and a sofa bed or a king-size bed along with a kitchenette and balcony. The resort also has 1– and 2-bedroom suites with full kitchens available. The new Intermezzo Spa, morning coffee hour, and a free weekly scuba lesson are some of the extras.

L. G. Smith Blvd. 330, Palm Beach. ☎ *800-992-2105 or 297-86-7700. Fax: 297-86-7271. Internet:* www.millresort.com. *Rack rates: Winter $180–$190 double; $200 junior suite. $320 1-bedroom apt.; $450 2-bedroom apt. Children up to 14 years old stay for free with their parents. AE, MC, V.*

Radisson Aruba Caribbean Resort
$$$$–$$$$$ Palm Beach

The resort sits on a 1,500-foot, less-crowded strand of Palm Beach's sugar-white sand with 50 shade palapas for guests (we didn't have a problem getting one, whereas at the Hyatt and Marriott guests stake out every inch of shade by 8:30 a.m., leaving late-risers to bake). Chill out on one of the comfortable cushioned lounges by one of the twin beachfront zero-entry free-form swimming pools. They are gargantuan and surrounded by ornamental grasses and swaying palm trees. Two bubbling whirlpools are hidden away at the property's far edge.

Radisson's elegant, 16,000-square-foot casino attracts a more upscale crowd than some of the others on the island. The 14-acre tropical landscaping is laced with lagoons and waterfalls, replete with parrots and macaws squawking from their gigantic cages. The stylish guest rooms, which are the most elegant on the island, have extra-roomy marble bathrooms with separate showers/tubs equipped with island-made aloe vera toiletries. Ultra-luxe comfortable, four-poster beds are plush with high-count linens. All rooms have spacious balconies with teak patio furniture — a big plus over the Hyatt. For sea views, you need to be above the fourth floor. Watch out for the high cost of breakfast here. It'll quickly push up your final tally.

This resort's extensive guest enrichment program is one of the best we've experienced. It helps visitors make the most of their Aruban vacation with fun extras like cooking classes to prepare local dishes, *papiamento* (the local language of Aruba) lessons, and family days (kite flying, sand castle–building lessons and more). Even though kids aren't as much of a focus as at some of the other resorts, kudos to the Radisson for not canceling its children's activities if only a few children show.

4400 J.E. Irausquin Blvd. 81, Palm Beach. ☎ *800-333-3333, 954-359-8002, or 297-86-6555. Fax: 297-86-3260. Internet:* www.radisson.com/palmbeachaw. *Rack rates: $340–$435 double. AE, DISC, DC, MC, V.*

Renaissance Aruba Beach Resort and Casino
$$$$–$$$$$ Oranjestad

If you like to be in the heart of the action, this busy hotel with a 24-hour casino and 130 shops adjacent will suit you. Located in downtown Oranjestad and within walking distance of fun discos and good restaurants, the Renaissance is good for couples and families looking for lots to do combined with a little privacy. The resort fronts a marina rather than a beach, but the Renaissance cleverly turned a negative into an asset by acquiring a small private island just five minutes away by motorboat and transforming it into a lovely alternative to Aruba's somewhat crowded beaches. You step off the elevator in the lobby to a waiting motorboat launch, which speeds you to Sonesta's island where full facilities await. All the usual water sports are offered. One path on the island leads to the adults-only section, where hammocks beckon, and couples can have their own private butler for the day. Another path takes you to an area reserved for families. The resort's regular Marina Tower guest rooms are on the small side (crowded for families taking advantage of the good children's program) and the tubs are liliputian. Go for the much roomier suites ($265 to $375 in high season) across the street, if budget permits.

L.G. Smith Blvd. 9, Oranjestad. ☎ *800-766-3782 or 297-83-6000. Fax: 297-83-4389. Internet:* www.arubasonesta.com. *Rack rates: $225 double; for MAP (two meals daily), add $50 per person a night. AE, DC, MC, V.*

Chapter 9

Settling into Aruba

By Echo and Kevin Garrett

● ●

In This Chapter

▶ Knowing what to expect when you arrive

▶ Getting around the island

▶ Discovering Aruba from A to Z

● ●

Aruba's declaration of independence from the Kingdom of the Netherlands on July 1, 1986, coincided with this small island's enthusiastic embrace of tourism as its future. Its warm, friendly people — among the Caribbean's most highly educated, because a quarter of the national budget is devoted to education — are known for their hospitality. In fact, many of them study at Europe's finest hotel schools before returning home to work in the tourism trade. In this chapter, we help you get settled into Aruba, and we cover all those essentials like arriving and getting around.

Arriving in Aruba

Arriving in the Caribbean just doesn't get any easier than this. Having welcomed more than 1 million visitors in 2001, tiny Aruba sure knows what it's doing. After you've gotten off the plane and whetted your appetite with the gorgeous sunshine, you'll whisk right through customs and passport control.

Thanks to a much-needed, $64 million expansion that tripled its capacity, Aruba's busy, busy Queen Beatrix International Airport (☎ 297-82-4800; E-mail: airportaruba@setarnet.aw) makes a much better first impression than it used to. It handles jumbo jets and charters that arrive from all over the world, disgorging tourists from the U.S., South America, and Europe amazingly well. The airport is clean, bright, and well-staffed.

You'll be presented immediately with armloads of tourist information — all free. Pick up copies of the excellent magazines *Aruba Experience* (☎ 297-83-4467; Internet: www.aruba-experience.com) and *Aruba*

Nights (www.nightspublications.com) — they're packed with coupons, and you may need them for a rental car. Cheerful tourist board representatives chirping *bon bini* (the Papiamento phrase for "welcome") patrol the orderly lines looking for tourists to assist.

Getting to Your Accommodations

Right after you've claimed your bags and cleared Customs, you'll find spiffy taxis lined up at the curb. Courteous drivers quickly approach when you beckon. The capital of Aruba, Oranjestad, is a five– to ten-minute ride from the airport and costs $10. The Aruba Marriott, an easy 20-minute, $22 ride, is the farthest hotel from the airport. The average tab runs $18 along the hotel strip. You can tip from 10 to 15% of the fare, but it's not mandatory.

If you rented a car, you can pick it up across from the airport building, along with easy-to-follow directions to your hotel.

Getting Around Aruba

Because most of the hotels are lined up along the island's fabulous beaches (see the "Aruba Accommodations" map in Chapter 8), you may not feel the need to wander far from the hotel pool and the milky teal blue calm of the Caribbean.

You definitely don't need a car to tour downtown Oranjestad. A leisurely stroll through the picturesque town with its charming Dutch architecture is all that's required to take in the entire shebang.

On foot

The hassle-free, pristine beaches of Aruba are perfect walks. Oranjestad is a good spot, too. Nature lovers and adventurers may want to take the easy hike around **Arikok National Park.** Ask your hotel to refer you to a guide, or contact the park at Piedra Plat 42 (☎ **297-82-8001**; Fax: 297-82-8961; E-mail: PNA@setarnet.aw).

By bus

Aruba has the Caribbean's most reliable public bus system, which runs hourly trips between the hotels fronting Palm and Eagle beaches and Oranjestad, as well as down the coast between Oranjestad and San Nicolas. Each trip costs $1 each way, and U.S. dollars are accepted. You can pick up a current schedule at your hotel's front desk. The terminal (☎ **297-82-7089**) is on Oranjestad's main drag across from the water-front, next to the Royal Plaza shopping center.

By taxi

Fixed fares are set by the government. After midnight, you pay an additional $1 surcharge for trips. Tell the driver where you want to go before you climb in, and he will tell you the fare. Make sure to ask for it in U.S. dollars.

Taxis are also available for sightseeing tours; an hour-long tour for one to four people costs $25. For the airport dispatch office, dial ☎ **297-82-2116** or 297-82-1604. Or ask your hotel to call a taxi for you. In town, you can easily flag one by raising your hand.

By car

Car rental companies on Aruba are eager for your business, and a free day's rental is often rolled into package deals, especially during generous summer promotions. We think that renting a car for a day here — especially if it's a freebie — is a fun idea, because this island is so safe and friendly. You'll likely also get extras like free pickup and delivery. Still, during high season, call ahead and reserve.

Whether you've reserved your car ahead of time or not, look for coupons in the handy tourist guides you grabbed when you got off the plane and present them when you start the transaction. Or simply ask about any special discounts. All rental companies offer unlimited mileage; with an island measuring 19 miles long by 6 miles wide, it's a no-lose proposition. Without a coupon, expect to spend about $50 a day. Local car rental agencies are sometimes slightly less expensive. You'll mainly see Toyotas and Suzuki Samurais on the road.

Here are some of the car rental operators: **Amigo** (☎ 297-86-0502); **Budget** (☎ 800-527-0700 or 297-82-8600); **Dollar** (☎ 297-86-0506); **Economy Car Rental** (☎ 297-83-0200 main office or 297-88-3208 at the airport); **Happy Island and Topless Car Rental** (☎ 297-87-5236); Hertz (☎ 800-654-3001 or 297-82-4545); **National** (☎ 800-227-7638 or 297-82-5451; at airport and Holiday Inn); and **Toyota Rent a Car** (☎ 297-83-4902).

Request a four-wheel-drive vehicle if you plan on touring the island's less-developed countryside, the *cunucu,* which is kind of like Australia's Outback. The weather's hot, so don't forget air-conditioning. Really, a day's rental is all you need to tour the entire island. (But a cheaper way to accomplish the same thing is to book one of the 4-x-4 tours of Aruba — see Chapter 11.)

All the roads in Oranjestad and toward the hotels are well-marked and in good shape. On other parts of Aruba, though, the signage quickly dwindles down to sketchy at best, and the same goes for the roads at certain points. In fact, locals often tack up homemade signs on the fences, made out of cactus, directing hopelessly lost tourists to the spot they're likely seeking.

You would think it'd be tough to get lost on such a small island, but we've even been with a few local drivers who appeared confused sometimes. Also, you may be unfamiliar with the road signs here, which use international symbols, and the European-style traffic lights. And speaking of signs, keep an eye out for one-way directionals in Oranjestad — the capital is a collection of one-way streets.

If you do rent a car, study the local rules of the road before setting out, bring a map (but feel free to ask directions), drive defensively, and remember that there are no right turns on red.

Parking is free, and traffic isn't bad. You get a few mild jam-ups in Oranjestad when people get off work or during a celebration, which, come to think of it, happens with great frequency, because Arubans love to celebrate. Aruba is safe, so if you do get lost, pull over and ask a local. Just be prepared to get directions in landmarks, rather than by street signs.

By bicycle, moped, and motorcycle

The flat terrain makes Aruba a fun place to bike or ride, but because of the ferocious intensity of the sun and wind, we recommend bicycles only for masochists or for those in good shape. Stay off Routes 1 and 2, which have busy traffic around the hotel strip and town. And take plenty of water and sunscreen.

Bicycles are available through many hotels. **Pablito Bike Rental** (☎ 297-87-0047) in Oranjestad rents mountain bikes for a full day for $12. Olympian triathlete Gert Van Vliet rents mountain bikes through his **Tri Bike Aruba** (☎ 297-85-0609) in Santa Cruz.

Motor scooters and motorcycles, which rent for $40 to $100 a day, can be found at **George's Scooter Rentals** (☎ 297-82-5975) or **Nelson Motorcycle Rentals** (☎ 297-86-6801). Motorcycle Mamas and Papas who want to go whole hog can rent Harleys at **Big Twin Aruba,** L.G. Smith Blvd. 124-A, (☎ 297-83-9322; Fax: 297-82-8660). Or at least have your picture taken with Big Twin's 1939 Harley Davidson Liberator.

Fast Facts: Aruba

ATMs

You'll find two ATMs at the airport. Several machines are available in town in the shopping areas: Noord Branch Palm Beach 4B; Seaport Marketplace, L.G. Smith Boulevard; Playa Linda Beach Resort, L.G. Smith Blvd. 87; Sun Plaza Building, L.G. Smith Blvd. 160. For a complete listing, look in the back of the handy guide you get at the airport. You can choose to get your money in either U.S. dollars or *florins* (Aruba's currency).

Baby-sitters

Most hotels are happy to help you arrange baby-sitting. The average cost per hour is $10.

Banks

Aruba Bank, Royal Bank of Trinidad and Tobago, and Caribbean Mercantile Bank are in Oranjestad. Hours are weekdays 8 a.m. to 4 p.m. (Banks do not close for lunch in Aruba.)

Credit Cards

Major credit cards and traveler's checks (with ID) are readily accepted.

Currency Exchange

The official currency is the Aruban florin (also called the Aruban *guilder*), written as Af or Afl. U.S. dollars are happily accepted everywhere: U.S. $1 = Afl $1.78. You really don't need to exchange money, unless you want pocket change for soda machines or a few coins to collect, because they're cool-looking.

U.S. dollars are the only foreign currency readily accepted on Aruba; however, other monies can be easily converted at any local bank. All exchange rates are posted in the bank, or check the Internet at www.xe.net/ucc/.

Doctors

Hotels have doctors on call.

Emergencies

For police dial ☎ **100**. For fire and ambulance dial ☎ **115**.

Hospitals

Horacio Oduber Hospital, J.E. Irausquin Boulevard, can be reached at ☎ 297-87-4300.

Information

You can find a tourist office in the airport. Prior to your visit, contact the Aruba Tourism Authority (1000 Harbor Blvd., Weehawkien, NJ 07087; ☎ 800-862-7822 or 800-TO-ARUBA in the U.S.; 416-975-1950 in Canada; 800-268-3042 in Quebec and Ontario; Internet: www.aruba.com).

Language

Dutch is the official language, but Arubans also speak English and Spanish. The everyday language of the people is Papiamento. Locals often mix three or four languages in the same conversation; keep your ears tuned for some interesting exchanges, even if you can't understand what's being said.

Maps

Maps are available throughout the island and in the back of free guides.

Newspapers/Magazines

Boulevard Drug and Bookstore (☎ 297-82-7385) in the Seaport Village Mall can keep you in touch with current events. The store sells stamps and road maps as well.

Pharmacies

For prescriptions and other needs, visit Boulevard Drug and Bookstore (☎ 297-82-7385) in the Seaport Village Mall.

Police

Call ☎ **100**.

Post Office

If you're ambitious, you can visit the post office at 9 J.E. Irasquin Blvd., Oranjestad (☎ 297-82-1900), but your hotel's front desk can also mail your letters and postcards.

Safety

Crime is extremely rare on Aruba, which is a prosperous island. You can walk about freely, but common-sense rules apply. Don't leave valuables wrapped in your towel on the beach or have your camera dangling behind you while you look at the shops along the waterfront.

Taxes

The government room tax is 7.6%, and hotels will sting you for an additional 10% service charge for room, food, and beverages. The Departure Tax is $23, plus $3.25 for those making use of the U.S. Departure terminal and, therefore, U.S. INS/Customs services in Aruba. The Departure Tax, officially referred to as the Passenger Facility Charge, is included in the airline ticket price.

Telephone

To call Aruba from the U.S., dial 011, then 297, and then the 6-digit local number.

International calls made from hotels carry heavy service charges resulting in a charge five times the normal rate. Walking or driving to a nearby SETAR teleshop is worth the time, resulting in a comparatively low cost of $1 per minute. In your hotel room, you can find a guide that lists the codes to reach the major carriers and also alerts you to which one the hotel deals with. Or you can call your hotel operator, who can usually quickly and efficiently connect you to the long-distance carrier you desire. You can reach AT&T at ☎ 800-462-4240; Sprint at ☎ 800-877-8000; and MCI at ☎ 800-888-8000.

Time Zone

Aruba is on Atlantic standard time year-round, so most of the year Aruba is one hour ahead of eastern standard time (when it's 10 a.m. on Aruba, it's 9 a.m. in New York). When daylight saving time is in effect in the United States, clocks in Aruba and New York show the same time.

Tipping

The standard is 10 to 15% if the tip is not already included, and $1 per day for maids and $1 per bag for bellhops. Many restaurants tack on 10 to 15% service charges to their bills, so check before you leave a double tip.

Water

The water is fine to drink; it comes from a desalinization plant on the island.

Chapter 10

Dining in Aruba

By Echo and Kevin Garrett

● ●

In This Chapter

▶ Sampling local cuisine

▶ Saving money on meals

▶ Locating the island's best restaurants

● ●

*I*n the mood for Indonesian food? How about a nice Argentinian steak? Or some sushi so fresh that it's practically swimming? You name it, you can expect it to be good here. Aruba is one of those islands where you'll really miss out if you just stick with the meals served at your all-inclusive resort. Many of the chefs on the island were trained in Europe's best hotel schools and restaurants. Some attained additional seasoning by working on cruise ships and in other hotels abroad. In other words, your palate reaps the full benefit of Aruba's melting pot.

Indeed, with more than 40 nationalities represented on this small island, finding a restaurant isn't the problem — you have more than 100 to choose from. Deciding on a restaurant is the hard part. We give you a head start in this chapter by reviewing some of our favorites.

Enjoying a Taste of Aruba

The local cuisine is a combination of Dutch and Caribbean. Dutch cuisine tends to use a lot of fine cheeses and meats with heavy sauces, and the Caribbean influence adds fresh seafood and curries. We love the result and urge you to try at least one local specialty while you're on the island, although sensitive stomachs may find local food too rich.

You'll also find a strong South American influence lending additional spice, because Aruba is so close to that part of the world. You'll have no problem getting a good steak here; the meat is imported from Argentina, which is noted for its terrific beef.

If you'll be visiting during high season, we strongly recommend that you e-mail reservation requests before you're on the island to avoid disappointment. Be aware that many of the restaurants follow the European custom of not presenting the bill until it's requested, and that your bill likely includes a 15% service charge, so be sure you don't overtip.

Although some of the best restaurants are at the hotels, several places are worth a taxi ride.

During Aruba's "One Cool Summer" celebration — May through September — the Watapana Food and Arts Festival allows you to sample specialties from several different restaurants while you browse works by local artists. Staged every Wednesday from 6:00 to 8:30 p.m. and located outdoors between the Allegro and Hyatt Regency on Palm Beach, the festival also features local entertainers.

Outrageous import taxes on wine render getting a decent bottle without paying sky-high prices virtually impossible. If you're a wine drinker, the excellent and more reasonably priced Chilean wines from nearby South America are your best bet. Beer drinkers are in luck: The local brew called Balashi (now you can get Balashi Light, too) just won an international gold medal, and Amstel and Heineken are brewed on neighboring Curaçao.

Two excellent liqueurs are brewed on the island: Ponche crema, which tastes kind of like eggnog, and Coe Coe, made from the agave plant. You'll find these two as ingredients in a number of tropical libations, lending them an Aruban spin.

Although some of the better restaurants are at the hotels, several places are worth a bus or taxi ride. Even if you're at an all-inclusive resort, the Dine-Around Program enables you to experience other restaurants at a reasonable price instead of eating at your hotel night after night.

Aruba's Best Restaurants

Brisas del Mar
$$–$$$ **Savanetta   Seafood/Traditional Aruban**

For expertly-prepared, spanking fresh seafood prepared down-home Aruban style, take the 20-minute drive ($1 bus or $24 cab ride) to get you to this locally-owned, open-air seaside restaurant. Housed in what was formerly a police station in the 1800s, this spot is nothing special in the looks department. But when we tasted the indigenously-flavored fish stew and classic Aruban fish cakes, called *kerri kerri,* from the old family recipes of dimunitive proprietress Lucia Rasmijn, we were hooked. She pops out of the kitchen throughout the evening to mingle with her guests, sharing an Aruban folk tale or island history with anyone who asks. Request a table right by the water overlooking Boca San Carlo where the

Dining in Aruba

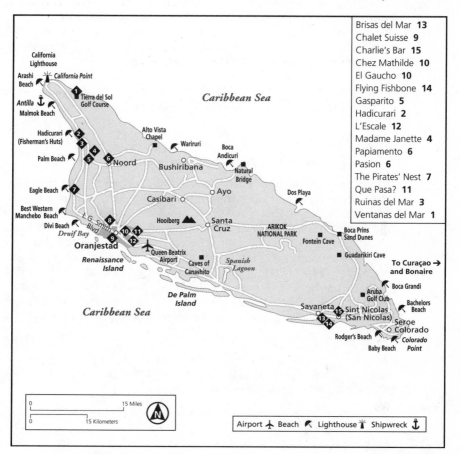

Brisas del Mar **13**
Chalet Suisse **9**
Charlie's Bar **15**
Chez Mathilde **10**
El Gaucho **10**
Flying Fishbone **14**
Gasparito **5**
Hadicurari **2**
L'Escale **12**
Madame Janette **4**
Papiamento **6**
Pasion **6**
The Pirates' Nest **7**
Que Pasa? **11**
Ruinas del Mar **3**
Ventanas del Mar **1**

Airport ✈ Beach ⚓ Lighthouse 🗼 Shipwreck ⚓

local fishermen arrive daily with their catches. You can order whatever they've brought to Lucia while enjoying the sounds of the sea. On the weekends live music brings in hordes of local families, and it's a fun place to bring your children, too.

Savanetta 22A. 20 minutes from downtown Oranjestad. ☎ *297-84-7718. Reservations required. Main courses: Lunch $5–$20; dinner $10–$29. AE, MC, V. Open: Tues–Sun noon to 2:30 p.m, and nightly 6:30–9:00 p.m.*

Chalet Suisse
$$$$ Eagle Beach   Swiss

We were caught off guard by the excellence of Chalet Suisse. (Okay, we confess right now that our knowledge of Swiss cuisine was nil.) The restaurant is conveniently located on Eagle Beach. Soothed by romantic lighting and an exceptionally attentive waitstaff, we enjoyed such scrumptious creations as the hot Chalet Suisse appetizer (shrimp, crab-meat, fish, lobster, and fresh mushrooms), lobster bisque, roast duck-ling with orange sauce, and a Caribbean seafood platter, which included lobster. Each dinner comes with fresh vegetables and home-baked bread. Save room for our fave: Toblerone chocolate fondue served with pound cake and fresh, perfectly ripened fruit.

J.E. Irausquin Blvd. 246. ☎ 297-87-5054. Reservations recommended. Main courses: $15–$42. AE, MC, V. Open: Mon–Sat 6:00–10:30 p.m.

Charlie's Bar

$–$$ **San Nicolas**   **Creole/International**

On the day you head to Baby Beach or Boca Grandi, stop in at Charlie's Bar, which has been operating since 1941 and is now run by the late Charlie's grandson Charlito. Forget about the food, you're here to soak up the atmosphere. While away an afternoon with the locals, artists, sailors, musicians, and other tourists drinking Amstels and nibbling on platters of Creole calamari and jumbo shrimp, accompanied by local bread and Aruban-style french fries (fat and freshly cut). The walls are cluttered with oddities left behind — from tennis shoes to license plates. Make a point of chatting with the friendly staff; you can pick up all kinds of fascinating island trivia. Kids are welcome at this authentic Caribbean-meets-Cheers hangout.

Zeppenveldtstr 56 (a 25-minute drive east of Oranjestad). ☎ 297-84-5086. Reservations not accepted. Main courses: $10–$18, daily soup $6. AE, MC, V. Open: Mon–Sat 11 a.m.–10 p.m. Closed on local holidays.

Chez Mathilde

$$$$ **Oranjestad**   **French**

If you're going to splurge, go for it at Chez Mathilde, one of the island's best restaurants. In an elegant house built in the 1800s — one of the few fine examples remaining on the island — you can enjoy French specialties focusing on fresh local seafood and imported aged beef. We suggest start-ing with the rich bouillabaisse and escargots escoffier. For a main course, try the mildly flavored sole with a delicious sauce or the *tournedos au*

Places for picky eaters

If your kids' favorite refrain is "Euuuw, Mom, do I have to eat that!?", try **Tony Roma's** (across from the Holiday Inn; ☎ **297-86-7427**) for ribs, or **Benihana** (Sasakiweg; ☎ **297-82-6788**) for good Japanese food prepared by chefs who entertain with their elaborate knife play while they prepare your dinner. Talk about playing with your food!

poivre (beef fillet with a pepper sauce). Make a reservation as soon as you're on the island and ask for a private nook in the ultra-romantic Pavilion Room, awash in tasteful beiges and decorated in Italian and French antiques. An elegant fountain serves as the tropical garden's centerpiece.

Havenstraat 23. ☎ 297-83-4968. Reservations required. Main courses: $17–$43. AE, DISC, MC, V. Open: Mon–Sat 11:30 a.m.–2:30 p.m. and dinner nightly 6–11 p.m.

El Gaucho
$$ Oranjestad   Argentinian Steakhouse

Located in an old town house infused with the traditional decor of Argentine *gaucho* (cowboy), this rustic, but cozy restaurant has become a prime stopover for steak lovers. These walls — half leather and half stone — talk, telling the legendary story of the Argentinian cowboy life. An upstairs dining room recently opened to expand the space. Celebrating its quarter century in Aruba, El Gaucho serves up thick slabs of juicy steaks charcoal-grilled Argentinian-style. The specialties of the house are an 18-ounce sirloin and a well-seasoned shish kebab called *Pincho Torro Caliente.* Of course, the food is paired with Argentinian wines. Cigar smoking is allowed in the cocktail lounge. Across the street at **Garufa,** El Gaucho's Cigar and Cocktail Lounge, an extensive variety of premium single malt scotch, cognacs, brandy, and the fine port wine, along with a selection of cigars (including Cubans) provide the topper for the evening.

Wilhelminastraat 80. ☎ 297-82-3677. Fax: 297-83-0123. Reservations required. Main courses: $16–$25. AE, D, MC, V. Open: Mon–Sat 11:30 a.m.–11:00 p.m. Closed the first two weeks of August.

Flying Fishbone
$$$ Savaneta   Seafood

If you're looking for romantic beachside atmosphere, this spot — located in the old fishing village — comes up a winner. This little gem, with just ten tables, is difficult to find but worth the 20-minute, $21 cab ride from Palm Beach (it's in the same area as Brisas Del Mar; look for the sign for Cosmos Day Spa and get good directions if you're driving yourself). Palm trees soar up through the roof, and we loved wiggling our toes in the sand at our water's-edge table. Make reservations for 6 p.m. to ensure you're settled at your table in time for sunset. Tropical cocktails are served in a hollowed-out coconut. Homemade bread is served with green pepper, garlic butter, and black olive spreads. Start with the creamy mushroom and celery red snapper soup. Seafood pots come steaming to the table in a hollowed-out cantelope. The filet mignon will melt in your mouth. The shrimp and blue cheese casserole is divine, too. Or you may want to spring for the Caribbean lobster in cognac sauce, which we recommend above the lobster in a wine, garlic, and butter sauce. Stellar service without being overbearing puts this place on our list of winners.

Savaneta 344. ☎ *297-84-2506. Reservations required. Main courses: $15–$33. D, MC, V. Open: Mon–Sat 5:30–10:00 p.m.*

Gasparito

$$$ Noord   Traditional Aruban

Across from the high-rise district in a traditional country house, a restaurant featuring works by local artists turns out some of the best local cuisine around. Relax and enjoy the excellent service while sampling such favorites as keshi yena, a wheel of Dutch gouda cheese filled with seafood, spiced chicken, or beef. (Trust us, it tastes much better than it sounds.) You'll see why the chef frequently wins awards in Caribbean cooking competitions.

Gasparito 3, near the high-rise hotel section. ☎ *297-86-7044. Reservations recommended. Main courses: $15–$33. AE, MC, V. Open: Mon–Sat 5:30–11:00 p.m., Sun 11 a.m.–4 p.m.*

Hadicurari

$ Palm Beach   Local

For years, this spot was a gathering place for local fishermen to anchor their colorful wooden boats and swap tales, but the development of the high-rise hotel district gradually encroached on their turf. Finally, the government agreed to give them this area to congregate, and it's also become an excellent casual dining spot in the heart of the action on Palm Beach. You can walk up and get the grilled catch of the day for $6, which gets you crioyo sauce (Aruba's version of Creole sauce), salad, and fried plantains. You also get a choice of either *funchi* (a cornmeal polenta), *pan bati* (a traditional Aruban flat bread), french fries, or rice. The proceeds go to help the local fishermen and the nonprofit center. Don't miss the generous Aruban-style barbeque grilled on the beach on Sunday. Just $8 nets you a plate groaning with food. Kids frolic on the playground equipment out front, while a collection of locals, windsurfers, and a few savvy tourists watch the sunset from the picnic tables next to the building brightly painted with scenes from the sea. This modest spot is also one of the most reasonably priced places to get a beer or tropical cocktail.

Centro di Pesca (The Fishery Center), L.G. Smith Boulevard. ☎ *297-86-0820. Reservations not accepted. Main courses: $6–$15. No credit cards. Open: Daily noon to 4 p.m., dinner 6:00–9:30 p.m.*

L'Escale

$$$$$ Oranjestad Harbor   French

Whether you've finished shopping downtown late or feel like trying your luck in the adjoining **Crystal Casino,** book dinner in this gracious, intimate French Empire–style restaurant. Overlooking Oranjestad's marina, this restaurant, with its formal service and strolling string Hungarian duo, delivers on the romance scale. Aruba-born Chef Calvert Cilie quit his day job at the local oil refinery to study cooking in Europe — a good career move for him and lucky for us. Using traditional French techniques, he skillfully blends local ingredients. Try any red snapper dish or the rack of lamb — or just put yourself in his capable hands and order the chef's choice. If you're in the mood to spring for a bottle of wine, L'Escale maintains one of the better selections on the island. It also puts on a fantastic champagne.

Request a table away from the bar and busy casino by the windows overlooking the seaport.

In the Renaissance Aruba Beach Resort and Casino, L.G. Smith Blvd. 82. ☎ ***297-83-6000**. Reservations recommended in winter. Main courses: $17–$50, Sunday champagne brunch $27.95 plus 15% service charge. AE, DC, DISC, MC, V. Open: Nightly 6–11 p.m.; Sat–Sun brunch 10 a.m.–2 p.m.*

Madame Janette
$$$ Cunucu Abao   International/Caribbean

A favorite hotspot with the hip, young windsurfing crowd, this restaurant was an instant hit in 1999 when it opened the doors of the casual, low-slung cunucu house it occupies a short drive from Palm Beach. Most of the tables are outside in the small desert courtyard, sparkling with strands of tiny white lights and candles. Request one at the outer edge for the most privacy. The casual mood and a guitarist who sings American folk classics (Wednesday through Sunday) make for a convivial evening. The courtyard can be a little warm on a still night, but that's the only drawback we found. European Master Chef and co-owner Karsten Gesing continues to generate a buzz with his creative menus, which make good use of the freshest seafood, herbs, vegetables, and fruit. Although trained in old-school ways, Gesing brings Caribbean flair to such appetizers as Madame's hot shrimps in petit casserole, and Caribbean rock lobster in a light creamy sauce with fine cognac. He employs his father's secret marinade on his savory rack of lamb. The well-trained service staff is friendly and lets patrons linger as long as they like. Settle in with the big wine list. It has a wide range veering from classic European to New World selections. For dessert, our favorite is "Mama Jamaica," fresh pineapple marinated in aged Appleton rum topped with vanilla ice cream and roasted coconut flakes.

Cunucu Abao 37. ☎ ***297-870-184** or 297-94-4223. Reservations strongly recommended. Main courses: $15–$33. AE, MC, V. Open: 6–10 p.m. except Tues.*

Papiamento

$$$$ Noord Local/Continental

If you're looking for a leisurely evening on a moonlit night, at Papiamento you feel as though you're dining in a grand country home at this elegant, family-owned and –run Dutch-style restaurant. The traditional Aruban and continental dishes (the menu changes nightly) are served poolside amidst riotous tropical gardens dotted with large terra-cotta pots. Tiny twinkling lights are twined through palms surrounding their private manor, built in the 1860s and filled with treasured antiques from Europe and Aruba. Chatêaubriand for two and Caribbean lobster are also winners.

Romantics should ask to be seated right by the pool.

Washington 61. ☎ *297-86-4544. Reservations required. Main courses: $24–$40. AE, MC, V. Open: Tues–Sun 6:30–10:30 p.m.*

Pasion

$$$$ Noord European/Asian Fusion

This trendy new spot, which features more than 250 wine selections in its wine cellar (the island's largest) offers beautifully presented dishes that are a clever blend of European gastronomic styles with an occasional dash of Japanese traditions. Candlelight plays off the vaulted, dark wood ceiling and textured walls, decorated with original art. The warm mood is further accentuated by mod music. For a special treat, book the Chef's Table or a table in the wine cellar equipped with wine lockers belonging to regular clients. Proven appetizers include smoked Salmon Boules (filled with crab meat and topped by Avruga caviar, served on a bed of lettuce with a dill and fennel emulsion) and the Tempura Shrimp Caesar Salad. For entrees, try veal tenderloin with a red pepper sauce and pasta with truffles and Porcini sauce. The best dessert is its decadently rich chocolate souffle with orange rum. On the ten-page wine list, you'll find Chateau Lafitte '96, Napa Valley's Montave Opus 1, and Concha y Toro's Alma Viva from Chile. A wine sommelier stands ready to help you pair wines with the creative menu.

Palm Beach Rd., 19-A ☎ *297-86-4752. Reservations advised. Main courses: $22–$38; AE, DC, DISC, MC, V. Open: Nightly 6–11 p.m.*

The Pirates' Nest

$$$ Eagle Beach Steaks/Seafood

At first glance, the kitschiness of this hotel restaurant may be a turnoff. The grand scheme is a fake Dutch galleon designed to look as if it's sinking in the sand. But it's also open air and situated on the best part of Eagle Beach. By day, this is a fun spot to come with the kids for good sandwiches and tasty salads. By night, the twinkling lights, moonlight, and torches transform the place. Chef Patrice Coste specializes in fresh seafood and U.S. steaks. We suggest Captain Kidd's shrimp treasure (jumbo Caribbean shrimp sautéed in a spicy chili sauce and flamed with cognac). For the best dinner deal, try the five-course chef's choice for two served away from the dining area on the beach. It includes a bottle of wine and cappuccino, coffee, or tea for $85 per couple. In the mornings you can get a lavish champagne buffet breakfast ($12.95) here, too, and during the happy hour (4 to 6 p.m.), live music entertains guests.

Bucuti Beach Resort, L.G. Smith Blvd. 55B. ☎ *297-83-1100. Reservations recommended. Main courses: Champagne breakfast $12.95, dinner $15–$26. AE, DISC, MC, V. Open: Daily for breakfast 7–11 a.m., lunch noon to 5 p.m., dinner 6:00–10:30 p.m.*

Que Pasa?

$$$ Oranjestad Casual   Caribbean/Aruban

This quaint, casual restaurant, tucked onto a downtown sidestreet, attracts a young, hip European crowd, along with locals and in-the-know U.S. tourists who like to dine here before an evening of dancing. Chef specials are scrawled on the blackboard, but the menu is an eclectic mix of Aruban favorites, spicy American appetizers, and Caribbean standards like jerk chicken. The wait staff here greets everybody like they're long, lost friends. The island art here and wildly colored interior is a hipper version of what you'll find at Gasparito, which has a charming old-fashioned feel to it.

Wilhelminastraat 2. ☎ *297-83-4888. Reservations recommended. Main courses: $15–$33. AE, DISC, MC, V. Open: Mon–Sat 5–11 p.m.*

Ruinas del Mar

$$$$ Palm Beach   Continental

For the hands-down best romantic ambience, head to the Hyatt Regency's Ruinas del Mar. Built to look like the old stone gold-mine ruins on the island and lit by torches and candlelight, this is an absolute stunner. Add to that the lush tropical landscaping, a lagoon complete with koi and black swans, and we're happily gazing into each other's eyes all evening. Executive Chef George Hoek, a native Aruban, spent time at the Hyatt Regency Beaver Creek in Colorado before returning home. His signature dish is a seafood mixed grill of locally caught fish and Caribbean lobster tail. His shrimp tempura with mango tequila salsa is a winner, too. Go with chocolate mousse tower for dessert. In the evenings, there's live entertainment.

One night on the weekend, a special table for two is set 15 feet from the shoreline and swathed by a white tent and surrounded by tiki torches. A waiter is assigned to serve you privately for the evening. Ask for the "Pampered in Paradise" table.

Hyatt Regency, J.E. Irausquin Blvd. #85. ☎ *297-86-1234. Reservations essential and resortwear requested. Main courses: $22–$38. AE, DISC, MC, V. Open: Daily for breakfast 7 a.m. to noon and dinner 5:30–10:00 p.m.*

Ventanas del Mar
$$$ Tierra del Sol   International

Not your basic clubhouse restaurant, the floor-to-ceiling windows of this elegant place, tastefully decorated with natural stone and warm terra-cotta finishes, yields stunning views of the California Lighthouse and this unique golf course with rolling sand dunes and the sea off the island's western tip. By day, golfers come here for the excellent breakfasts and hearty lunches (oversized sandwiches and gargantuan salads are a real bargain). For lunch we recommend the freshly grilled chicken Caesar salad and monster burgers. The real surprise is that dinner here is one of the most romantic spots on Aruba. Book an intimate table on the candlelit terrace where you'll be serenaded by a saxophonist. The sea bass in orange sauce is a must-try. The signature dish of the executive chef, who won Aruba's Chef of the Year in 2001, is a crispy fried whole snapper with stir-fried vegetables and a ginger soy sauce. Stellar service adds to the appeal.

Tierra del Sol Golf Course, Malmokweg. ☎ *297-86-7800. Reservations strongly recommended for dinner. Main courses: $20–$38. AE, DC, DISC, MC, V. Open: Breakfast daily 6:00–10:30 a.m., lunch daily 11 a.m.–3 p.m., dinner Tues–Sun 6–10 p.m.*

Chapter 11

Having Fun on and off the Beach in Aruba

By Echo and Kevin Garrett

• •

In This Chapter

▶ Soaking up the sun on Aruba's top beaches

▶ Diving into fun with water sports

▶ Satisfying the landlubber: Shopping and nightlife

• •

*I*n this chapter, our focus is on fun. We offer plenty of suggestions for activities that help you take advantage of Aruba's chief assets: water, sand, and sun. Aruba offers water sports galore, including world-class windsurfing and wreck scuba diving. If you prefer to be on solid ground, consider driving a four-wheeler through the desert, riding horses on the beach, or golfing on one of the Caribbean's most unique courses.

We wind up this chapter with a look at Aruba's nightlife scene, one of the most active among all the islands in this book. And in case this day-into-night excitement is not enough to keep you busy, we explain the ABCs of island hopping in this area of the Caribbean, giving you the scoop on Aruba's neighbors: Bonaire and Curaçao.

Hitting the Beaches

Aruba's main draws are its glorious powder-white beaches (all public) and its virtually guaranteed sunshine. The glossy photos that you've probably seen are accurate — impossibly white sand juxtaposed against the calm sea's turquoise and cobalt blues. The beaches are spotless, too. Locals and hoteliers alike understand the direct correlation between trash-free beaches and your willingness to visit their island.

Leaning toward the leeward side

You'll find Aruba's best-known beaches — Palm, Eagle, and Manchebo — on the leeward side. The low-rise and high-rise hotel districts are located here as well. Our favorite stretch of the famed Palm Beach — lined by the island's finest hotels and an abundance of imported palms — lies in front of the Aruba Marriott. Despite the constantly blowing trade winds, the Caribbean's clear, blue waters are remarkably smooth and boast visibility up to 100 feet. Even children can safely play in the gentle surf here.

Anywhere along Palm Beach, you can find beach and swim-up bars, casual restaurants, and public restrooms galore. If you decide to go for a long stroll, take along some money in case you work up a thirst.

A great place to stop and get a bite or an icy Amstel or Balashi (the local brew) is Hadicurari Fisheries Center, the fishermen's co-op right on Palm Beach. By law, the food prices must be low enough that the fishermen can afford to eat here, so you can get fresh fish (caught that day) at a great price. (See our review of Hadicurari in Chapter 10.)

You don't have to limit yourself to the beach right in front of your hotel. On Palm Beach, which gets pretty crowded during high season, you can jockey for a position in front of the larger hotels. Competition is especially fierce for shade-providing cabanas, which are reserved for the hotel's guests. Expect to pay about $5 a day for a beach chair if you aren't a guest at the hotel where you want to lounge, and during high season even guests sometimes find them in short supply.

On Arashi, parts of Eagle Beach, and Baby Beach, the government provides cabanas for visitors. The quietest and widest point of Eagle Beach is in front of the Bucuti Beach Resort. The surf here is a tiny bit rougher and the beach drops off much more quickly. If you aren't staying there, reserve lunch or dinner at its restaurant, The Pirate's Nest, and hang out at the beach before or after your meal. (See Chapter 10 for a review of The Pirate's Nest.)

On Fisherman's Hut Beach, littered with the battered remains of conch shells, several water-sport outfitters casually but expertly give windsurfing lessons. This spot is ideal for watching the neon-colored sails of the windsurfers as they skim across the aquamarine sea. You'll think you're watching a butterfly ballet.

At night, you can safely stroll along the beaches and hotel-hop until you settle on a "theme night" — pirates, anyone? — that best fits your mood. Holiday Inn's theme nights are kitschy fun and have been popular on the island for more than two decades.

Breezing toward the windward side

On the windward side of the island, the pounding waves and wild surf crashing against odd rock formations translate into only a few beaches that are worth investigating. But some of the beaches here offer a truly unique experience. On the southeastern tip of the island, **Boca Grandi** (Big Cove) is one of the prettiest and least crowded of Aruba's beaches. Skilled windsurfers and snorkelers love this beach, but you need to be a strong swimmer to go in the water here because the undertow can be fierce. **Dos Playa** is a good place for a quiet picnic and for swimming in the waves, but you should beware of the undertow here as well.

Wariruri, found near Alto Vista, is the island's hottest surfing/ bodyboarding spot. Extreme-sports enthusiasts also use the beach coves of **Boca Andicuri,** which is also an advanced shore dive site, meaning that you can wade to the dive site from the shore, instead of taking a boat. (Boca Andicuri is located near the Natural Bridge, which is described in the "Exploring Aruba" section later in this chapter.) Alto Vista, Dos Playa, and Boca Grandi are other great shore dive sites.

Terrific for families is the aptly named **Baby Beach.** Located on the southeast shore near San Nicolas, this beach makes a semicircular curve around bath-water calm, shallow waters sheltered by a promontory of rocks. You can buy cold drinks and food at the beach's concession stand, as well as rent snorkeling equipment. Baby Beach has a fun, festive vibe, thanks to the locals, who adore this spot.

On **Rodger's Beach** (just up the coast from Baby), you can find slightly better facilities with showers, restrooms, picnic tables, food vendors, and shade. Rodger's also has a shallow reef close to shore. Brave souls can venture farther out, where the coral reef offers decent snorkeling. A much greater abundance of marine life awaits in the waters surrounding either Curaçao or Bonaire. (See descriptions of these two islands later in this chapter.) You can rent snorkeling gear here for about $15 per day.

Picnicking Aruba-style

If you want to have a down-home picnic Aruba-style, try an Aruba barbeque. Every Sunday afternoon, home-style barbecue shops set up to sell a cholesterol jamboree: takeout platters groaning with slabs of ribs, chicken drumsticks and thighs, fish filets, and blood sausages, along with sides of rice, potato salad, and macaroni salad. If your hotel concierge desk can't direct you to a favorite stop, a quick drive around an Aruban neighborhood should turn up something. The average price is about $6.

Staying Active on Land and Sea

When you tire of soaking up the rays on the beach, Aruba offers plenty of other options for having a good time — in, on, and around the beautiful, bountiful beaches.

Putting wind in your sails

With its steady, strong trade winds (which average 15 knots year-round), Aruba is a natural location for windsurfing and one of the better places in the world to learn the sport. The calm waters off **Fisherman's Hut** (also known as Hadicurari) and the beaches of **Arashi** and **Malmok** are the most popular windsurfer hangouts. Fisherman's Hut is where the annual Hi-Winds World Challenge is held each June. But its waters aren't so crowded that beginners feel intimidated. Beginners stick close to the beach while more experienced surfers are much farther out.

When we took lessons, neither of us was much good. But the leather-tanned instructors, who all wore mirrored sunglasses (maybe so we couldn't see the laughter in their eyes) were immensely patient and skilled. Once, Echo thought her instructor was waving at her to let her know she was doing well. Actually, he was signaling her to come back in because she was headed to Venezuela. Nonetheless, we had a great time trying our hand at this sport. **Vela Windsurf Aruba** (Aruba Marriott Resort, ☎ **800-223-5443** or 297-86-9000; Internet: www.velawindsurf.com) rents boards for $60 a day. Beginner lessons run $55 an hour and include a board.

Good news for parents with adventuresome kids: Windsurfing instruction starts for children as young as age 4. The miniaturized boards for tots are adorable.

Both **Sailboard Vacations** (☎ 800-252-1070 or 617-829-8915 Stateside; Internet: www.sailboardvacations.com) and **Roger's Windsurf Palace** (☎ 800-225-0102) offer windsurfing and accommodations packages. Both are on Malmok Beach and have fully equipped shops with good instructors. This section of the beach has a little more of the surfer dude feel to it.

Dining and dancing onboard

The mood on Aruba is party, party, party. Reserve an evening for dirty dancing to live music on *Tattoo* (☎ 297-86-2010; Internet: www.aruba adventures.com/tattoo), a party boat with an unfortunately awful buffet dinner. It's $49 *a person* for a four-hour tour. But the big attraction is the $1 to $2 drinks, the fun dance scene, and the affable crew. If you're feeling frisky, wear your swimsuit under your clothes and take the plunge from the boat's rope swing.

Jolly Pirates (☎ 297-83-7355; Internet: www.jollypirates.com) has a $26 sunset cruise (5 to 7 p.m.) aboard a Brazilian teakwood 85-foot gaff-rigged sailing boat with an open bar and rope swing. Its starlight dinner cruise ($55) launches at 8:30 p.m. and ends at 11:30 p.m. Along the way, you get music, dinner, moonlight dips, and fun on the rope swing.

The *San Francesco* (☎ 297-93-8590), an authentic romantic wooden schooner built originally in Italy in 1870, recently made Aruba its home port and offers sails, too. Its owners sailed all over the Caribbean for several years before deciding on Aruba as their permanent base.

The *Sea Star* (☎ 297-86-2010) sails to a waterfront marina restaurant for a candlelit meal accompanied by island music. After dinner, you return to the boat for merengue and salsa dance lessons.

Diving right in

Aruba ranks right behind Bermuda for its wreck diving. For several years running, *Rodale's Scuba Diving* magazine has rated Aruba in the top five for the Best Wreck Diving in the Caribbean/Atlantic Region category. The magazine also notes that Aruba has one of the "World's Favorite Dive Sites," the *Antilla,* a hulking German freighter that sunk off Malmok Beach during World War II. It is one of the most remarkable sites in the Caribbean as well as the largest in the region, at 400 feet. The *Antilla* is now encrusted with coral and giant tube sponges, and its cathedral-like hold is easy even for a beginning diver. You'll often see schools of silver-sides, horse-eyed jacks, tarpons, and lobsters at the site. Check the cruise ship schedule because this site can get extremely crowded. The *Antilla* has also become extremely popular for night dives.

The California, a wooden cargo ship that sank while trying to deliver general merchandise from Liverpool to South America, is also a popular wreck dive. (In the midst of a midnight party, the California crew let the ship get a little too close to the dark Aruban coast.) If you're a qualified diver interested in wreck-diving, contact **De Palm Tours** (L.G. Smith Blvd. 142, ☎ 297-82-4400), and don't forget to bring your proof of certification. Another excellent operator, centrally located on Palm Beach between Holiday Inn and Playa Linda, is **Pelican Adventures N.V. Tours and Watersports** (P.O. Box 1194, Oranjestad, ☎ 297-87-2302; Fax: 297-87-2315; E-mail: pelican-aruba@setarnet.aw; Internet: www.pelican-aruba.com). Pelican has a PADI Gold Palm 5-Star Facility with custom-built dive boats and numerous dive packages (beginners scuba course, $70; PADI Open Water Certification, $350; one-tank dive, $35; two-tank dive, $55; night dive, $39). Other good operators include: **Unique Sports of Aruba** (third largest after Red Sail and Pelican) at L.G. Smith Blvd. 79 (☎ 297-86-0096); **Fly 'n Dive,** Shiribana 9-A Paradera (☎ 297-87-8759), which offers multi-dive sites on Aruba as well as those on neighboring islands; **Native Divers,** Koyari 1 (☎ 297-86-4763), a husband-and-wife team with personality plus that takes small groups (two to six divers) of experienced divers and offers far more flexibility than other operators; and **Aruba Pro Dive,** Ponton 88 (☎ **297-88-5520**).

We've heard from other scuba divers that **Red Sail Sports** (L.G. Smith Blvd. 83; ☎ **297-86-1603**; Internet: www.redsail.com), which caters to the cruise ship crowd, often repeats dives in the same week even though there are several other sites to visit. The staff appears to be on autopilot, with novice divers being virtually ignored, and the dive shop staff can be downright surly. We've always had a good experience with the same outfit on Grand Cayman, but the lesson learned: Don't presume a familiar dive operator is the same on every island.

Snorkeling adventures, ahoy!

Aruba yields some of our favorite snorkeling trips, too, although opportunities right off shore are limited. Your best bet is to take a snorkeling trip with one of the many boats offering excursions. They typically make three stops, including one at the *Antilla,* which is one of the few wrecks close enough to the surface for snorkelers to really enjoy. *Mi Dushi* (☎ **297-86-2010**; Internet: www.arubaadventures.com/midushi), a 78-foot Swedish sailing vessel built in 1925, which has a rope swing, specializes in four-hour guided snorkel trips crowned with an exceptional hot barbeque lunch (the trip is $48 per person). The crew is attentive, fun, and helpful with children. The first snorkeling stop at **Boca Catalina** is in the smoothest water, so if you're timid about trying snorkeling or have inexperienced youngsters with you, take the plunge at Catalina. The seas can be rough around the *Antilla,* but it's worth braving — though we wouldn't recommend it for young children unless they're confident swimmers. Silver sides, tarpons, and lots of macro life are visible on the coral-encrusted hull.

Another fun crew operates the *Jolly Pirates* (☎ 297-83-7355; Internet: www.jollypirates.com), a Brazilian schooner. It offers two snorkel expeditions to **Malmok Reef** (you can access this one from the beach, but you'll need water shoes because lots of rocks are at the entry), where you'll see giant brain coral and colorful barrel sponges; **Boca Catalina** (calm waters and lots of reef fish); and the *Antilla.* One goes out daily from 9:30 a.m. to 2:00 p.m. and costs $50 per person for a barbeque lunch, open bar, snorkeling gear, and use of the rope swing. The other sails Tuesday, Wednesday, Thursday, and Saturday from 3 to 6 p.m. You get time at the same three sites, but lunch isn't served. That trips costs $30 per person. Kids love the *Jolly Pirate,* too.

Another good snorkeling spot, especially for children, is at **De Palm Island.** The operator ferries you out to its private island from Balashi, about ten minutes from Oranjestad. The island has full facilities with volleyball and basketball, a tiny manmade beach, a kids' playground, fair food (nothing special), and a full bar. As soon as you step off the dock to snorkel, you'll encounter several large blue parrotfish, waiting for handouts. Snorkel beyond the crowd at the small pier and near the step ladder where the water gets really murky from the silt, and you'll find reefs in relatively good shape, teeming with six different types of parrotfish, as well as sergeant majors, squirrel fish, trunk fish, and much more. De Palm sells its island as "all inclusive" with additional charges for SNUBA (and a new Sea Trek option whereby you wear a helmet (in appearance, not unlike the old-time dive helmet) and walk along the sea floor. No dive certification is needed.

Swinging a round of golf

Aruba's deluxe hotels offer golf at the island's **Tierra del Sol** (Malmokweg; ☎ **297-86-0978;** E-mail: tierra.rent@setarnet.aw; Internet: www.tierradelsol.com), an 18-hole championship course designed by Robert Trent Jones, Jr., and one of the Caribbean's top courses. You can view the sea from an astounding 15 holes. Located near the California Lighthouse, this 6,811-yard, par-71 course allows you to admire the rugged beauty of Aruba's northwest coast. The sights include cacti, a saltwater marsh inhabited by egrets, a bird sanctuary with rare burrowing owls, and odd rock formations.

After playing this course, you may think the *A* in Aruba stands for *airball,* because the trade winds add an extra challenge to your swing. Fortunately, Tierra del Sol is not an overly difficult course, so it's still a lot of fun to play. Even beginners (like us) enjoy trying their hand at the game here. The surroundings are beautiful, and the pros have a sense of humor. (If you don't know your eight irons from your Tiger Woods, check out the club's "No Embarrassment" golf clinics.)

The $130 greens fee includes a golf cart. Club rentals are an extra $25 to $45. The golf clinic is a real bargain: $50 for a half day, which includes an excellent lunch at Ventanas del Mar, where floor-to-ceiling windows overlook the course.

During the low season, you can rent beautiful villas that surround the course (starting at $250 a night) and get free greens fees and cart fees as well as access to the club swimming pool. To book a villa, contact the Executive Office at ☎ **297-86-7800.** A fitness center overlooking the ocean is underway and should be completed by press time.

Exploring Aruba

If you just stick to the hotel strip, you'll think that Aruba's not much more than an overbuilt sandbar. Traveling across the island's unusual landscape or visiting its cultural attractions can paint an entirely different — and far more intriguing — tropical picture.

Traveling the cunucu by Jeep

Getting there is half the fun. That phrase certainly applies to Aruba's requisite island tour. Our favorite is the pink Jeep tour provided by **Eagle Jeep Tours** (☎ **297-83-9469**). You start out at the picturesque California Lighthouse. And yes, you actually do your own driving on this tour.

Here's the rub: You follow your leader along the rugged (and dusty) north coast, so try to get as close to the front of the line as possible. The big highlight is the **Natural Bridge,** a dramatic coral structure that stretches for 100 feet and hangs 25 feet above the wild surf that created it in the first place. If you look closely as you drive through the desert, you can see wild goats and lizards. Cacti and the weird divi-divi trees (growing at a 45-degree angle because of the trade winds) are everywhere. You'll get a good view from Alto Vista chapel. The remainder of the tour takes you through **Arikok National Park,** north of the road between Boca Prins and San Fuego and bound on the east by the coastline as far as Boca Keto. There, you'll see more cacti and birds such as *shoko* (owls) and *prikichi* (the Aruban parakeet). You may also see the almost extinct Aruban rattlesnake called *cascabel*.

Driving the rugged north coast can be a sunny, dusty trip. Bring some bottled water, sunglasses, extra sunscreen, and a bandana. Then get ready to eat some trail dust.

Taking in some Aruban culture

The **Bon Bini Festival** is held every Tuesday starting at 6:30 p.m. at small Ft. Zoutman (Zoutmanstraat Z/N, Oranjestad; ☎ **297-82-6099**), which houses an even smaller historical museum in its tower. The festival is well worth an hour or so of your time. The folkloric dancing and music will give you a feel for Aruba's warm-hearted people and their culture. The event is joyous and homespun, perfect for families, and only $3 per person. Skip the museum, though: The faded labeling is all in Dutch.

Sizing up the shopping scene

Aruba's tiny capital, Oranjestad, is a great place to stroll. Even better is the fact that its chief shopping strip, **Caya G. F. Betico Croes,** provides a whole afternoon's worth of browsing. Dutch porcelain, Dutch cheese, hand-embroidered linens, and skin creams made from the native aloe vera plant are all good buys and duty-free.

The high-end shops are tucked into **Royal Plaza Mall,** a colorful building designed in traditional Dutch architecture, rendering it as pretty as a wedding cake. You can find some cool shops across the street at the

90-shop **Seaport Village Mall** and the 60-shop **Seaport Marketplace.** The local market is right on the waterfront, too, but there's not much to it.

Because Aruba is so close to Central and South America, those with slightly offbeat tastes like us can find unique items in the boutiques. We found a store that was selling gorgeous long parreos (used as wraps over swimwear) for $8 to $12 each. At home, they'd cost at least four times that amount. Echo also bought a faux tortoise-shell bag for $15 (real tortoise-shell products cannot be brought back into the United States) and a Panamanian straw hat for $18 that still win compliments every time she uses them.

Living It Up After Dark

Feeling lucky? Almost every major Aruban hotel (11 at last count) comes with a casino attached. Most offer blackjack, poker, craps, roulette, baccarat, slot machines, and an island original called Caribbean Stud Poker, invented in 1988. This high-stakes game is like blackjack but tempts players with a progressive jackpot.

The Renaissance's **Crystal Casino** stays open all day and all night. We like it because it draws a more upscale crowd and is centrally located in downtown. It's also handy to the discos, in case we tire of blackjack. We'd recommend dinner at **L'Escale** (see review in chapter 10), also at the Renaissance, then gaming, then wind up the evening at whichever disco is the rage at the moment, or check out the best show in town, *Let's Go Latin.* This old Havana-style revue is the stunning work of famed Cuban art director Tomas Morales. The 26 dancers from Cuba go through 180 different costumes, each a work of art in themselves, as they twirl their way through different Latin dances to equally impressive music. Make reservations early, because the show is often a sellout. We'd also recommend being there when the doors open for seating at 8:30 p.m., in order to get a good view of the stage. The show runs Monday through Saturday at 9 p.m. at the **Crystal Theater,** at the Renaissance (☎ **297-83-6000**). Tickets are $37; children under 12, $18. However, some of the costumes are pretty revealing, so be forewarned. A package of the show with dinner at L'Escale is $64.

Other casinos worth checking out if you're feeling lucky include the following:

✔ **Casino Masquerade,** at the Radisson Aruba Caribbean Resort and Casino (J. E. Irausquin Blvd. 81, Palm Beach, ☎ **297-86-6555**), is one of the newest casinos on Aruba. On the lower-level lobby of the hotel, it's open from 10 a.m. to 4 a.m. daily. It offers blackjack, single deck, roulette, Caribbean stud, craps, and Let It Ride.

✔ **Royal Cabana Casino,** adjacent to La Cabana All-Suites Beach Resort and Casino (☎ **297-87-7000**). It's the Caribbean's largest casino — though it's not as upscale as the Crystal Casino, it's not full of tatty blue-haired ladies forlornly pumping quarters into the slots like in Atlantic City either. Its big claim to fame: the Tropicana Showroom, which has the island's longest running show, the *Jewel Box Revue,* with excellent impersonators doing their best Diana Ross, Madonna, Michael Jackson, and Tina Turner.

Put on your dancing shoes and your best resort wear for a night (or two) on the town. Most dance clubs don't require a cover charge, and alcohol isn't legal until you're age 21. Go late — the Latin influence means the action doesn't even get started until around 11 p.m. Aruban club hoppers are fickle, so check with your concierge before setting out. Here are some of the current hotspots:

✔ **Choose-a-Name** (Havenstraat 39 in Oranjestad, behind Royal Plaza; ☎ **297-88-6200**). Live music is featured almost nightly, Sunday through Saturday, and includes a "Karaoke Night" and happy hours.

✔ **Mambo Jambo** (Royal Plaza Mall, L. G. Smith Boulevard; ☎ **297-83-3632**). The crowd is a cosmopolitan blend of locals, as well as Dutch and Latino visitors, and the DJ plays lots of loud Latin rhythms. There's an array of specialty drinks.

✔ **Carlos and Charlies** (Weststraat; ☎ **297-82-0355**). On the second floor overlooking the main drag is this small, open-air restaurant, playing Latin music and disco for a young crowd of locals and visitors that spills onto the sidewalk outside. Casually dressed couples dance merengue and other fancy moves, but be prepared for a heavy party scene with many people extremely drunk.

✔ **Kukoo Kunuku** (☎ **297-86-2010; $55** a person). A favorite with 20-something visitors are these wildly-decorated party buses that blare festive Caribbean music and transport partiers from one bar to the next. The bus takes you to three local bars where the first drink is free, then $2 to $3 apiece. Of course, you start with dinner. "Sweet Daddy" Raymond is the most entertaining driver, so try to book with him.

Part IV
Barbados

"You and your big idea to vacation at one of the lesser known Caribbean islands! Whoever heard of St. Bronx anyway?"

In this part . . .

Before you pack your bags and head off for some royal treatment on Barbados, check out our recommendations for the best among a wide array of accommodations. We give you tips for arriving at your destination and for setting out to see the island's landscape.

On an island where food is an art form, you want to make the best of your dining experiences; our recommendations guide you to some prime choices. Finally, we show you how to live it up while the sun shines — and after it sets — with a guide to the best activities Barbados has to offer.

Chapter 12

The Lowdown on Barbados's Hotel Scene

By Echo and Kevin Garrett

. . . .

In This Chapter

▶ Sizing up hotel locations

▶ Focusing on top hotel picks

. . . .

*B*arbados boasts an impressive range of accommodations — villas, small boutique hotels, timeshares, small guesthouses, and a handful of all-inclusive resorts — along with some of the Caribbean's most over-the-top resorts, places that are luxurious to the point of absurdity. The ultra-exclusive **Sandy Lane** (☎ **246-432-2954**; Internet: www.sandy lane.com), which reopened in 2001, after being closed for more than three years of renovations — at a cost in excess of $350 million — leaps to mind. You won't find any big familiar-name chains here — although Hilton has announced plans to build a resort. The biggest operator on Barbados, with a total of 572 luxury rooms at six different resorts, is the **Elegant Hotels Group** (☎ **800-326-6898**), which owns Colony Club, Crystal Cove, Coconut Creek, Turtle Beach Resort, Tamarind Cove, and its newest property, The House, which opened in December 2001.

Barbados is not the place for romantic secluded retreats like you find on the British Virgin Islands or Jamaica. Nor is Barbados the place to find stunning structures; most hotels have fewer than 100 rooms, and, with few exceptions, the architects who designed them didn't go for the cutting-edge look. Most resorts have relied instead on Barbados's beautiful beaches and lush gardens to enchant visitors. Barbados can claim some of the region's more sophisticated and charming hoteliers. Many properties are exquisitely managed with a careful eye toward making guests feel welcome.

Figuring Out Where You Want to Stay

Barbados is developed, so don't expect to find a little gem tucked into the edge of jungle-like growth. Most of our recommendations are in fashionable St. James, St. Peter, or St. Michael parishes. (Parishes are like counties in the U.S.) All three are on Barbados's western shore, where Caribbean waters are calm. This area is nicknamed the Gold Coast — supposedly for the color of the sand, but we think it's because you need a bag of gold to pay your hotel bill. The resorts here tend to be self-contained. If you stay on the Gold Coast, don't expect to walk to a nearby restaurant; two-lane Highway 1 runs along the coast, and it's too busy to safely stroll for any distance.

Hotels on the south coast in Christ Church parish (near Bridgetown) tend to be a bit less pricey. If you like to restaurant-hop and enjoy nightlife, we recommend staying near here. On the scenic Atlantic side where the waves crash against the shoreline, you'll find a few rustic little places, popular with windsurfers. Villas, private homes, and condos are available south of Bridgetown, in the Hastings-Worthing area, and along the west coast in St. James and in St. Peter.

Many of the resorts, though on good beaches, are also near busy roads. If traffic noise bothers you, make sure you ask to be booked as close to the sea as possible. Unfortunately, some truck drivers on the island apparently find it great fun to merrily toot their horns as they roll by the hotels — especially in the wee hours of the morning.

Truth be told, if you're on a budget, Barbados isn't the best choice, unless you go during the summer low season. Ask for a room price for an approximate time in the distant future, and a reservationist is likely to tell you crisply, "Those rates haven't been set yet," or, "The rate will depend on availability." Translation: We'll charge as much as we possibly can, depending on how business shakes out. Best to have several exact dates in mind before you call to extract a quote.

Barbados does have some bargains, but you have to hunt for them. Try small efficiency condos where you can whip up your own meals. Or pick from a dozen or so guesthouses where you'll be treated to Bajan hospitality and traditional Bajan cooking.

Many Barbados hotels insist that you take their meal plans if you visit in winter. We find this limiting, especially because Barbados is known for having great restaurants.

You're always better off with at least a weeklong package. Hotel prices in Barbados are geared to the longer vacation times of Europeans, not the U.S. vacationers' habit of popping onto an island for three or four days. As a result, several per-night rates listed in this chapter may curl your hair — or even shock it into dreadlocks.

If you're thinking about a private home, contact the **Barbados Tourism Authority** (☎ **888-BARBADOS** or 246-427-2623; Fax: 246-426-4080; E-mail: btainfo@barbados.org; Internet: www.barbados.org). The BTA maintains a list of apartments and rates.

The **Barbados Super Saver Program** (☎ **246-228-4221**), which runs from April 15 through December 15, offers discounts on airfare, hotels, meals, car rentals, and attractions. Guests who book the package receive a range of information helpful for busy travelers including a full-color ticket-size voucher that includes a summary of the package, a list of discount specials, a 24-hour hotline number, a list of participating hotels, a full description of all the "Meet and Mingle" options, and reservation numbers to book any of the offers. The package also contains a sheet of tickets that can be redeemed for free meals and discounts when presented at participating vendors. The program includes round-trip air on American Airlines, Air Jamaica, or BWIA; transfers in Barbados; the first night free with a minimum five-night stay; full breakfast daily; and a "Bajan Meet-and-Mingle Meal Event." More than 20 hotels participate in the program.

Between Barbados's hefty room tax and the 10% surcharge, expect your final hotel bill to jump by about 18 to 25% of the subtotal.

Barbados's Best Accommodations

The rack rates listed in this section are in U.S. dollars and are for a standard double room during high season (mid-December through mid-April), unless otherwise noted. Lower rates are often available during the off-season and shoulder season (see Chapter 2 for information on travel seasons).

Other guidebooks and magazine articles consistently recommend and even trumpet some Barbados hotels that we have serious concerns about. With so many terrific places from which to choose, we'd hate for you to get stuck in one of these:

- ✔ **Atlantis Hotel,** a historic property that is literally crumbling into the sea and reeks of terrible smells

- ✔ **Edgewater Inn,** once a really cool little place that is now sadly dilapidated with broken furniture and lamp posts

- ✔ **Almond Beach Village,** a government-owned all-inclusive, packed wall-to-wall with families and honeymooners, where the service is some of the worst we've ever seen

- ✔ **Sam Lord's Castle,** way out from nowhere, where guests are stuck with bland food, iffy rooms, and far-from-royal treatment

At press time we heard that a rescue may take place for the first two. The latter two get staunchly defended as excellent choices by the largely British clientele, but we know there are much better places for the same money on Barbados.

Accra Beach Hotel and Resort
$$$ **Rockley**

In a West Indian "mega style," the three-story property is tastefully laid out, and it offers spacious rooms opening onto a view of the lovely pool or the sea. The units — the suites are good for families — have large balconies and wooden shutters, plus full-size bathrooms with tubs. The look is a bit sterile, more like a business person's hotel than a resort inn, and the rooms are showing some wear and tear. Steer clear of units marked "island view" — the panorama is of the parking lot. This is one of the best hotels on Barbados for those with disabilities. One drawback: Much of the hotel is open air, and the man-eating mosquitoes appreciate that fact. The food in the restaurants is lackluster, with breakfasts especially poor and pricey. Children under 12 stay free with a paying adult. A beauty salon, exercise room, squash court, and shops round out the facilities.

Highway 7 (Box 73W), Rockley, Christ Church. ☎ *800-223-6510 or 246-435-8920. Fax: 246-435-6794. Internet:* www.funbarbados.com/lodgings/accrabeach. cfm. *Rack rates: $160–$210 double, from $350 suite. Meal plans available. AE, MC, V.*

Bougainvillea Beach Resort
$$$$ **Christ Church**

This resort, on a broad sandy beach with good swimming and body surfing, is one of the best south-coast deals. A family favorite with friendly service, it's a low-rise timeshare with an assortment of studios and suites. It features all-suite first-class rooms and studios with one–, two–, or three-bedroom suites, each with a private balcony opening onto a seafront view; four units have plunge pools. However, be aware that all rooms face the pool and the popular swim-up bar, which stays open late, so it's pretty noisy day and night. Bedrooms are furnished along modern lines, a medley of pastels, comfortable and tasteful without being too exciting. Each unit has a small bathroom containing a shower unit. Deluxe suites have full kitchens, but no dishwasher. Waterfalls flow into the pools. Bougainvillea is just minutes away from the hip strip in St. Lawrence Gap with its many restaurants. This hotel participates in the Super Saver Program (see the "Figuring Out Where to Stay" section earlier in this chapter for more information).

Maxwell Coast Road, Christ Church. ☎ *800-223-6510, 800-988-6904, 800-742-4276, or 246-418-0990. Fax: 246-428-2524. E-mail:* centralres@sunbeach.net. *Internet:* www.funbarbados.com. *Rack rates: $240–$345 double; from $495 suite. AE, DC, MC, V, EP.*

Barbados Accommodations

Accra Beach Hotel & Resort **7**
Bougainvillea Beach Resort **10**
Casuarina Beach Club **8**
Cobblers Cove **1**
Coral Reef Club **5**
Divi Southwinds Beach Resort **9**
Glitter Bay **2**

Royal Pavilion **3**
Sandpiper **4**
Silver Rock Resort **11**
Tamarind Cove Hotel **6**
Time Out at The Gap **9**
Turtle Beach **8**

Airport ✈ Beach ☚ Church ☚ Lighthouse ☀

Casuarina Beach Club

$$$ St. Lawrence

Family-owned and –operated Casuarina Beach, which has won numerous awards for its environmental efforts, manages to be an oasis of calm in the midst of the frenetic south coast, 4 miles from Bridgetown and close to the Gap. Casuarina, which has wedding, honeymoon, and golf packages, is popular with honeymooners, families, and package groups from Canada and the U.K. Its oversized pool is perfect for doing laps, and the 1,500-foot strand of white, powder-soft sand it fronts has plenty of inviting lounge chairs for sunbathers. The surf can be a little rough, depending on the time of year. You can sit out on your balcony overlooking the tropical gardens and see a myriad of birds each morning. You may also catch a glimpse of a monkey climbing the palms in the early evenings. The hotel has tennis courts lit for night play and air-conditioned squash courts. All rooms and one– or two-bedroom suites have large balconies and kitchenettes, and several have interconnecting doors, making them good for familes. Scuba diving, golf, and other activities can be arranged. The hotel has a supervised children's playroom, and all facilities are wheelchair-accessible.

St. Lawrence Gap, Christ Church. ☎ *800-742-4276, 800-223-9815, or 246-428-3600. Fax: 246-428-1970. E-mail:* casbeach@bajan.com. *Internet:* www.casuarina. com. *Rack rates: $195–$210; 1 BR and 2BR $225–$390. Children under 12 stay free in parent's room. AE, DISC, MC, V, EP, CP.*

Cobblers Cove

$$$$$ St. Peter

Originally a plantation house, this intimate resort, shielded from traffic by a high coral stone wall, is adjacent to a small but pleasant crescent beach in a protected cove situated on Barbados's famed Gold Coast. Cobblers Cove, one of only five Caribbean hotels to achieve the vaunted designation of Relais and Chateaux, is a favorite of honeymooners, gourmands, and genteel U.K. visitors. The resort is not splashy, but it's ripe with a cozy elegance. The affable Antiguan-born General Manager, Hamish Watson, makes you feel like a welcome guest. Afternoon tea is served poolside. Situated on three lush and fragrant garden acres dotted with coconut and traveler's palms, ten two-story cottages house four suites each. Only bedrooms are air-conditioned. Suites have wide sitting areas with louvered shutters opening to furnished balconies or patios; spacious bathrooms with standard shower/tubs; and wet bars with a small fridge and hot pot. (Some suites are a bit too close to the busy highway; ask for suites 1 through 8, toward the sea.)

Road View, Speightstown, St. Peter. ☎ *800-890-6060 in the U.S., 01-81-367-5155 in London, 800-567-5327 in Canada, or 246-422-2291. Fax: 246-422-1460. E-mail:* cobblers@caribsurf.com. *Internet:* www.cobblerscove.com. *Rack rates: $740–$890 suite; $1,868–$2,115 Camelot/Colleton suites. For MAP (two meals daily) add $94 per person per night, including tax and service. AE, MC, V. Closed end of Jul–mid-Oct. Children under 12 are not allowed Jan 7–Mar 24.*

Coral Reef Club

$$$$$ St. James

This gracious luxury hotel is set on 12 elegantly landscaped acres beside a white-sand swath of beach that's ideal for swimming and snorkeling adjacent at the underwater marine park. At presstime, this Caribbean classic was closed for an extensive ten-month redo but was scheduled to be reopened for winter 2003. The plans are to transform existing cottage rooms into luxury junior suites — perhaps owing to the popularity of the ultra-luxe plantation suites introduced a few years ago — each with wraparound patio with dining area and a small private plunge pool in a natural rock-form setting. Vaulted pickled ceilings, living room, and bath with separate dressing room, tub, and shower will also be added. New garden rooms will be housed in Colonial-style buildings and will have combo tub/showers. A small full-service spa is being added, too. We recommend splurging on the ultra-spacious luxury plantation suites, if your budget allows. Each has a private bougainvillea-draped terrace or balcony and an open sundeck with a 9-x-12-foot private plunge pool. Canopied four-poster beds and oversized marble-decked tubs appeal to romantics. A beauty salon, a masseuse, three tennis courts, an exercise room, billiards, windsurfing, boating, and waterskiing are also available.

Highway 1, Holetown, St. James. ☎ *800-223-1108, 800-525-4800, or 246-422-2372. Fax: 246-422-1776. E-mail:* coral@caribsurf.com. *Rack rates: $520 double; from $665 junior suite; $1,950 luxury plantation suite. AE, MC, V.*

Divi Southwinds Beach Resort

$$$ St. Lawrence

Busy, busy Divi caters to couples who like being in the center of the action — the resort is a short stroll through a palm grove to a half-mile stretch of sandy white beach in the heart of St. Lawrence Gap's bustling and happening nightlife/restaurant district. The buildings on 20 lush acres are plain vanilla, but this newly-renovated-in-2001 Divi (much larger and more modern than sister property Divi Heritage) is the the sort of place where you don't spend much time in the room anyway. The friendly staff goes out of its way to make sure that you're having fun. Request a larger suite in the newer section with a full kitchen and a balcony overlooking the gardens and L-shaped pool. The older section is closer to the beach, but in this case, our vote goes to the roomier digs. The hotel has two restaurants and two bars, or you can cook in your room. On-site you also find two free-form pools, a beauty salon, a putting green, two lighted tennis courts, basketball, volleyball, a dive shop, and other shops.

St. Lawrence Gap, Christ Church. ☎ *800-367-3484 or 246-428-7181. Fax: 246-428-4674. E-mail:* reserve@diviresorts.com. *Internet:* www.diviresorts.com. *Rack rates: $210–$245. AE, DC, MC, V.*

Glitter Bay
$$$$$ Porters

In the case of this classy resort, all that glitters is . . . everything — from the accommodating staff to the polished suites to the sparkling Caribbean. In fact, this resort — not as formal as sister resort Royal Pavilion next door — remains such a favorite with repeat guests that you have to book nearly a year in advance to get a room during high season. You can select from one– and two-bedroom suites — which has helped make this place a favorite with well-heeled families — as well as duplex penthouses. All have king-size or two twin beds, plus private balconies or terraces. Some have full kitchens, and all have in-room safes and mini-bars. We prefer the beach house, which contains five garden suites. The grounds feature two pools with a waterfall and footbridge. A beauty salon, a masseuse, two lighted tennis courts, golf privileges, an exercise room, and shops are on-site. Guests can use facilities at Royal Pavilion. Glitter Bay's beachside hotel restaurant deserves high marks for romance.

Porters, St. James. ☎ *800-223-1818* or 246-422-4111. Fax: 246-422-3940. Internet: www.fairmont.com. Rack rates: $479 double; $759 1 BR suite. AE, DISC, DC, MC, V, EP, MAP.

Royal Pavilion
$$$$$ Porters

This elegant Spanish mission–style resort, located next door to its sister resort (the more casual though still pricey Glitter Bay), is tops with a well-traveled clientele who want an idyllic respite with a little water fun tossed in. Like Glitter Bay, it stays almost fully booked in the winter months. The same landscape architect from Glitter Bay is responsible for Royal Pavilion's equally breathtaking grounds. Splashing fountains and riotous blossoms soothe the senses. From the oceanfront suites, you walk ten steps to the sandy white beach.

Royal Pavillion shares amenities and a management company (Fairmont Hotels and Resorts) with Glitter Bay. Two lit tennis courts, nonmotorized water sports, 24-hour concierge, laundry, and limousine service are part of the eye-popping rates. Breakfast and lunch are served alfresco at the edge of the beach. Afternoon tea and dinner are in the Palm Terrace. Royal Westmoreland Golf Club is almost across the street. The welcome mat is yanked for children 12 and under. Housekeeping and the front desk could be snappier — especially at these prices.

Porters, St. James. ☎ *800-223-1818* or 246-422-4444. Fax: 246-422-3940. Internet: www.fairmont.com. Rack rates: $579–$1,400 suite. AE, DISC, DC, MC, V.

Sandpiper
$$$$$ Holetown

The Coral Reef Club (covered earlier in this section), owned by the same family, offers plusher digs, but may be full, so consider this more casual West Indian resort on a white-sand beach. Similar to Cobbler's Cove, it's a self-contained, intimate resort where a cascading waterfall greets arriving guests. It is set in a small grove of coconut palms and flowering trees, dramatically lit at night. A cluster of rustic-chic units surrounds the lushly landscaped pool ringed by cushioned wrought-iron chaise lounges; some rooms have fine sea views of the white-sand beach edged by mature palms. The newly redone rooms open onto little terraces that stretch along the second story, where you can order drinks or have breakfast. Accommodations are generous in size, consisting of superior rooms and one– or two-bedroom suites with white tile floors. All are beautifully furnished with tropical pieces. Each has a private terrace, luxurious bed, and small fridge. The medium-size bathrooms are equipped with combination tub/showers. The award-winning Mediterranean/ provincial cuisine with a Caribbean twist at the hotel restaurant ensures that diners won't be bored. Weekly buffets are offered in winter. The restaurant and bar have been handsomely redone with new artwork, lighting, and additional coral stone work.

Holetown (a 3-minute walk north of town), St. James. ☎ *800-223-1108 in the U.S., 800-567-5327 in Canada, or 246-422-2251. Fax: 246-422-0900. E-mail:* sandpiper@ caribsurf.com. *Rack rates: $495 double; from $735 1 BR suite; from $1,285 2 BR suite. Rates include breakfast. MAP available. MAP supplement of $135 a day for an adult; $70 a day for a child under 12. Children under 2 free. AE, MC, V.*

Silver Rock Resort
$$ Silver Sands

Ideal for professional windsurfers and adventure seekers, this beachfront hotel opened in January 2000. A range of beachfront, oceanview, and garden-view accommodations — some with soaring white pickled ceilings and louvered windows — are available. The hotel's open-air restaurant, Jibboom, serves tasty local and international dishes and has occasional theme nights. Guests frequently take part in the Friday Night Street Party at nearby Time Out at the Gap. Other sports popular with the hard-bodies who populate the Silver Rock Resort include scuba diving, snorkeling, boogie-boarding, surfing, hiking, beach volleyball, and sea kayaking. All guests receive reduced greens fees and preferential tee times at the newly opened Barbados Golf Club, the island's only public championship golf course.

Silver Sands, Christ Church. ☎ *246-428-2866. Fax: 246-428-3687. E-mail:* silver@ gemsbarbados.com. *Internet:* www.gemsbarbados.com. *Rack rates: $145–$180 double. AE, MC, V.*

Tamarind Cove Hotel
$$$$$ Paynes Bay

On 800 feet of prime beachfront, this flagship of a British-based hotel chain (St. James Properties) challenges the Coral Reef Club/Sandpiper properties, attracting the same upscale clientele, thanks to an $8 million restoration in the 1990s. Designed in Mediterranean style, with pale-pink walls and red terra-cotta roofs, the rambling resort occupies a desirable location on St. James Beach, 1½ miles south of Holetown. The stylish and comfortable rooms are in a series of hacienda-style buildings interspersed with vegetation. The well-appointed bathrooms boast dual basins, spacious Roman tubs, stall showers, and long marble counters. Each unit has a patio or balcony overlooking the gardens or ocean, which has a terrific reef with good snorkeling. The water-sports staff is friendly and helpful.

However, our praise stops there. Management overall has slipped, especially the concierge desk and exceedingly slow, uncaring service in the restaurants, which are extremely pricey. Make sure to request a room near the sea, otherwise you'll be disturbed by noise from the nearby highway. Room walls are somewhat thin, too, so you may also hear your neighbors.

Paynes Bay, St. James. ☎ *800-326-6898 or 246-432-1332. Fax: 246-432-6317. E-mail:* elegantna@earthlink.com. *Internet:* www.eleganthotels.com. *Rack rates: From $600. AE, MC, V.*

Time Out at the Gap
$$ St. Lawrence Gap

Across the road from Dover Beach, a wide white-sand beach, this hotel is extremely popular with an active, younger crowd looking for an affordable, yet happening place. The friendly staff adds to the party atmosphere that prevails, arranging water sports, submarine rides, cricket matches, and nature walks. Rooms, attractively furnished in neutrals with splashes of bright yellow and teals, are well arranged with tile floors and comfortable beds. They overlook the pool, surrounded by lush tropical plantings or the equally lush gardens. Children 12 and under are free of charge when sharing with two full-paying adults. Honeymoon suites and services are also available. Water-sports options are sometimes limited because the beach gets extremely windy. Food and drinks are excellent. On Friday nights, jazz plays at the popular Whistling Frog on site, and the hotel makes itself party central with lots of happenings throughout the week.

St. Lawrence Gap, Christ Church. ☎ *800-868-9429 or 246-420-5021. Fax: 246-420-5034. E-mail:* timeout@gemsbarbados.com. *Internet:* www.gemsbarbados.com. *Rack rates: $155–$165 double; $180 deluxe.*

Turtle Beach
$$$$$ Christ Church

Set on a wide, 1,500-foot-long white strand of beach on the south coast, this plush all-inclusive, three-story hotel opened in 1998 as the flagship of London-based Elegant Hotel Group. Guests from Great Britain account for 75% of the business, with many families coming on packages to take advantage of the Kids Club (for ages 3 to 11) running from 9 a.m. to 9 p.m. daily. The club has computer games and lots of activities for the pint-sized set. Included in the price, you get instruction and the equipment to participate in scuba diving, water-skiing, snorkeling, kayaking, sailing, and boogie boarding. Set in 6 acres of lush gardens, the hotel promises you ocean views from every suite. Tennis equipment is provided; golfers get special rates and times at Royal Westmoreland Golf Club. Ask about the hotel's excellent children's packages, which let one child between the ages of 2 and 12 stay free in the off-season. (Additional children stay at 50% off the adult rate.)

The restaurants here also have slow service and short hours, although the food quality is better than Almond Beach Village. Although birds aren't as much of a problem here, several stray cats wander around the grounds and in the restaurants.

Dover. ☎ *800-326-6898 or 246-428-7131. Fax: 246-428-6089. Rack rates: $288–$458 suite. Rates are all-inclusive. AE, DC, MC, V.*

Chapter 13

Settling into Barbados

By Echo and Kevin Garrett

. . . .

In This Chapter

▶ Knowing what to expect when you arrive

▶ Getting around the island

▶ Discovering Barbados from A to Z

. . . .

*B*arbados has steadily been gaining popularity with the U.S. market, though tourists from the States still only account for about 20% of the island's visitors. Because both of us have recently discovered that our Irish and Scottish ancestors immigrated to Barbados before entering the U.S. — in fact, many Americans, especially in the South, share that link to the Caribbean — we must confess that we've developed a soft spot for this island where polo and cricket are considered great fun.

It's by far the most urban of the islands covered in this book. Indeed, almost all of Barbados's population of more than a quarter million people live in and around the capital of Bridgetown. For the first hour you're on the island, you may be jangled at how crowded and congested it is. Relax. When you get away from the airport area and through Bridgetown, you'll start to find more of what you'd expect on a Caribbean island, and when you make it to your hotel and are offered a cool tropical punch (perhaps with a splash of rum), you'll know you're in the right place.

Arriving in Barbados

During high season when the Concorde whizzes in from London around 8 a.m. on Saturday mornings, its streamlined, high-tech silhouette doesn't seem out of place at thoroughly modern Grantley Adams International Airport, on the south coast about 8 miles east and a half-hour drive from the bustling, sprawling capital of Bridgetown. You won't find crinkly, sun-bleached tourist posters taped to the walls at this immaculate airport.

By 2005, Barbados will have plunked down upwards of $70 million to ensure its airport is oh-so-right. In addition, it has added air-conditioning to the Customs, baggage claim, and departure lounge areas, and it has doubled the airport's duty-free shopping area to more than 10,000 square feet. In fact, the Barbados airport is one of the few we've encountered that has an **Arrivals Duty-Free Shop** (☎ 246-430-2150), so that you don't have to wait till you're in a hurry at the end of your trip to pick up mementos.

Going through passport control and Customs takes far longer on Barbados than on most islands. Expect to spend at least a half hour in line if you're on a full flight. Plus, the paperwork is the most detailed we've seen and must be filled out in triplicate. Be sure to get it on the plane and fill it out en route to save time. The neatly uniformed Customs officials are crisply efficient. If you're carrying valuables like expensive jewelry and camera equipment, don't forget to register those items with the Customs officials as you're entering the country. Otherwise, you may find yourself paying an import duty on your belongings at the end of your stay.

The **Barbados Tourism Authority** operates welcome kiosks from 8 a.m. to 8 p.m. at both the airport terminal (☎ 246-428-5570) and the cruise terminal (☎ 246-426-1718). And for those who arrive cash-poor, ATMs are handily stationed at the kiosks.

More than half a million visitors — many of them making a return trip — come to Barbados each year, and another half million arrive via cruise ship. The Barbados Cruise Ship Terminal, located on Bridgetown's waterfront, is now one of the Caribbean's finest, thanks to a $6 million renovation. Bridgetown's Deep Water Harbour is on the northwest side of Carlisle Bay, and as many as eight cruise ships can dock simultaneously at its cruise ship terminal, whose interior features a faux island street scene with storefronts, brightly colored chattel houses, tropical flowers, benches, and pushcarts. Postal and banking facilities are also available at the terminal.

As soon as you clear Customs and immigration, you can whip out your plastic. The port facility now has 20 duty-free shops, more than a dozen retailers, and dozens of vendors. You can also find car and bike rentals, a florist, dive shops, and a communications center with fax and telephones. Downtown Bridgetown is an easy half-mile walk from the pier; a taxi costs about $5 each way.

Getting from the Airport to Your Hotel

A large sign at the airport announces the fixed rate for a taxi ride to each hotel or parish (district). Official taxis have a *Z* on their license plates, and they operate 24 hours a day. Rates are given in both Barbados and U.S. dollars. Count on about $24 to Speightstown, $20 to hotels on the west coast, and $16 to south-coast locations. Drivers are usually chatty and full of details about the island.

There's also a regular airport bus service into Bridgetown (Bds$1.50) that departs every 10 minutes, but it takes 45 minutes to get into town, and we have a feeling you'll be more than ready to get to your hotel.

This island is a good one on which to rent a car (see the next section for more details), but the roads are confusing. After a long day of travel and unless you're really good with a map, we'd suggest you take a cab to your hotel and have the rental car delivered the next day. Alternatively, if you're uneasy about driving yourself, several companies will provide you with a driver. One of the oldest companies on the island that provides the service is **Johnson's Stables & Garage Ltd.** (Hastings, Christ Church; ☎ **246-426-5181;** Fax: 246-429-3528), which has private cars and limousines as well as car rentals. For a private car to Glitter Bay, for example, the tab would run you $50 without tip.

If you're doing your own driving, get detailed directions on how to get to the Adams-Barrow-Cummins (ABC) Highway. It bypasses Bridgetown and saves you travel time to the west coast where most of the hotels are. Going along the coastal highway is much prettier, but it is much slower going, and because it'll likely be nightfall by the time you arrive, make it easy on yourself with the ABC.

Getting Around Barbados

After you've settled into your hotel, you'll probably want to check out the island's sites, shops, restaurants, and landscape. This section shares some sightseeing options.

By car

On the pro side for renting a car on Barbados is the fact that it's one of the most intriguing islands in the Caribbean to explore. It has historic Great Houses, practically deserted beaches, a bucolic countryside, unusual caverns, and riotous tropical gardens. The negatives include some of the most poorly-marked, confusing roads we've encountered in the Caribbean. The roads — most of which are paved but have potholes in the outlying areas — give new meaning to the word *narrow.* On the west coast and in the more urban areas, there's no shoulder, just a deep gulley between the road and the sidewalk. In the country, the dense sugar cane fields and lush growth can make it difficult to see around corners and at stop signs. And don't venture into the rural areas after dark — not because danger lurks, but because it's pitch black and you can barely see where you're going.

On top of all that, you're dealing with driving on the left, British style, the opposite of what U.S. drivers are accustomed to. In more rural areas, sheep and goats sometimes wander into the road. The only signs are tiny — sometimes hand-lettered — and vaguely point in a sometimes undecipherable direction. More than once, we had to pull over and debate exactly what the directional was telling us to do. Even after our discussion and looking at a map, we still got lost. Locals are generally helpful, though, when you ask for directions. We met one kind lady who insisted on leading us to the road we were searching for — even though it took her a good deal out of her way.

Prices are high even for the unimaginably miniscule mini-mokes, a putt-putt popular on the island. We reluctantly agreed to one on our most recent trip with our two sons in tow. At times, as we barely threaded our way past oncoming traffic, we were thankful that it was so small; at others, we all closed our eyes and prayed as huge construction trucks lumbered past. For a little more money, you can rent a four-wheel-drive Jeep or a convertible, which is what we'll do in the future.

All that said, if you want to rent a car, you must have a valid driver's license or an international driver's license, be 25 or older, and buy a $5 temporary driving permit for Barbados, obtainable at the airport, police stations, and car-rental firms. The permit will be valid for one year. You can pick up your vehicle at the airport. The rental process is smooth, but you may encounter another long line at the airport rental counters. We recommend having your vehicle brought to you where you're staying, which is a free service provided by companies. Be sure to request that it be tanked up with gas before it's brought to you. One was delivered to us at the airport recently, but the fellow gave it to us sitting on empty, which meant a stop at the gas station near the airport — another delay after a long travel day.

None of the familiar major firms offer rentals on Barbados, but about 30 local agencies — National is not the one U.S. visitors are familiar with — rent cars, Jeeps, or small open-air vehicles for $60 to $90 a day (or $250 to $325 a week), depending on the vehicle and whether it has air-conditioning. (We don't think air-conditioning is necessary.) The rental generally includes insurance. Before you turn down the collision damage waiver, be absolutely certain you're covered on either your auto insurance at home or by the credit card company with which you're paying. Proceed carefully with rentals on this island. Inspect the vehicle thoroughly, and point out even the smallest scratch before you drive away.

Among the car-rental agencies in Barbados are the following: **Coconut Car Rentals** (St. Michael; ☎ 246-437-0297); **Corbins Car Rentals** (St. Michael; ☎ 246-427-9531, 246-426-8336, or 246-426-8336); **Courtesy Rent-A-Car** (Grantley Adams International Airport; ☎ 246-431-4160); **Drive-a-Matic** (St. James; ☎ 246-422-4000); **National Car Rentals** (Lower Carlton, St. James; ☎ 246-422-0603: E-mail: bernmar@caribsurf.com); **P&S Car Rentals** (Pleasant View, Cave Hill, St. Michael; ☎ 246-424-2052); **Sunny Isle Motors** (Worthing; ☎ 246-435-7498); and **Sunset Crest Rentals** (St. James; ☎ 246-432-2222). Coconut Car Rentals gets high marks from travelers for friendly service and good prices.

The speed limit is 60km/h (roughly 37 mph) on the highway, 50km/h (about 30 mph) in the country, and 30km/h (20 mph) in town. Remember that kilometers per hour are the norm here; a shift in mental gears can keep you out of trouble if you're accustomed to miles per hour.

In Bridgetown and at The Gap on the south coast, where a great deal of construction is going on, parking can be virtually impossible. Near the waterfront, the roads are snarled with construction and several of them are one-way streets. Never turn your car over to a local who offers to find you a parking space for a small finder's fee. Tourists who have done so often find out the hard way that the space was illegal, which makes them the target of a ticket. Bridgetown's rush hour runs from 7:30 to 8:30 a.m. and 4:30 to 5:30 p.m.

By bus

Taking a bus in the Caribbean can be more hassle than the savings is worth, but Barbados (as well as Aruba and Grand Cayman) are exceptions. If you don't want to rent a car, you can explore this island easily and cheaply by relying on the bus system.

The fare is US75¢ (Bds$1.50) for any one destination, and you must have exact change in Barbados currency ready when you board. Barbados has a reliable bus system fanning out from Bridgetown, leaving from Fairchild Street for the south and east; from Lower Green and the Princess Alice Highway for the north going along the west coast, to almost every part of the island. The nationally owned buses (☎ **246-436-6820**) of Barbados are blue with yellow stripes. They're not numbered, but their destinations are marked on the front. On most major routes, they run between 6 a.m. and midnight about every 20 minutes.

Privately operated minibuses run shorter distances and travel more frequently. They are bright yellow, with their destinations displayed on the bottom-left corner of the windshield. Minibuses in Bridgetown are boarded at River Road, Temple Yard, and Probyn Street. The fare is US75¢ (Bds$1.50).

Small signs that say "TO CITY" or "OUT OF CITY" (meaning Bridgetown) are tacked on roadside poles to indicate bus stops. Ask a local to be sure you're heading in the right direction, if you're uncertain. Flag down the bus with your hand, even if you're standing at the stop or think you are. Drivers don't always stop automatically at the stops.

By taxi

Taxis aren't metered but operate according to fixed rates set by the government. They are allowed to carry up to five passengers, and the fare may be shared. Be sure to settle the rate before you start off and make sure you understand whether you're being quoted a rate in U.S. or Barbados dollars.

On a guided tour

A full-day guided tour is an excellent way to get your bearings. There's too much to see on this island to only do a half-day tour, although they are available. Several companies offer tours, and many specialize in specific areas like houses and gardens, arts and crafts, eco-tours, heritage, or black culture.

For those who are adventurous or for families, our pick is **Island Safari** (Bush Hall, St. Michael; ☎ **246-429-5337**; Fax: 246-429-8147), which offers a day-long Land/Sea tour for $95 per person, $50 for children 12 and under. You start out tooling around the Bajan countryside in a Land Rover and spend the afternoon on the *Tiami,* doing a sail/snorkel.

Boyce's Tours (Gazette Court, St. Michael; ☎ **246-425-5366**; Fax: 246-424-1455; E-mail: tours@boycetours.com) offers a craft tour ($30 per person) that takes visitors to some of our favorite artisans, a history and high-tea tour ($45 per person), and a photographer's dream tour ($35 per person) of Barbados's most dramatic vistas.

By scooter or bicycle

Scooters or bikes are a viable option for more adventurous travelers on this lush island — just be extremely careful in more urban areas. **Flex Bicycle Tours and Rentals** (☎ **246-419-2453** or 246-439-0829; E-mail: flexbikes@barbados.org) matches bikes and routes to rider's skills and preferences. Rates are $15 per day with a discount of two days free for every seven days of rental.

By helicopter

Bajan Helicopters (☎ **246-431-0069**; Fax: 246-431-0086) at the Bridgetown Heliport offers an eagle's-eye view of Barbados. The price per person ranges from $65 for a 20– to 25-minute "Discover Barbados" flightseeing tour to $122 for a 30– to 35-minute full "Island Tour" that makes a full circuit of the coastline.

Fast Facts: Barbados

ATMs

About 50 ATMs are available 24 hours a day at bank branches, transportation centers, shopping centers, and other convenient spots throughout the island. ATMs dispense Barbados dollars, of course.

Banks

Major banks are the following: Barbados National Bank (☎ 246-431-5700); Barclays Bank (☎ 246-431-5151); the Bank of Nova Scotia (☎ 246- 431-3000); Canadian Imperial Bank of Commerce (☎ 246-426-0571); and Royal Bank of Canada (☎ 246-431-6700). All have main offices on Broad Street in Bridgetown, plus branches in Speightstown, Holetown, and various towns along the south coast. The Barbados National Bank has a branch at the airport, and Canadian Imperial Bank of Commerce has a branch at the cruise ship terminal.

Business Hours

Bridgetown offices and stores are open weekdays 8:30 a.m. to 5:00 p.m. and Saturdays 8:30 a.m. to 1:00 p.m. Out-of-town locations may stay open later. Some supermarkets are open daily 8 a.m. to 6 p.m. or later. Banks are open Monday through Thursday from 8 a.m. to 3 p.m. and Friday from 8 a.m. to 5 p.m.

At the airport, the Barbados National Bank is open from 8 a.m. until the last plane leaves or arrives, seven days a week, even on holidays.

Credit Cards

Major credit cards and traveler's checks are widely accepted.

Currency Exchange

At press time, the Barbados dollar (Bds$1) was tied to the U.S. dollar at the rate of Bds$1.99 to US$1. U.S. dollars are readily accepted all over the island. Be sure that you know which currency you're dealing in when making a purchase. British pounds are not accepted; the currency exchange rate fluctuates daily and is posted at banks or online at www.xe.net/ucc.

Departure Tax

At the airport, before leaving Barbados, each passenger must pay a departure tax of US$12.50 (Bds$25), payable in either currency.

Doctors

Your hotel will have a list of doctors on call.

Electricity

Electric current on Barbados is 115/230 volts 50Hz. Hotels generally have adapters/transformers for use by travelers from countries that operate on 220-volt current.

Emergencies

In an emergency, call ☎ 211. For an ambulance, call ☎ 511; in case of fire, call ☎ 311. For a scuba diving accident, call **Divers' Alert Network (DAN)** at ☎ 246-684-8111 or 246-684-2948. The island has this region's only 24-hour hyperbaric chamber (Coast Guard Defence Force, St. Ann's Fort, Garrison, St. Michael; ☎ 246-427-8819; for nonemergencies, 246-436-6185).

Hospitals

Two modern facilities are on the island: Bayview Hospital, St. Paul's Avenue, Bayville, St. Michael (☎ 246-436-5446) or Queen Elizabeth Hospital, Martindales Road, St. Michael (☎ 246-436-6450).

Information

The Barbados Tourism Authority is on Harbour Road in Bridgetown (☎ 246-427-2623; Fax: 246-426-4080; E-mail: btainfo@barbados.org). Hours are 8:30 a.m. to 4:30 p.m. weekdays. Prior to your visit, contact the office of the Barbados Tourism Authority at 800 Second Ave., 2nd Floor, New York, NY 10017 (☎ 888-BARBADOS or 800-221-9831 or 212-986-6516; E-mail: btany@barbados.org; Internet: www.barbados.org). Barbados Hotel and Tourism Association (☎ 246-426-5041; E-mail: info@bhta.org) is also helpful. Another excellent resource is the annually published www.insandouts-barbados.com.

Language

The Queen's English is the official language, and the literacy rate on the island is 98%. The Bajan dialect is based on Afro-Caribbean rhythms tinged with an Irish or Scottish lilt.

Maps

You can pick up *Barbados in a Nutshell,* a free guide that contains a map, just about anywhere you travel across the island. Another free guide with a larger map is *The Sun Seeker.*

Pharmacies

Collins Pharmacy, Broad Street, Bridgetown (☎ 246-426-4515), is open from 8 a.m. to 5 p.m.

Police

In an emergency, call ☎ **211**; otherwise call ☎ 246-430-7100.

Post Office

The main post office, in Cheapside, Bridgetown, is open weekdays 7:30 a.m. to 5:00 p.m.; branches in each parish are open weekdays 8:00 a.m. to 3:15 p.m., except on Mondays when they close at 3 p.m. One branch is handily located at the airport.

Safety

Although Barbados is generally wealthy, poverty does exist here. Purse snatching, pickpocketing, armed robbery, and sexual assault on women have been reported. Most of the incidents have been around Bridgetown and St. Lawrence Gap. Take normal precautions: Don't leave cash or valuables in your hotel room, beware of purse snatchers when walking, exercise caution when walking on the beach (we'd avoid it at night altogether) or visiting tourist attractions, and be wary of driving in isolated areas of Barbados.

Taxes

A 7.5% government tax is added to all hotel bills. A 15% value-added tax (VAT) is imposed on restaurant meals, admissions to attractions, and merchandise sales (other than duty-free). Prices often include the tax, but if not, the VAT is added to your bill.

Telephone

Direct-dialing to the U.S., Canada, and other countries is efficient, and the cost is reasonable, but always check with your hotel to see if a surcharge awaits on the final bill. Remember that toll-free numbers aren't free from the Caribbean. To charge your overseas call on a major credit card without incurring a surcharge, dial ☎ 800-744-2000 from any phone.

All local calls are free if placed from private telephones. From pay phones, the charge is Bds25¢ for five minutes. Prepaid phone cards from Cable and Wireless (☎ 246-292-CARE), which can be used in pay phones throughout Barbados and other Caribbean islands, are sold at shops, tourist attractions, transportation centers, and other convenient outlets. For MCI dial ☎ 800-888-8000, for Sprint ☎ 800-877-4646, and for AT&T ☎ 800-872-2881.

For prepaid Internet access while you're on the island, contact Sunbeach (☎ 246-430-1569, Internet: www.sunbeach.net) for its Insta-Net card.

Time Zone

Barbados operates on Atlantic standard time year-round (same as eastern daylight time).

Tipping

A 10% service charge is usually added to hotel bills and restaurant checks in lieu of tipping. You can tip beyond the service charge to recognize extraordinary service. If no service charge is added, tip waiters 10 to 15% and maids $1 per room per day. Tip bellhops and airport porters $1 per bag. Taxi drivers expect a 10% tip.

Water

Tap water is safe to drink, naturally filtered through 1,000 feet of coral. It tastes better than what we find in the U.S.

Weather Reports

The average temperature ranges from 80 to 85 degrees Farenheit (27 to 29 degrees Celsius) with an average annual rainfall of 60 inches. Call ☎ 246-976-2376 for current conditions.

Chapter 14

Dining in Barbados

By Echo and Kevin Garrett

. . . .

In This Chapter

▶ Sampling the local cuisine

▶ Saving money on meals

▶ Locating the island's best restaurants

. . . .

Barbados, the easternmost island of the Lesser Antilles jutting out into the Atlantic, was often the first stop for ships carrying goods either from Europe or South America, so Bajans are used to having first pick of the bounty flowing into and out of the Caribbean. That long tradition of expecting the best of the best extends to food and has contributed to making this sophisticated island where the dining experience has been elevated to a fine art.

Want proof of Barbados's status in the world of cuisine? *Food & Wine*, American Express, and *Travel & Leisure* sponsored a chef exchange that saw some of New York's chic chefs trading aprons with chefs from the Barbados establishments Coral Reef Club, Turtle Beach, and Carambola — an event that is slated to become annual. Also, many of the zippy young chefs coming out of London to make a name in the food world come to the Caribbean — chiefly Barbados and the British Virgin Islands — to hone their talents. Gone are the days when English pub grub was about the most exciting thing coming out of the United Kingdom. These chefs, often trained in France and at the finest English country estates, design experimental and fun menus.

Like the island itself, however, eating out on Barbados is a study in contrasts. You can go as fancy (and pricey) as you want, with tuxedoed waiters at your elbow. Or you can get delicious down-home Bajan cooking at a funky little beachside cafe or at a weekly Friday night village fish fry for a reasonable price.

In this chapter, we give you a heads up about what tastes you can expect to experience on Barbados, and we list our favorite restaurants to make your dining decisions easier. During high season, many of the best places get booked up, so we suggest you e-mail reservation requests before you arrive.

Enjoying a Taste of Barbados

Interestingly enough, there's a strong culinary connection between Barbados and South Carolina, so if you're familiar with Low Country cooking, you'll have a good handle on the native cuisine of Barbados — lots of seafood and fresh vegetables like okra and tomatoes. Of course, catches from the Atlantic and Caribbean figure heavily into the menus here. Flying fish, the national bird — oops, we mean fish — leaps onto menus all over the island. Sides of rice and peas are important, as are spicy stews. Desserts are often made using fresh fruit.

Most restaurants here offer a strong taste of local flavor, and even franchises like KFC have adjusted their offerings to Bajan tastes. Get a side order of the Colonel's mashed potatoes, and you'll be served sweet potatoes spiked with local herbs. Chefette is the local answer to McDonald's, and the local chain has nearly two dozen locations around the island. It has playgrounds for kids at half a dozen locations. If you want a quick bite, it has good salads and burgers.

Pack your tiara and your jacket and tie for dining out on this island. Okay, okay, it's not quite that formal at most places, but on Barbados, you'll likely have the urge to dine at some swank spot at least once, and dressing up is the way it's done here. Shorts generally elicit raised eyebrows (at the least) in the evenings. Guys should wear collared shirts, and women should wear smart resort wear.

Following British custom, the waiters on this island do not bring your final bill until you signal that you're ready for it. Also, the service charge is usually already included, so make sure you don't overtip.

In-the-know tourists join the throng of locals at Oistin's Fish Fry on Friday nights where $12 and up gets you a whopping helping of crisply fried or grilled and deboned flying fish or chicken, macaroni pie, and a salad. Arrive by 7 p.m. and several vendors are frying up fish. Our pick is the one with the longest line: Fisherman's Net. It's a reasonable price for good food and a fun time with festive music blaring and locals scrambling to buy fresh-caught fish to cook at home.

A lot of locals and the media will steer you to the Atlantis Hotel in Bathsheba for a Sunday Bajan brunch. However, this once-classic spot has become dilapidated to the point of appearing unsanitary to us. On our last visit, one waiter was busily coating all the walls with bugspray and that wasn't the only bad odor we smelled. We had a similar experience at the once-exquisite Edgewater Inn. The buffet was a sad affair of overcooked food that looked like it had been sitting for hours.

For local fare (flying fish, pumpkin fritters, and the like) in Bathsheba, try the ultra casual but hip Bajan Surf Bungalow Guest House and Beach Grill (☎ **246-433-9920;** Internet: www.jorgen.com/surf) on the second-floor terrace overlooking the famed Soup Bowl, where surfers ride the waves, or the Round House Inn Restaurant and Bar (see the review later in this chapter), which also has that fab view. Another good Bajan spot that just opened in St. Joseph is Naniki at the Lush Life Nature Resort (☎ **246-433-1300;** E-mail: lushlife@sunbeach.net). If you're staying on the West Coast, stick to Brown Sugar's popular Planter's Buffet lunch (see the review later in this chapter).

Barbados's Best Restaurants

Bellini's Trattoria
$$ St. Lawrence Gap   Northern Italian

South of Bridgetown, this trattoria, on the main floor of Little Bay Hotel, evokes the Mediterranean in a beautiful setting that opens onto a veranda overlooking the water. The menu has a changing array of freshly made antipasti, plus well-prepared seafood dishes. The pasta menu with succulent sauces is extensive. After an appetizer — perhaps a small pizza — you can order tender and well-flavored beef tenderloin, chicken parmigiana, or jumbo shrimp in white wine, lemon, and garlic sauce. The Italian desserts, such as tiramisu, are velvety smooth.

Little Bay Hotel, St. Lawrence Gap, Christ Church. ☎ *246-435-7246. Reservations required. Main courses: $12–$23. AE, DC, MC, V. Open: Daily 6:00–10:30 p.m.*

Bombas Beach Bar
$$ Paynes Bay   Bajan/International

This colorful beach bar, tucked between Sandy Lane and Tamarind Cove hotels on the West Coast, serves tasty simple fare put out by Scottish Chef/Owner Gay Taaffe whose partner is a Bajan Rastafarian named Wayne Alleyne. Both locals and tourists favor this funky little place for dining alfresco on casual decking shaded by tall palm trees (lit by spotlights at night), right on the wide sandy beach. For lunch, it's beach-style snacks — jalapeno poppers and Bajan fishcakes, black and blue chicken sandwich (grilled with blue cheese). In front of Bomba's is a good place to swim in the sheltered bay, rent a beach chair and watch the sun go down. In the evening the chef cuts loose with lamb meatloaf with mint and apple chutney or chargrilled steakfish marinated in rum and lime with a hint of ginger. All main courses come with local veggies, rice, and crisp greens.

Paynes Bay Beach, St. James. ☎ *246-432-0569. Reservations not required. Main courses: $14–$17. MC, V. Open: Daily lunch noon to 4 p.m., snacks 4–7 p.m., dinner 7–10 p.m. Dinner only served Dec 15–Apr 15.*

Brown Sugar

$$ Bridgetown   Bajan

Brown Sugar, on the outskirts of Bridgetown, serves the tastiest Bajan specialties on the island. The alfresco restaurant, opened in 1977, is hidden behind lush foliage in a turn-of-the-century coral limestone bungalow. The latticed ceiling is punctuated with slow-turning fans, and on the open veranda you dine by candlelight beneath hanging plants, listening to waterfalls that feed into small ponds. We suggest starting with gungo-peak soup (pigeon peas cooked in chicken broth and zested with fresh coconut milk, herbs, and a touch of white wine). Among the main dishes we like, Creole orange chicken is the best, or you may like stuffed crab backs. A selection of locally grown vegetables is also offered. Only the lobster is expensive; most of the other dishes are reasonably priced. For dessert, we recommend walnut-rum pie with rum sauce. The restaurant is known for its buffet-style, three-course lunches, popular with local businesspeople for its good value, and it now offers takeout. Sometimes at night, live entertainment is offered.

Aquatic Gap, Bay Street, St. Michael. ☎ *246-426-7684. Reservations recommended. Main courses: $14.50–$50; lunch buffet $19 weekdays, $20 Sun. MC, V. Open: Sun–Fri 12:30–2:30 p.m. and daily from 6 p.m.*

Carambola

$$$$ Derricks   Classic French/Caribbean/Asian

Named for one of our favorite tropical fruits, Carambola is also one of our favorite Caribbean restaurants. Stationed beside the road that runs along the island's western coastline, this stunningly elegant restaurant, with crisp white linen topped tables and white canopies, sits atop a 20-foot seaside cliff and offers one of the most panoramic dining terraces in the Caribbean. The Cliff has the edge in the looks department, but both are stellar on all counts. The prize-winning cuisine is creative, with modern, French-nouvelle touches. Try the chef's lobster and spring rolls, or his grilled teriyaki of scallop and jumbo shrimp. Another spectacular dish is rack of lamb, coated in parsley and mustard with a truffle/sesame-seed/sweet-potato puree and caramelized root vegetables. The priciest items are the seafood platter and the grilled Caribbean lobster, but either is as succulent as you can imagine. Save room for one of the luscious desserts, such as lime mousse. Try to be seated by 6:30 p.m. to see the staff feed the manta rays that glide through the illuminated sea just below.

Derricks (1½ miles south of Holetown), St. James. ☎ *246-432-0832. Reservations recommended. Main courses: $24–$60. AE, MC, V. Mon–Sat 6:30–9:30 p.m. Closed Sun and Aug.*

The Cliff

$$$$$ St. James   International/Caribbean

Hands down this romantic restaurant is one of our all-time favorites in the Caribbean. Custom-made, wrought-iron torches and candelabras punctuate the already dramatic setting, a series of open-air terraces spilling

Dining in Barbados

Bellini's Trattoria **12**
Bombas Beach Bar **6**
Brown Sugar **9**
Carambola **5**
The Cliff **8**
The Emerald Palm **3**
Ile de France **4**
Jenner's at Cobbler Cove **2**
La Terra **4**
Luigi's Restaurant **12**
Mango's by the Sea **1**

Naniki **13**
Nico's Champagne Wine Bar
   & Restaurant **7**
Olives Bar & Bistro **4**
Pisces **12**
Ragamuffins **4**
Round House Inn Restaurant & Bar **14**
Shells **11**
The Ship Inn **12**
Waterfront Café **9**
X-Ray's **10**

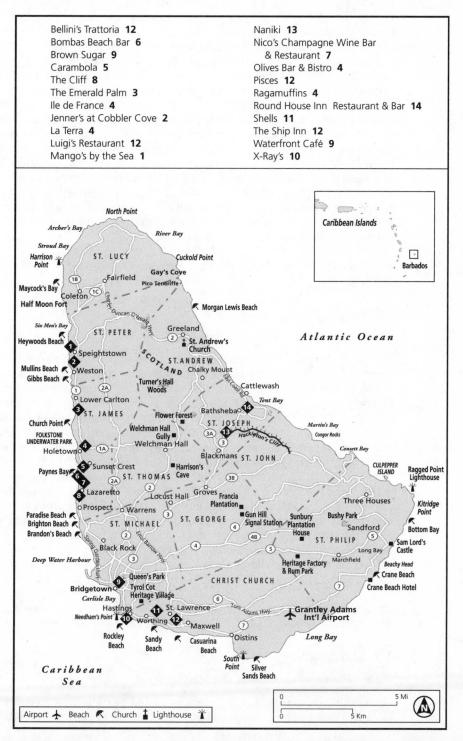

down to a 10-foot coral cliff, overlooking the illuminated sea, waves gently lapping the rocks below. Request a torch-lit table on the outer edge for the biggest wow factor. Flambeaus are rolled out to cover guests should it begin to rain. Ensconsed at our table we sipped a complimentary glass of Laurent Perrier Rose Champagne and watched fish glide by. Soothing Euro fusion music plays low in the background. Chef Paul Owens, whose *The Cliff, Barbados: Recipes by Paul Owens* topped Barbados's best-seller list in 2001, constantly changes the menu and offers nightly specials, too, making creative use of fresh local ingredients as well as imported ones. Of late his offerings have often had an Asian touch to them. Our starter was rocket salad with chargrilled vegetables, herbed goat's cheese, and balsamic vinaigrette and snow crab cake with coriander cream, and vinaigrette and red curry oil. We loved the seared tuna on wasabi mash with spicy Asian vinaigrette, Japanese ginger and soy as well as red snapper on jasmine rice with a Thai yellow curry coconut sauce. For dessert, keep cool with the assorted homemade sorbet served in a ginger basket. The snappy service equaled anything we've experienced at top restaurants in the U.S. We lingered because we didn't want the evening to end.

Derricks, St. James. ☎ 246-432-1922. Reservations required in winter. Main courses: $33–$37.50. AE, DC, MC. V. Open: Nightly from 6:30 p.m.

The Emerald Palm
$$$$ St. James   International

Escape from traffic noise and the congestion of this posh parish's coast to this 10-acre tropical oasis where the only noise is the trickling of waterfalls and the rustling of palms. The centerpiece: a massive coral stone country house, where you'll pass under an arbor and quickly be offered a drink to sip as you settle on one of the many comfortable lounges while your table — we suggest those in the fragrant garden — is prepared. You'll have to reserve early if you want the best table, the middle one of a trio of gazebos. The restaurant, which mainly attracts older Europeans, often has bookings a year in advance. Chef David Jones, who changes his menu three times a year, turns out flavorful and intriguing combinations. Begin with a marinated shrimp in soy and ginger served with a cucumber and pink grapefruit salad. Specialties include his grilled dolphin filet with a shrimp fritter, fondant potato and a grain mustard butter sauce or red snapper with fettucine, buttered bok choy, and red pepper cream. For the grand finale, go with the dark chocolate crème brûlée spiked with Mount Gay Extra Old Rum served with a clementine confit.

Porters, St. James (2 miles north of Holetown). ☎ 246-422-4116. Reservations required. Main courses: $20–$40. AE, MC, V. Open: Tues–Sun 6:30–9:30 p.m. Closed Mon.

Ile de France
$$$$ Holetown   Classic French/Seafood

From the terrace of this pleasantly casual restaurant just north of Holetown, diners have an entrancing view of Holetown Bay. Request one of the four prime, lantern-lit tables directly on the seafront, then place your-self in the capable hands of Michel and Martine Gramaglia, two French-born expatriates who handle their kitchen and dining room with grace and style. The classic French menu, heavy on seafood offerings, changes every three or four months, and the chef relies almost exclusively on locally grown pro-duce and locally caught seafood. Star starters are *escargots de Burgundy* and a classic seafood bisque with local fish and lobster. For the main course, go with the chef's take on the catch of the day — usually dorado, snapper, or kingfish, baked, grilled, or blackened, with a choice between two sauces. The well-seasoned seafood platter satisfies with half a lobster tail, a small portion of jumbo shrimp, scallops, and the catch of day. Other classic dishes include tournedos with a béarnaise sauce and roast rack of lamb. Although hardly innovative, each of these time-tested favorites is pre-pared with exactitude and refinement. For dessert, try the crème brûlée.

In the Settlers' Beach Hotel, Holetown, St. James (8 miles north of Bridgetown). ☎ *246-422-3245. Reservations recommended. Main courses: $20–$45. AE, MC, V. Open: Daily 8 a.m.–11 p.m.*

Jenner's at Cobblers Cove
$$$$ St. Peter   British Haute/Caribbean

This English country house on a beach is one of only six restaurant/hotels in the Caribbean to receive the Relais and Chateaux designation (recog-nizing excellent small hotels with top-notch restaurants). This elegant yet casual restaurant's open-air terrace allows sea breezes to waft through. Young English chef John Hardwick turns out his bold new take on English fare with a hint of the Caribbean. He's now consulting with the star chef of London's famed Jenner's. Start with the woodland mushroom soup or panfried smoked mackeral with sweet potato and lime pickle, raita, and basil oil. We also recommend grilled barracuda with Bajan seasoning with roast garlic mash, sauce vierge, and breadfruit crisps. Or you may want to go for the Table D'Hote menu. The chocolate decadence with brandy and Bailey's ice cream is worth the calories. On Tuesday evening, there's a barbecue buffet, and on Sunday a special curry lunch with steel-pan music (in winter only). On Tuesday, Thursday, and Saturday nights, a duo play-ing sax and guitar entertain.

If you have special dietary needs, this energetic cheery chef does back-flips to please his guests.

Cobblers Cove, St. Peter. ☎ *246-422-2291. Reservations required. Main courses: $24–$34. AE, MC, V. Open: Daily 8–10 a.m. and 12:30–9:30 p.m. Closed Jul 1–Oct 15.*

La Terra
$$$$ Baku Beach   Caribbean/Italian

Ascend to the second-floor terrace of the Baku Beach complex in Holetown, and you'll be transported at this culinary gem. Winner of an "Award of Excellence" from *Wine Spectator* as well as a nod from *Condé*

Nast Traveler as one of the world's "60 Hottest New Restaurants," La Terra blends classical Italian with contemporary dishes tinged with Caribbean flavors. The Cliff has the slight edge for sheer drama, but we'd be hard-pressed to choose between the two for our favorite meal. La Terra's Chef/Owner Larry Rogers's choice of jazz and classics from the 1940s, orchid sprays on the small tables, and the sound of tree frogs set the mood for romance, plus you also have the chic Casbah Nightclub conveniently located downstairs. Our appetizer of marinated and grilled calamari with a tomato herb vinaigrette was a perfect rendition of a familiar dish. We also savored baked barracuda in red wine, capers, and tarragon on fettuccine with steamed greens. Rogers and his wife, Michelle, who also own Olives, are a dynamic and creative force on the Bajan dining scene.

Baku Beach, Holetown. ☎ 246-432-1099. Reservations required. Main courses: $25–$40. AE, DC, MC, V. Open: Daily 6:30–10:00 p.m.

Luigi's Restaurant
$$ St. Lawrence Gap Italian

Since 1963, this open-air trattoria has operated in a Greenland-white building built as a private house. The feeling is contemporary, airy, and comfortable. Pizzas are offered as appetizers, along with more classic choices such as a half-dozen escargots or a Caesar salad (when available). Many pastas are available in half-orders as starters. The baked pastas (a creamy lasagna, for one) are delectable. Other dishes include the fresh fish or veal special of the day. For dessert, try the zabaglione and one of the wide selections of coffee, ranging from Italian to Russian or Turkish.

Dover Woods, St. Lawrence Gap, Christ Church. ☎ 246-428-9218. Reservations required. Main courses: $11.50–$24.50. MC, V. Open: Nightly from 6 p.m.

Mango's by the Sea
$$ Speightstown International

This romantic hideaway restaurant and bar overlooking the lapping waves is best known for its seafood: The owners, Montreal natives Gail and Pierre Spenard, buy the catch of the day directly from the fishermen's boats. The food is exceedingly good, and the seasonings aren't too overpowering. Market-fresh ingredients are used to good advantage. Appetizers may be anything from an intriguing green peppercorn pâté to pumpkin soup. If you don't want fish, opt for the 8-ounce U.S. tenderloin steak cooked to perfection or the fall-off-the-bone barbecued baby-back ribs. Top off your meal with passion-fruit cheesecake or star-fruit torte. There's live entertainment on some nights. After 10 p.m., cigar aficionados make their selection from a collection of Cubans from Pierre's humidor and puff away at the bar or their tables. It's also one of the few Caribbean restaurants to have a wine cellar.

2 West End, Queen Street, Speightstown, St. Peter. ☎ 246-422-0704. Reservations recommended. Main courses: $14–$32. MC, V. Open: Sun–Fri from 6 p.m. Closed June.

Naniki

$$ Suriname Caribbean/Organic

A little greenheart house in a valley outside the village of Suriname houses this new restaurant, emphasizing healthy cooking at the Lush Life Nature Resort. Tom Hinds, who is working to help his brainchild achieve Green Globe recognition, is committed to serving fresh vegetables, most of which are organic, along with Bajan and other Caribbean treats. Meticulous attention is paid to presentation of creations using delicacies like *lambie* (conch) and blue crab and grilled Bajan black belly lamb. Sweet potatoes, yams, and breadfruits are menu staples. This place is our top pick if you're heading to Bathsheba for the day. The Sunday Bajan buffet has become so popular that you need reservations.

The surroundings are refreshingly beautiful, too. Light streams through the mostly glass walls, making optimal use of the rolling hills, the stands of cabbage palms, and the Atlantic coast beyond. Greenheart paneling, floorboards and beams, and stone tiles were used in the construction. Pine furnishings are brightened with colorful plates and fresh anthuriums (Hinds grows them for commercial use).

Suriname, St. Joseph. ☎ *246-433-1300. Reservations recommended. Main courses: $11–$17. MC, V. Open: Tues–Sun noon to 5 p.m. Dinner served on moonlit nights only.*

Nico's Champagne Wine Bar and Restaurant

$$ Derrick's International

Set on the side of a road away from the sea that bisects some of the most expensive residential real estate on Barbados, Nico's is a great value with friendly service, a cozy, informal bistro inspired by the wine bars of London. In an atmospheric 19th-century building, originally constructed as the headquarters for a plantation, is its air-conditioned tropical bar. Meals are served at tables under a shed-style roof in the back garden. About a dozen wines are sold by the glass; the flavorful food is well-matched to the wines. The finest plates include deep-fried Camembert with passion-fruit sauce, chicken breasts stuffed with crab, and some of the best lobster (grilled simply and served with garlic butter) on Barbados.

Derrick's, St. James. ☎ *246-432-6386. Reservations recommended. Main courses: Lunch $9–$14, dinner $12–$36. AE, DISC, MC, V. Open: Mon–Sat 11:30 a.m.–9:30 p.m.*

Olives Bar and Bistro

$$ Holetown Mediterannean/Caribbean

Olive oil is used to prepare almost all the good-value, imaginative dishes here, and olives are the only snack served in the large breezy bar upstairs that has become a popular hangout. The street-level, air-conditioned, and unpretentious dining room (where no smoking is permitted) spills out from its original coral-stone walls and scrubbed-pine floorboards into a pleasant garden. (On a warm evening, stick to the inside air-conditioning.) The cuisine using fresh ingredients with a beautiful presentation celebrates the warm climates of southern Europe and the Antilles, and does so exceedingly well. Even some local chefs like to dine here on their nights off. Service is proficient and friendly. The best items include yellowfin tuna, marinated and seared rare and served with green peppercorn mustard cream sauce. Next door is a sandwich bar that serves light lunch fare, Monday through Friday from 8 a.m. to 4 p.m.

2nd Street, Holetown, St. James. ☎ 246-432-2112. Reservations required in winter. Main courses: $14–$33. AE, MC, V. Open: Light fare Mon–Fri 8:30 a.m.–4:00 p.m., dinner nightly 6:30–10:00 p.m.

Pisces
$$ St. Lawrence Gap   Bajan

This beautiful restaurant with a tropical decor offers alfresco dining at water's edge. Begin with one of the soups, perhaps split pea or pumpkin, or a savory appetizer like flying fish Florentine. Seafood lovers enjoy the Pisces platter — charcoal-broiled dolphin (mahimahi), fried flying fish, broiled kingfish, and butter-fried prawns. You may also be drawn to the seasonal Caribbean fish, which can be broiled, blackened, or panfried, and then served with lime-herb butter. A limited but good selection of poultry and meat is offered, including roast pork Barbados with a traditional Bajan stuffing.

From Bridgetown, take Highway 7 south for about 4 miles, then turn right at the sign toward St. Lawrence Gap. St. Lawrence Gap, Christ Church. ☎ 246-435-6564. Reservations recommended. Main courses: $14–$38. AE, DC, MC, V. Open: Nightly 6:30–9:30 p.m.

Ragamuffins
$$$ Holetown   Caribbean

This affordable, lively place — packed most nights — serves authentic island cuisine in a brightly colored, authentic chattel house, the humble abodes of the slaves and laborers who worked the sugar cane fields. The broiled T-bones, the most pricey menu item, are juicy and perfectly flavored. Vegetarians aren't ignored either. The cooks are always willing to stir-fry some vegetables with noodles, and a vegetarian stew is on the menu, too. On Sunday nights, it features the only drag show — often sold out, so reserve early — in Barbados. (Request seats in the garden for the best view.) Other menu highlights are blackened fish with garlic aioli, the local version of a spicy West Indian curry, and a zesty jerk chicken salad.

First Street, Holetown, St. James. ☎ 246-432-1295. Reservations required on Sunday and recommended on other days. Main courses: $16–$30. AE, MC, V. Open: Sun–Fri 7:30–9:30 p.m.

Round House Inn Restaurant and Bar
$ Bathsheba Bajan

This small historic inn, restored in 1997 by Robert and Gail Manley, is perched on a hill overlooking the dramatic Soup Bowl in Bathsheba where surfers like to battle the waves of the Atlantic. From the small tables beside the large open windows, you can watch families playing in the tidal pools at the water's edge. With stark curved white walls, tiles, and wood floors, this place has a small selection of Caribbean art on its walls. A small wood carved bar has surfboards hanging around it. The Round House attracts locals who love the Reggae and surf scene here. The Bajan food here is excellent, with tasty homemade bread, a decent selection of wines, and good, though casual, service. For lunch, go with the grilled flying fish sandwich served with breadfruit chips. The soups, served with saltbread, and the salads are good, too. Request some of the Bajan hot sauce on the side for an extra kick. At night go with the fisherman's with dolphin, flying fish, and shrimp, which comes with peas and rice. The homemade banana bread with ice cream is a great ender to the meal. In the evenings, live reggae bands are often playing. The rooms at the inn have been redone, too, and are a reasonably priced choice if you're into the surf scene or want to stay on this quiet coast.

Bathsheba, St. Joseph. ☎ *246-433-9678. Reservations required on Sunday and recommended on other days. Main courses: $8–$17. MC, V. Open: Daily 8 a.m.–9 p.m.*

Shells
$ Worthing Bajan/Continental

For cheap eats in a cool setting, you can't beat Shells on the south coast. It also offers dirt-cheap guest rooms that appeal to the young crowd that favors this end of the island. The small, open-air restaurant tucked on a side street is easily spotted by its electric blue and shocking pink accents. Dotted with potted palms and just off Sandy Beach, it's casual seaside dining at its best. Ten dollars will get you rotini pasta with cream curry sauce with shrimp and crab meat. Their secret sauce adds tang to their version of panfried flying fish. Top off your meal with coconut cream pie. When it gets super busy on the weekends, service can be slow.

First Avenue, Worthing. ☎ *246-435-7253. Reservation required for six or more. Main courses: $8–$12. MC, V. Open: Daily 5–10 p.m.*

The Ship Inn
$ St. Lawrence Gap English Pub/Bajan

South of Bridgetown between Rockley Beach and Worthing, The Ship Inn is a traditional English-style pub with an attractive, rustic nautical decor. You can also enjoy a drink in the garden bar's tropical atmosphere. Many guests come to play darts, to meet friends, and to listen to top local bands. The Ship Inn, which has a popular happy hour (4 to 6 p.m. and 10 to 11 p.m.), serves substantial bar food, such as homemade steak-and-kidney pie, shepherd's pie, and chicken, shrimp, and fish dishes.

St. Lawrence Gap, Christ Church. ☎ 246-435-6961. Reservations recommended for the Captain's Carvery only. Main courses: $8–$14.50; all-you-can-eat Carvery meal $12 at lunch, $21 at dinner, plus $9 for appetizer and dessert. AE, DC, MC, V. Open: Sun–Fri 12:15–3:00 p.m. and 6 p.m.–2 a.m.

Waterfront Cafe

$$ Bridgetown   International

This is your best bet if you're in Bridgetown shopping or sightseeing. In a turn-of-the-century warehouse originally built to store bananas and freeze fish, this cafe serves international fare with a strong emphasis on Bajan specialties. Try the fresh catch of the day prepared Creole-style, peppered steak, or the fish burger made with kingfish or dolphin. For vegetarians, the menu features such dishes as pasta primavera, vegetable soup, and usually a special of the day. Both diners and drinkers are welcome here for Creole food, beer, and pastel-colored drinks. Tuesday nights bring live steel-band music and a Bajan buffet. To see the Thursday night Dixieland bands, reserve about a week in advance. There's jazz on Friday and Saturday.

The Careenage, Bridgetown. ☎ 246-427-0093. Reservations required. Main courses: $14–$23. AE, DC, MC, V. Open: Mon–Sat 10 a.m–10 p.m.

X-Ray's

$$ Hastings   Bajan

Named after the popular Bajan D.J. X-Ray, who is present most nights as host and barfly, this casual little beachfront gem (formerly called Shak Shak) sports simple wooden chairs and small tables on a seaside deck next to a bright yellow traditional West Indian coral stone structure. It's surrounded by tropical flowering vines and palms and makes a good lunch spot or a romantic place for a low-key dinner. Menu highlights include the catch of the day, blackened salmon on a potato cake, shrimp simmered in Thai curry sauce served with rice, lamb shank seasoned with vegetables and pan gravy, and panfried dorado with tropical fruit salsa. At lunchtime, the pizzas and pastas are good picks. Most nights a live trio plays alternative rock and blues starting around 9 p.m., and the busy bar has become a popular hangout for tourists and locals alike.

Shak Shak Complex (next door to the Allamanda Beach Hotel), Hastings, Christ Church. ☎ 246-435-1234. Reservations recommended. Main courses: $13–$26. AE, MC, V. Open: Noon to 4 p.m and 6:30–10 p.m.

Chapter 15

Having Fun on and off the Beach in Barbados

By Echo and Kevin Garrett

. . . .

In This Chapter

▶ Soaking up the sun on Barbados's top beaches

▶ Diving into fun with water sports

▶ Satisfying the landlubber: activities, shopping, nightlife, and the arts

▶ Planning some super side trips

. . . .

George Washington (and his younger brother) slept here. Really. Lots of places make such a claim, but in this case, it's true. Indeed, Barbados has been giving the royal treatment to the wealthy and the famous for centuries — from the British royals to U.S. presidents, from the Rolling Stones to the Rockefellers. The upscale appeal comes from its outstanding golf courses (from the Royal Westmoreland to Sandy Lane), the historic Great Houses and gardens, its stellar dining scene (see Chapter 14), and the pampering of the Gold Coast's resorts with outstanding water sports in the calm Caribbean.

In the last several years, however, Barbados has become a popular holiday choice with common folks as well, especially younger Brits and Canadians, who come for the pub-hopping and dance scene on the south coast in an area known as The Gap, as well as for Barbados's rollicking music festivals. The younger set also likes the surfing on the rugged Atlantic side and the windsurfing on the south coast. Yes, you read that right: Surf's up in Barbados.

In this chapter, we guide you toward Barbados's best beaches and activities.

Hitting the Beaches

With more than 70 miles of coastline, the coral island of Barbados is ringed by a great selection of soft white to pale golden sand beaches with ample opportunities for water play from snorkeling to skiing to surfing. If you love nothing better than hanging out on the quintessential Caribbean beach, this island is a good pick. Most of the beaches — all are public, though you may have to cross a resort's property or find a small public path to access them — are relatively litter free. Although vendors selling pareos, shark-tooth necklaces, dolls, baskets, and carvings do approach you on the more populated beaches, they aren't overly aggressive. If you aren't interested in what they're selling, a simple but firm "No, thank you" should preserve your peace. You may also be approached by private boat owners who offer to take you water-skiing, parasailing, or snorkeling.

We discuss some of our favorite Bajan beaches in this section.

A euphemism that beach vendors who are selling drugs use is asking you if you're interested in any local pottery. Tell them you'll be checking out the wares at Earthworks, a well-known local maker of pottery.

West coast

If you're picturing the calm, clear kaleidoscope of blues that are the signature of the Caribbean, you'll likely find the beaches on the west coast — commonly referred to as the Gold Coast or Platinum Coast — to your taste. It's no accident that Barbados's toniest resorts and grand homes are located here, too. It's breathtakingly beautiful with tropical gardens, stands of palm trees, and little coves with shallow reefs close to shore for snorkeling. The Caribbean is often so smooth (especially early in the morning) that you can water-ski, and swimming conditions are generally excellent.

On this coast, you may encounter what looks like an apple tree with little green apples. There were several on Almond Beach Village's beach. Watch out and warn your children, too, because it's the fruit of the manchineel tree, and they're not only poisonous to eat but also toxic to the touch. Even taking shelter under the tree when it rains can give you blisters. Most manchineels are identified with signs or with a red ring painted on the tree trunk.

We recommend Mullins Beach, because it has a nice reef for snorkeling. Park on the main drag or take the bus. You can get food and drink at **Mullins Beach Bar** (☎ **246-422-1878**), which stays busy.

An even better spot for snorkeling is somewhat crowded but picturesque **Paynes Bay,** accessed from the Coach House, south of Holetown. It has good water sports. You can rent beach chairs and water-sports equipment at Bombas Beach Bar (see the review in Chapter 13), a color-ful gathering spot and watering hole. Famous for snorkeling on this side of the island is Folkestone Marine Reserve (see later in this chapter for more information). Sandy Lane's lovely strand offers excellent swimming conditions.

East coast

One bright morning during one of our visits, we set out in a rental car (reminding each other to drive on the left) to explore this coral island. Although the west coast of the island boasts white-sand beaches and calm, turquoise Caribbean water, we headed toward the crashing waves of the Atlantic pounding the east and craggy north coast. Our first stop: windswept Bathsheba/Cattlewash, where magnificent boul-ders frame crashing waves, to watch the sunrise. We were surprised to find a gaggle of surfers already there to catch the waves.

Bajans ride the waves here almost daily. (Barbados is the location of the Independence Classic Surfing Championships, held each November.) If you decide to try surfing, be sure to get advice from the experts at Bajan Surf Bungalow, who can also rent you gear.

On the sleepy east coast, you'll see miles of untouched beach along the island's wildest, hilliest, and most beautiful stretch. But swimming at Bathsheba or along the Atlantic coast can be extremely dangerous, so you may want to stick to sightseeing in these areas and save your swim-suit for the south or west coast beaches. If you like to stroll on the beach, the area north of Cattlewash is your best bet, and you can also find several beautiful spots — often deserted — for a picnic. You can get picnic fixings in Holetown, or stop by one of the local restaurants like the **Bajan Surf Bungalow Guest House and Beach Grill** (☎ **246-433-9920;** Internet: www.jorgen.com/surf) or the **Round House Inn Restaurant and Bar** (☎ **246-433-9678;** Fax: 246-433-9079) and ask for a boxed lunch.

If you're wading along the shore, watch out for sea urchins among the rocks. Locally called *cobblers,* these critters look like a small dark por-cupine underwater, about the size of a hockey puck. We always wear water shoes in the Caribbean, but if you're barefoot and step on one, its needle-sharp spines feel like a giant splinter imbedded in your foot. Apply vinegar immediately to neutralize the poison. The spines aren't life-threatening, just painful. And, yes, we do speak from experience.

South coast

Known for small waves and strong trade winds, the area, with its wealth of nightclubs, pubs, and reasonably priced seaside beach bars, attracts a young crowd looking for a good time. Windsurfers and body boarders head to this area, which is also good for swimming. Windsurfers are especially fond of wide, windswept **Casuarina Beach**, accessed from

Maxwell Coast Road, going across the property of the Casuarina Beach Hotel. You can order food and drinks at the hotel.

Silver Sands Beach, to the east of Oistins, is near the southernmost point of Barbados, directly east of South Point Lighthouse and near the Silver Rock Hotel. This white-sand beach is a favorite with many Bajans (who probably want to keep it a secret from as many tourists as possible). Drinks are sold at the Silver Rock Bar. Silver Rock is where the more-expert windsurfers come, primarily between November and June. Maxwell Beach (in front of the Windsurf Beach Hotel) is best for flat-water windsurfing.

Sandy Beach, reached from the parking lot on the main road in Worthing, has tranquil waters opening onto a lagoon, the epitome of Caribbean charm. A favorite of families, it's especially boisterous on weekends. We especially recommend getting your sustenance at Shell's (see Chapter 14 for a full review).

Carlisle Bay, which also has a new marine reserve and exceptionally calm waters for swimming, as well as changing facilities with restrooms, is popular with day-tripping cruise-ship passengers.

Ultra-popular Accra Beach in Rockley is a hotspot with body-boarders, and you can rent boards and snorkeling gear, as well as gear for other water-play. A wide interlocking brick promenade, several additional palms, and better parking facilities have made this area even prettier.

Southeast coast

The southeast coast is the site of the big waves, especially at **Crane Beach,** the white-sand strip set against a backdrop of palms that you've probably seen in all the travel magazines. It offers excellent bodysurfing and you can rent a board on the beach, but at times the waters may be too rough for all but the strongest swimmers. The beach is set against cliffs, with the Crane Beach Hotel, which has been completely redone, towering above it.

We suggest booking lunch at the **Crane's** beautiful restaurant (☎ 246-423-6220) overlooking the beach. On Sundays from 10 to 11 a.m., it sponsors a gospel brunch. Later that afternoon, it has a traditional Bajan spread with a steel-pan band playing. The prices are reasonable, the food good, and the view . . . pure heaven.

Bottom Bay, north of Sam Lord's Castle Resort, is one of our all-time Bajan favorites. Park on the top of a cliff, then walk down the steps to this much-photographed tropical beach with its grove of coconut palms; there's even a cave. The sand is brilliantly white against the aquamarine sea, a picture-postcard perfect beach paradise. Foul Bay is the longest beach on this coast, with dramatic cliffs framing either end of the white sandy beach. In the first half of the year, you'll often see sea turtles coming up for air just beyond the waves.

Finding Water Fun for Everyone

Though it's a coral island surrounded by fringing and banking reefs, Barbados hasn't become known among divers for good reason. First of all, fishing is still big business around this island, and you rarely see any large fish on its reefs. But if you're a beginning diver who wants to get in a few dives between rounds of golf or you're into wreck diving, you'll likely enjoy the experience. Snorkelers will find plenty to make renting the gear worth it. Visibility is generally around 80 to 90 feet, but during the rainy season, from June to January, it may be greatly diminished.

Locating dive and snorkeling sites

Many wrecks are submerged in the shallow waters off the south and west coasts. The most popular wrecks to explore are the south's *Berwyn,* a coral-encrusted French tugboat that sank in Carlisle Bay in 1916, which attracts photographers for its variety of reef fish, shallow depth, good light, and visibility. The **Carlisle Bay Marine Reserve** is newly established and now has eight wrecks — three shallow enough for snorkeling — in a concentrated area for divers to explore. The bay is noted as a place to see hawksbill turtles, elusive sea horses, and rare frogfish.

The most beautiful site on the west coast is **Dottin's Reef,** which stretches 5 miles from Bridgetown to Holetown. It's accessible at 40 feet, and is festooned with sea fans, gorgonians, and brain coral. You'll see parrotfish, barracuda, snappers, and maybe a sea turtle or two.

Also on the west is the *Stavronikita,* a 356-foot Greek freighter whose hull rests 130 feet under water with one mast just 20 feet beneath the surface. The freighter is often crowded with tourist divers, but it's a good wreck to explore. The ship was intentionally scuttled in 1978 a quarter of a mile off the west coast to become an artificial reef in **Folkestone Underwater Park,** north of Holetown.

At the **Folkestone Marine Park and Visitor Centre** (Church Point, Holetown, St. James; ☎ **246-422-2314;** admission 60¢), a Marine Museum has a large mini reef, saltwater aquarium, and marine artifacts and specimens. At the center, you can rent snorkeling gear and rent lockers for the day. The park also has an underwater snorkeling trail around Dottin's Reef. A glass-bottom boat ride allows youngsters and nonswimmers to get a good look, too, at the freighter. Open weekdays from 9 a.m. to 5 p.m.

Renting underwater gear

The good news for divers is that, because diving isn't as popular on this island, the dive-shop operators are eager to please. If they sense you're interested in a unique experience, dive masters will go out of their way to take you to interesting sites and point out the small marine life that you may otherwise overlook. The boats aren't overcrowded, so you can get more-personalized attention.

A one-tank dive on this island runs about $55; a two-tank dive costs about $90. All gear is supplied, and you can purchase multi-dive packages. You can rent gear for snorkeling for a small charge from most hotels. Snorkelers can usually accompany dive trips for $20 to $25 for a one– or two-hour trip.

Both **Dive Boat Safari** (Grand Barbados Beach Resort, Aquatic Gap, St. Michael; ☎ **246-427-4350**) and **The Dive Shop, Ltd**. (Aquatic Gap near Bay Street, St. Michael; ☎ **888-898-DIVE** or 246-426-9947; E-mail: hardive@caribnet.net; Internet: www.divebds.com) are located in the Carlisle Bay, with five wrecks and 15 reef sites nearby. The latter is the oldest dive shop on Barbados and teaches all levels of certification.

Dive Blue Reef Barbados (next to The Lone Star, St. James; ☎ **246-422-3133**; E-mail: bluereef@sunbeach.net; Internet: www.divebluereef.com) and **Hightide Watersports** (Coral Reef Club, St. James; ☎ **800-513-5763** or 246-432-0931; Fax: 246-432-0931; E-mail: hightide@sunbeach.net; Internet: www.divehightide.com), are both known for highly personalized dives catering to small groups. Hightide offers one– and two-tank dives, night reef/wreck/drift dives, the full range of PADI instruction, specialties including underwater photography, and free transportation. It also has a new custom-built, high-speed, 30-foot dive boat with dry storage and a camera table.

Snorkelers can sometimes see Hawksbill turtles in front of Dive Blue Reef. In an effort to conserve the magnificent sea turtles that were once plentiful around the island, local authorities launched the **Barbados Sea Turtle Project** in 1987. Turtles are tagged, monitored for disease and watched for nesting. The project relies on the public to notify them of any sighting. In fact, there's a 24-hour hot line that you can call to report any nesting activity (☎ **246-230-0142**).

Taking a ride under the sea

Atlantis Submarines (Shallow Draught, Bridgetown; ☎ **246-436-8929**; E-mail: contact-barbados@GoAtlantis.com; Internet: www.GoAtlantis.com) offers enormously popular mini-submarine voyages good for families with youngsters and those who are curious about what's under the sea but don't want to dive or snorkel. You have two choices on Barbados, both of which take about an hour and a half:

✔ The 48-passenger, 65-foot *Atlantis III* gives you a 50-minute tour of wrecks and reefs as deep as 150 feet. Special nighttime dives, using high-power searchlights, are spectacular. Adults, $80; children, $40; teens $52.

✔ Children enjoy the *Atlantis SEATREC* (Sea Tracking and Reef Exploration Craft), which essentially lets you experience the same views you'd get snorkeling without getting wet. The 36-passenger vessel has large viewing windows 6 feet below the surface, where you view the underwater marine life on a near-shore reef from the air-conditioned craft. Adults, $35; children, $17.

Make reservations before your trip if you'd like to go. These submarines do get booked up.

Water-skiing the Caribbean

We recommend water-skiing early in the day, because the waters can get a little rough in the afternoons. Many hotels on the west and south coasts of the island offer water-skiing, sometimes at no additional cost. If your hotel doesn't provide this service and you're staying on the west coast, book with **Hightide Watersports** (Coral Reef Club, St. James; ☎ **800-513-5763** or 246-432-0931; Fax: 246-432-0931; E-mail: hightide@ sunbeach.net; Internet: www.divehightide.com). It now has a Moomba World-Class, 300 horsepower mid-drive inboard tournament ski boat — the only one on Barbados — which gives a powerful pull. The friendly instructors offer lessons and work with kids, too. This outfit also rents gear for windsurfing, banana and biscuit rides, sea kayaks, Hobie Cats, Sunfish, and water bikes.

Private speedboat owners troll for business along the St. James and Christ Church waterfront, but you water-ski at your own risk with these operators.

Riding the wind

Experts say the windsurfing off Barbados is as good as any this side of Hawaii. Judging from the crowds that flock here, they're right. Windsurfing on Barbados has turned into big business between November and April, attracting windsurfers from as far away as Australia, Argentina, and Japan. The shifting of the trade winds between November and June and the shallow offshore reef of **Silver Sands** create unique conditions of wind and wave swells. This allows windsurfers to reach speeds of up to 50 knots and do complete loops off the waves. Silver Sands is rated the best spot in the Caribbean for advanced windsurfing. Barbados Windsurfing Championships are held in mid-January. Here's where to rent gear ($55 to $65 a day) or get instruction ($65 for an hour):

> ✔ **Beginners or less experienced windsurfers: Club Mistral Windsurfing School,** Grand Barbados Beach Resort in Carlisle Bay, south of Bridgetown (Aquatic Gap, St. Michael; ☎ **246-426-4000**).
>
> ✔ **Advanced: Silver Rock Windsurfing Club,** Silver Rock Hotel on Silver Sands Beach (Christ Church; ☎ **246-428-2866**).

Boards and equipment are often free of charge for guests at the larger hotels, and you may even get lessons kicked in as part of your package. Several smaller hotels specialize in windsurfing packages. Check out www.funbarbados.com/activities/sports/windsurging.cfm for links.

Telling fish tales

Barbados is deep-sea-fishing paradise. If you dream of hooking that big one, this island is a good place to book a full charter in your hunt for blue and white marlin, billfish, and sailfish — or a half-day if you're satisfied sticking closer to shore for dorado, tuna, wahoo, and barracuda. Charter fishing trips depart from the Careenage in Bridgetown.

You're in good hands with captain and owner Winston "The Colonel" White, who has been plying the waters around Barbados for more than a quarter of a century. His *Billfisher II* (Bridge House, Cavans Lane, the Careenage, Bridgetown; ☎ **246-431-0741**) is a 40-foot Pacemaker — with five rods and three chairs — that accommodates up to six people. Half-day charters get you drinks (rum, beer, and soft drinks) and sandwiches. Full-day charters include a full lunch, and the confident captain even guarantees fish. You can keep everything you catch, and the crew will clean and cook your catch for you at day's end.

The affable captain will match you with other people who would like to share the cost of the charter.

The Blue Jay (St. James; ☎ **246-429-2326**) is a 45-foot, fully equipped Sports-Fisherman with a huge cockpit and four fishing chairs. The fishing party is limited to four, guaranteeing that everyone gets to cast his line. Captain "Callie" Elton's crew knows the waters where the bigger game fish frolic. You may hook into such game fish as blue marlin, sailfish, barracuda, and kingfish. Each person fishing can invite a guest free of charge. Drinks and snacks are provided.

Sailing away

Most popular and fun are the **Jolly Roger "Pirate" Cruises** (☎ **246-436-6424**), operating out of Bridgetown Harbour. Passengers can rope-swing, swim, snorkel, and suntan on the top deck. Even mock weddings are staged. A buffet lunch with rum punch is presented Tuesday, Thursday, and Saturday from 10 a.m. to 2 p.m. Lunch cruises cost $61.50 per person. You can also sail on a catamaran lunch cruise, a four-hour cruise offered daily from 10 a.m. to 3 p.m., costing $65 per person. Children 12 and under sail for half price. Catamaran cruises are also available on *Limbo Lady* (☎ 246-420-5418), *Tiami* (☎ 246-430-0900), and *Tropical Dreamer* (☎ 246-427-7245). *Secret Love* (☎ 246-432-1972), a 41-foot Morgan sailboat, offers daily lunchtime or evening snorkel cruises.

Part cruise ship, part nightclub, the **M/V *Harbour Master*** (☎ 246-430-0900) is a 100-foot, four-story vessel with theme decks, a modern gallery, and three bars. It boasts a dance floor and a sit-down restaurant, and also offers formal buffets on its Calypso Deck. On the Harbour Master Deck, there's a bank of TVs for sports buffs. The showpiece of the vessel is an onboard semi-submersible, which is lowered hydraulically to 6 feet beneath the ship. This is, in effect, a "boat in a boat," with 30 seats. Lunch and dinner cruises cost $61.50 per person; the semi-submersible experience costs another $10.

Exercising On-Land Options

If your sea legs need a break from all that fun in and on the water, check out some of the options you'll find on dry land.

Hitting the links

Open to all is the Tom Fazio 18-hole championship golf course of the **Sandy Lane Hotel** (St. James; ☎ 246-444-2000; E-mail: mail@sandy lane.com), on the west coast. Greens fees are $135 in winter and $100 in summer for 18 holes, or $90 in winter and $60 in summer for its famed "Old Nine" holes, which winds through the estate grounds. Carts and caddies are available. In 2002, its new Green Monkey championship course, carved from a former quarry, was slated to open. The **Royal Westmoreland Golf and Country Club** (Westmoreland, St. James; ☎ 246-422-4653), has become the island's premier golf course. Designed by Robert Trent Jones, Jr., this $30 million, 27-hole course is spread across 500 acres overlooking the Gold Coast. It is part of a private residential community and can be played only by guests of the Royal Pavilion, Glitter Bay, Colony Club, Tamarind Cove, Coral Reef, Crystal Cove, Cobblers Cove, Sandpiper Inn, and Sandy Lane. It costs $115 for 9 holes, or $200 for 18 holes, including a cart.

Barbados Golf Club (Durants, Christ Church; ☎ 246-434-2121; Fax: 256-418-3131; E-mail: bgc@caribsurf.com; Internet: www.barbadosgolf club.com) on the south coast opened as Barbados's first public championship golf course in 2000. The 6,905-yard, par-72 course, designed by Ron Kirby, hosted the PGA Seniors Tournament in 2002. Greens fees for 18 holes are $119 in the high season ($79 low season) plus $13 for a cart and $20 for Callaway club rentals. A three-day unlimited golf pass during high season is $270 ($189 low season).

Taking a hike

The **Barbados National Trust** (☎ 246-426-2421) offers Sunday morning hikes throughout the year, often attracting more than 300 participants. Led by young Bajans and members of the National Trust, the hikes cover a different area of the island each week, giving you an opportunity to learn about the natural beauty of Barbados. The guides give brief talks on subjects such as geography, history, geology, and agriculture. The hikes, free and open to participants of all ages, are divided into fast, medium, and slow categories, with groups of no more than ten. All hikes leave promptly at 6 a.m., are about 5 miles long, and take about three hours to complete. There are also hikes at 3:30 and 5:30 p.m., the latter conducted only on moonlit nights. For the more fit, the Trust sponsors a three-hour trek through the Arbib Nature and Heritage Trail.

The **Arbib Nature and Heritage Trail**, which won *Islands* magazine's 1999 Ecotourism Award, takes you through Speightstown, once a major sugar port and even today a fishing town with old houses and a bustling waterfront; the mysterious gully known as "the Whim"; and the sur-rounding districts. The first marked trail is a 4.7-mile trek which begins outside St. Peter's Church in Speightstown, traverses the Whim, crosses one of the last working plantations in Barbados (Warleight), and leads to the historic 18th-century Dover Fort, following along white-sand beaches at Heywoods before ending up back in town. You must book a spot for the guided walk by 3 p.m. through the Barbados National Trust the day before you want to go. Hikes take place on Wednesday, Thursday, and Saturday starting at 9:00 a.m. and 2:30 p.m. The fee for adults is $15 and for children is $7.50.

Riding horses

A different view of Barbados is offered by the **Caribbean International Riding Centre**, St. Andrew, Sarely Hill (☎ 246-422-7433). With nearly 40 horses, Mrs. Roachford and her daughters offer a variety of trail rides for all levels of experience, ranging from a 1½-hour jaunt for $60 to a 2½-hour trek for $90. You'll ride through some of the most panoramic parts of Barbados, including the hilly terrain of the Scotland district. Along the way, you can see wild ducks and water lilies, with the rhythm of the Atlantic as background music.

Playing tennis and squash

Most of the larger hotels have tennis courts that can be reserved even if you're not a guest. In Barbados, most tennis players still wear traditional whites. **Folkestone Park**, Holetown (☎ 246-422-2314), is a public tennis court available for free on a first-come first-serve basis. The **National Tennis Centre**, Sir Garfield Sobers Sports Complex, Wildey Street, St. Michael (☎ 246-437-6010), charges $12 per hour; you must reserve in advance. Courts at the **Barbados Squash Club,** Marine House, Christ Church (☎ 246-427-7913), can be reserved for $12.50 for 45 minutes.

Watching from the sidelines

Barbados's spectator sports include several thoroughly British options.

Cricket

Not Jiminy Cricket — just plain cricket, which is the national sport and is played from May to late December. For information, call the Barbados Cricket Association (☎ 246-436-1397).

Horseracing

Horse races take place year-round (except April) every other Saturday, at the **Garrison Savannah** (☎ 246-426-3980; E-mail: barturf@sun beach.net; Internet: http://barbadosturfclub.com) in Christ Church. The track opens at 1:30 p.m. on race days, and admission is $5.

Polo

If you've never experienced a polo match, here's a great opportunity. Polo matches here are much more casual than at other places, so spectators are more than welcome — for a $2.50 fee. Matches are played at the **Barbados Polo Club** in Holders Hill, St. James (☎ 246-432-1802) on Wednesdays and Saturdays from October through April.

Touring historic sites

To encourage you to tour the island's many historic sites, the Barbados National Trust has designed the **Heritage Passport,** a free pass to some of Barbados's most popular attractions and historic sites, including Gun Hill Signal Station. When the holder pays full admission to visit some attractions, the passport will be stamped to validate free admission to other sights. Passports are free and can be picked up at displays in supermarkets, shops, hotels, and restaurants.

Every Wednesday afternoon from mid-January through mid-April, the Trust offers a bus tour of historic Great Houses and private homes open for public viewing, including Tyrol Cot Heritage Village (St. Michael); St. Nicholas Abbey (St. Peter); Francia Plantation, Drax Hall, and Brighton Great House (St. George); Villa Nova (St. John); and Sam Lord's Castle and Sunbury Plantation House (St. Philip). The cost is $18 per person, which includes transportation to and from your hotel. (If you want to visit the homes on your own, they're open on those Wednesday afternoons from 2:30 to 5:30 p.m.; entrance fees at each range from $1.25 to $5.)

History-rich Barbados has much to offer to those interested in the past. Thanks to the British influence, it also boasts some of the Caribbean's finest gardens. Here are our favorite picks to get a flavor for both aspects of Barbados:

- **Barbados Wildlife Reserve** (Farley Hill, St. Peter; ☎ 246-422-8826): Across the road from Farley Hill National Park, in northern St. Peter Parish, the reserve is set in a mahogany forest that's maintained by the Barbados Primate Research Center. Visitors can stroll through what is primarily a monkey sanctuary and an arboretum. Aside from the uncaged monkeys — watch your sunglasses, because these little thieves love to swipe them — you'll see wild hares, deer, otters, and wallabies (which were brought into Barbados). The best time to see the monkeys is in the afternoons after 3 p.m. The admission also allows you to visit Grenade Hall Forest, too. Walk through a rain forest with displays that explain why rain forests are important and what Barbados once looked like before its land was so heavily cultivated. The Grenade Hall Forest has a good snack bar with nice, shady tables for lunch. Admission is $12.50 adults, $6 for children age 12 and under. The reserve is open daily from 10 a.m. to 5 p.m.

- **Farley Hill National Park** (Farley Hill, St. Peter; no phone): Farley Hill surrounds what used to be one of the greatest houses of Barbados, Farley Hill, a mansion in ruins with a view of Barbados's Scotland District. The park lies in the north of the parish of St. Peter, directly across the road leading into the Barbados Wildlife Reserve. You can bring in a picnic and wander in the park, overlooking the turbulent waters of the Atlantic. You can enter the park for free if you're walking, but it costs $3.45 to bring a car in. The park is open daily from 8:30 a.m. to 6:00 p.m.

- **Andromeda Gardens** (Bathsheba, St. Joseph; ☎ 246-433-9384): We spent an entire afternoon here, admiring the fascinating collection of unusual and beautiful plant specimens from around the world assembled by the late Iris Bannochie and willed to the Barbados National Trust. Limestone boulders make for a natural 8-acre rock-garden setting for this impressive 6-acre garden, nestled among streams, ponds, and rocky outcroppings overlooking the sea above the Bathsheba coastline. It's one of our favorite gardens in all the Caribbean, and we don't tire of visiting it each time we return to Barbados. Thousands of orchids, hundreds of hibiscus and heliconia, and many varieties of ferns, begonias, palms, and other species grow here in splendid profusion. You'll occasionally see frogs, herons, lizards, hummingbirds, and sometimes a mongoose or a monkey. Spend at least an hour here — you'll likely have the gardens virtually all to yourself — and you may want to eat a picnic lunch from the Hibiscus Café. The well-stocked gift shop on site also offers some of the island's best prices. Admission is $6 for adults, $3 for children. The gardens are open daily from 9 a.m. to 5 p.m.

✔ **Harrison's Cave** (Welchman Hall, St. Thomas; ☎ 246-438-6640): The underground world here, the number-one tourist attraction of Barbados, is viewed from aboard an electric tram and trailer. On the tour, you'll see bubbling streams, tumbling cascades, and subtly lit deep pools, while all around stalactites hang overhead like icicles, and stalagmites rise from the floor. Visitors may disembark and get a closer look at this natural phenomenon at the Rotunda Room and the Cascade Pool. Although it's interesting, it may not impress Americans who have been to the far more spectacular Carlsbad Caverns. Tour reservations are recommended. Admission is $13 for adults, $6 children. The cave is open daily from 9 a.m. to 4 p.m. It's closed Good Friday, Easter Sunday, and Christmas Day.

Sizing up the shopping scene

Shopping in Barbados has improved a lot in the last few years. Bridgetown's Broad Street is the capital's primary shopping area, littered with signs advertising duty-free goods. We aren't big shoppers, but the upscale offerings here reminded us of Bermuda.

To get duty-free prices, you'll need to show your passport and airline ticket, so bring them with you on any shopping adventure.

Our idea of a fun shopping excursion was sampling Barbados's famed liquid gold — rum — after a fun tour of the **Mount Gay Rum Factory** (☎ 246-425-8757). The factory is a quick drive outside of Bridgetown, and we picked up a smattering of the island's history there. Island music was blaring over the loudspeaker while a gleeful bartender enjoyed pouring samples from Barbados's oldest distillery.

Typical Bajan crafts are pottery, woven floor mats and placemats, handprinted fabrics, dolls, needlecraft, shellwork, wood carvings, baskets and straw items, and artwork. **Best of Barbados** (☎ 246-421-6900) which has shops all over the island, gives you a good overall view of the handcrafts and art of the island. If you're short on time, find the nearest branch. The prices will be slightly higher than if you went directly to the artist, but not if you factor in the taxi fare or rental-car fee to do so.

Did Someone Say "Party"?

Just a quarter of a century after Barbados was settled in 1627, Bridgetown already had more than 100 bars. That tradition continues today. We've never seen a Caribbean island with so many watering holes — Barbados averages 12 per square mile. The nightclubs open around 9:30 p.m., but the action doesn't really heat up until at least 11:00 p.m. and may go on until 3:00 a.m. For most nightlife venues, women wear dresses or skirts, although nice pants are fine. Men can be found in khaki pants, collared shirts, and dress shoes.

Always exercise caution, especially if you're out late after the wallop of a few Planter's Punches has settled in. Take a cab back to your resort if you've had much to drink — the roads on Barbados are narrow and dark.

St. Lawrence Gap, called simply The Gap and situated on the south coast in the Worthing Area, has long had a reputation as the place for late-night limin'. Its "hip strip," which has been a construction zone of late, boasts a mind-boggling 40 bars, pubs, clubs, and restaurants. **Café Sol** (St. Lawrence Gap, Christ Church; ☎ **246-435-9531**) has a wrap-around terrace with a great view of the St. Lawrence Gap strip. One of the best-known nightspots is the **Ship Inn** (St. Lawrence Gap, Christ Church; ☎ **246-435-6961**), a friendly pub with live local bands every night for dancing.

On the south coast, the hot spot is **The Boatyard** (Bay Street on Carlisle Bay, five minutes from Bridgetown; ☎ **246-436-2622**). It has a pub atmosphere with both a DJ and live band music. From happy hours (twice daily: 3 to 6 p.m. and 10 to 11 p.m.) until the wee hours, The Boatyard is packed with mingling locals and visitors.

The Rusty Pelican (the Careenage, Bridgetown, St. Michael; ☎ **246-436-7778**) overlooks the bustling waterfront of the Careenage and features an easy-listening guitarist.

On the west coast, **Baku Beach** (Holetown, St. James; ☎ **246-432-BAKU;** cover charge $5 or $10, depending on the night) and its sister nightclub the **Casbah,** a Moroccan theme with Euro flair, are currently hot spots, though the action doesn't heat up until after 11 p.m. The trendy crowd at Baku, open nightly from 6:30 p.m., consists of locals and tourists alike. Some of the hottest bands on the island perform at its cocktail bar. The Casbah, open nightly from 10 p.m. to 3 a.m., resembles a New York City lounge with a DJ spinning tunes all night. Vintage Wine Bar, also at the Baku complex, serves light tapas, and a choice of champagnes, wines, and cigars.

Part V
The British Virgin Islands

The 5th Wave   By Rich Tennant

FEW MOMENTS IN SAILING COMPARE IN MAJESTY TO THE SHRINERS SUNSET REGATTA.

@RICHTENNANT

In this part . . .

Sailors love these peaceful, sparsely populated islands; if you're looking for a true getaway, you'll love them, too. We describe the best of the islands' accommodations and explain how to reach them by air and by sea.

Although seafood is the specialty on the BVIs, we offer recommendations for the best spots to experience a wide variety of cuisine. Finally, we give you the lowdown on the best ways to spend your time on the BVIs, including how to plan some island-hopping trips.

Chapter 16

The Lowdown on the British Virgin Islands' Hotel Scene

By Darwin Porter and Danforth Prince

. . . .

In This Chapter

▶ Sizing up hotel locations

▶ Focusing on top hotel picks

. . . .

*T*he British Virgin Islands, still in peaceful slumber, are what the United States Virgin Islands were some three decades ago before over-development. Only the Grenadines (owned by St. Vincent) are as favored by the yachting crowd. Sailing in the BVIs has been a tradition ever since the Arawak Indians first arrived back when Europe was getting through the Dark Ages.

You don't have to be a sailor, like former visitor Sir Francis Drake, to enjoy these idyllic islands. They seemed designed for R&R if you plan only to go to the beach.

In an overcrowded world, like the harbor at Charlotte Amalie on St. Thomas, the BVIs are sparsely populated. You may even have the beach all to yourself — especially if you find some hidden cove.

There are at least 40 islands (some people tally up a larger count, but they're including mere islets or rocks projecting up from the sea). Of these, no more than a dozen or so are inhabited. Some remain waiting for discovery. One, in particular, Norman Island, is so remote that it was said to have inspired Robert Louis Stevenson's novel, *Treasure Island*. For mega-resorts and around-the-clock entertainment, the USVIs should be your choice. But for the tranquil, laidback lifestyle, make it the BVIs. It's estimated that nearly half of the so-called rooms occupied in these islands are actually found on boats lying peacefully at anchor at night.

Figuring Out Where You Want to Stay

Except for some scattered accommodations on the remote islands such as **Anegada,** the choice narrows between **Tortola,** the island's capital, and **Virgin Gorda.** We tilt toward Virgin Gorda because it's even slower paced than Tortola, and it's also more beautiful. We're also drawn to Virgin Gorda's more secluded beaches — almost two dozen in all — and we like hiking its mountain peak. Don't write off Tortola, though. It has more activities than Virgin Gorda and some equally good inns and powdery beaches.

Many of the finest places to stay in either Tortola or Virgin Gorda are not on the beach. If that's a requirement of your vacation, you'll find such properties in the USVIs and most definitely in Aruba and Puerto Rico.

Instead of a beach location, you often get a panoramic view instead. The BVIs are mountainous islands, having been the tops of volcanoes in unrecorded times. From nearly every island inn or hotel, you can be on a good, white-sand beach within a ten-minute commute.

The greatest number of hotels, from barebones to first class, is found on Tortola. If you're shopping for villas to rent or seeking the lowest priced rooms available, you'll also do better on Tortola, as there are more low-rent choices here. Virgin Gorda is more exclusive, which translates into more money, of course.

For that ultimate escape, evocative of that old sitcom *Gilligan's Island,* we nominate Jost Van Dyke. This rugged 4-square-mile island is the West Indies as it used to be.

Because most inns are small, as are most island hotels, they fill up fast during the winter months, beginning around Christmas and lasting until mid-April. The Christmas holidays and February are the hardest times to get reservations.

From mid-April through mid-December, plenty of rooms are available and prices are slashed, usually around 20% but in some properties as much as 60%.

If you book into a resort on the MAP (breakfast and dinner) plan, you can save money. Renting a taxi every night to go to independently run restaurants on Tortola and Virgin Gorda is a lot of fun, but you can run up a big bill in a short time. The drawback to taking MAP is that you're confined to one hotel every night unless you can book on a "dine around plan."

Housing two to ten guests, private villas can be booked through **Virgin Gorda Villa Rentals Ltd.** (P.O. Box 63, The Valley, Virgin Gorda;

☎ **800-848-7081** or 284-495-7421; Fax: 284-495-7367; E-mail: `lbrecep tion@surfbvi.com`; Internet: `www.VirginGordaBVI.com`). Maid service, cooks, and staff are arranged. Efficiencies start at $850 a week in the winter.

The BVIs' Best Accommodations

The rack rates listed are in U.S. dollars and are for a standard double room during high season (mid-December through mid-April), unless otherwise noted. Lower rates are available in spring, summer, and fall. See Chapter 2 for more information on travel seasons.

Frenchman's Cay Resort Hotel

$$$$ **Tortola**

Ideal for honeymooners, this is a collection of first-class one– and two-bedroom condos opening onto the scenic Drake's Channel on a 12-acre site. On the windward tip of Frenchman's Cay, this nine-villa casual resort is a sleek retreat. Life revolves around an octagonal, peak-roofed structure, open to the breezes, that conceals everything from the restaurant to the library to the entertainment area, with a pool and tennis court nearby. Each with a shady terrace, accommodations come with full kitchens; all are imbued with a tropical motif with bamboo furnishings and one or two bathrooms. There is the aura of a barefoot elegance here. The downside? The adjoining beach is small, but the snorkeling is ideal.

P.O. Box 1054, West End, Tortola. ☎ *800-235-4077 or 284-495-4844. Fax: 284-495-4056. Internet:* `www.frenchmans.com`. *Rack rates: $260 villa, $390 two-bedroom villa for four. AE, DISC, MC, V.*

Guavaberry Spring Bay Vacation Homes

$$$ **Virgin Gorda**

This is a special property in a tropical setting of flowers and trees. From here, you can walk right over to **The Baths,** the top sightseeing attraction of Virgin Gorda with its giant boulders and tranquil pools (ideal for a swim). You're also near the golden sands of Spring Bay. Guests occupy one of 18 redwood-built hexagonal houses, with louvered windows open to catch the tradewinds. Each accommodation is a home away from home, with one or two bedrooms, a living room with a combined kitchen and dining area, a private bathroom with shower, a kitchenette, daily maid service, and an open sun deck with views of Sir Francis Drake Channel. For emergency supplies, there's an on-site commissary.

Spring Bay, Virgin Gorda (P.O. Box 20). ☎ *284-495-5227. Fax: 284-495-5283. Internet:* `www.guavaberryspringbay.com`. *Rack rates: $185–$265 one– or two-bedroom home. No credit cards.*

Leverick Bay Resort
$$ **Virgin Gorda**

Less well known than Guavaberry (see the preceding listing) and not as dramatically situated, this complex of 18 spacious hillside villas lies at the southern edge of Virgin Gorda's North Sound. There are two small beaches here, but it's only a ten-minute ride to the far superior beach at Savannah Bay. The units are breeze-swept and comfortable with their waterfront balconies or patios. Each comes with such essentials as a refrigerator and safe. Furnishings are far more luxurious, but they're designed for comfort and easy living. You can cool off in a small pool. On-site is a little spa offering the usual — massage, both manicures and pedicures, and body treatments.

The Valley, Virgin Gorda (P.O. Box 63). ☎ *800-848-7081 or 284-495-7421. Fax: 284-495-7367. Internet:* www.leverickbay.com. *Rack rates: $149 double. AE, MC, V.*

Little Dix Bay
$$$$$ **Virgin Gorda**

Those who want a posh retreat, the original creation of Laurance Rockefeller himself in 1964, head for this winning choice, far superior to all the first-class hotels on Tortola. The 98-unit resort opens onto a half-moon-shaped private bay with a white-sand beach, set against a backdrop of a 500-acre preserve. Surprisingly, only 80% of the accommodations are air-conditioned; the rest are equipped with ceiling fans. Units are spacious and breezy, decorated with Caribbean style, and some of the rooms — our favorites — are in two-story rondavels like tiki huts on stilts, very South Pacific. If you like a lot of facilities, such as fitness centers, tennis courts, snorkeling, and Sunfish sailing, this resort is for you. You even get a daily *New York Times* fax. The children's program here is the best in the BVIs.

P.O. Box 70, Virgin Gorda. ☎ *888-ROSEWOOD or 284-495-5555. Fax: 284-495-5661. Internet:* www.littledixbay.com. *Rack rates: $450–$875 double. Discounts for children. AE, MC, V.*

Nail Bay Resort
$$ **Virgin Gorda**

Nestled beneath Gorda Peak National Park, this 25-room resort lies on the site of a 19th-century sugar plantation. The enclave is comprised of luxurious rooms, apartments, and two– to five-bedroom villas, all with sweeping views of the water. You'll feel at home with its array of amenities such as CD/cassette/radios, TV/VCRs, fridges, microwaves, toaster ovens, and coffeemakers; a few feature espresso machines. Facilities include pools replete with a waterfall and swim-up bar (a rarity in the laid-back BVIs), a tennis court, and bocce and croquet lawns. Three crescent beaches are within easy walking distance of the 147-acre estate. If you don't want to cook, a chef can come to your villa and prepare meals.

Accommodations in the British Virgin Islands

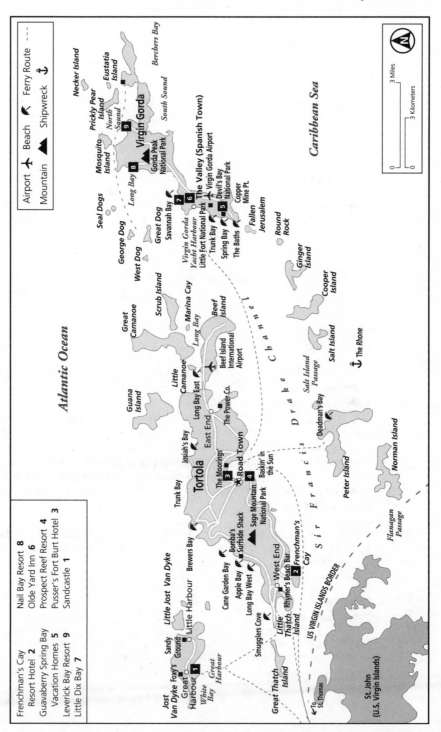

Frenchman's Cay Resort Hotel **2**
Guavaberry Spring Bay Vacation Homes **5**
Leverick Bay Resort **9**
Little Dix Bay **7**
Nail Bay Resort **8**
Olde Yard Inn **6**
Prospect Reef Resort **4**
Pusser's Fort Burt Hotel **3**
Sandcastle **1**

Airport ✈ Beach ↖ Ferry Route ---
Mountain ▲ Shipwreck ⚓

P.O. Box 69, Virgin Gorda. ☎ *800-871-3551 or 284-494-8000. Fax: 284-495-5875. Internet:* www.nailbay.com. *Rack rates: $125–$145 double. Packages available. AE, DISC, MC, V.*

Olde Yard Inn
$$–$$$ Virgin Gorda

This 15-room charmer is our top choice for a B&B in the BVIs. This tranquil retreat is the kind of place you seek in the Caribbean but rarely find. Its drawback is that Savannah Bay with its good white-sand beach is a difficult 20-minute walk away. A free hotel shuttle takes you there. A mile from the airport, the inn is set in tropical gardens with a beautiful pool, an open-air health club, and a Jacuzzi. You can live in the main house or, more privately, in two bungalows with more spacious bedrooms. Some of the rooms are air-conditioned, the others cooled by trade winds and ceiling fans. Excellent meals are served alfresco, often to the sound of music. The library, open to guests, contains the largest private collection of books in the BVIs.

P.O. Box 26, Virgin Gorda. ☎ *800-653-9273 or 284-495-5544. Fax: 284-495-5986. Internet:* www.oldeyardinn.com. *Rack rates: $195 double. AE, MC, V.*

Ole Works Inn
$ Tortola

On Tortola, the premises of a three-century-old sugar mill, this 18-room inn is a good alternative to Tortola's pricey resorts. Across the road from a wide, well-maintained, white-sand beach, it is not for the demanding but is a worthy choice. In a setting of foliage and flowers, the bedrooms are in a lackluster modern structure of wood, glass, and stone, and units range from hillside accommodations with air-conditioning and refrigerators to simple, older yet comfortable doubles. A honeymoon suite nestles in an old tower. The hotel's owner, Quito Rhymer, is a famous island recording star, and it's always party time at the on-site bar, a hush settling only when Quito performs.

P.O. Box 560, Cane Garden Bay, Tortola. ☎ *284-495-4837. Fax: 284-495-9618. Internet:* www.bviguide.com/ole.html. *Rack rates: $95–$200 double. MC, V. Closed Sept.*

Prospect Reef Resort
$$$ Tortola

Spread across 44 acres rising above a private yacht harbor, this is the largest resort in the BVIs, with 137 rooms. Less than a mile south of Road Town, the low-rise hotel makes up for its lack of a beach with a lot of facilities, including three restaurants, three bars, three pools, six tennis courts, and a fitness center and spa (the best on the island). A hotel van transports you to the beach. Water sports such as snorkeling and sailing round out the agenda, as do children's programs (yes, there's babysitting). Families enjoy the large units with kitchenettes and the separate bedrooms or sleeping lofts. There's a wide range of options for living here from the regular guest rooms to villas.

Drake's Highway (P.O. Box 104), Road Town, Tortola. ☎ *800-356-8937 or 284-494-3311. Fax: 284-494-5595. Internet:* www.prospectreef.com. *Rack rates: $150–$310. AE, MC, V.*

Pusser's Fort Burt Hotel
$$ Tortola

Pusser's, famous for its rum, operates this 12-room unit on the site of a fort constructed by the Dutch in the 17th century. Near Prospect Reef, it offers no beach but does have a freshwater pool with a panoramic view of the harbor. It's only a three-minute stroll to two of the island's best beaches: Garden Bay Beach and Smuggler's Cove. Bedrooms are set at a higher elevation than any others around Road Town. The regular doubles have recently been renovated and are spacious. The on-site Fort Burt Restaurant and Pub is popular with both visitors and Road Towners.

P.O. Box 3380, Fort Burt, Road Town, Tortola. ☎ *284-494-2587. Fax: 284-494-2002. Rack rates: $99–$165 double. AE, MC, V.*

Sandcastle
$$$ Jost Van Dyke

Those with fantasies of being Robinson Crusoe retreat here. Six cottages, set in tropical gardens with views of the sea, are built to open onto a white-sand beach. This colony of octagonal cottages is the ultimate retreat for escapists. Only two units are air-conditioned, but all are furnished in a simple but comfortable Caribbean motif, each with a large, tiled bathroom. This is only for self-sufficient types who bring their own amusement with them, although there is complimentary windsurfing and snorkeling. On-site is one of our favorite hangouts, **The Soggy Dollar Bar** (see Chapter 18).

White Bay, Jost Van Dyke. ☎ *284-495-9888. Fax: 284-495-9999. Internet:* www.sandcastle-bvi.com. *Rack rates: $200–$250 double. AE, MC, V.*

Chapter 17

Settling into the British Virgin Islands

By Darwin Porter and Danforth Prince

- -

In This Chapter

▶ Knowing what to expect when you arrive

▶ Getting around the islands

▶ Discovering the British Virgin Islands from A to Z

- -

San Juan, a half hour flight to Tortola, is the main gateway into the British Virgin Islands. There are more flights to San Juan from the U.S. mainland than anywhere else in the Caribbean. New York and Miami have the most frequent flights into Puerto Rico. Another gateway is Charlotte Amalie, the capital of the U.S. Virgin Islands. You can fly to St. Thomas, then make another connection into Tortola. There are no direct flights to Tortola from the U.S. mainland.

Arriving in the BVIs by Plane

Although recently expanded, **Beef Island Airport** (☎ 284-494-3701) on Tortola is relatively modest. There is often congestion when several flights are scheduled to take off within 20 to 30 minutes of each other. If you've checked into a major hotel, you'll often find a welcome desk right at the airport to make your transition easy. If you've booked more modest digs, you'll see a fleet of taxis waiting to take you either to your hotel in Tortola or to one of the ferry departure points if you're going on to another island such as Virgin Gorda. The little Queen Elizabeth Bridge connects Beef Island with "mainland" Tortola.

By a quick phone call, e-mail, or fax, you can alert your hotel of your arrival time. All reception desks know the easiest transportation link, especially important if you're staying on one of the islands other than Tortola. Transfer costs, most often by ferry service, may be included in your hotel bill, with you signing a voucher or two en route to your final destination.

To enter Tortola, you must pass through Customs and passport control (☎ 284-495-2235). No large jets land here, but the line at Customs can take a long time because officials are thorough, often insisting that arriving passengers open up all their luggage for a detailed search.

Arriving in the BVIs by Ferry

Even though a plane is quicker and more efficient, many passengers prefer the sea route from St. Thomas or St. John in the USVIs. A sail from island to island becomes part of the Caribbean experience. From Charlotte Amalie (on St. Thomas) or Cruz Bay (on St. John), public ferries ply these sometimes choppy waters to Road Town and the West End on Tortola.

Unless sailing conditions are bad, ferries depart daily at 6:15 a.m. Depending on the season, departures are scattered throughout the day until the last ferries leave at 5:30 p.m. A one-way fare is $25 per person or $45 round trip. Everything depends on the weather, so schedules are subject to change. You often have to check boat departures upon your arrival at St. Thomas.

Here are the major ferry operators, in the BVIs:

- ✔ **Native Son, Inc.** (☎ 284-495-4617) connects St. Thomas (Red Hook) and St. John to Road Town and West End, Tortola, daily.

- ✔ **Smith's Ferry Services** (☎ 284-494-4454 or 284-495-4495) operates daily to connect St. Thomas (Red Hook) and St. John to Road Town and West End, Tortola. It also connects Tortola to Virgin Gorda.

- ✔ **Inter-Island Boat Services** (☎ 284-495-4166) connects St. John (Cruz Bay) and West End, Tortola, daily.

From either St. Thomas or St. John, ferries traverse the Sir Francis Drake Channel, named after the fabled English seafarer the Spanish still call a "pirate." Waters can be choppy or downright rough, especially in winter, and the ferries are relatively stable. Even so, sea sickness is commonplace, and many prudent passengers take Dramamine to ward off this malady.

While based in the BVIs, many visitors become day-trippers to the USVIs. Don't go just in your bikini; take photo ID. You are, in effect, crossing through international waters. If you've left your identification in your hotel room in the BVIs, you may not be able to get back into the country.

BVI patrol boats from the Port Authority monitor local waters and may demand to see your passport when traveling between the two sets of

Virgins. The three main entry ports into the BVIs where Customs and immigration booths are set up are at the ferry docks on Tortola, Virgin Gorda, and Jost Van Dyke.

Getting from the Airport to Your Final Destination

Getting around the BVI archipelago is part of the fun of making a trip here. Ferryboats or *puddle-jumpers* (small prop planes) are the way to go for both locals and visitors. Except for some remote islands you aren't likely to visit anyway, the major stopovers in the chain lie in close proximity to each other. Many visitors, for example, often like to go to a different island every day during their stay to sample the beaches on a nearby neighbor — for example, sailing from Tortola to Jost Van Dyke in the morning with a return in the late afternoon.

By car

The taxi lobby is powerful enough in Tortola to have pickup of rental cars banned at the Beef Island Airport. After you clear customs, a fleet of taxis or open-air shuttles await you to take you anywhere on the island. Taxis are often shared, the cabbie crowding in as many passengers and as much luggage as he can. After you're at your hotel, you can make arrangements for picking up a rented car if you want one.

By taxi

Don't let the name of the company scare you away. **Deadman's Taxi Service** (☎ **284-495-2216** at the office, 284-496-7979 on the cellular, or 284-496-6555) is your best deal for hooking up with the island's best and most knowing driver, James Pickering. You get not only where you want to go but learn a lot about the legend and lore of Tortola from this cabbie. Your hotel desk can also call you a taxi.

Taxis from the Beef Island airport travel to Road Town, the capital of Tortola, in about 20 minutes. The entire taxi costs $18, and, as mentioned, is often shared, which cuts down the tariff per person, of course. The taxi driver will often make you wait until he corrals more customers to share the ride.

By ferry

Many arriving passengers at the Beef Island Airport are actually going to a hotel on neighboring Virgin Gorda. Open-air shuttle buses await incoming flights and will transport you over to the North Sound Express (☎ **284-495-2138**; Fax: 284-495-1639). You could walk this route if you didn't have luggage. A small, high-speed ferry will drop you either at Bitter End or Biras Creek's dock. Along the way, you get a panoramic look at some of the islands. You'll see why Virgin Gorda is often compared to a large pregnant woman lying prone on her back.

You need a reservation to take the **North Sound Express Ferry,** which departs daily at 6:15 a.m., 10:30 a.m., 3:30 p.m., 5:30 p.m., and 7:15 p.m.; it costs $22 each way and takes about 45 minutes. If you arrive after 7:15 p.m., you can still get to Virgin Gorda, but you have to arrange in advance and fork over a $30 surcharge per person.

If you're going to Virgin Gorda's Spanish Town or a resort nearby, take a taxi to Road Town's ferry dock and board **Smith's Ferry Services** (☎ 284-495-4495) or **Speedy's** (☎ 284-495-5240) for the half-hour ride, which costs $15 to $23 each way.

By plane

If you're going to one of the remote islands, such as Jost Van Dyke or Anegada, you can board a small puddle-jumper or sea plane for a quick flight. But you should make such arrangements with the hotel of your choice before your arrival in the BVIs.

If you don't mind a small aircraft and want to skip the ferryboat, you can arrange a booking on one of these local carriers:

- ✔ **Clair Aero Services** (☎ 284-495-2271) offers scheduled flights from Tortola to Anegada on Monday, Wedneday, Friday, and Sunday.

- ✔ **Cape Air** (☎ 800-352-0714 or 284-495-2100; Internet: www.fly capeair.com) features hourly service from Tortola to San Juan and St. Thomas.

- ✔ **Air Sunshire** (☎ 800-327-8900 or 284-495-8900) takes you from Tortola to the miniscule Virgin Gorda Airport, which closes at dusk. The trip's so brief it's virtually a takeoff-and-land flight.

When you're on Virgin Gorda, **Mahogany Taxi Service** (☎ 284-495-5469) or **Potter's Taxi** (☎ 284-495-5329 or 284-495-5960) meet you at the airport for the ten-minute, $22 roller-coaster ride to the North Sound, where your hotel's launch will pick you up and ferry you across a small bay.

Getting Around the BVIs

You'll quickly get the hang of island-hopping in the BVIs. It's a way of life for the locals, many of whom work on one island but commute by ferryboat to their home on another island in the late afternoon.

By ferry

The former pirates' haven of the BVIs is not only the Caribbean's favored sailing grounds for yachties, but it's also the most practical means of getting around. Because public ferries are the main transportation link for the islanders themselves, they're the cheapest and easiest way to get from island to island or even to St. Thomas or St. John. See "Arriving in the BVIs by Ferry" earlier in this chapter, for a list of the major ferryboat operators.

Arrive at the ferry dock at least 15 minutes before departure time to get the best seat. Unless the weather is bad, ferries leave on time. Some of the larger resorts, such as Little Dix Bay, have their own ferry boats, a point that can be clarified when you're making arrangements with your hotel for your arrival in the BVIs.

If you miss the boat and there isn't another one for a long time, or even until the next day, you still can get to where you're going by renting a private water taxi at a fare to be negotiated. You can be certain that it will be at least ten times the rate of the public ferry.

On foot

Until the muggers learn about the BVIs, it's still one of the safest places to walk either day or night in the Caribbean. That advice, incidentally, doesn't go for the streets of Charlotte Amalie on St. Thomas where muggings are commonplace.

Hiking is rather tame fare here — nothing like Jamaica's Blue Mountains. It's a rather tame undertaking except for the national parks such as the Sage Mountain National Park on Tortola or Gorda Peak National Park on Virgin Gorda. For recommendations of the best hikes, refer to Chapter 19.

By taxi

The local government dictates taxi rates so you won't have to negotiate them as you will have to do in most islands of the Caribbean. The good news is that the cabbies in the BVIs are the most honest we've ever encountered in the islands. Taxis meet incoming planes at the Beef Island Airport and at all the ferry docks at Road Town and West End. Cabbies also operate like tour guides and can take you to all the major beauty spots on Tortola in about three hours for a cost of $50. Your hotel will book you a taxi, which will come to your front door, or else you can call directly, either **Turtle Dove Taxi Service** (☎ **284-494-6274**) or **B.V.I. Taxi Association** (☎ **284-495-1982** or 284-294-2322).

Cheaper than a taxi are the so-called open air *safari buses,* which are ideal for a group of people sharing a ride. It's the least expensive way to get around Tortola or Virgin Gorda for a look at either island. For details, call the **B.V.I. Taxi Association** (☎ **284-495-1982** or 284-494-2322).

By car

The roads — that is, when they have roads — are a disaster; driving is on the left; and there's not much to see on an actual driving tour. Usually, you can get by on a visit by using taxis when needed. Those who plan to spend part of their vacation hopping from island to island won't have much need for an auto anyway. You'll probably be on the beach most of the time or else out on the waters in a boat. Our advice is to save your money on a car rental during your BVI trip.

If you feel you must always have wheels wherever you go, and you rent a car, you'll rarely encounter a traffic jam except in Road Town when people are going to work or getting off from work, or when cruise ship arrivals generate more traffic two or three times a week. If you're staying in a remote villa or hotel on Tortola, you may feel a car is best. Check first with your hotel to see if a rental car can be included in a package deal. Some hotels will also rent you a car (though perhaps not in state-of-the-art condition).

You'll need your own driver's license from back home, and you'll also have to pay $10 for a temporary BVI permit. Most car rentals cost around $55 per day. Make reservations before arriving on the island, especially from Christmas through February when rental cars are in short supply. Sticking with international firms is safer than dealing with some underfinanced and often unreliable local companies. On Tortola the choices are:

- ✔ **Avis** (☎ **800-331-1212** or 284-494-3322)
- ✔ **Itgo** (☎ **800-527-0700** or 284-494-2639)
- ✔ **Hertz** (☎ **800-527-0700** or 284-495-4405)
- ✔ **National** (☎ **800-227-7368** or 284-494-3197)

As a holdover from British colonialism, you drive on the left. But, as in the States, most vehicles have the steering wheel on the left. It can be disconcerting unless you're used to it — another reason not to rent a car.

By motorcycle or bicycle

Tortola's terrain is mountainous or at least hilly — no problem if you're an Olympic athlete but a bit difficult for most folks. Mountain bikes and helmets for $20 a day are rented at **Boardsailing B.V.I.** (☎ **284-495-2447**) at Nanny Cay and Trellis Bay, and **Last Stop Sports** (☎ **284-494-0564**; Internet: www.laststopsports.com) in Road Town on Tortola. Last Stop also arranges bike/hike excursions.

Motor scooters at $40 a day are available at **Shane's Scooters** (☎ 284-494-0976) in Road Town.

Fast Facts: The BVIs

ATMs

Only Tortola and Virgin Gorda have ATMs. On Tortola, try Banco Popular (☎ 284-494-2117) on Main Street next to the customs office in Road Town, or the Bank of Nova Scotia at Wickhams Cay (☎ 284-494-2526), also at Road Town.

Baby-sitters

Most hotels will make arrangements for baby-sitters at $10 an hour and up.

Banks

You get the best exchange rates at banks. (see ATMs). Hours vary but in general are Mondays through Thursday 8:00 a.m. to 4:30 p.m. and Friday until 5:30 p.m.

Currency

The U.S. dollar is the official currency of the BVIs, much to the surprise of many a Brit who view the archipelago as a "colony." You'll have no problem spending Yankee greenbacks.

Doctors

Check with your resort for a referral; serious emergencies may require an airlift to St. Thomas or San Juan. The nearest decompression tank is in St. Thomas.

Emergencies

For fire, police, and ambulance, dial **999** or **911.**

Festivals

April's Spring Regatta is a sailor's dream; the two-week BVI Emancipation Festival starts at the end of July and goes until August; in December the best local fungi bands compete at the Scratch/Fungi Band Fiesta on Tortola.

Hospitals

Peebles Hospital (☎ 284-494-3497), Porter Road in Road Town, Tortola, is the only hospital in the BVIs.

Hurricanes

The season swirls from June through November. September is the dreaded month in which a storm is most likely to hit.

Information

The British Virgin Islands Tourist Board office is above the FedEx office on the AKARA Building's second floor in Wickham's Cay in Road Town (☎ 800-835-8530 from the U.S., or 284-494-3134). You can also e-mail bvitourb@caribsurf.com with specific questions about the BVIs. The official Web site is www.bviwelcome.com. On the island, pick up the latest copy of *The British Virgin Islands Welcome Tourist Guide,* published bimonthly. For a good read on the beach, you can devour *Treasure Island* by Robert Lewis Stevenson, supposedly based on the BVIs' Norman Island.

Language

It may not be the Queen's English, but it is English, often spoken in a patois.

Maps

The colorful pocket-sized map published by the tourist board is everywhere — and it's free: at the airport, by the ferry docks, at your hotel, and in gift shops.

Newspapers/Magazines

The more deluxe resorts offer *The New York Times* by fax. Otherwise, you'll be hard pressed to find either the *Times* or *USA Today.* Most hotels — if they have televisions — offer CNN.

Pharmacies

J.R. O'Neal Drugstore is at 80 Main St., in Road Town, Tortola (☎ 284-494-2292). Closed Sunday.

Police

Dial **999** or **911** for emergencies.

Post Office

Where else? Main Street in Road Town, Tortola (☎ 284-468-3701 or 284-494-3701, ext. 4996). Hours are Monday through Friday 8:30 a.m. to 4:00 p.m. and Saturday 9 a.m. to noon. Fun fact: There are no zip codes in the BVIs.

Safety

Take normal precautions in town, but crime is rare on these islands. You can walk about freely, but don't leave valuables wrapped in your towel on the beach or dangle your camera behind you while you look at the shops along the waterfront. There are still a few hotels that don't even have locks on their doors.

Taxes

Room tax is 7%; departure tax is $10 by air and $5 by sea (not included in the price of your ticket).

Taxis

Call the B.V.I. Taxi Association (☎ 284-494-2875, 284-494-2322, or 284-495-2378).

Telephone

To reach the BVIs directly, dial 1, then 284, then the seven-digit local number. You can make a credit card call from the BVIs by dialing 111 from any phone and following the recorded instructions on completing your call. For North America, dial 1, plus the area code, plus the number; dial 011, plus the country code, plus the number for Europe.

At your resort, dial your hotel operator and get exact instructions on how to dial direct using your calling card. Instructions vary all over the place, so ask.

Time Zone

The BVIs are on Atlantic standard time year-round, which means that they are an hour ahead of eastern standard time during fall and winter when the U.S. goes on daylight saving time.

Tipping

Restaurant service calls for 10 to 15%, if not already included in your tab; $1 per bag for bellhops, and $1 a day for maid service. No tip is required for taxi drivers unless they help you in some special way.

Weather and Surf Reports

The Web site www.caribwx.com offers updated reports three times a day. The British Virgin Islands receive little annual rainfall. The temperature ranges from 75 to 85 degrees, and a steady trade wind helps you keep cool.

Chapter 18

Dining in the British Virgin Islands

By Darwin Porter and Danforth Prince

● ●

In This Chapter

▶ Sampling the local cuisine

▶ Locating the islands' best restaurants

● ●

The British Virgin Islanders have lived from the sea for centuries. Fresh fish is still the focus of most menus, including grouper as good as that in the Bahamas. The lobster caught off the island of Anegada is justly fabled among foodies, and is imbued with a sweet flavor, more so than the coveted lobsters from Maine.

Except in a few restaurants in Tortola and on Virgin Gorda, cookery is rather straightforward, because there is no real native cuisine. In general, there are far grander restaurants in St. Croix and St. Thomas than anywhere in the BVIs.

Most visitors dine at their hotel, especially at night, when traveling around the islands on badly lit roads is difficult. For the most part, at least for our recommendations, the food is competently prepared. Because the BVIs don't grow much of their foodstuff, and nearly everything in the larder has to be imported, prices tend to be high.

Dress has become casual but not totally laid-back. That is, men are asked to wear shirts with collars, but no one requires a jacket. A man's tie is a memory of yesterday. Women appear in fashionable resort wear at the finer places. Out at the funky little beach shacks, show up dressed as you would to clean up the backyard on a hot summer day.

Relishing a taste of the islands

Unlike the old days, more and more places take credit cards. But in some of the smaller joints, bring along some dollars. Many local cooks set up little dives offering amusing dining, calling their places "Naughty Thelma's," or whatever (and they may not take plastic). They make for a sense of adventure when dining out if you can escape from your hotel dining room for the night.

Making your own discoveries, finding those little treasures like **Mrs. Scatliffe's** famous baked chicken in coconut served with her own garden vegetables, is fun. You can locate this treasure on the second-floor terrace of Mrs. Scatliffe's home, a yellow-and-white building across from Carrot Bay in Road Town (☎ **284-495-4556**; lunch Monday through Friday; dinner nightly 7 to 9 p.m.; reservations essential; prix-fixe menu $25 to $30). A lively fungi band performs some evenings. Another delight is the **Sandcastle** (☎ **284-495-9888**) on Jost Van Dyke, a candlelit beachside restaurant where four-course menus like duck l'orange and stuffed grouper are regularly served. (See our complete review of Sandcastle later in this chapter.)

Of course, fresh seafood seasoned with local herbs is invariably part of the menu on these islands. You'll also find spicy West Indian cooking, with curries of every description, at small, locally owned places.

The Best Restaurants

In this archipelago, you can't always dine where you want at night unless you're willing to take a boat or a puddle-jumper, and few want to do that just for dinner. Most guests opt for at least the MAP (breakfast and dinner) plan at their hotel (see Chapter 16 for more details on that). Some of the restaurants recommended in this section are ones you'll want to visit only for lunch as you're hopping about the islands. The first-class resorts employ either the most talented of local chefs or else cooks trained in America or Europe (mostly Britain).

If you're on a boat, you can still make reservations at many of the restaurants in the BVIs by contacting them via radio on VHF (very high frequency) Channel 16. Ask the captain to call ahead for you.

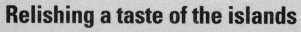

Bath and Turtle Pub
$ Virgin Gorda   Pub Grub/International

The most frequented pub in Virgin Gorda, this local favorite lies at the end of the waterfront shopping plaza in Spanish Town. You can come here to drink, to listen to the live music on Wednesday and Sunday nights, or to select an indoor or courtyard table to fill up on the grub of the day. Portions are large and affordable. The spiciest chicken wings on

Dining in the British Virgin Islands

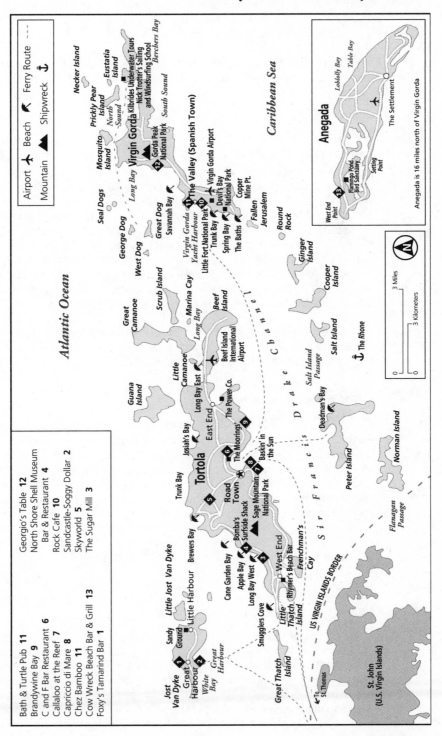

Bath & Turtle Pub **11**
Brandywine Bay **9**
C and F Bar Restaurant **6**
Callaloo at the Reef **7**
Capriccio di Mare **8**
Chez Bamboo **11**
Cow Wreck Beach Bar & Grill **13**
Foxy's Tamarind Bar **1**

Georgio's Table **12**
North Shore Shell Museum
Bar & Restaurant **4**
Rock Cafe **10**
Sandcastle-Soggy Dollar **2**
Skyworld **5**
The Sugar Mill **3**

Airport ✈   Beach ⚓   Ferry Route - - -
Mountain ▲   Shipwreck ⚓

Atlantic Ocean

Caribbean Sea

Anegada

Anegada is 16 miles north of Virgin Gorda

D r a k e   C h a n n e l

S i r   F r a n c i s

US VIRGIN ISLANDS BORDER

Tortola

Virgin Gorda

The Valley (Spanish Town)

↓ The Rhone

3 Miles
3 Kilometers

the island are made here and flavored with ginger and tamarind. The chili is spicy, as is the barbecue chicken. Steak, lobster (prepared as you wish), and daily seafood temptations round out the menu. The bartender's mango coladas are addictive.

Virgin Gorda Yacht Harbour, Spanish Town. ☎ *284-495-5239. Reservations recommended. Main courses: $10–$20. AE, MC, V. Open: Daily 7:30 a.m.–11:00 p.m.*

Brandywine Bay
$$$$ Tortola Tuscan

With tables opening to a panoramic view of Sir Francis Drake Channel, this is your best bet for romantic dining. The location is a ten-minute ride by car or taxi east of Road Town. You arrive at an elegant hillside house where the chef and owner, David Pugliese, welcomes you like a private guest in his house. This is not a discovery — gourmet magazines such as *Bon Appétit* have already discovered it. As a former fashion photographer, Pugliese believes in presentation, and he sets an elegant table. Begin, perhaps, with his homemade mozzarella served with fresh basil and tomatoes, going on to grilled grouper graced with fresh herbs or a succulent homemade pasta. Beautifully sauced duck is a regular feature. One of the island's finest wine *cartes* is presented to you.

Just outside of Road Town on Sir Francis Drake Highway, Brandywine Bay. ☎ *284-495-2301. Reservations recommended. Main courses: $20–$33. AE, MC, V. Open: Mon–Sat from 6:30 p.m. Closed Aug–Oct.*

C and F Bar Restaurant
$$ Tortola West Indian

Near The Moorings (see Chapter 19 for details on this yachtie haven), this is one of Tortola's most laid-back eateries. Chef Clarence enjoys a local following. Here is an excellent place to order that sweet Anegada lobster that everyone talks about lovingly. Locally caught fish is prepared as you like it. Try Clarence's spicy curried conch or his zesty barbecue chicken, finishing off with a piece of his real homemade key lime pie.

Purcell Estate. ☎ *284-494-4941. Reservations not necessary. Main courses: $12–$22.50. AE, MC, V. Open: Nightly 6:30–11:00 p.m.*

Callaloo at the Reef
$$$$ Tortola Modern Caribbean

At the Prospect Reef Resort, sailors and visitors mingle at night to be cooled off by trade winds through large open windows at this second-floor dining room that opens onto a marina with a panoramic view of Sir Francis Drake Channel. You can select from an à la carte menu or else enjoy the prix-fixe dinner, which is changed nightly. Lead off, perhaps, with the seafood and pumpkin bisque, or scallops sautéed in honey and spices and topped with a ginger wine zabaglione. Oven-baked snapper is given real island flavor and is served with a passion fruit–butter sauce. Side dishes include very typical West Indian fare such as green gungo peas and rice breadfruit gratin, or mashed yams and potatoes in a medley.

Waterfront Drive, Road Town. ☎ *284-494-3311. Reservations recommended. Main courses: $22–$28. Four-course, prix-fixe menu $37.50. AE, DISC, MC, V. Open: Daily 7 a.m.–10 p.m.*

Capriccio di Mare
$–$$ Tortola   Italian

Brandywine Bay Restaurant (see the listing earlier in this chapter) is more upmarket, but its developers, in what they called "a flight of fancy," opened this laid-back, informal *caffé,* which almost overnight became a favorite with both islanders and visitors. There is no more authentic Italian *caffé* in the Virgin Islands. You can stop in to refresh yourself from early morning through supper time. So, from the cappuccino consumed in the morning until you down the last succulent pasta or zesty pizza at night, this is a good address with which to be familiar. For lunches, the sandwiches are well stuffed, and the salads are made of fresh greens. You can also stop in here and get the fixings for a picnic on your favorite beach.

Waterfront Drive, Road Town. ☎ *284-494-5369. Reservations not necessary. Main courses: $8–$14. No credit cards. Open: Mon–Sat 8 a.m.–9 p.m. Closed Sun.*

Chez Bamboo
$$$ Virgin Gorda   Cajun/Creole

This is as close as Virgin Gorda comes to evoking a New Orleans supper club. Make a night of it. It lies a five-minute walk north of the Virgin Island Yacht Club. Here you can enjoy food prepared with zesty flair, full of flavor as evoked by the conch gumbo. Nassau grouper comes *en papillotte* (baked in foil), and there is also New Orleans strip steak in a creamy Worcestershire sauce. The crème brûlée is the island's best. Friday night on the terrace, you can listen to live blues or jazz music.

Near the Virgin Gorda Yacht Club, Spanish Town. ☎ *284-495-5752. Reservations recommended. Main courses: $19.50–$28. AE, MC, V. Open: Tues–Sun 5–10 p.m.*

Cow Wreck Beach Bar and Grill
$$$ Anegada   West Indian

Flat as a johnny cake, the remote island of Anegada is fabled for its lobsters. Here they're kept in a cage underwater, waiting their turn to do service in the pot. Informal and funky, this family-owned eatery is laid-back and a lot of fun. A straw roof shelters you from the elements, and rough wood tables are placed on a terrace with an ocean view. At lunch you can snorkel before eating, or at night enjoy a "sundowner" or two. Those who drop in for lunch often order sandwiches. But if you're here in the evening, go for that lobster. There's none better in the West Indies.

Lower Cow Wreck Beach, Anegada. ☎ *284-495-8047. Main courses: $18–$25. Reservations necessary for dinner. Open: Lunch daily 10:30 a.m.–3:00 p.m.; dinner seatings daily 6–7 p.m. (Open daily unless there are no reservations, in which case the restaurant closes, so be sure to make a reservation.)*

Foxy's Tamarind Bar
$$$ Jost Van Dyke   West Indian

"Foxy," or Philicianno Callwood, is a legend among yachties in the Virgin Islands. It's always party time here, especially on New Year's Eve when it's the hottest and most happening place in the BVIs. Known for more than three decades for his little bar and restaurant, Foxy will feed you well. Drop in at lunchtime and he'll tempt you with *rotis* (flat African-styled bread stuffed with curried fillings). He also grills a mean burger. If you're dining, reserve a table by 5 p.m. Grilled meats and freshly caught seafood such as lobster are prepared with zest and flair. Foxy also has a way with barbecue. Bands play from Thursday to Saturday nights when the joint jumps.

Great Harbour. ☎ *284-495-9258. Main courses: $18–$25. AE, MC, V. Reservations required for dinner. Open: Lunch daily noon to 2:30 p.m.; dinner daily 6:30–9:00 p.m. — but you must reserve by 5 p.m. The bar is open from 9:30 a.m. "until everybody goes home."*

Giorgio's Table
$$$$ Virgin Gorda   Italian

A 15-minute drive north of Spanish Town, Giorgio's is the only authentic Italian restaurant on Virgin Gorda. The interior evokes a yacht, but most guests ask for a table on a large covered terrace, where the stars will get in your eyes. Giorgio is proud that he cooks Italian as opposed to Italian-American. He seeks flavor in all his dishes from the succulent pastas to the freshly caught fish. He gets the pick of the catch the fishermen bring in. You can also stop in for lunch, filling up on pizzas and sandwiches.

Mahoe Bay. ☎ *284-495-5684. Reservations recommended. Main courses: $25–$35. AE, DISC, MC, V. Open: Lunch daily noon to 2:30 p.m.; dinner daily 6:30–9:00 p.m.*

North Shore Shell Museum Bar and Restaurant
$$$ Tortola   West Indian

Mrs. Scatliffe (see "Relishing a taste of the islands" earlier in this chapter) is the most celebrated local chef in the BVIs. Her daughter, Mona, took her recipes with her when she married Egberth Donovan and opened this West Indian tavern where they serve a savory Caribbean cuisine. We like to drop in early for breakfast, sampling the island's best pancakes, which are made with such ingredients as guava, mango, and coconut. For dinner we also arrive early for one of those soursop daiquiris (there are none better). From the authentic island menu, you can enjoy such main dishes as grilled lobster, barbecued chicken, and spicy conch fritters, along with some zesty chicken and tender ribs. Her mama taught Mona well. After dinner an impromptu fungi band entertains in this concrete-block building with its modest museum of shells.

Carrot Bay, North Shore, Tortola. ☎ 284-495-4714. Reservations recommended at dinner. Main courses: $17–$22. AE, MC, V. Open: Daily 8:00 a.m.–9:30 p.m.

Rock Cafe

$$$ Virgin Gorda   Italian/Caribbean

Unlike the name suggests, this is not some island clone of the ubiquitous Hard Rock Cafe. It's even better in our view than that overrated international chain. You can stop for a drink in the bar before going to the rear where a different world unfolds. The setting is amidst boulders like the ones at The Baths, the number-one sightseeing attraction on Virgin Gorda. The recessed lighting and boardwalks add to the theatrical allure at night. Fortunately, the chefs don't depend just on the setting. The menu is wisely balanced, the dishes well prepared and consumed with affordable wine from a respectable list whose vintages range from Italy to California. Freshly caught red snapper comes in a tangy marinade, and we're especially fond of the chicken piccata.

The Valley. ☎ 284-495-5482. Reservations strongly recommended. Main courses: $16–$28. AE, MC, V. Open: Nightly 4 p.m. to midnight. Special Tequila bar upstairs.

Sandcastle–Soggy Dollar

$$$$$ Jost Van Dyke   West Indian

Corporate escapees Debby Pearse and Bruce Donnath came to run this small resort in 1996. Until then, the only access to the bar-restaurant was via a small dinghy, and invariably guests took a dunk up to their waists, thus the name. By day, flying fish sandwiches, rotis, and jumbo burgers keep guests sated at the unassuming open-air spot. On Sunday afternoons calypso and reggae tunes draw charter yachts to the small beach. By night at the beachfront dining room, you're treated to linen-and-silver-set tables by candlelight and a four-course affair accompanied by home-made bread. The menu is changed daily but may include such dishes as mahimahi Martinique (marinated in citrus juice and cooked with fresh dill, onions, and fennel). The sesame-coated snapper is also excellent, as are the fresh pastas.

White Bay, Jost Van Dyke at Sandcastle Resort. ☎ 284-495-9888. Reservations for dinner must be made by 4 p.m. for 7 p.m. seating. Prix-fixe dinner $32. MC, V. Open: Daily for a bar lunch 11 a.m.–4 p.m. and for dinner at 7 p.m. (one seating).

Skyworld
$$$$ **Tortola** **International**

The equal of Brandywine, maybe even better on some nights, Skyworld is aptly named, because it commands the grandest view of any restaurant on the island, at a windswept 1,337 feet. You can even see the U.S. Virgins from here if the weather is clear. You can dine in a more formal section or in a casual, laid-back atmosphere in a garden. The menu is the same in both places, and over the years we've found this restaurant the most reliable choice for dining on the island. We always go for the fresh catch of the day, preferably grilled. We like to begin with a savory fresh fish chowder or such delightful appetizers as mushrooms stuffed with conch meat. For dessert, the chef makes the best key lime pie on the island.

Ridge Road, Road Town. ☎ 284-494-3567. Reservations required for dinner. Main courses: $24.75–$36. Open: Daily 11 a.m.–3 p.m. and 5:30–8:30 p.m.

The Sugar Mill
$$$$ **Tortola** **Caribbean/Californian**

Have you ever wished those food critics would just put down their laptops, pick up their sauté pans, and launch their own restaurant if it's all so easy? Former *Bon Appétit* columnists Jeff and Jinx Morgan did just that when they bought The Sugar Mill, a 350-year-old former plantation in Apple Bay, which they subsequently transformed into Tortola's most atmospheric restaurant. Candles cast a golden glow on the thick walls of ballast stone and coral of what was a former rum distillery, and fine examples of Haitian art decorate the walls.

The handful of menu offerings rotates nightly and includes wine pairings recommended by Jeff. The West Indian influence is evident, but the experimental duo doesn't stop there. Standouts are the Cajun oyster étouffée (stew), grilled mahimahi in banana leaves with a peppery Creole sauce, and Jamaican jerk pork roast with pineapple chipolte sauce. The liberally used vegetables and herbs come from the hotel's garden. The mango and pineapple mousse or banana crepes are a sweet and scrumptious delight to end the meal.

Apple Bay. ☎ 284-495-4355. Reservations required. Main courses: $22–$28. AE, MC, V. Open: Dinner nightly 7:00–8:30 p.m; lunch daily at the Islands Beach Bar noon to 2 p.m.

Chapter 19

Having Fun on and off the Beach in the British Virgin Islands

By Darwin Porter and Danforth Prince

. . . .

In This Chapter

▶ Soaking up the sun on the BVIs' top beaches

▶ Diving into fun with water sports

▶ Satisfying the landlubber: activities and nightlife

. . . .

You'd have to go to the South Pacific to find sailing waters to equal those of the British Virgin Islands. Places for swimming and snorkeling are found around every bend on every island and in every small bay or hidden cove.

If you don't sail, you can always delight in the beaches, many of which you can have all to yourself, because most of them are uncrowded. Visitors, some of whom return year after year, come here mainly for sun, sea, and nature. There is little to see in man-made attractions, just what nature left.

Without any casinos, hotel chains, grand restaurants, and shopping malls, this chain of islands attracts those seeking a tranquil retreat from the world. They are strictly for R&R — there is less to do here than on any island chain in the Caribbean. But it is for that very reason that most visitors seek them out, because they are in complete contrast to the bustling and more commercialized islands of the USVIs.

 Because the postal system in the BVIs is notoriously slow, we've not included addresses here. Link up with an outfitter through an e-mail or a phone call. Or else you may go for a vacation and return home before you receive a reply.

Hitting the Beaches

Sometimes on a remote beach in the BVIs you won't have the golden sands all to yourself. You may have to share the beach with a family of iguanas out for some late morning sun. Some of the best beaches are on deserted islands appealing to the Robinson Crusoe in you. These are reached only by boat trips, which can be arranged with locals in both Tortola and Virgin Gorda.

Even on the remotest beach, signs of encroaching civilization crop up unexpectedly. Our party of eight had booked an island all to ourselves. One day as we were sunning ourselves, a boatload of some 100 gay male tourists arrived and took over the beach, running nude up and down its long stretches. Getting into the spirit of it, our party ordered kegs of beer brought over for the men and invited them to our own hastily arranged "Octoberfest." Chances are that won't happen to you. You'll probably wander for miles without encountering another beachcomber.

Though practiced, nudity on the beaches is not officially endorsed. Some people do go nude, but it's against the law. If you want to show off your assets, you'd be more comfortable going to Negril, Jamaica, or one of the French islands such as Martinique. Most British Virgin Islanders are deeply religious, and are offended by public nudity.

All beaches are public in these islands, and that includes such exclusive enclaves as the 850-acre island, **Guana Island Club,** or the 74-acre hideaway **Necker Island.** We don't recommend going to either one of them unless someone like Bill Gates and his family invited you. You're allowed to use the beaches, but they don't really want you there — in fact, a security guard may ask you to move on.

If you want to sample the high life, the nearest beach to Tortola that will give you a preview of it is **Deadman's Bay** on the exclusive **Peter Island.** In spite of its name, this 1,800-acre island is one of the most beautiful and romantic palm-fringed beaches in the BVIs, as well as the setting for the most expensive resort in the BVIs, **Peter Island Resort** (☎ **800-346-4451** or 284-495-2000). The beach of the resort is easily reached by boat from Tortola.

On Tortola

West of Road Town, **Cane Garden Bay Beach** is the island's finest strip of fine white sands with sheltering palm trees, a Caribbean movie cliché. This is also the best beach for facilities — you'll find kiosks renting kayaks, sailboards, and Hobie Cats. Windsurfing is also possible. It is a favorite anchorage for the yachting crowd and is the site of food shacks, bars, and shops. If a cruise ship is in port, avoid this beach, because passengers invariably are taken here.

On cruise-ship days, you may want to head to remote **Elizabeth Beach,** with its wide, palm-fringed sands. This beach, only recently accessible by road, lies off Ridge Road. Also reached along Ridge Road is the never-crowded **Josiah Bay Beach** in the east end.

A small, sandy beach at the west end, **Smuggler's Cove,** opposite the offshore island of Great Thatch, is one of our favorites. A "half moon" of white sand, it lies at the end of the bumpy Belmont Road and is a popular spot for snorkelers because of its great visibility and its under-water parade of rainbow-hued fish and brain and elkhorn corals.

Another good beach, **Brewers Bay Beach,** lies east of Cane Garden Bay along the hilly Brewers Bay Road and is the site of a campground. Both snorkelers and windsurfers come to this beach of white sands. It's a popular spot in the late afternoon when beach buffs gather for their "sundowners" at one of the two beach bar shacks found here.

For the most fun beach party in all the Virgins, both U.S. and British, head for **Bomba's Surfside Shack** (☎ **284-495-4148**). Its construction of flotsam and jetsam *du jour* looks like a train wreck. Both visitors and locals in equal numbers flock to this rollicking haven of reggae music and the most lethal rum punches on the island. Revelers dance bare-foot in the sands all night. Its "Full Moon" parties are legendary, and local fungi bands entertain on Wednesday and Sunday nights. The free house tea is spiked with hallucinogenic mushrooms, and the barbecue isn't bad either.

On Virgin Gorda

First, the good news. Called the "Stonehenge of the BVI," **The Baths** are the most fabled spot in all the Virgin Islands for swimming and spectac-ular beauty. The boulders here are massive, in some cases like a mam-moth truck, and no one knows how they got here, although scientists speculate that volcanic explosions pushed them to the surface in dim, unrecorded times.

Tranquil pools and grottoes are flooded with sea water, and the snor-keling can be excellent. What's the downside? Because The Baths are so magnificent, they're on everybody's itinerary, including the cruise-ship charters from St. Thomas and St. John, which start rolling in by 10 a.m. You'll have to hang out until 4 p.m. before the crowds thin out.

We like to come here for a swim shortly after the sun comes up when we can enjoy the mysticism and surreal beauty of this place before the hordes invade.

Even if you arrive during overcrowded periods, you can look around, then retreat to **Spring Bay Beach,** a nearby strip of white sands and turquoise clear water. This beach, which you can walk to from The Baths, is rarely crowded because it's not known. The snorkeling is also idyllic here. For even more privacy, you can take a difficult 15-minute trail to **Trunk Bay Beach,** another wide, sandy beach nearby.

Another good beach is **Mahoe Bay Beach** at the Mango Bay Resort (☎ 284-494-5672), a complex of villas set on landscaped grounds fronting the islets of the Sir Francis Drake Channel. The sands are good here, and the waters have great visibility for snorkelers. Swimming conditions are also ideal.

There are also good beaches on the northern end of Virgin Gorda at the very pricey **Bitter End Yacht Club** (☎ 284-494-2746), which is far too expensive for the average pocketbook. Windsurfers are especially fond of this spot, and it also offers the best water-sports rentals on the island, including Sunfish and Boston Whaler rentals. The offshore reefs feature some of Virgin Gorda's best snorkeling opportunities. Via a foot-path from Bitter End, you can explore **Bercher's Bay Beach,** which attracts the shellcomber, with its delicately hued shells found among the rocks here.

On Jost Van Dyke

Getting more discovered every year, this 4-square-mile island is named for a Dutch pirate. It didn't get electricity until the early '90s. Because it is one of the most favored spots in the BVIs by yachties, a series of ramshackle bars and food joints have been opened to cater to this burgeoning trade. Our favorite of these is the justifiably famous **Foxy's** (see Chapter 18), known for its New Year's Eve parties but a lively venue throughout the year.

The best beach, reached by a little road, is **White Bay Beach,** on the southern rim of the island, lying west of the only real settlement here, pompously called "Great Harbour." Lined with palm trees, the beach also has some real funky bars; in some of these a Rasta man may try to sell you *ganja* (marijuana).

A local boatman, for a fee to be negotiated, may take you over to the uninhabited **Sandy Cay,** a beach of perfect white sands and clear waters with some of the best snorkeling we've found in the BVIs.

On Anegada

Home of the Caribbean's sweetest lobsters, Anegada is the most remote and the most northerly of the British Virgins, lying at a point 30 miles east of Tortola. Most of the BVIs are hilly or even mountainous, but Anegada is so flat that ships or boats don't even see it on the horizon until they're almost upon it.

It's estimated that some 500 ships went down on Anegada's dangerous Horseshoe Reef. There are reports of vast sunken treasures to be found here. At its loftiest point, Anegada manages to rise 28 feet. The island itself is 3 miles wide and 11 miles long.

The best beaches lie at its northern and western tiers, and it's because of these white sands that most visitors come here in the first place. There's little else except the bird sanctuary of the **B.V.I. National Parks Trust** with its colorful flamingo colony.

The best beach of white sands facing beautiful living coral reefs is found at the amusingly named **Loblolly Bay,** with its funky little food joints and raffish bars. Snorkelers swim among the caverns offshore to see the rainbow-hued marine life. Sea turtles and the unwelcome barracuda can also be found here. We've never done a scientific experiment, but we've found that the sands here are whiter and more powdery than elsewhere in the BVIs.

The greatest delight is to order a freshly caught lobster cooked on the beach. We like to head over to **Big Bamboo** at Loblolly (☎ **284-495-2019**) for this succulent treat. The wafting aromas from the grill will entice you. If you've downed too much beer, a hammock is waiting.

 Another amusing place is the **Cow Wreck Bar and Grill** on Lower Cow Wreck Beach (see Chapter 18 for more details). "Cow Wreck?" you ask. A century or so ago a boat loaded with cow bones to be used in making buttons ran afoul on these notorious reefs and split apart, those bovine bones scattering into the sea. For years to come, cow bones washed ashore.

Water Fun for Everyone

There is no place in the Caribbean where you're likely to spend more time on the water than in the BVI archipelago. Whether swimming at the boulder-strewn Baths or island-hopping from Virgin Gorda to Tortola, or from Cooper Island to Guana, the island chain is your best chance to live that mermaid (or merman) fantasy.

Sailing away

The BVIs, especially Tortola and Virgin Gorda, are imbued with the best marinas and shore facilities of any other country in the West Indies. Tortola is the charter-boat center of the Caribbean. It's estimated that about 65% of all visitors come here for the sailing, with the added allure of swimming, diving, and snorkeling — a virtual water wonderland.

Instead of long overnight sea jaunts, you can sail with ease from island to island in a short time. With island outcroppings everywhere, there are rarely major waves (good news for those prone to sea sickness), and most of the waters are tranquil. You're in sight of some land mass virtually wherever you sail in the BVI chain.

The island nation caters to both the first-time sailor who will need a captain and a small crew, and the veteran sailor going bareboat and hauling his own anchor.

The premier charter-boat operator in the Caribbean is **The Moorings** (☎ **800-535-7289** or 888-724-5273; Fax: 727-530-9747; Internet: www. moorings.com), which has a flagship base on the protected side of Tortola in Road Town. It's home to 18 crewed yachts and 150 bareboats (including 32– to 50-foot sloops and catamarans). Bareboats run $2,700 to $9,555 a week; crewed yachts cost $9,744 to $19,320 for six people per week.

Other outfitters on Tortola that may put you out to sea include **Catamaran Charters** (Nanny Cay, just west of Road Town; ☎ **284-494-6661**), which charters catamarans with or without captains. **BVI Yacht Charters** (Inner Harbour Marina, Road Town; ☎ **284-494-4289**) offers 38– to 51-foot sailboats for charter.

Old salts and beginning sailors flock to the **Bitter End Yacht Club** (☎ **800-872-2392** or 284-494-2745; Fax: 284-494-4756), which operates in the tranquil waters of the North Sound. This is the most idyllic place to learn to windsurf or sail in the BVIs. At the yacht club, seek out **Nick Trotter's Sailing and Windsurfing School.** The staff here is the best on island; they're patient with neophytes. You can also charter boats here.

Windjammer's 208-foot, three-masted barkentine *Flying Cloud* specializes in 6- and 13-day sails through the island chain. Prices range from $1,000 to $2,975 (☎ **800-327-2601**; Fax: 305-674-1219; Internet: www.windjammer.com).

Paddling your own kayak

You can wave at the yachties as you go by piloting your own kayak at a fraction of the cost. A typical kayak itinerary starts at Peter Island, site of the BVIs' most exclusive resort, and goes to Norman Island, said to have been the inspiration for Stevenson's novel, *Treasure Island.* The jaunt by sea continues on to Tortola before reaching the more remote Jost Van Dyke, coming to an end at St. John, the most beautiful of the USVIs. Five-day trips, costing $995 per sailor, are booked with Arawak Expeditions (www.gorptravel.com) through **Gorp Travel Wilderness Experience, Inc.** (☎ **800-444-0099**).

Seeing the BVIs from under the water

The BVIs are number one for sailing but not for diving. If you want a strictly diver's holiday, head for Grand Cayman (see Chapter 23) or the Dutch island of Bonaire, adjacent to Aruba (see Chapter 11). But if you'd like to work some diving into your vacation, the BVIs are a potent underwater attraction, mainly because of its chief dive site, the wreckage of the **RMS _Rhone._** This 310-foot royal mail steamer sank in 1867 in waters near the western point of Salt Island. _Skin Diver_ magazine called it "the world's most fantastic shipwreck dive," teeming with a wide variety of marine life and stunning coral formations. A film based on Peter Benchley's _The Deep_ was shot at this site.

The second most intriguing dive site is the wreck of the **_Chikuzen,_** a 270-foot, steel-hulled refrigerator vessel that went down on Tortola's east end in 1981. It lies in 80 feet of water, home today to an array of tropical fish, including black-tip sharks and octopus. Off Ginger Island is another premier dive site, **Alice in Wonderland,** known for its coral wall that slopes from 40 feet to a sandy bottom of 100 feet. Monstrous overhangs and mammoth corals, plus an array of graceful sea animals from the garden eel to the long-nose butterfly fish, make it a diver's favorite.

In addition to the celebrated dive sites mentioned, the island chain also has more than two dozen other popular dive sites filled with coral formations and abundant marine life. The BVIs are especially known for their wreck diving, because before Doppler weather reports, hurricanes could sweep in without warning, sending ships to watery graves. Visibility underwater is among the clearest in the Caribbean.

Nearly all dive sites are within a 35-mile reach so you can have a varied underwater program without boating over long stretches of sea. Even the most distant dive sites lie within a 30-minute boat ride of either Tortola or Virgin Gorda.

Norman Island, the legendary setting for Stevenson's _Treasure Island,_ is eagerly sought out by divers for its series of four sea caves, one idyllic for snorkelers at Treasure Point. Bring the fixings for a picnic and make a day of it. The aptly named **Angelfish Reef** lives up to its promise. You can also see schools of eaglerays here.

The clear visibility underwater makes the BVIs a mecca for snorkelers as well. Snorkelers can even see some of the _Rhone,_ because its rudder lies in shallow water about 15 feet below the surface.

For snorkelers marine life is abundant, and the living reefs are in better shape than in the USVIs. You'll find thousands of brilliantly colored fish such as parrot fish, queen angelfish, damselfish, wrasses, and a variety of soft corals and incredible sponges in all shapes and sizes. A purple tube sponge that was nearly 5 feet long was discovered on Norman Island.

If waters get choppy, as they often do, snorkelers can easily move on to a neighboring cove or even sail to another island nearby. Waters, of course, are more tranquil in summer. All dive operators and all resorts have snorkeling gear, including **Bitter End Yacht Club** (North Sound, Virgin Gorda; ☎ **800-872-2392**), near prime snorkeling sites with gear to rent to nonguests.

Also on Virgin Gorda, you can learn your history lesson on the RMS *Rhone* wreck from **Kilbrides Underwater Tours** (Bitter End Yacht Club; ☎ 800-932-4286 or 284-495-9638; Internet: www.sunchaserscuba.com), which takes divers to 50 different sites and offers resort dive courses and PADI certification. Rates are $65 for a one-tank dive and $85 for a two-tank dive.

PADI five-star **Dive B.V.I. Ltd.** (☎ 800-848-7078 or 284-495-5513; Fax 284-495-5347; E-mail: info@divebvi.com) operates out of Leverick Bay, Virgin Gorda Yacht Harbour, Peter Island, and Marina Cay. Owner Joe Giacinto has been diving the BVIs for more than three decades, charging $85 for a two-tank dive.

Back on Tortola, the leading outfitter is **Baskin' in the Sun** (Prospect Reef, Tortola; ☎ 800-233-7938 or 284-494-2858; Fax: 284-494-4303; Internet: www.dive-baskin.com), which charges $65 for a one-tank dive, $95 for a two-tank dive, and $30 for a snorkel trip. Its programs emphasize reef ecology in both its beginning and advanced diving courses. Trips leave daily at 8:30 a.m.

Underwater Safaris at The Moorings, Tortola, and Cooper Island (☎ 284-494-3535 or 284-494-3965) offers resort and advanced diving courses and both day and night dives. Rates are $68 for a one-tank dive, $94 for two tanks, and $100 for a resort course.

Reeling in the big one

When fishermen talk about whoppers in the BVI, they don't mean burgers. The waters washing up on the BVI are some of the richest game-fishing channels in the world, especially the 50-mile so-called Puerto Rican Trench near Anegada. Record catches of tuna, marlin, sailfish, shark, bluefish, and wahoo have been recorded.

Blue Ocean Adventures (Road Town, Tortola; ☎ 284-494-2872), charges $650 for a half-day charter, or try the **Bitter End Yacht Club** (see contact information in the previous section). For a special treat, ask if your resort's chef will prepare your catch for you, too. Most will happily accommodate your request.

Bonefishing (fishing for small but feisty catches in the saltwater flats) is a popular sport. Be warned: These fish are skittish — one wrong move can send the school fleeing. Try your hand at snagging these elusive critters on Anegada. **Anegada Reef Hotel** at Setting Point (☎ 284-495-8002) can "hook" you up.

Exercising On-Land Options

If your sea legs need a break from all that fun in and on the water, check out some of the options you'll find on dry land.

Hiking in the hills

In spite of its tiny size, the BVIs offer more nature reserves and national parks than any other island nation in the Caribbean except Jamaica.

Our favorite trails are in the hilly remnants of a primeval rain forest in the 92-acre **Sage Mountain Park** on Tortola where the BVIs reach their loftiest citadel at 1,780 feet. A trio of trails lead up to the summit, as you make your way along lush growth such as the elephant-ear philodendron, prickly ferns, and hanging vines.

You'll see plenty of white cedar, the country's national tree, and such stunning plants as the red palicourea, with its tiny red flowers and black fruit.

Trails begin west of Road Town. Secure the makings of a picnic before setting off. As you enjoy your picnic, you can take in the same view enjoyed by Sir Francis Drake of Ginger Island, Peter Island, Jost Van Dyke, Sandy Cay, and Salt Island.

On Virgin Gorda, the 265-acre **Virgin Gorda Peak National Park** is riddled with well-marked trails. Here you can climb the "belly" of the woman that suggests the geographic shape of Virgin Gorda — that is, a pregnant woman lying flat on her back. The "navel" in the belly is reached at 1,370 feet. Laurance Rockefeller built the lookout point at the summit, which is a continuation of the paved road to Little Dix Bay.

On Virgin Gorda, you can also hike through the **Devil's Bay National Park** in the southwest corridor of the tiny island. This area embraces the much-touted Baths with their mammoth boulders. If it's not too crowded, you can explore these caverns, labyrinths, and passageways created by these huge rocks. As the waves surge and retreat, shimmering pools are created where you can enjoy a cool splash — hence, the name of The Baths. The granite stones, incidentally, are not native to the Caribbean. Perhaps the last glacial age deposited them here. The trails through this park begin south of The Baths.

Contact the **British Virgin Islands Tourist Board** for more information. The office is above the FedEx office on the AKARA Building's second floor in Wickham's Cay in Road Town (☎ **800-835-8530** or 284-494-3134; Internet: www.bviwelcome.com).

No-shopping zone

If you were born to shop, you need not leave the bazaars of Charlotte Amalie on St. Thomas. They're the best in the Caribbean. But if you like to purchase "little things," shopping is mildly amusing in the BVIs.

Most shops are centered along Main Street in Road Town on Tortola. The shopping here is not duty-free. If you make a purchase, it is the same as if you'd bought an item in London.

You can look for imports from the U.K. and can often find some bargains in such items as Wedgwood china. This is not a place to bargain, however.

What's for sale? Pusser's Rum, island spices and herbs, local handcrafts, certain botanical skin-care products, terra-cotta pottery, and plenty of T-shirts and sandals. Those Cuban cigars for sale have to be smoked before you return to the U.S., because they aren't allowed entry by U.S. Customs.

Living It Up After the Sun Goes Down

For glittering casinos and night life, go to San Juan. Night life in the BVIs often means lot of rum drinking, dinner, and early retirement to bed.

Many locals — and visitors, too — eagerly anticipate happy hour, when all bars offer two drinks for the price of one. Sometimes free snacks are included. In general, happy hours are from 4 to 7 p.m., but this can vary.

On Tortola, you can tank up on the BVIs' "Painkiller," made from the local Pusser's Rum at **Pusser's Road Town Pub** on Waterfront Drive in Tortola (☎ **284-494-3897**). Orange and pineapple juice and a dash of coconut crème are added to the libation. You can stick around for some English pub grub such as fish 'n chips or shepherd's pie.

The hottest spot on island is **Rhymer's Beach Bar**, in Tortola's west end (☎ **284-494-4639**). At this beach bar and restaurant, you meet the most convivial gang of locals and visitors of any age hanging out in the BVIs, enjoying the camaraderie, the tropical rum punches, and the native menu of conch chowder, tasty ribs, and the like. Steel-drum bands entertain in the evenings.

Funky little beach bars are found throughout the inhabited islands. Our favorites include the **Soggy Dollar** at White Bay on Jost Van Dyke (see Chapter 18). It has a clothesline strung out front where you can dry your paper money. Why? Because patrons frequently get caught by sea swells getting to this place and wind up waist deep in water. Sunday nights are devoted to calypso and reggae. Otherwise you'll find us at **Foxy's** (see Chapter 18), our favorite watering hole in all the BVIs. Come here for a limin' time (*limin'* means "hanging out" — and that is just what you do here, for hours on end).

Part VI
Grand Cayman

The 5th Wave
By Rich Tennant

"Your serve is basically good, it's just you're doing something funny right at the very end."

In this part . . .

If you have your eye on this peaceful, laid-back diving
mecca, we have some tips for spotting the best accommodations and saving a penny or two during your stay. We
show you how to navigate toward your destination and
how to find your way around the island after you arrive.

You have a wide variety of dining options on Grand
Cayman; we share the restaurants that top our list of
favorites. Finally, we let you know some of the best ways
to soak up fun and sun in, around, and under the water.

Chapter 20

The Lowdown on Grand Cayman's Hotel Scene

By Echo and Kevin Garrett

. . . .

In This Chapter

▶ Sizing up hotel locations

▶ Focusing on top hotel picks

. . . .

Grand Cayman is a curious place. Although tourism is huge here, and its famous Seven Mile Beach (like Aruba's hotel strip) features a lineup of every type of hotel and condo imaginable, the island still manages to exude a certain laid-back charm. Maybe that's because its residents by-and-large have the security of wealth — they're glad you're vacationing here, but nobody's desperate for your money. In fact, Grand Cayman's wealth isn't based just on tourism. It's built on banking, and with the prices you pay for the privilege of staying on this island (unless you get a great low-season package or dive package), islanders may need to build more banks to hold all the dough rolling in.

This peaceful, safe, and upscale island takes all the work out of your vacation if you just want to hang at the beach or swim with the fishes. That's why it's become a favorite with honeymooners, cruise ship passengers, and seniors — despite warnings from previous tourists to "take half as many clothes as you think you'll need and twice as much money."

Families with young children have discovered that huge summer discounts make the cost of a week on this clean, safe island about the same as a week at Disney World. So if your kids can entertain themselves in the water, and if you'll be happy with a sanitized version of the Caribbean, Grand Cayman is a good choice. If we were going to Grand Cayman with our two sons, we'd go during Pirate's Week in October (for more details, see Chapter 2).

Despite its British ways, Grand Cayman has veered toward being too Americanized for some tastes. In recent years, many fast-food chains, cutesy little boutiques in restored buildings in George Town (the capital), and homogenized timeshares have increased the Florida-come-to-the Caribbean look. You can find local color, thanks to some of the quirky artists who live on the island, but you have to look for it.

You'll find about as broad a range of accommodations here — from big chains to condos, villas, and modest guesthouses — as on the much larger islands of Puerto Rico, Jamaica, and St. Thomas. In fact, the Cayman Islands (islanders hate to hear them called "the Caymans") have more than 2,000 hotel rooms and an equal number of units in condos (timeshares), guesthouses, and dive lodges. You'll see tons of "For Sale" signs on the island, and you'll probably be pitched to buy a timeshare at least once if you're on the island for more than a day. A new wave of construction is going on, bringing even more timeshares and condos.

If you have the patience, you can take a look at one of these timeshares and get rewarded for listening to the spiel. For example, when we were at **Morritt's Grand Resort** (☎ **345-947-7449**; Internet: www.morritt.com), those who took a tour were getting a free lunch and drinks for two, a North Wall dive for two, and $40 cash.

What the Cayman Islands don't have is a predominance of mega all-inclusives. Although a few resorts offer this option, the European Plan (EP) and Modified American Plan (MAP) are more popular, as are the many dive packages. Traditionally, this trio of islands have lacked ultra-deluxe, five-star resorts, but with The Ritz-Carlton, Grand Cayman, a 366-room hotel coupled with a 71-room condominium residence being built to the tune of $350 million, the tide will finally turn. Until it opens — now scheduled for October 2003 — if you're looking for the lap of luxury, head to Barbados, Jamaica, St. Thomas, or Puerto Rico.

About a third of the 1 million visitors who come to Grand Cayman annually are here for the scuba diving, but Grand Cayman also gets loyalists (not to the Crown) who use their timeshares the same week year after year.

Gays and lesbians avoid this island, which has a reputation for homophobia (see Chapter 4).

Before you spring for a dive package up front, make sure you know what you're buying with your bucks. Some dive operators are more geared toward experienced divers, whereas others are better suited to beginners.

During the summer months, when Grand Cayman's resorts offer big price breaks, many families tour the island. We've heard grousing from teens who are bored because of the dearth of nighttime activities. For families with young children, though, the gentle waters are ideal; your little wannabe mermaids and mermen won't be disappointed. Both the Hyatt and the Westin have strong children's programs.

Figuring Out Where You Want to Stay

As with Aruba, almost all 50 of Grand Cayman's hotels and condos are crowded along the island's famous Seven Mile Beach. Even if you go to the island for diving, you may want to be close to this lovely beach. From here, you have broad dining options; you can walk to town from many resorts.

Hard-core divers like to stay on the East End, near Grand Cayman's best diving. If you want to skip the crowds and Cayman Cowboys (as the dive operators who pack people on their boats are derisively called), head to the much more secluded north side, which also offers good diving.

Divers who want more of an escape will do better on Cayman Brac or Little Cayman, which we describe at the end of this chapter. But if you think nightlife is limited on Grand Cayman, you'll be bored out of your wetsuit on those quiet islands.

Food is one of your bigger expenses when you vacation on Grand Cayman; restaurants here charge top dollar, compared with costs on other Caribbean islands. So that you don't have to eat out all the time, we recommend booking into a resort with a meal plan. But make sure that the resort has more than one good restaurant; otherwise, you'll be ready to mutiny by the time your stay is over.

If you don't mind making your own meals, you can save a bundle by renting one of this island's many condos or guesthouses with kitchens. You can easily spend as much on one dinner out on Grand Cayman as it would take to stock up enough groceries for a week. Two well-stocked grocery stores are **Hurley's Supermarket** (in Red Bay just beyond the intersection of Crewe Road and South Sound Road; ☎ 345-949-8488), which spans 30,000 square feet with a bakery, deli, and sandwich and salad bar, and **Fosters Food Fair** (The Strand on Seven Mile Beach and at the Airport; ☎ 345-945-4748 or 345-949-5155).

Remember that you can't bring in any fresh fruit or vegetables from outside the island. Also, request an advance list from management detailing what's already stocked in the kitchen, so you don't waste precious suitcase room on basics (such as spices). You'll need a rental car to haul groceries if you decide to prepare food on your own.

Grand Cayman's Best Accommodations

Because Grand Cayman doesn't have extensive nightlife, shopping, or even much sightseeing, you'll probably spend much of your time around the property at which you're staying. Therefore, the amenities and what your room, pool, and particular stretch of beach are like are very important.

Guesthouses may be some distance from the beach and short on style and facilities, but in addition to being a good bargain, they're a great choice for families with older children. (With babies and toddlers, we'd stick to the hotels with established children's programs.) Some guesthouses have outdoor grills and picnic tables.

Most guesthouse owners do not accept personal checks or credit cards but do take reservations through the **Cayman Islands Reservation Service** (6100 Blue Lagoon Dr., Suite 150, Miami, FL 33126; ☎ **800-327-8777**). This service can also describe and book most condominiums and villas on the islands. **Cayman Villas** (☎ **800-235-5888** or 345-947-4144; Fax: 345-949-7471) and **Hospitality World Ltd.** (☎ **800-232-1034** or 345-949-3458; Fax: 345-1949-7054) are local agencies that make reservations.

The rack rates listed in this section are in U.S. dollars and are for a standard double room during high season (mid-December through mid-April), unless otherwise noted. Lower rates are often available during the off season and shoulder season (see Chapter 2 for more information on travel seasons).

The Avalon
$$$$$ Seven Mile Beach

One of the best condo options on Seven Mile Beach, the Avalon has one of the plum spots on the famed strand. We like the oversized tub and separate shower in the spacious baths, as well as the tropical decor of the roomy units. It also has daily maid service except on Tuesdays. The handsome property consists of 27 three-bedroom/three-bathroom units (15 of which can be rented and book up fast; call at least six months in advance to avoid disappointment). All are located right on the Caribbean. Only a short distance from restaurants and a five-minute drive from George Town, the Avalon has style that's disappointingly rare on Grand Cayman. Each condo has a fully equipped open kitchen and a large, screened lanai overlooking the glorious beach. Fitness buffs are bound to be pleased with the tennis court, fitness center, swimming pool, and hot tub.

Grand Cayman Accommodations

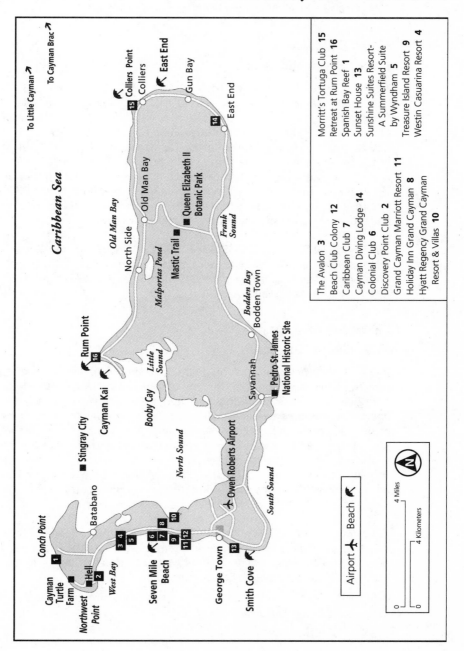

Caribbean Sea

To Little Cayman ↗
To Cayman Brac ↗

Colliers Point
Colliers
East End
Gun Bay
East End

Old Man Bay
Old Man Bay
North Side
Queen Elizabeth II
Botanic Park
Frank Sound
Mastic Trail
Malportas Pond

Rum Point
Cayman Kai
Little Sound
Booby Cay
Bodden Bay
Bodden Town
Savannah
Pedro St. James
National Historic Site

Stingray City
North Sound
Owen Roberts Airport
South Sound

Conch Point
Batabano
Cayman Turtle Farm
Hell
Northwest Point
West Bay
Seven Mile Beach
George Town
Smith Cove

The Avalon **3**
Beach Club Colony **12**
Caribbean Club **7**
Cayman Diving Lodge **14**
Colonial Club **6**
Discovery Point Club **2**
Grand Cayman Marriott Resort **11**
Holiday Inn Grand Cayman **8**
Hyatt Regency Grand Cayman Resort & Villas **10**

Morritt's Tortuga Club **15**
Retreat at Rum Point **16**
Spanish Bay Reef **1**
Sunset House **13**
Sunshine Suites Resort-A Summerfield Suite by Wyndham **5**
Treasure Island Resort **9**
Westin Casuarina Resort **4**

Airport ✈ Beach ↙

N

0   4 Miles
0   4 Kilometers

West Bay Road (P.O. Box 31236). ☎ *345-945-4171. Fax: 345-945-4189. Rack rates: $680–$755 (higher at Christmas and Easter holidays). AE, MC, V.*

Beach Club Colony
$$$$$ **Seven Mile Beach**

Three miles north of George Town, the Beach Club — with its 41 rooms, built in the early 1960s — snagged one of the finer spots on Seven Mile Beach. Over the years, the Club has established a loyal following among divers, who return year after year. Unfortunately, the cruise ship day-trippers have also discovered the strand of beach in front of the hotel. So on days when the ships are in, you'll wish you were somewhere else. The center of activity is designed like a large colonial plantation villa with a formal Doric portico. A popular beach bar featuring Grand Cayman staples of calypso and rum draws both guests and outsiders. The resort has a dive shop on-site and offers all types of water sports.

West Bay Road (P.O. Box 903G). ☎ *800-482-DIVE or 345-949-8100. Fax: 345-945-5167. Internet:* www.caradonna.com. *Rack rates: $500 double. Rates are all-inclusive. Children 6 and under stay free in parent's room; ages 7–17 $85 daily. Honeymoon and dive packages available. AE, MC, V.*

Caribbean Club
$$$$ **Seven Mile Beach**

If you like potluck dinners, you'll like the homey feel of this cluster of 18 one– and two-bedroom condos, six of which are right on lovely Seven Mile Beach. Each is individually owned, so you never know what you'll get when it comes to decor. All have their own patios with barbeque grills. The condos, all with air-conditioning, direct-dial phones with voice mail, and premium cable TV, are set in tropical gardens and offer some seclusion. Nothing fancy, but pleasant. There's no pool, but the beach is terrific. Tennis courts are on-site. These condos are wheelchair accessible and draw a low-key crowd looking for a quiet, comfortable, beachside escape. Foster's Supermarket is across the street.

Seven Mile Beach (P.O. Box 30499). ☎ *345-945-4099. Fax: 345-945-4443. E-mail:* reservations@caribclub.com. *Internet:* www.caribclub.com. *Rack rates: $260–$525. Rates include MAP (two full meals daily). AE, MC, V. No children under age 12 are accepted during high season.*

Cayman Diving Lodge
$$$$$ **East End**

If you care more about gazing at the creatures of the deep than eating them at fancy restaurants, you'll like this remote spot east of George Town (20 miles from the airport). The rooms here are 30 feet from the water's edge. The pace is slow, like the Grand Cayman of 20 years ago. The two-story lodge sits amidst tropical palms on a private coral-sand beach. A live, horseshoe-shaped coral barrier reef just offshore — about 4 to 10 feet deep and great for macro shots of the critters — means that the continually available diving and snorkeling equipment gets a good workout. Three ample squares a day are served family-style, ensuring that the dive crowd gets refueled. (The menus are heavy on seafood.) The rather worn rooms, which have only showers, are no great shakes, but good service and housekeeping help make up for the lack of ambience. Internet and e-mail connections are recent additions to the in-room offerings.

East End (P.O. Box 11). ☎ *800-TLC-DIVE or 345-947-7555. Fax: 345-947-7560. E-mail:* divelodge@aol.com. *Internet:* www.divelodge.com. *Rack rates: $651 diving package for three nights. Rates are all-inclusive and include two 2-tank dives. AE, MC, V.*

Colonial Club
$$$$$ Seven Mile Beach

Pretty-in-pink Colonial Club occupies a highly desirable stretch of Seven Mile Beach. Built in 1985, the main appeal of these 24 standard condos is the good upkeep and service of the neat-as-a-pin accommodations. The three-story building is conveniently located ten minutes from the airport and 4 miles north of George Town. Your choices are units with two bedrooms and three bathrooms or units with three bedrooms and three bathrooms. Besides a pool, you have a tennis court (lit at night) and Jacuzzi at your disposal. One drawback: There's no on-site restaurant.

West Bay Road (P.O. Box 320W). ☎ *345-945-4660. Fax: 345-945-4839. Rack rates: $364–$416 apartment for two; $416–$468 apartment for three to four; $468–$520 apartment for four to five. Minimum stay five nights Dec 16–Apr 15. AE, MC, V.*

Discovery Point Club
$$$$ Seven Mile Beach

This ultra-secluded complex, at the far north end of Seven Mile Beach in West Bay (6 miles from George Town), has a lovely beach and great snorkeling in the protected waters of nearby Cemetery Reef. It's a great place for families and often offers some good deals during the low season. The suites and villas are freshly redone with sunny yellow and marine blue accents. If you're the independent type who wants to stay far off the beaten path, you're assured of a quiet spot here. There's no nightlife and no restaurant. You'll need to rent a car. But what you do get is a screened patio, coin laundry, tennis courts, a hot tub, and a pretty pool.

West Bay (Box 439). ☎ *800-327-8777 or 345-945-4724. Fax: 345-945-5051. Rack rates: $225–$455 double. Wedding and honeymoon packages available. Kids 6 and under stay free April–Dec. AE, DC, MC, V.*

Grand Cayman Marriott Beach Resort

$$$$$ **Seven Mile Beach**

Hurricane Michelle took a swipe at this resort's already dwindling sliver of Seven Mile Beach. Many recent guests have been taken aback by how narrow the strip is. The resort was busing its guests to the Holiday Inn where the beach is much wider. Eventually Mother Nature will likely return some of the sand, but beach bunnies should probably go elsewhere for now. The other drawback to this resort is that "ocean view" can often be debatable. Our room's view gave us a mere sliver of the water. Make sure to double-check when making reservations, if a view is important to you. All rooms have large balconies, and most are angled to make the most of the promised seaside view. The oversized adjoining rooms draw families to this five-story property, just 1 mile from George Town. It offers all the usual water sports through Red Sail Sports. It also has the island's largest conference center, as well as 309 rooms, and it's extremely popular with conventioneers and sales incentives groups, so it'll probably strike most vacationers as too corporate.

Seven Mile Beach (Box 30371). ☎ **800-228-9290** *or 345-949-0088. Fax: 345-949-0288. E-mail:* marriott@candw.ky. *Internet:* www.marriott.com. *Rack rates: $375–$411 double; from $800 suite. AE, DISC, DC, MC, V.*

Hyatt Regency Grand Cayman Resort and Villas

$$$$$ **Seven Mile Beach**

Hugging one of the best sections on famed Seven Mile Beach and housed in grand, low-slung British Colonial–style buildings amid beautifully landscaped gardens with tall royal palms, this elegant Hyatt Regency has no real competition on the island. Of the choices in this book, we'd put it in our Top 20 for its great beach location, some of Grand Cayman's best restaurants (see Chapter 22 for reviews of Bamboo and Hemingways), over-the-top water sports (the top-notch Red Sail Sports even caddies your gear for you), fantasy-inducing water oasis (seven pools, rooftop sundeck, a footbridge, and two swim-up gazebo bars), full-service spa (the only one on Grand Cayman), two health clubs, and breathtaking Britannia Golf Club. The international staff, attentive without being fussy, makes you feel like you're part of a fun global village. Guests in the Regency Club are treated to VIP service, and now you can also rent a villa or one of the beachfront suites (built to the tune of $15 million). The suites look out over the beautiful pool area and are mere feet from the beach.

The children's program is top-notch, as is customary with Hyatt resorts we've visited, but with the food and beverage prices here, we think a condo with kitchen facilities is a better choice for families. Under age 18, kids stay free if they share a room with their parents. This resort is more suitable for couples on a getaway or a honeymoon.

West Bay Road (P.O. Box 1588). ☎ *800-55-HYATT or 345-949-1234. Fax: 345-949-8528. E-mail:* hyatt@candw.kyor. *Internet:* www.hyatt.com *or* www.britanniavillas.com. *Rack rates: $375–$575 double; $735 two-bedroom villa. Additional fee for meal plans. AE, DC, MC, V.*

Holiday Inn Grand Cayman

$$$$ Seven Mile Beach

This new, less budget-busting option lies across the street from its portion of Seven Mile Beach. It's not within walking distance of restaurants and shopping, so you'll need to either take the bus or rent a car. That's the bad news. The good news is that the beach here is wide and rock-free, with decent snorkeling and fine swimming. Best of all, the beach is typically not very crowded — yet. Word will probably be out soon. The rooms — definitely request an ocean view — are basic but nice. It has a full-service dive shop and two restaurants, e-mail and Internet access, and on-site laundry facilities.

1590 West Bay Rd. (P.O. Box 30364-SMB). ☎ *800-HOLIDAY or 345-946-4433. Fax: 345-946-4434 E-mail:* hicayman@candw.ky. *Rack rates: $240–$280. AE, MC, V.*

Morritt's Tortuga Club

$$$ East End

These plantation-style, three-story condos, about half timeshares, are about 30 feet from the water. The surrounding eight beachfront acres are on the idyllic East End, about 26 miles from the airport and known for some of Grand Cayman's best diving. Some people would say this location is isolated, and that's exactly what the clientele here is after. Nothing is within walking distance, unless you count the scuba diving, snorkeling, and windsurfing. A rental car is an absolute must. Home to Tortuga Divers, which offers resort courses, and Cayman Windsurfing, which offers snorkeling and windsurfing and rents sailing craft and catamarans, this well-managed complex is perfect for athletic types eager to get the most from sun, sand, and surf in a laid-back atmosphere. The snorkeling off the dock here is terrific thanks to a protective outer reef about a quarter-mile offshore. One of the two pools has a swim-up bar and a waterfall. Each of the comfortably furnished one- and two-bedroom townhouses — most facing one of two pools — has a fully equipped kitchen, but many guests eat at the restaurant on-site (where the food is pricey). The next closest restaurant is about 2 miles away.

Morritt's has a metered electricity charge, which averages about $50 extra for a week's stay (unless you do something silly like leave the sliding door open with the air-conditioning running).

East End (P.O. Box 496GT). ☎ *800-447-0309 or 345-947-7449. Fax: 345-947-7669. E-mail:* reservations@morritt.com. *Internet:* www.morritt.com. *Rack rates: $225 studio; $255 one-bedroom apartment; $295–$350 two-bedroom apartment. Five night minimum booking. Dive packages available. AE, DISC, MC, V.*

Retreat at Rum Point
$$$$$ North Side

On the north central tip, you'll find a well-kept collection of villas and condos stationed along a sandy, narrow peninsula fringed with casuarina trees, far from the madding crowds swarming Seven Mile Beach. Up to six people can rent a two-bedroom villa here; a group of two or three will be comfortable in a one-bedroom unit. The decor is potluck, but the units are spacious with fully equipped kitchens, washers and dryers, and cable TV. Dive facilities with Red Sail Sports or Ocean Frontiers are nearby, as well as three good restaurants. Divers love the superb offshore diving, including the famed North Wall. On-site you have a restaurant, bar, pool, sauna, tennis court, exercise room, and racquetball court.

A rental car is a must: The Retreat is a 35-minute drive from town or the airport.

North Side (Box 46). ☎ *345-945-9135. Fax: 345-945-9058. E-mail:* retrempt@candw.ky. *Internet:* www.theretreat.com.ky. *Rack rates: $300–$595 double. It often has Internet specials. AE, DISC, MC, V.*

Spanish Bay Reef
$$$$$ North West Bay

One of Grand Cayman's few all-inclusive resorts, Spanish Bay Reef, which was closed for renovations and then damaged by Hurricane Michelle, reopened, much improved, in January 2002. It's on sliver of sandy beach at the island's northwest tip. The reef out front has a steep drop-off, which make for superior diving and good snorkeling. The outdoor bar/dining area surrounds the pool and has views of the ocean; the indoor bar/dining area is spacious and made of coral-stone. Fishing charters are available.

North West Bay (P.O. Box 903). ☎ *800-327-8777 or 345-949-8100. Fax: 345-949-1842. Rack rates: High season $460 double. Children 6 and under stay free in parent's room; ages 7–17 $85 daily. Honeymoon and dive packages available. Rates include meals, Jeep rental, bicycles, introductory scuba/snorkel lessons, and snorkeling equipment. AE, MC, V.*

Sunset House
$$$ Seven Mile Beach

Low-key describes this spartan diver's resort with rooms — okay, so they look like 1950s-era strip motels — on the ironshore (sharp, hard, calcified black coral) south of George Town and about 4 miles from Seven Mile Beach. Some rooms have kitchenettes, and all have dataports and e-mail access. The congenial staff, a happening bar, and a terrific seafood restaurant match with the full-service dive operation (including six dive boats) to make this place extremely popular with scuba divers. Full dive services include free waterside lockers, two– and three-tank dives with its fleet of six dive boats, and use of the excellent Cathy Church's Underwater Photo Centre. Perhaps to make up for not being on the beach, the hotel has two pools (one right by the sea), plus a whirlpool. It's a five-minute walk to a sandy beach and a ten-minute walk to George Town. All-inclusive dive packages are the way to go here with great rates via Cayman Airways and American Airlines.

South Church Street (P.O. Box 479). ☎ *888-854-4767 or 345-949-7111. Fax: 345-949-7101. E-mail:* sunsethouse@sunsethouse.com. *Internet:* www.sunset house.com. *58 rooms. Rack rates: $165–$300 double. Meal plans available for extra charge. Dive packages. AE, DISC, MC, V.*

Sunshine Suites Resort — A Summerfield Suites by Wyndham
$$$$ **Seven Mile Beach**

This newly-built all-suites hotel is in the heart of Seven Mile Beach and offers one of the best values on this pricey island. Since the former Comfort Suites was taken over by Wyndham, it has been offering an introductory rate that includes continental breakfast and a room upgrade. The surprisingly roomy rooms — white walls with gray tiled floors and louvered windows — all come with kitchens and have sea views. Suites have dual phone lines with dataports. Laundry facilities and an exercise room are on-site. Don Foster Dive operation is on-site, too. Stingers, the poolside restaurant and bar, has already begun to draw a crowd.

West Bay Road. ☎ *800-WYNDHAM or 345-945-7300. Fax: 345-945-7400. Internet:* www.wyndham.com. *Rack rates: $245–$325. 10% discount for booking online. AE, MC, V.*

Treasure Island Resort
$$$$ **Seven Mile Beach**

This sprawling, five-story complex — a Ramada in a previous incarnation — is one of the largest resorts on the island and has excellent snorkeling right in front of its reef beach. The entry is rocky, so you'll need watershoes. This southern stretch of Seven Mile Beach isn't the wide sand strand, leaving guests to walk gingerly on its rocky strand. Just a few resorts up, the beach greatly improves. The resort's strong suit? Above-par entertainment six nights a week, shopping and good restaurants within walking distance, a plethora of activities, and a caring staff that tries hard. It's popular with families. But in the looks department, we're talking late-1960s-apartment-building grim. We'd compare Treasure Island to a nice Days Inn in the U.S. It's a good moderate pick for active types who are watching their budgets and plan to spend most of their time enjoying water sports or scuba diving. The 278 guest rooms, which are worn and sometimes have sloppy housekeeping, surround a courtyard with two large pools, a Jacuzzi, and a waterfall.

Consider yourself forewarned: The term *air-conditioning* is used loosely here. What we call air-conditioning and what Treasure Island calls it are two different animals. The rooms do have refrigerators so you can at least keep your sodas or beer cold.

269 West Bay Rd. (P.O. Box 1817). ☎ ***800-203-0775*** *or 345-949-7777. Fax: 345-949-8672. Internet:* www.treasureislandresort.net. *Rack rates: $260 double. AE, DC, MC, V.*

Westin Casuarina Resort
$$$$$ Seven Mile Beach

Like the Hyatt, the low-slung Westin has 700 feet on palm-fringed Seven Mile Beach. This beautiful and large (343-room) British Caribbean–style resort, which we'd rate second to the Hyatt, occupies one of the better stretches of Seven Mile Beach. A new full-service spa came on-line in November 2001. The staff is cheerful and energetic. Like many other hotels on Grand Cayman, the Westin offers a plethora of water sports including the biggie — scuba diving — through Red Sail Sports. You'll find a challenging 18-hole golf course across the street, as well as a salon and a spa. Camp Scallywag is available for kids ages 4 to 12. Bright, airy rooms (on the small side) with private balconies face either the Caribbean or the lovely gardens. This elegant resort is one of those places where the sea view is worth the extra money, so go for it. You'll thank us when you're watching the sunset from your balcony. Two free-form pools with a happening swim-up bar, and poolside decks (5,000 square feet of them) are appealingly lined with palm and date trees. Cruise-shippers sometimes try to crash the scene.

If you love the nightlife, you aren't going to love the Westin. This resort is the kind of place where everybody goes to bed early. Oh, but what a bed it is! If you haven't slept in Westin's Heavenly Bed (yes, the company gave its specially designed and manufactured mattress a name), you're in for a treat. We've slept in a lot of hotel rooms, but the double-pillow-topped mattress with premium sheets here are amazing.

Seven Mile Beach Road (Box 30620). ☎ ***800-WESTIN-1*** *or 345-945-3804. Internet:* www.westin.com. *Rack rates: $410 to $525 double. AE, MC, V.*

Chapter 21

Settling into Grand Cayman

By Echo and Kevin Garrett

- -

In This Chapter

▶ Knowing what to expect when you arrive

▶ Getting around the island

▶ Discovering Grand Cayman from A to Z

- -

*I*f you come to Grand Cayman expecting to encounter an upper-crust attitude to coincide with the island's reputation as an offshore banking mecca, you'll be pleasantly surprised. Despite its wealth and status as a British Overseas Dependent Territory — we know, even the designation sounds stuffy — Grand Cayman is relaxed and casual. In fact, Kevin says it reminds him of his tiny hometown in Georgia where you have to buy a car with an automatic transmission so you can have one hand free to wave to people.

The cost of living is about 20% higher in Grand Cayman than in the United States; one U.S. dollar is worth only about 80 Cayman cents. Nonetheless, many of the 40,000 islanders are wealthy, and they wear their millionaire status without any ostentation. If you run into any problem while on the island, the warm and friendly folks on Grand Cayman are happy to point you in the right direction.

 In 2003, the Cayman Islands celebrate their 500th anniversary on the world map, so look for special celebrations and join in the birthday party. For details, e-mail info@cayman500.ky.

Arriving in Grand Cayman

With more than 100 flights landing at **Owen Roberts International Airport** (☎ 345-949-5252) weekly — 70 direct flights from Miami alone — officials are adept at handling a continuous stream of visitors. This clean, modern airport with its good air-conditioning system is one of the more comfortable in the Caribbean. Even if you're coming in on a packed flight, you'll likely encounter few lines and barely feel that you're entering a foreign country.

The customs of the Cayman Islands

Here are a few tips to help you fit in:

✔ **Language:** The Caymanians will know that you've just arrived if you make either of two faux pas: mispronouncing Grand Cayman (it's pronounced K-man) or referring to it as "the Caymans." Islanders either say "The Cayman Islands," or "Cayman" but never "the Caymans."

✔ **Clothing:** Even though this island is laid-back, you won't see women sans bathing-suit tops or even women in thong bikinis strolling the beach. No form of public nudity is tolerated. Even jokey T-shirts are suspect. One way islanders can tell who has come off the cruise ships is by observing the number of logo'ed tank tops in the group.

✔ **Etiquette:** You'll hear older people's first names preceded by "Mr." or "Miss" (for example, Mr. Sam) as a sign of respect.

The airport is centrally located for points east and west. After you clear Customs and gather luggage, you'll note stacks of free tourist information. Grab a copy of everything you see — especially useful is **"Key to Cayman,"** available at the airport, hotels, and shops. These giveaways often contain coupons for meals, attractions, and car rentals.

No cash? No problem. ATMs are everywhere. (What else would you expect on an island 22 miles long and 8 miles wide with more than 500 bank offices?) But you'd better look like you can afford your vacation when you arrive on Grand Cayman. Otherwise, you're likely to be questioned by Customs officials to determine whether you've got the bank account to bankroll your fun on the island.

Flights going onto Cayman Brac land at Gerrard-Smith Airport; flights to Little Cayman land at Edward Bodden Airfield. Air service from Grand Cayman to Cayman Brac and Little Cayman is offered via **Cayman Airways** (☎ **800-422-9626** or 345-949-2311; Internet: www.caymanairways.com) and **Island Air** (☎ **345-949-5252;** Internet: www.islandaircayman.com), which has four flights daily.

The other way to travel to Grand Cayman is by ship. Most major cruise lines call in Grand Cayman, docking in George Town. However, the Cayman Islands limit cruise visitors to a maximum of 6,000 cruise passengers or three ships per day, whichever is greater. Tuesdays, Wednesdays, and Thursdays tend to be the busiest days.

Best-selling mystery writer and former jockey Dick Francis told us over drinks one afternoon that he fell in love with the island after taking a cruise through the Caribbean and docking here. He makes Grand Cayman his home.

Getting to Your Accommodations

Check with your hotel ahead of time to see if it offers free pickup at the airport. All arriving flights are met by taxis, which line up neatly, awaiting an agent to assign them to deplaning passengers.

Taxis are usually vans (capable of transporting divers and all their accompanying gear) or Toyota Corollas. Taxi rates are fixed, and you can get fare information from the dispatcher at the curb. Drivers are generally charming and happy to share island lore. Typical one-way fares from the airport to Seven Mile Beach range from $16 to $24, depending, of course, on which end of the beach you're travelling to.

Taxis are also readily available from all resorts and from the taxi stand at the cruise ship dock in George Town. A sign with current rates is posted at the dock.

Local minibuses run along main routes between 7 a.m. and 6 p.m. from George Town parallel to Seven Mile Beach. The fare is $2.

If you've rented a condo but not a car and you need provisions, have **McCurley's Tours** (☎ **345-947-9626**) pick you up at the airport. The driver will gladly take you by a grocery store en route.

If you rent a car, getting to your hotel from the airport should be easy on this flat island. The roads are well marked and in good shape, and your car-rental agent can pencil in the route for you on the map. The major car-rental companies all have offices in a plaza across from the airport terminal, where you can pick up and drop off vehicles.

Getting Around Grand Cayman

This island is one of the easiest in the Caribbean to navigate. The terrain is flat, and the easy-going locals are ready to help if by some weird happenstance you get lost. (We can't imagine such a thing on this island, but you never know.)

By car

You'll have to pay for a $7.50 rental permit to drive any vehicle on the island. You can get a permit from either the rental agent or the central police station in George Town if you have a valid driver's license. You must have a credit card and be at least 21 years of age — 25 with some companies — to rent a car.

Rates range from $35 to $75 a day; remember to use coupons and ask about special promotions. Car-rental companies include **Budget** (☎ 800-472-3325 or 345-949-5605), **Cico Avis** (☎ 800-331-1212 or 345-949-2468),

Coconut (☎ 800-262-6687 or 345-949-4377), **Economy** (☎ 345-949-9550), **Hertz** (☎ 800-654-3131 or 345-949-2280), **Soto's 4X4** (☎ 345-945-2424), and **Thrifty** (☎ 800-367-2277 or 345-949-6640). Some agencies offer additional discounts for booking via the Internet.

Most firms have a range of models, from compacts to Jeeps to minibuses. Divers who are staying a bit farther afield and have gear to haul will definitely need a larger vehicle; we suggest a Jeep or van with plenty of sprawl room. Whatever kind of car you choose, you're sure to encounter lots of other people who have rented the exact same model. Put something in your car window, so that you'll be able to distinguish your car easily. Otherwise, you may find yourself staring at a sea of small, white, four-door Toyotas the way we did one morning when we came out of our hotel.

Everyone drives on the left side of the road — British style — and the steering wheel is on the right, so when pulling out into traffic, look to your right. The car's setup may be slightly different in other ways, too. The local joke is to watch out for tourists with their windshield wipers on, because they're about to make a turn.

When you get away from the airport and heavy traffic along Seven Mile Beach, traffic thins out and driving is simple. You can't get lost, because you'll travel Grand Cayman's one main road, a route that offers a few little offshoots. George Town has several one-way streets marked with international signs. Ask the rental agent to show you what the signs look like.

If you're behind a bus that stops to let off passengers, be sure to stop or else you may run over a fellow traveler — the exit doors swing out into traffic. Always watch for pedestrians; Grand Cayman attracts visitors from around the world, and you never know what the pedestrian rules are on their home turf.

You may want to tour the island for a day; you won't need more than that for a complete tour. For that day, rent a car — unless it's really important to you to pick up local history and color from a taxi driver, who will gladly serve as a guide. If you tour by taxi, though, the tab will likely exceed what you'd pay for a one-day car rental.

On foot

If your accommodations are in the midst of Grand Cayman's Seven Mile Beach, your feet will get you where you need to go. You can walk to the shopping centers, restaurants, and entertainment spots along West Bay Road. George Town is small enough to see on foot.

By bicycle, moped, and motorcycle

Biking is popular on this flat, safe island where drivers tend to take it easy; bikes, mopeds, and motorcycles are good means to explore. When renting a motor scooter or bicycle, don't forget to wear sunscreen. Also remember to drive on the left. Bicycles ($10 to $15 a day) and scooters ($25 to $30 a day) can be rented from **Bicycles Cayman** (☎ **345-949-5572**), **Cayman Cycle** (☎ **345-945-4021**), and **Soto Scooters** (☎ **345-945-4652**). Some resorts also offer free bicycles.

Ask whether your speedometer is in kilometers per hour or miles per hour. They're often in kilometers, but the speed signs (circles with 25, 30, 40, or 50) are posted in miles per hour.

Fast Facts: Grand Cayman

ATMs

ATMs are available universally on this bank-riddled island.

Baby-sitters

Hotels can readily help you arrange baby-sitting, but don't wait until the last minute. Expect to pay at least $7 an hour. Unemployment on the island is low, so plan in advance.

Banks

The main banks are Barclays Bank, Cayman National Bank, Royal Bank of Canada, Bank of Nova Scotia, Canadian Imperial Bank of Commerce, and Washington International Bank. Bank hours are Monday through Friday 9 a.m. to 4 p.m. Banks are closed on weekends.

Business Hours

Shops in George Town are open from 9 a.m. to 5 p.m. Monday through Saturday. Shops are usually closed Sundays except in hotels.

Credit Cards

Major credit cards are widely accepted.

Currency Exchange

Although the U.S. dollar is accepted everywhere, you'll save money if you go to the bank and exchange U.S. dollars for Cayman Island (CI) dollars, worth about US$1.20 at press time. The Cayman dollar is divided into a hundred cents with coins of 1¢, 5¢, 10¢, and 25¢ and notes of $1, $5, $10, $25, $50, and $100 (no $20 bills). Prices are often quoted in Cayman dollars, so it's best to ask. You'll also be given change in Caymanian money. All prices quoted in this book are in U.S. dollars, unless otherwise noted.

Doctors

Health care on the island is excellent. Ask your hotel concierge for a referral, or call Cayman Medical and Surgical Centre's 24-hour physician referral hotline at ☎ 345-949-8150.

Electricity

Electricity is the same in the Cayman Islands as it is in the United States (110-volt, 60 cycle).

Emergencies

For an ambulance/police/fire, call ☎ **911**.

Hospital

The Cayman Islands Hospital (☎ 345-949-8600) in George Town on Hospital Road has a state-of-the-art accident and emergency unit, staffed 24 hours a day. George Town Hospital (Hospital Road, George Town;

☎ 345-949-4234 or 555) has a two-man double-lock hyperbaric chamber; it's manned on a 24-hour on-call basis by trained staff from the Cayman Islands Divers chapter of the British Sub Aqua Club, and it's supervised by a doctor trained to treat diving injuries.

Information

The main office of the Department of Tourism is in the Pavilion (Cricket Square and Elgin Avenue, P.O. Box 67; ☎ 345-949-0623 or 345-914-1270; Fax: 345-949-4053; Internet: www.caymanislands.ky). You can find information booths at the airport (☎ 345-949-2635), at the Cruise Landing at Spotts when cruise ships are in port during rough seas, or in the kiosk at the cruise ship dock in George Town (☎ 345-949-8342). Grand Cayman also maintains an islands-wide tourist hot line (☎ 345-949-8989).

You can contact the Tourist Information and Activities Service (☎ 345-949-6598 or 345-945-6222) day or night for complete tourist information and free assistance in booking island transportation, tours, charters, cruises, and other activities.

Language

English is the official language.

Maps

You can pick up a good map at any tourist information kiosk or at the hotels. Look for the "The Cayman Islands Map and Tourist Guide" or "Key to Cayman," both free publications.

Pharmacies

Island Pharmacy (☎ 345-949-8987) is in West Shore Centre on Seven Mile Beach.

Police

In an emergency, call ☎ 911.

Post Office

Post offices are generally open weekdays from 8:30 a.m. to 5:00 p.m. and Saturday from 8:30 to 11:30 a.m. Beautiful stamps are available at the General Post Office in downtown George Town and at the philatelic bureau in West Shore Plaza.

Safety

This island doesn't suffer from the crime that plagues some other Caribbean islands. You can walk wherever you like. Nonetheless, don't tempt fate: Don't leave valuables in plain sight in rental cars, be sure to lock your hotel room when you leave, and don't leave valuables unattended on the beach.

Frankly, Caymanians are law-and-order types. They're more concerned about you breaking the law than they are about islanders taking something or harming another person. Penalties for drunk driving or for drugs include jail time and large penalties.

One of the few dangers comes from the manchineel trees that have fruit that look like little green apples. They're poisonous to touch. Even raindrops dripping from them can cause painful blisters if they hit your skin. Most of these trees are marked with a red ring on the trunk or a small warning sign. Caution your children not to touch the fruit.

As for sharks, we were assured that they don't hang around the popular dive sites; they generally prefer deeper water. However, at Stingray City, an 8½-foot hammerhead swam right underneath Kevin.

Taxes

All accommodations add a 10% government tax, and you'll encounter a departure tax of $10 when you leave the island. Otherwise, there is no tax on goods or services. But most hotels and restaurants tack on a 15% service charge to your bill.

Telephone

For international dialing to Cayman, the area code is 345 (changed from 809). To call outside, dial 0+1+area code and the number.

You can call anywhere, anytime, through the cable and wireless system and local operators. To make local calls, dial the seven-digit number.

To place credit card calls, dial ☎ 800-744-2000. AT&T USA Direct (☎ 800-872-2881), Sprint Direct (800-366-4663), and MCI Direct (☎ 800-888-8000) can be used from any public phone and most hotels. This wealthy island offers good Internet connections with several Internet cafes and kiosks if you just can't stand to be away from your laptop.

Time Zone

The islands are on Atlantic standard time, one hour ahead of eastern standard time.

Tipping

The norm is 15% across the board at hotels and restaurants, but note that many places automatically put it on your final bill. Check so you don't overtip. Taxi drivers expect a 10 to 15% tip.

Water

Water is safe to drink, but please conserve for the island's sake.

Weather and Surf Reports

Check out the following Web sites: www.weather.com or www.gobeach.com/hurr.htm.

Chapter 22

Dining in Grand Cayman

By Echo and Kevin Garrett

● ●

In This Chapter

▶ Sampling the local cuisine

▶ Locating the island's best restaurants

● ●

*I*n culinary schools, students are sometimes asked to create a meal with a box of miscellaneous ingredients — in a limited amount of time. Many days, chefs on Grand Cayman are forced to perform that same drill. The small coral island doesn't produce much in the way of fresh fruits and vegetables. About the only fruit around here is *las frutas del mar:* fish, conch, lobster, turtle (farmed on the island), octopus, and squid.

Although the local ingredients may be limited, your restaurant choices aren't. Like Aruba, this small island boasts a surprising number of restaurants — more than 200 all told — featuring everything from Caribbean classic to New World, Thai, Asian, and American cuisine.

 Hurricane Michelle caused a few old standards to shutter. Several others that you may see recommended elsewhere have been left off our short list of new favorites. Some have stumbled, others have just gotten tired or too touristy. For example, Cracked Conch By the Sea and the Lobster Pot were good choices for many years, but not any more. They're both overdone and overcooked — and we're not just talking about the seafood.

Using what they have on hand, Caymanian cooks have created their own distinctive cuisine, which prominently features a version of conch fritters, spicy pepperpot soup, Cayman patties (filled with lobster, chicken or other meat, or vegetables), fish "rundown" (fresh catches simmered in coconut milk), and the national dish of turtle stew. (Turtle, which tastes somewhat like beef and is slightly chewy, is farmed here.) Local lobster is in season from summer's end until January.

Dining out on Grand Cayman can put a serious dent in your budget, so consider whether some sort of meal plan at your hotel would make sense for you. You can easily blow $20 or more per person at breakfast. To cut costs, many people bring their own groceries from home or buy them on the island and cook for themselves in their condos. There are several fast-food chains, too, if you aren't looking for anything fancy.

For fast, low-cost Internet, hot coffee, and good cheesecake, head to **Café del Sol** (Marquee Shopping Centre, Harquail Bypass; ☎ 345-946-2233; Internet: `www.cafedelsol.ky`).

For the best and cheapest hearty brunch (opens at 10:30 a.m.) on the island, head to **Fidel Murphy's Irish Pub Restaurant** (Queens Court Plaza, Seven Mile Beach, West Bay Road; ☎ 345-949-5189), which has an Irish breakfast with bacon, sausage, tomato, black and white pudding, baked beans, and two fried eggs for $8.95.

Despite the high prices and British influence, you won't have to spend money on fancy duds for dinner. Casual attire is suitable at most places.

Grand Cayman's Best Restaurants

Bamboo
$$ Seven Mile Beach Sushi/Japanese

The hippest thing to hit Grand Cayman in a long time is this swank sushi joint where a bleached-blonde sushi master named Kaz presides over the festivities like an MTV host. The handsome wait crew pads around in sleek, all black attire, and appears just as you need the next rainbow roll. In a room with walls paneled in warm woods and with recessed colored lighting, Kaz cheerfully whips out the most succulent sushi and sashimi we've ever tasted. We are true sushi connoisseurs, and we were astounded at the quality and his creativity. We especially liked the white snake, a special hand roll with BBQ freshwater eel, cucumber, tobiko, and thinly sliced avocado. The drink of the house is sakatini — sake-meets-martini. Try the red dragon (vodka, plum sake, and cranberry juice). Every Wednesday night Hi Tide plays live from 6:30 to 10:30 p.m.

On some nights, Kaz gives lessons on how to make sushi while New Age Japanese music plays softly in the background. It's a fun, don't-miss experience.

West Bay Road at the Hyatt. ☎ 345-949-1234. Reservations essential. Main courses: $17–$45. AE, DISC, MC, V. Open: Mon–Fri 5 p.m.–1 a.m., Sat 5 p.m. to midnight.

Grand Cayman Dining

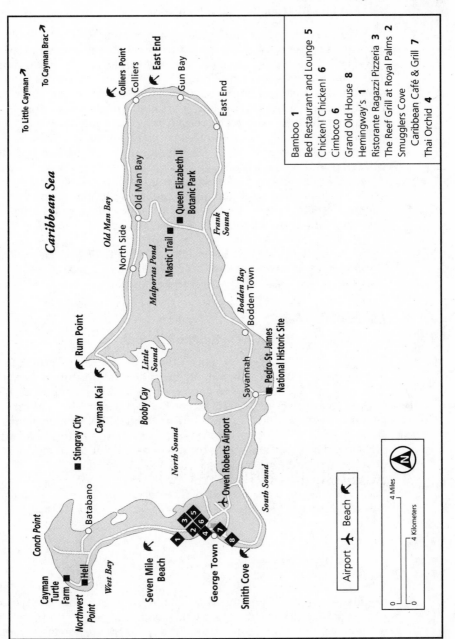

Bamboo **1**
Bed Restaurant and Lounge **5**
Chicken! Chicken! **6**
Cimboco **6**
Grand Old House **8**
Hemingway's **1**
Ristorante Ragazzi Pizzeria **3**
The Reef Grill at Royal Palms **2**
Smugglers Cove
Caribbean Café & Grill **7**
Thai Orchid **4**

Bed Restaurant and Lounge

$$ Seven Mile Beach   Eclectic Global

Low lighting, Moroccan indigo blues and orange reds with funky high-color modern art hint at the young sophisticates that have discovered this edgy cosmopolitan hangout, fashioned after the one in South Beach. The ambitious menu delivers on its promise, with the chefs bringing a sure hand to dishes suitable to the wildly eclectic tastes of the diners Bed attracts. Sharing several appetizers is a popular way to sample many items, and the prices are pretty reasonable (for Grand Cayman) given the portions. Most main courses are under $20. This atmosphere — servers don pajamas — sparks new friendships started at the bar and ending with shared dinners. The Uruguayan rack of lamb gets our vote along with the white chilean seabass encrusted with pistachio and a roasted garlic saffron cream or grilled marinated local grouper in spicy chipolte coconut cream sauce. Vegetarians will enjoy the vegetable curry or lasagna. Bed has one of the only wine cellars on Grand Cayman.

Islander Complex, Seven Mile Beach. ☎ *345-949-7199. Dinner reservations recommended. Main courses: $12–$27. AE, MC, V. Open: Dinner nightly 6–11p.m; lounge open Mon–Fri. 6 p.m.–1 a.m., Sat 6 p.m. to midnight.*

Chicken!Chicken!

$ Seven Mile Beach   Caribbean Chicken

Known as one of the best values on the island for tasty Caribbean-style wood-roasted chicken, this super busy little shop offers daily lunch specials until 3 p.m. that give you an entire meal for $5 to $7.25. It's the Caribbean's answer to Boston Market, but lots better. The chicken is marinated in citrus and herbs, then slow roasted. Sides include jicama cole slaw, sweet tarragon carrots, buttermilk mashed potatoes, and several other good dishes. Takeout makes the perfect solution when you want a picnic lunch for beach-hopping.

West Shore Centre. ☎ *345-945-2290. No reservations needed. Children's menu available. Main courses: $8–$10. AE, MC, V. Open: Daily 11a.m.–10 p.m.*

Cimboco

$ Seven Mile Beach   Caribbean

The exhibition-style kitchen of this place — dolled up in Caribbean brights — turns out creative fire-roasted pizzas, Caribbean-style sandwiches (roti and jerk chicken), rustic pastas and simply prepared catch-of-the-day seafood, all well-priced. The appetizers are equally as creative: plaintain wrapped callaloo with a Cayman sauce and coconut or Caribbean fire-roasted shrimp with local greens, bacon, tomatoes, and blackeye peas. It's one of the best bargains on the Grand Cayman.

Next to the Cinema, Seven Mile Beach. ☎ *345-947-2782. No reservations. Main courses: $8–$13. AE, MC, V. Open: Daily 11 a.m.–10 p.m.*

Grand Old House

$$$ George Town   Caribbean/New World

Although the dining scene on Grand Cayman has changed considerably in the last few years, this Grand Dame, set in a former early-20th-century plantation house where legend has it that you can spot a *duppy* (island-speak for "ghost"), still lives up to its own legend. Reserve a romantic table in one of the seaside gazebos with fans swirling lazily overhead. Chef Mathai, who counts presidents and royalty among his guests, adds Caribbean flair to his fun-to-read menu with offerings like Cayman-style turtle steak in spicy tomato sauce with bermuda onions and bell peppers or baked shrimp "Grand Old House" with local herbs, white wine, and hollandaise sauce with mousseline potato ring. The starter can be the classic conch fritter or something a little more exotic like terrine of fresh foie gras and smoked wild boar. He's equally good with both. The restaurant just garnered *The Wine Spectator* award for the 13th year straight. A Cuban pianist performs nightly (except Sundays) starting at 6:30 p.m.

648 S. Church St. ☎ 345-949-9333. Dinner reservations essential. Children's menu available. Main courses: $19–$29. AE, MC, V. Open: Mon–Fri 11:45 a.m.–2:00 p.m, nightly 6–10 p.m. Closed Sun May 15–Nov 15.

Hemingway's

$$$ Seven Mile Beach   Nouvelle Caribbean

We love the amber glow emanating from this romantic, right-on-the-beach place with French doors giving view to the sea beyond. Diners don elegant resortwear for this retreat where the air-conditioning is welcome after a day in the sun. A classical guitarist serenades diners. The paella with broiled Caribbean lobster and pan-fried snapper with vanilla sweet potato cake, goat cheese, and thyme brulee are winners. If you want a tropical drink, try the Seven Mile Meltdown, with dark rum, peach schnapps, pineapple juice, and fresh coconut. Or try the Papa Doble, a daiquiri fashioned like those Hemingway preferred in Havana. Some grouse about the high prices here, but you'll find the experience, the food, and the price you pay comparable to other restaurants we've recommended. At lunch the salads are generous and well-priced.

West Bay Road, on the beach in the Hyatt complex. ☎ 345-945-5700. Reservations a must during high season. Main courses: $22–$32. AE, DISC, MC, V. Open: Daily 11:30 a.m.–2:30 p.m. and 6:00–9:30 p.m.

Ristorante Ragazzi Pizzeria

$$$ Seven Mile Beach   Casual Italian

The warmth of the golden burnished woods in the interior matches the warmth of the service and the homemade Italian fare served up at this popular place. It has the only wood-burning brick oven on the island and turns out delicious thin-crust pizzas and homemade breads. It has dining outside but the interior with cobalt blue accents, bold art, and wines behind glass, making up one wall, is enough to lure us in.

Ragazzi's gets really booked up, and even if you have a reservation, you may have to wait 30 minutes or so.

In front of the Hyatt on West Bay Road, Buckingham Square Center. ☎ *345-945-5595. Reservations essential. Main courses: $18–$36. AE, MC, V. Open: Daily for lunch 11:30 a.m–4:30 p.m and dinner 4:30–11:00 p.m.*

The Reef Grill at Royal Palms
$$$ Seven Mile Beach   Seafood

The current hotspot for dining and one of our top five picks, this seaside restaurant — where live local bands like CoCo Red play on the beach — has deservedly earned a reputation as one of the best places for spanking fresh fish. The honey soy glazed sea bass with Thai curry and tuna sashimi over a rice cake with wasabi ponzu dipping sauce rate among our most memorable dishes from Grand Cayman. Meat eaters rave about the grilled rib eye. Go with the coconut ice cream or mango sorbet for dessert. The wine list has 20 selections, and the service is great. You can dine in the elegant, air-conditioned bistro with flickering candles and sconces, but we suggest a garden patio table where the mood is more casual.

Seven Mile Beach (between the Hyatt and the Marriott). ☎ *345-945-6358. Reservations essential. Main courses: $16–$28. AE, DISC, MC, V. Open: Daily 6–10 p.m.*

Smugglers Cove Caribbean Café and Grill
$$$ Georgetown Harbour   Caribbean New World

Tucked away on a secluded cove, you can sit seaside and listen to the waves against the ironshore at this romantic spot. It has supplanted the Lobster Pot as the place to come for grilled Caribbean lobster. We also loved its lobster ravioli with grilled lobster, served with creamy lobster sauce with a hint of cognac. The extensive wine list is a veritable world tour, with everything from Classic French to New World wines that go with the chef's inventive cuisine. A particularly nifty starter was the jerked baby duck on a bed of greens.

Seaside Georgetown Harbour. ☎ *345-949-6003. Reservations essential. Main courses: $19–$28. AE, MC, V. Open: Nightly 5:30–10:30 p.m.*

Thai Orchid
$$$ Seven Mile Beach   Thai

Don't let the bare-bones Thai decor — the rich red of the interior walls is about the only thing that stands out — dissuade you from this unassuming spot. Our test was its perfect rendition of our fave, panang curry.

Thai Orchid passed with flying colors. It also offers an extensive vegetarian menu. We love Thai food as much as we love diving, and this spot is the place to tank up.

Dive masters and savvy tourists flock to a bountiful all-you-can-eat lunch buffet on Tuesdays and Thursdays.

Queens Court Shopping Plaza. ☎ *345-949-7955. Main courses: $15–21. $11.95 lunch buffet. AE, MC, V. Open: Mon–Sat 11:30 a.m.–2:30 p.m. and 6–10 p.m.*

Chapter 23

Having Fun on and off the Beach in Grand Cayman

By Echo and Kevin Garrett

● ●

In This Chapter

▶ Soaking up the sun on Grand Cayman's top beaches

▶ Diving into fun with water sports

▶ Satisfying the landlubber: activities, shopping, and nightlife

● ●

*I*f Grand Cayman is your vacation pick, we're assuming you love the water the way we do. And when it comes to activities centered around (and in) the sea, Grand Cayman makes a great choice.

Besides scuba diving, Grand Cayman is noted for other water sports like windsurfing and deep-sea fishing, as well as for interesting golf and decent shopping. In this chapter, we help make sure that you don't miss a thing Grand Cayman has to offer, and we take away any remaining stress factors. Hassle-free fun is what we're going for, and we're sure that's what you're seeking, too.

Heading for the Sand and Surf

Grand Cayman's **Seven Mile Beach** — one of the Caribbean's finer bands of sand — begins north of George Town, the capital. This famed stretch, which is actually only 5½ miles long (but who's counting?), boasts sparkling white sands edged by casuarina pines and a variety of palms. Toward the southern end, the landscape becomes quite rocky, a condition worsened by Hurricane Michelle, which struck in October 2001. Low-rise deluxe resorts, condos, and small hotels are strung all along the beach, much like Aruba's immensely popular but crowded Palm Beach.

The surf is that milky teal color that invites you to loll on a raft. You don't have to worry about being swept out to sea either. The wave action along this beach mirrors the calm of the island, and the bath-warm water barely laps at your ankles.

Thankfully, you don't have to be a guest at a particular hotel to use the beach, and you're welcome to use the beach bar and restroom facilities at most spots. The Hyatt gets understandably persnickety about nonguests overtaking its pools and beach chairs. And Hyatt security can spot nonguests a mile away. (For starters, you won't have the plush Hyatt-issued blue beach towel tucked under your arm.) We somehow managed to stay below security's radar, but a Ralph Cramden lookalike sporting blue zinc oxide on his nose and a "Will Work for Beer" tank top was immediately tossed.

Be discreet if you're not a registered guest and you decide to venture beyond a hotel's beach bar or restroom facilities. We wouldn't recommend trying to use the pool at a place where you're not staying; however, if you eat lunch at the hotel restaurant, that's your meal ticket to splash in the pool if you like.

About the only time Seven Mile Beach gets crowded is when the cruise ships dock; no more than 6,000 passengers are allowed per day, but that's still a lot of folks. You'll never see the crush of people you find on the most popular beaches in Puerto Rico or Aruba, though. You also don't have to worry about vendors asking to braid your hair or inviting you to toss out the toll for cheap jewelry and tie-dyed T-shirts like you do in Jamaica or Puerto Rico. And panhandling is outlawed, so forget about being hassled. In fact, Grand Cayman, with one of the lower crime rates in this hemisphere, is among the few islands where we could actually visualize ourselves napping on the beach without worrying about what would be gone when we woke up. Of course, the annoying buzz of jet skis plying the waters off Seven Mile Beach makes snoozing unlikely, but we can dream.

The rockier beaches on the east and north coasts, a good 20- to 30-minute drive, are protected by an offshore barrier reef and offer good snorkeling. They're much less congested, and their reefs are in better shape than Seven Mile Beach, which has suffered from its popularity. On the southwest coast you can find small sandy beaches, but they're better for sunning than snorkeling because blankets of ribbonlike turtle grass have proliferated in the water.

Having Fun in and on the Water

What they lack in nightlife — though that's getting better, too — the Cayman Islands make up for in water sports. The diving, fishing, swimming, and water-skiing are among the finest in the Caribbean.

Observing some underwater rules

Underwater life is sensitive and we should all do our best to respect this fragility. When you're underwater remember to observe the following rules:

✔ **Look, but don't touch.** Coral reefs are extremely sensitive, and some coral grows less than an inch per year. Breakage by careless divers can take decades for Mother Nature to repair. Please don't bump, stand on, break, or even touch the coral.

✔ **Don't feed the fish (or the stingrays).** We know you'll see other people doing it, but marine research has demonstrated that feeding by humans is doing serious damage to the fish population by throwing off the delicate balance of the coral reefs. Besides, you may wind up with a "stingray hickey." These graceful, buttery soft creatures vacuum the food out of your hands (their mouths are in the middle bottom part of their bodies), and sometimes the suction can be uncomfortable. We saw one fellow who had been giving the rays squid handouts wipe his hands on his swim trunks. He immediately got much closer to these creatures than he'd intended. Not a good move.

Diving right in

First things first. Grand Cayman, ringed by glorious coral reefs teeming with marine life, has earned its reputation as a world-class diving destination. Underwater visibility often exceeds 100 feet in these crystalline teal waters where you can indulge your Jacques Cousteau fantasies at more than 130 sites — everything from wall dives and wreck dives to cave dives, coral garden dives, and shore dives. The island has won kudos from every diver's publication and is the Caribbean's premier dive spot.

Grand Cayman's diving is literally a mountaintop experience. The coral island sits at the top of an underwater mountain, the side of which — known as the **Cayman Wall** — plummets straight down for 500 feet before becoming a steep slope falling away for 6,000 feet and eventually plunging 23,000 feet to the ocean floor.

We'd heard rumors that Grand Cayman isn't what it used to be and that the popular dive sites have been overrun. So off we went to check it out ourselves. We're happy to report that you can still find gorgeous corals, diverse marine life, and great wall diving, but if you want more pristine diving, you need to go to the east or north of the island. Sadly, the diving hordes have damaged the corals, particularly to the west of the island.

Yes, divers seem to be everywhere. (When a tiny island has more than 60 dive operators, what do you expect?) But thanks to the good practices of the ultra-professional operators and vigorous conservation efforts, the diving experience here rates a definite thumbs-up. (The Grand Cayman operators make sure divers' professed expertise really is up to snuff and that a diver has a current card from one of the national diving schools. We've been on islands where dive operators didn't even ask about those things.)

If something does go wrong during a dive, the island has a decompression chamber; most cases of decompression sickness (or "the bends") can be successfully treated locally (see Chapter 21).

Taking a scuba course

If you've never tried scuba diving, Grand Cayman is a great place to get your feet wet. You can take a *resort,* or introductory, course in the morning and make your virgin dive that afternoon. You won't have to worry about strong currents, and the (usually) patient dive instructors are used to dealing with beginners. A resort course allows you to sample the sport (which is expensive) without committing to the much more costly and lengthy process of getting certified.

One resort course designed to teach the fundamentals of scuba to beginners who already know how to swim costs $120. It requires a full day: The morning is spent doing some classroom work and learning skills in the pool; the afternoon incorporates a one-tank dive. All necessary equipment is included. Contact **Bob Soto's Diving Ltd. (☎ 800-BOB-SOTO** or 345-949-2022) or **Red Sail (☎ 877-RED-SAIL** or 345-945-5966) at the Hyatt or Treasure Island Resort. For more information on these companies, see the following section.

If you aren't in good physical shape, or if you have a great deal of anxiety about the prospect of being under the sea, we wouldn't recommend a resort course. Unless you're the type who catches on quickly, you'll feel pushed, and we wouldn't want a bad initial experience to sour you on a great sport. If you have any sort of medical condition that may preclude you from diving, such as high blood pressure, frequent ear infections, or sinusitis, you'll need to obtain clearance from a doctor on-island who specializes in dive medicine. The dive shop will give you a referral.

If you're interested in becoming a certified diver, we strongly urge you to do all your coursework at home. Otherwise, you may be certifiable after you realize how much precious beach and dive time you have to waste so close and yet so far from the Caribbean. Your local YMCA probably teaches a certification course with necessary pool work. Then you can simply do your check-out dives in Grand Cayman and get official.

Peeking into an underwater world

What if you're not a diver? Snorkeling on Grand Cayman allows you to see much of the same scenery thanks to the incredible clarity of the water. More than 400 species of fish and more than 100 species of coral have been identified in these reefs. Popular spots where you can snorkel right off the beach include the **West Bay Cemetery Reef, Public Beach, Wreck of the Cali, Smith's Cove, Devil's Grotto,** and **Eden Rock.**

The snorkeling is excellent off the north coast. Many fish have taken to the Russian warship that was scuttled offshore. (Look for the beautiful queen angelfish that make their home between two of the guns.)

All the dive operators listed in the previous section offer snorkeling trips, but one of our favorites is **Captain Marvin's Water Sports** (☎ **800-550-6288,** ext. 3451, or 345-945-4590; Fax: 345-945-5673; E-mail: CAPTMVN@candw.ky). Octagenarian Captain Marvin Ebank, who has been in business since 1951 and who unofficially founded Stingray City (see the following section), is still operating an all-day snorkel tour of the north shore, taking guests out on his 40-passenger *Miss Jackie* every day except Sunday. The boat leaves at 9 a.m. for Conch Point, where you can see live queen conch (pronounced *conk* — as in what you'll get on the head if you try to remove any of these shells). The second stop is at a colorful shallow barrier reef. Lunch is Caymanian fare on Kaibo Beach. After lunch, it's full-speed ahead to Stingray City, with a final stop at Coral Gardens.

Swimming with the stingrays

If you book a tour to **Stingray City,** which is 2 miles east of Grand Cayman's northwestern tip, forget walking shoes — you'll need your swimsuit. At this unusual underwater attraction (accessible via an easy dive in the 12-foot waters of North Sound or by snorkeling across the surface), you'll see hordes of graceful creatures. (We're talking stingrays, not tourists.) We absolutely love this place. Seeing all these beautiful creatures flitting about is surreal.

In the mid 1980s, when local fishers cleaned their catches and dumped the leftovers overboard, they noticed swarms of southern stingrays (which usually eat marine crabs) feeding on the debris, a phenomenon that quickly attracted local divers and marine zoologists. Today, between 30 and 70 relatively tame stingrays hover for daily handouts of squid from increasing hordes of snorkelers and scuba enthusiasts.

Treasure Island Divers (☎ **800-872-7552** or 345-949-4456) charges divers $45 and snorkelers $25 to visit this unusual attraction. The trip starts Monday, Wednesday, Friday, and Sunday at 1:30 p.m.

During the summer, Captain Sterlin Ebanks of **Stingray City Tours** (call ☎ **345-949-9200,** ext. 71, and ask for the "Summer Special") gives half off the three-hour Stingray City snorkel trip, which stops at Stingray City, Coral Garden, and the shallow barrier reef. For $20, you get snorkeling equipment, refreshments, and a free pickup from Seven Mile Beach. Trips depart daily at 10:00 a.m. and 1:30 p.m. You must reserve in advance and pay cash to get this price.

Enjoying the Waves without Getting Wet

If you're yearning for a peek under the sea but don't want to dive, you still have plenty of options. *Atlantis XI* on Goring Avenue (☎ **800-253-0493** or 345-949-7700) is a $3 million submersible that's 65 feet long, weighs 80 tons, and was built to carry 48 passengers. You can view the reefs and colorful tropical fish through the 26 two-foot-wide windows as the vessel cruises at a depth of 100 feet through a coral garden maze. *Atlantis XI* dives Monday through Saturday; reservations are recommended 24 hours in advance.

You have two options when boarding the *Atlantis XI:*

✔ *Atlantis Odyssey* features such high-tech extras as divers communicating with submarine passengers by wireless underwater phone. This 45-minute dive costs $82.

✔ *Atlantis Expedition* lets you see the famous Cayman Wall, lasts 55 minutes, and costs $72 for adults, $49 for ages 13 to 18, and $36 for kids 4 to 12; no children under age 4 allowed.

Seaworld Explorer, which costs $24, is a semi-submarine that introduces viewers to the marine life of Grand Cayman. Children 4 to 12 are charged $19; younger children are free. The *Deep Explorer*, which takes two passengers, is a submersible that goes 200 yards offshore and then drops to 800 feet ($345 per person) or 1,000 feet ($450 per person).

Telling fish tales

Sport fishers come to Grand Cayman from all over the world for a chance at reeling in one of the big ones: tuna, wahoo, and marlin. Most hotels can make arrangements for charter boats; experienced guides are also available. We recommend **Captain Frank Ebanks** (Frank's Watersports, Coconut Place on West Bay Road; ☎ **345-945-5491** or 345-949-3143). With three decades of experience, he offers deep-sea fishing excursions in search of tuna, wahoo, and marlin on a variety of air-conditioned vessels. Half-day tours depart at 7 a.m. and 1 p.m. and cost $400; full-day tours cost $575. The fee can be split. He also takes people out for reef, bone, and tarpon fishing (half day $300; full day with seafood lunch $450).

Navigating the waves

The best-known water-skiing outfitter is **Red Sail Sports** in the Hyatt Regency Cayman on West Bay Road (☎ 345-945-5966). Water-skiing outings can be arranged for $75 per hour, with the cost divided among several skiers. Parasailing, which yields a great view of George Town, is offered for $50 per ride. Other outfitters are found at the **Westin Casuarina** (☎ 345-949-8732), **Rum Point** (☎ 345-947-9203), and the **Marriott Grand Cayman Beach Resort** (☎ 345-949-6343), all charging comparable prices.

Speed freaks looking for some thrills will be glad to know that jet-skiing is allowed off Seven Mile Beach, where you can skip over the surf at more than 30 mph. You'll be several yards off shore. After a quick lesson in operating the watercraft and a review of some safety tips, you'll be on your way. We personally don't like these things, and we'd like to see them eliminated from rental options, particularly in a spot known for its reefs. Many islands have banned jet skis because of the damage they wreak on the reefs, not to mention the noise they produce. Check with your resort's front desk for the nearest watersports operator offering jet-skiing — if you must.

Some jet-skiers ignore swimmers and divers in the area and come too close — we know you won't be that careless.

If you prefer a gentler approach to the waves, you can glide quietly along the water enjoying the warm Cayman breezes from your rented sailboat. Anchor in a shallow spot and snorkel or swim to cool off. Red Sail Sports rents 16-foot Prindle catamarans for $28 per hour, depending on the time of day.

Living It Up on Dry Land

The underwater delights are the main attraction on Grand Cayman, but sea-based exploration only scratches the surface of available activities on this island. Check out a few other options for your vacation pleasure.

Teeing off

Grand Cayman offers an unusual golf experience at the **Britannia Golf Club** (☎ 345-949-8020), next to the Hyatt Regency on West Bay Road. The course, the first of its kind in the world, was designed by Jack

Nicklaus. It incorporates three different courses in one: a 9-hole championship layout, an 18-hole executive setup, and an 18-hole Cayman course. The last was designed for play with the Cayman ball, which goes about half the distance of a regulation ball.

The Britannia's greens fees run $60 to $90 in season, $40 to $65 off-season, depending on the configuration of the course you intend to play. Mandatory cart rentals go for $15 to $25; club rentals, $25. Hyatt guests receive a discounted rate and can reserve 48 hours in advance; the Britannia accepts reservations from everyone else no earlier than 24 hours ahead.

The Links at SafeHaven (☎ 345-949-5988 for tee times) — Grand Cayman's only 18-hole championship course — is a 6,605-yard, par-71 course with panoramic views of the north coast. It bears a resemblance to the old, windswept Scottish coastal courses known as Links, from which it takes its name. Call for prices and more information.

Exploring George Town

The good news on Grand Cayman is that you can feel safe walking anywhere on the island. The bad news? You won't have much to look at in your wanderings. The tiny capital of George Town can be explored easily in an afternoon. About the most exciting thing here is the post office on Edward Street where you can buy Cayman Islands' beautiful and highly collectible stamps.

Originally built as a house in 1833, the **Cayman Islands National Museum,** at Harbour Drive (☎ 345-949-8368), was used as a courthouse, a jail (now the gift shop), a post office, and a dance hall before reopening in 1990 as a museum. It's a good entry point to the island's history and way of life. The museum is small but fascinating with good displays and videos that illustrate local geology, flora, and fauna. Admission is $5, and it's open weekdays from 9 a.m. to 5 p.m. and Saturdays from 10 a.m. to 4 p.m.

Pick up a walking-tour map of George Town at the museum gift shop before leaving.

Going to Hell and back

Hell really does exist on Grand Cayman. And we don't mean being caught on a dive boat on a rough day without Dramamine. On Grand Cayman, Hell is a surreal craggy landscape at the far northwest end of West Bay Beach Road, about a half-hour from George Town. When you've reached Hell, that's the end of the line — er, road, we mean. The area got that nickname in the 1930s thanks to the otherworldly rock formation of dolomite and limestone. Caymanians, always looking for a business opportunity, turned the natural sculpture into a tourist attraction. If you want to thrill your friends back home, the postmaster will stamp your postcard with "Hell, Grand Cayman" — a certain hit with those who envied your travel plans.

You'll only want to spend 15 minutes tops in Hell. There's not much to do, and the biggest excitement is getting the postmarked proof that you've been there.

Ivan Farrington, the proprietor of the **Devil's Hangout Gift Shop,** dresses up like the demon himself. While you're buying your postcards, he'll crack lots of jokes about the place — "It's a hell of a town, isn't it? But it's hotter than hell here." He'll also tell you where to go when you leave.

The **Cayman Turtle Farm** (☎ **345-949-3894**; Internet: www.turtle.ky), on Northwest Point near Hell, is the only green sea turtle farm of its kind in the world. However, it was severely damaged by Hurricane Michelle, and at presstime, plans for a new farm (across the road from the old site) had just been hatched. (Many of the turtles were swept out to sea during the hurricane.) Attracting more than a quarter of a million visitors annually, it had been the most popular land-based tourist attraction in the Cayman Islands. On previous visits, we saw turtles ranging in size from smaller than our hand to larger than the floats that people loll on at Seven Mile Beach.

Once the Cayman Islands' surrounding waters were teeming with turtles. (Columbus called the islands Las Tortugas because of them.) Today, these creatures have dwindled alarmingly in numbers; the green sea turtle is now an endangered species.

The turtle farm has a twofold purpose: to provide the local market with edible turtle meat and to replenish the waters with hatchling and yearling turtles. You cannot bring turtle products back into the United States. By the time you read this book, the farm should be well on the road to recovery.

Book the **Turtle Release Eco Tour** and you can participate in a program where you tag and release the endangered creatures. It costs $125 including the rental of snorkel or dive gear. For more info, go to www.turtle.ky or www.divetech.com or contact **Divetech** (☎ **345-949-1700**; E-mail: divetech@candw.ky).

Enjoying a Dose of Local History

At the end of a quiet, mango and mahogany tree-shaded road in Savannah, Grand Cayman, high atop a limestone bluff, lies one of the Caribbean's most spectacular historic restorations. The **Pedro St. James Historic Site** (☎ **345-947-3329**) is an historically accurate reconstruction of a 1780 Great House, which was the birthplace of democracy on the Cayman Islands and its first national landmark. The visitor center offers a 20-minute film that gives a zippy overview of the Cayman Islands' 200-year history. It's a 20-minute ride from George Town. Hours are 8:30 a.m. to 5:00 p.m. daily. Admission is $8 for adults, $4 for children 6 to 12 years old, and free for children under 6.

Hop in your rental car or onto the ferry at the Hyatt Regency dock and head to **Rum Point** on Grand Cayman's quiet north side, a favorite destination for both residents and visitors. Experience island atmosphere the way it used to be (Rum Point was first documented on a 1773 map, and you one can only speculate how it got its name!) in a scenic spot known for its clear, calm waters and tall pines. Swim, snorkel, sink into a hammock (tough to snag during high season) or a lounge chair with a book, or try a glass-bottom boat trip. **The Wreck Bar and Grill** (☎ 345-947-9412), a Rum Point landmark, serves lunch and frosty drinks at picnic tables on the beach, and the **Rum Point Club Restaurant** (☎ 345-947-9412) is a good spot for a beachfront dinner.

Communing with the wildlife

For a terrific walk, do it up royally at **Queen Elizabeth II Botanic Park** (☎ 345-947-9462 or 345-947-3558; for information call 345-947-7873 or e-mail guthrie@candw.ky) at Frank Sound Road on the North Side, about a 45-minute drive from George Town. The short trail (less than a mile long) slices through 60 acres of wetland, swamp, dry thicket, mahogany trees, orchids, and bromeliads. The trail is easy enough for children, and you could easily see it all in under an hour. You may spend two hours if you want to meander through the Heritage Garden and other new additions.

Time your visit for early in the day when the animals are more active. You'll probably see *hickatees,* the freshwater turtles found only on the Caymans and in Cuba. Occasionally you'll spot the rare Grand Cayman parrot or the anole lizard with its cobalt-blue throat pouch. Even rarer is the endangered blue iguana, but you can see 40 of them here. Your best chance to see them in motion is from 8:30 to 10:30 a.m. on a sunny day.

The park is open daily from 9:00 a.m. to 5:30 p.m.; guests are admitted until 4:30 p.m. Admission is $6.25 for adults, $3.15 for children, and free for children 5 and under.

A visitor center offers changing exhibitions, a good gift shop, and a canteen for food and refreshments. We like the new **Heritage Garden** with its restoration of a traditional early-19th-century Caymanian home, garden, and farm, and its floral garden with 2½ acres of flowering plants and traditionally grown fruit trees (mango, breadfruit, tamarind, plum, cherry, and ackee). Around the small lake you'll find many birds.

If you're more athletic and an eco-hound to boot, don't miss one of Grand Cayman's newer attractions: the **Mastic Trail** (west of Frank Sound Road, a 45-minute drive from George Town). This restored

200-year-old footpath winds through a 2-million-year-old woodland area leading to the North Sound. *Islands* magazine gave this site one of its top eco-preservation awards. Named for the majestic mastic tree, the rugged 2-mile trail showcases the reserve's natural attractions, including a native mangrove swamp, traditional agriculture, and an ancient woodland area, home to the largest variety of native plant and animal life found in the Cayman Islands.

The hike is not recommended for children under 6, the elderly, or persons with physical disabilities. Wear comfortable, sturdy shoes and carry water and insect repellent. For reservations, call ☎ 345-945-6588 Monday through Friday.

For $50 per person, you can take a guided tour of **Mastic Trail** that includes transportation and cold soft drinks. For more information and reservations, call ☎ **345-949-1996,** fax 345-949-7494, or write Mastic Trail, P.O. Box 31116 Seven Mile Beach, Grand Cayman. Two-and-a-half-hour guided tours, limited to eight participants, are offered Monday through Friday at 8:30 a.m. and 3:00 p.m., and on Saturday at 8:30 a.m.

Shopping away

The duty-free shopping in George Town encompasses the types of luxury items that you'll also see in the USVIs: silver, china, crystal, Irish linen, and British woolen goods. Unfortunately, you'll also run into such local crafts as black coral jewelry. (We're disappointed to see this sold, especially on an island that relies on pristine corals to entice visitors.)

The prices on many items are not that much better than in the United States. Our advice is to comparison shop before you come so you'll know if you're truly being offered a deal. Don't purchase turtle products or any shells. They cannot be brought into the United States.

Longing for Some Nightlife

Okay, okay . . . you have to understand. Divers expend a lot of energy on their sport, plus some of them would rather see nature's nighttime light show on the coral reefs than hang out in a disco. That means if you're looking for a cranking nightlife, you're on the wrong island.

Barhopping is about as crazy as it gets here, particularly during happy hour (usually from 5 to 7 p.m.). Watching the sunset and trying to see the mysterious green flash that people say they see on the horizon right at the moment the sun sizzles into the sea is the big entertainment. Bars close at 3 a.m. weeknights and at midnight on Saturday and Sunday nights (seems odd that the bar would close at midnight on Saturdays — but it's true). Many are shuttered on Sundays. For other options, look at the freebie magazine *What's Hot* or check the Friday edition of the *Caymanian Compass*.

Sports nuts who can't live without ESPN head to the **Lone Star Bar and Grill** (☎ 345-945-5175) on West Bay Road. There, they can see sports events simultaneously on 15 different TV screens and sip lime and strawberry margaritas. This popular watering hole is a favorite gathering spot for local dive masters, too. Mondays and Thursdays are fajita nights — all-you-can-eat affairs. Tuesday is all-you-can-eat lobster night, virtually unheard of in the Caribbean.

A few nightclubs with dancing have opened recently. Current hotspots are: **O bar** (☎ 345-943-OBAR), a sleek night club at Queen's Court lair on Seven Mile Beach; **Matrix Nite Club and Lounge** (☎ 345-949-7169; dress up), in the Islander Complex behind World Gym, which plays high-tech, high-energy dance music, with Friday being the most packed night; **Bed Restaurant and Lounge** (☎ 345-949-7199), fashioned after the too-hip-for-words nightspot in Miami's South Beach; and old standby **Sharkey's** (☎ 345-947-5366), in the Falls Shopping Centre, Seven Mile Beach, a popular disco and bar filled with rock 'n' roll memorabilia from the 1950s that draws an older, more sedate crowd.

Part VII

Jamaica

The 5th Wave   By Rich Tennant

JAMAICA'S ESCALATOR FALLS

In this part . . .

_J_amaica has something for everyone, from the seasoned traveler to the first-timer in the Caribbean. We sort through the vast array of accommodation choices to highlight our favorites. We also show you how to get to the island and how to safely explore it after you arrive.

The cuisine on this island has a kick; we list some of our favorite spots to experience the fiery variety of local fare. Finally, whether you're looking for water sports or nightlife, we show you how to make the most of your time on Jamaica.

Chapter 24

The Lowdown on Jamaica's Hotel Scene

By Darwin Porter and Danforth Prince

. . . .

In This Chapter

▶ Sizing up hotel locations

▶ Focusing on top hotel picks

. . . .

*N*owhere else in the Caribbean will you find such an array of accommodations. Whatever your needs are, there is probably a bed waiting for you in Jamaica at a price you can afford. You can live here for $20 a night or $1,000 a night — the choice is yours.

Honeymooners fly in by the planeload to stay at the all-inclusive mega-resorts, which were pioneered here before sweeping across the West Indies to such islands as St. Lucia. Some resorts cater to families; others, especially all the Sandals properties, to couples only, defining a loving duo as male and female. Some resorts, especially those in Montego Bay, attract the poshest and most demanding traveler. After staying at Half Moon, the first President Bush recommended it to Junior and his wife, Laura.

Jamaica also rents some of the grandest villas in the West Indies. Harrison Ford or Eddie Murphy may have warmed your bed before you checked in. Some beds for the night are found in funky shacks on the beach, others in palaces like the new Ritz-Carlton at Mo Bay (the nickname the locals use for Montego Bay). And some places in Jamaica (not our recommendations) are so bone-bare that only the most die-hard backpacker doing Jamaica on $5 a day would contemplate a stopover.

Many visitors winging into the fourth largest island in the West Indies let their choice of hotel determine the type of stay they're going to experience. That is especially true of persons who plans to spend nearly all their time at an all-inclusive, venturing out for some shopping or sightseeing before returning to the safety of their compound, where they also take most, if not all, of their meals.

If you're going to Half Moon in Mo Bay, you may want to take along a casually elegant collection of resort wear, especially for dining or entertainment at night, whereas if you're heading for a hedonistic resort in Negril, all you need to bring are a bathing suit, a bed sheet for toga night, and not a lot of luggage.

Figuring Out Where You Want to Stay

The largest concentration of hotels is in Montego Bay, Negril, and Ocho Rios/Runaway Bay, with Port Antonio on the north coast running a distant fourth. Most visitors don't venture outside these large resorts, although a few offerings, such as Jake's on the southern coast, or a Hilton stopover for a business or cultural trip to Kingston, are worth considering, depending on your interest. When you see what each resort has to offer in the pages ahead, you can determine which place you're going to honor with your business.

Montego Bay

If you arrive like most visitors, your plane will land outside Montego Bay, your gateway into the troubled but fascinating island of Jamaica.

The party crowd rushes through the airport and on to Negril in the southwest. Those who stay behind can sample Jamaica's second largest city (Kingston is number one).

A cruise-ship mecca and a growing industrial base, it is also the major resort on the island, with more hotels, more restaurants, and more sightseeing attractions, especially on its periphery, than any other resort. In that regard, it's rivaled only by Ocho Rios. Negril has few sightseeing attractions other than its Seven Mile Beach, which is all it needs.

Montego Bay is the most cosmopolitan and sophisticated of the island's resorts, and it has been ever since its touristic future was launched back in the 1940s when rich travelers came to test the spring-fed waters at **Doctor's Cave Beach** (see Chapter 27), still Mo Bay's number-one beach.

Mo Bay never won any port city beauty contests, like the panoramic harbor at Charlotte Amalie on St. Thomas or the historic, restored old city of San Juan. It is completely undistinguished architecturally, yet it's the center for exploring the most historic sights in western Jamaica. It also has some of the Caribbean's finest golf courses, dwarfing all other competition on the island. It offers the island's best shopping and opens onto a marine park of turquoise waters and stunning underwater formations along its coral reef.

Romantic bargains

Jamaican resorts such as SuperClubs or Sandals compete like Olympic athletes for the honeymoon, anniversary, or even "Romantic Duo" business. All of these chain resorts are all-inclusives centered at Negril, Mo Bay, or Ocho Rios/Runaway Bay. Offerings can change from year to year.

Currently, **SuperClubs** (☎ 800-859-SUPER) is presenting the wedding for free if you stay at one of their hotels. If you book a honeymoon package, the staff handles the paperwork of the actual wedding arrangements. If you book six nights, you get a seventh night free. A wedding cake, champagne, even a nondenominational marriage officer, and the flowers are part of the deal.

Also touting honeymoon packages, **Sandals** (☎ 888-SANDALS) consistently wins as the "world's number one-all inclusive honeymoon destination" from *Brides Magazine*. Sandals also features a package for "renewal of marriage vows." Subject to change, prizes such as a free 20-piece Royal Doulton china set is offered to couples who book for six nights or more. The basic wedding package is free, though restrictions may apply. This could represent a savings of up to $1,500.

Kingston may be rioting and killing policemen, the countryside languishing in poverty, but Mo Bay puts on a smiling face for its visitors, the mainstay of its economy.

College students started coming here for spring break during the first few weeks of March. But when word spread about the nudity and ganja smoking in Negril, there was a rush to the southwest.

Negril

Kick-back-'n-groove Negril, on the arid western tip of the island, lies a 50-minute drive southwest of Mo Bay (usually a two-hour drive) but is a world apart.

This once-sleepy fishing village was discovered by the hippies of the 1960s, who took to its ganja smoking and nudity, two cultural pastimes of that era that still flourish here. In those days, the counter-culture press heralded Negril as a "groovy outpost," with no phones, no electricity, and plenty of free sex.

Old reputations take a long time to die, and there is still somewhat of a '60s aura about Negril, especially at a handful of raunchy resorts such as Hedonism II.

There is also another, more sophisticated Negril, evoked by its first-class resorts that are bringing a more mature dimension to Negril, even attracting the family trade.

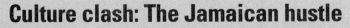

Culture clash: The Jamaican hustle

If you're going to walk along any resort in Jamaica on your own, chances are you'll acquire an unwanted companion or two. Hustlers hawking everything from ganja to sex, or else offering their services as a "guide," attach themselves to you like those leeches that clung to Bogie in the film classic *The African Queen.* Getting rid of them can take some powerful persuasion on your part — a simple "no" rarely turns off these battle-hardened veterans. You may have to call one of the resort police (if you can spot one) to get rid of these uninvited walking companions.

Negril's Seven Mile Beach of white sand is what put it on the tourist map in the '60s and keeps it there — that and three sheltered bays, including Negril Harbour (still nicknamed Bloody Bay from its whale-slaughtering days), Orange Bay, and Long Bay.

There are two faces to Negril. The beachfront is home to the mega-resorts, which lie along Norman Manley Boulevard. This two-lane high-way is flanked by restaurants, shops, and hotels and is bordered by the seemingly endless sands, some of which are for nudists.

The West End, where Stella went to get her groove back, lies south of Negril River and is a journey back to the resort's '60s heyday. Here the little inns are more intimate and raffish. Instead of a beach, visitors swim off the limestone cliffs honeycombed with caves.

As Negril moves into the 21st century, it is improving and becoming more of a world-class resort, although it is leagues away from overtaking Mo Bay in exclusivity. Negril has none of the world-class resorts that Mo Bay has — nothing like Half Moon (covered later in this chapter) for example.

From the end of February and over the Easter weekend, thousands of students from America's East Coast colleges descend on Negril for one massive hell-raising good time. It's called "Don't Stop the Carnival," with action around the clock, including reggae concerts, wet T-shirt competitions, dancing in foam flavored with piña-colada, whatever. If you're not a spring breaker, you may want to clear out of Negril at this time. You'll be in the minority. "When the students leave," a local vendor, Cosmos, told us, "our fields are stripped of ganja, and all the Red Stripe beer and Appleton Rum are gone."

Ocho Rios/Runaway Bay and Port Antonio

A trio of resorts lure visitors to the lush north coast of Jamaica, which records far more rainfall than the arid south, part of which evokes cactus-studded Arizona.

Nicknamed Ochi, Ocho Rios is the cruise capital of the Jamaica, drawing more visitors by sea than Mo Bay. It is not named for eight rivers, as its name suggests. The Spanish called the section of flowing rapids *los chorreros,* which was corrupted by the English into "ocho rios." There aren't eight rivers anyway. The resort lies about a two-hour drive east of Mo Bay.

The satellite resort of Runaway Bay is first approached as you drive in from the west in car, van, or bus from Mo Bay. Runaway Bay is the site of several all-inclusive resorts but is removed from most of the action and the cruise-ship hordes dominating the center of Ocho Rios.

The tiny little banana and fishing port of Ocho Rios itself has virtually disappeared in a sea of bad commercial architecture and mega-resorts, most of which extend to the east of the center. Ocho Rios opens onto Ocho Rios Bay, dominated by a decaying bauxite-loading terminal evocative of Ohio's Rust Belt.

Many hip jazz aficionados who would head for the more fun-loving resort of Negril instead of Ocho Rios go here anyway for the most important jazz festival in the Caribbean. The week-long **Ocho Rios Jazz Festival** presented at various venues takes place annually during the second week in June. Some of the biggest names in jazz from both America and the West Indies perform at this time. For details, call ☎ **323-857-5358** or go to www.ochoriosjazz.com.

The busy port town of Ocho Rios may be meager on attractions within its central core, but it's set against a lush section of the north coast. Easy half– or full-day trips are possible east, west, or south. Waterfalls, grottoes, some of Jamaica's most luxuriant gardens, and old plantations can occupy your time when you're not on the beach.

Most of the all inclusives lie on the beach-studded coast east of Ocho Rios. If you demand a hotel on the beach, these are for you. Others prefer to be more remotely located, and there are properties on the hillsides, most of which are within a 10– to 15-minute commute of a good beach. There are also various secret nooks and crannies where you can stay, places not known to the masses who descend on the center.

One such "secret" address is an apartment over the **Coyaba River Garden and Museum** (see Chapter 27 for more details). In the heart of these beautiful gardens you can rent an apartment year-round for $100 a night. Decorated in a Caribbean tropical motif with wood furnishings, the rental comes with one bedroom, a large living room, and a veranda, with air-conditioning, TV, kitchenette, and a private phone line.

The beach strip between Ocho Rios and Port Antonio to the east put the north coast on the tourist maps of the world when they were discovered by such celebrated figures as Sir Noel Coward. He and his lover, Graham Payn, erected a home, Firefly, here that attracted everybody from the Queen Mother of England to Sir Winston Churchill, along with his "bloody loved ones" such as Katharine Hepburn. Errol Flynn claimed that he personally "discovered" the glories of Port Antonio when his yacht washed ashore in a storm. In time, Ian Fleming in 1946 constructed "Goldeneye" at Oracabessa, where he created the character of "007," James Bond, in 1952. Today this property (☎ **800-688-7678** or 876-975-3354) is open to the "public" — that is, those who can afford it, and we're talking the likes of Jim Carey or Martha Stewart, who shell out 6,000 big ones a night for the entire property.

The all-inclusive: A safe haven or not for you?

Of all the resorts of Jamaica, the all-inclusive has virtually taken over Ocho Rios, although Mo Bay and Negril have their fair share. The concept was pioneered by Jamaica's Butch Stewart with his Sandals properties (☎ **888-SANDALS**) and has since swept the Caribbean, including such islands as St. Lucia. Sandals caters only to couples (male/female), although most other resorts welcome all known couplings.

All-inclusives are not for the independent traveler. At the all-inclusive, you get all your meals and most activities paid for as part of a package. Some dine-around plans help you break the monotony of eating at the same resort every night. With their 24-hour security force, these all-inclusives give you more protection than the smaller, independent inns without such expensive patrolling.

If you're an adventure traveler, you may not want such womb-like security. You may prefer to stay at a small inn or little hotel where you're free to roam throughout the day, returning to your bed after a night of rum and reggae on the town.

Like a mother hen, the all-inclusive will pamper you during your entire stay, even pick you up at the airport and haul you back there for your return flight. At the little independent inn or small hotel, you're more or less on your own. The choice is yours.

If you don't want to stick to the all-inclusives, one of the best travel agencies specializing in hotel deals is **Changes in L'Attitudes** (☎ **800-330-8272**; Internet: www.changes.com). Its Web site is fast loading and informative. For villas in Mo Bay, Ocho Rios, and Port Antonio, contact **Elegant Resorts International** (P.O. Box 80, Montego Bay, Jamaica; ☎ **800-237-3237**; Fax: 876-953-9563).

To the east of Ocho Rios, Port Antonio is still an elite retreat for some film stars, such as Harrison Ford and Eddie Murphy, although it no longer has the cache it did in the '50s and '60s when some of the golden-age movie stars showed up.

Still used as a film site every year or so, Port Antonio positively slumbers when compared to the other resorts just previewed, and it is for this reason we like it so.

Set against a lush background with some of the best beaches in Jamaica, the hotels here suffer a low occupancy rate. That means that many of the glamour addresses of yesterday aren't kept in state-of-the-art condition, because the hotels can't generate enough money to maintain them properly. Still, there's a lovely, nostalgic, and evocative decay over the place that can make for a charming interlude for those who require tranquility on their holiday and who want to escape the masses who overrun the other resorts.

Jamaica's Best Accommodations

The rack rates listed are in U.S. dollars and are for a standard double room during high season (mid-December through mid-April), unless otherwise noted. Lower rates are available in spring, summer, and fall. See Chapter 2 for more information on travel seasons.

Banana Shout
$ **Negril**

The owner of this resort, Detroit-born Mark Conklin, a psychologist, wrote the best novel yet on Negril. *Banana Shout* is a racy story of hippies, voodoo, drug smugglers, and a displaced wild counterculture. A colony of seven handsomely furnished cottages are set on 2½ acres of tropical gardens with waterfalls and fruit trees opening onto a cliff in the West End. Concrete steps crossing tiered decks lead down to the garden. All the bedrooms, furnished with handcrafted pieces, contain kitchenettes and ceiling fans.

4 West End Rd. (P.O. Box 4), Negril. ☎ *876-957-0384. Fax: 876-957-0384. Internet:* `http://theone.negril.com/bananashout`. *Rack rates: $45–$100 double. MC, V.*

Charela Inn
$$$ **Negril**

On a choice 3-acre plot of landscaping on Seven Mile Beach, this 49-room resort was designed to evoke an Iberian hacienda. It has long been the market leader in the moderately priced field and caters to an independent traveler not wanting to book into one of the all-inclusives. Close to

Jamaica Accommodations

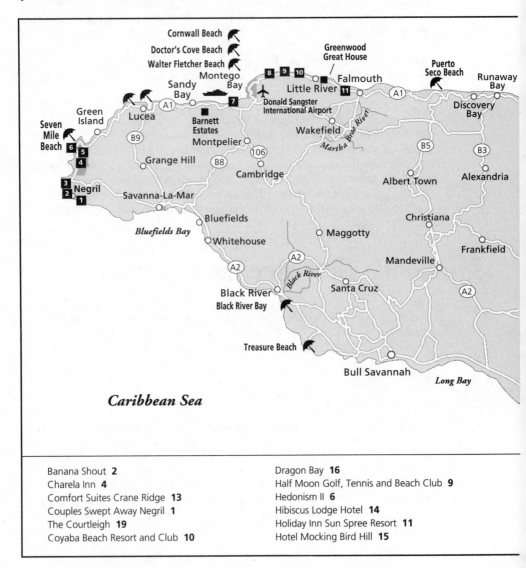

Cornwall Beach
Doctor's Cove Beach
Walter Fletcher Beach
Greenwood Great House
Puerto Seco Beach
Runaway Bay
Montego Bay
Sandy Bay
8 **9** **10**
Falmouth
Little River **11**
Donald Sangster International Airport
Discovery Bay
Green Island
Lucea
A1
Barnett Estates
Wakefield
Martha Brae River
Seven Mile Beach
6 **5**
4
B9
Montpelier
B5
B3
Grange Hill
B8
106
Cambridge
Albert Town
Alexandria
3
2 Negril
1
Savanna-La-Mar
Bluefields
Maggotty
Christiana
Frankfield
Bluefields Bay
Whitehouse
Mandeville
A2
A2
Black River
Black River
Black River Bay
Santa Cruz
A2
Treasure Beach
Bull Savannah
Long Bay

Caribbean Sea

Banana Shout **2**	Dragon Bay **16**
Charela Inn **4**	Half Moon Golf, Tennis and Beach Club **9**
Comfort Suites Crane Ridge **13**	Hedonism II **6**
Couples Swept Away Negril **1**	Hibiscus Lodge Hotel **14**
The Courtleigh **19**	Holiday Inn Sun Spree Resort **11**
Coyaba Beach Resort and Club **10**	Hotel Mocking Bird Hill **15**

Sandals, it is a world apart in aura from that couples-only resort (covered later in this section). A self-reliant guest checks in here into one of the rooms overlooking the water or the garden. Accommodations are full of character, often with a four-poster bed. We try to avoid the rooms on the ground floor with their barred patios. The on-site Le Vendôme restaurant serves one of the finest prix-fixe meals in Negril, and offers live music on Thursday and Saturday nights. Children under 10 stay free in their parents' rooms. On site is a pool; windsurfing and Sunfish sailing can be arranged.

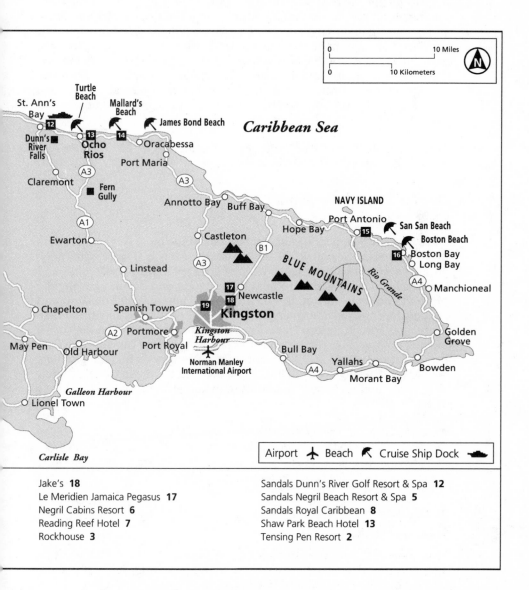

St. Ann's Bay
Turtle Beach
Mallard's Beach
James Bond Beach
Dunn's River Falls
Ocho Rios
Oracabessa
Port Maria
Claremont
Fern Gully
Caribbean Sea
NAVY ISLAND
Annotto Bay
Buff Bay
Port Antonio
San San Beach
Ewarton
Castleton
Hope Bay
Boston Beach
Boston Bay
Long Bay
Linstead
BLUE MOUNTAINS
Rio Grande
Manchioneal
Chapelton
Spanish Town
Newcastle
Kingston
Kingston Harbour
Portmore
Port Royal
Golden Grove
May Pen
Old Harbour
Norman Manley International Airport
Bull Bay
Yallahs
Bowden
Morant Bay
Galleon Harbour
Lionel Town
Carlisle Bay

Airport ✈ Beach 🏖 Cruise Ship Dock ⛴

Jake's **18**
Le Meridien Jamaica Pegasus **17**
Negril Cabins Resort **6**
Reading Reef Hotel **7**
Rockhouse **3**

Sandals Dunn's River Golf Resort & Spa **12**
Sandals Negril Beach Resort & Spa **5**
Sandals Royal Caribbean **8**
Shaw Park Beach Hotel **13**
Tensing Pen Resort **2**

Norman Manley Boulevard (P.O. Box 33), Negril. ☎ **800-423-4095** in the U.S. or 876-957-4648. Fax: 876-957-4414. Internet: www.charela.com. *Rack rates:* $158–$210 double. AE, MC, V.

Comfort Suites Crane Ridge
$ **Ocho Rios**

Okay, so it's no Sandals or even Shaw Park (covered later in this section), but where can you stay in comfort in a suite in Ocho Rios at $50 per person in the dead of winter? Its location on 7 acres of landscaped grounds is admittedly not on the beach, but a free hotel shuttle will take you to some golden sands in just ten minutes. All the well-furnished and comfortable accommodations are suites, either one or two bedrooms, each with air-conditioning and with a kitchenette. Independently minded travelers who shun the all-inclusives like it here, and it's also a favorite with families who prefer to prepare some of their own meals. Onsite is a fairly standard restaurant and two bars, plus a pool, but most sports and activities you plan for yourself.

17 Da Costa Dr., Ocho Rios. ☎ *800-221-2222 in the U.S., or 876-974-8050. Fax: 876-974-8070. Rack rates: $100 double. AE, MC, V.*

Couples Swept Away Negril
$$$$$ Negril

Midway along Seven Mile Beach, this is one of the most elegant of the all-inclusive properties in Negril. A special feature is a 10-acre adult play-ground across the boulevard, featuring Negril's best health club and tennis courts along with aerobics classes, yoga, and the like. Locally the place is known for attracting "health nuts," whereas Hedonism II and Sandals lure the most sexually active. A total of 134 well-furnished bedrooms are spread across 26 two-story villas with large balconies over-looking the water. At the beach is a grill offering spicy Jamaica fare, and there is also a veggie bar. Water sports are strong here, including sailing, scuba, windsurfing, water-skiing, kayaking, and snorkeling. In all, there's more taste and style here than that reflected at the other all-inclusives along the strip.

Norman Manley Boulevard, Long Bay (P.O. Box 77), Negril. ☎ *800-COUPLES in the U.S. and Canada, or 876-957-4061. Fax: 876-957-4060. Internet:* www.sweptaway.com. *Rates: $1,665–$2,050 per couple. Rates are for three nights and are all-inclusive, including airport transfers. AE, MC, V.*

The Courtleigh
$-$$ Kingston

More personal and welcoming than the Pegasus (covered later in this section), this 126-unit, six-story hotel is also more affordable. It is sand-wiched between the Jamaica Hilton and the Pegasus in the heart of the business and diplomatic district of New Kingston, a lot safer place to be at night than the historic quarter bordering the waterfront. Bedrooms are well furnished, often with hardwood pieces such as mahogany and the occasional four-poster bed. The suites are especially recommended, because they have walk-in closets and large desks. The on-site restau-rant, Alexander's, is a worthy choice for dining, and there are also two bars, a swimming pool, and a gym.

85 Knutsford Blvd. ☎ *876-929-9000. Fax: 876-926-7744. Internet:* www.courtleigh.com. *Rack rates: $125–$145 double. AE, MC, V.*

Coyaba Beach Resort and Club

$$$$–$$$$$ **Montego Bay**

Only a 15-minute ride east of Mo Bay, but a world apart, Coyaba opens
onto a beautiful strip of white sands along a private beach. All-inclusive,
the 50-unit gem evokes a colonial atmosphere with its plantation-style
decor and Great House. Personally managed by the Robertson family, it
offers well-furnished units in the main structure or, even better, in a three-
floor complex near the beach. Mahogany furnishings and hand-carved
bedsteads are grace notes, and junior suites come with refrigerators. A
fishing dock with a cabana juts out into the bay. Children are welcome and
have their own programs and video library with baby-sitter arranged.
Good food is served at two restaurants, and facilities also include a pool,
three bars, tennis court, health club and spa, plus water sports.

Mahoe Bay, Little River (P.O. Box 88), Montego Bay. ☎ *877-COYABA-8 or
876-953-9150. Fax: 876-953-2244. Internet:* www.coyabajamaica.com. *Rack
rates: $290–$390 double. Meal plans $105 per person. Three-night minimum stay
required in winter. Honeymoon packages available. Kids ages 12 and under stay
and eat free in parents' room. AE, MC, V.*

Dragon Bay

$$$ **Port Antonio**

So maybe it's a little battered here and there, but the 90-unit Dragon Bay
is still an appealing choice, its bungalows and villas opening onto a pri-
vate sandy beach. Many Europeans check in for long stays, enjoying the
location on the water and the grounds that front 55 acres of lush forest.
The setting is so idyllic that filmmakers have used the resort as a back-
drop for such flicks as the remake of the *Lord of the Flies.* The world may
have forgotten the Tom Cruise movie, *Cocktail* (even the actor himself
wants to forget that one), but the film is immortalized here at the Cruise
Bar, one of three on-site bars. Most units contain kitchens, although on
site are a pair of restaurants and a grill on the beach. Two tennis courts
and a good dive shop round out the facilities.

P.O. Box 176, Port Antonio. ☎ *876-993-8751. Fax: 876-993-8971. Internet:* www.
dragonbay.com. *90 units. Winter $175–$205 double; $240–$270 1-bedroom suite;
$360 2-bedroom suite; $440 3-bedroom suite. Off-season $120–$150 double; $200 1-
bedroom suite; $250 2-bedroom suite; $320 3-bedroom suite. AE, MC, V.*

Half Moon Golf, Tennis, and Beach Club

$$$$$ **Montego Bay**

For the visitor seeking a deluxe resort without the stuffiness of some of
Mo Bay's grand dames, this is the finest choice in all of Jamaica. This
well-landscaped, sprawling 419-unit colony is set on 400 acres with a half-
mile of white crescent-shaped sandy beach 8 miles east of the center of
Mo Bay. It is consistently ranked as one of the world's leading resorts, a
luxurious hideaway of refinement and style. It's one of those amazing

compounds that can appeal to everybody from golfers or horsemen (or –women), to honeymooners or families. Golfers flock to its Robert Trent Jones, Sr.–designed 18-hole golf course. Everyone from the queen of Jamaica (Elizabeth II of England) to the first President Bush has temporarily called Half Moon home. Villas with private pools are the posh way to go, but even the standard doubles are luxuriously furnished, often with Queen Anne or Chippendale reproductions.

The on-site Sugar Mill serves the resort's finest food, but there are 5 other restaurants as well, along with 6 bars and 13 tennis courts. Sports such as horseback riding or deep-sea fishing are arranged.

Children view Half Moon as a Shangri-La, with their special pool, playhouses, tennis courts, and donkey rides.

Rose Hall, Montego Bay. ☎ *800-626-0592 or 876-953-2211. Fax: 876-953-2731. Internet:* www.halfmoon.net. *Rack rates: $390–$490; from $590 suite. Breakfast and dinner $70 per person. Wedding and honeymoon packages available. AE, MC, V.*

Hedonism 11
$$$$$ Negril

It's called the "human zoo." Nowhere in the Caribbean is there such an aptly named resort, 280 units filled with a hell-raising crew intent on fun in the sun, naked or otherwise. For revelers, it's Ground Zero. Located 2 miles east of the town center, the resort colony lies at the northern tip of Negril Beach. Racy, wild, and woolly, the resort invites you to go "wicked for a week." The notorious toga parties would make Nero feel right at home. Singles (mostly male) coexist with couples on the beach with its nude and prude sides. Its five bars stay busy day and night, and a trio of restaurants serves standard fare — but plenty of it. Other facilities include two pools and six tennis courts, plus a dive shop and fitness center. As for the rooms, the more time you spend outside the better. They're not special, with tired furnishings and beds that have seen much gymnastics in their day.

Negril Beach Road (P.O. Box 25), Negril. ☎ *800-859-7873 in the U.S. or 876-957-5200. Fax: 876-957-5289. Internet:* www.superclubs.com. *Rack rates: $2,040–$2,280 double. Rates are all inclusive for 4 days/3 nights. AE, DC, DISC, MC, V.*

Hibiscus Lodge Hotel
$$ Ocho Rios

Long the choice of the frugal traveler, this venerated old inn is built on a cliff three blocks from the Ocho Rios Mall and overlooking the wide sands of Mallards Bay Beach. Run in a personable, welcoming way, it's near the center of town, with its shops and restaurants, although the on-site restaurant itself (see Chapter 26) is one of the finest in the area and is known for its Jamaican fare. The bedrooms are large and well furnished, and many are suitable for trios. Units open onto the sea, and on site is a pool suspended over the cliffs and enveloped by a spacious sundeck.

83 Main St. (P.O. Box 52), Ocho Rios, St. Ann. ☎ *876-974-2676. Fax: 876-974-1874. E-mail:* mdoswald÷jamaica.com. *Rack rates: $115–$126 double. AE, DC, MC, V.*

Holiday Inn SunSpree Resort
$$$$ Montego Bay

This family friendly, all-inclusive lies on a half-mile of white-sand beach set on 12 landscaped acres. After a $13 million renovation, it is shipshape once again, especially in its 76 oceanfront rooms. The 523-unit hotel is one of the island's largest and is housed in a seven-floor structure. Rooms are tastefully and comfortably furnished, ranging from midsize to spacious and opening onto balconies. Nonstop action is the keynote here so try to book away from the dining and nightlife sections. Kids are favored here with their own play area with splashing fountains and children's programs. The resort offers standard but well-prepared food in its restaurants, and its four bars are always active. Four tennis courts, a dive shop, three pools, a fitness center, and other facilities, plus entertainment and nearby golf, add to its allure.

P.O. Box 480, Rose Hall (5 miles east of Montego Bay). ☎ *800-HOLIDAY or 876-953-2485. Fax: 876-953-2840. Internet:* www.sixcontinentshotels.com/holiday-inn. *Rack rates: $280–$540 double. Rates all-inclusive. AE, MC, V.*

Hotel Mocking Bird Hill
$$ Port Antonio

For the eco-conscious traveler, this is the number-one choice in Jamaica. This welcoming ten-room inn lies a five-minute drive from the golden sands of Frenchman's Cove Beach and 6 miles east of Port Antonio in the foothills of the Blue Mountains. On 7 "natural" acres of land, 600 feet above the coastline, two women with a vision, Barbara Walker and Shireen Aga, created this little charmer, which is like a B&B. Rooms have either air-conditioning or ceiling fans, and the water is solar heated. The furniture is locally made from bamboo. The on-site restaurant, Mille Fleurs, is worth a special trip even if you're a nonguest (see the review in Chapter 24). Don't expect phones or TVs in the bedrooms — it's not that kind of place. Drop into the on-site art gallery for a look at some of Ms. Walker's art along with that of other artists.

If you don't like dogs, or are allergic to them, better book elsewhere. The owners' lovable but large mutts have the run of the joint and add to the cozy charm of the place — that is, for those who, like us, love dogs.

Mocking Bird Hill, East of Port Antonio on North Coast Highway (P.O. Box 254), Port Antonio. ☎ *876-993-7267 or 876-993-7133. Fax: 876-993-7133. Internet:* www.hotelmockingbirdhill.com. *Rack rates: $180–$230 double. AE, MC, V.*

Jakes

$–$$$ Treasure Beach

This is the ultimate escapist's retreat, lying on the undeveloped and arid south coast of Jamaica east of Negril. Constructed on a cliff overlooking a scenic bay, this special, 15-room retreat lies adjacent to a rocky beach below. It's funky and fun; its colony of buildings seemingly inspired by some Moroccan Casbah. Sally Henzell, a Jamaican of British ancestry, and her husband, director/producer of that reggae classic, *The Harder They Come,* created this hip joint, finding inspiration from anyone, but especially from Antoní Gaudí, the controversial Barcelona architect. If you like outdoor showers, painted concrete floors, saltwater pools where guests appear in "the minimum" if that, and green glass bottles embedded in stucco, this is your kind of place. It's too laid-back for the crowd that books into such resorts as Sandals. Even if you don't stay here, try to visit for its restaurant on a day trip down from Negril. If ever an inn in Jamaica deserved to be called rustic chic, it's Jake's. It's our kind of place.

If you need to live in a refrigerator when visiting Jamaica, Jake's is not for you. This is cactus country, and its hot ceiling fans are not adequate at times. Mosquito nets are provided for good reason, because those sand flies will find you a tasty morsel.

Treasure Beach, Calabash Bay P.A., Saint Elizabeth. ☎ *800-OUTPOST or 876-965-0635. Fax: 876-965-0552. Internet:* www.islandoutpost.com. *Rack rates: $95–$225 double. AE, MC, V.*

Le Meridien Jamaica Pegasus

$$$ Kingston

For the business traveler or for the visitor who wants to absorb some of the cultural attractions of Jamaica's capital, this is the finest choice in New Kingston, overtaking its closest rival, the almost as good nearby hotel, the Kingston Hilton, 77 Knutsford Blvd. (☎ **876-926-5430**). A 17-floor, 343-room high-rise (at least in Kingston skyscraper terms), the hotel lies at the core of the business and diplomatic center of Kingston, offering the finest dining and leisure facilities in the city, with a trio of restaurants, two bars, two tennis courts, a swimming pool, and a gym. From its pizzas to its seafood, the Pegasus is a good dining choice even for nonguests visiting New Kingston. The accommodations are medium in size but well equipped with such amenities as safes and coffeemakers. Try for a guest room with a balcony overlooking the bay or the Blue Mountains in the distance. The staff here is better trained than at any other hotel in Kingston.

81 Knutsford Blvd., off Oxford Road, Kingston. ☎ *876-926-3690. Fax: 876-929-5855. Internet:* www.jamaicapegasus.com. *Rack rates: $190–$205 double. AE, MC, V.*

Negril Cabins Resort

$$$$$ **Negril**

Set on a 10-acre site of tropical gardens, this cabin colony lies across from a wide sandy beach at Bloody Bay. An 84-unit complex, it features wood-built cabins constructed on stilts in a setting of mango trees, royal palms, and bull thatch. From your tree-level balcony you can look into the garden or at the ocean beyond. The finest accommodations here, called "executive suites" for some reason, contain a sunken living and dining section and air-conditioning. Other units are cooled by ceiling fans. The hotel offers a good kids' program, a fitness center, a pool, and tennis courts, and serves fairly decent Jamaican fare in its on-site restaurant. Children under 12 stay free in their parents' room.

Rutland Point, Manley Boulevard (P.O. Box 118), Negril. ☎ *800-382-3444 or 876-957-5350. Fax: 876-957-5381. Internet:* www.negril-cabins.com. *Rack rates: $360–$510 double for 3 nights. AE, MC, V.*

Reading Reef Hotel

$$ **Montego Bay**

A 15-minute drive west of Montego Bay, this informal 28-unit resort is imbued with class and comfort, lying on 2½ landscaped acres and fronting a small but idyllic sandy beach. The colony opens onto scenic reefs once visited by the master himself, Jacques Cousteau. Bedrooms are furnished with first-class appointments, the two– or three-bedroom suites coming with kitchenettes. The restaurant is a worthy choice even if you're not a guest.

Route A1, Bogue Lagoon, Long Hill Road (P.O. Box 225), Reading, Montego Bay. ☎ *876-952-5909. Fax: 876-952-7217. Internet:* www.montego-bay-jamaica. com/jhta/reefclub. *Rack rates: $115–$450 double, from $265 in suite. AE, MC, V.*

Rockhouse

$$ **Negril**

The Rolling Stones checked out in 1970, but under its new Aussie owners this funky 28-unit "boutique inn" is better than ever. With its thatched roof, it looks like something on a remote South Pacific island. Opening onto a small cove, you're perched on a cliffside in Negril's West End. A ladder leads down to the cove for snorkeling and swimming, and there is also a cliffside pool. Hedonism II (covered earlier in this section) isn't really hip. This place is, and so are the outdoor showers for showing off your physical assets. You sleep in a four-poster bed romantically draped in mosquito neeting in the colonial style. Four cottages offer sleeping lofts. Zesty Jamaican food featuring freshly caught fish is served at the on-site restaurant.

West End Road (P.O. Box 3024), Negril. ☎ *876-957-4373. Fax: 876-957-4373. Internet:* www.changes.com/rockhouse. *Rack rates: $130 studio, $210 villa. AE, MC, V.*

Sandals Dunn's River Golf Resort and Spa
$$$$$ Ocho Rios

One of the best members of the Sandals chain in Jamaica, this couples-only (read that "male and female") resorts opens onto a wide beach of white sands lying between Ocho Rios and St. Ann's Bay. The 256-unit complex is set on 25 landscaped acres and is very activity oriented, with complimentary use of an 18-hole, par-71 championship course, the largest hotel pool in Jamaica, 12 tennis courts, and a health club and spa. It's estimated that three-fourths of the guests are young honeymooners, but this Sandals also attracts the silver-haired, some of whom are celebrating a 25th anniversary or whatever. The decor evokes the Mediterranean, with marble columns in its Italian palazzo-syled lobby and in the design of its architecture. This Italianate motif is also carried out in the spacious bedrooms with their walk-in closets and panoramic balconies. The food is superior to many Sandals resorts and is widely varied, ranging from the Caribbean to Japan.

Mammee Bay, Route A3 (P.O. Box 51), Ocho Rios. ☎ *888-SANDALS in the U.S. and Canada, or 876-972-1610. Fax: 876-972-1611. Internet:* www.sandals.com. *Rack rates start at $915 for 2 per night. Three-night minimum stay required. Rates are all-inclusive. AE, MC, V.*

Sandals Negril Beach Resort and Spa
$$$$ Negril

Entrepreneur Butch Stewart long ago invaded Negril with his couples (male/female only) concept of an all-inclusive vacation. Occupying a prime location on Negril's Seven Mile Beach, this 21-acre, 223-unit resort attracts many first-timers to Jamaica, some booked in here on a honeymoon package. The resort is strong on water sports, such as scuba and snorkeling. The best rooms open right onto the sands or have balconies with a sea view. The aura is casual and laid-back, not as raunchy as the notorious Hedonism II (covered earlier in this section). Four restaurants, including a Japanese teppenyaki cuisine prepared at table, give you some variety for on-site dining. With its five bars, Sandals attracts the drinking crowd.

Norman Manley Boulevard (Box 12), Negril. ☎ *888-SANDALS in the U.S. and Canada, or 876-957-5216. Fax: 876-957-5338. Internet:* www.sandals.com. *Rack rates start at $290 per person per night. Three-night minimum stay required. Rates are all-inclusive, including airport transfers. AE, MC, V.*

Sandals Royal Caribbean
$$$$$ Montego Bay

The flagship of all the on-island Sandals Resorts, this couples-only (male/female) all-inclusive is a tiny resort on its own private beach. Some of its former British colonial aura remains, and this is a more refined resort than its sibling, Sandals Montego Bay (☎ 876-952-5510), which has a better beach than the Royal Caribbean but unfortunately lies at the edge of the airport. The 190-unit RC attracts more of an international crowd than the more American-oriented Sandals Montego Bay. The *luxe* beachfront accommodations with their private balconies or patios are preferred, but all the units are well kept and comfortably furnished. There is a variety of cuisine at its four restaurants, including Bali Hai, on a private offshore islet, Sandals Cay. Four bars, three pools, a trio of tennis courts, water sports, entertainment, and a health club keep you action-oriented.

Mahoe Bay, North Coast Highway (Box 167), Montego Bay. ☎ *888-SANDALS or 876-953-2232. Fax: 876-953-2788. Internet:* www.sandals.com. *Rack rates: $1,620–$2,280 per couple for 4 days/3 nights. Rates all inclusive. AE, MC, V.*

Shaw Park Beach Hotel
$$$ Ocho Rios

Constructed around a wide beach of white sands at a private cove, this 106-unit resort is an old favorite that draws many repeat guests. Opening onto Cutlass Bay, one of Jamaica's most panoramic, it lies 2 miles east of the center of Ocho Rios and a 4-mile drive from Dunn's River Falls. You'll recognize its Georgian colonial-style architecture on a hill that's the center of a 25-acre estate. There is still the allure of the 1950s here, although the resort has kept abreast of modern times. There is no frantic activity agenda here as there is in the Sandals property at Dunn's River (covered earlier in this section), although some water sports and a fitness center are found along with a pair of tennis courts. Entertainment ranges from fashion shows to reggae dancing, and reef tours provide daytime amusement. Families with children are welcomed, and there's a kiddies program, a playground, and a pool for the young ones. Without ever rising to greatness, the food is better than the ususal resort fare. Bedrooms are medium sized to roomy, and the preferred ones have a private balcony or terrace fronting the bay.

Cutlass Bay (P.O. Box 17), Ocho Rios. ☎ *800-377-1126 in the U.S. or 876-974-2552. Fax: 876-974-5042. Internet:* www.shawparkhotel.com/main.htm. *Rack rates: $182–$200 double. Free breakfast and dinner for children up to 12 sharing room with parents. Rates include buffet breakfast. Prix-fixe dinner $33 per person extra. MC, V.*

Tensing Pen Resort
$$ Negril

Along West End Road, a 10-minute taxi from Seven Mile Beach, this is an inn of character and a certain raffish charm. Ther 12-unit colony is set in a botanical garden with orchids and bromeliads among other luxuriant growth. An independent-type traveler is attracted to the beautifully furnished bedrooms with tile floors, beds of tropical wood, and refrigerators. Muslin netting drape some of the beds in an evocative touch.

You sleep in a rustic hut bungalow or a cut-stone cottage with outdoor showers. A Great House sleeps friendly groups or families. Guests meet fellow guests when using the large communal kitchen.

West End Road (P.O. Box 13), Negril. ☎ *876-957-0387. Fax: 876-957-0161. Internet:* http://caribbean.wheretostay.com/property/103.html. *Rack rates: $110–$120 double, $420 Great House. AE, MC, V.*

Chapter 25

Settling into Jamaica

By Darwin Porter and Danforth Prince

• •

In This Chapter

▶ Knowing what to expect when you arrive

▶ Getting around the island

▶ Discovering Jamaica from A to Z

• •

Sailing around the lush coasts of Jamaica, Christopher Columbus got it right when he said, "It is the fairest island eyes have beheld; mountainous and the land seems to touch the sky." That was way back in 1494, but the words are still true today.

Except for the island of Grenada, Jamaica is the most lush island in the West Indies, its Blue Mountains reaching a peak at 7,400 feet. It is a land of countless cascading waterfalls (such as Dunn's River in Ocho Rios) and of more than 150 rivers, the most fabled of which is the Rio Grande near Port Antonio on which you can go river rafting.

For such a relatively small land mass — about the size of the state of Connecticut — the terrain is widely varied, from tropical rain forests to an arid southern coast that evokes in parts an African savanna. Jamaica is blessed with some of the best sandy beaches in the Caribbean, most often golden, but sometimes white, and, on occasion, black volcanic sand (found on the south coast).

No one knows exactly how many people inhabit the island of Jamaica, but estimates put the population at 2½ million, of which some 850,000 live in the capital of Kingston. Of these, some 95% claim Africa as their ancestral home.

Although dominated by persons of African descent, Jamaica has such a large polyglot population that its national slogan is, "Out of Many, One People." Thousands of Germans, Irish, Welsh, and English live on the island along with Chinese, Middle Easterners, and East Indians. The Middle Easterners are called "Syrian" by locals. The leader of the Jamaican Labour Party, Edward Seaga, a former prime minister, is Lebanese.

In the West Indies, Jamaicans are known for their sardonic wit and their humor, often using sarcasm as the ultimate putdown, especially of pretentious people. The humor is often lusty, tinged with sexual connotations.

Arriving in Montego Bay or Kingston

Most resort-bound foreign visitors land at the **Donald Sangster International Airport** (☎ 876-952-3124), 2 miles east of the center of Montego Bay, the island's leading resort. This airport not only serves Mo Bay itself, but all the other major resorts, including Ocho Rios and Runaway Bay to the east, and Negril to the southwest, and even such remote south coast villages as Treasure Beach.

Visitors who seek more of an experience with Jamaican culture or else have business there wing into the **Norman Manley International Airport** (☎ 876-924-8235) at Kingston. The Kingston airport is also the closest to those planning a hiking tour of the Blue Mountains or a stay at the small north coast resort of Port Antonio.

Landing in Mo Bay

After you deplane on the tarmac, you walk into the burning heat of the terminal of Jamaica's most efficient airport, which has been expanded and improved in recent years for your convenience. You head directly down a long, air-conditioned corridor to Jamaican Customs and Immigration.

Surprisingly, winter visitors often clear the rather thorough Jamaican Customs faster than summer visitors. The summer months are virtually homecoming months for Jamaicans living abroad. They often arrive with massive luggage, which local officials insist on probing thoroughly. The wait can seem endless, particularly if disputes arise about what Jamaicans are trying to bring back home.

With many exceptions, you can usually clear Customs in less than half an hour. While you wait, a live band will often serenade with everything from reggae to calypso. At a desk of the Jamaican Tourist Board, meager literature on the island is dispensed. There are plenty of coupons touting discounts at attractions, restaurants, bars, and car-rental outfitters.

After you're given the green light by Customs and Immigration, a currency exchange office awaits you. Here is where you can exchange the Yankee dollar for the Jamaican dollar. U.S. money is widely accepted in Jamaica, although sometimes the Jamaican dollar will come in handy. It's wise to exchange at least US$100 into Jamaican dollars for those times you'll need the local coin of the realm.

The currency exchange kiosk at the airport offers better exchange rates than at most banks. Your hotel invariably offers the worst exchange rates. There are some ATMs at the airport, but don't count on these. Readers report that the machines are either out of order or out of cash.

After you've secured your checked luggage, your problems aren't over yet. Guard it carefully both within the airport and when leaving the airport to get into some form of transport. Stolen luggage is a commonplace occurrence, so keep your eagle eye on alert.

Flying into Kingston

Montego Bay is the international airport in the west of Jamaica, with the Norman Manley airport, 11 miles southeast of Kingston, receiving visitors to the eastern shores of Jamaica. Domestic flights — say, from Mo Bay to Kingston — fly into the smaller **Tinson Pen Airport** (☎ **876-987-8068**), to the west of the center of Kingston.

The Norman Manley International Airport lies on the Palisadoes, a narrow strip of land that projects into the Caribbean Sea. After going through Customs and Immigration, which is much tighter than ever following the September 11, 2001, terrorist attacks on the U.S., you enter the main terminal.

On site are a rental desk for Island Car Rentals (covered later in this chapter) and one for Jamaica Union of Travelers Association (JUTA), the official taxi company for Kingston. There is usually a small kiosk of the Jamaican Tourist Board here, which opens to meet major international flights and dispenses *Discover Jamaica,* a booklet with an island-wide map.

As in Mo Bay, keep your eye out for your luggage. Many visitors report having their luggage stolen after they clear Customs and during the time they're arranging ground transportation — either taxi or car — into the center of Kingston.

Getting to Your Accommodations

When your luggage has been inspected at the Donald Sangster airport at Mo Bay, you're officially cleared to enter Jamaica. If you're staying at one of the mega-resorts or the all-inclusives, chances are a hotel van will be waiting to take you to its grounds and check you in. You should have notified your resort of choice in advance before your arrival in Jamaica. The big resorts will have desks at the airport and you can go to the staff there or else look for your resort's name on a placard held up by a hotel van operator.

The attendant for the resorts will have a list of all the arrivals due in at the same time as you, and you won't roll until everyone has been accounted for. Baggage handlers will hoist your luggage onto the hotel bus or into the van. Tip them $1 per bag and watch to be sure that all your luggage makes it on the bus or van. This process for all passengers can take another 20 to 30 minutes.

If you're arranging to rent a car or taxi, be prepared for the "Mo Bay" hustle. Don't hand your luggage over to anyone who comes up to help you. Only deal with an official baggage handler with a badge. The so-called "porter" could actually be a thief, and you'll never see your baggage again. Many pirate taxi drivers in unmarked and uninsured cars will also try to hustle you into their vehicles. Don't go for it. You may leave the airport and head down some back street where a robber — prearranged with the "innocent" taxi driver — will suddenly emerge and steal your possessions from the pirate cab.

By taxi

If you're staying at one of the smaller, more affordable hotels, you'll have to get where you're going on rented wheels. Use only taxis or buses operated by **JUTA** (☎ **876-952-0813;** Fax: 876-952-5355). The union's emblem, a red license plate with the initials PPV (for "public passenger vehicle") indicates an official cab. Unlike pirate cabs, these air-conditioned taxis are insured and licensed to carry you.

An airport taxi dispatcher in front of the terminal holds a clipboard and arranges a ride to where you're going in the Greater Montego Bay area.

By air

The wild rides in speeding vehicles along bumpy, pot-holed roads leading either to Negril or Runaway Bay/Ocho Rios have, over the years, earned notoriety among travelers to Jamaica. You can skip them by taking a small domestic commuter plane to the landing strips at Negril or Ocho Rios.

Flights are aboard **Air Jamaica Express** (☎ 800-523-5585) with local offices in Montego Bay at ☎ **876-952-4300;** in Kingston at ☎ **876-922-4661;** in Negril at ☎ **876-957-5251;** and in Ocho Rios at ☎ **876-975-3254.**

Flights are small and often fully booked, so make reservations before you leave home, either directly through Air Jamaica or through a travel agent. Your departure has to be confirmed a full 72 hours in advance, so be duly warned.

More than 50 scheduled flights per day are flown cross-island by Air Jamaica Express. The airline will fly you to all the air strips at the major resort areas, including Montego Bay, Ocho Rios/Runaway Bay, and Negril. If you land in the west at Mo Bay and want to fly east, Air Jamaica will also take you to Port Antonio, a resort on the northeastern coast, and even Kingston itself. On most flights, you're airborne for only 20 to 30 minutes. A typical one-way fare on the most popular air route, Mo Bay to Negril, costs $60 one-way, with no reduction if you book round-trip.

Sometimes getting a booking aboard Air Jamaica Express isn't possible — either the flight departed without you or you didn't make a reservation far enough in advance. In that case, **Jamaica AirLink** (☎ 877-359-5465 in the U.S. or 876-365-0763 in Jamaica), like Superman, may come to your rescue. This little charter carrier flies between Mo Bay, Negril, Ocho Rios, and even more remote Port Antonio. Alert the airline of your arrival in Mo Bay, and a staff member will meet you and help you through Customs, guiding you to the aircraft. Although charter planes can be wickedly expensive, Jamaica AirLink is reasonable if you can collect a party of four. The airline will do that for you. If there are two of you, the staff can quickly arrange for another couple to fly on the same trip. In that case, a one-way fare is $65 per person from the Mo Bay airport to Negril, or $85 per person from Mo Bay to the more distant Ocho Rios.

By bus

Two major outfitters operate buses from the Mo Bay airport to Negril and Runaway Bay/Ocho Rios, and this is the cheapest way to go to either major resort. Both **Tour Wise** (☎ 876-952-4943) and **Caribic Vacations** (☎ 876-953-2600 or 876-952-2565) run buses from the Mo Bay airport and will drop you off right at the doorstep of your hotel, not a mile or two away. Fares are affordable: A one-way fare from Mo Bay to a resort on Negril's Seven Mile Beach costs $21 per person for the two-hour trip. You can even be taken to a little inn at the West End cliffs in Negril for $25 per person.

The ride to Negril or Ocho Rios by bus from Mo Bay can be your introduction to Jamaica, and chances are you'll have a story to tell the folks back home. Bus rides in Jamaica are not for the faint-of-heart. Surely no one in the Caribbean drives like a Jamaican driver, who is king of the road, wildly overtaking vehicles, dodging cows or schoolchildren, and playing hopscotch with fellow buses.

A long line of cars in front of your bus is approaching a blind curve. That's "no problem, Mon" for a battle-hardened Jamaican driver who will attempt the daredevil folly of passing as your knuckles turn white. Only India and Ethiopia have more auto fatalities than Jamaica.

By car

If you routinely rent a car and race across Nigeria, or drive through Calcutta without a blink, driving around Jamaica will be like eating a piece of island rum cake. But if you're a first-timer to Jamaica, not used to the Jamaicans' own rules of the road (or lack of them), try to avoid a car rental.

Many veteran visitors to Jamaica, however, rent a car at the airport and head out for Ocho Rios, some 75 miles to the east, or Negril, 65 miles to the southwest. But we don't recommend it for the timid driver for these reasons:

- ✔ Bad roads
- ✔ Bad drivers
- ✔ Bad characters
- ✔ Bad directions
- ✔ Bad vibes

Jamaica has dozens of car-rental companies, including some U.S. nationals. The major ones have branches at the Mo Bay airport. Rentals should be arranged before you leave home. You often get a better deal that way and have some guarantee that a car will be waiting for you — arranging rentals after you've arrived may be difficult, especially in winter when bookings are heavy. Even with a reservation, you won't always be able to get the vehicle of your choice because of overbookings.

Because they don't have to pay the added cost of an airport rental desk, car-rental agencies outside the airports are less expensive, but these rentals are much more difficult to arrange because of their lack of accessibility.

In general, car rentals in Jamaica are more expensive than in the average U.S. city. Travelers from such countries as England won't be surprised at the high tariffs, which may well match those they pay back home.

Many car-rental agencies offer unlimited mileage. If yours doesn't, you should look for one that does. Inspect your car carefully before taking off, and note that any dents are recorded. In Jamaica, you'll often have to pay for any damage or scratch discovered on a vehicle even though you rented it that way. The slightest mark on a car can mean extra charges for you.

Getting Around Jamaica

Navigating yourself in a rental car across the wilds of Jamaica can be an offbeat adventure, filled with uncertainty.

By taxi

Island taxis, even the official ones, have no meters, and, if they do, they rarely work, having long ago been tampered with. The official transport agency is **JUTA,** with offices in all the major resorts and at the two international airports at Mo Bay and Kingston. JUTA prices its tariffs by the car, not by the passenger, and adds a one-quarter jump to fares between midnight and 5 a.m. (For more information, see the "Traveling from the Airport to Your Accommodations" section earlier in this chapter.)

Pirate taxis — called *robots* on the island — will also solicit your business, often aggressively. Many people, especially locals, ride these cabs successfully. They stop at random and pick up as many passengers as they can fit in. You'll often have some stranger piled right on top of you. Pickpockets often work these illegal cabs, and keeping control of your belongings is often difficult. Robots almost invariably lack three elements: seatbelts, air-conditioning, and car insurance.

JUTA drivers are also trained to take you on sightseeing tours at a resort, including Mo Bay, Negril, and Ocho Rios. Depending on where you want to go and for how long, half-day to full-day tours range from $50 to $100 per vehicle, a cost that can be split among three or four passengers.

The staff at your hotel reception desk can call you a cab. If you're staying in one of the major resorts, such as Mo Bay, and patronizing certain first-class restaurants, a private van will often be provided by the establishment, picking you up, taking you to dinner, and bringing you back. Call the restaurant of your choice to see if such a luxury is offered. If so, you save all that transport money. If you do rent a taxi, it is customary to ask the driver to return for you at a certain time and haul you back to your hotel. Most drivers easily agree to that, because it's a guaranteed fare for them.

JUTA taxi drivers can also be flagged down on the street. Agree on the fare before getting in, however.

For longer jaunts such as trips from Mo Bay to Ocho Rios, or for half– or full-day tours, you may be quoted what sounds like ridiculously high tariffs. Often they are. Regrettably, you can't always trust the tour desk or even the reception desk of your own hotel. Sometimes staff members or desk personnel, especially at some of the all-inclusives such as Sandals, have made deals with drivers, perhaps one of their cousins. If you agree to the inflated rate, the cabbie often gives a kickback to the hotel staff member who booked the deal. This is a widely practiced scam.

On foot

Even though you may be hassled by hustlers trying to make some sort of deal with you, you still may want to explore the heart of your resort on foot. If you do, go walking during the daytime and keep your guard up. Avoid, whenever possible, wandering around at night, even in a small group. If you ever need some street smarts and a keen eye, it's walking the teeming streets of Jamaican towns, especially Kingston. Except for some annoying vendors or volunteers wanting to be your "guide," the following districts should not be a problem for strollers:

- ✔ Mo Bay's Gloucester Avenue or "hip strip," where you'll find lots of restaurants, clubs, shopping, and beaches
- ✔ Ochi's shopping district, near where the cruise ships unload their passengers
- ✔ Negril's Seven Mile Beach or its West End

These sections are tourist zones and are often patrolled by security police. Even so, taking out a fat wallet to make a purchase, carrying around expensive camera equipment, or wearing pricey jewelry puts you at risk. Wandering off and getting lost on some back street, especially in a slum, is done at your own risk.

The most dangerous place for a stroll is downtown Kingston near the waterfront, although this district is not without its fascination. Even the cruise-ships had to stop coming here because of muggings. Yet many visitors walk around unmolested every day, taking in the sights in this history-rich part of Kingston. The choice is yours, and it depends on how adventurous you are. Our only advice is that it's better done with a guide, which can be arranged through your hotel. And stay out of the district at night. Many Kingstonians avoid downtown Kingston after dark.

Wherever you are, be aware of your surroundings at all times and don't walk around alone — especially if you're a woman. Jamaican men apparently have heard about the book and movie *How Stella Got Her Groove Back* (the story of an author who falls in love with a young Jamaican man while she's on vacation). You'll get lots of offers if you're walking unaccompanied. Just say no, firmly but politely, and stride on.

By bus

Only the most diehard world-traveled backpackers ride on local buses, especially those linking one Jamaican town with another. Many Jamaicans themselves won't ride these buses. The only good thing about public bus travel in Jamaica, as distinguished from privately arranged bus travel for visitors, is that fares are remarkably cheap. Buses and private minibuses, called *coasters,* traverse the island.

Buses are invariably overcrowded, drivers often take dangerous chances, they are a haven for pickpockets, possessions are easily lost as they're carelessly thrown on top of the bus and held together by rope, people hang out from open doors because of overcrowding, and latrine stops are so foul you can smell the toilets a mile away. Not only that, but drivers routinely overcharge foreign visitors. If you disregard our advice and ride buses anyway, don't be surprised to find yourself sharing a seat with a woman carrying a little pig to market, or perhaps a plump chicken. The Jamaican government is slowly attempting to make improvements in bus travel. It's an uphill journey for them.

By car

When you've gone through the hassle of arranging a car rental, some 10,000 miles of roads await you in Jamaica. Of those, only a third are likely to be paved, if that's what you call it. Many of the others, especially in the hard-to-reach hinterlands, don't seem to have been worked on since the Arawaks blazed these trails hunting for some wild animal for the nightly roast.

The creator of "007," Ian Fleming, lived on the north coast of Jamaica and hatched the character of his master spy. James Bond, according to all those movies, would have no trouble driving in Jamaica. But you may be challenged by it, and it is for that reason that we don't recommend renting a car, even though Jamaica has considerable charms that you may not see unless you have your own wheels for exploring on your own.

To make matters worse, accidents are a routine occurrence, and break-ins of cars are commonplace. The potholed roads and the British-imported custom of driving on the left with a steering wheel also on the left make driving a bit chancy.

If you still want to rent wheels after all our heads-ups, here's the scoop. At most agencies, a driver has to be at least 25 years old; a few may rent you a car if you're 21, although insurance will be higher. You must also possess a valid driver's license (those from home are fine for short-term visits) and a credit card, and you'll also have to put down a security deposit — not in cash but as a guarantee on your credit card. If the car is returned undamaged, that security deposit is refunded or rather removed from your credit card charge.

Toyota Corollas and Suzuki Sidekicks are the most popular rentals. Rates average $50 to $150 a day, but on top of that several agencies also insist that you carry their pricey insurance (as much as $50 a day), even if your home auto insurance covers rentals. You'll also get socked with a 15% government tax on your car rental. If you need a baby seat or anything special, be sure to ask when you reserve.

A few tour operators offer good fly/drive packages that include rental cars. If you're determined to have your own wheels, consider that route to conserve funds.

If you hold a private auto insurance policy in the U.S., check to see if you're covered in Jamaica for loss or damage to the car, and liability in case a passenger is injured. The credit card you used to rent the car also may provide some coverage. Policies vary widely from holder to holder. Most American Express cardholders, for example, don't need a damage waiver option, because most Jamaican car-rental agencies recognize AmEx's policy, especially if you're dealing with a U.S.-affiliated firm such as Hertz. Many local car-rental companies in Jamaica don't recognize the policy; therefore, you may feel safer in dealing with a U.S. affiliate than a domestic car-rental agency.

Car-rental insurance probably does not cover liability if you caused the accident. Check your own auto insurance policy, the rental-company policy, and your credit card coverage for the extent of coverage: Is Jamaica covered? Are other drivers covered? How much liability is covered if a passenger is injured? (If you rely on your credit card for coverage, you may want to bring a second credit card with you, because damages may be charged to your card and you may find yourself stranded with no money.)

Car-rental insurance costs about $20 a day. Hiring a guide at a daily rate for sightseeing works out much cheaper. Plus, you'll be with someone who knows where the potholes are; where school children tend to congregate right by the road; where persnickety farm animals tend to be on the loose, grazing with their hindquarters occupying half the lane; and where construction goes on for miles and for years with no end in sight.

Because disputes often break out about whether you've actually reserved a car during seasons when they get snapped up quickly, we strongly recommend booking through a familiar company before you leave your home country and insisting on a confirmation number. Several agencies offer free delivery and pickup of your vehicle to your hotel or villa.

Budget International (☎ **800-527-0700** or 876-952-3838 at the Montego Bay Airport, or ☎ **876-924-8762** in Kingston) is a good choice. With Budget, a daily collision-damage waiver costs another $15 and is mandatory.

Other U.S.-based operators on Jamaica include:

- ✔ **Dollar International** (☎ **800-800-4000** in the U.S.)

- ✔ **Hertz International,** which operates branches at both airports (☎ **800-654-3001** for reservations; Mo Bay's Donald Sangster airport ☎ **876-979-0438;** or Kingston's Norman Manley airport ☎ 876-924-8028)

- ✔ **Avis** with branches at the two major airports — in Montego Bay (☎ **876-952-4543**) and in Kingston (☎ **876-924-8013**)

✔ **Thrifty Car Rental** (opposite the Mo Bay airport at ☎ 876-952-5825; Fax: 876-952-2679)

✔ **Kemwel Holiday Auto** (☎ 800-678-0678)

Local car-rental companies include:

✔ **Island Car Rentals** (☎ 876-952-7225 in Montego Bay; ☎ 876-926-5991 in Kingston)

✔ **Jamaica Car Rental** (☎ 876-952-5586 in Montego Bay)

✔ **Prospective Car Rentals** (☎ 876-952-0112 in Montego Bay)

✔ **United Car Rentals** (☎ 876-952-3077 in Montego Bay)

✔ **Vernon's Car and Jeep Rental** (☎ 876-957-4354 in Negril; Fax: 876-957-4057), which rents convertible Jeeps

Driving time for the 50 miles from the center of Montego Bay to Negril is 2 hours. From Montego Bay to Ocho Rios, expect a minimum drive of 2½ hours; from Ocho Rios to Port Antonio, 2½ hours; and from Ocho Rios to Kingston, 2 hours. Be especially cautious at night. Speed limits in town are 30 mph, 50 mph outside towns. Speed traps are common.

Gas stations are open daily; few accept credit cards, and most of them require payment in Jamaican dollars. Gas costs roughly $2.50 a gallon and is measured in the Imperial gallon (a British unit of measure that is 25% larger than a U.S. gallon).

By bicycle, moped, and motorcycle

Most hotels' concierge or tour desks can arrange the rental of bicycles, mopeds, and motorcycles. Daily rates run from about $50 for a moped to $85 (helmets and locks included) for a Honda 550. Deposits of $100 to $300 or more are required. However, we highly recommend that you don't rent a moped or motorcycle, because of Jamaica's status, as mentioned, as the country with the third-highest accident rate in the world combined with the hassle-factor of fending off aggressive vendors and drug dealers at traffic lights.

If you ignore our advice, at least check on your medical insurance before you leave and have proper identification handy in case you land at a health-care facility (see Chapter 7).

Mountain biking has become popular around the Blue Mountains, Negril, Port Antonio, and the rural Treasure Beach area on the south coast where traffic and other hazards aren't as pronounced. You'll need your valid driver's license to rent anything motorized.

Tykes Bike Rental and Tours (West End Road near Rick's Café and at the Visitor Information office in Negril; ☎ **876-957-0388**) offers free pickup and drop-off service.

If you're staying at a resort in Mo Bay or Ocho Rios, you can sometimes arrange a rental at your hotel. Independent outfitters open and shut down so frequently no guidebook can keep abreast. Because bike and motor scooter rentals in these resorts are not popular, few independent operators can make a go of it.

Fast Facts: Jamaica

ATMs

Traveler's checks, no longer used by some visitors, are still in wide use in Jamaica because few ATMs accept U.S. bankcards. Cash advances can be made using credit cards — that is, if the ATM is working. The dollars spilling out will be Jamaican, of course.

Baby-sitters

Most charge about $7 an hour for one child. Sitters are easily arranged at your hotel, and we've found that caregivers on Jamaica are among the best in the Caribbean. If you stay out late, though, please tip extra and ask how the sitter plans to get home.

Banks

One of the most convenient banks is the Bank of Nova Scotia at the following addresses: Sam Sharpe Square, Montego Bay (☎ 876-952-4440); Main St., Ocho Rios (☎ 876-974-2081); Negril Square, Negril (☎ 876-957-3040); and 35 King St., Kingston (☎ 876-922-1420). Banks island-wide are open Monday through Thursday from 9 a.m. to 2 p.m. and Friday from 9 a.m. to 4 p.m. A few are open on Saturday morning. Be aware, however, that the banks often don't have computers, and you're likely to encounter at least a half-hour wait in line. Many hotels and resorts offer currency exchange.

Credit Cards

MasterCard and Visa are the most popular, followed by American Express. Some places also accept Discover and Diners Club.

Currency Exchange

The unit of currency on Jamaica is the Jamaican dollar, represented by the same symbol as the U.S. dollar ($). Both U.S. and Jamaican currencies are widely accepted. Always clarify which currency is being quoted. There is no fixed rate of exchange for the Jamaican dollar. At press time, the exchange rate was about J$43 to US$1.

Jamaican currency is issued in banknotes of J$10, J$20, J$50, J$100, and J$500. Coins are available in denominations of 5¢, 10¢, 25¢, 50¢, J$1, and J$5. We recommend carrying small change in Jamaican or U.S. dollars for tips, beach fees, and other incidentals.

Bank of Jamaica exchange bureaus are located at both international airports (Montego Bay and Kingston), at cruise-ship terminals, and in most hotels. Immigration cards, needed for bank transactions and currency exchange, are given to visitors at the airport arrivals desks. Exchanging currency outside of the banking system is illegal.

Customs

On virtually every flight returning to the United States, Jamaican Customs with their "nosy" dogs catch some visitors returning with *ganja* (marijuana) in their luggage. Although at times it seems that half the people of Jamaica are "going up in smoke," this drug is illegal here. If arrested, you can be subjected to stiff fines or even jailed. Expulsion from the country without your ganja is the easiest "sentence."

Doctors

Hotels have doctors on call. If you need any particular medicine or treatment, bring evidence, such as a letter from your own physician.

Electricity

Most places have the standard 110 volts AC (60 cycles), same as the United States. However, a few establishments operate on 220 volts AC (50 cycles). If your hotel is on a different current from your U.S.-made appliance, ask for a transformer and adapter.

Emergencies

To report a fire or call an ambulance, dial ☎ **110**. For the police and air rescue, dial ☎ **119**.

Festivals

The big annual event is Carnival throughout Jamaica, admittedly not as spectacular as the one staged in Trinidad. Islanders dance in the street and the air is filled with music — reggae, of course. Kingston makes the biggest splash, with Ocho Rios and Montego Bay tying for second. Carnival takes place in these cities in April. Negril, with the wildest costumes (or lack of them), holds its carnival in May. During the first week in August, Bob Marley fans and reggae aficionados in general "Catch a Fire" at the annual Sumfest. The big event on the fishermen's calendar is the Blue Marlin Tournament in October in Port Antonio.

Hospitals

For dire situations, seek help in San Juan or Miami. St. Ann's Bay Hospital, St. Ann's Bay

(☎ 876-972-0150) has a hyperbaric chamber for scuba-diving emergencies. In Kingston, the University Hospital is at Mona (☎ 876-927-1620); in Montego Bay, the Cornwall Regional Hospital is at Mount Salem (☎ 876-952-5100 or 876-952-6683); and in Port Antonio, the Port Antonio General Hospital is at Naylor's Hill (☎ 876-993-2646). Negril only has minor-emergency clinics.

Homework

The most amusing novel about Jamaica in many a year is Terry McMillan's *How Stella Got Her Groove Back.*

Information

You'll find the Jamaican Tourist Board offices at the international airports and at 2 St. Lucia Ave., Kingston (☎ 876-929-9200); Cornwall Beach, St. James, Montego Bay (☎ 876-952-4425); Shop no. 29, Coral Seas Plaza, Negril, Westmoreland (☎ 876-957-4243); in the Ocean Village Shopping Centre, Ocho Rios, St. Ann (☎ 876-974-2582); in City Centre Plaza, Port Antonio (☎ 876-993-3051); and in Hendriks Building, 2 High St., Black River (☎ 876-965-2074).

Before you fly down, you can contact the Jamaican Tourist Board at 801 Second Avenue, 20th Floor, New York, NY 10017 (☎ 800-233-4582 or 212-856-9727; Fax: 212-856-9655).

Language

English is the official language, but it's not the Queen's English. Like everything else on the island, Jamaicans have given English their own distinctive patois. In fact, the English language as spoken in Jamaica has been the subject of learned studies, such as *Jamaica Talk* by Frederic G. Cassidy. Just to give you a preview of *Jamaica Talk,* here are some common words. A *batty boy* is a gay male; a *higger* is a market vendor; *I-ital* means natural foods; a *mule* is a childless woman; and to *skin-out* is to abandon whatever you're doing for sex.

Nudity

Nude bathing is allowed at a number of hotels, clubs, and beaches (especially in Negril), but only where signs indicate that swimsuits are optional. Elsewhere, English sensibilities prevail, and the law does not even allow topless sunbathing.

Maps

Good maps are widely available at the airport, tourist information offices, and resorts.

Newspapers and Magazines

Resort gift shops carry a decent selection, including *USA Today,* and many hotels offer *The New York Times* via fax at no charge. However, serious news junkies will find the cover price on foreign magazines and newspapers extremely inflated.

Pharmacies

Local pharmacies will not accept a prescription unless issued by a Jamaican doctor. The best all-around pharmacy in Montego Bay is Rosehall Village Pharmacy, Shop 22, Half Moon Bay (☎ 876-953-2399). In Ocho Rios, you'll find the Great House Pharmacy, Brown's Plaza (☎ 876-974-2352); and in Kingston, Moodie's Pharmacy, in the New Kingston Shopping Centre (☎ 876-926-4174).

Police

For the police and air rescue, dial ☎ 119.

Post Office

Jamaica issues stamps highly praised by collectors. The Montego Bay post office (☎ 876-952-7389) is at 122 Barnett St., and is open weekdays from 8 a.m. to 5 p.m. As you leave Negril Square, the post office is on the Lighthouse Road.

Safety

Most hotels and resorts, and even some villas, have private security guards, so you probably won't run into any problems. However, beaches are public, so if you go for a stroll, you can expect to be approached by people selling everything from wood carvings and shells to drugs and sex to tours of the "real Jamaica." Safeguard your valuables and never leave them unattended on a beach. Likewise, never leave luggage or other valuables in a car or in the trunk. The U.S. State Department has issued a travel advisory about crime rates in Kingston, so don't go walking around alone at night. Caution is also advisable in many north coast tourist areas, especially remote houses and isolated villas that can't afford security.

Drugs (including marijuana) are illegal, and imprisonment is the penalty for possession. Also, you may well be buying ganja from a police informant, many of whom target visitors so that they aren't turning on their hometown buddies. Don't smoke pot openly in public, no matter who you see doing it. You may be the one who gets caught. Above all, don't even consider bringing marijuana back into the United States. Drug-sniffing dogs are stationed at the Jamaican airports, and they will check your luggage. U.S. Customs agents pay keen attention to all those arriving from Jamaica, and they easily catch and arrest those who try to take that sort of souvenir home.

Shopping Hours

Hours vary widely, but as a general rule most establishments are open Monday through Friday from 8:30 a.m. to 4:30 or 5:00 p.m. Some shops are open on Saturday until noon.

Taxes

Jamaica charges a general consumption tax of 15% on all goods and services, which includes car rentals and telephone calls. Additionally, the government imposes a 6.25% tax on hotel rooms. You'll also encounter a J$1,000 (US$23) departure tax at the airport, payable in either Jamaican dollars or in its equivalent in U.S. dollars. Don't count on getting the cash at the airport, because few ATMs accept U.S. bankcards, and the machines are often out of money or service.

Telephone

To call direct from the United States, dial the area code 876, then the local number. Likewise, to call the U.S., simply dial the area code and number. But the best idea is to call collect. Otherwise, you'll pay about $3 a minute plus hefty surcharges, including the 15% general consumption tax. To make on-island calls, simply dial the seven-digit phone number. Coin-operated phones are rare. If you need to make many calls outside of your hotel, purchase a World-Talk card at the post office or other outlets advertising it. Local and international calls made with these cards are cheaper than operator-assisted calls.

Time Zone

Jamaica is on eastern standard time year-round; it does not observe daylight saving time. So, when the United States is on daylight saving time and it's 6 a.m. in Miami, it's 5 a.m. in Jamaica.

Tipping

Tipping is expected everywhere. Generally, hotels and restaurants expect 10 to 15%, and the same goes for tour guides and drivers. Some places add a service charge to the bill. Tipping is not allowed in the all-inclusive hotels.

Water

Water is safe to drink, because it's filtered and chlorinated. But, as always, you're more prudent to drink bottled water if it's available. Negril has had problems with water shortages.

Weather and Surf Reports

The local newspaper is the most reliable source.

Chapter 26

Dining in Jamaica

By Darwin Porter and Danforth Prince

- -

In This Chapter

▶ Sampling the local cuisine

▶ Locating the island's best restaurants

- -

*F*rom curried goat to jerk pork, the pungent and aromatic cuisine of Jamaica borrowed freely from all its settlers, creating a unique "pepperpot stew" of savory dishes. Some of the ethnic dishes would grow hair on your chest, even if you're a woman, but others are undeniably excellent and inventive.

From Africa, slaves brought recipes in their memories along with *yabbas,* or clay pots, in which to cook their stews. Some of the "descendants" of those clay pots are still in use in the Jamaica of today.

East Indians brought their hot curries, and immigrants arriving from the Middle East and China, especially Hong Kong, added more flavor and spice to the cuisine. Some of the dishes were inspired by the Arawak and Taíno Indians. And the Rastafarians have added their *I-tal* cuisine of natural ingredients. No meat, no liquor, not even salt — and still the Rasta cuisine tastes marvelously good. For a survey of the dishes fed to reggae great Bob Marley, head for **Minnie's Vegetarian and Seafood Restaurant** in Ocho Rios (see the listing later in this chapter). She was Marley's cook but now shares her secret *I-tal* recipes with you.

Even if a dish is fiery hot, Jamaicans often sprinkle their own Pickapeppa Sauce over it, making it even hotter. This sauce can be addictive, and the formula for making it is a closely guarded secret. We've detected the taste of onions, raisins, tomatoes, mango, tamarind, red-hot peppers, cane vinegar, spices such as thyme or "whatever."

Nyam-ing around the Island

Nyam was a word the slaves brought from Africa. It means "to eat," and that is what you can do rather well throughout the island. Yes, you can find McDonald's, Burger King, and even KFC franchises, but the island has oh-so-much more to offer.

Many hotels still offer a bland international cuisine, although more and more island dishes appear on menus. On a recent swing through Jamaica, we even saw listed on a Sandals restaurant menu such soups as red pea (actually bean) and pepperpot, the latter a legacy of the Taínos with salt pork, okra, salt beef, and leafy callaloo, the local "spinach."

If pepperpot is the national soup, then akee (also ackee) is the national dish. The red-skinned akee is poisonous until Mother Nature pops its open, releasing the dangerous gases. The lobes of the fruit are boiled, then blended with salt cod, peppers, and onions. This is a breakfast favorite; the akee resembles scrambled eggs when cooked. Akee and sal' (salt) fish is the way many a Jamaican fortifies himself or herself for the day — that and some bammies (cassava cakes), green bananas, or fried plantain.

Some of the truly local dishes you'll taste only in lowly food shacks, not in hotels. These include red beans cooked with pig's tail or salt beef and dumplings. Jamaicans have given their own colorful names to their most famous dishes — Solomon Gundy for spiced pickled herring; stamp and go for batter-fried saltfish fritters; rundown for salt cod or mackerel boiled in coconut milk; dip and fall back, a salty stew made with bananas and dumplings; and matrimony for a dessert "wedding" star apple pulp with orange segments in cream.

Internationally, Jamaica's most famous dish is jerk pork. Bottles of jerk pork seasonings now line the shelves of American grocery stores. The pork is marinated in a "wake-up-your-tongue" hot sauce, then slowly barbecued over an open pit (usually in an oil drum). The fire is from pimento wood (allspice to most people), giving the meat its character-istic zest. Chicken, fish, and even lobster can also be "jerked."

Jamaican beef is tough and is often ground into patties. The tender, juicy steaks served on the island are from the U.S. Go for fresh fish whenever you can, especially snapper, kingfish, grouper, and marlin. A typical offering is escoveitched fish, which is pickled, then fried with onions and peppers.

Side dishes include the likes of the starchy breadfruit, whose seedlings were brought to Jamaica by Captain Bligh; rice and peas, or the *cho-cho,* called *christophine* in most of the West Indies, a squash-like vegetable that grows on the vine like a cucumber.

Wandering in a Jamaican Garden of Eden, Eve would not have settled for a mere apple. Instead she may have selected lush mangos, the yellow-rose papaya, the dark-purple star apple, the pink-fleshed and grape-like guinep, the fragrant soursop, or the musky sweet guava. The sight of the ugli, like a warty, mottled, and deformed citrus may have turned her off — that is, until she sampled its gushingly juicy golden pulp.

and tropical flowering gardens. You're also just a 15-minute drive from El Yunque National Park, the only rain forest in United States territories. Rising seven floors, the 694-room mega-resort also takes in the Rio Mar Country Club with its two 18-hole golf courses, and has a vast array of facilities, including 8 restaurants, 6 bars, a casino, a health club and spa, and 13 tennis courts. It also offers water sports and can arrange sailing and deep-sea fishing. Its children's programs make it a family favorite. The best and most expensive accommodations are on the top floor with enhanced service and amenities, but all the units are exceedingly comfortable and well equipped, opening onto private balconies or terraces, and furnished with a restful decor of Caribbean wicker, rattan, and painted furniture.

Avoid suites 5099 and 5101 — the balconies overlook the hotel's noisy air-conditioning ducts.

6000 Rio Mar Blvd. (P.O. Box 6100), Rio Grande. ☎ 800-WESTIN-1 or 787-888-6000. Fax: 787-888-6600. Intermet: www.westinriomar.com. *Rack rates: $395–$675 double, $900 suite. AE, DISC, DC, MC, V.*

Wyndham El Conquistador Resort and Country Club
$$$$$ Fajardo

Mitsubishi, at a cost of $250 million, has given this old property a new lease on life in the 21st century. With 915 rooms, it's set on 500 acres of forested hillside. To reach the hotel's private beach, you take a hotel ferry to the little fantasy island of Palomino, with its white sands, caverns, horseback riding, nature trails, and such water sports as scuba diving, windsurfing, and snorkeling. The mega-resort is also a favorite among yachties because of its 32-slip marina. Accommodations come in five different sections, each with a Mediterranean theme. You stay in Spanish-style "villages," such as Las Olas or Las Casitas. If you'd like a room with a balcony overhanging the water, ask for an accommodation in La Marina Village. A stylish tropical decor prevails, and rooms are handsomely equipped, often with kitchens. The resort's Golden Door Spa is the finest outside San Juan, and the 6,700 yard, par-72, 18-hole golf course, the creation of Arthur Hills, is one of Puerto Rico's finest. A vast array of facilities include six restaurants, seven bars, a night club, a casino, six pools, six tennis courts, children's programs, and a dive shop for water sports.

1000 Avenue El Conquistador (P.O. Box 70001), Fajardo. ☎ 800-468-8365 (direct to hotel), 800-WYNDHAM, or 787-863-1000. Fax: 787-863-6500. Rack rates: $455–$765 double, from $1,375 suite. AE, DC, DISC, MC, V.

Wyndham El San Juan Hotel and Casino
$$$$–$$$$$ Isla Verde, San Juan

One of the grandest hotels in Puerto Rico, this is the favored hotel along the beachfront extending from Condado to Isla Verde moving toward the airport. It opens onto one of the island's best golden-sand beaches and is

To finish a meal, it can only be Blue Mountain coffee. Ian Fleming had his master spy, "007" himself, proclaim it the most aromatic, exotic, and finest coffee in the world.

Almost no place in Jamaica requires men to wear ties at night, although a limited few request a jacket. More and more, even in the fanciest joints, a collared shirt for men will suffice. Women appear in fashionable resort wear ranging from a sundress to slacks and a blouse. If a restaurant or dining room is air-conditioned, women should bring a wrap, perhaps a shawl or sweater. If a Jamaican has air-conditioning, he believes in turning it on at full blast.

Jamaica's Best Restaurants

It takes a sense of adventure to go out at night and sample cuisine at the local taverns. Taxis are expensive, and there is always a certain danger of wandering around after dark.

For that reason, many guests prefer to stay at their hotel at night. If it's an all-inclusive, dinner comes as part of the package. You'll be safe and secure in your Sandals or SuperClubs dining room, but will you eat well? You'll certainly get heaping amounts of food. Although Jamaican resorts have improved their cuisine in recent years, offering more variety, even Japanese food, they still lag behind comparable food served at top-rated American or European resorts. Much of the foodstuff, such as beef, served in these resort hotels is imported from the U.S. or elsewhere, including Mexico.

Because more and more guests are staying in their hotel at night, or booked into an all-inclusive where they've already paid for their meals, a death pallor has fallen over many an independent restaurant. The independent restaurant used to prosper in resorts such as Ocho Rios before the all-inclusives came in and virtually "ate up" all the customers. A few (see our recommendations) struggle valiantly on in the face of the all-inclusive onslaught.

To survive, some of these restaurants have raised their prices, which does little to attract customers. It's a vicious cycle with no sign of relief on the way.

To break the monotony of dining at the same resort every night, some of the all-inclusives offer a dine-around plan. Sandals features the most, allowing a guest to dine at a different restaurant every night, providing it falls under the vast Sandals umbrella of resort restaurants.

Because so many potential diners resist paying an expensive taxi there and back, many upmarket restaurants have their own minivans, taking you to the restaurant and back to your hotel at night. That makes it easy for you, and has greatly increased business to some independents. We

Jamaica Dining

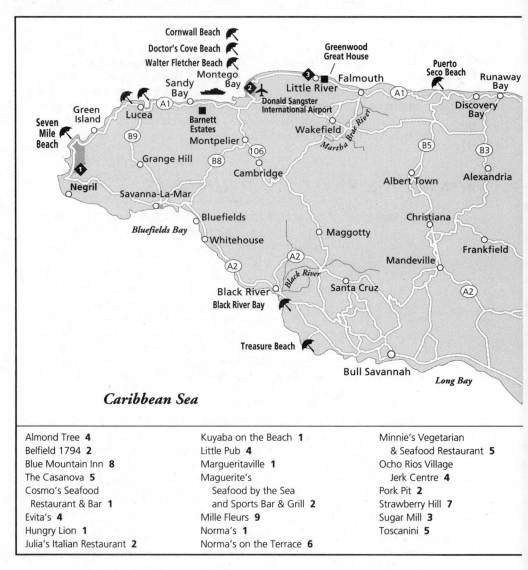

Almond Tree **4**	Kuyaba on the Beach **1**	Minnie's Vegetarian
Belfield 1794 **2**	Little Pub **4**	& Seafood Restaurant **5**
Blue Mountain Inn **8**	Margueritaville **1**	Ocho Rios Village
The Casanova **5**	Maguerite's	Jerk Centre **4**
Cosmo's Seafood	Seafood by the Sea	Pork Pit **2**
Restaurant & Bar **1**	and Sports Bar & Grill **2**	Strawberry Hill **7**
Evita's **4**	Mille Fleurs **9**	Sugar Mill **3**
Hungry Lion **1**	Norma's **1**	Toscanini **5**
Julia's Italian Restaurant **2**	Norma's on the Terrace **6**	

feel, however, that they've handled the cost of the "free" transportation by raising their menu prices.

Reservations in winter are important at the top-ranked restaurants. Even if you're staying at an all-inclusive, you may not find a free table at the hotel's best restaurant. Guests quickly learn which on-site restaurant serves the best food and book a table. To guarantee that you, too, have a table, make dinner reservations when booking your room.

St. Ann's Bay · Turtle Beach · Mallard's Beach · James Bond Beach · *Caribbean Sea* · Dunn's River Falls · **Ocho Rios** · Oracabessa · Port Maria · Claremont · Fern Gully · A3 · A3 · Annotto Bay · Buff Bay · Hope Bay · Port Antonio · NAVY ISLAND · San San Beach · Boston Beach · A1 · Ewarton · Castleton · B1 · *BLUE MOUNTAINS* · *Rio Grande* · Boston Bay · Long Bay · A4 · Manchioneal · Linstead · A3 · Newcastle · Chapelton · Spanish Town · **Kingston** · *Kingston Harbour* · A2 · Portmore · Port Royal · Bull Bay · Golden Grove · May Pen · Old Harbour · Norman Manley International Airport · Yallahs · Bowden · Morant Bay · A4 · *Galleon Harbour* · Lionel Town · *Carlisle Bay*

0 — 10 Miles
0 — 10 Kilometers
N

Airport ✈ Beach 🏖 Cruise Ship Dock 🚢

Almond Tree
$$$ Ocho Rios   Jamaican/International

The restaurant at this small and affordable inn is named for the almond tree that grows through its roof. It is especially dramatic at night when you can enjoy the twinkling lights and trade winds from its cliffside location overlooking the sea below. For years, it was considered almost mandatory for visitors to come here and have a drink in one of the swinging rope chairs in the terrace bar. Candlelit dinners are served alfresco on the little pavilions set into the cliffside. Roast suckling pig is the specialty enjoyed by everybody from Keith Richards of the Rolling Stones to movie stars traveling incognito. Some habitúes claim the food isn't as good as it used to be (what is?), but it's still well flavored and prepared, everything from medallions of beef Anne Palmer named after the "white witch" of Rose Hall to a savory serving of Jamaican plantation rice. No one in the area does lobster Thermidor better than this chef.

In the Hibiscus Lodge Hotel, 83 Main St., Ocho Rios. ☎ *876-974-2813. Reservations essential. Main courses: $12–$30. AE, DC, MC, V. Open: Daily noon to 2:30 p.m. and 6:00 –9:30 p.m.*

Belfield 1794
$$$ **Montego Bay International/Jamaican**

Owned and operated by the Half Moon Resort, this former 18th-century plantation home lies in the hills above Mo Bay. Arrive early for a drink at the bar, carved out of the former threshing floor of an antique sugarcane mill. Afterward you can look at the nearby Great House on a 15-minute tour before settling down to enjoy the polished cuisine. The food is served on a carved wooden platter covered with a breadfruit leaf or in a "Dutchie," a shallow cast-iron pot. The cuisine is international, but the use of island seasonings and ingredients gives it Jamaican zest and flair. Try the curried goat, a jerk combination platter, or our all-time favorite, filet of fish with a medley of butters made from lime, orange, and grapefruit. Shuttle buses run back and forth from Half Moon.

Barnett Estate, Granville. ☎ *876-952-2382. Reservations needed. Main courses: $15–$20. AE, MC, V. Open: Mon–Sat 6:30–11:00 p.m.*

Blue Mountain Inn
$$$$ **Kingston Caribbean/International**

This is the most romantic place to escape Kingston at night other than Strawberry Hill (see the listing later in this chapter). In only a 30-minute drive north of Kingston, you can enjoy the setting of the Blue Mountains in a former 18th-century coffee plantation on the banks of the Mammee River. Kingston, in all its squalor, looks beautiful here at night with the twinkling lights, and on chilly nights a log fire burns. With its sparkling glass and gleaming silver, you get old-fashioned service here evocative of colonial Jamaica. The cuisine, refined over many a year, is not imaginative but presents well-prepared dishes from a changing menu of fresh seafood, island-grown vegetables, and mostly imported meats. The recipes haven't changed much since the '50s, but they were good then, so why not now?

Gordon Town Road, Kingston. ☎ *876-927-1700. Reservations required. Main courses: $20–$40. AE, MC, V. Open: Mon–Sat 7:00–9:30 p.m.*

The Casanova

$$$$$ Ocho Rios   French/International

At least one night of your vacation you'll want to step out in grand style. Put on your finest resort duds and head over to the tony Grand Lido Sans Souci where you, as a nonresident, can purchase a night pass, which entitles you to all the food and drink you can partake of before 2 a.m. The cuisine here is in general far superior to that served at the Sandals restaurants. Top-quality ingredients go into the finely honed cookery, with some of the dishes based on those served at the fabled Harry's Bar in Venice, so beloved by Hemingway. Typical dishes include smoked chicken breast in a continental berry sauce as an appetizer, or a small vegetable mousse with a fontina cheese sauce. For your main course, try a perfectly roasted Cornish hen with citrus and mild spice. Desserts are sumptuous. You can also sample one of the house's four special coffees.

In the Grand Lido Sans Souci. Along Route A3, 3 miles east of Ocho Rios. ☎ 876-994-1353. Reservations required. Nonresident evening pass of $95 per person includes dinner and all drinks and is valid from 6 p.m.–2 a.m. Tues and Fri evenings there is a beach buffet, entertainment, and drinks. AE, DC, MC, V. Open: Daily 6:30–9:30 p.m.

Cosmo's Seafood Restaurant and Bar

$$ Negril   Seafood/Jamaican

The first time we dropped in at this East End dive, the owner and local character, Cosmo Brown, rushed over with a cup of conch soup. "Taste it," he said. "It's the best on the island." We must have agreed with him because we've been coming back ever since. He's not only a whiz with conch, which he also prepares stewed or curried, but with any number of seafood dishes, including grilled lobster. You eat under a thatched roof hut, and may be tempted to use the beach facilities with changing rooms, costing $3 per person.

Norman Manley Boulevard, Negril. ☎ 876-957-4784. No reservations. Main courses: $7.50–$18.50. AE, MC, V. Open: Daily 9 a.m.–10 p.m.

Evita's

$$$ Ocho Rios   Italian

No, Evita Peron isn't alive and well and dispensing savory Italian food in Ocho Rios. The local Evita is actually the sophisticated international blonde-haired hostess, Eva Myers. When a hurricane blew down her place in Mo Bay, she moved her pots and pans to Ocho Rios and has been ensconced ever since, dispensing her cuisine to appreciative diners. She even grows her own herbs, which enhance many of her dishes such as homemade pastas that range from a Rastafarian version (no meat) to a "Viagra pasta" (oysters are the aphrodisiac). If not pasta, try one of the fresh fish dishes. We recommend the enticingly prepared snapper stuffed with crabmeat. Lobster and scampi in a buttery white cream sauce is another memorable dish. Come here early for a sundowner, taking in the dramatic view from this hilltop 19th-century gingerbread West Indian house overlooking Mallards Bay. Half orders of pasta are available, and kids under 12 eat for half price.

Mantalent Inn, Eden Bower Road, Ocho Rios. ☎ 876-974-2333. Reservations recommended. Main courses: $10–$29. AE, MC, V. Open: Daily 11a.m.–11 p.m.

Hungry Lion
$$ Negril   Italian/Rastafarian

This hip local eatery draws the Bob Marley wannabe to its laid-back perch, an open-air hangout on the cliffs of the West End, far removed from the frenetic, organized activities of the mega-resorts directly east. If you don't go in for Jamaican Red Stripe beer or a rum punch, a juice bar awaits you, turning out the most soothing, freshly squeezed drinks in Negril. For the first-time visitor, some of the fruit juice flavors may be a first for you. That staple choice of pub grubbers around the world, shepherd's pie, is all veggie here, as is the lasagna with the spinach-like leafs of the callaloo plant. Don't believe the waiter when he tells you the green is from the marijuana plant. Some Rastas don't eat seafood, but it's served here. Especially recommendable are the pan-fried snapper, freshly caught that day, and the kingfish steak grilled just right. King lobster is prepared almost any way you want it. Save room for the pineapple-carrot cake, even better than mama used to make.

West End Road, Negril. ☎ 876-957-4486. Main courses: $8.50–$24. AE, MC, V. Open: Daily 5:30–10:30 p.m.

Julia's Italian Restaurant
$$$$$ Montego Bay   Italian/International

Reached by a jolting ride up a hilly, rocky road, Julia's serves the best Italian cuisine in Mo Bay in a former private home once built in 1840 for the Duke of Sutherland. The views of Mo Bay at night compete with the cuisine. Although fine in every way, Julia's still takes second billing to Evita's (see the listing earlier in this chapter) or Toscanini (see the listing later in this chapter), both competitors in the Ocho Rios area. A finely honed prix fixe is served nightly by Neville and Gisela Roe, a Jamaican-German couple who combine some of the best of continental cuisine with Jamaican flair. Look for about ten different types of pasta at night, even such Germanic dishes as pork schnitzel and goulash with noodles. The desserts are some of Mo Bay's best, especially the cheesecake of the day or Black Forest cake.

Julia's Estate, Bogue Hill. ☎ 876-952-1772. Reservations essential. Prix-fixe dinner $50–$55 per person. AE, MC, V. Open: Daily 5:00–10:30 p.m. Private van transportation provided.

Kuyaba on the Beach
$–$$ Negril   International

Right near De Buss Nightclub, one of the most popular reggae joints in Jamaica, is another joint projected out into the water. Laidback, raffish, funky, it is the most evocative of those casual eateries that put Negril on the tourist map. People come here for the fun almost as much as they do for the food, finding a favored table on the wooden deck over the beach or a hammock seat at the bar and slugging down some of the tropical punches like screaming banana or Kuyaba rainbow. After a few of these, you'll be seeing more than rainbows. If an Arawak were left on the island (these Indians were killed off), he'd tell you that Kuyaba in his speak means "feasting, drinking, and dancing," so the eatery is aptly named. A mento band plays on some nights, and you can often hear Cuban salsa. Stop in for breakfast or stick around for a lunch of meal-sized, freshly made salads or big, juicy burgers. At night the cook gets more serious, grilling freshly caught red snapper, maybe even swordfish. Steaks from the U.S. are grilled to perfection, and sometimes lamb chops appear on the menu.

If you'd like to sleep in a party atmosphere, you can rent one of the nine simply-furnished bedrooms that affordably cost $75 to $103 for a double per night.

In the Hotel Kuyaba, Norman Manley Boulevard, Negril. ☎ *876-957-4318. Main courses: $10–$23. Burgers, sandwiches, and salads: $6–$9. AE, MC, V. Open: Daily 8 a.m.–11 p.m.*

Little Pub
$$ Ocho Rios   Jamaican/International

This is your best bet for combining drink, entertainment, and pub grub all under one roof. With its sports bar and a West Indian review on most nights, this is a lot of fun, featuring outdoor dining. Reggae bands enliven the scene on some nights. If you like steak and seafood, and plenty of it, all at an affordable price, come here. As the waiter told us, "We don't get the fancy diners, but we feed you well." Dig into the barbecued chicken, the grilled kingfish, the freshly caught lobster, and, most definitely, the jerk pork, the curried chicken, or one of the succulent pastas. The pub also serves one of the heartiest breakfasts in town, and many locals like to stop in for a big burger with fries at lunch.

59 Main St., Ocho Rios. ☎ *876-974-2324. Reservations recommended. Main courses: $13.50–$28.50. AE, MC, V. Open: Daily 7:00 a.m.–10:30 p.m.*

Margueritaville
$$$ Negril   American/International

Inspired by the Jimmy Buffet song, it's party time here day or night. A cousin of its sibling in Mo Bay, Margueritaville is the leading sports bar of Negril, even luring some of the gang from Sandals and Hedonism II. It's relatively tame during the day, but the action begins after sundown. The complex is both a bar and a restaurant, plus an on-site gallery, gift shop, and dive center — very touristy but fun if you're in the mood. Live music rocks the joint after 9 p.m. When management doesn't want to pay for live entertainment, they give the entertainment job to you with karaoke. Oh, yes, the food. It's better than you may have expected. During the day you get good burgers and well-stuffed sandwiches here. At night, try such good-tasting dishes as the southern fried chicken or their "Pacific paella." The drink of choice? A margarita, of course, and the bartenders make a great selection, at least four dozen (we lost count after sampling 38) different varieties.

Norman Manley Boulevard, Negril. ☎ *876-957-4467. Main courses: $10–$26. Burgers and sandwiches: $6.25–$9.75. AE, MC, V. Open: Daily 9 a.m.–11 p.m.*

Marguerite's Seafood by the Sea and Sports Bar and Grill
$–$$ Montego Bay International/Seafood

Across from the Coral Cliff Hotel, this two-in-one restaurant and bar is both the best known sports bar in Mo Bay and also one of the choice dining spots for fresh seafood. On a terrace swept by the trade winds, you can eat and drink either in the sports bar and grill, with its straightforward menu of seafood, sandwiches, pastas, and pizzas, or in the more formal restaurant. The cuisine doesn't rate a rave, but it is competently prepared if you stick to the flambéed grilled dishes.

Gloucester Avenue. ☎ *876-952-4777. Reservations needed only for restaurant. Main courses: $10–$42. Snacks and platters: $6.50. AE, DC, MC, V. Restaurant open: Daily 6:00–10:30 p.m. Sports bar open: Daily 10 a.m.–3 a.m.*

Mille Fleurs
$$$ Port Antonio International/Caribbean

With the scent of jasmine perfuming the air cooled by the distant Blue Mountains, and the sound of the sea below, this is not only a romantic interlude, but a refined place to sample a well-prepared cuisine made with fresh ingredients. A delightful couple, artist Barbara Walker and her friend, Shireen Aga, welcome you into this homelike environment. Arrive early to enjoy one of their smooth tropical punches. Drawing largely a European clientele, they are becoming increasingly known to Americans thanks to the likes of us. Mille Fleurs in recent times has emerged as the number-one dining choice in the Greater Port Antonio area. By candlelight you're served your dinner ending with a selection from a trolley of Sangster's Jamaican liqueurs. Some of the vegetables and herbs used are from the hotel's own gardens. The menu is forever changing but includes a generous number of vegetarian dishes. If featured, we'd recommend the coconut and garlic soup, followed by fresh fish in a spicy mango-shrimp sauce. Breads, most jams, and ice creams are homemade. There's lots of New Age charm here.

Mocking Bird Hill, East of Port Antonio on North Coast Highway, Port Antonio. ☎ *876-993-7267 or 876-993-7134. Reservations required. Main courses: $12–$25. Lunch platters: $8.50–$25. AE, MC, V. Open: Daily noon to 2 p.m. and 7:00–9:30 p.m.*

Minnie's Vegetarian and Seafood Restaurant
$$ Ocho Rios   Vegetarian/Rastafarian

"Minnie" Phillips, a Rastafarian herself, was the personal chef to the late Bob Marley, reggae artist extraordinaire. At her little restaurant, you can sample the same dishes that she prepared for this superstar. His favorites were curried tofu, gunga pea stew, vegetarian patties, vegetable soups (or stews), and whatever the local fishermen brought to her door that day. She does a delectable grilled grouper, for example. Dishes are enjoyed under the shade of an alfresco patio. The little eatery enjoys a setting on 3 tropical acres with its own beach and running stream. Before lunch we suggest a swim in the spring-fed pool.

Adjacent to the Carib Inn, at the east end of Main Street. ☎ *876-974-0236. Reservations not needed. Main courses: $4–$13 at lunch, $14–$20 at dinner. No credit cards. Open: Daily noon to 3 p.m. and 6–10 p.m.*

Norma's
$$–$$$ Negril   International/Jamaican

Norma Shirley is not only the best female chef in Jamaica, she's called the Caribbean's Julia Child. Once she ran a popular restaurant in New York, but she moved back to Kingston to open the best restaurant there (see Norma's on the Terrace later in this chapter). At this Negril outpost, she established this new outlet for herself, using her same recipes and flair for cookery. It's a sort of franchise. Because most visitors to Negril don't make it on to Kingston, she wanted local tastebuds to know what a delight she is in the kitchen. Even without Norma on the premises all the time, you feel her culinary presence in the rich, bountiful dishes created here from the products of the Jamaican countryside. Seasonally adjusted, the menu offers beautifully prepared fare such as delicately poached salmon, a perfectly cooked and very tender rack of lamb, enticingly tasty lobster cocktails, and a well-sauced Cornish game hen. No one does grilled deviled crab backs better than Norma.

In the Sea Splash Resort, Norman Manley Boulevard. ☎ *876-957-4041. Reservations recommended. Main courses: $5.95–$21 at lunch, or $12.50–$24.95 at dinner. AE, DC, MC, V. Open: Daily 11:00 a.m.–10:30 p.m.*

Norma's on the Terrace
$$–$$$ Kingston   Jamaican

The celebrated woman chef Norma Shirley welcomes guests to the finest restaurant in the center of Kingston. For food not quite as good, you have to head to the Blue Mountains and dine at Strawberry Hill. Her culinary wares are showcased in Devon House, a striking, classic building erected in 1991 by George Stiebel, a Jamaican who became one of the first black millionaires in the Caribbean. Ms. Shirley changes her menus with the seasons, but you can always get something good here on her carefully balanced menu with well-chosen ingredients given her own innovative flair and zest for cooking. Her Jamaican chowder with crabmeat, conch, lobster, and shrimp is the finest we've ever had in Jamaica. You can dine in grand style if you order her grilled whole red snapper encrusted with herbs and served in a sauce studded with capers and laced with fresh thyme. The intense flavor of a grilled smoked pork loin is only enhanced by its ginger-laced teriyaki sauce with a side of caramelized apples.

In Devon House, 26 Hope Rd. ☎ *876-968-5488. Reservations recommended. Main courses: $14.95–$41.50. AE, MC, V. Open: Mon–Sat 11 a.m.–11 p.m.*

Ocho Rios Village Jerk Centre
$ **Ocho Rios   Jamaican**

This dive, frequented by locals, is one of the best places to sample jerk pork on home turf, even if you're just visiting from a cruise ship in the afternoon. Jamaican jerk seasonings are used at their best to create hot, spicy dishes — both chicken and pork. All of these main courses are consumed with a frosty Red Stripe beer (maybe more than one). From the chalkboard menu, you can learn of the specials of the day, perhaps tangy barbecue ribs, also heavily spiced, or a freshly caught red snapper grilled to perfection.

Da Costa Drive. ☎ *876-974-2549. Jerk pork $3 for a quarter-pound, $11 per pound. Whole jerk chicken $14. MC, V. Open: Daily 10 a.m.–11 p.m.*

Pork Pit
$ **Montego Bay   Jamaican**

Locals and adventuresome visitors flock to this laid-back joint for a taste of the celebrated jerk pork and jerk chicken, said to have been a culinary gift of the Maroons, those slaves who escaped and fled into the hinterlands to escape bondage. If so, we owe them a debt. The jerk meats are fiery and full of zest and cooked in the old-fashioned method of barbecuing. It's served on picnic tables. It's best to come here with a group if you can corral one, ordering the food at picnic tables along with such "sides" as baked yam or baked potato. As a change of pace, roast fresh fish of the day is also featured. Everything is washed down with Red Stripe beer.

27 Gloucester Ave., a half-mile past the brewery and Walter Fletcher Beach, Montego Bay. ☎ *876-952-1046. One pound of jerk pork $9.50. Open: Daily 11 a.m.–11 p.m.*

Strawberry Hill

$$$$ Blue Mountains   Modern Jamaican

The setting is as equally charming as that of the Blue Mountian Inn, and the cuisine is even better in the sense that it's more lighthearted and modern. At this previously recommended outpost, a favorite retreat for off-the-record celebrities, a refined cuisine is served to those who take in the twinkling lights of Kingston at night. On chilly nights in the mountains, a bar with a crackling fire is a magnetic attraction. Diners prefer tables on the second-story enveloping porch or else in the Great House with its tall ceilings and wrought-iron chandeliers. This is a restaurant for a long, leisurely meal — not fast service. Every dish is given island flavor, such as the freshly grilled catch of the day with a jerk mango and sweet pepper salsa, or rotis stuffed with herb-infused curried goat. Shrimp is perfectly grilled, its flavor enhanced by fresh cilantro. The Irish Town potato cakes with a passion-fruit salsa and mango chutney may precede a velvety crème caramel with a dash of Grand Marnier for an enticing aroma. The fashionable set from Kingston journeys into the hills for the big spread Sunday brunch.

Irish Town, Blue Mountains. ☎ *876-944-8400. Reservations needed. Main courses: Lunch $20–$25; 3-course prix-fixe dinner $49; Sun brunch $45. DC, MC, V. Open: Daily noon to 3 p.m. and 6–10 p.m.*

Sugar Mill

$$$–$$$$ Montego Bay   International/Caribbean

As you sit at a private table by the waterfall, know that you've selected one of the most romantic places for dining in Mo Bay. You'll also get a more polished cuisine here than anywhere else at the resort. The restaurant is named for its former role when it was the site of a water wheel making sugar from cane for a nearby plantation. If you visit for lunch, you can sample what may be a first for you, an akee burger with bacon. Before ordering that, you can sample a velvety pumpkin soup. To finish? There's nothing finer than the homemade rum/raisin ice cream. For dinner, there's even a refined version of jerk pork, fish, or chicken. The smoked marlin is one of the chef's specialties and is something to savor. The cookery is superbly crafted, and there's always something bubbling in the curry pot of the day, even curried goat served with a fruit-studded chutney.

At Half Moon Golf, Tennis, and Beach Club, 7 miles east of Mo Bay, Rose Hall. ☎ *876-953-2314. Dinner reservations essential. Main courses: $19.50–$44. AE, MC, V. Open: Daily noon to 3 p.m. and 7–11 p.m.*

Toscanini
$$$ Harmony Hall Italian

We're still loyal to Evita's (see the listing earlier in this chapter), but unknown to her, we like to head east on some nights to sample the savory, succulent cuisine served here. The restaurant is run by a family from Parma, one of the gastronomic centers of Italy, or according to the people of Parma, "the gastronomic center of Italy," and to hell with Bologna's claims. Emanuele and Lella Guilivi, and her brother, Pierluigi Ricci, welcome you, bringing their continental sophistication and flair to the cuisine. The setting, in a revived 19th-century mansion, is part of a complex that includes an art gallery. Much of their cuisine is classic Italian, and much of it adapted to local ingredients and tastes. The chef, for example, caters to vegetarians. Even a Rasta man could dine securely here. The homemade pastas are the best along the coast, and a special appetizer we've enjoyed more than once is marinated marlin. Fresh lobster and the finest of seafood are featured nightly at one of the candlelit tables on a small terrace. To avoid a long taxi ride from Ocho Rios at night, many diners visit at lunch during a tour of the area.

Harmony Hall, Towers Isle, Route 3, 4 miles east of Ocho Rios. ☎ 876-975-4785. Main courses: $10–$35. Pastas: $9–$16. AE, MC, V. Open: Tues–Sun noon to 2:30 p.m. and 7:00–10:30 p.m.

Chapter 27

Having Fun on and off the Beach in Jamaica

By Darwin Porter and Danforth Prince

• •

In This Chapter

▶ Soaking up the sun on Jamaica's top beaches

▶ Diving into fun with water sports

▶ Satisfying the landlubber: activities, shopping, and nightlife

• •

*W*ith all its political turmoil, a possible sense of danger, and a lot of hassle from the local vendors and hustlers, you may reasonably ask, "Why Jamaica?"

For all its faults, it remains the most exotic island in the West Indies, with the possible exception of Haiti. Some islands even have prettier beaches, but Jamaica's allure, ever since its swashbuckling days, has drawn a steady stream of visitors to this "Island in the Sun," and many came to visit and stayed forever.

As one old salt from England told us, "All islands in the Caribbean have sunsets. But carnal red sunsets?"

There is a diversity here unequalled in the Caribbean, with Jamaica's polyglot population and its landscapes that range from rain forests to arid, desert-like flatlands, to towering mountain peaks, to a bustling city (Kingston), to a remote mountain village where you go to buy Blue Mountain coffee.

You get the finest golf courses in the Caribbean at Mo Bay; some of the best scuba diving and water sports; the most varied program of outdoor activities including river rafting, mountain biking, and swimming in blue lagoons seemingly waiting for the movie cameras.

When the sun goes down, it's party time in Jamaica, more so than in any of the other islands. The sound of reggae fills the night air.

In this chapter, we can only give you some reasons to go to Jamaica. Many, many other reasons you'll discover for yourself once you're there.

Heading for the Beaches

Jamaica offers a dazzling choice of beaches. Whoever it was took a ruler and measured off 200 miles of beaches from white sand to black sand encircling the island. Many of these are so secluded you'll have them all to yourself. Others such as those at Mo Bay and Ocho Rios are overrun, especially when cruise ships arrive.

Most of the beaches of Jamaica need not concern you. You'll happily settle for the strip of sand in front of your resort. For the most part, the mega-resorts, including the all-inclusives, have grabbed up the best sands.

Pick and choose carefully if a beach is the reason you're coming to Jamaica. Montego Bay, Jamaica's second largest city, has more hotels but only some relatively modest public beaches. Ocho Rios, site of

The culture club

This land of the perennial summer is not a mere beachfront but the most culturally diverse nation in the West Indies. Its people for the most part are poor, but the island is rich, with some 3,000 species of flowering plants alone (more than 800 found nowhere else); slithery reptiles like the endangered American crocodile; more than 250 species of birds; more botanical gardens than any other island, and some of the grandest national parks in the Caribbean Sea's archipelago, including the Blue Mountains/John Crow National Park.

Thanks to Bob Marley and other stars, reggae music is now played around the world, and Jamaican art — still deep-rooted in African tradition — hangs in some of the most prestigious galleries in Europe and America, even Japan.

Yes, there is racial tension here — a lot of it at times, which is to be expected as a holdover from the legacy of slavery. Even the Queen of Jamaica (Elizabeth II of England) was snubbed on a royal visit by some Jamaican politicians in 2002, as the representative of a European nation that once championed slavery.

To see all this island wonder requires quite a bit of movement, a lot of hassle, and a slight uneasiness, especially when you venture into the country's cultural capital, Kingston. If you feel uneasy, ask your hotel to book you a guide (they charge reasonable rates), and set out to sample for yourself what all the excitement is about.

Or not. No one said you had to visit any "must see" sights. There's nothing wrong with going to Jamaica and lying on the beach for a week. There are far worse things to happen to you in this world.

the second conglomeration of hotels, has only two beaches, and they're crowded.

For a beach holiday, make it Negril. No beach on the island can match its 7 miles of white sand.

If you like to take it all off, Negril is the place to flaunt your charms. Some parts of its beachfront are clothing optional, dividing the "prudes" from the "nudes."

The XXX-rated beach attraction for Negril is **Booby Cay**, a tiny islet that the Walt Disney people used in their film *20,000 Leagues Under the Sea.* Today it's more likely to attract the cameramen from *Playboy* (or *Playgirl* as the case may be). This is the nude island of Jamaica, reached after a half-mile boat ride from Rutland Point. First-time visitors assume the "booby" refers to a woman's breasts, because there are many of those on exhibit here. Actually it's called "Booby" because of its original inhabitants, a colony of blue-footed booby birds. The crowd from Hedonism II is especially fond of visiting for the day. Barbecues are staged, and boatloads arrive, some of whose passengers have taken off their swimsuits before hitting the sands. If you visit, take plenty of suntan lotion to protect your vital assets.

Robinson Crusoe types may shun all these public and overrun beaches. For that uncrowded beachfront, you can head for the south coast, an easy drive east of Negril along A2. After leaving the dreary port city of Savanna-La-Mar, the first good beach you'll approach is **Bluefields Beach,** where the famous reggae star Peter Tosh used to live. At the western fringe of Bluefields Bay is **Paradise Park,** a cattle and dairy farm with waters ideal for swimming and picnic tables and barbecue grills on site.

Farther down the coast, past the settlement of Black River, you come to relatively undiscovered **Treasure Beach,** with its long black sandy beaches flanked by rocky limestone headlands, suitable for mountain biking and hiking. Local fishermen along the shoreline, for a reasonable fee to be negotiated, will take you out either for fishing or cruising on the bay. In the evening, have dinner at our favorite stopover, Jake's (see Chapter 24), check in and drink and dance the night away in the moonlight.

The public beaches in Montego Bay are good but small and usually crowded. They lie right in the center of the resort opening off Gloucester Avenue or "Hip Strip" as it's known. The 5-mile-long **Doctor's Cave Beach** (☎ 876-952-2566) launched Mo Bay as a resort in the 1940s. Popular with families, it is the best all-around beach in Mo Bay. Also opening onto Hip Strip is **Cornwall Beach** (☎ 876-952-3463), a long stretch of white sand with excellent swimming all year. Both beaches have dressing cabañas and water-sports kiosks. You can rent chairs, umbrellas, and rafts from 9 a.m. to 5 p.m. daily, and admission to either beach is $3 for adults or $1.50 for children 12 and under. Regrettably, vendors and hustlers annoy you throughout the day.

In the heart of Mo Bay, the third-most-popular strip of sand is **Walter Fletcher Beach** (☎ 876-979-9447), a family favorite because of its tranquil waters. Many beach buffs picnic here for lunch, although there's an on-site restaurant, along with changing rooms and a lifeguard. Open daily from 10 a.m., it charges $2.30 for adults and $1.15 for children.

You'll pay more but can escape the hordes by going to **Rose Hall Beach Club** (☎ 876-680-0969), 11 miles east of Mo Bay. Here you get a half mile of private white-sand beach and turquoise waters, better facilities, and a finer restaurant, along with clean toilets and changing rooms, even a full water-sports program. The cost is $6 for adults or $3 for kids any time daily from 10 a.m. to 6 p.m.

In spite of its many all-inclusive mega-resorts, Ocho Rios is not great beach country. Ochi, as it's called, is also the major cruise-ship entry port for Jamaica, and beaches are even more crowded when these mammoths dock. In the center of the resort is **Mallards Beach,** always overrun although the sands are idyllic here. To the south, the white sands of **Turtle Beach** are even more alluring but it, too, is busy. Locals themselves, with children in tow, also swim here, and it gets very crowded on weekends.

We like to escape Ocho Rios entirely and follow 007's trail to **James Bond Beach** (☎ 876-975-3663), lying at Oracabessa east of Ochi. This is near the former home of Bond's creator, Ian Fleming. The sandy strip is open Tuesday through Sunday, charging $5 for adults and $2.50 for children. On site is a water-sports concession as well.

It rains a lot in Port Antonio but its beaches are among the most beautiful and most secluded in Jamaica. Elizabeth Taylor and Richard Burton have long left the beach at **Frenchman's Cove,** 5 miles east of Port Antonio, but this beach is still a romantic romp. It's a beach of white sand with a freshwater stream, costing $3 to enter it daily from 9 a.m. to 5 p.m.

While at Port Antonio you can also go for a dip in the **Blue Lagoon** where the 14-year-old Brooke Shields swam nude in the movie of the same name. There's no beach here but the always stunning waters are fed by a natural amphitheater, and it's one of the finest places for a refreshing dip in all of Jamaica — without your bikini, of course.

Taking the Plunge with Water Fun

Jamaica is hardly the scuba center of the Caribbean, and islands such as the Caymans or Bonaire have far more spectacular underwater worlds. Even so, there are diving adventures to enjoy, especially at Negril.

Hurricanes have severely damaged many of Jamaica's once stunning reefs — that and careless boaters, overzealous fishermen, and young boys robbing the shore of its shells and sea fans to hawk to tourists.

In spite of that, there is still plenty of marine life. The following outfitters feature dive trips and certification courses and will also rent the snorkeler gear for the day:

In Montego Bay

Dive Jamaica (☎ 876-953-2021) is run by PADI-certified instructor Ben Baker who offers everything from resort courses to specialty certification, with outings to a variety of sites, including the Basket Reef, where you'll see basket sponges, sea fans, parrot fish, and perhaps even a turtle or dolphin if you're lucky. **North Coast Marine Sports** (☎ 876-953-9266), located at the Half Moon Golf, Tennis, and Beach Club, offers everything from scuba-diving to Sunfish, snorkel gear, kayaks, and more. They can arrange for deep-sea fishing trips and snorkel cruises, too.

In Negril

The best area for snorkeling is off the cliffs in the West End, where you can see stingrays, sergeant majors, and several parrot fish on the reef at a depth of about 10 to 15 feet. You can find dozens of shops along West End Road, where you can rent snorkeling equipment at modest prices.

Ochi and Runaway Bay offer good snorkeling, too, on its shoreline east of Ocho Rios to Galina Point, which is fringed by a colorful reef. The reef fish are making a slight comeback, and marine life is varied. Although some reefs are accessible from the shore, you can avoid the boats and beach activity if you take a short boat ride to the better reefs further offshore. The best outfitter is **Resort Divers**, centered at Shaw Park Beach Hotel, Cutglass Bay (☎ 876-974-2552). They know the north coast better than anyone, including the infamous Devils Reef, a pinnacle that drops some 200 feet into the deep, luring only experienced divers. The outfitter also specializes in a variety of water sports — not just diving — including deep-sea fishing, snorkeling, and parasailing. Their prices are competitive: a glass bottom and snorkeling cruise costing $25, parasailing at $55, jet-skiing at $30 per run, a banana boat ride at $15 per person, a sunset cruise at $25, and deep-sea fishing beginning at $350 for a half day. A one-tank boat dive goes for $40, a two-tank boat dive for $70, and a night dive for $60. All dive packages include tanks, weights, and belt. Fins, snorkels, and masks can be rented ($5 per day for all three).

If you're going to Port Antonio, snorkel with **Lady Godiva's Dive Shop** in Dragon Bay (☎ 876-993-8988), 7 miles from Port Antonio. Lady Godiva offers two excursions daily to San San Bay, a colorful reef off Monkey Island, for $12 per person. Snorkeling equipment costs $9 for a full day's rental, and dive prices range from $40 to $60 per person.

Negril Scuba Centre (Negril Beach Club Hotel, Norman Manley Boulevard ☎ 800-818-2963 or 876-957-9641), is the best-equipped scuba facility in Negril. Beginner's dive lessons are offered daily, as well as multiple-dive packages for certified divers. Full scuba certifications and specialty courses are also available. A resort course, designed for first-time divers with basic swimming abilities, includes all instruction and equipment, a lecture on water and diving safety, and one open-water dive. It begins at 10 a.m. daily and ends at 2 p.m. The price is $75. A one-tank dive costs $30 per dive plus $20 for equipment rental. More economical is a two-tank dive, which includes lunch; you must complete your dive in one day. It costs $55, plus the (optional) $20 rental of all equipment. This organization is PADI-registered, although it accepts all recognized certification cards. It specializes in night dives and has been in business for two decades.

Enjoying the Water without Getting Wet

Even if you don't know how to swim, you can enjoy "close encounters" with the water on this plush island known for its tranquil rivers and cascading waterfalls.

Rolling down the river on a raft

One of the more unusual ways to enjoy the water in Jamaica is to take one of its famed river raft rides, popularized by the late Errol Flynn, the dashing, womanizing actor who used to challenge his friends to raft races.

Although a fading Hollywood memory, Flynn was spoofed by Mel Brooks as "the man in the green tights" — Flynn was known for his swashbuckling roles, including Robin Hood. He is still known and talked about in the Port Antonio area.

Here's how to hook up with this amusing sport. A Jamaican raftsman will pole you down the Rio Grande. We're not talking Texas here — Jamaica's Rio Grande is only 8 miles long, stretching like a snake from Berrydale to Rafter's Restaurant. The trip takes three hours, and you can bring along a picnic to enjoy on the river's bank. Plenty of vendors will be on hand to hawk a frosty Red Stripe. Or else you can wait and order lunch at Rafter's.

The following companies arrange rafting trips:

> ✔ **Rio Grande Tours,** Rafter's Restaurant, St. Margaret's Bay (☎ 876-993-5778), provides a fully insured driver who will take you in your rented car to the starting point at Grants Level or Berrydale, where you board your raft. The rafts, some 33 feet long and only 4 feet

wide, are propelled by stout bamboo poles. The raised double seat about two-thirds of the way back accommodates two passengers. The skipper guides the craft down the river, between steep hills covered with coconut palms, banana plantations, and flowers, through limestone cliffs pitted with caves, past the "Tunnel of Love" (a narrow cleft in the rocks), then on to wider, gentler water. Trips last two to three hours and are offered from 9 a.m. to 5 p.m. daily at a cost of $45 per raft, which is suitable for two people. The trip ends at the Rafter's Restaurant, where you collect your car, which has been returned by the driver.

✔ **Martha Brae's Rafters Village** (☎ 876-952-0889) lies 28 miles to the east of Mo Bay at a point 3 miles inland from Falmouth. The rafts are similar to those on the Rio Grande. You sit on a raised dais on bamboo logs. It isn't necessary to wear a swimsuit because you're seated in dry comfort. The cost is $45, with two riders allowed on a raft, plus a small child if accompanied by an adult (but use caution). The trips last 1¼ hours and operate Monday through Saturday from 9 a.m. to 4 p.m. Along the way, you can stop and order cool drinks or beer along the banks of the river. There's a bar, a restaurant, and two souvenir shops in the village.

✔ **Mountain Valley Rafting** (Lethe, ☎ 876-956-4920) runs trips down the River Lethe, approximately 12 miles southwest of Mo Bay. The hour-long trip is about $45 per raft (two per raft) and takes you through unspoiled hill country. You can also book through your hotel tour desk.

✔ If you're staying in Negril or on the South Coast, we recommend **South Coast Safaris** (1 Crane Rd., ☎ 876-965-2513) where you can take a boat ride up Jamaica's largest river, navigated through mangrove swamps in savanna country. You'll see egrets and other water birds, as well as Jamaica's crocodiles. Locals call them alligators. The one-hour safari costs $15 per person.

Also in that area, you should check out the **Y.S. Falls**; a *jitney* (small bus) will drop you near the falls. It's an idyllic place to play in the cool waters and have a picnic. The site is not nearly as touristy as **Dunn's River Falls** in Ocho Rios. The estate is open daily from 9:30 a.m. to 4:30 p.m.

✔ **Dunn's River Falls** (☎ 876-974-2857) is Ocho Rios's biggest attraction — and its most touristy — and is to be avoided when cruise ships are in port. Forming a daisy chain, you climb to the top of the falls with a guide (tip expected, of course). After the climb, you "stairstep" down through tiers of cascades and cooling pools until you reach the beach. Admission to the falls is $6 for adults and $3 for children ages 2 to 11. They're open daily from 8:30 a.m. to 5:00 p.m.

Wear old tennis shoes or sports sandals to protect your feet from the sharp rocks and to prevent slipping. Although very small children are allowed to climb the falls, consider carefully whether you want to take a risk, especially with toddlers.

✔ A morning spent at Dunn's River Falls can be followed by the most scenic drive in the area, reached by heading down A3 south into a lush gorge called **Fern Valley.** Originally a riverbed, the main road thorugh the valley now passes a profusion of wild ferns, a rain forest, hardwood trees, and lianas. The road runs for 4 miles, taking in a profusion of more than 600 species of ferns. You can stop at any point at one of the roadside stands inspecting carved wood souvenirs and basketwork or perhaps picking up some fresh fruit at one of the stands.

Angling

Seaworld Resorts, whose main office is at the Cariblue Hotel, Rose Hall Main Road, Montego Bay (☎ 876-953-2180), operates flying-bridge cruisers, with deck lines and outriggers, for fishing expeditions. A half-day fishing trip costs $380 for up to four participants.

Sticking to Dry Land

From horseback riding to wilderness hiking, from golf to tennis, the resorts of Jamaica and its hinterlands offer many chances for an "athletic vacation" for those who don't want to spend all their time lying on a beach.

Riding the range on horseback

For the horseback rider, the best stables, even the best trails, are found near the resort of Ocho Rios.

Chukka Cove Farm (☎ 876-972-2506) lies at Richmond Llandovery, 4 miles to the east of Runaway Bay. These are the best stables in Jamaica, with hour-long trail rides costing $30, or a three-hour beach ride going for $55. During weekends in winter, polo players, often from Britain, visit here.

In the same area you can also go horseback riding along a trio of scenic trails at **Prospect Plantation**, Route A3, 3 miles east of Ocho Rios (☎ 876-994-1058). A one-hour horseback ride goes for $20, although longer trail rides can be arranged. You can also tour a working plantation, at a cost of $12 per person (it's free for ages 12 and under). Tours are conducted Monday through Saturday at 10:30 a.m., 2:00 p.m., and 3:30 p.m., and on Sunday at 11:00 a.m., 1:30 p.m., and 3:00 p.m.

In Negril, you can go riding through the Negril Hills to the south of the resort. Several outfitters in the area can rent you a horse, but your best bet is **Country Western Horse Rental** (☎ 876-957-3250), adjacent to the police station on Sheffield Road in the center of town. A two-hour ride follows the rocky coastline before heading into the Negril Hills.

In Montego Bay, the area around the resort is heavily built up, but the people at **Rocky Point Riding Stables**, Half Moon Club, Rose Hall (☎ 876-953-2286), know the best trails. Their 30 horses are housed in Jamaica's most beautiful stables, where you can arrange for a 1½-hour beach or mountain ride costing $50 per rider.

Exploring the lush interior

The best guided hikes and the best guided ATV tours are offered along the lush north coast, which gets more rain than elsewhere in Jamaica. In Port Antonio, Valley Hikes (% 876-993-3881) features a variety of hikes of various difficulties through the Rio Grande Valley, that luxuriant area between the John Crow Mountains and the Blue Mountains. The easiest trail is a $1^1/_2$-hour waterfall tour for $35. You can also take a 4-mile hike into the Blue Mountains, taking in its flora and fauna at a cost of $35 per person.

You can also go on wheels on a guided ATV tour arranged by **Wilderness Resort**, St. Mary (☎ 876-974-5189), which will take you into a rain forest in the hinterlands of Ocho Rios. Their tours through the wilds, which include some time out for fishing, go for $60 per person.

Linking up with a round of golf

The game of golf was imported from Scotland in the late 19th century, and it's been a firmly entrenched sport ever since. Today Jamaica offers some of the finest golf courses in the Caribbean, the best centered at Mo Bay.

Caddies are required, and rates are $12 to $25, but you'll get extra entertainment: They carry your golf bag and clubs balanced sideways on their heads.[1]

Some of the best courses are in Mo Bay. The following are our favorites:

- ✔ **White Witch of Rose Hall Golf Course**, part of the new Ritz-Carlton Rose Hall grounds (☎ 876-953-2204), lies east of Montego Bay and is Jamaica's newest and most spectacular course. Designed by Robert von Hagge, it is set on 200 landscaped acres, charging $175 for hotel guests, $225 for nonguests.

- ✔ The **Half Moon Golf, Tennis, and Beach Club**, Rose Hall, 7 miles east of Mo Bay (☎ 876-953-2560), has a championship Robert Trent Jones–designed 18-hole course. Greens fees are $90 for guests, $130 for nonguests.

- ✔ **Ironshore**, at Ironshore, 3 miles east of the airport (☎ 876-953-3681), is an 18-hole, par-72 course. The greens fee is $80.

✔ **Tryall Golf, Tennis, and Beach Club**, 15 miles west of Mo Bay on North Coast Highway (☎ 876-956-5660), has an 18-hole championship course on the site of a 19th-century sugar plantation. Guests of Tryall pay $80 in winter, $40 in the off-season. Nonguests can play only in the off-season, paying $150 for the privilege.

✔ **Wyndham Rose Hall**, at Rose Hall, 4 miles east of the airport on North Coast Highway (☎ 876-953-2650), has a challenging seaside and mountain layout. Fees run $100 for guests, $125 for nonguests.

✔ **Ocho Rios has the Sandals Golf and Country Club**, 2 miles east of Ocho Rios (☎ 876-975-0119), whose adjacent 18-hole course is known for its panoramic scenery, 700 feet above sea level. The greens fee is $100 for nonguests.

✔ **SuperClub's Runaway Golf Course**, North Coast Highway, Kingston (☎ 876-973-7319), is a challenging 18-hole course that has witnessed many championship tournaments. The greens fee is $80 for nonguests; guests of SuperClubs play for free.

✔ **Negril Hills Golf Course**, Sheffield Road (☎ 876-957-4638), is Negril's only golf course. Although it doesn't have the prestige of such Montego Bay courses as Tryall, it's the only golf course in western Jamaica. The 225-acre course lies in the foothills of Negril at Sheffield, 3 miles east of the center of the resort, bordering the Great Morass. Opening in 1994, the course is known for its water hazards and its undulating fairways. This is one place where if your ball goes into the water, you don't try to retrieve it unless you want to fight over it with a crocodile. On site is a restaurant (mediocre food) and a pro shop.

Having a ball with tennis or squash

The mega-resorts offer tennis courts, which are free to their guests. Most of them, except for the all-inclusives, will let nonguests play if they reserve court space and "pay to play." Nonguests are charged from $6 to $8 per hour. Tennis pros on site will usually give lessons for about $14 per hour.

What follows is a sampling of some of the best courts:

✔ **Wyndham Rose Hall Golf and Beach Resort,** Rose Hall (☎ 876-953-2650), outside Montego Bay, is an outstanding tennis resort, though it's not the equal of Half Moon or Tryall (covered later). Wyndham offers six hard-surface courts, each lit for night play. As a courtesy, nonguests are sometimes invited to play for free, but permission has to be obtained from the manager.

✔ **Half Moon Golf, Tennis, and Beach Club,** outside Montego Bay (☎ 876-953-2211), has the finest courts in the area, even outclassing Tryall. Its 13 state-of-the-art courts, 7 of which are lit for night games, attract tennis players from around the world. Lessons cost

$25 to $35 per half hour, $50 to $65 per hour. Residents play free, day or night.

✔ **Tryall Golf, Tennis, and Beach Club,** St. James (☎ 876-956-5660), offers nine hard-surface courts, three lit for night play, near its Great House. Day games are free for guests; nonguests pay $30 per hour.

✔ In Negril, tennis buffs book into **Couples Swept Away Negril,** Norman Manley Boulevard (☎ 876-957-4061), which offers ten courts, more than any other in the area. Half of these are clay, the others hard courts.

✔ At Ocho Rios, **Beaches Grand Sport at Ciboney,** Main Street (☎ 876-974-1027), focuses more on tennis than any other resort in the area. It offers three clay-surface and three hard-surface courts, all lit for night play. Guests play free, day or night, but nonguests must call and make arrangements with the manager.

Climbing every mountain

Reaching its peak at 7,400 feet in the Blue Mountains, Jamaica offers the Caribbean's most dramatic mountain scenery and its most varied, with cascading waterfalls, roaring rivers, and vast, almost jungle-like rain-forests filled with stunning flora. To watch the sun come up at the towering peak of the Blue Mountains is the goal of many a hiker in Jamaica. Even if you don't want to get up that early, you can enjoy organized hikes through this lush terrain. Many of the trails were first chopped out of the wilderness by British soldiers. Today they are more likely to be used by farmers carrying coffee by mule trains (sometimes the crop is ganja).

At the end of the trail, know that a steaming cup of Blue Mountain coffee — "the java of kings" — is waiting for you. Sometimes locals use wildflower honey instead of sugar to sweeten the brew.

You could get lost, mugged, or whatever, wandering around these Blue Mountain trails on your own. We recommend that you set out only with a guide. You can go with a group or else on your own with one or two other people in your party, but always, *always* with a guide.

You can book with Kingston's best-known specialists in eco-sensitive tours, **Sunventure Tours**, 30 Balmoral Ave., Kingston (☎ 876-960-6685). The staff here can always arrange an individualized tour for you and your party, but it also has a roster of mainstream offerings. The **Blue Mountain Sunrise Tour** involves a camp-style overnight in one of the most remote and inaccessible areas of Jamaica. For a fee of $150 per person, participants are retrieved at their Kingston hotels, driven to an isolated ranger station, Wildflower Lodge, that's accessible only via four-wheel-drive vehicle, in anticipation of a two-stage hike that begins at 2 p.m. A simple mountaineer's supper is served at 6 p.m. around a campfire at a ranger station near Portland Gap. At 3 a.m., climbers hike by moonlight and flashlight to a mountaintop aerie that was selected for its view of the sunrise over the Blue Mountains. Climbers stay aloft until around noon that day, then head back down the mountain for an eventual return to their hotels in Kingston by 4 p.m.. A four-hour trek, costing from $25 to $30 per person, can also be arranged.

Cycling is another option for touring the Blue Mountains. **Blue Mountain Bike Tours** in Kingston (☎ 876-974-7075) offers all-downhill bike tours through the Blue Mountains — you peddle only about a half dozen times on this several-mile trip. Visitors are driven to the highest navigable point in the Blue Mountains, where they are provided bikes and protective gear. Lunch, snacks, and lots of information about coffee, local foliage, and history are provided. The cost is about $85 per person.

Going to the birds

Birdies "flock" to Jamaica, which offers some serious opportunities to observe our feathery friends. There are more than 250 different species on the island including the verrain hummingbird, which can be seen in the Blue Mountains. Only the famous "bee" hummingbird found in some places in Cuban forests is smaller.

Some 50 species of birds are found only in Jamaica, and in no other habitat in the world. Many of the species you are likely to see, including the Jamaican blackbird, are endangered.

In the 20th century many exotic birds in Jamaica went the way of the dodo. If you're with a guide, don't be surprised if he shows fright at the sound of the *patoo,* an African word for owl. Superstitious Jamaicans believe the screech of the owl is a signal that the Grim Reaper is on his way.

The best place for concentrated bird-watching is at the **Rocklands Wildlife Station**, about a mile outside Anchovy on the road from Montego Bay, St. James (☎ 876-952-2009). It's a unique experience to have a Jamaican "doctorbird" perch on your finger to drink syrup, to feed small doves and finches millet from your hand, and to watch dozens of other exotic birds flying in for their evening meal. Don't take children age 5 and under to this sanctuary, because they tend to bother the birds. Admission is $6.90; open daily from 2 to 5 p.m.

At **Marshall's Pen cattle estate and private nature reserve**, near Mandeville, guided bird-watching tours of the scenic property and other birding spots on Jamaica may be arranged in advance. Six persons are taken on a tour for $60. Self-catering accommodation is sometimes available for bird-watchers only, but arrangements must be made in advance. For information, contact Ann or Robert Sutton, Marshall's Pen, P.O. Box 58, Mandeville, Jamaica, W.I. (☎ **876-904-5454**). Robert Sutton is co-author of *Birds of Jamaica,* a photographic field guide published by Cambridge University Press.

Exploring the island's past

Like Tara in *Gone with the Wind,* the Great House in Jamaica was a large house at the center of a sugar plantation where "the master" lived with his wife and family, waited upon by house slaves. Some of these Great Houses are still preserved in Jamaica today, although islanders disdain their evocation of the days of slavery. The two most intriguing Great Houses lie outside Mo Bay.

Once the grandest Great House in Jamaica, **Rose Hall** (☎ 876-953-2323) is the stuff of legend and lore, fabled as the former abode of the notorious "White Witch of Rose Hall." If you believe all those bodice-ripping Gothic novels, "the witch," Annie Palmer, murdered at least three husbands and various lovers. Actually this libel may be just so much paperback fodder. The real Annie Palmer died peacefully at the age of 72 (she wasn't murdered in her bed) after a long and apparently happy marriage. The vastly restored Rose Hall was originally built between 1778 and 1790 as the center of a 6,000-acre plantation with more than 2,000 slaves. Frankly, the legend of Annie Palmer overrides the decoration and architecture here, but it's well worth a visit to see how the landed gentry lived. On the outskirts of Mo Bay, Rose Hall lies 2 miles east of the little town of Ironshore across from the Rose Hall resorts. Admission is $15 per person, or $10 for those 11 and under. Hours are daily from 9 a.m. to 6 p.m.

Greenwood Great House, lying 15 miles east of Montego Bay (☎ 876-953-1077), also has literary associations, these for real. The Georgian style Great House was the former abode of Richard Barrett, whose cousin was the famous poet Elizabeth Barrett Browning. The house was built between 1780 and 1800, when the Barrett family was the largest landholder in Jamaica, owning 84,000 acres and 3,000 slaves. The house has been restored, and you can visit it, seeing its library and antiques, although the interior is not as ornate as Rose Hall. Guides in costumes offer a narrated tour. The house charges $12 admission, or $6 for children under 12; open daily from 9 a.m. to 6 p.m.

Checking out what's land-based

Not all the attractions of Jamaica are on the beach or in the water. The island offers a number of land-based attractions for those who'd like to dip into its interior or take driving tours along its coastlines.

At an elevation of 420 feet, the **Coyaba River Garden and Museum** (☎ 876-974-6235) lies 1½ miles south of Ocho Rios at the Shaw Park Estate on Shaw Park Ridge Road. Meaning "paradise" in Arawak, Coyaba is set on 3 acres of beautifully landscaped gardens with some of the most evocative of the island's flora. The grounds are filled with cascades, carp pools, and streams. In a villa on-site, artifacts trace the history of Jamaica from the early Arawaks to independence from Britain. Taking about an hour, tours are conducted daily from 8 a.m. to 5 p.m., costing $4.50 for ages 13 and up (free for others).

Celebrities, many from the golden age of Hollywood, frequented the north coast of Jamaica in the '50s and '60s, and one of them, **Sir Nöel Coward**, liked the island so much he erected a "retreat from the world" at **Firefly** (☎ 876-725-0920), lying in St. Mary, 20 miles east of Ocho Rios overlooking the little town of Oracabessa. Sir Nöel, along with his longtime companion, Graham Payn, lived here until Nöel's death in 1973. His friends, from Katharine Hepburn to the Queen Mother of England, dropped in for a visit. A closet still contains his Hawaiian-print shirts, and in his bedroom rests the original four-poster bed he once occupied. The library contains his collection of books, and there are two grand pianos where he composed some of his famous show tunes. Coward is buried on the grounds. The house is open Monday through Thursday and Saturday from 9 a.m. to 5 p.m., charging an admission of $10.

On the same day you visit Firefly, you can also drop in at **Harmony Hall** (☎ 876-975-4222), lying at Tower Isles on Route 3, 4 miles east of Ocho Rios. Built in the 19th century as the center of a sugar plantation, the restored complex is today the site of an art gallery showcasing some of the best paintings and sculpture by island artists. Seek out, in particular, the "Starfish Oils" by Sharon McConnell. Arts, crafts, and "reggae" resort ware are also sold. The complex is also the home of Toscanini, one of the best restaurants in Greater Ocho Rios (see Chapter 26 for details). Harmony Hall is also the site of the Garden Café for informal food and drink.

Kingston is not only the political capital of Jamaica, but also the island's cultural center. The **National Gallery**, Roy West Building, Kingston Mall (☎ 876-922-1561), showcases the most important art collection on the island. It's a treasure trove of the nation's most talented sculptors and painters, the most famous of which is Edna Manley, a sculptor, who was married to Norman Manley, a former prime minister. In the entryway, you're greeted with a large statue of the late Bob Marley. Admission is $1.25 and hours are Tuesday through Thursday 10:00 a.m. to 4:30 p.m., Friday 10 a.m. to 4 p.m., and Saturday 10 a.m. to 3 p.m.

While in Kingston, you can also see its most visited attraction, the **Bob Marley Museum**, 56 Hope Rd. (☎ 876-927-9152), the reggae singer's former home and recording studio where he lived until his death on May 11, 1981, in a Miami hospital. You can tour the house, filled with Marley memorabilia, Monday through Saturday from 9:30 a.m. to 4:00 p.m., paying $9.20 for adults, $6.90 ages 13 to 18, and $4.60 ages 4 to 12.

The Jamaican marketplace

You literally can't go anywhere in Jamaica, even if lying on the beach, without some vendor coming around and hawking locally made crafts to you, much of dubious taste. Not only that, but every town, village, or hamlet has vendors along the roadsides, including Fern Gully, south of Ocho Rios. Hardwood carvings of Bob Marley are pure kitsch, and bead jewelry comes in Rasta colors of yellow, green, and red. If you're interested, remember to bargain. The asking price is merely the beginning of the negotiation. You can often get an item for about 25 percent less than what was first asked.

Here's a thing or three you may want to bring back with you — all duty-free:

- Jamaican rum
- Tia Maria, Jamaica's world-famous coffee liqueur
- Blue Mountain coffee
- Hot sauces
- Wood carvings
- Fine handmade Macanudo cigars

Most duty-free merchandise is sold at the major shopping plazas in Ocho Rios and Mo Bay. In Mo Bay, most of the duty-free shops are at **City Centre** or the **Holiday Village Shopping Centre.** Even better is **Half Moon Plaza,** on the coastal road 8 miles east of Mo Bay.

In Ocho Rios, all the major duty-free markets, easy to find, lie in the center of town, including **Ocean Village Shopping Centre, Coconut Grove Shopping Plaza,** and **Pineapple Place Shopping Centre.**

If you'd like to escape the hassle of the marketplace and shop in ease and comfort, you can visit the **Gallery of West Indian Art,** at the exclusive Round Hill Hotel, Route 1A, west of Mo Bay (☎ **876-952-4547**). Here the boutique owner has acquired some of the finest Jamaican and Haitian paintings, along with some painted locally made pottery.

The best Jamaican art on the island is showcased at two galleries in Kingston: **Frame Gallery,** 10 Tangerine Place (☎ **876-926-4644**), with more than 300 works on exhibit, and its main competitor, **Mutual Life Gallery,** Mutual Life Centre, Oxford Rd. (☎ **876-929-4302**), a constantly changing showcase of the island's finest artists, both known and unknown.

Limin' after dark

When the sun goes down, the sounds of reggae fill the air, and the blenders whirl in the tropical bars mixing those lethal rum punches. For such large resorts, nightlife in Mo Bay and Ocho is a bit skimpy, except for staged entertainment at the hotels such as limbo dancers, reggae bands, and the like. There's more happening in Kingston after dark (not the safest place to be) and Negril than anywhere else on island. Because running around at night on your own is a bit risky, many visitors staying at one of the smaller inns can visit one of the all-inclusives just for the night with a purchase of a night pass, usually valid from 6 p.m. to 2 a.m. The cost varies but averages around $95 per person. Once inside, you're entitled to all the food and drink you can consume, with the entertainment thrown in as well.

One of the hottest new venues after dark in Kingston is **Asylum,** 69 Knutsford Blvd. (☎ **876-929-4386**), where the program changes nightly. Some nights are devoted only to reggae music, other nights to various contests, sometimes to the old hits of the '70s and '80s. A crowd mainly of locals in their 20s to 30s flock here to enjoy the music, the dance, the entertainment and even karaoke. It's very tropical and very happening, open Tuesday through Sunday from 5 p.m. to 2 a.m., charging a cover ranging from $4.60 to $6.90.

In Negril, **De Buss,** found on Norman Manley Boulevard (☎ **876-957-4405**), is the most popular and versatile hangout on Negril Beach and is large enough to accommodate everything from major reggae concerts to simple rums and cola on the beach. You can also dance on the sands if this is your idea of a good time. It was named after the decaying wreck of a double-decker bus, a long-ago part of Kingston's mass-transit system, that was hauled to this site in the 1960s. Nearby is an imposing-looking courtyard area flanked with a stage that was bashed together from 2-x-4s and plywood, and brightly painted in Rastafarian colors, where live bands perform every Thursday and Saturday in the off-season, and virtually every night in winter. It's open daily from 9:00 a.m. to at least 11:00 p.m. and during show nights till at least 1:30 a.m.

In Ocho Rios, the place to head after dark is **Jamaic'N Me Crazy,** at the Renaissance Jamaica Grande (☎ **876-974-2201**), which has the best lighting and sound system in Ocho Rios (and perhaps Jamaica). The crowd includes everyone from the passing yachter to the curious tourist, who may be under the mistaken impression that he is seeing an authentic Jamaican nightclub. It charges nonguests $30 to cover everything you can shake or drink. Open nightly from 10 p.m. to 3 a.m.

In Montego Bay, **The Brewery,** Gloucester Avenue (☎ **876-940-2433**), is one of the city's most popular nightlife hangouts, evoking a mixture of an English pub and an all-Jamaican jerk pork pit. There's a woodsy-looking bar where everyone is into Red Stripe and reggae, lots of neo-medieval memorabilia à la Olde England, and a covered veranda in back where clients overlook the traffic on busy Hip Strip. This place mixes a "brew" of locals and visitors, usually in their 20s to 30s, and does so exceedingly well.

Part VIII
Puerto Rico

The 5th Wave By Rich Tennant

"Oh quit looking so uncomfortable. It's the Caribbean! No one wears a cape and formal wear in the Caribbean."

In this part . . .

*P*uerto Rico is a big island, and the range of accommodations available is stunning. We try to keep things simple by narrowing down our recommendations to the best of the best. Although this island is one of the easier ones to access in the Caribbean, we share tips for ensuring a smooth arrival and for planning some successful sightseeing.

From cutting-edge preparations to simple down-home meals, we point you toward the best dining options on Puerto Rico. Finally, we give you ideas for how to spend your time on the island, from lounging at the beach to exploring the beauty of Old San Juan.

Chapter 28

The Lowdown on Puerto Rico's Hotel Scene

By Darwin Porter and Danforth Prince

● ●

In This Chapter

▶ Sizing up hotel locations

▶ Focusing on the top hotel picks

● ●

The room with your name on it that may be waiting for you in Puerto Rico could be in a high-rise opening onto San Juan's Condado Beach, most famous in the Caribbean, or else in a restored convent in the historic old city of San Juan. In that same Old Town in San Juan, it may be in an artist's studio, or else somewhere out on the island — perhaps in a parador that was created out of a former coffee plantation or else a "glitz-and-ritz" type of place, the Hyatt Dorado Beach on a 1,000-acre estate with two 18-hole golf courses. If you want a hotel with a casino, you'll find those, too, both in San Juan or in one of the satellite resorts out on the island.

Figuring Out Where You Want to Stay

When stacked up against such larger islands of the Caribbean as Jamaica or Cuba, Puerto Rico is small, measuring 110 miles from east to west and 35 miles from north to south. The smallest of the easternmost islands known as the archipelago of the Greater Antilles, it opens onto a 275-mile coastline rimmed with beaches, although it has a mountainous interior.

Chances are you'll book a room on the north coast in or around San Juan, because most resorts are centered here. The southern coast of Puerto Rico is relatively undeveloped. We'll provide our picks to help you keep your options simple.

Unlike such islands as Jamaica, the all-inclusive hotel — operating on the "American Plan" with all meals — has not overtaken Puerto Rico. Most of the island's hotels function on the European Plan (EP) — that is, a room but no meals. Nonetheless, you can still book into a meal plan at most of the island's resorts, and you can save money this way — it works out cheaper than if you dine à la carte at every meal.

Under a meal plan, we recommend the Modified American Plan (MAP), which gives you breakfast and dinner at your hotel but leaves you free to eat elsewhere at lunch. Under MAP, you'll at least get out every day to sample some of the island's restaurants and won't be obligated to take every meal at the resort of your choice.

For more information on dining plans, see Chapter 6.

San Juan: A tale of two cities

If Charles Dickens were writing about San Juan, instead of London and Paris, he could still call it *A Tale of Two Cities,* because Puerto Rico's capital divides into two radically different zones.

The seven-block square known as *Viejo San Juan,* or Old Town, is the most historic and architecturally pure in all the Caribbean. Today a protected World Heritage site, Old Town has buildings that date back 500 years ago, although vastly restored. The Spanish architectural style of carved wood or iron balconies prevails. Old Town not only offers some of the Caribbean's most historic museums, forts, and sightseeing attractions, but also is one grand shopping bazaar. It is also the site of El Convento, Puerto Rico's most venerated landmark hotel. With very few exceptions, accommodations are scarce in Old Town; it's much better as a dining choice.

The hotels stretch to the east of Old Town, beginning along the Condado beach strip, long called "the Waikiki of the Caribbean." Beach resort life began at the Condado mainly in the 1920s, but now Isla Verde, lying farther east close to the airport, is challenging the Condado, many of whose hotels are looking stale.

Gamblers, families, commercial travelers, and cruise-ship passengers in San Juan for a brief layover prefer this long San Juan beachfront, with its high-rises, many dating from the dull architectural era of the 1960s. All the mega-resorts open onto the beachfront.

All the large resorts also feature casinos. San Juan is hardly Las Vegas but only Aruba equals it in gambling in the Caribbean. One big difference: In Las Vegas gamblers often get liquor served free. In San Juan, you have to pay not only your gambling debts, but your scotch bill as well.

Elsewhere on the island

Outside of San Juan, luxury resorts are found at Dorado, with two Hyatts lying 18 miles west of San Juan. Two other large resorts, the

Renting a villa or condo

For families or friends traveling together, a short-term villa or condo is an attractive alternative to a hotel, especially when the daily or weekly rental can be shared. Here are some contacts to make if you want to investigate this lodging choice:

✔ For rate information about upmarket rentals in San Juan's Isla Verde Beach–bordering section, contact **Condo World,** 4230 Orchard Lake Rd., Suite 5, Orchard Lake, MI 48323 (☎ **800-521-2980;** Fax: 248-683-5076).

✔ For information on nearly 200 properties in San Juan's Condado and Isla Verde, contact **Puerto Rico Vacation Apartments,** Marabella del Caribe Oeste S-5, Isla Verde, San Juan, PR 00979 (☎ **800-266-3639** or 787-727-1591; Fax: 787-268-3604).

✔ For weekly and monthly rentals in Rincón, contact **Island West Properties,** Rte. 413, Km 1.3, Box 700, Rincón, PR 00677 (☎ **787-823-2323;** Fax: 787-823-3254).

✔ For rentals on Vieques, try either **Connections,** Box 358, Esperanza, Vieques, PR 00765 (☎ **787-741-0023**), or **Acacia Apartments,** Box 1211, Esperanza, Vieques, PR 00765 (☎ **787-741-1856**).

Westin Rio Mar Beach and Wyndham El Conquistador, lie to the east of San Juan. Other than those mega-resorts, and with the exception of Horned Dorset Primavera at Rincón in the west, most hotels in Puerto Rico are relatively modest affairs. For small villas, inns, and condos, you can always escape to the offshore island of Vieques.

As an option to a sprawling mega-resort, you can book into one of the rural inns of Puerto Rico, some of them government-sponsored paradores. Most of them are modest but the prices are very affordable. Paradores usually charge from $55 to $135 a night for a double room.

You can make reservations for all paradores by contacting the tourist board's **Paradores of Puerto Rico,** Box 4435, Old San Juan, PR 00902 (☎ **800-443-0266** or 800-866-7827 for all of Puerto Rico).

In hotels outside of San Juan, rates don't often include airport transfers. Be sure to ask when you book.

Puerto Rico's Best Hotels

The rack rates listed in this section are in U.S. dollars and are for a standard double room during high season (mid-December through mid-April). Rates are lower during the off-season and shoulder season; see Chapter 2 for advice on when to go. Purchasing a package tour is another way to save money on accommodations; see Chapter 5 for details.

At Wind Chimes Inn

$ Condado, San Juan

Lying only a short block from the Condado's sandy beaches, this 17-room hotel is one of the best and most affordable along the ocean-bordering strip. There's a real tropical feel here, as evoked by the patio where you can sit out and enjoy a rum punch while shaded by swaying palm trees and flowering bougainvillea. The wind chimes hung about the patio and playing breeze-induced melodies give the inn its name. Bedrooms are well furnished with tropical styling and contain both ceiling fans and air-conditioning, even kitchens. The tiled bathrooms are small, with showers. A good breakfast is served every morning on the patio, and for other meals many restaurants are within a short walk of the Wind Chimes.

1750 McLeary Ave., Condado, San Juan. ☎ *800-946-3244 in the U.S. or 787-727-4153. Fax: 787-728-0671. Internet:* www.atwindchimesinn.com. *Rack rates: $80–$129 double, $125–$140 suite. AE, DISC, MC, V.*

Copamarina Beach Resort

$$$ Guánica

This 106-unit resort set on 18 acres is a mecca for divers but attracts everybody from honeymooners to families as well. Between the sea and Guánica Dry Forest in a UNESCO-designated world biosphere reserve, it lures nature lovers as well. The reserve is home to more than 100 species of birds. The resort opens onto a wide public beach set against a back-drop of palms. Of the two pools, one comes with a Jacuzzi and the other is for kids. Much improved after a $5.5 million overhaul, the rooms are in one– and two-story wings radiating from a central core. They're very tropical, with tile floors and louvered doors and screens opening toward private terraces or verandas. A favorite of visiting *sanjuaneros,* the resort's two restaurants serve one of the finest cuisines along the south coast. Hot tip: Join one of the $4 snorkeling excursions to an offshore cay called Gilligan's Island (after the long-running TV sitcom). Two tennis courts and two bars are part of the facilities, and you can rent bikes, kayaks, and snorkeling gear.

Rte. 333, Km 6.5, Caña Gorda (P.O. Box 805), Guánica. ☎ *800-468-4553 (direct to hotel) or 787-821-0505. Fax: 787-821-0070. Internet:* www.copamarina.com. *Rack rates: $165–$260 double. AE, DC, DISC, MC, V, EP.*

Hotel El Convento

$$$$$ Old San Juan

This is the most historic hotel in Puerto Rico, housed in what was the New World's first Carmelite convent, which was restored and opened in 1997, each bedroom costing $275,000. Replete with a Spanish courtyard and a splashing fountain, it evokes old Spain. A total of 59 well-furnished rooms lie on the top three floors, each one different and individually decorated, and furnished for the most part with restored mahogany antiques. Suites

Puerto Rico Accommodations

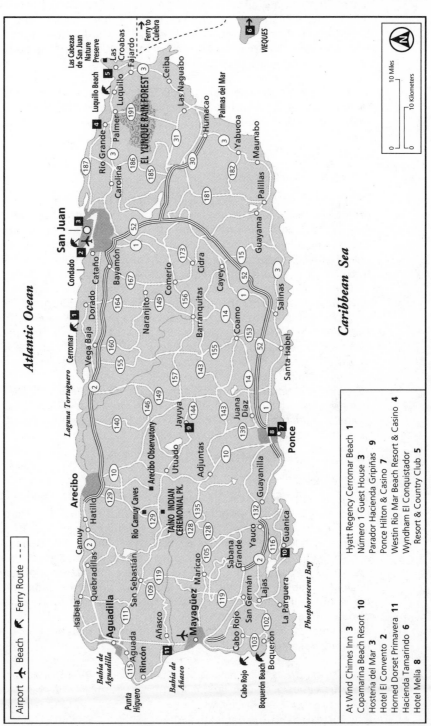

Atlantic Ocean

Caribbean Sea

Airport ✈ Beach ☈ Ferry Route ---

San Juan

Arecibo

Mayagüez

Ponce

Las Cabezas de San Juan Nature Preserve

EL YUNQUE RAIN FOREST

VIEQUES

Ferry to Culebra

At Wind Chimes Inn **3**
Copamarina Beach Resort **10**
Hosteria del Mar **3**
Hotel El Convento **2**
Horned Dorset Primavera **11**
Hotel Melia **8**

Hyatt Regency Cerromar Beach **1**
Número 1 Guest House **3**
Parador Hacienda Gripiñas **9**
Ponce Hilton & Casino **7**
Westin Rio Mar Beach Resort & Casino **4**
Wyndham El Conquistador Resort & Country Club **5**

Phosphorescent Bay

are even more splendid with marble floors, colonial antiques, and black marble bathrooms, all with Jacuzzi. A swimming pool on the fourth floor overlooks the historic port, and you're a 15-minute walk from the nearest beach. Even if you're not a guest, consider dining here in one of four restaurants (or have a drink in a pair of bars). We like to begin our evening with a tropical punch at El Picoteo Tapas Bar.

100 Cristo St., Old San Juan. ☎ *800-468-2779 or 787-723-9020. Fax: 787-721-2877. Internet:* www.elconvento.com. *Rack rates: Rooms $315–$375 double; suites from $550. AE, DISC, DC, MC, V.*

Gallery Inn
$$$–$$$$ **Old San Juan**

This private home turned 22-room inn, the former abode of an aristocratic Spanish family, is not for everyone, especially those who want a mega-resort with casino. The most whimsically bohemian inn in the Caribbean, it is also an art studio and gallery, the domain of Jan D'Esopo and Manuco Gandia. Macaws and cockatoos are on hand to welcome you to this hilltop location in Old San Juan with panoramic views. You are a 15-minute ride to the nearest beach. Quirky details such as winding, uneven stairways give the inn its bohemian charm. Bedrooms are full of comfort and individually furnished. Lovers or honeymooners book into the top-floor suite with a panoramic view of El Morro, the fortress. At night, as the sun sets, the rooftop deck is the most romantic spot in Old Town.

204–206 Calle Norzagaray, Old San Juan. ☎ *787-722-1808. Fax: 787-724-7360. Internet:* www.thegalleryinn.com. *Rack rates: $145–$270 double, includes continental breakfast. AE, MC, V, CP.*

Horned Dorset Primavera
$$$$$ **Rincón**

The most elite retreat on the west coast of Puerto Rico, this intimate, 31-unit resort is one of the special inns of the Caribbean. It's designed in the style of a Spanish hacienda and is set among lush gardens overlooking the sea with a secluded beach, a small strip of narrow golden sands. The rooms deliberately don't have phones or TVs, because guests come here for a total retreat. Kids under 12 aren't even allowed. Bedrooms are beautifully furnished, often with mahogany four-posters evoking plantation days. In the bathrooms are brass-footed tubs and marble walls. The choice units are the eight suites in the separate Casa Escondida villa, some with their own private pools. The on-site restaurant is one of the finest in western Puerto Rico.

Rte. 429, Km 3 (Box 1132), Rincón. ☎ *800-633-1857 or 787-823-4030. Fax: 787-823-5580. Rack rates: $380–$440 double, from $540 suite. AE, MC, V.*

Hacienda Tamarindo
$$–$$$ Vieques

Built around a mammoth tamarind tree, two centuries old, this intimate, 16-unit inn was created by two Vermonters, Burr and Linda Vail who gave it the look of a Spanish colonial hacienda. Less than a mile west of Esperanza, the inn is ⅛ mile inland from the ocean, with a footpath leading to a pool and the beach. Bedrooms have tiled floors and reflect Linda's decorating skills. Each is spacious and eclectically furnished, with a medley of art and antiques. It's suggested that families with children under 12 book elsewhere. There's a convivial bar on site, but for dinner, guests walk five minutes down the hill to the Inn on the Blue Horizon, which serves some of the best food on the island.

Rte. 996, Km 4.5 Barrio Puerto Real (P.O. Box 1569), Vieques. ☎ *787-741-8525. Fax: 787-741-3215. Internet:* www.enchanted-isle.com/tamarindo. *Rack rate: $155–$180 double. AE, MC, V.*

Hosteria del Mar
$–$$ Ocean Park, San Juan

At Ocean Park, lying between the two major beachfronts of Condado and Isla Verde, is one of the finer affordable guesthouses in this residential seaside colony. Try for one of the attractively furnished bedrooms on the second floor, because they have private balconies open to the tradewinds and views of the ocean. Those at ground level come with private patios. The eight bedrooms are done in a tropical motif with wicker furnishings and ceiling fans, although there is air-conditioning as well. Children 11 and under stay free in their parents' room. There is no pool but with the ocean close, you don't need one. On site is a much-frequented local restaurant that serves a tasty Puerto Rican cuisine and some vegetarian and macrobiotic specialties.

1 Tapia St., Ocean Park, San Juan. ☎ *877-727-3302 in the U.S. or 787-727-3302. Fax: 787-268-0772. Internet:* www.travelguides.com/inns/full/PR/1704/html. *Rack rates: $75–$125 double without ocean view; $165–$185 double with ocean view. AE, DC, DISC, MC, V.*

Hotel Meliá
$ Ponce

Before the inauguration of the Ponce Hilton (covered later in this chapter), this was the traditional favorite, lying in the bull's-eye center near the Ponce Cathedral and the landmark Parque de Bombas with its famous red-and-black firehouse. Not connected with the international hotel chain of Meliá, this is a 75-unit hotel like that found in some small provincial town in Castile. Spanish tiles of Moorish design reinforce that image. Upstairs the rooms are a bit cramped but tidily kept and well furnished.

The only thing special about them is their affordable rates. At least you don't have far to go for dinner. Under separate management, the on-site restaurant, Mark's at the Meliá, is one of the finest dining spots in town. You're a 20-minute ride from the beach and there is no pool.

2 Calle Cristina (P.O. Box 1431), Ponce. ☎ *800-742-4276 or 787-842-0260. Fax: 787-841-3602. Internet:* www.homecoqui.net/melia. *Rack rates: $82–$131 double. Rates include continental breakfast. AE, MC, V.*

Hyatt Regency Cerromar Beach
$$$$–$$$$$ Dorado

This is one of the Caribbean's grandest family resorts, lying 22 miles west of San Juan and sheltered in a seven-floor building on the 1,000-acre estate it shares with the Hyatt Dorado 1½ miles away. Golfers are attracted to its two courses designed by Robert Trent Jones, Sr., and kids splash in the 1,776-foot-long "fantasy pool," the longest freshwater pool in the area, with 14 "waterfalls." The children's program here is the best on the island. The resort also contains one of the best spas and health clubs on the island. The Dorado beach is also one of the finest in Puerto Rico when you tire of that pool. Bedrooms are of good size and attractively decorated and maintained, most of them opening onto private balconies. There's a choice of four good restaurants, three bars, a dance club, and a casino, along with 14 tennis courts. An older type of patron is attracted to the sibling Hyatt Dorado, which is more elegant and subdued, and also more expensive.

Rte. 693, Km 11.8 (Box 1351), Dorado. ☎ *800-233-1234 or 787-796-1234. Fax: 787-796-4647. Internet:* www.hyatt.com. *Rack rates: $375–$535 double. AE, DISC, DC, MC, V.*

Número 1 Guest House
$–$$ Ocean Park, San Juan

Even more inviting than Hosteria del Mar (covered earlier in this chapter), this is an intimate, 13-room, low-rise inn in the Ocean Park Beach section of San Juan, between the mega-resorts of Condado to the west and Isla Verde to the east. A stylish boutique hotel evocative of Laguna Beach, California, it attracts more repeat clients than any other in Ocean Park, both gay and straight. The atmosphere is laid-back and relaxed. The inn lies behind a walled-in compound with a beautiful garden with its splashing fountains and swimming pool. The owner has made all the well-furnished bedrooms comfortable and pleasing to the eye with white tile on the floors and West Indian furnishings in wicker or rattan. For those seeking some charm at an affordable price for their beach holiday, the inn is aptly named "number one."

Calle Santa Ana, Ocean Park, San Juan. ☎ *866-726-5010 in the U.S., or 787-726-5010. Fax: 787-725-5482. Rack rates: $135 double, $265 apartment. Rates include continental breakfast. AE, MC, V.*

Parador Hacienda Gripiñas
$$ Jayuya

In just a 2½-hour drive southwest of San Juan you can find yourself resting on the front porch of an Old World hacienda that was at the center of a former coffee plantation. This 20-room inn is one of the most atmospheric of the government-linked paradores of Puerto Rico, a chain of country inns scenically located. There are still 20 acres of aromatic coffee bushes here that produce coffee beans, and the atmosphere itself evokes island life of long ago, with its landscaped gardens and whirling ceiling fans. On the open-air porch, a hammock is waiting for you. The small rooms are modest, but each comes with a shower-only private bathroom and a comfortable bed. Away from the main house are two pools. Warning: The mountain-fed pools are chilly. The staff will arrange boating or fishing trips for you at Lake Caonillas, a 30-minute drive from the parador, which is also situated near a major island attraction, Río Camuy Cave Park. On site is a typical restaurant serving mainly a Puerto Rican cuisine. When you reach Jayuya, head east via Route 144. At the junction with Route 527, go south for 1½ miles until you see the parador signposted.

Rte. 527, Km 2.5 (P.O. Box 387), Jayuya. ☎ ***787-828-1717.*** *Rack rates: $125 double. AE, MC, V.*

Ponce Hilton and Casino
$$$ Ponce

Even though it's not on a beach, this 148-unit hotel is the most luxurious along the southern coast of Puerto Rico, lying on 80 landscaped acres, a ten-minute drive north of the city of Ponce. A five-minute trip by private car or taxi will deliver you to the closest beach of volcanic black sand, or else in 20 to 30 minutes you'll be delivered to far more alluring golden sandy beaches west of Ponce. The island's new Hilton is also the best equipped along the coast, with two restaurants, three bars, a small casino, four tennis courts, a fitness center, a lagoon-shaped pool, water sports, and a summer camp and playground for children, as well as a business center. Bedrooms are midsize to spacious, and typically attired in West Indian furnishings, each one exceedingly comfortable and opening onto a private terrace or balcony.

1150 Avenida Caribe (P.O. Box 7419), Ponce. ☎ ***800-HILTONS*** *or 787-259-7676. Fax: 787-259-7674. Rack rate: $185–$280 double, $475 suite. AE, DC, DISC, MC, V.*

Westin Rio Mar Beach Resort and Casino
$$$–$$$$$ Rio Grande

The Westin chain made an impressive debut in the Caribbean with this $180 million resort set on 481 landscaped acres near Rio Mar Beach and just a five-minute ride to Luquillo, the best and most popular beach in Puerto Rico. You're coddled in comfort here, in a setting of artificial lakes

a monument to opulence and the good life. Sheathed in red marble and hand-carved mahogany paneling, the public rooms are luxurious, centered around a magnificent lobby with a massive chandelier where it's always party time. From cigar bars to live salsa music, this grand lobby of the hotel is the most glittering place to be at night along the beach strip. Accommodations come in a bewildering number of choices and locations, ranging from bungalows on the outer reaches of the gardens — they're called *casitas* — to oceanfront-bordering suites in the 17-story tower with an eagle's view of Greater San Juan. The facilities are impressive, with three bars, two pools, tennis courts, a health club and spa, water sports, and a children's club. What makes this hotel special is its selection of eight different restaurants, all serving a different type of cuisine, ranging from Mexico to Japan, from the Caribbean to Italy.

Avenue Isla Verde (P.O. Box 2872), Isla Verde. ☎ *800-WYNDHAM or 787-791-1000. Fax: 787-791-0390. Rack rates: $415–$565 double, from $625 suite. AE, DC, MC, V.*

Chapter 29

Settling into Puerto Rico

By Darwin Porter and Danforth Prince

. . . .

In This Chapter

▶ Knowing what to expect when you arrive

▶ Getting around the island

▶ Discovering Puerto Rico from A to Z

. . . .

More airplanes arrive from the United States in San Juan, the capital of Puerto Rico, than on any other island in the Caribbean. San Juan is, in fact, the gateway to the northern Caribbean, and flights are not only frequent but more affordable with many deals available.

Even though you've flown from Miami, New York, or wherever, when you land in Puerto Rico you're still in the United States, or at least an American territory. Flying time from Miami is only two hours.

San Juan is the major hub for American Airlines, which through that carrier or its subsidiary, American Eagle, offer more flights throughout the Caribbean than any other carrier.

Arriving in Puerto Rico

The main airport for Puerto Rico, and the major air terminal in all of the Caribbean, is **Luís Muñoz Marin International Airport** (☎ **787-791-4670**), lying east of Isla Verde and east of the resorts of the Condado and the Old Town of San Juan. The airport is one of the finest in the Caribbean, evoking the Miami airport in some aspects. Half of all the flights to and from the Caribbean pass through here, making it a busy, bustling place.

American Airlines isn't only the only carrier flying into the Luís Muñoz Marin International Airport, although for many travelers that airline offers the most frequent and the largest number of flights from cities on the U.S. mainland, including New York, Newark, Miami, Baltimore, Boston, Chicago, Dallas/Fort Worth, Tampa, Fort Lauderdale, and Washington (Dulles). **Delta** is the most convenient connection from

Atlanta and points in the southeast, and **United Airlines** wings in from such cities as Detroit, Memphis, and Minneapolis. **US Airways** flies down from Charlotte, North Carolina; Pittsburgh; and Philadelphia.

Because Puerto Rico is a territory of the United States, its citizens can fly in and out without a passport, although some photo ID is required. If your flight originated on the U.S. mainland — perhaps in Miami — you do not have to clear U.S. Customs and Immigration. If you're flying into San Juan from somewhere else in the Caribbean, perhaps Barbados or Jamaica, you will have to clear Customs and Immigration because you have been outside the United States. Otherwise, an American citizen can walk through the airport, following the signs leading to ground transport such as a taxi.

Many passengers arriving in San Juan, often from a long trip, or others who face difficult waits for their next air connection, avail themselves of the **Diamond Point International Massage** (☎ 787-253-3063), lying near gates 4 and 5. Here a highly trained staff offers massages at the rate of $1 for each minute. Relaxing foot massages go for $25 for a 15-minute session, or, for the same price, you get 15 minutes of aromatherapy. The parlor is open daily from 9 a.m. to 6 p.m. and MasterCard and Visa are accepted.

Families with children arriving at San Juan with a layover between flights will find a centrally located video arcade, with games such as Cruisin' USA, Marvel Superheroes, and X-Men. A change machine dispenses quarters.

Those meeting scheduled flights soon learn that Puerto Rico is an hour ahead of the U.S. mainland when it's on eastern standard time. The only time clocks in Puerto Rico and the East Coast are coordinated is when the mainland goes on daylight saving time.

Getting from the Airport to Your Hotel

Some hotels such as the mega-resorts will have a van waiting for you at the airport to take you the final distance to your hotel of choice. You will need to alert your hotel of your arrival when making a reservation. If you're staying at one of the smaller, independent operators, you'll have to get to your hotel or resort on your own steam. Here's how you do it.

By taxi

Taxi drivers line up at the airport, meeting all incoming flights, so there is rarely a wait. Fares are about the same as in most major U.S. cities such as Miami. When you're on the sidewalk in front of the terminal with your luggage, tell the official dispatcher (he or she is in uniform and wears a badge) where you're going. You'll be presented with a slip of paper with the amount of your fare written on it. Give this to your driver, who is obligated to follow the fixed tariffs.

Airport taxis, called **Taxi Turísticos,** assess rates based on zones. The hotels of Isla Verde are close to the airport so you're charged $8 per person. Heading to a hotel on the Condado costs $12. In the unlikely event you're staying in Old Town, the fare is the most expensive at $16.

If you're carrying more than two pieces of luggage, you'll pay an additional 50¢ per bag and another dollar for use of the trunk.

Bracero Limousine Ltd. (☎ 787-253-1133) offers limousine transport from the airport to various neighborhoods of San Juan for prices that are much higher than those offered by taxis (although the limousines are much more luxurious than taxis). The fare for transport (with luggage) to any hotel in Isla Verde or Condado is $105 and to Old San Juan is $125.

By car

If you reserved a car before you left the mainland, you are more likely to get a better rate and you have the convenience of having your vehicle waiting for you at the airport. All major U.S. car-rental firms have desks at the airport. Look for your choice in the ground transportation section adjoining the baggage claim area. See "Moving Around Puerto Rico," later in this chapter, for more information on auto rentals.

If you need a wheelchair-accessible van, you can get such a vehicle via **Wheelchair Getaway (☎ 800-868-8028).**

Moving Around Puerto Rico

San Juan offers the best and most varied means of getting about in the Caribbean. If you want to see the island itself, public transportation is woefully inadequate.

By car

If you're staying only in San Juan, you can get about by public transportation, foot, hotel shuttle, or taxi. But if you want to tour the island in any depth, especially that hidden beach or that mountain retreat, a car is necessary.

As the Caribbean goes, the highways or even smaller arteries of Puerto Rico are well marked and in passable or even good condition for the most part. Distances are posted in kilometers and not in miles. Surprisingly, speed limits are posted in miles. Night driving is to be avoided when possible because of poor lighting.

Compared to Jamaica, motorists in Puerto Rico are practically driving-school instructors. That being said, they do have a tendency to indulge in dangerous passing and seem to hog the center of the road.

 If you plan to veer off the main highways on the island and head for remote destinations in the mountainous interior, the maps handed out by car-rental agencies are not adequately detailed. The maps sold at gasoline stations, such as those published by Rand McNally, are worth the investment. See "Quick Concierge," later in this chapter, for more on maps.

A valid driver's license from your country of origin can be used in Puerto Rico for three months. All major U.S. car rental agencies are represented on the island, including **Avis** (☎ 800-874-3556 or 787-253-5926), **Budget** (☎ 800-527-0700 or 787-791-0600), **Dollar** (☎ 800-800-4000 or 787-791-5500), **Hertz** (☎ 800-654-3030 or 787-791-0840), **National** (☎ 787-791-1805), and **Thrifty** (☎ 787-253-2525). Local rental companies, sometimes less expensive, include **Tropical** (☎ 877-791-2820 or 787-791-2820).

Most car-rental agencies in Puerto Rico offer unlimited mileage. If yours doesn't, seek out a firm that does. Rental rates start as low as $40 per day, plus insurance. Check with your local insurer to see if you're covered in Puerto Rico. Extra insurance is often waived for those with American Express or certain gold bank credit cards. Many discounts with coupons are featured in tourist literature handed out at the airport information desks. Sometimes your AAA membership will get you a discount. Often if you reserve three days or more in advance, you'll also get a discount.

The major car-rental firms such as Hertz or Avis offer a free shuttle service from the airport to their car depots where you can pick up your car.

 Gasoline stations in Puerto Rico sell by the liter, not by the gallon. Credit cards are accepted at stations along major highways. After you veer into the mountains, carry the Yankee dollar to purchase your fuel.

By taxi

Taxis are plentiful in San Juan, more difficult to secure out on the island. In San Juan, the major operator, **Taxi Turísticos,** are painted white and are marked with the company's logo on its doors. These official taxis charge fixed tariffs based on the zones in which you travel. Depending on where you're going in San Juan, fares in general range between $8 and $16.

All authorized taxis, falling under the umbrella of the **Public Service Commission** (☎ 787-756-1919), should have a working meter. If not, agree on the price before getting in. Expect a minimum charge of $3, plus an extra charge of $1 at night. You're assessed 10¢ for each $1\frac{1}{3}$ mile and 50¢ for every piece of luggage. You can call a cab in San Juan by dialing **Major Taxicabs** at ☎ 787-723-2460, or in Puerto Rico's second city of Ponce by dialing **Ponce Taxi** at ☎ 787-840-0088.

Taxis are lined up outside the entrances to most hotels, and if not, a staff member can almost always call one for you. But if you would like to arrange a taxi on your own, call **Rochdale Radio Taxi** (☎ 787-721-1900).

On foot

If you stay in one of the major tourist zones in San Juan, you can walk about, especially in Old Town. If you get tired, you can always hop on Old Town's free trolley, described later in this chapter.

Self-guided walking tours of Old San Juan are outlined in copies of *Qué Pasa,* the official information booklet issued by the tourism authority. You probably picked up a copy at the airport. If not, your hotel will have one. If you want a more penetrating look at the city, you can book a tour from **Colonial Adventure** (201 Recinto Sur; ☎ 787-793-2992). The company offers a variety of informative walking tours for groups of ten or more; rates range from $18 to $24 per person.

By bus

If your vacation money is lean, you can rely on the *guaguas* or buses run by the **Metropolitan Bus Authority** (☎ 787-729-1512). They're very crowded at rush hours; be careful of pickpockets who also ride these buses. The fare is really cheap, costing 25¢ on a standard bus or 75¢ on the more modern and comfortable Metrobus.

Most of the large hotels of the Condado and Isla Verde maintain an air-conditioned bus that makes free shuttle runs into Old San Juan. Clients are usually deposited at the Plaza de Colón. Public buses also make the run along the Condado, stopping at clearly designated bus stops placed near the major hotels. Public buses usually deposit their clients at the Plaza Colón and the main bus terminal across the street from the Cataño ferryboat pier. This section of Old San Juan is the starting point for many of the city's metropolitan bus routes.

Tren Urbano in 2003: The way to go

San Juan will be linked to its major suburbs such as Santurce, Bayamón, and Guaynabo in the summer of 2003 by a $1.25 billion urban train called "Tren Urbano." This will be the first mass-transit project in the history of Puerto Rico. The new train system is designed to bring a fast and easy mode of transportation to the most congested areas of metropolitan San Juan. Trains will run every four minutes during peak hours in morning and afternoon. The line is expected to carry some 115,000 passengers daily. For more information, call ☎ 787-765-0927.

A cheap way to get to Puerto Rico's second city, Ponce, or its third largest city, Mayagüez, is aboard a *público* (public car). With fares fixed by the Public Service Commission, these *públicos* are spotted by their yellow license plates, which end in a P or PD. They carry about 18 passengers in vans running during the day and can be boarded in San Juan's Old Town at the Plaza Colón or at the airport.

Information about *público* routes between San Juan and Mayagüez is available from **Linea Sultana,** Calle Esteban González 898, Urbanización Santa Rita, Rio Piedras (☎ 787-765-9377). Information about *público* routes between San Juan and Ponce is available from **Choferes Unidos de Ponce,** Terminal de Carros Públicos, Calle Vive in Ponce (☎ 787-764-0540) or **Linea Boricua** (☎ 787-765-1908).

Fares from San Juan to Mayagüez run $16 to $30; from San Juan to Ponce, $15 to $25. Although prices are low, the routes are slow, with frequent stops, an often erratic routing, and lots of inconvenience.

By trolley

When you tire of walking around Old San Juan, you can board one of the free trolleys that run through the historic area. Departure points are the Marina and La Puntilla, but you can hop aboard along the route by flagging the trolley down (wave at it and signal for it to stop) or by waiting at any of the clearly designated stopping points. Relax and enjoy the sights as the trolleys rumble through the old and narrow streets.

By ferry

Ferry de Cataño (☎ 787-788-1155) crosses San Juan Bay between Old San Juan (Pier 2) and costs only 50¢ one-way. It departs every 30 minutes from 6 a.m. to 10 p.m. If you'd like to visit one of the offshore islands of Puerto Rico — Culebra or Vieques — you can go to the eastern seaport of Fajardo. Here the **Fajardo Port Authority** (☎ 787-863-0705) runs a 400-passenger ferry to Vieques three times daily, costing $2 one-way (trip time: 1½ hours). It takes the same time to cross between Fajardo and Culebra, with ferries departing two times a day Monday through Friday and three times on weekends. A one-way fare costs $2.25.

Fast Facts: Puerto Rico

ATMs

These machines are called ATH on Puerto Rico, but they operate the same as ATMs and are widely available on the island. You'll find one at the St. Thomas airport near Gate 4.

Baby-sitters

Expect to pay at least $8 and up per hour.

Banks

Many major U.S., Canadian, and European banks have branches in San Juan and are open Monday through Friday from 8:30 a.m. to 2:30 p.m. and Saturday from 9:45 a.m. to noon.

Credit Cards

All major credit cards, especially MasterCard and Visa, are widely accepted on the island.

Currency Exchange

The Yankee dollar is the coin of the realm.

Departure Tax

There is none.

Doctors

Puerto Rico has an excellent health-care system. Ask your hotel for a referral if necessary.

Electricity

Puerto Rico uses a 110-volt AC (60-cycle) electrical system, the same as in the United States. European guests who have traveling appliances that use other systems can call ahead to confirm that their hotel has adapters and converters.

Emergencies

For ambulance, police, and fire, call ☎ 911.

Hospitals

If you need hospital care, contact one of the following: Ashford Presbyterian Community Hospital, 1451 Av. Ashford, Condado, San Juan (☎ 787-721-2160); Bella Vista Hospital, Cerro las Mesas, Mayagüez (☎ 787-834-6000 or 787-834-2350); the clinic Eastern Medical Associates, 267 Av. Valero, Fajardo (☎ 787-863-0669); or San Juan Health Centre, 200 Av. de Diego, San Juan (☎ 787-725-0202).

Homework

Listen to native son Ricky Martin's latest release.

Information

Contact the Puerto Rico Tourism Company, P.O. Box 902-3960, Old San Juan Station, San Juan, PR 00902-3960 (☎ 800-223-6530, from the United States, or 787-721-2400; Internet: www.prtourism.com). Other branches are located at: 3575 W. Cahuenga Blvd., Suite 560, Los Angeles, CA 90068 (☎ 323-874-5991) and 901 Ponce de León Blvd., Suite 601, Coral Gables, FL 33134 (☎ 305-445-9112).

Government and tourism-company information offices are also found at Luis Muñoz Marín International Airport in Isla Verde (☎ 787-791-1014 or 787-791-2551) and La Casita (☎ 787-722-1709) at Plaza Darsenas near Pier 1 in Old San Juan (open until 8 p.m. Monday, Tuesday, Thursday, Friday, and Saturday).

Further out on the island, information offices are in Ponce, Plaza Las Delicias (☎ 787-843-0465); Aguadilla, Rafael Hernández Airport (☎ 787-890-3315); Cabo Rojo, Rte. 100, Km 13.7 (☎ 787-851-7070); and in many town halls on the main plaza. Offices are usually open Monday through Saturday 8 a.m. to noon and 1:00 to 4:30 p.m.

Language

Puerto Rico's official language is Spanish, although the island is bilingual. Nearly all young people speak English. If you travel in the mountainous interior, and especially if you try to converse with older people, you'll find that a Spanish phrase book may come in handy if you're lost and seeking directions.

Maps

The Puerto Rico Tourism Company, Paseo de la Princesa, Old San Juan, PR 00901 (☎ 787-721-2400) is an excellent source for maps and printed materials. Be sure to pick up a free copy of *Qué Pasa* and *Bienvenidos,* the official visitors guide.

Newspapers/Magazines

Getting publications from all over the world is easy on this island. You'll find excellent newsstands at the airport. The *San Juan Star* comes out daily in English and Spanish.

Pharmacies

The most common and easily found pharmacies are Puerto Rico Drug Company, 157 Calle San Francisco, Old San Juan (☎ 787-725-2202) and Walgreens, 1330 Av. Ashford, Condado, San Juan (☎ 787-725-1510). Walgreens operates more than 30 pharmacies on the island. The one located in Condado is open 24 hours a day.

Police

For police assistance with an emergency, call ☎ **911.**

Post Office

Post offices in San Juan have Express Mail next-day service to the mainland.

Major post office branches are located at 153 Calle Fortaleza in Old San Juan, 163 Avendia Fernandez Juncos in San Juan, 60 Calle McKinley in Mayagüez serving western Puerto Rico, and 102 Calle Garrido Morales in Fajardo serving eastern Puerto Rico. Post offices are open Monday through Friday 7:30 a.m. to 4:30 p.m. and Saturday 8 a.m. to noon.

Safety

At night, exercise extreme caution when walking along the back streets of San Juan, and don't venture onto the unguarded public stretches of the Condado and Isla Verde beaches at night. All these areas are favorite targets for muggings. Out on the island it's much safer, but you should always take the usual precautions. As your mama told you, don't leave any property unattended on a beach. Before heading to the beach, put your valuables in the hotel safe (many first-class hotels have safes in your room). Storing valuables in your car or trunk is never wise, even if you lock the vehicle securely.

Store Hours

Street shops are usually open Monday through Saturday 9 a.m. to 6 p.m. (9 a.m. to 9 p.m. during Christmas holidays). Mall stores tend to stay open later, until 8 or 9 p.m. in most cases.

Taxes

Many hotels and restaurants add a 10 to 15% service charge. Check to make sure you don't end up tipping twice. In the little hotels, especially those in small beach towns or in the mountains, don't be surprised to see a surcharge for air-conditioning, often $5 a day, added to your tab. Hotel rooms are taxed by Puerto Rico at the rate of 11% in casino hotels, 9% in standard hotels, and 7% in paradores.

Telephone

The area code is 787. For Americans, dialing Puerto Rico is the same as dialing another state in the U.S. or a province in Canada. When making a call on the island, just dial the seven-digit number.

Time Zone

Puerto Rico is on Atlantic standard time, one hour ahead of eastern standard time and the same as eastern daylight time. For the current time of day, call ☎ 800-866-5829.

Tipping

Many islanders depend on your tip for their living. If service isn't added to your bill, tip waiters 15 to 18% of the bill. Hotel porters get $1 per bag, and most maids get $1.50 to $2 per day. For a cabbie, tip 15% of the fare.

Water

Tap water is generally fine on the island; just avoid drinking it after storms, when the drinking-water supply may become mixed with sewage. Thoroughly wash or peel produce that you buy in markets before eating it.

Weather Reports

Log on to the Caribbean Weather Man at www.caribwx.com/cyclone.html or listen to Radio WOSO (1030 AM), an English-speaking station.

Chapter 30

Dining in Puerto Rico

By Darwin Porter and Danforth Prince

. . . .

In This Chapter

▶ Sampling the local cuisine

▶ Locating the island's best restaurants

. . . .

*I*ts restaurant scene hardly equals Miami, but in the Caribbean the cookery of Puerto Rico makes it *numero uno*. Even serious foodies agree. To create their unique *cocina criolla* (Creole cuisine), island chefs owe a debt to just about everybody, even the Taíno Indians, the original settlers.

The Spanish brought their own savory recipes as did African slaves. The end result makes for a tantalizing *asopao* (the island's national soup, a delectable gumbo) of different delights to your palate. Puerto Rican cuisine, like that soup itself, can "feature a little bit of any and everything," a wise old island cook once told us.

Many Puerto Ricans, unlike many other parts of the Caribbean, follow the Spanish tradition in that they like to dress up when they go out at night, either to the clubs or to the top-rated restaurants. Men should wear their best-looking resort wear, and women in general appear in high heels and a sporty looking dress or pantsuit. You're still welcomed in most places regardless of your dress, but most visitors feel more comfortable when they're dressed to fit in with the other diners. At the best restaurants, reservations are always preferred during the busy winter season.

In most of the Caribbean, we recommend that, if possible, you escape from your hotel dining room unless you're booked at an all-inclusive resort. Over the years we've come to believe that the best and more varied dining is outside the hotels in the independently operated little restaurant.

In Puerto Rico, either in San Juan or out on the island, that isn't always true. Many of the finest restaurants are found at hotels. Weekends at these hotels can be particularly busy, as well-heeled islanders pack into hotel restaurants, savoring the same cuisine as visitors.

Enjoying a Taste of Puerto Rico

Along with a cold beer or a glass of rum, Puerto Ricans like to begin their meal with some savory appetizers, such as crunchy cod fritters (called *bacalaitos*) or perhaps *empanadillas,* crescent-shaped turnovers stuffed with lobster, crab, conch, or beef. A basket of *tostones* is likely to your rest on your table. Puerto Ricans eat *tostones* the way Americans devour potato chips. They are twice-fried plantains, sometimes delectably coated with honey. Ripe plantains are also baked to make *amarillos* (fried in sugar and red wine, and flavored with cinnamon).

Called *arroz con habichuelas,* rice and beans accompany nearly every meal, lunch or dinner. Rice is often a main dish, especially when it's the national soup *asopao,* most often cooked with shrimp, lobster, chicken, or even octopus.

The aroma that wafts from kitchens throughout Puerto Rico comes from *adobo* and *sofrito* — blends of herbs and spices that give many of the native foods their distinctive taste and color. *Adobo,* made by crushing together peppercorns, oregano, garlic, salt, olive oil, and lime juice or vinegar, is rubbed into meats before they are roasted. *Sofrito,* a potpourri of onions, garlic, and peppers browned in either olive oil or lard and colored with *achiote* (annatto seeds), imparts the bright yellow color to the island's rice, soups, and stews.

Most visitors to the island prefer the fresh fish and shellfish. A popular dish is *mojo isleno* (fried fish with Puerto Rican sauce). The sauce is made with olives and olive oil, onions, pimentos, capers, tomato sauce, vinegar, and a flavoring of garlic and bay leaves. Fresh fish is often grilled, and perhaps flavored with garlic and an overlay of freshly squeezed lime juice — a very tasty dinner indeed. Caribbean lobster is usually the most expensive item on any menu, followed by shrimp. Puerto Ricans often cook *camarones en cerveza* (shrimp in beer). Another delectable shellfish dish is *jueyes hervidos* (boiled crab).

If you're a frugal traveler, dining out on the island, you'll think that every meal in Puerto Rico serves *flan* (caramel custard) for dessert, and most of them do. Other popular desserts include a coconut pudding, *tembleque,* or another pudding, *dulce de leche,* which is really "candied milk." Served with an island white cheese, a fruit paste made of guava is another popular dessert beloved by locals.

It is customary for most Puerto Ricans to finish their meal with the strong, black aromatic coffee grown here. Originally imported from the nearby Dominican Republic, coffee beans have been produced in the island's high-altitude interior for more than 300 years and still rank among the island's leading exports.

Rum is the national drink, and you can buy it in almost any shade. Because the island is the world's leading rum producer, it's little wonder that every Puerto Rican bartender worthy of the profession likes to concoct his own favorite rum libation.

As you travel around the island, look for restaurant signs indicating that an establishment is one of the *mesones gastronómicos,* or preferred dining establishments designated as such by the Puerto Rico Tourism Company. These restaurants are known for serving *comidas criollas* (traditional Puerto Rican and Creole food). Although we can't always guarantee top-quality food in every one of these places, they invariably offer good value. There are some 40 of these *mesones* island-wide.

Puerto Rico's Best Restaurants

Any one of the following restaurants will give you a taste of the best the island has to offer.

Ajili-Mójili
$$$ Condado, San Juan   Puerto Rican/Creole

Sanjuaneros come here to dine on the food they learned in their *mamacita*'s kitchen, but the chefs have elevated this *comida criolla* (traditional Puerto Rican and Creole food) to new highs, lightening the recipes and making island dishes more refined and sophisticated. Set against old brick walls, the restaurant and bar are evocative of a Spanish *taberna* (tavern) of long ago. The food is a delight, and the waiters are helpful in explaining any concoction with which you may be unfamiliar. The *arroz con pollo* (stewed chicken with saffron rice) shows a solid technique, as does the *mofongos* (green plantains stuffed with chicken, shrimp, pork, or veal). The kitchen takes full advantage of the island's bounty, especially in its meat dishes such as *medallones de cerdo encebollado* (pork loin sautéed with onions) and *carne machada* (rib eye of beef stuffed with ham). The chefs will also regale you with *lechon asado con maposteado* (roast pork with rice and beans). The dish sounds ordinary, but the kitchen knows how to enliven it with real flair and flavor.

1052 Av. Ashford (at the corner of Calle Joffre). ☎ *787-725-9195. Reservations required. Main courses: $16–$35. AE, MC, V. Open: Mon–Fri 11:30 a.m.–3:00 p.m. and Mon–Sat 6–10 p.m.*

Amadeus
$$–$$$ Old San Juan   Contemporary Puerto Rican

A long-enduring favorite of both visitors and locals in Old Town, this restaurant lies in a restored 18th-century structure that was once the home of a rich merchant. More so than Ajili-Mójili (see the preceding listing), this restaurant gives a totally modern interpretation to classic island dishes. One appetizer alone, Amadeus dumplings with guava sauce and arrowroot fritters, will spark your palate for what's ahead. The chef creates a palette of flavors and originality in such dishes as pizza with smoked salmon and caviar or tender pork scaloppini in a sweet and sour sauce that had us asking for the recipe. The grilled fish such as mahimahi is given real Cajun authenticity and is an excellent choice for a main course.

106 Calle San Sebastián. ☎ 787-722-8635. Reservations recommended. Main courses: $12–$26. AE, MC, V. Open: Tues–Sun noon to midnight, Mon 6 p.m. to midnight.

Back Street Hong Kong

$$$$ Isla Verde, San Juan   Mandarin/Szechuan/Hunan

Looking like a stage set with the cameras getting ready to roll, this is one of the Caribbean's leading Chinese restaurants. The props were dismantled from a pavilion at the 1964 New York World's Fair and brought here to San Juan and reassembled under the roof of this deluxe hotel. You dine beneath a soaring redwood ceiling, feasting on some of the delights of Asia. The chefs take special care with all the dishes, which explains their large repeat clientele. Perhaps they'll dazzle you with their pineapple fried rice served in an actual pineapple. They also do an admirable job with scallops in a bitter orange sauce. Some of their zestiest concoctions are their fiery Szechuan and chicken dishes. A medley of bracingly fresh lobster and shrimp is called "Dragon and Phoenix."

In Wyndham El San Juan Hotel and Casino, Isla Verde Avenue. ☎ 787-791-1000. Reservations recommended. Main courses: $18–$29. AE, MC, V. Open: Mon–Sat 5 p.m. to midnight, Sun 1 p.m. to midnight.

Le Belle Epoque

$$$–$$$$ Condado, San Juan   Fusion/French

For two years in a row at the beginning of the millennium, master chef Jeremie Cruz has reigned as "Caribbean Chef of the Year." If you're dining on the Condado, this is the preferred choice, an elegant setting of Murano chandeliers and hand-painted, custom-made plates, plus formal service. The restaurant, with good reason, is a favorite of visiting celebrities to San Juan. Cruz has evolved a distinctive style all his own, even if he is making something as classic (or as common) as onion soup or lobster bisque. For an appetizer, he prepares a perfect seafood mousse resting under a brown potato crust. On our latest visit, we enjoyed a classic *coq au vin* (chicken with wine) with wild mushrooms and a divinely poached salmon with "lobster potatoes." His desserts win the chef's surprise award — take the lemongrass soup with sorbet, pieces of fresh fruit, and candied carrots.

Casabella Building, 1400 Magdalena Ave., Condado, San Juan. ☎ 787-977-1765. Reservations required. Main courses: $17–$22. AE, MC, V. Open: Mon–Sat noon to 3 p.m. and 5–11 p.m.

Old San Juan Dining

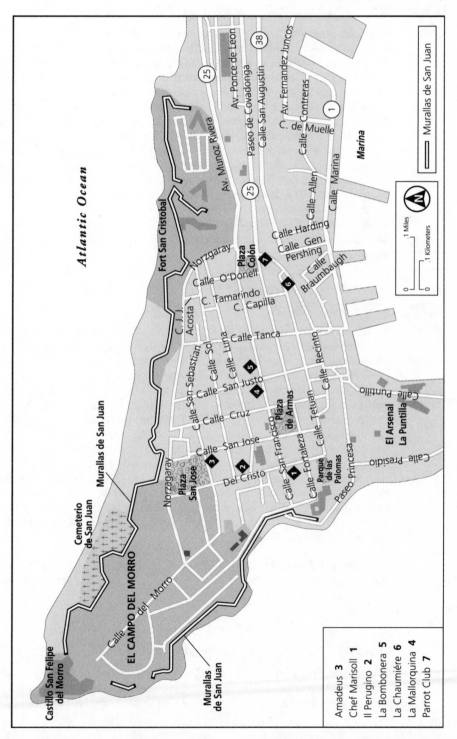

Amadeus **3**
Chef Marisoll **1**
Il Perugino **2**
La Bombonera **5**
La Chaumiére **6**
La Mallorquina **4**
Parrot Club **7**

Chef Marisoll

$$$$ Old San Juan   Continental

Marisol Hernández is the reigning queen of the kitchen in Puerto Rico, one of the top chefs island-wide where male cooks have long dominated with the pots and pans. In an elegant setting in an Old Town Spanish colonial building, with a courtyard patio for dining, Ms. Hernández dazzles you with her culinary creations. Her cookery is marked by fresh ingredients and a polished technique. Her appetizers are Old Town's finest selection, especially her peppers stuffed with codfish or her creamy Italian polenta with a wild mushroom fricassée. Bravo for the Cajun-spiced blackened shrimp and andouille sausages served on a bed of linguine. The loin of veal medallions with shiitake mushrooms and oven-dried tomatoes won our hearts until our fickle palates tasted the curried chicken breast with basmati rice and a tangy homemade mango chutney.

202 Calle Cristo. ☎ *787-725-7454. Reservations required. Main courses: $25–$40. AE, MC, V. Open: Lunch Thurs–Sat noon to 2:30 p.m, dinner Tues–Sun 7–10 p.m. Closed Mon.*

Horned Dorset Primavera

$$$$–$$$$$ Rincón   French/Caribbean

The poshest restaurant in western Puerto Rico, which also serves the finest cuisine, is elegantly sheltered under the roof of this previously recommended Relais et Châteaux. If you're touring the west it makes a perfect luncheon stopover even if you're not a guest. At night the intimate lighting, the elegant service, and the sound of the ocean can put you in the mood for romance. Changed nightly, the menu is based on the inspiration of the chef that day and what he found fresh and good at the market. Once the produce is secured, he comes back to the kitchen to concoct intelligent, imaginative dishes of subtle flavors, including, for example, an unusual chilled parsnip soup or perhaps a fricassée of wahoo with wild mushrooms. A magnificent lobster comes in medallions in an orange-flavored "white butter" sauce, and the grilled loin of beef is perfectly flavored in a zesty pepper sauce. A winning blend of flavors materialized in the mahimahi in a ginger-laced cream sauce served on a bed of *al dente* cabbage.

Rte. 429, Km 3, Rincón. ☎ *787-823-4030. Reservations recommended. Main courses: $22–$35, prix-fixe dinner for two $136. AE, MC, V. Open: Daily noon to 2 p.m. and 7–9 p.m.*

Il Perugino

$$$–$$$$ Old San Juan   Tuscan/Umbrian

This restaurant pleased Luciano Pavarotti, one of the world's most discerning palates (he can also sing) and is likely to enchant you, too. Come here for the best Italian food in Old San Juan. Only La Piccola Fontana (covered later in this chapter) does it better, and it's a close race. The setting is in the courtyard of a former private townhouse built three centuries ago, close to the Old Town Cathedral. Owner/chef Franco Seccarelli brought many of the most treasured recipes from his homeland of Perugia, deep in the heart of Umbria, a gastronomic center of Italy. The skillful cookery swoops from the classic to the inspired in such perfectly balanced dishes as marinated fresh salmon, medallions of beef flavored with balsamic vinegar, and a "black pasta" made with crayfish and eels that should be awarded some honor. As in Umbria, black and white truffles appear on the menu, but, as always, they are lethal in price.

105 Calle Cristo. ☎ 787-722-5481. Call for reservations after 4 p.m. Main courses: $18–$39. AE, MC, V. Open: Daily for dinner 6:30–11:00 p.m.

La Bombonera
$ Old San Juan   Cafe

An Old San Juan tradition for 100 years, this cafe and restaurant is still going strong. Some of its oldest habitués have been eating here for 60 years. We like to join the throngs for breakfast — the pastries are unmatched in San Juan — where portions served are so large that they'll practically fortify you for the day. The old men who hang out here order endless refills of *café con leche* (coffee with milk). You can return for lunch or dinner, enjoying a selection of flavorful and well-prepared island dishes such as rice with squid as good as your mama made for you. The tantalizing and aromatic roast legs of pork emerging from the oven move quickly. For decades, the chefs have pleased with their savory kettle of seafood *asopao* (a gumbo-like soup). How about a prune pie for dessert? Don't knock it till you've tried it.

259 Calle San Francisco. ☎ 787-722-0658. Reservations recommended. Main courses $6.95–$14.95. AE, MC, V. Open: Breakfast, lunch, and dinner daily 7:30 a.m.–8:00 p.m.

La Chaumière
$$$$ Old San Juan   Classic French

The location is in back of the Tapía Theater, but once inside you will think you're somewhere in the countryside of France. Francophiles delight in this place, and if you're young you'll get to sample some of the classic French dishes your parents enjoyed when they toured Europe in the '60s. A good country-style pâté, filled with richness, can get you started — that, or a perfectly made fish soup in the style of Provence. Our recently sampled rack of lamb had flavor, aroma, and texture, as did the filet mignon served with a classic Béarnaise sauce. A meltingly tender Dover sole meunière was also enjoyed at our table, and we'd award a star to the magret of duckling.

Calle Tetuán 367. ☎ 787-722-3330. Reservations required. Main courses: $25–$32. AE, DC, MC, V. Open: Mon–Sat 6 p.m. to midnight. Closed Jul–Aug.

La Mallorquina

$$–$$$ Old San Juan   Puerto Rican

Puerto Rico's oldest restaurant dates from 1848, and little has changed, certainly not the recipe for that savory *paella* (the famous saffron rice dish) or one of Old Town's best *asopaos* (the gumbo-like soup that comes with expensive lobster or more democratically priced chicken). The most ordered dish over the years? The classic *arroz con pollo* (chicken with rice). For a starter, the garlic soup will leave you with an aromatic taste in your mouth — and the breath to go with it. On a summer day, you may prefer the more soothing gazpacho. Nearly everyone finishes their meal with an order of the chef's flan or caramel custard. It's a tradition here, and tradition is what this place is all about.

207 Calle San Justo. ☎ *787-722-3261. Reservations not accepted for lunch, recommended for dinner. Main courses: $12–$20 for lunch, $17–$29 at dinner. AE, DC, MC, V. Open: Lunch and dinner Mon–Sat noon to 3 p.m. Closed Sun and in Sept.*

La Piccola Fontana

$$$$$ Isla Verde, San Juan   Northern Italian

This is not only the best Italian restaurant along the beach strip of San Juan, it is one of the leading Italian restaurants of the Caribbean. Even if you've "dined Italian" in New York, or gone to Italy, the chefs at La Piccola can hold their own against some stiff competition. The setting is off the lobby of this magnificent *luxe* mega-resort in two neo-Palladian rooms with frescoed walls of Italy's ruins and landscapes, a bit corny perhaps. But that's all that is corny here — certainly not the exquisite cuisine. Even if it's simply grilled veal chops, the chefs get it right. They also grill fresh filets of fish perfectly too. Our favorite pasta — and it's a succulent one — is tortellini San Daniele, made with tender veal, prosciutto, cream, and sage. Try also the grilled medallions of filet mignon served over a bed of freshly braised arugula. We applaud this restaurant for its fresh flavors, heady perfumes, and decisive seasonings.

In Wyndham El San Juan Hotel and Casino, Isla Verde Ave. ☎ *787-791-0966. Reservations required. Main courses: $28.95–$39.95. AE, DC, MC, V. Open: Dinner daily 6–11 p.m.*

Mark's at the Meliá

$$–$$$ Ponce   International/Puerto Rican

The finest dining along the island's south shore in its "second city" is found at the Meliá Hotel (see Chapter 28). The viands here are tastier and better than even at the Ponce Hilton's best restaurants. The master chef here is Mark French (yes, that's his real name, ideal for a chef). His cookery is not French but international. Although he roams the world for his repertoire, he is inspired by much of the produce of Puerto Rico, which he fashions into many dishes. For example, he serves fried green plantains, but his version comes with sour cream and a dollop of caviar. His tamarind-barbecued lamb with a yucca mojo deserves high praise because it's delectable, as is his corn-crusted red snapper with yucca purée, or his tempura jumbo shrimp with an Asian salad. Count yourself lucky if you saved room for his vanilla flan layered with rum sponge cake and topped with a caramelized banana.

In the Meliá Hotel, Calle Cristina. ☎ *787-284-6275. Reservations recommended. Main courses: $14–$30. AE, MC, V. Open: Lunch Wed–Sat noon to 3 p.m. and Sun noon to 5 p.m., dinner 6:00–10:30 p.m.*

Parrot Club
$$$ Old San Juan   Contemporary Puerto Rican

If you're taking the mayor of San Juan or the governor of Puerto Rico out to dinner, head here to Old Town's hottest restaurant. In what was a hair tonic factory from a hundred years ago, a beautiful restaurant has been installed to tempt you into a long, lush evening of refined food and good times. The chefs are skilled at Nuevo Latino cuisine, blending elements of Spanish, Taíno, and even African influences into their tasty repertoire. Meals are consumed against a backdrop of live music, classic Cuban, wild salsa, or Latino jazz. The intensely flavored ceviche of halibut is rich in texture, as are the crabcakes *caribeños,* one of our all-time favorites. The seared pork medallions with a sweet plantain chorizo or the sugar-cured skewered lamb with couscous will win you over, as will the pan-seared tuna served with a sauce made from dark rum and essence of oranges. The bartender's special drink is Parrot Passion, made from lemon-flavored rum, triple sec, and fresh oranges and passion fruit.

363 Calle Fortaleza. ☎ *787-725-7370. Reservations not accepted. Main courses: Lunch $12–$20, dinner $17–$29. AE, MC, V. Open: Lunch daily 11:30 a.m.–3:00 p.m., dinner Mon–Sat 7–11 p.m., Sun 6:30–10:30 p.m. Closed for two weeks in July.*

Chapter 31

Having Fun on and off the Beach in Puerto Rico

By Darwin Porter and Danforth Prince

● ●

In This Chapter

▶ Soaking up the sun on Puerto Rico's top beaches

▶ Diving into fun with water sports

▶ Satisfying the landlubber: activities, shopping, and nightlife

▶ Planning some super side trips

● ●

*R*ivaled only by Jamaica, Puerto Rico is the most diverse destination in the Caribbean. From its 258 miles of sandy beaches to its lush inland forest, Puerto Rico is a happy wedding of natural beauty and historical sights.

Its restored Old Town of San Juan is the Caribbean's greatest living history book, far excelling its nearest rival, Santo Domingo of the Dominican Republic. From whale-watching to golf courses, from mammoth caves to windsurfing, Puerto Rico is a year-round destination.

Cruise ships also make it the busiest port in the Caribbean, even more so than the clogged harbor of Charlotte Amalie on St. Thomas. If you're hungry for a good time, Puerto Rico has something on its menu for you.

On a whirlwind tour, we give you the lay of the land (and sea) of Puerto Rico's beaches, followed by a guide to water sports, from diving to deep-sea fishing. You can, of course, spend all your time on the beach (or beaches). But if you're an active, adventurous traveler, you can do everything from horseback riding to hiking in the mountains, golfing to spelunking, snorkeling to scuba diving. We wind up with a look at Puerto Rico's rollicking fiesta of a nightlife scene, a tempest and trendsetter among all the islands of the Caribbean. Finally, we go island-hopping to explore Puerto Rico's Spanish Virgin Islands.

Spending a Day (Or More) at the Beach

Puerto Ricans share with their visitors a love of their beaches, and on weekends, winter or summer, they flock to their strips of golden sand to share space with the tourists. We'd dare to say that Puerto Ricans are the most beach-loving people of any country in the Caribbean. Because there are so many beaches — some crowded, some so isolated you'll have the sands all to yourself — there is room for everyone.

On the northern coast, the Atlantic waters are more turbulent than those along the more tranquil southern shore. Some stretches near San Juan and the major resorts are incredibly crowded, but you can still find a quiet, remote beach. The big resorts have claimed the most ideal beaches, but even so, they're still open to the public. Public bathing beaches in Puerto Rico are called *balnearios*. These are government-run, with lifeguards, parking, and dressing rooms.

All the *playas* (beaches) on the island are open to the public, even those bordering the most expensive mega-resorts. Of course, if you use any of the facilities of a resort, you'll have to pay. Admission is free to all beaches, but parking is generally $2.

Public beaches usually shut down on Monday but are open Tuesday through Sunday from 9 a.m. to 5 p.m. If Monday is a holiday, the *balnearios* are closed on Tuesday. For a report or any information on the island's beach, call the Department of Recreation and Sports (☎ 787-722-1551 or 787-728-5668).

If you're booked a hotel on San Juan's Isla Verde or the Condado, chances are you can take off your mainland clothes, put on a swimsuit, and be on a white sandy beach within 30 minutes. Even if your hotel is not right on the sands, it's probably no more than two or three blocks away.

The **Condado/Isla Verde** beaches are the best and most frequented in Greater San Juan. Good snorkeling is possible from either beach, and rental equipment is available at various kiosks. Condado Beach, where beach tourism to Puerto Rico began in the 1920s, evokes Miami Beach with its high-rises. Set near San Juan, this lively beach is punctuated with tall coconut palms and jammed with city folk mingling with resort guests. Boom boxes blare, young women dare with their barely-theres, and vendors sell colorful *pareos* (island wraps), anklets, T-shirts, and cheap eats.

Near the airport, **Isla Verde Beach** is a favorite of locals who share the golden sands with guests of the high-rise resorts found here. Isla Verde has picnic tables, so you can pick up the makings of a lunch and spend the day at the beach. This strip is also good for snorkeling because of its calm, clear waters. Isla Verde Beach extends from the end of Ocean Park to the beginning of a section called Boca Cangrejos. Most sections of this long strip have separate names, such as El Alambique, which is often the site of beach parties, and Punta El Medio, bordering the new Ritz-Carlton, also a great beach and very popular even with the locals. If you go past the luxury hotels and expensive condos behind the Luís Muñoz Marín International Airport, you arrive at the major public beach at Isla Verde. Here you'll find a *balneario* with parking, showers, fast-food joints, and water-sports equipment. The sands here are whiter than the golden sands of the Condado and are lined with coconut palms, sea-grape trees, and even almond trees, all of which provide shade from the fierce noonday sun.

One of the most attractive beaches in the Greater San Juan area is **Ocean Park,** a mile of fine gold sand in a neighborhood east of Condado. This beach attracts both young people and a big gay crowd. Access to the beach at Ocean Park has been limited recently, but the best place to enter is from a section called El Ultimo Trolley. This area is ideal for volleyball, paddleball, and other games. The easternmost portion, known as Punta La Marias, is best for windsurfing. The waters at Ocean Park are fine for swimming, although they can get rough at times.

One of the best beaches for windsurfers is at Rincón, 100 miles west of San Juan. Surfers from all over the world flock to the beach at **Punta Higuero,** along Route 413. Swells from the Atlantic Ocean in winter form waves averaging 5 to 6 feet in height, with rideable rollers sometimes reaching 15 to 25 feet. This beach is also a winter venue for watching for the endangered humpback whales, which pass in review off the coast from December through February. Some of the best snorkeling on the island is also possible offshore.

Rivaling Condado and Isla Verde beaches, **Luquillo Public Beach** is the grandest in Puerto Rico and one of the most popular. It's 30 miles east of San Juan near the town of Luquillo. Here you'll find a mile-long half-moon bay set against a backdrop of coconut palms. This is another of the dozen or so *balnearios* of Puerto Rico. Saturday and Sunday are the worst times to go, because hordes of *sanjuaneros* (San Juan residents) head here for fun in the sun. Water-sports kiosks offer everything from windsurfing to sailing. Facilities include lifeguards, an emergency first-aid station, ample parking, showers, and toilets. You can easily have a local lunch here at one of the beach shacks offering cod fritters and tacos.

Luquillo has a unique wheelchair-accessible program called Mar Sin Barreras or "sea without barriers," which allows physically challenged people to bask in the warm ocean waters. For more information, call ☎ 787-889-4329.

Some of the best snorkeling in Puerto Rico is in and around Fajardo lying to the east of Luquillo. Its beach, **Playa Seven Seas,** is not as hotsy-totsy as Playa Luquillo, but it's an attractive and sheltered wide strip of sand shaded by coconut palms. The beach lies on the south-western shoreline of Las Cabezas peninsula and is very crowded on weekends. The best snorkeling, however, is not here. Walk along this beach for about half a mile to another beach called **Playa Escondido** or "Hidden Beach." Beautiful coral reefs, ideal for snorkeling in clear waters, lie right off this *playa*.

We'll let you in on an even more alluring secret. East from Las Cabezas is a marine wildlife refuge known as **La Cordillera** or "The Spine." Off the mainland of the island, these are the most gin-clear and the most tranquil waters we have yet to find in Puerto Rico. They are teeming with wildlife, including several species of fish such as grouper, but also lobster, moray eels, and even sea turtles. On these islets you may even see a rare crested iguana. **Aqua Sports** in Fajardo (☎ 787-888-8841) will take you here.

Lying 18 miles west of San Juan, the two **Dorado Beaches** are flanked by the Hyatt Dorado Beach Hotel and the larger Hyatt Regency Cerromar Beach Hotel. These are among the most desirable white sandy beaches on the island.

Whetting Your Appetite for Water Fun

Puerto Ricans look to their enveloping coastline as both a source of food and a source of fun. Here's how you can join them in this under-water world.

Diving Puerto Rican waters

Frankly, the diving is better in Bonaire and the Cayman Islands than it is in Puerto Rico. If you want a strictly diver's vacation, head to one of those outposts. But if you want to include some diving in an otherwise full vacation agenda, Puerto Rican waters can tempt you. What makes Puerto an interesting dive site is that a continental shelf envelops it on three sides, creating coral reefs, sea walls, caves, and trenches.

Check out your dive operator thoroughly. Reaching some of the better sites requires a lengthy boat trip. Some operators have acquired a rep-utation for trying to pawn off more accessible sites with little marine life when a little more effort would transport divers to pristine reefs with far more marine action. Plus, you don't want to be on an old boat spewing fumes if you have to travel far.

The best diving is offshore, with some fairly pristine sites. Looking like it's from that long-running musical *South Pacific,* the 360-acre **Isle**

Desecheo lies 15 miles off the coast of Rincón in the west. It is a wildlife preserve; its fringe reefs are among Puerto Rico's finest and are filled with coral and tropical fish, including rock "terraces" and caves.

Also in western Puerto Rico, diving is spectacular off the offshore **Isla Mona,** which is called Puerto's Rico's "Jurassic Park" because of all the wildlife found there, including gigantic rock iguanas with their big heads and powerful jaws. A 14,000-acre nature preserve 50 miles off the coast, Mona offers overfished waters but visibility of 150 feet, with reef dives, wall dives, and nearly ten different kinds of living coral.

In eastern Puerto Rico, some two dozen of the best dive sites lie south of the fishing port of Fajardo within a 5-mile radius offshore. One of the best known and the most dramatic is called **The Cracks,** just off the coast from the town of Humacao. There are large fissures in the reef in which rainbow-hued fish and other marine life feed.

Savvy divers also flock to the offshore island of **Culebra,** 18 miles east of the port of Fajardo (reached by ferry). A favored site here is called "Magical Mystery Tour," with a maze of tunnels and varied coral, lying in depths of 40 feet with good visibility.

A number of outfitters on the island will take you on a half-day dive costing $70 to $90 for one– and two-tank dives, with all equipment thrown in. You can arrange some dive packages, including lunch, beginning at $60. Night dives will generally cost twice as much. Most snorkeling excursions start at $33, including boat transport (usually a sailboat), equipment rental, and maybe lunch. Either snorkelers or scuba divers can hook up with an outfitter by contacting one of the following, each a specialist: **Caribbean School of Aquatics** (San Juan Bay Marina; ☎ **787-823-6429;** Internet: www.tainodivers.com), **Descheco Dive Shop** (Rincón; ☎ **787-823-0390**), or **Dive Copamarina** (Guánica; ☎ **787-821-0505**).

Hook up with one of these outfitters is always wiser than diving or snorkeling on your own, because you can easily become disoriented. Windsurfers also need to take precautions. At Steps, Dogman's, and Tres Palmas, three major windsurfing sites just north of Rincón in western Puerto Rico, several surfers have drowned in waves that shot up for at least 24 feet.

Advanced divers can head to the **Parguera Divers Training Center,** Parador Posada Por la Mar, Route 304, La Parguera (☎ **787-899-4171**). Dive master Angel Rovira has been diving the walls for more than a decade and knows every crevice of the wall diving. Angel and his wife, Roberta, put a premium on customer service, and they make sure that repeat guests don't repeat sites. Under their watchful eyes, you'll likely see nurse sharks, Atlantic spadefish, queen angelfish, and more.

Boarding the surf

Winter storms in the north Atlantic Ocean have made the western city of Rincón a mecca for windsurfers from November through April. There is no land mass to break the swells. These gnarly waves roll into Rincón sometimes dangerously high at some 25 feet.

The best surfing beaches are along the Atlantic coastline from **Borinquén Point** south to Rincón, where you'll find several surf shops, including **West Coast Surf Shop** (2 E. Muñoz Rivera St., Rincón; ☎ 878-823-3935) where you can rent surfboards for $20 and up for a full day. The reefs and rocks here mean that this "Surf City" is better for the experienced surfer. Beginners can check out Aviones in Piñones east of San Juan, La Concha beaches in San Juan, and Casa de Pesca in Arecibo, all summer surfing spots that have surf shops.

Having Fun on the Water without Getting Wet

If you can't imagine a trip to Puerto Rico without some close encounter with the sea, check out the ways you can take to the water — without jumping in.

Wandering the water's surface

Puerto Rico's waters are not the sailor's Valhalla that the British Virgin Islands are (see Chapter 19), but they're often idyllic. From the fishing port of Fajardo on the east coast, a boater can reach such offshore, unspoiled cays as Icacos and Palomino in only an hour or two. Also lying to the east of Fajardo are the resort islands of Culebra and Vieques, and beyond that the islands that form the archipelago of the Lesser Antilles.

Unless you go far astray into the ocean, navigation is relatively easy because you're always in site of a land mass.

Marinas and charter boats are found all around the island, but the biggest concentration is in the vicinity of Fajardo. Catamarans, know for their stability, are especially popular. A typical charter starts from 9:30 a.m. for a leisurely sail to Icacos. (Prices begin around $70 per person. Many outfitters will arrange your transportation to Fajardo if you're staying in San Juan.)

Ocean kayaking along lagoons and through mangrove channels is yet another fun way to have an encounter with the island's waters without getting wet.

The mega-resorts spread across the beachfront from the Condado (closest to Old Town San Juan) to Isla Verde in the east near the airport and rent all sorts of equipment: Sunfish, windsurfers, paddleboats, and kayaks. The waves here can be turbulent from November through April, but the constantly blowing trade winds delight sailors.

In San Juan, contact the **Condado Plaza Hotel and Casino Water-Sports Center** (999 Av. Ashford; ☎ 787-721-1000) or the **Wyndham El San Juan Hotel and Casino Watersports Center** (Av. Isla Verde; ☎ 787-791-1000). Boating and sailing trips of all kinds are offered by **Caribbean School of Aquatics** (San Juan Bay Marina; ☎ 878-728-6606) and **Castillo Watersports** (ESJ Tower, Isla Verde; ☎ 787-791-6195 or 787-725-7970).

Moving east of San Juan, **Iguana Water Sports,** Westin Rio Mar Beach Resort and Country Club, 6000 Rio Mar Blvd., Rio Grande (☎ 787-888-6000) stocks a wide selection of small craft. Sailing instruction is available at the **Palmas Dive Center,** Candelero Resort at Palmas del Mar, Rte. 906, Humacao (☎ 787-852-6000). **East Wind II Catamaran,** Fajardo (☎ 787-860-3434), can fix you up with a catamaran snorkeling excursion.

To experience an oddity on the water at night, head for the little beach resort of La Parguera, lying in the southwestern sector of the island, reached by heading south of San Germán along Route 304. La Parguera is west of Ponce. This part of the island has been likened to Louisiana's bayous, with its mangrove swamps, secluded coves, and "islets." The attraction is *Bahía Fosforescente,* or Phosphorescent Bay, where marine plankton, formally known as microscopic dinoflagellates, light up the waters when disturbed, but only on a moonless night. It's like looking at thousands of lightning bugs under the sea. Several boats leave from La Parguera for the hour-long trip nightly from dusk to midnight. The standard fee is $10 per person.

Hooking the big one

In Puerto Rico, you can feel like you're in Hemingway's *The Old Man and the Sea,* pursuing the giant blue marlin. Puerto Rico's Annual Billfish Tournament is the world's largest consecutively held competition of its kind. Puerto Rico's clear waters are home to game fish such as blue and white marlin (most prevalent in late summer), wahoo, dorado (best from November through early April), yellow and blackfin tuna, and barracuda. Catches have set more than 30 world records.

Boats range from 34 to 61 feet in length. Half-day (four hours in the morning or four hours in the afternoon) and full-day, charters can be arranged through **Benitez Deep-Sea Fishing,** Club Nautico de San Juan, San Juan (☎ 787-723-2292; Fax: 787-725-4344). Other options include **Castillo Watersports,** Isla Verde (☎ 787-791-6195).

Outside of San Juan, try **Parguera Fishing Charters,** La Parguera
(☎ **787-899-4698** or cellular 787-382-4698) and **Tropical Fishing
Charters,** Av. El Conquistador, Fajardo (☎ **787-860-8551** or
787-759-1255).

Food and drink are provided by your skipper, but it may not be what
you want to drink or eat. Check in advance. If you don't like what's at
the bar or on the menu, bring your own provisions. Fortunately, Puerto
Pico doesn't hit you with extra taxes, nor does it require you to take
out a fishing license.

Enjoying Your Time on Dry Land

The rich, lush island of Puerto Rico, from its mountainous interior to
its seascapes, can be enjoyed by everyone from the horseback rider to
the golfer, from the hiker to the biker. Here's the best way to hook up
with these active sports.

Hitting that ball

The comparison is a bit far-fetched, but Puerto Rico is often called "the
Scotland of the Caribbean." It and Jamaica (see Chapter 27) have the
best golf course in the West Indies.

In recent years, the island has hosted the LPGA tour and the Hyatt PGA
Matchplay Challenge. You can pick from 18 courses on the island, 14 of
which are championship links designed by golf legends Greg Norman;
Robert Trent Jones, Sr.; George Fazio; Arthur Hills; Greg Player; and, of
course, home-island hero Chi Chi Rodríguez. Call ahead to reserve tee
times. Some resorts limit their players to guests only (or at least favor
guests). Greens fees begin at $45 but can run up to $185.

Some of Puerto Rico's best golf is found at the two Hyatt resorts at
Dorado, 18 miles west of San Juan. The quartet of 18-hole golf courses
here were designed by Robert Trent Jones, Sr. The two original
courses, known as East and West (☎ 787-796-8961 for tee times), were
carved out of a jungle and offer tight fairways bordered by trees and
forests, with lots of ocean holes. The somewhat newer and less noted
North and South courses (☎ 787-796-8915 for tee times) feature wide
fairways with well-bunkered greens and an assortment of water traps
and tricky wind factors. Each course has a 72 par. The longest is the
South course at 7,047 yards. Although open to nonguests, these four
courses are owned by **Hyatt Dorado Beach** and the **Hyatt Regency
Cerromar Beach Hotels** at Route 693, Km 10.8 and Km 11.8, Dorado.

Competing with the golf courses at Dorado is Chi Chi Rodríguez's
own signature course, **Dorado del Mar Golf Club,** 200 Dorado del Mar
(☎ 787-796-3070). This course affords panoramic scenery, water on

12 holes, and tropical trade winds. Chi Chi's own favorite hole is 10, a long uphill par-5. A host of the Honda Classic, the 6,937-yard, 18-hole course opened in 1998. Playing the course costs $85 Monday through Friday or $95 on weekends.

Giving the Dorado courses serious competition these days are two world-class championship courses at **Westin Rio Mar Beach Resort and Country Club,** 6000 Rio Mar Blvd., Rio Grande (☎ **787-888-6000**). They're as easily accessible from San Juan as the Dorado courses. Rio Grande is 19 miles east of San Juan. The older of the two, the Ocean Course, was designed by George and Tom Fazio as part of the original resort, and has been a staple on Puerto Rico's professional golf circuit since the 1960s. In 1997, Westin opened the property's second 18-holer, the more challenging River Course, the first Greg Norman–designed course in the Caribbean. Both courses are sandwiched between the ocean and the foot of El Yunque, the only tropical rain forest in the U.S. National Forest system.

Few other real-estate developments in the Caribbean devote as much attention and publicity to their golf facilities as the **Palmas de Mar Golf Club** (☎ **787-285-2256**). Today, both the older course (the Gary Player–designed Palm Course) and the newer course (the Reese Jones–designed Flamboyant) have pars of 72 and layouts of around 6,800 feet each. Crack golfers consider holes 11 to 15 of the older course among the toughest five successive holes in the Caribbean.

Engaging in a game of tennis

If you're staying at one of the large resorts, certainly if that hotel is outside of San Juan, there's a good chance your hotel will have its own tennis courts. If you're in a smaller inn in San Juan or even out on the island, your hotel probably won't have a tennis court. Most hotels will allow nonguests to play for a fee, but you have to call to book a court time, and hotel guests naturally are given preference. The city of San Juan offers 17 lighted courts at **San Juan Central Municipal Park** (Calle Cerra, exit on Route 2; ☎ 787-722-1646). Fees run $4 per hour from 8 a.m. to 6 p.m. and $5 per hour from 6 p.m. to 10 p.m. Two tennis courts are available at the **Condodo Plaza Hotel and Casino** (999 Av. Ashford; ☎ 787-721-1000). Fees for nonguests range from $10 to $20 per hour.

Other island-based tennis facilities include the following:

- ✔ Seven courts at the **Hyatt Dorado Beach** (Rte. 693, Km 10.8, Dorado; ☎ **787-796-1234**)

- ✔ Eight courts at the **Hyatt Regency Cerromar Beach** (Rte. 693, Km 11.8, Dorado; ☎ **787-796-1234**)

- ✔ Four courts at the **Ponce Hilton and Casino** (Rte. 14, 1150 Av. Caribe, Ponce; ☎ **787-259-7676**)

✔ Twelve courts at the **Westin Rio Mar Resort and Country Club** (6000 Rio Mar Blvd., Rio Grande; ☎ 787-888-6000)

✔ Twenty courts at **Doral Resort at Palmas de Mar** (Rte. 906, Humacao; ☎ 787-852-6000)

Rooting for the home team

When it comes to baseball, Puerto Ricans reach a fever pitch. If you have any fans in your family, consider taking in a ball game on the island that's given birth to such greats as Roberto Clemente, Roberto and Sandy Alomar of the Cleveland Indians, and their father, Sandy Alomar, a former league player and coach of the San Diego Padres. The island's season runs from October through February. Stadiums are in San Juan, Santurce, Ponce, Caguas, Arecibo, and Mayagüez; the teams also play once or twice in Aguadilla. Contact the **Puerto Rico Tourism Company** (☎ 800-223-6530) for details or call **Professional Baseball of Puerto Rico** (☎ 787-765-6285).

Hiking the island

The best place for hiking in the entire Caribbean is the Caribbean National Forest, nicknamed **El Yunque**, the only tropical rain forest in the U.S. National Park Service. The United Nations has designated El Yunque a Biosphere Reserve. It is riddled with 28,000 acres of trails, lying only a 45-minute drive east of San Juan. It's entered at the **El Portal Tropical Forest Center**, Highway 3, then right on Route 191 (☎ 787-888-1810 or 787-888-1880).

Granted national park status by President Theodore Roosevelt, it's an ideal spot for a picnic among rare flora and fauna, including 240 species of tropical trees, 20 kinds of orchids, and varied wildlife including millions of tiny tree frogs whose distinctive cry of *coquí* (pronounced *ko-kee*) has given them their name. Other tropical birds include the greenish blue–and-red-fronted Puerto Rican parrot, once nearly extinct and now making a comeback. Other rare animals include the Puerto Rican boa, which grows to 7 feet (but it's very unlikely that you'll encounter one). More than two dozen animal species found here live nowhere else in the world.

As you hike along the terrain, with its ropelike vines and feathery primeval ferns, you will think you've entered "Me Tarzan, You Jane" country. Towering over El Yunque is El Toro, its highest peak at 3,523 feet. At least 200 inches of rain fall on El Yunque annually, and islanders thank the Indian god, Yukiyú, the namesake of the forest, for this showering abundance of water, the envy of many a "dry" island in the Caribbean, such as Aruba.

Because it's likely to rain down on you at any minute, bring along a lightweight rain slicker and some sturdy hiking boots. Along your trails, you'll find sheltered picnic tables and observation towers.

El Portal Tropical Forest Center features displays that explain El Yunque and tropical forests around the world. A theater presents video shows in English and Spanish. The visitor center is open daily from 7:30 a.m. to 5:00 p.m. (6:00 p.m. on Saturday and Sunday). El Portal charges a $3 entry fee. For more information, you can contact the **Department of Natural Resources (☎ 787-724-3724)** and the U.S. Forest Service (☎ 787-724-3724). We suggest planning a full day of exploring this preserve. If you have kids along, you'll find plenty of easy trails for them to tackle.

Most San Juan hotels have a tour desk that can make arrangements for you to hike the forests. All-day tours ($35 to $60) can include a trip to Ponce, a day at El Comandante Racetrack, or a combined tour of the San Juan and El Yunque rain forest. Leading tour operators include **Normandie Tours, Inc. (☎ 787-722-6308)**, **Rico Suntours (☎ 787-722-2080** or 787-722-6090), **Tropix Wellness Tours (☎ 787-268-2173)**, and **United Tour Guides (☎ 787-725-7605** or 787-723-5578).

Horsing around

Puerto Ricans not only love baseball (see "Rooting for the home team," earlier in this chapter), they also have a passion for betting on the horses. In just a 20-minute taxi ride or drive east of San Juan, **El Comandante Racetrack,** Route 3, Km 15.3, Canovanas (☎ 787-724-6060), is one of the major racetracks of the Caribbean. Post time is 2:15 p.m. The on-site restaurant is open on race days: Monday, Wednesday, and Friday through Sunday from 12:30 to 5:30 p.m.

If you'd rather ride a horse than watch one race, you've also arrived on the right island. Many locals are avid horsemen (or –women), and Puerto Rico is known in equestrian circles for its *paso fino* horses. These well-bred, graceful animals have a distinctive gait. You should always call to reserve before arriving at one of the stables.

One of the most convenient stables, and our favorite, is **Hacienda Carabali,** Route 992, Km 4, Luquillo (☎ 787-889-5820 or 787-889-4954). This outfitter features the best of both worlds: rides along Puerto Rico's best beach at Playa Luquillo and rides through El Yunque, the rain forest (see "Hiking the island," earlier in this chapter).

While still in the eastern part of the island, you can also be linked up with forest trails and beach rides at the **Palmas de Mar Equestrian Center** at Doral Resort, Route 906, Humacao (☎ 787-852-6000). A unique place for riding is **Hacienda Campo Alegre**, Route 127, Km 5.1,

Yauco (☎ **787-856-0381**). Here you can ride the trails of a 200-acre island ranch. There's a restaurant on site, and this is a family favorite because it has playgrounds.

Pedaling around Puerto Rico

If you generally bike around New York City, then San Juan should be no daunting challenge. Not only San Juan, but the major arteries along the north coast are filled with cars and their fumes, no fun for bikers at all. In much of the interior, including the mountain-bike trails across the Cordillera Central, biking is for those in training for the Olympics.

The best areas we've found are along the small roads on the island's southern coastline, both east and west of Ponce. This coastal plain area makes biking more fun than a challenge. If you like to bike along a wide beach, we suggest the one fronting the town of Boquerón in the southwest.

In the southwest, you can rent bikes at **Boquerón Balnearios,** Department of Recreation and Sports, Route 101, Boqueron (☎ **787-722-1551** or 787-722-1771) and the **Ponce Hilton,** Route 14, 1150 Av. Caribe, Ponce (☎ **787-259-7676**). In the Dorado area, west of San Juan, on the north coast, you can rent bikes from the **Hyatt Dorado Beach,** Route 693, Km 10.8 (☎ **787-796-1234**) or the **Hyatt Regency Cerromar Beach,** Route 693, Km 11.8 (☎ 787-796-1234).

Going on a shopping spree

If you, like us, feel you were "born to shop," San Juan is your kind of city. For those bargains in imported perfumes or expensive electronics, head for Charlotte Amalie, the capital of St. Thomas (see Chapter 35). Because, as a territory of the United States, U.S. import taxes have been paid, in Puerto Rico you can take back all you want in merchandise without extra duty. Because the duty has been paid, it is reflected in the merchandise. Even so there are bargains; San Juan shops grant heavy discounts. Boutiques and specialized stores line the narrow streets of Old San Juan.

The Puerto Rico Tourism Company's Artisan Center (☎787-721-2400) or the **Fomento Crafts Project** (☎ **787-758-4747,** ext. 2291) offer advice about where to purchase high-quality works by island craftspeople.

Puerto Rican rum is the best in the world — just ask any local rum producer. Most visitors who like rum punches pick up a bottle or two before flying back or returning by ship to the mainland. Prices are lower than in the States, and you can bring back as many bottles as you want without paying duty. *Ron,* as it's called locally, is the national drink of Puerto Rico, the world's largest producer. To many rum drinkers, there is no other brand than the famous Bacardi. No contest, it is the smoothest rum we've ever drunk. To a lesser degree, we're also fond of Ronrico, Castillo, Don Q, and, for variety, a spiced rum called Captain Morgan.

The most impressive of the island's crafts are the *santos,* carved religious figures that have been produced since the 1500s. Craftspeople who make these are called *santeros.* Using clay, gold, stone, or cedar wood, they carve figurines representing saints, usually from 8 to 20 inches tall.

Another Puerto Rican craft has undergone a big revival just as it seemed that it would disappear forever: lace. Originating in Spain, *mundillos* (tatted fabrics) are the product of a type of bobbin lace-making. This craft, five centuries old, exists today only in Puerto Rico and Spain. The first lace made in Puerto Rico was called *torchon* (beggar's lace). Early examples of beggar's lace were considered of inferior quality, but artisans today have transformed this fabric into a delicate art form, eagerly sought by collectors. Lace bands called *entrados* have two straight borders, whereas the other traditional style, *puntilla,* has both a straight and a scalloped border.

The most popular of all Puerto Rican crafts are the frightening *caretas-* papier-mâché masks worn at island carnivals. The menacing horns, fang-toothed leering expressions, and bulging eyes of these half-demon, half-animal creations send children running and screaming to their parents. At carnival time, they are worn by costumed revelers called *vejigantes. Vejigantes* wear bat-winged jumpsuits and roam the streets either individually or in groups.

Puerto Rico, like the States, has its share of shopping malls. The greatest concentration of specialty stores is in Old San Juan, where you can get about on a free trolley if you don't want to walk. The best shops are on Calle Cristo, Calle San Francisco, and Calle Fortaleza, although dipping into the smaller side streets is fun as well.

Here are some unique shops to seek out:

- ✔ **El Alacazar** (Calle San Jose 103; ☎ 787-723-1229), established in 1986, is the largest emporium of antique furniture, silver, and art objects in the Carribean.

- ✔ **Galeria Palomas** (Calle del Cristo 207; ☎ 787-725-2660) is one of the leading art galleries of Puerto Rico, carrying some of the major painters in Latin America, although prices begin at $75.

- ✔ **Butterfly People** (Calle Fortaleza 152; ☎ 787-723-2432) sells unique mounted butterflies that will last forever. Some are sold as wall murals.

✔ **La Calle** (105 Calle Fortaleza 105; ☎ 787-725-1306) is the best emporium selling brightly painted papier- mâché carnival masks.

✔ **Club Jibarito** (Calle Cristo 202; ☎ 787-724-7797) sells Puerto Rico's own excellent cigars, which some aficionados prefer to the more famous Cuban cigar.

✔ **Spicy Caribbee** (Calle Cristo 154; ☎ 787-725-4690) offers Old Town's best selection of Puerto Rican coffee.

Our favorite brands of coffee are Café Crema, Café Rico, Rioja, and Yaucono, in that order.

Living la vida loca

Wherever you find *sanjuaneros,* you'll find a party going on. Puerto Ricans love their social life, and tops on their lists are dancing and dressing up. Women should wear their killer heels (just watch the ballast stone streets), and men should show up decked out, too.

Like New York, the whirling club scene of San Juan can be tough to keep up with. *Qué Pasa,* the official visitor's guide, tries to keep abreast. Also, pick up a copy of the *San Juan Star, Quick City Guide,* or *Bienvenidos.* If your hotel has a concierge, he or she is usually a font of information about what's hot after dark.

Fridays and Saturdays are big nights in San Juan when clubs are their most crowded, and the only way you'll get into some of them without a reservation is if you're Ricky Martin or Jennifer Lopez. If you're staying at an upscale hotel, ask the concierge if he or she can reserve a good table at the most happening spots. The hottest action doesn't start until 10 p.m. or after.

Old San Juan's cobblestone streets are closed to auto traffic on Friday and Saturday nights, making the area perfect for a romantic stroll. If you're looking for more action, walk to Calle San Sebastian, lined with trendy bars and restaurants where you'll see lines of people waiting to get through the doors. Outside of San Juan, nightlife is hard to come by beyond the resorts.

Some of the best clubs in San Juan are in hotels, including **Babylon,** in Wyndham El San Juan Hotel and Casino, 6063 Isle Verde Ave., Isla Verde (☎ 787-791-1000), imposing a $10 cover. Attracting an age group of 25– to 45-year-olds, it offers hot dancing and one of the best sound systems in the Caribbean. In neighboring Santurce, a trendy hot spot to hear live music is **Unplugged Café,** 365 De Diego Ave. (☎ 787-723-1423). Its repertoire is like a "musical magazine" — jazz, blues, R&B, rock, even comedy shows and karaoke.

East of Isla Verde along the Condado strip, **Houlihan's,** 1903 Ashford Ave., Condado (☎ 787-723-8600), is the best place to hear merengue, Spanish rock, or salsa. It imposes a $10 to $20 cover charge, and attracts a young, fun-loving crowd, an equal mix of locals and visitors.

Favorite after-dark spots in Old San Juan are **Rumba,** Calle San Sebastian 152 (☎ 787-725-4407), which is the best place for salsa dancing, attracting some of the island's best bands. **Club Lazer**, Calle del Cruz 251 (☎ 787-725-7581), is a dance club sprawling across three floors of an antique building. Charging an $8 to $10 cover, it lures with its merengue and salsa beat.

The most popular gay bar in San Juan is the **Beach Bar** on the ground floor of the Atlantic Beach Hotel, Calle Vendig 1 (☎ 787-721-6900), an open-air bar that reaches its cruisy peak on a Sunday afternoon. Drag shows often take place on its terrace. Patterned after dance emporiums in New York, **Eros,** 1257 Ponce de Leon, Santurce (☎ 787-722-1131), offers cutting-edge music in a fantasy-charged, erotic atmosphere. Catering exclusively to lesbians, **Cups,** 1708 Calle San Mateo, Santurce (☎ 787-268-3570), offers on occasion live music and cabaret; it attracts both the lipstick lesbian and the butch.

Many visitors come to Puerto Rico on package deals and stay at one of the posh hotels at the Condado or Isla Verde just to gamble.

Nearly all the large hotels in San Juan/Condado/Isla Verde offer casinos, and there are other large casinos at some of the bigger resorts outside the metropolitan area. The atmosphere in the casinos is casual, but still you shouldn't show up in bathing suits or shorts. Most of the casinos open around noon, closing often at 2, 3, or 4 a.m. Patrons must be at least 18 years old to enter.

The casino generating all the excitement today is the 18,500-square-foot Casino at **The Ritz-Carlton**, 6961 State Rd., Isla Verde (☎ 787-253-1700), the largest in Puerto Rico. It combines the elegant decor of the 1940s with tropical fabrics and patterns. This is one of the plushest and most exclusive entertainment complexes in the Caribbean. It features traditional games such as blackjack, roulette, baccarat, craps, and slot machines.

One of the splashiest of San Juan's casinos is at the **Wyndham Old San Juan Hotel and Casino**, Calle Brumbaugh 100 (☎ 787-721-5100), where five-card stud competes with some 240 slot machines and roulette tables. You can also try your luck at the **Caribe Hilton** (one of the better ones), Calle Los Rosales (☎ 787-721-0303), **Wyndham El San Juan Hotel and Casino** (one of the most grand), 6063 Isla Verde Ave. (☎ 787-791-1000), or the **Condado Plaza Hotel and Casino**, 999 Ashford Ave. (☎ 787-791-1000). There are no passports to flash or admissions to pay.

Exploring Old San Juan

There is no city of the West Indies more historic or more beautiful than Old San Juan, a 7-block-square zone that is best explored on foot or by the free Old Town Trolley, which you can hop on board and get off any time something catches your fancy. Once encircled by a fortress wall, it is now a protected area, both a UNESCO World Heritage Site and a U.S. National Historic Site.

To stroll the lamp-lit cobblestone streets of Old San Juan is to walk back in history 500 years. The Spanish founded "Rich Port" (its English name) back in 1521. In the oldest capital city under the U.S. flag, there are at least 400 buildings that are restored to their colonial splendor. Many are adorned with iron balconies filled with potted plants in the Spanish tradition. Some of the *adoquines,* or bluish stones, that go to make the streets originally arrived in port as ballast aboard Spanish galleons.

Churches, museums, shops, historic forts, hotels (a rather meager lot), restaurants (more than you'll even need), bars, nightclubs, and taverns — it's all here to amuse you. Exploring the major streets of Old San Juan takes about three or four hours (not counting any interior visits). Absorbing all of Old Town's unique atmosphere would take weeks.

We recommend that you walk the streets of Old San Juan in both day and after dark, because the mood and atmosphere are remarkably different. You can see more during the day, but nighttime strolls are more romantic.

Here are some highlights of Old San Juan:

- **Casa Blanca,** 1 Calle San Sebastian (☎ **787-725-5584**): The "White House" of Old San Juan is sometimes mistaken as the residence of Ponce de León. Actually it was built in 1521 after the famed explorer died in Cuba. His son-in-law, Juan García Troche, ordered the house to be erected on land given to Ponce by the Spanish Crown for services rendered. Two years after it was built, it was destroyed by a hurricane, and the present masonry home is a reconstruction. The descendants of Ponce de León occupied the house for 250 years until the Spanish government took it over in 1779 as a residence for military commanders. There's an attractive garden with a refreshing fountain in the courtyard, and the Juan Ponce de León Museum on the second floor, exhibiting antiques, paintings, and artifacts from the 16th to the 18th centuries. Admission is $2. Open Tuesday through Saturday from 8 a.m. to noon and 1 to 5 p.m.

- **Cathedral de San Juan,** 153 Calle Cristo (☎ **787-722-0861**): This is the ecclesiastical center of Puerto Rico, its most venerated religious edifice. A wood building with a thatched roof stood here

Old San Juan Attractions

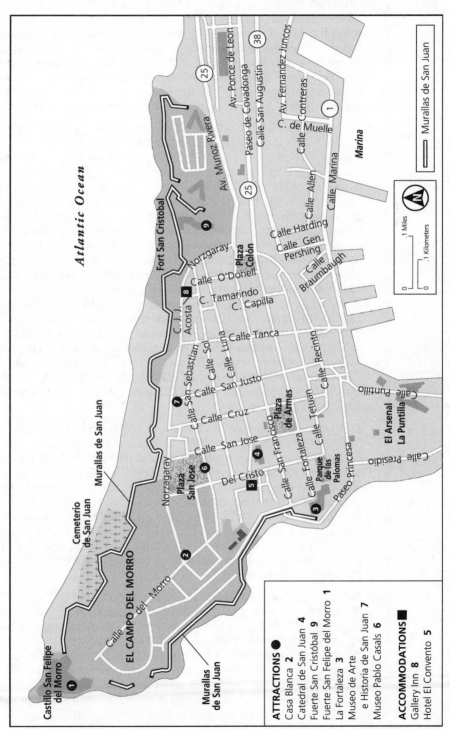

Atlantic Ocean

Castillo San Felipe del Morro

Cemeterio de San Juan

Murallas de San Juan

EL CAMPO DEL MORRO

Calle del Morro

Murallas de San Juan

Fort San Cristobal

Norzgaray

Plaza Colón

Calle O'Donell

C. Tamarindo

C. Capilla

C. J. Acosta

Calle San Sebastián

Calle Sol

Calle Luna

Calle San Justo

Calle Cruz

Calle San Jose

Norzagaray

Plaza San José

Del Cristo

Plaza de Armas

Calle San Francisco

Calle Fortaleza

Calle Tetuan

Parque de las Palomas

Paseo Princesa

Calle Tanca

Calle Recinto

Calle Puntilla

El Arsenal

La Puntilla

Calle Presidio

Av. Muñoz Rivera

Av. Ponce de Leon

Paseo de Covadonga

Calle San Augustín

Av. Fernandez Juncos

38

25

25

1

Calle Contreras

C. de Muelle

Calle Allen

Calle Marina

Marina

Calle Harding

Calle Gen. Pershing

Calle Braumbaugh

Murallas de San Juan

9

8

7

6

5

4

3

2

1

.1 Miles

.1 Kilometers

0

0

Murallas de San Juan

ATTRACTIONS ●
Casa Blanca **2**
Catedral de San Juan **4**
Fuerte San Cristóbal **9**
Fuerte San Felipe del Morro **1**
La Fortaleza **3**
Museo de Arte
e Historia de San Juan **7**
Museo Pablo Casals **6**

ACCOMMODATIONS ■
Gallery Inn **8**
Hotel El Convento **5**

until a hurricane blew it away in 1529. The present church was launched in 1529, although the building has undergone many architectural changes over the years. Many of its once-treasured relics have been looted over the centuries. Most of what you see today is from the 19th century, although a quartet of vaulted rooms remain from the original structure. The greatest relic is the marble tomb of Ponce de León resting near the transept. Nearby is an alleged relic of San Pío, the Roman martyr. Open Monday through Saturday 8:30 a.m. to 4:00 p.m. Masses held daily.

✔ **Museo d'Arte,** 299 Av. José de Diego, Santurce (☎ 787-977-6277): Puerto Rico's most important gallery, which opened in 2000 and was constructed at a cost of $55 million, is a state-of-the art showcase for the island nation's rich cultural heritage as reflected mainly through its painters. Housed in a former city hospital in Santurce, the museum features both a permanent collection and temporary exhibitions. Prominent local artists are the star — for example, Francisco Oller (1833–1917), who brought a touch of Cézanne or Camille Pissarro to Puerto Rico (Oller actually studied in France with both of these Impressionists). Another leading star of the permanent collection is José Campeche, a late 18th-century classical painter. The museum is like a living textbook of Puerto Rico, beginning with its early development and going on to showcase camp aspects such as the poster art created here in the mid-20th century. All the important modern island artists are also presented, including the best known, the late Angel Botello, but also such contempories as Rafael Tufiño and Arnaldo Roche Rabell. Admission $5 adults, $3 children under 12. Open Tuesday, Thursday, and Saturday 10 a.m. to 5 p.m., Wednesday 10 a.m. to 8 p.m., Sunday 11 a.m. to 6 p.m.

✔ **La Fortaleza,** Calle Recinto Oeste (☎ 787-721-7000, ext. 2211, or 787-721-7000, ext. 2211 or 2323): The oldest executive mansion in continuous use in the western hempishere is today both the office and residence of the governor of Puerto Rico. Governors come and go, but this mansion seems to endure forever, having been the seat of government for centuries. The original structure that stood here dates from the mid-16th century. Guided tours conducted on the hour in English take you through the mansion, where you get to view the Moorish gardens, the dungeon, and a chapel. Informal but "proper" attire is required. Admission is free. Open Monday through Friday 9 a.m. to 4 p.m.

✔ **Fuerte San Filipe del Morro,** Calle Norzagaray (☎ 787-729-6960): "El Morro" (its local nickname), a U.S. National Historic Site, still stands guard on the rocky promontory overlooking the entrance to San Juan's harbor. With its round tower still intact, it's been guarding the bay since its founding in 1540. Built on six levels, about 150 feet above the sea, the fort contains walls up to 15 feet thick. This is the oldest Spanish fort in the so-called New World, still an attraction with its tunnels, turrets, dungeons, ramps, and barracks. On site is a small museum tracing the fort's history, and a video is shown; tours are offered in English. You can also visit on your own. Admission is $2. Open daily from 9 a.m. to 5 p.m.

✔ **Museo de Arte y Historia de San Juan,** Calle, Norzagaray at Calle MacArthur (☎ 787-724-1875): A bustling marketplace in 1855, this handsome building is now the modern San Juan Museum of Art and History. You'll find exhibits of Puerto Rican art and audiovisual shows that present the island's history. Concerts and other cultural events take place in the huge courtyard. Admission is free. Open Monday through Saturday 9 a.m. to 4 p.m.

✔ **Museo Pablo Casals,** 101 Calle San Sebastián, Plaza de San José (☎ 787-723-9185): The famed cellist lived in Puerto Rico for the last 16 years of his life. He came here in 1956 as a protest against the dictatorship of Federico Franco in Spain. Almost at once he became a major cultural figure on the island, and contributed in part to a renaissance of music and the arts in Puerto Rico. Videotapes of major Casals Festival concerts are shown if requested. The museum displays much memorabilia of the great artist, including pictures, manuscripts, letters, and his favorite cellos. Even his beloved old sweater is exhibited. Admission is $1. Open Tuesday through Saturday 9:30 a.m. to 5:00 p.m.

✔ **Fuerte San Cristóbal,** Calle Nozagaray (☎ 787-729-6960): The other major fort on the island in addition to El Morro (see earlier in this list) is this formidable fortress from the 18th century that protected Old San Juan from land-based attacks. Begun in 1634 and reconstructed in the 1770s, it is one of the largest forts ever built in the Americas by Spain, its walls rising more than 150 feet above sea level. On 27 acres, it was linked to El Morro by a series of monumental walls and bastions riddled with cannons. You can visit on your own, although park rangers sometimes lead free tours. Admission is $2. Open daily 9 a.m. to 5 p.m.

Exploring the Rest of the Island

The only way to see Puerto Rico in any depth is to rent a car and get a good road map — and, even so, you may end up getting lost, but you can often make some fascinating discoveries that way. Many of the roads, especially those around the coastline, are kept in good shape. The north shore around San Juan is clogged at rush hours in the morning and again in the late afternoon.

Families can bank on fun and education when they visit **Parque Zoologico de Mayagüez,** Route 108 at Barrio Miradero (☎ 787-834-8110), a 45-acre tropical compound that's home to exotic animals from around the world. Admission is $6; parking $2. Open Wednesday through Sunday from 8:30 a.m. to 4:00 p.m.

Mona Island, lying 50 miles across the treacherous Mona Passage, is called the "Galapagos of the Caribbean," because it is home to several endangered or unique indigenous species. The nearest town for embarkation is Puerto Rico's "third city" of Mayagüez. The heart-shaped island is 7 miles long. Once inhabited by the Táino Indians, it was later used by pirates to stash their booty. Limestone cliffs reach a height of 200 feet on the north coast, and there are some pristine beaches where you may disturb one of the mammoth iguanas or perhaps a nesting hawksbill turtle. In the coral reefs offshore, visibility is good up to 150 feet. Camp sites are available, but otherwise Mona is uninhabited, except for that wildlife. Private boats from the west coast of Puerto Rico visit the island daily. Contact the **Department of Natural Resources** (☎ 787-723-1616 or 787-721-5495) for data about the island or to reserve a camp site if you'd like to stay overnight.

If E.T. phones home, the scientists at **Observatorio de Arecibo,** Route 625 (☎ 787-878-2612; Internet: www.naic.edu), will pick up the phone. Some of the coolest scenes of James Bond's movies, as well as the Jodie Foster film *Contact,* were filmed here. This is the world's largest radio telescope, with a 20-acre curved reflector installed over a natural karst sinkhole. Lying 41 miles to the west of San Juan, it is dubbed "the ear to heaven." At this base, scientists can monitor natural radio emissions from distant galaxies, pulsars, and quasars. If some form of extraterrestrial intelligence is trying to send us a message, the scientists here are waiting. This facility searching for life in outer space was launched on October 12, 1992, the 500th anniversary of Columbus arriving in the New World. You can take a self-guided tour through the observatory, including a look at the visitor center where you can see exhibits on the planetary systems. Admission is $4. Open Wednesday through Friday noon to 4 p.m., Saturday and Sunday 9 a.m. to 4 p.m.

Allow a half-day to tour this site — especially if you have budding astronomers in your family. This facility is part of the National Astronomy and Ionosphere Center of Cornell University.

Even if you don't like caves, there is fascination to be experienced at the 300-acre **Río Camuy Cave Park,** Route 129, Km 18.9 (☎ 787-898-3100 or 787-756-5555), set on a 250-acre site just to the southwest of Arecibo Observatory. You can visit both Arecibo and Río Camuy on the same day-trip west of San Juan. The caves contain the third-largest underground river in the world, and were known to the Taíno Indians. For years the caves lay undiscovered until their rediscovery in the 1950s. Visitors descend into the cool caverns 200 feet underground on a trolley. At the entrance to the Clara Cave of Epalme, visitors are let out for a 45-minute nature walk where they view stalagmites, stalactites, and large natural "sculptures" formed over the centuries. Tours change slightly in the off-season. Admission is $10, parking $2. Open Wednesday through Sunday 8:00 a.m. to 3:45 p.m.

Don't expect Stonehenge or any monumental ruins if you visit **Parque Ceremonial Indígena — Caguana,** Route 111, Km 12.3 (☎ 787-894-7325).

But this ceremonial site at Tibes, near Ponce, is one of the few reminders left by the early settlers of the island, the Taino Indians. In a natural botanical garden, the Indians used these ball courts (called *batey*) as many as eight centuries ago. Stone monoliths still stand outlining many of the former courts, and a few weigh up to a ton. The Taínos used the 13-acre site for both recreation and worship, and they left behind some petroglyphs to intrigue future generations. What exactly was the ball game played here? Some archaeologists have suggested that it was the mother of soccer; others view it like playing volleyball without a net. Admission is free. Open daily from 9:00 a.m. to 4:30 p.m.

The city of Ponce, second largest in Puerto Rico, makes for one of the island's most interesting stopovers, lying 75 miles southwest of San Juan. A once-decaying city, it has undergone a Renaissance; hundreds of its buildings have been restored and given a new lease on life for the 21st century. Buildings ranging in style from European neoclassical to Spanish colonial are called *Ponce Créole,* a kind of colonial architecture with both interior and exterior balconies.

Ponce's Calle Reina Isabel is a virtual textbook of the different Ponceño styles. Many of the most historic buildings are on streets radiating from the stately **Plaza Las Delicias** (Plaza of Delights). The **Cathedral of Our Lady of Guadalupe**, Calle Concordia (☎ 787-842-0134), dates from 1660 and stands on the western edge of the Plaza Las Delicias. The present building is Gothic inspired.

The major attraction of the city is **Museo de Arte de Ponce,** Av. De Las Americas 25 (☎ 787-848-0505). Donated to the people of Puerto Rico by Luís A. Ferré, a former governor, this museum has the finest collection of European and Latin American art in the Caribbean. The building itself was designed by Edward Durell Stone, who also designed the John F. Kennedy Center for the Performing Arts in Washington, D.C., and has been called the "Parthenon of the Caribbean." Its collection represents the principal schools of American and European art of the past five centuries. Among the nearly 400 works on display are exceptional pre-Raphaelite and Italian baroque paintings. Visitors will also see artworks by other European masters, as well as Puerto Rican and Latin American paintings, graphics, and sculptures. On display are some of the best works of the two "old masters" of Puerto Rico, Francisco Oller and José Campéche. The museum also contains a representative collection of the works of the old masters of Europe, including Gainsborough, Velázquez, Rubens, and van Dyck. Admission is $4 adults, $1 children under 12. Open daily 10 a.m. to 5 p.m.

The oldest cemetery in the Antilles, the **Tibes Ceremonial Center** is on Route 503 at Kilometer 2.2 outside Ponce (☎ 787-840-2255). Bordered by the Rio Portuguéz and excavated in 1875, it contains some 186 skeletons, dating from A.D. 300, as well as pre-Taíno plazas from A.D. 700. The site also includes a re-created Taíno village, seven rectangular ball courts, and two dance grounds. The arrangement of stone points on the dance grounds, in line with the solstices and equinoxes, suggests a

pre-Columbian Stonehenge. Here you'll also find a museum, an exhibi-
tion hall that presents a documentary about Tibes, a cafeteria, and a
souvenir shop. The museum is open Tuesday through Sunday from
9:00 a.m. to 4:30 p.m. Admission is $2 for adults, $1 for children. Guided
tours in English and Spanish are conducted through the grounds.

Better known as *El Faro* or "The Lighthouse," **Reserva Natural las
Cabezas de San Juan** in the northeastern corner of the island, north
of Fajardo off Route 987, is one of the most beautiful and important
areas on Puerto Rico. Here you'll find seven ecological systems and a
restored 19th-century Spanish colonial lighthouse. From the lighthouse
observation deck, majestic views extend to islands as far off as St.
Thomas in the U.S. Virgin Islands. Surrounded on three sides by the
Atlantic Ocean, the 316-acre site encompasses forestland, mangroves,
lagoons, beaches, cliffs, offshore cays, and coral reefs. A boardwalk
trail winds through the fascinating topography. Ospreys, sea turtles,
and an occasional manatee are seen from the windswept promontories
and rocky beach. Under the tutelage of Las Cabezas guides, every visitor becomes a naturalist for a few absorbing hours. You have to call
and make a reservation to tour the reserve, either at ☎ **787-722-5882**
or 787-860-2560. Tours in English are Friday through Sunday at 2 p.m.
The location is on Route 987, Km 6.8.

Venturing to Offshore Islands

They still may be virtually unknown to many visitors, but the offshore
islands of Vieques and Culebra are where Puerto Ricans go for their
own vacations. Sandy beaches and low prices are the powerful attractions of both islands. Culebra still slumbers in the early 1950s, but
Vieques is fast becoming one of the hottest tropical destinations in the
Caribbean. The unspoiled beaches and stylish inns of Vieques have created quite a buzz. Vieques, with more tourist facilities than Culebra, lies
7 miles off the eastern coast of Puerto Rico. It is visited today mainly for
its 40-odd white-sand beaches. The island had been occupied at various
times by both the French and the British before Puerto Rico acquired it
in 1854. The ruins of many sugar and pineapple plantations testify to its
once-flourishing agricultural economy. The U.S. military took control of
two-thirds of the island's 26,000 acres in 1941 and still uses the area for
military training.

The U.S. Navy named some of the beaches, such as **Green Beach,** a
beautiful, clean stretch at the island's west end. **Red Beach** and **Blue
Beach** are great jumping-off points for snorkelers. **Sun Bay** (Sombé) is
also a very beautiful white-sand beach, which offers picnic tables, a
bathhouse, tent sites, and good snorkeling offshore. Other popular
beaches are **Navia, Half Moon, Orchid,** and **Silver,** but if you continue
along the water, you may find your own nameless secluded cove with a
fine strip of sand. You may even see a wild *paso fino* horse galloping in

the surf. The visitor information center (☎ 787-741-5000) is in the fishing village of Esperanza.

A tranquil, inviting little island, **Culebra** lies in a mini-archipelago of 24 chunks of land, rocks, and cays, 18 miles east of Puerto Rico's main island and halfway to St. Thomas, U.S. Virgin Islands. It's just 7 miles long and 3 miles wide and has only 2,000 residents. The landscape is dotted with everything from scrub and cacti to poincianas, frangipanis, and coconut palms. Today vacationers and boaters can explore the island's beauty, both on land and under water. Culebra's white-sand beaches (especially Flamenco), its clear waters, and its long coral reefs invite swimmers, snorkelers, and scuba divers.

More isolated is **Playa Zoni,** a 1-mile strip of sand flanked by large boulders and scrub. Located on the island's northeastern edge, about 7 miles from Dewey (Puebla), it's one of the most beautiful beaches on the island. Snorkelers, but not scuba divers, find it particularly intriguing, despite the surf that makes underwater visibility a bit murky during rough weather. Known for its beautiful corals, unspoiled underwater vistas, and the absence of other divers, Culebra is what the Caribbean used to be before crowds of divers began exploring the sea. At least 50 dive sites, on all sides of the island, lure you into a water wonderland.

Part IX
The U.S. Virgin Islands

The 5th Wave   By Rich Tennant

"Don't worry, they may be called St. Croix, St. Thomas, and St. John but you're not required to act like a saint while you're there."

In this part . . .

*W*hether your destination is St. Thomas, St. Croix, or St. John, and whether your taste runs toward chain resorts or private villas, we list the best accommodations choices available. We also show you how to travel to and among the islands by air and by sea.

Local seafood takes center stage in USVI restaurants, and we guide you toward the best dining options. Finally, we offer suggestions for ways to while away your day in paradise, from snorkeling to shopping.

Chapter 32

The Lowdown on the U.S. Virgin Islands' Hotel Scene

By Darwin Porter and Danforth Prince

● ●

In This Chapter

▶ Sizing up hotel locations

▶ Focusing on top hotel picks

● ●

The U.S. Virgin Islands, especially the most-visited St. Thomas, offer one of the densest concentrations of hotels in the Caribbean. Island promoters like to boast that there's a bed waiting for you whatever your requirements — Grand Palazzo living or B&B. Supplementing the regular hotels and inns is a vast array of timeshares, condos, and private villas. The familiar chains such as Ritz-Carlton, Marriott, and Westin show their shining faces in the USVIs, but there are also simpler West Indian inns for the frugal traveler. The good news for the eco-sensitive traveler is that little St. John offers more award-winning campgrounds than anywhere else in the Caribbean. It's also a safe destination. Except for the British Virgin Islands, we consider safety a problem while camping in much of the Caribbean, especially in Jamaica. St. John's campgrounds should be reserved as early as possible in winter.

Figuring Out Where You Want to Stay

The widest choice of accommodations are east and north of Charlotte Amalie, the capital of St. Thomas. To the east, you'll find the mega-resorts, including two hotels run by Marriott. Most of these large-scale resorts open directly onto the beach.

If a having direct access to a beach is not your top priority, and if money is tight, consider staying at one of the smaller inns in Charlotte Amalie itself. You're only about a ten-minute ride from a good beach at any of these properties, and you can walk to shops, nightlife, and the little dives of adjoining Frenchtown.

On neighboring St. John, there are few large hotels, the biggest being the Westin Resort (see the listing later in this chapter). If you're not renting a car, staying at Cruz Bay, where the ferryboat docks, is most convenient. That way, you can walk to shops and restaurants. Otherwise, most of the camp sites and villas lie above Cinnamon Bay.

On the island of St. Croix, the largest cluster of hotels and inns is found near the waterfront in the historic capital of Christiansted, where you can take a ferry across the water to a good beach. Most of the finest accommodations lie outside Christiansted, in some cases in the "second city" of St. Croix, Frederiksted. Some of the best and largest hotels are scattered along the coastline opening directly onto golden sandy beaches.

Not all our picks are on a beach, but all have access to some of the best beaches in the Caribbean.

The USVIs' Best Accommodations

The rack rates listed in this section are in U.S. dollars and are for a standard double room during high season (mid-December through mid-April), unless otherwise noted. Lower rates are available during the off season and shoulder season; see Chapter 2 for information on travel seasons.

Blackbeard's Castle
$$ Charlotte Amalie, St. Thomas

Not to be confused with Bluebeard's Castle (see the next listing), Blackbeard's is far more intimate and private, more like a restored home, whereas Bluebeard's is a full-service resort. Because of its charm and friendliness, we infinitely prefer our beards "black." On a hillside over-looking the harbor of Charlotte Amalie, the so-called castle grew up on the site of a 1679 tower erected by the Danish governor of the island. Blackbeard himself once may have used the site as a lookout post for unfriendly ships. We rank the gay-friendly Blackbeard's as the most atmospheric of all the small inns on St. Thomas, offering a total of 11 handsomely furnished bedrooms. The least expensive are the garden units, which are small and have no balconies. The larger rooms, actually junior suites, are more spacious and open onto balconies; many contain four-poster beds.

St. Thomas Accommodations

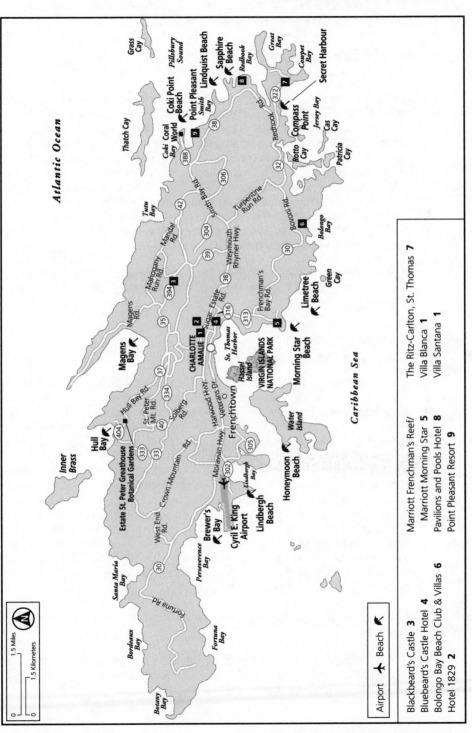

Airport ✈ Beach ⬋

Blackbeard's Castle **3**
Bluebeard's Castle Hotel **4**
Bolongo Bay Beach Club & Villas **6**
Hotel 1829 **2**

Marriott Frenchman's Reef/
Marriott Morning Star **5**
Pavilions and Pools Hotel **8**
Point Pleasant Resort **9**

The Ritz-Carlton, St. Thomas **7**
Villa Blanca **1**
Villa Santana **1**

Blackbeard's Hill, P.O. Box 6227, Charlotte Amalie, St. Thomas, USVI 00801. ☎ *800-344-5771 or 340-776-1234. Fax: 340-776-1234. Internet:* www.blackbeards castle.com. *Rack rates: $115–$220. AE, MC, V.*

Bluebeard's Castle Hotel

$$$ **Charlotte Amalie, St. Thomas**

The days when this was the island's number-one hotel have long since passed, but the 170-unit resort still remains the best choice for those who want to be close to Charlotte Amalie and not in one of the East End resorts. Bluebeard's is not on a beach but operates a free hotel shuttle to Magens Bay. If you feel you were "born to shop," this is also your best bet because you can walk to the leading shops of St. Thomas or at least take a taxi if the hill climb is too steep. The view is panoramic here, and bedrooms are priced according to their vista. All units come with terraces. Standards are the less attractive rooms and without a view. Deluxe gives you a panoramic sweep of the harbor. A small pool, two tennis courts, and three restaurants add to its allure.

Bluebeard's Hill (P.O. Box 7480), St. Thomas, USVI 00801. ☎ *800-524-6599 or 340-774-1600. Fax: 340-774-5134. Rack rates: $169–$275 double. Additional person $25 extra. AE, DISC, MC, V.*

Bolongo Bay Beach Club and Villas

$$$$ **South Shore, St. Thomas**

A 15-minute drive from Charlotte Amalie, this beachfront resort is casual and fun, because it's heavy on activities. Its white-sand beach, set against a backdrop of palm trees, is one of its biggest assets. Over the years, this resort, operated by the Doumeng family, has offered decent value and the widest array of choices for lodging on the island. The majority of rooms are in three-floor wings opening onto the beach and graced with a small terrace or upper balcony. Efficiency kitchens come with many of the accommodations. For families, some two-bedroom units are an option. In all, there is a rather confusing array of both living arrangements and package deals, so you'll need to talk directly to the hotel or with a good travel agent to see what is best for your vacation needs. If you're a very frugal traveler, the cheapest deal is a room at the Bayside Inn across the street. Bolongo's water-sports program ranks among the island's best. There are two restaurants and bars, three pools, two tennis courts, a large health club, and a dive shop.

Kids age 12 and under stay free year-round and eat free during the summer.

7150 Bolongo, St. Thomas, USVI 00802. ☎ *800-524-4746 or 340-775-1800. Fax: 340-775-3208. Internet:* www.bolongo.com. *Rack rates: $245 double with no meals, $450 all-inclusive double. AE, MC, V.*

St. Croix Accommodations

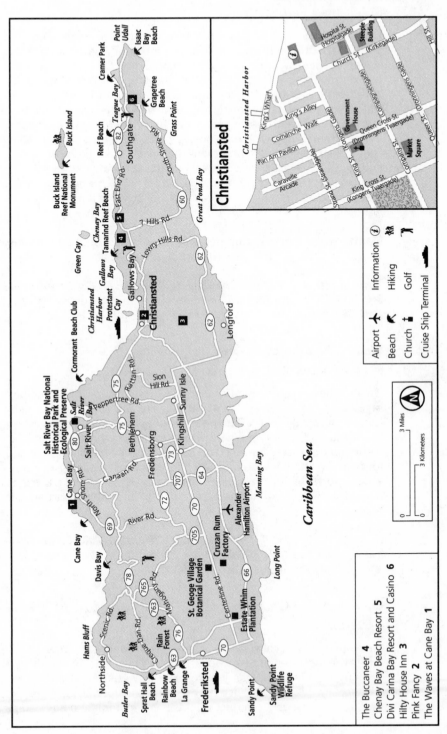

Christiansted

Christiansted Harbor

Hospital St. (Hospitalgade)

Steeple Building

Church St. (Kirkegade)

Hill St.

King's Wharf

King's Alley

Comanche Walk

Government House

Queen Cross St. (Dronningens Tvaergade)

Pan Am Pavilion

Caravelle Arcade

King Cross St. (Kongens Tvaergade)

Queen St. (Dronningens Gade)

Company St.

King St. (Kongens Gade)

Strand St. (Strandgade)

Market Square

Point Udall

Isaac Bay Beach

Cramer Park

Grapetree Beach

Teague Bay **6**

Grass Point

Buck Island

Buck Island

Buck Island Reef National Monument

Reef Beach

Southgate **82**

South Shore Rd.

East End Rd.

Great Pond Bay

60

Chenay Bay Tamarind Reef Beach **5**

7 Hills Rd.

Green Cay

Lowry Hills Rd. **4**

62

Gallows Bay

Christiansted Harbor

Protestant Cay

Christiansted **2**

Longford

3

62

Cormorant Beach Club

Sion Hill Rd.

Rattan Rd.

Sunny Isle

Salt River Bay National Historical Park and Ecological Preserve

Salt River Bay

Peppertree Rd. **75**

Kingshill

Manning Bay

Cane Bay **80** **75**

Salt River

Bethlehem

Fredensborg

73

707

64

Canaan Rd.

North Shore Rd.

1

69

72

70

Alexander Hamilton Airport

Cane Bay

Davis Bay

River Rd.

705

Cruzan Rum Factory

Manning Bay

Long Point

Caribbean Sea

78

St. George Village Botanical Garden

Centerline Rd.

66

Northside

Scenic Rd.

765

763

Mahogany Rd.

Creque Dam Rd.

76

Rain Forest

63

Estate Whim Plantation

Hams Bluff

Butler Bay

Sprat Hall Beach

Rainbow Beach

La Grange

Frederiksted

70

Sandy Point

Sandy Point Wildlife Refuge

Airport ✈

Information ⓘ

Beach 🏊

Hiking 🚶

Church ✝

Golf ⛳

Cruise Ship Terminal

N

3 Miles

3 Kilometers

0

The Buccaneer **4**
Chenay Bay Beach Resort **5**
Divi Carina Bay Resort and Casino **6**
Hilty House Inn **3**
Pink Fancy **2**
The Waves at Cane Bay **1**

The Buccaneer

$$$$$ **East End, St. Croix**

Lying 2 miles east of Christiansted, this family-owned resort is the island's traditional luxury choice, with a trio of white-sand beaches and featuring the best sports program in St. Croix. On the 340-acre site of a cattle ranch and a sugar plantation, the property has roots back in the 17th century. Both honeymooners and upmarket families find it ideal. After taking a palm tree–lined private road to a pink hilltop colonial building, you're shown to a spacious bedroom with a Mediterranean and West Indian motif, along with four-poster beds, tile floors, and marble bathrooms. Families book the cottages, honeymooners preferring one of the suites with private terraces overlooking the water. Buccaneer's eight tennis courts are the best on the island, as is its children's program. The resort is also the choice for golfers because of its first-rate, 18-hole course.

Many couples marry at this elegant property. The Doubloon rooms, with whirlpool tubs, are the best and are right on the water.

Route 82 (P.O. Box 25200), Gallows Bay, St. Croix, USVI 00824. ☎ *800-255-3881 or 340-773-2100. Fax: 340-778-8215. Internet:* www.thebuccaneer.com. *Rack rates: $280–$660 double. Rates include full breakfast. AE, DISC, DC, MC, V.*

Chenay Bay Beach Resort

$$$–$$$$ **East End, St. Croix**

On a wildlife preserve 4 miles east of Christiansted, this is the best cottage colony in St. Croix. Fifty cottages are scattered over the site of a former sugar plantation. The beachfront is one of the best on the island for swimming, snorkeling, and windsurfing. Chenay Bay is our favorite resort for families. Not only are the spacious accommodations suitable for families, there is also a good children's program and free tennis and water sports, including snorkeling and kayaking. You take a gravel path to the sea where you'll find a big pool, picnic tables, and an informal restaurant.

Route 82 (P.O. Box 24600), Christiansted, St. Croix, USVI 00824. ☎ *800-548-4457 or 340-773-2918. Fax: 340-773-6665. Internet:* www.chenaybay.com. *Rack rates: $215–$330 cottage for one or two. AE, MC, V.*

Cinnamon Bay Campgrounds

$–$$ **St. John**

Enveloped by tropical vegetation and opening onto Cinnamon Bay Beach, this is the most complete camp site in the Caribbean. In winter, getting a booking is difficult unless you reserve way ahead of time. The campgrounds are popular because they're good and contain far more facilities than similar properties in the Caribbean except for Maho Bay Camps (see

St. John Accommodations

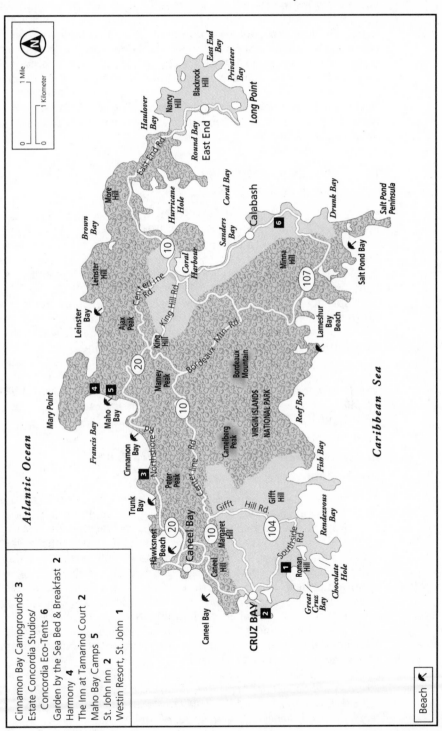

Cinnamon Bay Campgrounds **3**
Estate Concordia Studios/
Concordia Eco-Tents **6**
Garden by the Sea Bed & Breakfast **2**
Harmony **4**
The Inn at Tamarind Court **2**
Maho Bay Camps **5**
St. John Inn **2**
Westin Resort, St. John **1**

listing), which is equally fine. The cheapest rental is a bare site; for that, you must bring in your own tent and equipment. A more comfortable way to stay here is to rent a tent (10 x 14 feet with a floor), including such extras as linen and cooking equipment. The most luxurious offering is one of the cottages, consisting of a 15-x-15-foot room with two concrete walls and two screen walls. Cottages come with kitchen facilities and four twin beds. In an outbuilding are the toilets and the cool-water showers.

Route 20 (P.O. Box 720), Cruz Bay, St. John, USVI 00831. ☎ *800-539-9998 or 340-776-6330. Fax: 340-776-6458. Rack rates: $130 beachfront; $110 cottage; $80 tent; $25 bare site. AE, MC, V.*

Divi Carina Bay Resort and Casino
$$$$ Christiansted, St. Croix

Here's where the high-rollers stay. Over many objections, this resort introduced casino gambling to the USVIs. As a resort, it's a fine choice even if you don't go to the tables at night. The hotel opens onto 1,000 feet of white-sand beach and, to make it more alluring, Divi operates "The Spa," the finest such facility on the island. If you don't want to go to the beach, you can take advantage of one of the five pools on site. The most desirable accommodations are the ocean-fronting rooms and villa suites. All the rooms here, however, are good sized and completely modern, with excellent bathrooms and such grace notes as balconies. You're faced with three restaurants for your dining options, and such facilities as a water-sports center and a children's program.

25 Estate Turner Hole, St. Croix, USVI 00820. ☎ *888-823-9352 or 340-773-9700. Fax: 340-773-6802. Internet:* www.divicarina.com. *Rack rates: $225–$250 double. AE, DC, MC, V.*

Estate Concordia Studios/Concordia Eco-Tents
$$ St. John

A developer, Stanley Selengut, is known as the most eco-sensitive man on St. John. On some 50 sea-bordering acres at Salt Pond Bay, a 45-minute drive from St. John's "capital," Cruz Bay, he has created a series of 20 studios and 11 tent-cottages, which provide an alternative choice for those who find Maho Bay and Cinnamon Bay camps fully booked in winter. The cottages are sold solar– and wind-powered, each opening onto a panoramic view. Cooled by trade winds, the cottages can sleep two guests in comfort, and each unit is provided with a kitchen. Nine studios are encased in six cottages, each connected with boardwalks. The eco-tents are also a comfortable way to camp, because each one comes with a kitchen and a small private shower along with a composting toilet. Tents can hold up to six campers.

20–27 Estate Concordia, Coral Bay, St. John, USVI 00830. ☎ *800-392-9004 or 212-861-6210. Fax: 212-861-6210. Rack rates: $135–$190 studio for two; $110 eco-tent for two. Additional person $25 extra. AE, MC, V.*

Garden by the Sea Bed and Breakfast
$$$ Cruz Bay, St. John

A ten-minute walk south from the port at Cruz Bay where the ferry docks, this is the best B&B on the island. It is ideally located as well, lying within easy reach of some of the best beaches between Turner and Frank bays and only a minute's walk along a little trail by Audubon Pond, which will take you to the white sands of Frank Bay Beach. The house with three bedrooms to rent was built in the 1970s with West Indian gingerbread trim and high ceilings. Bedrooms are a bit exotic, decorated with objects from all over the globe, such as fountains from Tokyo or elephant bamboo canopied beds from Thailand. Served on the terrace, the breakfast equals that of the finest B&Bs in America.

P.O. Box 1469, Cruz Bay, St. John, USVI 00831. ☎ *340-779-4731. Internet:* www. gardenbythesea.com. *Rack rates: $180–$200 double. No credit cards.*

Harmony
$$$ Maho Bay, St. John

Stanley Selengut, St. John's most eco-sensitive developer (see Concordia listing), does it again at this hillside site above Maho Bay Camps. A dozen first-rate studios were created in six two-story houses, with some of the island's most panoramic views. The entire resort operates on solar and wind power. Not only that, even the building materials were created from recycled discards — old tires, scrap lumber, yesterday's newspaper. Glass bottles and plastic were reconstituted to make inviting, livable materials, perhaps a sign of the future. The recycling was carried out beautifully. To see these materials at Harmony, you'd never know they had a previous incarnation. A computer monitors energy consumption in each studio, which comes with a bathroom with shower, a kitchenette, and an outdoor terrace. Guests are allowed to use the water-sports facilities at Maho Bay Camps (see lisiting). The closest beach is near Maho Bay Camps as well.

Maho Bay (P.O. Box 310), Cruz Bay, St. John, USVI 00831. ☎ *800-392-9004, 340-776-6240, or 212-472-9453. Fax: 340-776-6504. Internet:* www.maho.org. *Rack rates: $185–$210 studio for two. Additional person $25 extra. Seven-night minimum stay in winter. MC, DISC, V.*

Hilty House Inn
$$ Christiansted, St. Croix

In the 1700s, sugarcane was brought to this site and turned into rum. Today the grounds contain one of the best B&Bs in St. Croix. On the east side of St. Croix in a hilly area, the house lies a 15-minute ride from the airport. If you want to be on the water, look elsewhere, because the nearest beach is a ten-minute drive away. The house itself is two centuries old, though modernized and perfectly restored. The plantation era is evoked by its high-ceiling living room and a large fireplace. The most evocative unit is the master bedroom with its four-poster bed and a sunken shower. Accommodations are handsomely furnished, each coming with a bathroom with shower. On the grounds are two self-catering cottages that are ideal for families. On very hot days when the trade winds are asleep, you'll miss air-conditioning.

Queste Verde Road (P.O. Box 26077), Gallows Bay, St. Croix, USVI 00824. ☎ and fax 340-773-2594. E-mail: hiltyhouse@worldnet.att.net. *Rack rates: $120 double-occupancy house; $145 cottage. Three-night minimum stay in cottages. Extra person $25. No children under 12. Rates include continental breakfast. No credit cards.*

Hotel 1829
$$ Charlotte Amalie, St. Thomas

Having far more atmosphere and charm than Bluebeard's Castle, this 15-room inn is yet another option for those who want to stay close to Charlotte Amalie and its bevy of shops. You're not at a beach, the hotel pool is much too small, and it's a steep climb from town back to the hotel, but those are minor drawbacks for those seeking an old-fashioned inn. Registered as a National Historic Site, the hotel was a former home, said to have been built by a French sea captain for his new bride. You get what you pay for here. If you'll settle for a "cozy" bedroom (that means small) and one that doesn't get much sunlight, you can live like a frugal traveler. Costing more, the accommodations in the main house are spacious and often filled with antiques such as four-posters evoking the colonial era. Try to get a room with a balcony overlooking the harbor, one of the grandest panoramas in the West Indies. Be warned: You'll climb a lot of steps here to reach the various levels (there is no elevator). Magens Bay Beach lies a 15-minute drive or taxi ride away.

This is not a good pick if you have children or are physically challenged in any way.

Kongens Gade (P.O. Box 1567), St. Thomas, USVI 00804. ☎ 800-524-2002 or 340-776-1829. Fax: 340-776-4313. Internet: www.hotel1829.com. *Rack rates: $100–$180 double. Rates include continental breakfast. AE, DISC, MC, V.*

The Inn at Tamarind Court
$$ Cruz Bay, St. John

If you're carrying light luggage, you can walk to this inn right from the ferryboat dock. Long a fan of the budget traveler, it is a 20-room West Indian hostelry and enjoys a repeat clientele who know they get good value here. The bedrooms are small but reasonably comfortable, and they are well maintained, 14 of them coming with a tiny bathroom with shower. Four units don't have a bathroom, although the hall plumbing is adequate. There are no phones in the rooms. The bar in the patio is an island favorite and a good place to meet locals, and there is also a reasonably priced restaurant on site. From the hotel, you can walk to shuttles that take you to the beaches.

P.O. Box 350, South Shore Road, Cruz Bay, St. John, USVI 00831. ☎ *800-221-1637 or 340-776-6378. Fax: 340-776-6722. Internet:* www.tamarindcourt.com. *Rack rates: $108–$138 double. Rates include a continental breakfast. AE, DISC, MC, V.*

Maho Bay Camps
$$ St. John

Surrounded by the Virgin Islands National Park, this is the most luxurious camping site in the Caribbean, slightly better than the also highly rated Cinnamon Bay Campground. It is part of the string of eco-sensitive resorts in St. John, including the Harmony. From its site, an 8-mile drive northeast of Maho Bay, it lies above a good sandy beach, which you can walk to. At the beach, kayaking, sailing, and windsurfing can be arranged, and the waters have good visibility and quite a bit of marine life, attracting the snorkeler in you. The tents are linked by steps, walkways, and ramps. Covered with screens and canvas, the tent-cottages can sleep as many as four campers, who quickly learn to use the electric lamps and propane stoves. Linen, an ice chest, and cooking and eating utensils come with the tent.

Maho Bay (P.O. Box 310), Cruz Bay, St. John, USVI 00831. ☎ *800-392-9004, 340-776-6226, or 212-861-6210. Fax: 340-776-6504. Internet:* www.maho.org. *Rack rates: $108–$123 double. AE, MC, DISC, V.*

Marriott Frenchman's Reef/Marriott Morning Star
$$$$$ South Shore, St. Thomas

Three miles east of Charlotte Amalie, two of the grandest resorts in St. Thomas are really a pair of twins. Of the two, we find Morning Star more luxurious, tranquil, and intimate. A glass-enclosed elevator takes guests down to a white-sand beach. On a bluff overlooking both the harbor and the sea, Frenchman's Reef offers a total of 408 units — it's been called a "human zoo" here in winter — and Morning Star boasts only 96 units housed in five-cottage buildings containing between 16 and 24 units. The Frenchman offers the most facilities — five restaurants and nine bars — but guests at Morning Star are free to walk next door and use them, along with their tennis courts, pools, and the finest and most state-of-the-art spa of any hotel on the island. There's also a children's program, and the twins boast the best hotel entertainment on the island.

Estate Bakkeroe, Flamboyant Point (P.O. Box 7100), St. Thomas, USVI 00801. ☎ *800-524-2000 or 340-776-8500. Fax: 340-715-6191. Internet:* www.marriott.vi. *Rack rates: $339–$529 double. Wedding packages available. AE, DISC, DC, MC, V.*

Pavilions and Pools Hotel

$$$$ Estate Smith Bay, St. Thomas

Ideal for a honeymoon, this 25-room resort, 7 miles east of Charlotte Amalie, is a string of tastefully rebuilt and furnished condominium units. It is near Sapphire Bay, which boasts one of the island's best beaches and water-sports concessions, although the well-known hotel that stands there is in decline and in need of renovation. At P&P, you're given your own villa, with floor-to-ceiling glass doors opening directly onto your own private swimming pool. After checking in, you don't have to see another soul until you leave. The fence and gate are high, and your space opens onto greenery. Around your own pool is an encircling deck. Inside, a high room divider screens a kitchen, and each bedroom offers ample closet space behind louvered doors. The little pavilion has a garden shower where you can bathe Adam and Eve–style surrounded by greenery, while being screened from Peeping Toms. A small bar and barbecue area sit against a wall on the reception terrace, where the hotel hosts rum parties and cookouts. Informal, simple meals are served nightly, and occasionally a musician or singer entertains. Free snorkeling gear is offered. Honeymoon packages are available.

6400 Estate Smith Bay, St. Thomas, USVI 00802. ☎ *800-524-2001 or 340-775-6110. Fax: 340-775-6110. Internet:* www.pavilionsandpools.com. *Rack rates: $250–$275 double. AE, DISC, MC, V. Rates include continental breakfast in winter only.*

Pink Fancy

$ Christiansted, St. Croix

Those seeking an evocative West Indian inn, as opposed to a resort, will take a "fancy" to this pink complex. Its core is a historic 1780 Danish-style town house from the colonial era. But it wasn't until the 1950s that it gained a lot of publicity as a hangout for writers and artists, attracting playwright and actor Nöel Coward among other celebrities. The famous and fabled have long checked out, but the 12-unit complex is as good as ever. It's the most atmospheric little hotel in town, filled with antiques, comfortable furnishings, and tropical motifs such as rattan. In the best and larger rooms are canopied or iron beds in the plantation style. For the beach, guests have to take a three-minute launch to the Sands on the Cay, an islet that lies in the harbor of Christiansted.

27 Prince St., Christiansted, St. Croix, USVI 00820. ☎ *800-524-2045 or 340-773-8460. Fax: 340-773-6448. Internet:* www.pinkfancy.com. *Rack rates: $95–$150. Extra person $20. Rates include continental breakfast. AE, DC, DISC, MC, V.*

Point Pleasant Resort

$$$$ St. Thomas

This private, unique resort sits on Water Bay, on the northeastern tip of St. Thomas, just a five-minute walk from Stouffer's Beach but far-removed from the bustle of Charlotte Amalie. The 95 villa-style suites are rented when their owners are not in residence. From your living room gallery, you look out on the islands of Tortola, St. John, and Jost Van Dyke. The complex sits on a 15-acre nature preserve lush with flowering shrubbery, century plants, and frangipani trees. Waiting for your discovery are secluded nature trails, old rock formations, and lookout points. Some of the villas have kitchens, and the furnishings are light and airy, mostly with rattan and floral fabrics. The restaurant, Agavé Terrace, one of the finest on the island, offers three meals a day. The cuisine, featuring seafood, is a blend of nouvelle American dishes with Caribbean specialties. Locals entertain several nights a week There's also a dining and shopping shuttle daily. Three freshwater swimming pools, a lit tennis court, snorkeling equipment, and Sunfish sailboats round out the offerings.

6600 Estate Smith Bay #4, St. Thomas, USVI 00802. ☎ *800-777-1700 or 340-775-7200. Fax: 340-776-5694. Internet:* www.pointpleasantresort.com. *Rack rates: $255–$275 double; $525 two-bedroom villa. Packages available for families, honeymoons, and anniversaries. AE, DC, DISC, MC, V.*

The Ritz-Carlton, St. Thomas
$$$$$ Charlotte Amalie, St. Thomas

If money is no object and you want to live in the grandest style the USVIs have to offer, make it the 152-room Ritz-Carlton. Opening onto white-sand beaches, this is a luxury hotel set on a 15-acre oceanfront estate at the eastern end of St. Thomas, 4½ miles southeast of Charlotte Amalie. In landscaped gardens, it evokes a grand Italian palazzo, with its array of fountains, courtyards, and columns. At the heart of the resort is a 125-foot lagoon (actually a pool). You'll need to check in to a European hotel to find appointments like these handcarved furnishings, elegant linens, and tasteful fabrics along with spacious marble-clad bathrooms. Those staying here and spending the least money opt for a room on the ground floor with a tiny peek of an ocean view. The magnificent and spacious oceanview rooms open onto views of St. Thomas's neighboring island of St. John.

6900 Great Bay Estate, St. Thomas, USVI 00802. ☎ *800-241-3333 or 340-775-3333. Fax: 340-775-4444. Internet:* www.ritzcarlton.com. *Rack rates: $545–$695 double. Honeymoon packages available. AE, DISC, DC, MC, V.*

St. John Inn
$$ Cruz Bay, St. John

For years this was a closely guarded address among frugal travelers to St. John. This 13-room inn overlooking Enighed Pond was called Cruz Inn. Now rechristened as St. John Inn and much rejuvenated, it is better than ever, even though its rates have gone up. There's more flair here now, and in some ways it evokes one of the small inns found in Northern California. Some bedrooms are tiny, but others are of generous size. An occasional antique or a wrought-iron bed adds a decorative touch. For the highest rate, you get a junior suite with a kitchenette and a sitting area.

P.O. Box 37, Cruz Bay, St. John, USVI 00831. ☎ *800-666-7688, or 340-693-8688. Fax: 340-693-9900. Internet:* www.stjohninn.com. *Rack rates: $120–$195 double. AE, DISC, MC, V.*

Villa Blanca
$$ Charlotte Amalie, St. Thomas

Inn hunters (as opposed to resort hoppers) often seek out this cozy, 14-room charmer lying immediately to the east of St. Thomas's capital, Charlotte Amalie. It occupies a hilltop site on 3 landscaped acres with a panoramic view of one of the most scenic harbors in the Caribbean, most often filled with cruise ships. Guests are housed in two rooms in the main core of the house (these larger units are preferred) or in one of the rooms in the annex opening onto the garden. Units range from small to midsize and come with a small kitchenette and a balcony or patio. There's a fresh-water pool on site, but the nearest beach is Morning Star Bay, a distance of 4 miles by car or taxi.

Raphune Hill, Route 38, Charlotte Amalie, St. Thomas, USVI 00801. ☎ *800-231-0034 or 340-776-0749. Fax: 340-779-2661. Internet:* www.st-thomas.com/villa blanca. *Rack rates: $115–$145. Rates include continental breakfast. AE, DC, MC, V.*

Villa Santana
$$ Charlotte Amalie, St. Thomas

More luxurious than its major competitor, Villa Blanca (see the previous listing), this is an island villa that dates from the 1850s when it was constructed by a Mexican general. Beautifully restored, it lies a 5-minute walk from Charlotte Amalie but a 15-minute drive from the nearest good beach at Magens Bay. Long an island favorite for those clients who prefer inns, the property opens onto one of the grand vistas of the ship-clogged harbor. Guest rooms are installed in a wide range of places from the former library of the general to what was once a wine cellar. A bedroom has even been fitted into a lookout tower, La Torre, which was the old pump house. Accommodations are handsomely and comfortably furnished with kitchenettes. Much of the decor, in honor of the founder of the place, is Mexican inspired, including the clay tiles. On-site is a pool.

Denmark Hill, Charlotte Amalie, St. Thomas, USVI 00802. ☎ *and fax 340-776-1311. Internet:* www.st-thomas.com/villasantana/. *Rack rates: $125–$195. AE, MC, V.*

The Waves at Cane Bay
$$–$$$ East End, St. Croix

One of the best-run condo properties — rented to visitors when the owners aren't in residence — is between Christiansted and Frederiksted on the ocean at Cane Bay Beach. The beach itself is rock strewn and at high tide seems to drop out of sight, although there's good scuba diving and snorkeling here with a dive shop on the grounds. The resort lies a 20-minute drive west of Christiansted and a 5-minute drive east of the golf course at the Sunterra Resort. Mostly the resort attracts divers. The rooms, in two-story buildings with verandas overlooking the water, are spacious and come with kitchens, tile floors, and neat little bathrooms with showers. Families often check in here preparing light meals and sometimes hardly leaving the premises during their vacation. You'll need a car if you stay at this remote north-shore location.

Route 80 (P.O. Box 1749), Kingsbill, St. Croix, USVI 00851. ☎ *800-545-0603 or 340-778-1805. Fax: 340-778-4945. Internet:* www.canebaystcroix.com. *Rack rates: $140–$195 double. AE, MC, V.*

Westin Resort, St. John
$$$$$ Great Cruz Bay, St. John

This posh retreat is set on 34 oceanfront acres in the southwest of St. John. The lushly planted property lies a 10-minute drive south of Cruz Bay. St. John is noted for its small inns and villas; this sprawling mass of a mega-resort is anything but. It's just what many visitors like: a flashy, architecturally appealing property with the largest array of facilities on St. John, including four restaurants, three bars, a fitness center, a dive shop, and six tennis courts. It's also a family favorite because of its spacious accommodations and its children's programs. The pool, in fact, is the largest in the Virgin Islands, and when you tire of it there's always that 1,200-foot white-sand beach.

Route 104 (P.O. Box 8310), Great Cruz Bay, St. John, USVI 00831. ☎ *800-808-5020 or 340-693-8000. Fax: 340-693-4500. Internet:* www.westinresortstjohn.com. *Rack rates: $379–$559. AE, DISC, DC, MC, V.*

Chapter 33

Settling into the U.S. Virgin Islands

By Darwin Porter and Danforth Prince

. . . .

In This Chapter

▶ Knowing what to expect when you arrive

▶ Getting around the islands

▶ Discovering the USVIs from A to Z

. . . .

*E*xcept for San Juan, it is easier by air or sea from the U.S. mainland to reach Charlotte Amalie, capital of St. Thomas, than any other destination in the Caribbean. From St. Thomas, you can make easy connections by air to St. Croix or by ferryboat to St. John.

All the U.S. Virgins, especially St. Thomas, are major stopovers for cruise ships as well. St. Thomas can also serve as your gateway to the British Virgin Islands (see Part V), because the BVIs aren't serviced by direct flights from the U.S. mainland.

Arriving in St. Thomas

You land on narrow St. Thomas (12 miles long and 3 miles wide) at its western edge, right outside the capital of Charlotte Amalie. **Cyril E. King Airport** (☎ 340-774-5100) is modest but handles a lot of traffic, including continuing flights to St. Croix and as well as the British Virgin Islands.

If you live in such East Coast cities as Miami or New York, you can fly out in the morning and within three to four hours be resting on the beach in St. Thomas. You're speeded on your way because you don't have to go through long lines at U.S. Customs. You walk right into the airport and head for ground transportation.

Before leaving the airport, pick up a free copy of *What to Do: St. Thomas & St. John.* This helpful little magazine is kept up to date with news on island happenings. Not only that, but it contains several coupons for discounts to use later for restaurants, tours, sightseeing, and whatever.

Getting from the Airport to Your Hotel

Because most visitors to the USVIs arrive on St. Thomas, this section guides you either directly to your hotel or to means for making your way to your next destination.

If you're staying on **St. Thomas:**

✔ **By taxi:** Unlike Jamaica, most resorts on St. Thomas will not have a hotel van waiting to take you for free to your hotel. Regulated by the Virgin Island Taxi Commission, taxi vans meet all incoming flights. A ride into the capital, Charlotte Amalie, takes 20 minutes unless you run into morning or late-afternoon rush-hour traffic. The commission sets fees: The typical fare for two or more sharing a taxi is $10 to Bluebeard's Castle or $12 to Marriott Frenchman's Reef. You're charged $1 extra for each piece of luggage. Most of the resorts are in the island's East End, which you can reach in 30 minutes, unless there's heavy traffic (then 45 or more minutes).

✔ **By car:** The major car-rental firms from the U.S. are ready and waiting for you at the airport. Giving them serious competition are a number of island-based, smaller car-rental outfitters where you can sometimes make a good deal. These independents on St. Thomas are more reliable than any of the similar firms throughout the Caribbean. Even before you go, you can often make a good deal with one of the four national "biggies," especially in the off-season. A midsize vehicle costs about $350 per week. Nearly all cars are rented with air-conditioning and automatic transmission. In summer, many hotel packages include a rental car, at least for a day or two, and many private villas also include the price of your auto.

If you're uncertain of your home car-insurance policy and feel you need extra collision damage insurance, the daily costs range from $15 to $20 in most cases. Check local policies carefully. Even with this extra insurance you could still get hit with a huge deductible. This policy varies from rental company to rental company — nothing at Budget, $250 at Avis, and the full value of the car at Hertz.

Even though part of the U.S. territories, driving is still on the left, dating from the days of the Danish occupation. In town, the speed limit is 20 mph, rising to only 35 mph out on the island. When you see local roads, you wouldn't want to speed anyway. Nighttime driving is hazardous because of poorly lit, narrow, curvy roads — and that left-handed driving mentioned.

If you're staying on **St. Croix:**

✔ **By air:** It's now easier than ever before to travel between St. Thomas and St. Croix. **American Eagle** (☎ **800-433-7300** in the U.S.) has three flights a day, costing $90 to $120 one-way. In addition,

> **Seaborne Seaplane** (☎ 340/773-6442) offers 10 or 11 round-trip flights daily, going for $75 to $150 one-way. Flight time is 30 minutes.

✔ **By ferry:** A ferry service between Charlotte Amalie in St. Thomas and Puerto Rico, with a stop in St. John, is available about once every two weeks (sometimes more often in high season). The trip takes about two hours, costing $60 one-way or $100 round-trip, including ground transportation to the San Juan airport or Condado. Children pay $60 round-trip. For more information, call ☎ 340-776-6282.

If you're staying on **St. John:**

✔ **By ferry:** The easiest and most common way to get to St. John is by ferry (☎ 340-776-6282), which leaves from the Red Hook landing pier on St. Thomas's eastern tip; the trip takes about 20 minutes each way. Beginning at 6:30 a.m., boats depart more or less every hour. The last ferry back to Red Hook departs from St. John's Cruz Bay at 11 p.m. The service is frequent and efficient enough that even cruise-ship passengers temporarily anchored in Charlotte Amalie can visit St. John for a quickie island tour. The one-way fare is $3 for adults, $1 for children age 12 and under. Schedules can change without notice, so call in advance.

To reach the ferry, take the Vitran bus from a point near Market Square (in Charlotte Amalie) directly to Red Hook. The cost is $1 per person each way. In addition, privately owned taxis will negotiate a price to carry you from virtually anywhere to the docks at Red Hook.

If you've just landed on St. Thomas and want to go straight to the ferry dock, your best bet is to take a cab from the airport (Vitran buses run from Charlotte Amalie but don't serve the airport area). After disembarking from the ferry on St. John, you'll have to get another cab to your hotel. Depending on the traffic, the cab ride on St. Thomas is about 30 to 45 minutes and costs about $14.

✔ **By boat:** You can also board a boat for St. John directly at the Charlotte Amalie waterfront for a cost of $7 each way. The ride takes 45 minutes. The boats depart from Charlotte Amalie at 9 a.m. and continue at intervals of between one and two hours, until the last boat departs around 5:30 p.m. (The last boat to leave St. John's Cruz Bay for Charlotte Amalie departs at 3:45 p.m.) Call ☎ 340-776-6282 for more information.

Traveling Inland from the Docks

From Carnival lines to Princess cruises, all the major ships call at Charlotte Amalie in St. Thomas. Some lines feature stopovers at the satellite island of St. John, and a few ships also call on St. Croix, anchoring at the pier at Fredriksted and not at that island's capital of

Christiansted. Island tours are usually booked by a ship's staff before you disembark. If so, your designated van will be waiting. If not, taxis meet every arriving ship along St. Thomas's Havensight and Crown Bay docks if you'd like to negotiate your own independent island tour, taking a "breather" from your fellow cruise-ship passengers.

Air-conditioned vans and open-air safari buses will take you to Charlotte Amalie for shopping or the beach. The cab fare from Havensight to Charlotte Amalie is $4; you can, however, walk the 1½ miles to town in about 30 minutes, along the waterfront. From Crown Bay to town, the taxi fare is $3 per person whether you travel solo or share; it's a 1-mile walk, but the route passes along a busy highway. Transportation from Havensight to Magens Bay for swimming is $6.50 per person ($4 per person if you share a ride).

In St. Croix, taxis greet arriving cruise ships at the Frederiksted Pier. All the shops are just a short walk away, and you can swim off the beach in Frederiksted, where snorkeling is good. Most ship passengers visit the capital at Christiansted on a tour. A taxi to Christiansted will cost $20 for one to two people.

Some cruise ships stop at St. John to let passengers disembark for a day. The main town of Cruz Bay is near the ship terminal. If you want to swim, the famous Trunk Bay is an $8 taxi ride (for two) from town.

Getting Around the USVIs

Roads on St. Croix are easy to navigate because the island is flat. Narrow routes going through hillsides and far too much traffic make driving in St. Thomas less than a pleasure. Except for a few main arteries, roads on St. John are very difficult — blind curves; narrow, hilly terrain; and some potholed dirt roads that even a motorist with a four-wheel-drive will find all but impossible. Businesses and residents are accustomed to handling visitors, so if you're confused, just ask for directions or other information.

By ferry

This is a great way to see the Virgin Islands. Not only do you get to where you're going, but you can enjoy a scenic boat ride — all for an affordable price. If you're staying on St. John, you fly first to the airport outside Charlotte Amalie. From there, you can take a taxi to the nearby dock at Charlotte Amalie or else to Red Hook in the East End. Used for public transport by the islanders themselves, ferries ply across the waters to Cruz Bay, the major settlement on St. John. Ferry service, however, has been discontinued from St. Thomas to St. Croix.

Ferries also leave from St. Thomas plying the waters to the "other Virgins," the British Virgin Islands.

The most frequented ferry routing in the Virgin Islands is from St. Thomas to Cruz Bay on St. John. You have a choice of taking a ferry from the Charlotte Amalie waterfront, lying west of the Coast Guard's dock, or from the funky little community of Red Hook in the east end where you can arrive early and have a beer or soda in one of the raffish taverns and perhaps order a fish patty or two from one of the local vendors.

Depending on weather conditions or mechanical failures, schedules can vary, so check with the ferry services themselves if you're trying to keep an appointment such as an airplane connection.

From the dock at Charlotte Amalie, St. John–bound ferries sail daily at 9 and 11 a.m., and at 1:00, 3:00, 4:00, and 5:30 p.m. The ferry leaves Cruz Bay for returns to Charlotte Amalie at 7:15, 9:15, and 11:15 a.m., and at 1:15, 2:15, and 3:45 p.m. Trip time is 45 minutes, with one-way tickets costing $7 for adults or $3 for children. From the dock at Cruz Bay, daily departures are at 6:30 and 7:30 a.m., and then from 8 a.m. hourly until midnight. On St. John, ferries heading back to Red Hook sail on the hour beginning at 6 a.m. The last one pulls out at 11 p.m. The Red Hook linkup takes from 15 to 20 minutes, costing adults $3 one way or children under 12 $1.

Two ferry services, **Smith's Ferry** (☎ **340-775-7292**) and **Native Son, Inc.** (☎ **340-774-8685**), link St. Thomas with Tortola in the British Virgin Islands. Ferries leave from both Charlotte Amalie and Red Hook on St. Thomas, landing at Road Town or West End on the island of Tortola. Smith's Ferry also provides service to Virgin Gorda, the second main island of the BVIs. Call for schedules, because hours of departure can vary from day to day. The cost of a one-way ticket is $22, $40 round trip. From Charlotte Amalie to Tortola's West End takes any-where from 45 minutes to 1 hour, the trip to Road Town 1½ hours. The Red Hook–to–Road Town run is only 30 minutes. The journey from Charlotte Amalie to Virgin Gorda sails only two times a week, costing $28 one way or $40 round trip. From the island of St. John, you can ferry to Tortola's West End on the *Sundance* (☎ **340-776-6597**); the 30-minute trip costs $21 one-way.

To get to the East End of St. Thomas from the Charlotte Amalie water-front without the hassle, you can hop aboard the 26-passenger skiff known as *The Reefer* (☎ **340-776-8500,** ext. 445). The boat takes you to Marriott Frenchman's Reef Beach Resort (see Chapter 32) every 30 minutes daily from 8:30 a.m. to 5:00 p.m. Returns from the East End are daily from 9:00 a.m. to 5:30 p.m. Even if you're not staying at one of Marriott's resorts, this is the easiest way to reach the highly desirable Morning Star Beach. A one-way ticket costs $5 (trip time: 15 minutes).

To enter the British Virgin Islands you'll need proof of citizenship. A valid passport is always best, although a birth certificate or voter's registra-tion card with photo ID usually does the trick.

By plane

If your final destination is not St. Thomas, following are some common carriers who fly to other nearby islands:

- **American Eagle** (☎ **800-433-7300** or 340-778-2000) offers frequent flights daily from St. Thomas to St. Croix's Henry E. Rohlsen Airport.

- **LIAT** (☎ **340-774-2313**) has service from St. Thomas and St. Croix to Caribbean islands to the south.

- **Cape Air** (☎ **800-352-0714**; Internet: www.flycapeair.com) offers hourly air service to St. Croix and Tortola.

- **The Seaborne Seaplane** (☎ **340-773-6442**), which you catch from a terminal on the waterfront across from Charlotte Amalie's main drag, also flies between St. Thomas and St. Croix several times daily, as well as to Tortola. A round-trip ticket to St. Croix costs $150. One child can fly free per accompanying adult.

Make reservations for the seaplane and check your luggage early, noting the strict weight limit of 40 pounds of luggage per passenger. Your baggage may be on the next flight if you don't check in early. The 20-minute flight to St. Croix is scenic, and you're dropped off right at the dock, a five-minute walk from Christiansted. If you do get caught waiting for your luggage, you can wander around and look at the little shops or grab a bite at one of the waterfront restaurants there.

On foot

The most interesting towns for walks are Charlotte Amalie on St. Thomas and both Frederiksted and Christiansted on St. Croix. A good self-guided tour of Charlotte Amalie's central district is found in the freely distributed *St. Thomas–St. John Vacation Handbook*. The St. Thomas Historical Trust also issues a self-guided tour of the historic sector (this one available for $1.95 in bookstores).

On St. Croix, the best deal is to hook up with one of the **St. Croix Heritage Tours** (☎ **340-778-6997**), offering informative walks through the history-rich sections of Christiansted and Frederiksted.

By public transportation

The public bus service on St. Thomas is better than on most Caribbean islands but woefully inadequate for those coming from metropolitan centers in the United States. Vitran buses, charging 75¢ for runs in Charlotte Amalie, or $1 to outlying places on the island, run about every half hour from town to the East End. Buses also run to western St. Thomas, with more limited service to northern outposts.

On neighboring St. John, more limited service is offered by Vitran buses, which make the run from the Cruz Bay ferry dock to Coral Bay and to the eastern end of the little island at Salt Pond. Some locals use this bus and there are endless stops, so it's not a convenient way to get anywhere fast. Vitran fares are still $1, as on St. Thomas.

In St. Croix, there are independently operated minivans, which cross the island frequently, mostly going along Route 70 between the capital of Christiansted to the "second city" of Frederiksted. A one-way fare is $1.50 for the 20-mile run, with many stops along the way. The slow-moving Vitran buses are mostly used by the locals, and the average fare is $1.

By taxi

Taxis are the most convenient way to travel on all three islands, and fares are generally lower than in mainland U.S. cities. Taxis aren't metered, but tariffs are set by the government. Rates are posted at the airport and in hotel lobbies. It's the law for the driver of a cab to show you the published rates if requested. Rates are also printed in the widely distributed *St. Thomas This Week* and *St. Croix This Week* booklets.

Even with the rates government controlled, it's still wise to settle on the charge before getting in the cab. Rates are per person. Cabbies often take more than one passenger, charging you a lower fee than if you book the taxi just for yourself.

On St. Thomas, taxis respond to phone calls. Try one of the following:

- ✓ **Islander Taxi** (☎ 340-774-4077)
- ✓ **The VI Taxi Association** (☎ 340-774-4550)
- ✓ **East End Taxi** (☎ 340-775-6974)

Taxis are plentiful on St. Croix and St. Thomas, less so on St. John. Cabs can be hailed on the street. They are especially plentiful along the waterfront in Charlotte Amalie. Stands lie across from Emancipation Garden. On St. Croix taxis cluster at the airport and at the Frederiksted pier when cruise ships arrive; they are also easily available in the center of Christiansted. Try the **St. Croix Taxi Association** (☎ 340-778-1088) at the airport and **Antilles Taxi Service** (☎ 340-773-5020) or **Cruxan Taxi and Tours** (☎ 340-773-6388) in Christiansted.

Taxis on St. John are not only a convenient way to get about, they are also a lot of fun, because most are in open-air "safari buses." Taxis meet ferries arriving at the Cruz Bay ferry dock coming either from Charlotte Amalie or Red Hook. They also are available at the two major island hotels, and you can flag one down whenever you see one. Just because other people are in the cab doesn't mean they won't stop for you if there is room; shared taxis are commonplace. Cabbies on St. John don't respond to calls as efficiently as drivers on St. Thomas and St. Croix. On St. John they may show up — then again, they may not. It's more laid back here.

By car

Driving is on the left side of the road, although the steering wheel will be on the left as well. Seat belts are mandatory, and the roads are narrow and hilly in St. Thomas and even worse on St. John.

A valid U.S. driver's license is good for a 90-day stay. The minimum age is 18 years. Even so, many car-rental firms don't rent to anyone under 25.

In-depth explorations of St. Thomas and St. Croix require a private vehicle. On St. John, you can usually get around without a car unless you're staying at a private villa far from Cruz Bay. Then you're pretty isolated and a car will come in handy.

Because of winding, narrow roads, the government wisely limits speed to 20 to 35 mph. Gasoline is very expensive in the USVIs. If you have a breakdown, call the car-rental outfitter. All three islands have garages that will tow in broken-down vehicles.

Driving in St. Thomas

Try to avoid driving in and out of Charlotte Amalie Monday through Saturday from 7 to 9 a.m. and from 4:30 to 6:30 p.m. Traffic is bumper to bumper, and no one seems to be moving. Drivers' patience wears thin, but there is little "road rage" like you'd find in California.

You can rent a car on St. Thomas from the following companies:

- ✔ **Budget** (☎ **800-626-4516** or 340-776-5774)
- ✔ **Cowpet Rent-a-Car** (☎ **340-775-7376**)
- ✔ **Dependable Car Rental** (☎ **800-522-3076** or 340-774-2253)
- ✔ **Discount** (☎ **340-776-4858**)
- ✔ **Sun Island Car Rental** (☎ **340-774-3333**)

Driving on St. Croix

Because the island is mainly flat, the roads here are better than on hilly St. Thomas or St. John. Speed limits are higher too, especially at 55 mph along the four-lane Melvin H. Evans route linking Christiansted with Frederiksted. Elsewhere on the island speed limits are 35 to 40 mph.

Occasionally, all the rental companies run out of cars at once. To avoid disappointment, make your reservations early. Call one of the following:

✔ **Avis** (☎ **800-331-1084** or 340-778-9355)

✔ **Budget** (☎ **888-227-3359** or 340-778-9636)

✔ **Olympic** (☎ **888-878-4227** or 340-773-2208)

✔ **Thrifty** (☎ **800-367-2277** or 340-773-7200)

Driving on St. John

St. John has the most beautiful landscape of the USVIs, but it's the most difficult to navigate by car. If you're going into the interior, especially the national park, a four-wheel-drive vehicle is needed. The very limited major routes are paved and passable. When you veer from them, however, expect dirt roads that are potholed and sometimes impassable after heavy rainfalls.

At the height of the winter season, finding a car may be difficult. Reserve well in advance to ensure that you get the vehicle of your choice. Call one of the following:

✔ **Cool Breeze** (☎ **340-776-6588**)

✔ **Delbert Hill Taxi Rental Service** (☎ **340-776-6637**)

✔ **Denzil Clyne** (☎ **340-776-6715**)

✔ **St. John Car Rental** (☎ **340-776-6103**)

✔ **Spencer's Jeep** (☎ **888-776-6628** or 340-693-8784)

By helicopter

This is the most expensive but the most dramatic way to see the U.S. Virgins. The best deal is offered by **Seaborne Seaplane Adventures**, 5305 Long Bay Rd. (☎ **340-777-1227**), featuring narrated "flightseeing" bird's-eye views. A half-hour "'Round the Island" tour costs $99 per person, with other tours available from their base at the Havensight Mall on St. Thomas. Deluxe copter tours are a feature of **Air Center Helicopters** (☎ **340-775-7335**), from their base at the Charlotte Amalie waterfront. A half-hour tour for four passengers is $400, the cost divided among the group. Longer flights to the BVIs can be arranged.

Fast Facts: USVIs

ATMs

On St. Thomas, the branch of First Bank (☎ 340-776-9494) near Market Square or the Banco Popular (☎ 340-693-2777) and Chase Manhattan Bank (☎ 340-775-7777) have ATMs. On St. Croix, contact Banco Popular (☎ 340-693-2777) or Chase Manhattan Bank (☎ 340-775-7777) for information on branch and ATM locations. On St. John, Chase Manhattan Bank (☎ 340-775-7777) has the island's only ATM.

Baby-sitters

You can find sitters easily, but try to reserve 24 hours in advance. Expect to pay $8 or more per hour.

Banks

Bank hours are generally Monday through Thursday from 9 a.m. to 3 p.m. and Friday 9 a.m. to 5 p.m. A handful have Saturday hours (9 a.m. to noon). Walk-up windows open at 8:30 a.m. on weekdays.

Credit Cards

Credit cards are widely accepted in the USVIs. Visa and MasterCard are the cards of choice at most local businesses, although American Express and, to a lesser extent, Diners Club are also popular. Discover is accepted but very rarely.

Currency Exchange

The U.S. dollar is used throughout the territory, as well as in the neighboring BVIs. All major credit cards and traveler's checks are generally accepted.

Doctors

On St. Croix, a good local doctor is Dr. Frank Bishop, Sunny Isle Medical Center (☎ 340-778-0069). On St. Thomas, Doctors-on-Duty, Vitraco Park (☎ 340-776-7966) in Charlotte Amalie is a reliable medical facility. On St. John, contact St. John Myrah Keating Smith Community Health Clinic, P.O. Box 8312, Susannaberg 3B (☎ 340-693-8900).

Emergencies

On all USVIs, call ☎ **911** for ambulance, fire, and police.

Hospitals

St. Thomas Hospital (☎ 340-776-8311) has a decompression chamber. On St. Croix, outside Christiansted there's the Gov. Juan F. Luis Hospital and Health Center, 6 Diamond Ruby, north of Sunny Isle Shopping Center on Route 79 (☎ 340-778-6311). You can also try the Frederiksted Health Center, 516 Strand St. (☎ 340-772-1992). On St. John, visit the Myrah Keating Smith Community Health Center, Route 10, about 7 minutes east of Cruz Bay (☎ 340-693-8900).

Homework

Read Herman Wouk's dated but still amusing *Don't Stop the Carnival*.

Information

Before you visit the island, contact the USVI Division of Tourism at #1 Tolbod Gade, St. Thomas, USVI 00802 (☎ 800-372-USVI or 212-332-2222; Fax: 212-332-2223; Internet: www.usvi.net).

On St. Thomas, the USVI Division of Tourism has an office in Charlotte Amalie (Box 6400, Charlotte Amalie 00804; ☎ 800-372-8784 or 340-774-8784). You'll also find a visitor center in downtown Charlotte Amalie and a cruise ship welcome center at Havensight Mall. The National Park Service operates a visitor center across the harbor from the ferry dock at Red Hook.

On St. Croix, the USVI Division of Tourism has offices at 53A Company St. in Christiansted (Box 4538, Christiansted 00822; ☎ 340-773-0495) and on the pier in Frederiksted (Strand St., Frederiksted 00840; ☎ 340-772-0357).

On St. John, there's a branch of the USVI Department of Tourism (Box 200, Cruz Bay 00830; ☎ 340-776-6450) in the compound between Sparky's and the U.S. Post Office in Cruz Bay. The National Park Service (Box 710, 00831; ☎ 340-776-6201) also has a visitor center at the Creek in Cruz Bay.

Language

English is official, but islanders often speak it with a Creole accent and use words known only to themselves. Even so, you should have no language problem anywhere in the Virgin Islands.

Maps

If you plan to do extensive touring of the island, purchase *The Official Road Map of the U.S. Virgin Islands,* available at island bookstores and free at the Christiansted office of the Department of Tourism.

St. Thomas This Week, distributed free by the visitor center and usually on cruise ships stopping on St. Thomas, contains a good two-page map with a clear, easy-to-follow street plan of Charlotte Amalie, plus the locations of important landmarks and all of Charlotte Amalie's leading shops.

The St. John Tourist Office (☎ 340-776-6450) is located near the Battery, a 1735 fort that is a short walk from where the ferry from St. Thomas docks. You'll find plenty of travel information here, including a free map of Cruz Bay and the entire island that pinpoints all the main attractions. Hours are Monday through Friday 8 a.m. to noon and 1 to 5 p.m.

St. Croix This Week, which is distributed free to cruise-ship passengers and air passengers, includes detailed maps of Christiansted, Frederiksted, and the entire island, pinpointing individual attractions, hotels, shops, and restaurants.

Newspapers/Magazines

Copies of U.S. mainland newspapers, such as *The New York Times, USA Today,* and *The Miami Herald,* arrive daily in St. Thomas and are sold at hotels and newsstands, but the markup is high. The latest copies of *Time* and *Newsweek* are also for sale. *St. Thomas Daily News* covers local, national, and international events. Pick up *Virgin Islands Playground* and *St. Thomas This Week;* both are packed with visitor information and are distributed free all over the island.

Newspapers such as *The Miami Herald* are flown into St. Croix, which also has its own newspaper, *St. Croix Avis. Time* and *Newsweek* are widely sold as well. Your best source for local information is *St. Croix This Week,* which is distributed free by the tourist offices.

On St. John, copies of U.S. mainland newspapers arrive daily and are for sale at Mongoose Junction, Caneel Bay, and the Westin. The latest copies of *Time* and *Newsweek* are also for sale. Complimentary copies of *What to Do: St. Thomas/St. John* contain many helpful hints, although this publication is a commercial mouthpiece. It is the official guidebook of the St. Thomas and St. John Hotel Association and is available at the tourist office and at various hotels.

Pharmacies

On St. Thomas, Havensight Pharmacy (☎ 340-776-1235) in the Havensight Mall is open daily from 9 a.m. to 6 p.m. Kmart (☎ 340-777-3854) operates a pharmacy inside the Tutu Park Mall; it's open from 8 a.m. to 9 p.m. Sunrise Pharmacy (☎ 340-775-6600), in Red Hook, is open daily from 9 a.m. to 6 p.m.

On St. Croix, most drugstores are open daily from 8 a.m. to 8 p.m. Off-season hours may vary; call ahead to confirm times. Kmart (☎ 340-692-2622) operates a pharmacy at its Sunshine Mall store. People's Drug Store, Inc., has two branches: on the Christiansted Wharf (☎ 340-778-7355) and at the Sunny Isle Shopping Center (☎ 340-778-5537), just a few miles west of Christiansted on Route 70. In Frederiksted, try D&D Apothecary Hall, 501 Queen St. (☎ 340-772-1890).

On St. John, the St. John Drug Center (☎ 340-776-6353) is in the Boulon shopping center, up Centerline Road in Cruz Bay. It's open Monday through Saturday from 9 a.m. to 5 p.m.

Post Office

Hours may vary slightly from branch to branch and island to island, but on weekdays they generally open between 7:30 and 8:00 a.m. and close between 4:00 and 5:30 p.m.;

on Saturday, they generally open between 7:30 and 8:00 a.m. and close between noon and 2:30 p.m.

The main U.S. Post Office on St. Thomas is near the hospital, with branches in Charlotte Amalie, Frenchtown, Havensight, and Tutu Mall. There's a post office at Christiansted, Frederiksted, Gallows Bay, and Sunny Isle on St. Croix, and one at Cruz Bay on St. John.

Safety

St. John is relatively safe, even at night, but St. Thomas, especially around its capital, Charlotte Amalie, has the highest crime rate in the Virgin Islands. You may want to avoid it at night. St. Croix has less crime than St. Thomas but caution is advised, especially if you plan night visits to the dives of Frederiksted or Christiansted where muggings may occur.

Shops

Shopping hours vary from establishment to establishment, but on St. Thomas most stores along Main Street in Charlotte Amalie, the major shopping center, are open Monday through Saturday from 9 a.m. to 5 p.m. Most of the shops near Havensight Mall where cruise ships dock keep the same hours. If cruise ships arrive on a Sunday, many owners — not wanting to face such a massive loss of business — will also open their stores.

On St. Croix, hours are the same as on St. Thomas, the only difference is that many retailers in Christiansted stay open at night until about 9 p.m. St. John is more laid-back and so are its shopkeepers, most of whom open at 9 a.m. (or 10 a.m. if they had a big night the evening before). Most stores close at 5 or 6 p.m. Shops are concentrated either at Mongoose Junction or Wharfside Village in Cruz Bay, and some of these stay open in the early evening.

Telephone

The area code for all of the USVIs is 340, and you can dial direct to and from the mainland as well as to and from Australia, Canada, New Zealand, and the United Kingdom. Local calls from a public phone cost 25¢ for five minutes.

On St. John, the place to go for telephone or message needs is Connections in Cruz Bay (☎ 340-776-6922) or in Coral Bay (☎ 340-779-4994).

Time Zone

The USVIs are on Atlantic time, which places the islands one hour ahead of eastern standard time. However, during daylight saving time, the USVIs and the East Coast are on the same clock.

Tipping

Most hotels add on a 10 to 15% service charge; ask if it's already included when you're initially quoted a price. A 10% service charge is often (but not always) added on to restaurant bills; you can leave another 5% if you thought the service was unusually good. You usually don't need to tip taxi drivers, because most own their own cabs, but you can tip 15% if they've been unusually helpful.

Water

There is ample water for showers and bathing in the Virgin Islands, but conserving is always wise. Many visitors drink the local tap water with no harmful aftereffects. To be prudent, especially if you have a delicate stomach, stick to bottled water.

Weather and Surf Reports

All three islands receive both cable and commercial TV stations. Radio weather reports can be heard at 8:30 a.m. and 7:30 p.m. on 99.5 FM.

Chapter 34

Dining in the U.S. Virgin Islands

By Darwin Porter and Danforth Prince

. . . .

In This Chapter

▶ Sampling the local cuisine

▶ Saving money on meals

▶ Locating the island's best restaurants

. . . .

*T*he good news is that the U.S. Virgin Islands are home to the largest cadre of skilled chefs in the Caribbean, even outdistancing Puerto Rico, another capital of cuisine. The bad news is that the prices charged are familiar to those who've just visited Miami or New York.

From the most elegant, refined cuisine of France, to the casual deli food, the USVIs have it all, with a lot of emphasis on international fare such as Mexican, Chinese, and Italian. In many places such as little taverns and shanties near the beach, you can also sample local island dishes. As one old-time Virgin Islander woman cook told us, "We like to show some of you visitors how to escape from hamburger hell from time to time."

The large resorts of the USVIs have long recognized that good food is an integral part of your vacation experience. They have hired some of the best chefs from both the United States and Europe to tempt you to stay on their premises at night and not venture out on badly lit, narrow roads heading for some distant independent restaurant. The larger resorts offer a widely varied cuisine on their grounds, giving you several choices for dining, ranging from simple fare to more elaborate menus with generally excellent wine lists.

Those high prices mentioned become easier to tolerate when you consider that most of your meals will be taken at a table where you'll have a panoramic view of the sea and a tropical atmosphere. Hopefully, a cool, soothing trade wind will be blowing when the waiter presents your check.

For those on the tightest of vacation budgets, we've also included many little taverns where you can't dine on haute cuisine, but you can eat reasonably well — all at an affordable price.

A Taste of the USVIs

Most of the foodstuff is imported from the U.S. mainland, and the added cost of shipment is reflected on the right side of the menu (the price list of course). If you're a fish fancier, your best bet is locally caught fish, which can range from yellowtail to grouper, from red snapper to mahimahi and wahoo. Virgin Islanders often serve it grilled with a hot lime sauce, and we view this as the tastiest of island specialties.

Way back when, locals gave colorful names to the various fish brought home for dinner, everything from "ole wife" to "doctors," both of which are whitefish. "Porgies and grunts," along with yellowtail, kingfish, and bonito, also show up on many dinner tables. Fish is usually boiled in a lime-flavored brew seasoned with hot peppers and herbs and is commonly served with a Creole sauce of peppers, tomatoes, and onions, among other ingredients. **Salt fish and rice** is an excellent low-cost dish, the fish flavored with onion, tomatoes, shortening, garlic, and green pepper.

Conch Creole is a savory brew, seasoned with onions, garlic, spices, hot peppers, and salt pork. Another local favorite is chicken and rice, usually made with Spanish peppers. More adventurous diners may try **curried goat,** the longtime classic Virgin Island dinner prepared with herbs, cardamom pods, and onions.

If you want a light meal of local food, order a ***johnnycake*** (an unleavened cornbread/flour treat), a ***pate*** (a small pastry filled with meat or fish), or a thick slice of ***dumb bread*** (a round loaf cut into pieces and stuffed with cheese) from any of the mobile food vans you see around the islands.

For a *belonger* experience (as locals call themselves), stop at a local restaurant for goat stew, leg of lamb with guava, curry chicken, or fried pork chops. Local cooks pile on the sides, so dining is akin to eating at a "meat-'n'-three" in the southern U.S. Nearly all locals eat peas 'n rice with their main dishes. Pigeon peas, the most common Virgin Island vegetable, are called *gunga* or congo peas. They are often flavored with ham, salted meat, onions, tomatoes, fresh herbs, and even an occasional slice of pumpkin.

The most varied cuisine is found on St. Thomas, which has a wider selection of restaurants and better trained kitchen staffs than all the other islands. Almost anything you want can be found on the island. If you crave deli food like that served on Miami Beach or in New York, it's here, too. If you remember fondly that little bistro you discovered on the Left Bank of Paris, it is entirely possible that the French chef is taking a winter hiatus to cook in St. Thomas at night while enjoying the beach during the day.

St. Croix has had many invaders, with a total of seven flags of different nationalities having flown over the island. That culinary heritage remains in its cuisine today. The food ranges from Danish to American, with a lot of fusion recipes in between, plus a strong focus on French and Italian. Some smaller places serve West Indian dishes. Although they will feed you well, St. Croix restaurants don't have the scope of those on St. Thomas.

As the smallest of the islands, St. John has the least number of restaurants, but, even so, the range is varied from shacks to the most formal and elegant of *luxe* dining rooms at the two major hotels. St. John is said to have more artists than all the other islands combined, and that creative diversity is also reflected in the imaginative cuisine served here.

Each year dining in the USVIs seems to grow more and more relaxed, informal, and laid-back as top restaurant owners have long ago abandoned their demand that men wear jackets and ties. Many visitors, at least at the dives, eat in their shorts and a tank top.

At the top-rated restaurants, it's better for men to show up in slacks and a shirt with buttons, whereas women will feel comfortable in the evenings in a tailored pants suit or a stylish sundress. After all, you don't want the maître d' to take one look at what you're wearing and seat you in a dark corner, a potted palm hiding you from view.

The USVIs' Best Restaurants

When you visit one of the USVIs, you're likely to stay put, perhaps popping over to one of the other islands for a day or so. We arranged our dining favorites to reflect the ways you're most likely to experience the USVIs — island by island. We start with St. Thomas, with the widest selection of dining places. We follow with St. Thomas's biggest rival for the vacationer's dollar, the larger island of St. Croix. Even though bigger in land mass, it doesn't have the offerings of St. Thomas, but what St. Croix does have is choice. Most of St. Croix's restaurants, except for a few favorites "out on the island," are found in the capital of Christiansted. We wind up with St. John, where you'll find a surprisingly sophisticated scene, for such a small, laid-back island.

On St. Thomas

Here's what you can expect to find to satisfy your appetite for a variety of fare.

Agavé Terrace

$$$–$$$$ East End Seafood/Caribbean

Perched high above a steep and heavily forested hillside on the eastern tip of St. Thomas, this outstanding restaurant offers a sweeping panorama of St. John and the BVIs at night. The chefs serve inventive fresh fish prepared as you like it. The fare has gleaned six gold medals in Caribbean cooking competitions. At the Lookout Lounge, you can order the house drink, Desmond Delight, a combination of rum, pineapple juice, and a "secret ingredient." The extensive wine list won a *Wine Spectator* award. A live steel-drum band draws listeners Tuesday and Thursday nights.

Point Pleasant Resort, 6600 Estate, Smith Bay. ☎ *340-775-4142. Reservations recommended. Main courses: $18–$32. AE, MC, V. Open: Daily 6–10 p.m.*

Alexander's Café

$$$ Frenchtown Austrian/Italian/Seafood

Small, intimate Alexander's, west of Charlotte Amalie, has just a dozen tables in an air-conditioned room with picture windows overlooking the harbor. The Teutonic dishes are the best on the island, especially when they involve seafood such as a pasta with an array of mussels, shrimp, clams, crab, and the catch of the day. A delectable conch schnitzel — cooked as you would a breaded veal cutlet — often appears on the menu. Many newer dishes are showing more of an Italian slant to the menu, including marinated tuna steak or penne in a basil pesto cream sauce. One of our favorites is a pan-seared and herb-crusted tenderloin of lamb with a mint-flavored port sauce. The apple strudel is the island's best. At lunch you can dine on light fare including sandwiches (even a veggie burger), quiches, and crêpes, plus the chef's hot specials of the day.

24A Honduras. ☎ *340-776-4211. Reservations essential. Main courses: $12–$24.95. AE, DISC, MC, V. Open: Mon–Sat 11:30 a.m.–5:00 p.m and 5:30–10:00 p.m.*

Banana Tree Grille

$$$ Charlotte Amalie International/Caribbean

The choice dining spot at this recommended hilltop hotel is this smoothly run restaurant overlooking romantic-at-night panoramic views of the Charlotte Amalie harbor. When making a reservation, try for a table at the edge of the multi-tiered restaurant. The Grille offers a real aura of the tropics, with lights winking at you in palm trees, a hip waitstaff in Hawaiian shirts, tropical drinks being blended at the bar, and flickering candlelight. Start with the bacon-wrapped horseradish shrimp, going on to such main events as lobster tail tempera with an orange sambal sauce or mustard-glazed salmon. Meat aficionados gravitate to a shank of lamb slowly braised in Chianti and served with an aïoli sauce over white beans and garlic-mashed potatoes. Desserts are justifiably called "decadent."

Bluebeard's Castle, Bluebeard's Hill, Charlotte Amalie. ☎ *340-776-4050. Reservations recommended. Main courses: $16–$31. AE, V, MC. Open: Tues–Sun 6:00–9:30 p.m.*

St. Thomas Dining

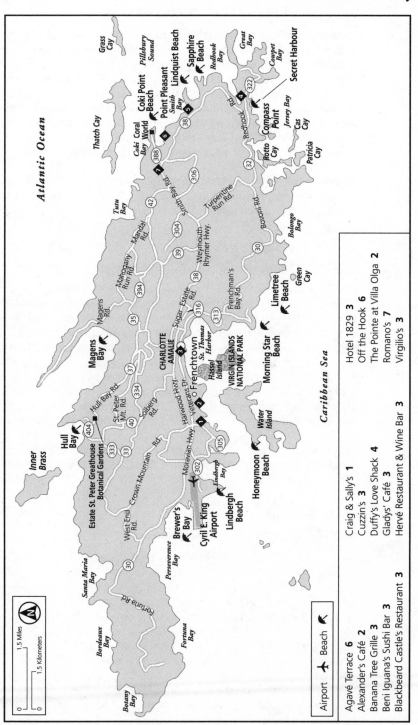

Airport ✈   Beach ⬏

Agavé Terrace **6**
Alexander's Café **2**
Banana Tree Grille **3**
Beni Iguana's Sushi Bar **3**
Blackbeard Castle's Restaurant **3**

Craig & Sally's **1**
Cuzzin's **3**
Duffy's Love Shack **4**
Gladys' Café **3**
Hervé Restaurant & Wine Bar **3**

Hotel 1829 **3**
Off the Hook **6**
The Pointe at Villa Olga **2**
Romano's **7**
Virgilio's **3**

Beni Iguana's Sushi Bar
$–$$ **Charlotte Amalie** **Asian/Japanese**

Across from Emancipation Park, this is the restaurant that brought the cuisine from Japan to St. Thomas. The bar and restaurant are installed in a former cistern with an open-air courtyard. The old Danish colonial doors are still in place, and the interior has been given a coating of red and black Chinese lacquer. Sushi comes in familiar packaging here, and the tuna or salmon sahimi is a delight. If you're uncertain of menu terms, all you have to do is look at the pictures of the various dishes. Combo plates for four to five diners can be served, costing $25.50 to $35.50. The savory "green-lipped" mussels come from Australia.

In the Grand Hotel Court, at Norre Gade and Tolbod Gade. ☎ *340-777-8744. Reservations recommended. Main courses: $8–$17; sushi: $4–$15 per portion (two pieces). AE, MC, V. Open: Mon–Sat 11:30 a.m.–9:30 p.m.*

Blackbeard Castle's Restaurant
$$$ **Charlotte Amalie** **Continental/Asian**

Here you can enjoy "tower dining," eating while taking in the most stunning view of the port of Charlotte Amalie. The castle's open-air tower has been turned into the setting for a romantic gourmet dinner. It is said that the pirate Blackbeard once kept watch for invaders from this tower. Chefs roam the world for inspiration, and try to pack a lot of flavor into every dish without destroying an item's natural goodness. Try the orange and sugarcane marinated duck with mashed sweet potatoes, or dig into the grilled tuna with chile and tomatillo sauces. Those old American favorites such as filet mignon or stuffed Caribbean lobster appear on the menu, but we gravitate more to the red snapper baked with a nut crust.

In Blackbeard's Castle, Blackbeard's Hill. ☎ *340-776-1234. Reservations needed 1 week in advance. Main courses: $19–$28. AE, MC, V. Open: Lunch daily 11 a.m.–2 p.m.; dinner Mon–Sat 6–10 p.m.*

Craig & Sally's
$$–$$$ **Frenchtown** **International**

Islanders, often with kids in tow, as well as savvy visitors make their way to this St. Thomas favorite to sample the culinary skills of Chef Sally Darash, who's the best woman chef on the island. She runs this place with husband, Craig, who is in charge of the wine cellar. Always inventive, Sally is a fusion chef, borrowing from Asia, the West Indies, and the Mediterranean, but giving all the dishes her special touch, as evoked by such starters as an eggplant "cheesecake" with a pinenut and garlic breaded crust. For main dishes, we go for her sautéed Chilean sea bass with a tangy mango barbecue glaze and a fresh mango couscous. Or you may opt for her baked halibut in a Mexican mole sauce with rice and a jalapeño black bean quesadilla. Nothing is finer for dessert than her white chocolate cheesecake.

22 Estate Honduras. ☎ *340-777-9949. Reservations recommended. Main courses: $15–$28. AE, MC, V. Open: Lunch Wed–Fri 11:30 a.m.–3:00 p.m.; dinner Wed–Sun 5:30–10:00 p.m.*

Cuzzin's
$$ Charlotte Amalie   West Indian

For a "taste of the islands," head to this local eatery in a 250-year-old yellow brick building close to most of the major shops in Charlotte Amalie. Once a livery stable, the place has been transformed into a comfortable dining room that still adheres to oldtime Virgin Island recipes. Conch, lobster, and various fish — caught daily by local fishermen — are prepared by West Indian chefs, who turn out delectable stews (try the savory conch version), lobster, and other native dishes. The best pasta is Cuzzin' Nemo, a mélange of shrimp, conch, lobster, and scallops over pasta. Some of the dishes here, such as stewed mutton, rarely appear anymore on island menus. Many oldtime drinks are still served here, including ginger beer and sea moss (milk, ginger, seaweed, and nutmeg).

7 Backstreet. ☎ *340-777-4711. Reservations recommended. AE, MC, V. Open: Lunch Mon 11 a.m.–4 p.m. and Tues–Sat 11 a.m.–5 p.m.; dinner Tues–Sat 5:00–9:30 p.m.*

Duffy's Love Shack
$–$$$ East End   Eclectic

This is a funky local dive that's somewhat of an island legend. Near the Red Hook ferry dock, Duffy's became known when the Mamas and the Papas came over from St. John to entertain. They proved such an island favorite the group went on to glory in the States. Theme parties on Thursday night still keep the entertainment memory alive at this open-air "shack," with lots of bamboo and a thatched roof over the bar. The bar is more popular than the dining room, because the bartenders here are known for their lethal rum drinks, including a 50-ounce flaming extravaganza. A standard American cuisine is combined with recipes with West Indian flair, including everything from "cowboy steak" to "junkanoo" chicken in a coconut and pineapple sauce. Habitués praise the chef's "blackened shark" if that's your idea of good eating. If not, we recommend the jerk tenderloin. After 10 p.m., a more limited menu appears, mainly sandwiches.

650 Red Hook Plaza. ☎ *340-779-2080. Main courses: $8–$16. No credit cards. Open: Daily 11:30 a.m.–2:00 a.m.*

Gladys' Café
$ Charlotte Amalie   West Indian/American

When Gladys Isles arrived here from her native Antigua, she brought her local island recipes with her, and today she concocts some of the best West Indian fare in Charlotte Amalie. Her breakfast is the biggest in town, served with unlimited coffee. If you come back for lunch (no dinners are served), you can dig into her hearty fare, including pan-fried whitefish, a savory conch in a lemon butter sauce, and various rotis (like stuffed crepes). She also makes such old island favorites as saltfish 'n dumplings or a robust red bean soup. As you're leaving, you can buy her special bottles of hot sauce costing $5 to $10, depending on size.

Royal Dane Mall. ☎ 340-774-6604. Main courses: Breakfast $8.95, lunch $8–$15. AE, DC, MC, V. Open: Mon–Sat breakfast 7–11 a.m., lunch 11 a.m.–5 p.m.; Sun brunch 8 a.m.–2 p.m.

Hervé Restaurant & Wine Bar
$$$–$$$$ Charlotte Amalie   American/Caribbean/French

Hervé Chassin is arguably the island's best chef, operating next to (and surpassing) the viands served at that classic landmark, Hotel 1829. Opening onto panoramic view of yacht-clogged Charlotte Amalie, Chassin attracts with an innovative menu of top-quality ingredients and a romantic atmosphere with flickering candles and beautifully served tables. You can dine on a large open-air terrace or in the intimate wine room. Start with the pistachio-encrusted brie, shrimp in a stuffed crab shell, or conch fritters with mango chutney. From here, you can let your taste buds march boldly forward with red snapper poached with white wine, or a delectable black-sesame-crusted tuna with a ginger/raspberry sauce. Well-prepared nightly specials of game, fish, and pasta are features. Desserts here are equally divine — you'll rarely taste a creamier crème caramel or a lighter, fluffier mango or raspberry cheesecake.

Government Hill. ☎ 340-777-9703. Reservations necessary. Main courses: $5.50–$16.50 at lunch, $19–$26 at dinner. AE, MC, V. Open: Daily lunch 11 a.m.–3 p.m., dinner 6–10 p.m.

Hotel 1829
$$$$$ Charlotte Amalie   Continental/Caribbean

We suggest you make an evening of it here by arriving early for a "sunset cocktail" in the darkly atmospheric bar tavern still haunted by the ghosts of yesteryear when it was a celebrity favorite and you never knew who you were likely to encounter here, perhaps Edna St. Vincent Millay or Mikhail Baryshnikov. They are long gone but the romantic aura lingers on. Although it has long ceased to be the finest restaurant on the island — the competition today is too fierce for that — it does offer the most elaborate prix-fixe menu in St. Thomas, backed up by an award-winning wine list, the island's finest. The menu is changed nightly and adjusted seasonally, and the cookery is first rate with a solid technique. There's a distinctively European twist to the menu, with many of the dishes prepared and served from trolleys beside your table. The chefs are long known for their delectable and feathery light soufflés: chocolate, Grand Marnier, coconut, and a marvelous raspberry one.

Kongens Gade (at the east end of Main Street). ☎ 340-776-1829. Reservations essential but not accepted more than 1 day in advance. Prix-fixe dinner $50–$75. AE, DISC, MC, V. Open: Nightly 6–10 p.m.; closed Jun 1–Dec 1.

Off the Hook

$$–$$$ East End   Asian/Caribbean

Diners enjoy an eclectic medley of specialties inspired by Asia, although the chefs concoct dishes using some of the freshest and finest ingredients of the West Indies. In an open-air dining room near the American Yacht Harbor, close to the departure point for the ferry to St. John, the fresh catch of the day — hauled off the little fishing boats just pulling in — is delivered to the kitchen where it's grilled to perfection. The yellowfin tuna keeps us coming back. The chef is also adept at preparing a tuna and salmon sushi platter. The black Angus steak is always a pure delight. The decor is rustic, with outdoor dining and wooden tables.

6300 Estate Smith Bay. ☎ 340-775-6350. Reservations required. Main courses: $16–$25. AE, MC, V. Open: Nightly 5:30–10:00 p.m.; closed Sept 15–Oct 15.

The Pointe at Villa Olga

$$$ Frenchtown   Steaks/Seafood

This upscale restaurant is known for serving the finest cut of prime rib on the island. But it also features grilled seafood, which on occasion is even better. The stripped-down 19th-century villa that contains the Chart House was the Russian consulate during the island's Danish administration. It lies a short distance beyond the most densely populated area of Frenchtown village. The dining gallery is a spacious open terrace fronting the sea. Cocktails start daily at 5 p.m., when the bartender breaks out the ingredients for his special Bailey's banana colada. Calamari, pasta dishes, coconut shrimp, and Hawaiian chicken are part of the expanded menu. For dessert, order the famous mud pie.

Villa Olga, Frenchtown ☎ 340-774-4262. Reservations recommended. Main courses: $17–$29; prix-fixe menu $19.95. AE, DC, MC, V. Open: Nightly 6–10 p.m.

Romano's

$$$–$$$$ East End   Northern Italian

In a setting near Coral World, a New Jersey-born chef, Tony Romano, brings the savory cuisine of Northern Italy to St. Thomas. The dishes served here would even please the late Frank Sinatra, who was known to toss a plate of spaghetti across the room if it wasn't cooked to his specifications. Tony's dishes are full of flavor and beautifully spiced with lots of herbs. We delight in his linguine with pesto and find his lasagne, made with four different kinds of cheese, velvety and creamy. You can have fish if you want it, perhaps a perfectly broiled salmon, although we suggest his classic Italian meat dishes, especially osso buco and scaloppini flavored with Marsala. Romano's has been an island tradition since it opened in 1988.

97 Smith Bay Rd. ☎ *340-775-0045. Reservations required. Main courses: $19–$30; pastas $14.95–$21. MC, V. Open: Mon–Sat 6:00–10:30 p.m; closed Sun. Closed August and 1 week in April for Carnival.*

Virgilio's

$$$–$$$$ Charlotte Amalie   Northern Italian

For Northern Italian cuisine even better than Romano's (see the preceding listing), you can stay right in Charlotte Amalie and head for the domain of Virgilio del Mare. Under heavy ceiling beams and brick vaulting, you can dine in a soothing atmosphere under crystal chandeliers with soft Italian background music. Virgilio has taught his chefs well, and they invariably feature fresh-tasting ingredients that are handled with a razor-sharp technique. The *cinco peche* (clams, mussels, scallops, oysters, and crayfish simmered in a saffron broth) is a delectable house special, while the alfredo fettuccine here is the best on the island. Classic dishes are served with a distinctive flair — the rack of lamb, for example, is filled with a porcini mushroom stuffing and glazed with a roasted garlic aïoli. The marinated grilled duck is served chilled. You can even order an individual margarita pizza.

18 Dronningens Gade (entrance on a narrow alleyway running between Main Street and Backstret). ☎ *340-776-4920. Reservations recommended. Main courses: $11–$23 lunch, $16–$35 dinner. AE, MC, V. Open: Mon–Sat lunch 11 a.m.–3 p.m., dinner 6:00–10:30 p.m.*

On St. Croix

The largest of the USVIs, St. Croix dishes out rich dining opportunities.

Blue Moon

$$$ Fredricksted   International/Cajun

Your best bet for dining in St. Croix's "second city" of Frederiksted is this waterfront bistro that draws big crowds on Friday night for its live jazz. In a two-century-old stone-built house, it's a bit funky with its homemade art, including a trash-can lid advertising its name. In an informal, and laid-back atmosphere, you can begin with the "lunar pie," with feta, cream cheese, onions, mushrooms, and celery in phyllo pastry, or the artichoke-and-spinach dip. Main courses include the catch of the day and, on occasion, Maine lobster. The clams served in garlic sauce are also from Maine. Vegetarians opt for the spinach fettuccine. There's also the usual array of steak and chicken dishes. Save room for the yummy apple spice pie.

17 Strand St. ☎ *340-772-2222. Reservations recommended. Main courses: $17.50–$31.50. AE, DISC, MC, V. Open: Lunch Tues–Fri 11:30 a.m.–2:00 p.m. and Sun 11 a.m.–2 p.m.; dinner Tues–Sat 5:00–9:30 p.m. and Sun 6–9 p.m.*

St. Croix Dining

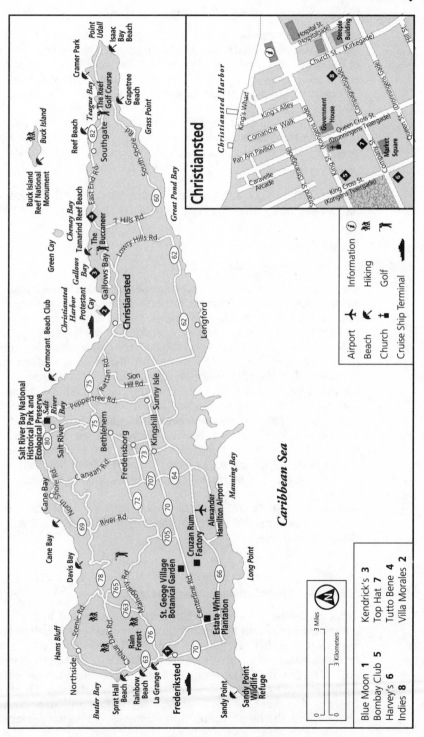

Christiansted

Information

Beach

Church

Cruise Ship Terminal

Airport

Hiking

Golf

Caribbean Sea

Blue Moon **1**
Bombay Club **5**
Harvey's **6**
Indies **8**

Kendrick's **3**
Top Hat **7**
Tutto Bene **4**
Villa Morales **2**

Bombay Club
$–$$$ Christiansted   Eclectic

In a historic townhouse, this eatery — popular with locals — serves pub fare and daily specials, all at affordable prices. The cooks prepare "dishes of the day," which may be your best bet because they include fresh fish, succulent pastas, conch in various ways, along with chicken cutlets or filet mignon. We prefer their linguini alfredo with shrimp, sautéed conch, and lots of garlic and butter. A grilled prime rib is a choice order — it comes with a brandied demi-glace. You can, of course, eat lighter, ordering big, freshly made salads, buffalo wings, and burgers. The cooks also prepare some of the town's best stuffed crabs. There's a lot of heavy drinking, or as an habitué put it, "We like our suppers liquid here."

5A King St. ☎ *340-773-1838. Reservations recommended. Main courses: $7.75–$20. MC, V. Open: Lunch Mon–Fri 11:30 a.m.–4:00 p.m.; dinner daily 5:30–10:00 p.m.*

Harvey's
$ Christiansted   West Indian

Sarah Harvey is mistress of those pots and pans at this friendly, casual eatery where life-sized murals honor Tim Duncan, island-grown basketball hero of the San Antonio Spurs. Locals and an occasional visitor quickly fill up the dozen tables, partaking of the island-inspired cuisine based on recipes handed down through the generations. No one bothers to print a menu, and daily specials are listed on the blackboard. The ambience is of the 1950s with plastic and flowery tablecloths. Try one of Sarah's homemade soups, especially the callaloo (similar to spinach) or the chicken. For an appetizer, we go for the conch in butter sauce. For a main dish, it's hard to beat the broiled kingfish or red snapper, although you can opt for the savory barbecue spareribs. Sarah is also known for making the best curried goat stew in town. Main dishes come with seasoned rice and beans, local sweet potatoes, fried plantain, and fungi. Homemade pies are made with guava, pineapple, or coconut.

11B Company St. ☎ *340-773-3433. Reservations not required. Main courses: $4–$10. No credit cards. Open: Monday through Saturday 11:30 a.m.–4:00 p.m. Closed Sunday.*

Indies
$$$–$$$$ Christiansted   Caribbean/Creole

Some of the island's most refined cuisine is served in a 19th-century courtyard where Dan Finnegan quickly established himself as among the very best chefs in Christiansted shortly after his arrival on the island. He fashions imaginative menus from the island's fresh fish, fruit, vegetables, and other produce. The menu changes depending on what's fresh. The fresh fish and lobster are caught in Caribbean waters, and local seasonal fruits and vegetables are featured. Try the swordfish with fresh artichokes, shiitake mushrooms, and thyme, or perhaps the baked wahoo with lobster curry and fresh chutney and coconut. Soup choices may include an excellent island lobster and shrimp bisque or a spicy black-bean soup. A different pasta dish is offered nightly. All the desserts are freshly made.

55–56 Company St. ☎ 340-692-9440. Reservations recommended. Main courses: $18–$28. AE, DISC, MC, V. Open: Mon–Fri lunch 11:30 a.m.–2:30 p.m., dinner 6–10 p.m.

Kendricks

$$$$ **Gallows Bay**   **French/Continental**

The staff of *Bon Appétit* — and justifiably so — have discovered the succulent, finely honed cuisine served at the historic Quin House complex at Company and King Cross streets in the center of town, with both an up– and downstairs dining room. To learn of the culinary prowess of the chefs, we recently enjoyed some of the house specialties, including pan-seared Thai shrimp with cucumber relish and a coconut-infused rice. The signature appetizer that night was seared scallops and artichoke hearts in a lemon-cream sauce. There was no finer dish we discovered than the pecan-crusted roast loin of pork with a ginger-laced mayonnaise.

2132 Company St. ☎ 340-773-9199. Reservations required for dinner upstairs. Main courses: $22–$29. AE, MC, V. Open: Mon–Sat 6–10 p.m.

Top Hat

$$$$ **Christiansted**   **Continental/Danish**

For years this restaurant was the "top hat" on St. Croix. Newer and more innovative restaurants such as Kendricks or Indies have challenged its supremacy, but it's still going strong under the chef/owner Bent Rasmussen. It is the only Danish restaurant on the island, evoking memories of the long Danish occupation of St. Croix. This second-story restaurant turns out a notable continental-inspired cuisine with such old favorites as crisply roasted duck stuffed with apples and prunes, chilled cucumber soup, local mahimahi sautéed with a butter and lime sauce, and the town's best Wiener schnitzel. Smoked eel appears with scrambled eggs, and the *frikadeller* (those savory Ping-Pong sized meatballs) are always a delight.

52 Company St. ☎ 340-773-2346. Reservations needed. Main courses: $18–$30. AE, DISC, MC, V. Open: Mon–Sat 6–10 p.m. Closed May–Aug.

Tutto Bene

$$$ **Christiansted**   **Italian**

In the center of town, this trattoria is the domain of Smokey Odom and Kelly Williams, who are known for their robust and hearty Italian recipes. "We feed you well here," Williams accurately told us. Nothing is fancy and service is on wooden tables covered with painted tablecloths. The place attracts an equal number of visitors and locals, who feast on the succulent pastas and the perfectly grilled fish. A signature dish is the chef's special, *tutto di mare* with mussels, clams, and shrimp in a white wine and pesto sauce spread over linguine. We also recommend the juicy veal chop with sun-dried tomatoes.

2 Company St. ☎ 340-773-5229. Reservations accepted only for parties of five or more. Main courses: $14.95–$26.95. AE, DISC, MC, V. Open: Daily 5–10 p.m.

Villa Morales
$ Fredriksted Puerto Rican

At a location 2 miles from Frederiksted you can select a table either indoors or outdoors to enjoy some real island cookery. If you come early you can mix with the locals in the cozy bar. Those with a taste for Hispanic cuisine will be richly rewarded here with all those favorite dishes your Puerto Rican mama (assuming you had one) prepared for you. Savory examples include fried snapper with white rice and beans, stewed conch, roasted or stewed goat, and stewed beef. Meal platters are garnished with beans and rice. Most of the dishes are at the lower end of the price scale. About once a month, the owners transform the place into a dance hall, bringing in live salsa and merengue bands (the cover ranges from $5 to $15).

Plot 82C (off Route 70), Estate Whim. ☎ 340-772-0556. Reservations recommended. MC, V. Main courses: $7–$14 at lunch, $8–$25 at dinner. Open: Thurs–Sat 8 a.m.– 10 p.m.

On St. John

Treats for the eyes and palate await you on St. John, an expanse of 20 square miles that is far from diminutive in its tasty offerings.

Asolare
$$$–$$$$$ Cruz Bay Asian/French

At night our favorite retreat on the island is this refined restaurant, where you can linger at a table on a balcony perch overlooking Cruz Bay with a panorama of the moonlit water. This is one of the best places in St. John at which to arrive early for a sundowner, perhaps waiting for the moment when the sun sinks to see the legendary "green flash" that Hemingway wrote about. The chef roams the world for inspiration, and cooks with flavor and flair, using some of the best and freshest ingredients available on the island. To begin, try the grilled Asian barbecued shrimp and scallion wonton or the marinated vegetable spring rolls. For a main course, you may be tempted by crispy Peking duckling with sesame glaze or the peppercorn dusted filet of beef. Two truly excellent dishes are the lime-sautéed chicken with yellow curry sauce and sashimi tuna on a sizzling

St. John Dining

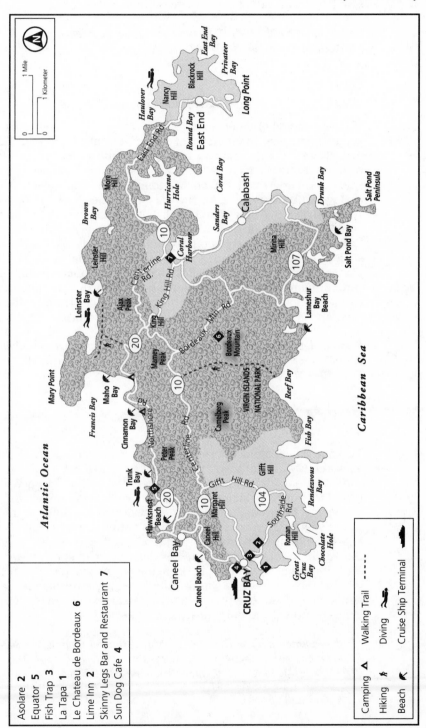

Asolare **2**
Equator **5**
Fish Trap **3**
La Tapa **1**
Le Chateau de Bordeaux **6**
Lime Inn **2**
Skinny Legs Bar and Restaurant **7**
Sun Dog Cafe **4**

Camping ⛺   Walking Trail - - - - -
Hiking 🥾   Diving 🤿
Beach 🏖   Cruise Ship Terminal ⚓

plate with plum–passion fruit–sake vinaigrette. For dessert, try the frozen mango guava soufflé or chocolate pyramid cake.

Caneel Hill. ☎ *340-779-4747. Reservations required. Main courses: $27–$35. AE, MC, V. Open: Daily 5:30–10:00 p.m.*

Equator
$$$$–$$$$$ St. John Caribbean/Fusion

On the grounds of a deluxe hotel, the retreat of the wintering wealthy, you can dine near the remains of an 18th-century sugar mill. Take stairs to a circular dining room with a wraparound porch. In its center, the restaurant grows a giant poinciana-like Asian tree of the *Albizia lebbeck* species. Islanders call it "woman's tongue tree." The cuisine is the most daring on the island, and for the most part, the chefs pull off their transcultural dishes. A spicy and tantalizing opener is lemongrass and ginger cured salmon salad (get *Gourmet* magazine on the phone). A classic Caribbean callaloo soup is offered, and the salads use fresh ingredients such as tomatoes and endive. Daily Caribbean selections are offered, or you can opt for such fine dishes as seared Caribbean mahimahi with a lentil or pumpkin mélange or penne pasta with shiitake mushrooms and roasted tomatoes in an herb garlic cream sauce. There's always a dry, aged Angus steak or a grilled veal chop for the more traditional palate.

In the Caneel Bay Hotel. ☎ *340-776-6111. Reservations required. Main courses: $22–$32. AE, MC, V. Open: Winter daily 6:30–9:30 p.m; off-season Wed, Thurs, and Sun 6:00–9:30 p.m.*

Fish Trap
$$$ Cruz Bay Seafood

This aptly named place serves St. John's best seafood. It's a casual, laid-back atmosphere with tables placed on a covered patio open to the trade winds, an easy walk up from the ferry dock. Chef Aaron Willis is the island's favorite, bringing his New York culinary training with him but showing a total familiarity with West Indian seasonings and flavors. Nobody on St. John does conch fritters better than this skilled cook, and he's been praised by such national magazines as *Vogue* and *Gourmet.* Depending on the catch of the day, six fresh fish specials are featured nightly, most likely wahoo, shark, mahimahi, or snapper. The grilled tuna, for example, comes in a wasabi sauce and the swordfish is made more appetizing by the use of lemongrass. An array of steaks, tasty pastas, chicken cutlets, and burgers are always served.

In Town Center, next to Our Lady of Mount Carmel Church. ☎ *340-693-9994. Reservations not accepted unless parties include six or more. Main courses: $7.95–$22.95. AE, DISC, MC, V. Open: Tues–Sun 4:30–9:30 p.m.*

La Tapa

$$$–$$$$ **Cruz Bay**   **Tapas/International**

An equal mixture of local habitués and visitors flock here at night to sample *tapas,* Spanish-inspired bite-size morsels of fish, meat, or marinated vegetables, accompanied by pitchers of sangria. There's a tiny bar with no more than five stools, a two-tiered dining room, and lots of original paintings (the establishment doubles as an art gallery for emerging local artists). Menu items are thoughtful and well conceived, and include fast-seared tuna with a Basque-inspired relish of onions, peppers, garlic, and herbs; a steak soaked with rum, and served with a cracked pepper sauce and mashed potatoes; and linguine with shrimp, red peppers, and leeks in peanut sauce.

Centerline Road. ☎ 340-693-7755. Reservations recommended. Tapas from $4. Main courses: $19–$27. AE, MC, V. Open: Fri–Wed 5:30–10:00 p.m.

Le Chateau de Bordeaux

$$$$–$$$$$ **Bordeaux Mountain**   **Continental/Caribbean**

Patrons are always comparing the romantic setting at night to dining in a "treehouse." Close to the geographical center of the island and the loftiest restaurant on St. John, the "chateau" lies 5 miles east of Cruz Bay. Panoramic views are seen in every direction from one of its terrace tables. Chefs have a talent for sauces and combining flavors, and their namesake, Bordeaux reds, are heavily featured on the wine *carte*. A lunch grill on the patio serves burgers and drinks daily from 10:00 a.m. to 4:30 p.m. In the evening, amid the Victorian decor and lace tablecloths, you can begin with a house-smoked chicken spring roll or velvety carrot soup. After that, move on to one of the saffron-flavored pastas or savory West Indian seafood chowder. Smoked salmon and filet mignon are a bow to the international crowd, and the wild-game specials are more unusual. The well-flavored Dijon mustard and pecan-crusted roast rack of lamb with shallot port reduction is also a good choice. For dessert, there's a changing array of cheesecakes, among other options.

Junction 10, Centerline Road. ☎ 340-776-6611. Reservations recommended. Main courses: $22–$36. AE, MC, V. Open: Lunch daily 11 a.m.–3 p.m.; dinner nightly with two seatings at 5:30–6:30 p.m. and 8–9 p.m. Closed Sun and Mon in summer.

Lime Inn

$$ **Cruz Bay**   **Seafood/American**

This eatery enjoys a devoted local following because of its fresh fish and seafood dishes prepared in many ways. Most diners will be pleased with the affordable fish dinners, especially the Wednesday night feast with all the shrimp you can eat. In a tropical garden setting in the heart of Cruz Bay, steaks, Caribbean lobster, juicy burgers, and charcoal-grilled fish emerge beautifully cooked from the outdoor grill. These dishes are backed up by an array of homemade soups and fresh salads.

Lemon Tree Mall, Kongens Gade. ☎ *340-776-6425. Reservations not needed. Main courses: Dinner $13–$25, lunch $7–$15. AE, MC, V. Open: Lunch Mon–Sat 11 a.m.– 3 p.m; dinner Thurs–Tues 5:30–10:00 p.m. Closed 3 weeks in July.*

Skinny Legs Bar and Restaurant
$ Coral Bay   American

This is a funky eatery that serves good food and can show you a good time while you're enjoying its convivial atmosphere. It is said, and we concur, that Skinny attracts the largest number of Willie Nelson look-alikes in the West Indies. The dive is also known as the best restaurant and bar for meeting the locals. The place is really a shack, known for cooking the best burgers on the island, which are downed with St. John's own home brew, Blackbeard Ale. A lot of the fare is pub grub, such as sandwiches, salads, grilled chicken, and daily specials — perhaps pot roast.

Route 107 (near the Coral Bay dinghy dock). ☎ *340-779-4982. Reservations not needed. Main courses: $6–$10. No credit cards. Open: Daily 11 a.m.–10 p.m.*

Sun Dog Cafe
$ Cruz Bay   Eclectic

If you're shopping at Mongoose Junction, a fun place for lunch is this courtyard eatery located upstairs above the shoppers. Tables are shaded, and you can enjoy a menu of freshly made salads, well-stuffed sandwiches, and such delights as chicken with Jamaican "jerk" season-ings or the triple cheese quesadilla. Pizzas are also served, including the cook's signature white-artichoke pizza studded with roast garlic.

Mongoose Junction Shopping Center. ☎ *340-693-8340. Reservations not needed. Main courses: $4.75–$11. No credit cards. Open: Daily 11 a.m.–6 p.m.*

Chapter 35

Having Fun on and off the Beach in the U.S. Virgin Islands

By Darwin Porter and Danforth Prince

● ●

In This Chapter

▶ Soaking up the sun on the USVIs' top beaches

▶ Diving into fun with water sports

▶ Satisfying the landlubber: activities, shopping, and nightlife

▶ Planning some super side trips

● ●

*L*ying 1,000 miles from the southern tip of Florida, the trio of U.S. Virgin Islands — St. Thomas, St. Croix, and St. John — are billed as the "American Paradise." The islands are populated with a blend of American "expats" and native-born islanders who live more or less in harmony.

Either by the cruise-ship passenger or the vacationer winging in, **St. Thomas** is the most visited of the islands in the U.S. archipelago. Its panoramically scenic harbor at Charlotte Amalie is rivaled only by San Juan, as the most active cruise port in the Caribbean. It's also the shopping mecca of the West Indies, and most cruise-ship passengers arrive to shop, which, to many of them, is more important than the beaches.

Our favorite of the island trio, tiny **St. John,** lies only a short ferry ride from Charlotte Amalie. Two-thirds of this island is a national park, and there is a laid-back, casual feel to this place that attracts a lot more artists than any other island in the Caribbean.

The largest of the Virgin Islands, **St. Croix** is often overlooked, yet its atmosphere is unique. There are plenty of beaches to explore here, and it has two towns known for their colonial architecture, the capital at Christiansted and the "second city," Frederiksted where cruise ships arrive.

White-sand beaches or golden sands can be found on all these islands. If you visit one island, you haven't seen the others — each of the three is remarkably different from the rest. In the pages ahead, we spell out the major attractions of each, from shopping to beaches. It's the lucky visitor who has planned a trip long enough to sample all three. Even if you're visiting only St. Thomas, in just a day or even a half day if you're rushed, you can take the ferry over to St. John for a tour in a "safari bus."

Hitting the Beaches

"We're from Canada, and we came here for the beaches," a husband-and-wife team recently told us in February. That couple came to the right place. Some beaches of the Caribbean are made of black volcanic sand. Not those in the USVIs. They rank near the top of all the beaches in the Caribbean.

On St. Thomas

Depending on who's counting, St. Thomas boasts nearly 50 beaches, and all of them are open to the public, even those in front of the mega-resorts. Sometimes you have to walk across a hotel's grounds to reach a beach. Although the sands belong to all of us, you'll have to pay extra if you use any of the resort's equipment such as chaise longues. The major St. Thomas beach is **Magens Bay** (Route 35 and 42; the beach charges a $3 entrance fee; 25¢ per child under 12; open daily from 8 a.m. to 6 p.m.), known for its heart-shaped shoreline and crystal-clear waters ideal for snorkeling around the rocks. It lies 3 miles north of Charlotte Amalie. Lined with lush green palms and equipped with showers and changing rooms, this beach is a good place to spend a whole day. **Virgin Island Eco-Tours** (☎ 340-779-2155) features a kayak tour that launches from this beach.

Magens Bay gets very crowded when a lot of cruise ships are in port. It's especially busy on Saturday and Sunday and on all holidays. Bathhouses are found here along with snack bars and rum bars. It's a tradition at some point during your visit to Magens to drop in for a drink at the little **Udder Delight** (☎ 340-777-6050), a stand serving tasty milkshakes laced with Cruzan rums. Your kid can enjoy one of the fruit-flavored shakes. ("Dad, what's a soursop milkshake?")

Coki Point Beach, in the northeast near Coral World, is good but often very crowded. It's noted for its warm, crystal-clear water, ideal for swimming and snorkeling (you'll see thousands of rainbow-hued fish swimming among the beautiful corals). Locals even sell small bags of fish food, so you can feed the sea creatures while you're snorkeling. From the beach, there's a panoramic view of offshore Thatch Cay. Concessions can arrange everything from water-skiing to parasailing.

An East End bus runs to Smith Bay and lets you off at the gate to Coral World and Coki. Watch out for pickpockets.

Sapphire Beach is set against the backdrop of the Sapphire Beach Resort and Marina, where you can have lunch or order drinks. There are good views of offshore cays and St. John, a large reef is close to the shore, and windsurfers like this beach a lot. You can rent snorkeling gear and lounge chairs. Take the East End bus from Charlotte Amalie, going via Red Hook. Ask to be let off at the entrance to Sapphire Bay; it's not too far of a walk from here to the water.

Small and special, **Secret Harbour** is near a collection of condos. With its white sand and coconut palms, it's the epitome of Caribbean charm. The snorkeling near the rocks is some of the best on the island. No public transportation stops here, but it's an easy taxi ride east of Charlotte Amalie heading toward Red Hook.

Morning Star Beach (also known as Frenchman's Bay Beach) is near the Marriott Frenchman's Reef Beach Resort, about 2 miles east of Charlotte Amalie. Here, among the often-young crowds (many of whom are gay), you can don your skimpiest bikini. Sailboats, snorkeling equipment, and lounge chairs are available for rent. The beach is easily reached by a cliff-front elevator at Frenchman's Reef.

On St. Croix

The most celebrated beach is offshore **Buck Island,** part of the U.S. National Park Service network. After a snorkeling trip here in the early '60s, President Kennedy declared it a government-protected marine park. Buck Island is actually a volcanic islet surrounded by some of the most stunning underwater coral gardens in the Caribbean. The white-sand beaches on the southwest and west coasts are beautiful, but the snorkeling is even better. The islet's interior is filled with such plants as cactus, wild frangipani, and pigeonwood. There are picnic areas for those who want to make a day of it. Boat departures are from Kings Wharf in Christiansted; the ride takes half an hour.

Your best choice for a beach in Christiansted is the one at the **Hotel on the Cay.** This white-sand strip is on a palm-shaded island. To get here, take the ferry from the fort at Christiansted; it runs daily from 7 a.m. to midnight. The four-minute trip costs $3; it's free for guests of the Hotel on the Cay. Five miles west of Christiansted is the **Cormorant Beach Club,** where some 1,200 feet of white sand shaded by palm trees attracts a gay crowd. Because a reef lies just off the shore, snorkeling conditions are ideal.

We highly recommend both **Davis Bay** and **Cane Bay,** with swaying palms, white sand, and good swimming and snorkeling. Because they're on the north shore, these beaches are often windy and their waters are not always tranquil. The snorkeling at Cane Bay is spectacular; you'll see elkhorn and brain corals, all lying some 250 yards off the "Cane Bay Wall." Cane Bay adjoins Route 80 on the north shore. Davis Beach doesn't have a reef; it's more popular among bodysurfers than snorkelers. There are no changing facilities. It's near Carambola Beach Resort.

On Route 63, a short ride north of Frederiksted, lies **Rainbow Beach,** which offers white sand and ideal snorkeling conditions. Nearby, also on Route 63, about five minutes north of Frederiksted, is another good beach, called **La Grange.** You can rent lounge chairs here, and a bar is nearby.

Sandy Point, directly south of Frederiksted, is the largest beach in all the U.S. Virgin Islands. Its waters are shallow and calm, perfect for swimming. Try to concentrate on the sands and not the unattractive zigzagging fences that line the beach. Take the Melvin Evans Highway (Route 66) west from the Alexander Hamilton Airport.

On St. John

Most visitors flock to the north shore bordering the 11,560-acre national park. Like all USVI beaches, these sandy strips are the most crowded during cruise-ship arrivals and on Saturday, Sunday, and holidays. If you're seeking more secluded beaches, head for the eastern and southern shorelines.

The best beach, hands down, is **Trunk Bay**, the biggest attraction on St. John. To miss its picture-perfect shoreline of white sand would be like touring Paris and skipping the Eiffel Tower. One of the loveliest beaches in the Caribbean, it offers ideal conditions for diving, snorkeling, swimming, and sailing. The only drawback is the crowds (watch for pickpockets). Beginning snorkelers in particular are attracted to the underwater trail near the shore; you can rent snorkeling gear here. Lifeguards are on duty. This is the best-equipped beach on St. John, with the best facilities such as changing rooms and lockers. Its facilities and calm waters make it idyllic for families. Admission is $4 per person for those over age 16. If you're coming from St. Thomas, both taxis and "safari buses" to Trunk Bay meet the ferry from Red Hook when it docks at Cruz Bay.

Caneel Bay, the stamping ground of the rich and famous, has seven beautiful beaches on its 170 acres, and all are open to the public. **Caneel Bay Beach** is open to everyone and easy to reach from the main entrance of the Caneel Bay resort. A staff member at the gatehouse will provide directions. **Hawksnest Beach** is one of the most beautiful beaches near the Caneel Bay properties. It's not a wide beach, but it is choice. Because it lies near Cruz Bay, where the ferry docks, it is the most overpopulated, especially when cruise ship passengers come over from St. Thomas. Safari buses and taxis from Cruz Bay will take you along Northshore Road.

The campgrounds of **Cinnamon Bay** have their own beach, where forest rangers sometimes have to remind visitors to put their swim trunks back on. This is our particular favorite, a beautiful strip of white sand with hiking trails, great windsurfing, ruins, and wild donkeys (don't feed or pet them!). Changing rooms and showers are available, and you can rent water-sports equipment. Snorkeling is especially popular; you'll often see big schools of purple triggerfish. This beach is best in the morning and at midday, because afternoons are likely to be windy. A marked **nature trail,** with signs identifying the flora, loops through a tropical forest on even turf before leading straight up to Centerline Road.

Maho Bay Beach is immediately to the east of Cinnamon Bay, and it also borders campgrounds. As you lie on the sand here, you can take in a whole hillside of pitched tents. This is also a popular beach, often with the campers themselves.

Soaking Up Some Water Fun

If you want to get your feet wet with cool Caribbean-style underwater exploration, consider the possibilities on the USVIs.

On St. Thomas

With its 30 spectacular reefs, *Skin Diver* magazine rates St. Thomas as one of the best waterworlds in the Caribbean for both snorkeling and scuba diving. The best scuba-diving site off St. Thomas, especially for novices, is **Cow and Calf Rocks,** off the southeast end (45 minutes from Charlotte Amalie by boat); here you'll discover a network of coral tunnels riddled with caves, reefs, and ancient boulders encrusted with coral. The *Cartanser Sr.,* a sunken World War II cargo ship that lies in about 35 feet of water, is beautifully encrusted with coral and home to a myriad of colorful resident fish. Another popular wreck dive is the *Maj. General Rogers,* the stripped-down hull of a former Coast Guard cutter.

One of the island's best outfitters is **Aqua Action,** 6501 Red Hook Plaza (☎ 340-775-6285), a full-service, PADI, five-star dive shop at Secret Harbour Beach Resort. Owner Carl Moore, a certified instructor for the Handicap Scuba Association, teaches scuba to visitors with disabilities. **Chris Sawyer Diving Center** (☎ 877-929-3483 or 340-775-7320), at Compass Point Marina, is a PADI five-star outfit that specializes in dives to the 310-foot-long RMS *Rhyne* in the British Virgin Islands (see Chapter 19). (Don't forget your passport and your C-card if you take this trip.) This center also has a NAUI certification center. If you'd like a bird's-eye view of the reefs without getting your hair wet, that too is possible at **Caribbean Parasail and Watersports**, 6501 Red Hook Plaza (☎ 340-775-9360). You can be picked up at your hotel and taken to the lift-off point. You sit in a harness linked to a parachute and are airborne from the dock. Like an eagle, you soar for a ten-minute aerial view, costing $55 per person. The outfitter also rents all sorts of water-sports equipment such as kayaks and jet skis.

Surfers find the conditions on St. Thomas generally idyllic, and equipment can be rented at most mega-resorts in the East End. Figure on paying $60 for a one-hour lesson. The best outfitter for this is **West Indies Windsurfing,** Vessup Beach, No. 9 Nazareth (☎ **340-775-6530**).

On St. Croix

Sponge life, black coral (the finest in the West Indies), and steep drop-offs into water near the shoreline make St. Croix a snorkeling and diving paradise. The island is home to the largest living reef in the Caribbean, including the fabled north-shore wall that begins in 25 to 30 feet of water and drops to 13,200 feet, sometimes straight down.

Buck Island is a major scuba-diving site, with a visibility of some 100 feet. It also has an underwater snorkeling trail.

Other favorite dive sites include the historic **Salt River Canyon** (northwest of Christiansted at Salt River Bay), which is for advanced divers. Submerged canyons walls are covered with purple tube sponges, deep-water gorgonians, and black coral saplings. You'll see schools of yellowtail snapper, turtles, and spotted eagle rays. We also like the gorgeous coral gardens of **Scotch Banks** (north of Christiansted), and **Eagle Ray** (also north of Christiansted), the latter so named because of the rays that cruise along the wall there. **Cane Bay** is known for its coral canyons.

Davis Bay is the site of the 12,000-foot-deep Puerto Rico Trench. **Northstar Reef,** at the east end of Davis Bay, is a spectacular wall dive, recommended for intermediate or experienced divers only. The wall here is covered with stunning brain corals and staghorn thickets. At some 50 feet down, a sandy shelf leads to a cave where giant green moray eels hang out.

St. Croix is home to the best scuba-diving outfitters in the USVIs. Most one-tank dives cost $60, going up to $80 for a two-tank dive, with all equipment and an underwater tour included. The best outfitter for trips over to Buck Island is **Dive St. Croix** (☎ **800-523-3483**), based at Christiansted Wharf. It also takes divers to some three dozen different dive sites offshore. A competitor, offering almost as many tours, is **V.I. Divers Ltd.** (☎ **877-773-6045** or 340-773-6045), lying in the vicinity of Pan Am Pavilion. This is a PADI five-star facility. Another PADI outfitter is **Anchor Five Center,** Salt River Marina, Route 801 (☎ **800-523-3483** or 340-778-1522); the staff here are experts on dives at the wall of Salt River Canyon, already mentioned.

Windsurfing on St. Croix is no match for Rincón, Puerto Rico (see Chapter 31). But if you're in St. Croix and want to go windsurfing, you'll find that most resorts have equipment for hire, especially **Tradewind Surfing,** located in Hotel on the Cay (☎ **340-773-7060**), lying on a little cay offshore at Christiansted Harbor. You can also hook up with sailing here, plus avail yourself of a lot of water-sports gear such as kayaks and jet skis.

On St. John

The best beaches for good snorkeling are **Watermelon Cay** at Leinster Bay and **Haulover Bay,** the latter a favorite among local divers. **Cinnamon Bay** is another much-favored spot among divers. To escape the hordes such as those that flock to **Trunk Bay** on the north shore, you'll need a boat to reach the best dive places and the greatest snorkeling spots. All of the water-sports outfitters recommended here will take you to the little places of enchantment, including **Johnson Reef** on the north coast, both **Fishbowl** and **Steven Cay** at Cruz Bay, and **South Drop** and **Horseshoe** on the southern tier. Along the sandy coves of Caneel Bay at its **Honeymoon Beach,** you can see the rare spotted eagle ray — called the "flying saucers of the deep blue sea." Other good locations include the ledges at **Congo Cay,** the wreck of the *General Rogers,* and the "tunnels" at **Thatch Cay.**

The largest outfitter — and the best — is **Cruz Bay Watersports** (☎ **340-776-6234**), a PADI and NAUI five-star diving center, charging $70 for a one-tank dive or $80 for a two-tank dive, including equipment and an underwater tour. They also offer snorkeling tours, as does **Low Key Watersports** at Wharfside Village (☎ **340-693-8999**). This outfitter is known for its wreck dives, and can also hook you up with snorkeling and an array of water sports including parasailing and kayak tours.

Windsurfers head for the **Cinnamon Bay Campground,** Route 20 (☎ **340-776-6330**), with rentals costing from $12 to $15 per hour. A two-hour introductory lesson goes for $45.

Enjoying the Waves Without Getting Wet

Sailors, fishermen, and those who just plain love to hang out on the sea are drawn to this trio of islands.

On St. Thomas

With more than 100 vessels to choose from, St. Thomas is the charterboat mecca of the USVIs. You can go through a broker to book a private sailing vessel with a crew, or you can contact a charter company directly.

Island Yachts, 6100 Red Hook Quarter, 18B (☎ **800-524-2019** or 340-775-6666) is a charter boat company in Red Hook. **Nauti Nymph,** 6501 Red Hook Plaza, Suite 201 (☎ **800-734-7345** or 340-775-5066) has a large selection of powerboats for rent. Rates range from $220 to $350 a day and include snorkel gear.

If you want to enjoy water fun while sea-kayaking, the best operator is **Virgin Islands Ecotours,** 2 Estate Nadir on Route 32 (☎ **340-779-2155**), which knows every mangrove swamp at the marine reserve on the island's southeastern shoreline. The outfitter takes you on a two-and-a-half-hour guided kayak jaunt, with time out for snorkeling and splashing about in the water. It also offers a tour starting in Magens Bay (see the earlier section, "Hitting the Beaches"). Many of the resorts on St. Thomas's eastern end have kayaks, too.

St. Croix

The big sailing adventure here is over to **Buck Island Reef National Monument,** a 300-acre volcanic islet surrounded by 550 acres of underwater coral gardens. Most charter-boat outfitters operate out of the Green Cay Marina along the waterfront in Christiansted. All captains sailing over to the island will drop anchor and allow you ample time for hiking, swimming, or snorkeling. Most visitors also plan to have a picnic lunch here.

One of the most reliable operators is **Mile Mark Watersports** in the King Christian Hotel, 59 King's Wharf, Christiansted (☎ **800-523-DIVE** or 340-773-2628), which conducts two different types of tours. The first option is a half-day tour aboard a glass-bottom boat departing from the King Christian Hotel, daily from 9:30 a.m. to 1:00 p.m. and 1:30 to 5:00 p.m.; it costs $35 per person. The second is a full-day tour, offered daily from 10 a.m. to 4 p.m. on a 40-foot catamaran, for $65. Included in this excursion is a small picnic on Buck Island's beach.

Captain Heinz (☎ **340-773-3161** or 340-773-4041) is an Austrian-born skipper with more than 25 years of sailing experience. His trimaran, *Teroro II,* leaves Green Cay Marina "H" Dock at 9 a.m. and 2 p.m., never filled with more than 23 passengers. This snorkeling trip costs $50 for adults, $30 for children age 10 and under. The captain is not only a skilled sailor but also a considerate host. He will even take you around the outer reef, which the other guides do not, for an unforgettable underwater experience.

St. John

With most operators found at Cruz Bay on St. John, sailing opportunities are plentiful, especially to secluded beaches or offshore islets, and on even longer jaunts to the British Virgin Islands where a passport is needed. Cruises allow time-out for snorkeling and swimming.

Many outfitters are waiting to carry you away, including the most luxurious one, **Proper Yachts** (☎ 340-776-6256), which can arrange for short day-sails or else more prolonged trips on deluxe yachts leaving from the swank Caneel Bay Resort. Shorter and cheaper trips are offered by **Ocean Runner** (☎ 340-693-8809), leaving from the waterfront in Cruz Bay in a little one– or two-engine craft. A block up from the pier at Cruz Bay, **Connections** (☎ 340-776-6922) is the outfitter to hook you up with a sailboat.

Sea kayaking is as popular on St. John as it is in St. Thomas (see the preceding section). Here the people to guide you along coastal waters and across secluded bays is **Arawak Expeditions** (☎ 800-238-8687 or 340-693-8312), charging $45 per passenger for a half-day jaunt.

Telling Fish Tales

Several world records have been set in these waters, legendary locations for sportfishing and catches of monumental proportions.

On St. Thomas

Nineteen world records — eight for blue marlin — have been chalked up in recent years. The legendary catches such as 1,000-pound blue marlins have been nabbed at the North Drop, lying some 20 miles off the northern coast of the island. Big catches of dolphin, wahoo, tuna, skipjack, and sailfish also turn up.

To book a boat, contact the **Charter Boat Center,** 6300 Red Hook Plaza (☎ 800-866-5714 or 340-775-7990) or **Sapphire Beach Marina,** Sapphire Bay (☎ 340-775-6100). Or, to find the trip that will best suit you, walk down the docks at either American Yacht Harbor or Sapphire Beach Marina and chat with the captains.

On St. Croix

Blue marlin is also caught in record catches in the waters off St. Croix, with the best sportfishing at **Lang Bank** off the north coast. Bonito, sailfish, wahoo, and tuna turn up in large catches.

The best outfitter who can arrange fishing trips in its 38-foot powerboat, *Fantasy,* is **Mile Mark Watersports**, based at Gallows Bay (☎ 340-773-2628).

On St. John

The famous North Drop, mentioned earlier, can also be reached in a fishing charter sailing out of St. John. Deep-sea fishing, however, is illegal in the waters of the island's National Park. What is allowed is rod-and-reel fishing from St. John's beaches. **American Yacht Harbor** (☎ 340-775-6454) offers sport-fishing trips, and though it's based in Red Hook on St. Thomas, the operator will pick you up on St. John. On St. John itself, the best local outfitter catering to visiting fishermen is **St. John World Class Anglers** (☎ 340-779-4281), which lives up to its name in its series of half– and full-day fishing trips to offshore cays.

Exercising Other Onshore Options

If you need a change of pace after so much spectacular water adventure, try one of the following dry-land activities.

Teeing off

If a holiday on the golf course is the way you want to spend your vacation, you'll find far greater courses in Montego Bay, Jamaica (see Chapter 27) or on the island of Puerto Rico (see Chapter 31). St. Thomas has only one course, St. Croix three, and St. John none.

On St. Thomas

Mahogany Run, on the north shore at Mahogany Run Road (☎ 800-253-7103), is an 18-hole, par-70 course. This beautiful course rises and drops like a roller coaster on its journey to the sea; cliffs and crashing sea waves are the ultimate hazards at the 13th and 14th holes. Former President Clinton pronounced this course very challenging. Greens fees are $115 for 18 holes, reduced to $90 in the late afternoon. Carts are included, and club rental costs $35.

On St. Croix

St. Croix has the best golf in the USVIs. Guests staying on St. John and St. Thomas often fly over for a day's round on one of the island's three courses. The **Carambola Golf Course,** on the northeast side of St. Croix (☎ 340-778-5638), was created by Robert Trent Jones, Sr., who called it "the loveliest course I ever designed." It's been likened to a botanical garden. The par-3 holes here are known to golfing authorities as the best in the tropics. The greens fee of $100 in winter, or $58 in summer, allows you to play as many holes as you like. Carts are included. **Buccaneer,** Gallows Bay (☎ 340-773-2100, ext. 738), 2 miles east of Christiansted, has a challenging 5,810-yard, 18-hole course with panoramic vistas. Nonguests of this deluxe resort pay $65 in winter or $45 off-season, plus $15 for use of a cart. The **Reef,** on the east end of the island at Teague Bay (☎ 340-773-8844), is a 3,100-yard, 9-hole course, charging greens fees of $20 including carts. The longest hole here is a 579-yard par-5.

Taking up tennis

Finding a place to break out your tennis whites is easy on these islands. Because the noonday sun is fierce, tennis buffs like to play before 10 a.m., or after 5 p.m. Most courts are lit for matches at night, and nonguests who call and reserve space are welcomed at the various resorts.

On St. Thomas

Several tennis facilities are available here. To make reservations, try one of the following:

- **Mahogany Run Tennis Club,** Route 42 (☎ 340-775-5000)

- **Marriott Frenchman's Reef Tennis Courts,** Estate Bakkeroe (☎ 340-776-8500, ext. 444)

- **Renaissance Grand Beach Resort,** Smith Bay Road (☎ 340-775-1510)

- **The Ritz-Carlton, St. Thomas,** 6900 Great Bay Estate (☎ 340-775-3333)

- **Sapphire Beach Resort,** Sapphire Bay (☎ 340-775-6100)

The government of St. Thomas offers two public courts at the Sub Base, adjacent to the Water and Power Commission. Courts are open daily until 8 p.m. You can't reserve space; you just have to show up and wait your turn.

On St. Croix

Tennis buffs will be tempted to tuck into **The Buccaneer,** with its eight courts (two lighted), plus a pro and a full tennis pro shop (Route 82; ☎ 340-773-2100). You'll also find three courts (one lighted) at **Club St. Croix,** Route 752 (☎ 340-773-4800), and four courts (two lighted) at the **Carambola Beach Resort,** Route 80 (☎ 340-778-5638).

On St. John

The Westin Resort, St. John 104 (☎ 340-693-8000), offers six lighted courts, and nonguests can play on them for $15 per hour. In Cruz Bay, the local government maintains some public courts adjacent to the St. John Fire Department. Courts are lit until 9 p.m. and you don't need reservations. You just show up and wait your turn.

Using your pedal power: Bicycling

To get a feeling for rural and flat St. Croix, let the pedals be your guide on a biking adventure. St. Thomas doesn't offer good biking options; St John's roads are steep, and no one rents bikes here anymore.

The best outfitter is **St. Croix Bike and Tours**, Pier 69 Courtyard at Frederiksted (☎ 340-772-2343). For a cost of $35 each, you're taken on one of two tours, not only around this historic town itself, but on a good and relatively flat route ending at Hamm's Bluff. Another bike tour goes on a fairly easy route through the island's only rain forest. The price includes all equipment — helmet and everything — and the services of a guide.

Taking a gallop: Horseback riding

Try a unique view of the Virgin Islands from the saddle.

On St. Croix

The largest stables are **Paul and Jill's Equestrian Stables**, Route 58 (☎ **340-772-2880** or 340-772-2627), at Sprat Hall, the island's oldest plantation Great House, lying near Frederiksted. The operator, Jill Hurd, is an island character from one of St. Croix's best-known families. For $50, she offers two-hour rides through the rain forest and along the shore. She also conducts moonlit rides. Reserve at least a day in advance.

On St. John

For $55 for a one-hour ride, the staff at **Carolina Corral** (☎ **340-693-5778**) will take you horseback riding along St. John's most scenic trails. You can mount a donkey if you prefer. Riding lessons are also offered.

Taking a hike

Get a ground-level view of all the flora, fauna, and other attractions by strapping on your most comfortable shoes and setting out to explore. (St. Thomas doesn't rate high scores for cool hiking sites.)

On St. Croix

The island's western district contains a 15-acre "**Rain Forest**" with a network of footpaths offering some of the best nature walks in the USVIs. The nonprofit **St. Croix Environmental Association**, Arawak Building, Suite 3 at Gallows Bay (☎ **340-773-1989**), at a cost of $25 per hiker, will take you through this treasure emerging at Salt River, where Columbus first sighted land here. Hikes are from December through March.

On St. John

St. John has the most rewarding hiking in the Virgin Islands. The terrain ranges from arid and dry (in the east) to moist and semitropical (in the northwest). The island boasts more than 800 species of plants, 160 species of birds, and more than 20 trails maintained in fine form by the island's crew of park rangers. Much of the land on the island is designated as **Virgin Islands National Park** (☎ 340-776-6201). Visitors are encouraged to stop by the **Cruz Bay Visitor Center,** where you can pick up the park brochure, which includes a map of the park, and the *Virgin Islands National Park News,* which has the latest information on park activities. Be sure to carry a lot of water and wear sunscreen and insect repellent when you hike.

St. John is laced with a wide choice of clearly marked walking paths. At least 20 of these originate from Northshore Road (Route 20) or from the island's main east-west artery, Centerline Road (Route 10). Each is marked at its starting point with a preplanned itinerary; the walks can last anywhere from ten minutes to two hours. Maps are available from the national park headquarters at Cruz Bay.

One of our favorite hikes, the **Annaberg Historic Trail** (identified by the U.S. National Park Service as trail 10), requires only about a half-mile stroll. It departs from a clearly marked point along the island's north coast, near the junction of routes 10 and 20. This self-guided tour passes the partially restored ruins of a manor house built during the 1700s. Signs along the way give historical and botanical data. Visiting the ruins costs $4 per person for those over age 16. One of the most popular hikes is the guided 2½-mile **Reef Bay Hike.** Included is a stop at the only known petroglyphs on the island and a tour of the sugar-mill ruins. A park ranger discusses the area's natural and cultural history along the way. The hike starts at 10 a.m. on Monday, Thursday, and Friday and costs $15 per person. Reservations are required and can be made by phone.

Shop 'til you drop

Duty-free shopping has made St. Thomas the shopping bazaar of the West Indies. Even if you're going only to St. Croix and skipping St. Thomas, you'll still find a huge array of similar shops, but not as many as on St. Thomas. St. John, on the other hand, is the home of little specialty shops, often featuring hand-crafted items.

It's possible to find well-known brand names here at savings of up to 60% off mainland U.S. prices. But be warned: Savings are not always so good. Before you leave home, check prices in your local stores if you think you may want to make a major purchase, so you can be sure that you are, in fact, getting a good deal. Having sounded that warning, we'll mention some St. Thomas shops where we have found good buys.

The best buys include china, crystal, perfume, jewelry (especially emeralds), Haitian art, fashion, watches, and items made of wood. Cameras and electronic items, based on our experience, are not the good buys they're reputed to be. St. Thomas is also the best place in the Caribbean for discounts on porcelain, but remember that U.S. brands may often be purchased for 25% off the retail price on the U.S. mainland. Look for the imported patterns for the biggest savings.

Most shops, some of which occupy former pirate warehouses, are open Monday through Saturday from 9 a.m. to 5 p.m. Some stores open Sunday and holidays if a cruise ship is in port. *Note:* Friday is the biggest cruise-ship day at Charlotte Amalie (we once counted eight ships in port at once), so try to avoid shopping then. It's a zoo.

Shoppers with U.S. passports can take advantage of a generous $1,200 per person duty-free allowance. Remember to save your receipts. A final bit of good news: There is no sales tax in the USVIs.

Exploring the USVIs

These islands each have something very different, but all share a rich history. Here we hit the high points.

St. Thomas

The capital, Charlotte Amalie, where most visitors begin their sightseeing, has all the color and charm of an authentic Caribbean waterfront town. In days of yore, seafarers from all over the globe flocked here, as did pirates and members of the Confederacy, who used the port during the American Civil War. (Sadly, St. Thomas was the biggest slave market in the world.)

The old warehouses once used for storing pirate goods still stand, and today, many of them house shops. In fact, the main streets are now a virtual shopping mall and are usually packed. Sandwiched among these shops are a few historic buildings, most of which can be covered on foot in about two hours:

✔ **Government House,** Government Hill (☎ **340-774-0001**). This is the administrative headquarters for the U.S. Virgin Islands. It's been the center of political life in the islands since it was built around the time of the American Civil War. Visitors are allowed on the first two floors. Some paintings by former resident Camille Pisarro are on display, as are works by other St. Thomas artists. Admission is free. Open weekdays from 8 a.m. to 5 p.m.

✔ **American Caribbean Museum,** 32 Raadets Gade, between Waterfront and Main streets (☎ **340-714-5150**). The cultures of the U.S. and the Caribbean are united in this museum, whose exhibits trace the history of the Virgin Islands from their volcanic beginnings through the Indian settlements and the discovery of the archipelago by Christopher Columbus. The museum also traces Danish colonization of the islands. Memorabilia concerns Alexander Hamilton, who was reared on St. Croix. Displays also show the transfer of the Virgin Islands from Denmark to the United States under President Wilson in 1917. You learn that this transfer of landmass was the result of a tortured 50-year negotiation starting with President Lincoln. Lincoln was assassinated by John Wilkes Booth just three months before he was to begin negotiations for the purchase of the islands. The museum also traces the impact of the American Revolution on the Virgin Islands, including Benedict Arnold's link to the islands, and the impact of the Civil War. Finally, the museum shows what happened when the United States bought the islands, with visits by presidents ranging from Hoover to Clinton. Admission is $8 for adults, $4 for children. Open daily from 9 a.m. to 3 p.m.

✔ **Synagogue of Beracha Veshalom Vegmiluth Hasidim,** 16 Crystal Gade (☎ **340-774-4312**). This is the oldest synagogue in continuous use under the American flag and the second oldest in the western hemisphere. It was erected in 1833 by Sephardic Jews, and it still maintains the tradition of having sand on the floor, commemorating the exodus from Egypt. The structure was built of local stone, along with ballast brick from Denmark and mortar made of molasses and sand. To the rear of the synagogue, the Weibel Museum showcases Jewish history on the island. Open weekdays from 9 a.m. to 4 p.m.

Outside of Charlotte Amalie, check out the following:

✔ **Coral World Marine Park and Underwater Observatory,** Coki Point — turn north off Route 38 at sign approximately 20 minutes from Charlotte Amalie (☎ **340-775-1555;** Internet: `www.coral worldvi.com`). This is the best marine park on the islands. The only thing close to it is the Seaquarium on Curaçao, but we give this one the edge because of Coral World's multi-level offshore underwater observatory. The Predator Tank here is one of the world's largest coral reef tanks. An aquarium with two dozen portholes offers views of marine life in the West Indies. Activities include daily fish and shark feedings and exotic bird shows. Admission is $18; $9 for children 3 to 12. Open daily from 9 a.m. to 5 p.m. Expect to spend at least three hours here, especially if you have kids.

✔ **Frenchtown.** Route 30 (Veterans Drive) will take you west of Charlotte Amalie to this colorful little settlement. Early French-speaking settlers arrived on St. Thomas from St. Barts after they were uprooted by the Swedes. Many island residents today are the direct descendants of those long-ago immigrants, who were known for speaking a distinctive French patois. This village contains a number of restaurants and taverns. Because Charlotte Amalie has become somewhat dangerous at night, Frenchtown has picked up its after-dark business and is the best spot for dancing and other local entertainment.

✔ **Mountain Top.** For the most panoramic view of St. Thomas, both its land– and seascape, head here and stand on its observation deck at a point 1,500 feet above sea level. It's also a custom to order a banana daiquiri at the bar. A number of shops are here as well, but they're very touristy. To reach it, drive north (or take a taxi) along Route 33, following the signposts.

✔ **Paradise Point Tramway,** Route 30 at Havensight (☎ **340-774-9809**). This contraption affords visitors a dramatic view of Charlotte Amalie harbor, with a ride to a 697-foot peak. The tramway, similar to those used at ski resorts, operates four cars, each with a ten-person capacity, for the 15-minute round-trip ride. It transports customers from the Havensight area to Paradise Point, where they can disembark to visit shops and the popular restaurant and bar. Admission is $15 round trip; $7.50 for ages 6 to 12; free for children 5 and under. Open daily from 9:00 a.m. to 5:30 p.m.

St. Croix

One of the most historic and well-preserved towns in the Caribbean, **Christiansted** is an old, handsomely restored (or at least in the process of being restored) Danish port. On the northeastern shore of the island, on a coral-bound bay, the town is filled with Danish buildings erected by prosperous merchants in the booming 18th century. These red-roofed structures are often washed in pink, ocher, or yellow. Arcades over the sidewalks provide shade for shoppers. The whole area around the harbor front has been designated a historic site, which is looked after by the U.S. National Park Service.

The Heritage Trail

A trail that leads into the past, **St. Croix Heritage Trail,** launched at the millennium, helps visitors relive the Danish colonial past of the island. All you need are a brochure and map, available at the tourist office in Christiansted (53A Company St.; ☎ **340-773-0495**), and you can set out on this 72-mile road, which is teeming with historical and cultural sights. The route, among other of the trail's historic sites, connects the two major towns of Christiansted and Frederiksted, going past the sites of former sugar plantations. The trail traverses the entire 28-mile length of St.Croix, passing cattle farms, suburban communities, even industrial complexes and resorts. So it's not all manicured and pretty. But much of it is scenic and worth the drive. Allow at least a day for this trail, with stops along the way. Nearly everyone gets out of the car at Point Udall, the easternmost point under the U.S. flag. You'll pass an eclectic mix of churches and even a prison. The route consists mainly of existing roadways, and that pamphlet you picked up will identify everything you're seeing. The highlight of the trail is the Estate Mount Washington, a strikingly well-preserved sugar plantation. Another highlight is Estate Whim Plantation, one of the best of the restored Great Houses with a museum and gift shop. Another stop along the way is along Salt River Bay, which cuts into the northern shoreline. This is the site of Columbus's landfall in 1493.

For information on Christiansted or the island itself, stop in at the **Visitor's Center** at 53A Company St. (☎ 340-773-0495), which is open Monday through Saturday from 8 a.m. to 5 p.m., dispensing guidance, maps, and brochures.

These sites in Christiansted may interest you:

- **Fort Christiansvaern** (☎ 340-773-1460). This fortress overlooking the harbor is the best-preserved colonial fortification in the Virgin Islands. It's maintained as a historic monument by the U.S. National Park Service. Its original four-pronged, star-shaped design was in accordance with the most advanced military planning of its era. The fort is now the site of the St. Croix Police Museum, which has exhibits on police work on the island from the late 1800s to the present. Admission is $2. Open daily from 8:00 a.m. to 4:45 p.m.

- **Steeple Building,** on the waterfront off Hospital Street (☎ 340-773-1460). This building's full name is the Church of Lord God of Sabaoth. It was built in 1753 as St. Croix's first Lutheran church, and it was deconsecrated in 1831; the building subsequently served at various times as a bakery, a hospital, and a school. Today, it houses exhibits relating to island history and culture. Admission is $2 (including admission to Fort Christiansvaern). Open Monday through Friday from 8:30 a.m. to 4:30 p.m.

- **St. Croix Aquarium,** 13 Caravelle Arcade, Christiansted (☎ 340-773-8995). This aquarium has expanded with many exhibits, including one devoted to "night creatures." In all, it houses some 40 species of marine animals and more than 100 species of invertebrates. A touch pond contains starfish, sea cucumbers, brittle stars, and pencil urchins. The aquarium allows you to become familiar with the marine life you'll see while scuba-diving or snorkeling. Admission is $5, $2.50 for children under 12. Open Tuesday through Saturday from 11 a.m. to 4 p.m.

- **Estate Whim Plantation Museum,** Route 70, Centerline Road, 2 miles east of Frederiksted (☎ 340-772-0598). This restored Great House is unique among those of the many sugar plantations whose ruins dot the island. It's composed of only three rooms. With 3-foot-thick walls made of stone, coral, and molasses, the house resembles a luxurious European château. A division of Baker Furniture Company used the Whim Plantation's collection of models for one of its most successful reproductions, the "Whim Museum–West Indies Collection." A showroom here sells the reproductions, plus others from the Caribbean, including pineapple-motif four-poster beds, cane-bottomed planters' chairs with built-in leg rests, and Caribbean adaptations of Empire-era chairs with cane-bottomed seats. Admission is $6. Open Wednesday through Monday from 10 a.m. to 4 p.m.

✔ **Fredriksted.** This former Danish settlement at the western end of the island, about 17 miles from Christiansted, is a sleepy port town that comes to life only when a cruise ship docks at its shoreline. Frederiksted was destroyed by a fire in 1879. Its citizens subsequently rebuilt it with wood frames and clapboards on top of the old Danish stone and yellow-brick foundations. Most visitors begin their tour at russet-colored **Fort Frederik,** at the northern end of Frederiksted next to the cruise-ship pier (☎ **340-772-2021**). This fort, completed in 1760, is said to have been the first to salute the flag of the new United States. When a U.S. brigantine anchored at port in Frederiksted hoisted a homemade Old Glory, the fort returned the salute with cannon fire, violating the rules of neutrality. Also, it was here on July 3, 1848, that Governor-General Peter von Scholten emancipated the slaves in the Danish West Indies, in response to a slave uprising led by a young man named Moses "Buddhoe" Gottlieb. The fort has been restored to its 1840 appearance and is today a national historic landmark. You can explore the courtyard and stables. A local history museum has been installed in what was once the Garrison Room. Admission is free. It's open Monday through Friday from 8:30 a.m. to 4:30 p.m. To the south of the fort is the **Visitors' Bureau,** at Strand Street (☎ **340-772-0357**), where you can pick up a free map of the town.

✔ **St. Croix Leap,** Mahogany Road, Route 76 (☎ **340-772-0421**). If you're on western St. Croix, near Frederiksted, visit St. Croix Leap for an offbeat adventure. In this open-air shop, you can see stacks of rare and beautiful wood being fashioned into tasteful objects. This is a St. Croix Life and Environmental Arts Project, dedicated to manual work, environmental conservation, and self-development. The end result is a fine collection of local mahogany serving boards, tables, wall hangings, and clocks. Sections of unusual pieces are crafted into functional, artistic objects. St. Croix Leap is 15 miles from Christiansted, 2 miles up Mahogany Road from the beach north of Frederiksted. Large mahogany signs and sculptures flank the driveway. Visitors should bear to the right to reach the woodworking area and gift shop. The site is open daily from 9:00 a.m. to 5:30 p.m.

✔ **St. George Village Botanical Gardens,** 127 Estate St., just north of Centerline Road, 4 miles east of Frederiksted, Kingshill (☎ **340-692-2874**). This is a 16-acre Eden of tropical trees, shrubs, vines, and flowers. The garden is a feast for the eye and the camera, from the entrance drive bordered by royal palms and bougainvillea to the towering kapok and tamarind trees. It was built around the ruins of a 19th-century sugarcane-workers' village. Self-guided walking-tour maps are available at the entrance to the garden's great hall. Facilities include restrooms and a gift shop. Admission is $6. Open daily from 9 a.m. to 4 p.m.; closed holidays.

St. John

The government inaugurated route numbers in the '90s but no one seems to bother with them or remember them. Therefore, you'll need a good map if you get lost (and you probably will). Carry a bathing suit because you'll be passing along a shoreline of some of the loveliest beaches in the USVIs. Expect narrow, steep, winding, potholed roads, which means you should allow plenty of time to get to where you're going. See our recommendations in Chapter 34 for some of the best luncheon stopovers along the way. Gathering the makings for a picnic at Cruz Bay before heading out is even more fun. If you really want to see the island in any depth, you need to rent a car. If you're uneasy about driving on bad roads, you can generally hook up with a safari bus at Cruz Bay with a load of passengers trailblazing it around the island. Here are some favorite spots to visit:

✔ **Annaberg Plantation,** Leinster Bay Road (☎ **340-776-6201**). Constructed in 1780, this plantation — now in ruins — was once the most important in that century when the smell of boiling molasses permeated the air for miles around. Partially restored, Annaberg is the best preserved plantation on the island. The other Great Houses were burned during slave uprisings. Plaques placed here by the National Park Service identify and describe the ruins of each building and their former functions. You just wander about, because there are no set visiting hours. Seek out the St. John National Park Service Visitor's Center. Park Service tours cost $4.

✔ **Bordeaux Mountain,** Route 10. For a panoramic view of the island, the best lookout point is on this mountain, which we visited previously for dining (see our recommendation of Le Chateau de Bordeaux in Chapter 34). Centerline Road runs almost to the pinnacle at 1,277 feet, the loftiest point on St. John. The most panoramic scenery is viewed at the aptly named Picture Point. The Park Service Visitor's Center (see the preceding bullet) distributes free maps.

✔ **Catherineberg Ruins,** Route 70. A scenic drive along Centerline Road will lead to what remains of the Catherineberg Sugar Mill. The decaying remains of a windmill here evoke this plantation's heyday in the 18th century, when it was the nerve center for a thriving sugar plantation. A slave revolt in 1733 brought an end to this prosperity.

Having Fun After Dark in the Islands

Among the USVIs, St. Thomas offer the most choices as far as nightlife is concerned. St. Croix offers the only gambling casino in the USVIs. On St. John, the idea of a fun night is to head to one of the raffish saloons for some heavy drinking.

St. Thomas

Charlotte Amalie is no longer the swinging town it used to be. Many of the streets are dangerous after dark, so visitors have mostly abandoned the town except for a few places. Much of the action has shifted to **Frenchtown,** which has some great restaurants and bars. However, just as in Charlotte Amalie, some of these little hot spots are along dark, badly lit roads. The big hotels, such as Marriott's Frenchman's Reef Beach Resort and Bluebeard's, have the most lively after-dark scene.

- ✔ **Greenhouse,** Veterans Drive (☎ **340-774-7998**). This is the most popular spot after dark in Charlotte Amalie, not the safest place to wander around at night. You may want to take a taxi here. The restaurant and bar lie directly on the waterfront and offer entertainment ranging from live reggae to recorded dance music. When it's live reggae on Wednesday and Friday nights, a $5 to $10 cover is imposed.

- ✔ **The Old Mill,** 193 Coutant (☎ **340-776-3004**). This is the biggest and newest entertainment hot spot on the island. Its trio of offerings include a sports bar for the Bud and Marlboro crowd with four pool tables, a wine and champagne bar in a restored 18th-century sugar mill, and a spacious dance club with a sunken floor and a superb lighting and sound system. The club is open Thursday through Sunday.

- ✔ **Iggies,** 50 Estate Bolongo (☎ **340-775-1800,** ext. 2540). As darkness falls, this is one of the most active sports bars on the island, and it also presents karaoke and offers pool tables and night volleyball.

- ✔ **Agave Terrace,** Point Pleasant Resort, Smith Bay (☎ **340-775-4142**). If you're planning to dine at this recommended restaurant, you may want to make it on a Tuesday or Thursday night to hear some West Indian steel-pan bands.

St. Croix

Christiansted has a lively and casual club scene near the waterfront.

- ✔ **Divi Casino,** Divi Carina Bay Resort, 25 Estate Turner Hole (☎ **340-773-9700**). The big nightlife news of St. Croix is the opening of this casino, the first on St. Croix, at the Divi Carina Bay Resort. After much protest and controversy, gambling was introduced in spring 2000. The 10,000-square-foot casino boasts 12 gaming tables and 275 slot machines. St. Croix has traditionally taken a backseat to St. Thomas when it comes to tourism, and it is hoped that the casino will bring more visitors to the island.

✔ **Cormorant,** 4126 La Grande Princesse (☎ **340-778-8920**). On Thursday night during the winter season, this gay-friendly club dishes up a West Indian cuisine with a small local band.

✔ **Hotel on the Cay,** Protestant Cay (☎ **340-773-2035**). If you're in Christiansted on a Tuesday night, the place to be is not there but on a ferryboat taking you across the harbor to this hotel with its big West Indian buffet and native folkloric shows.

✔ **Indies,** 55–56 Company St. (☎ **340-692-9440**). On Thursday and Saturday nights, this previously recommended restaurant presents jazz evenings.

✔ **2 Plus 2 Disco,** 17 La Grande Princesse (☎ **340-773-3710**). This is a real Caribbean disco. It features the regional sounds of the islands, not only calypso and reggae but also salsa and *soca* (a hybrid of calypso and reggae). Usually there's a DJ, except on weekends when local bands are brought in. The place isn't fancy or large. Come here for *Saturday Night Fever.*

St. John

Unless you count lots of drinking in the local taverns, this is not a party island. Yet St. John is a pleasant place to be at night, especially when Cruz Bay is lit up. Locals listen to music, talk, drink, and often dance. Two local papers, *St. John Times* or the *Tradewinds,* keep you tuned to anything that's happening, which often isn't very much.

✔ **Ellington's,** Gallows Point Suite Resort (☎ **340-693-8490**). Drop in for a sunset drink on the panoramic upper deck, and watch the twinkling lights go on across Cruz Bay. You may like the place so much you'll stick around for dinner.

✔ **Caneel Bay Bar,** Route 20, at the Caneel Bay Resort (☎ **340-776-6111**). This bar presents live music nightly from 8:00 to 10:30 p.m. The most popular drinks here include the Cool Caneel (local rum with sugar, lime, and anisette) and the trademark of the house, Plantation Punch (lime and orange juice with three different kinds of rum, bitters, and nutmeg).

✔ **Fred's,** Cruz Bay (☎ **340-776-6363**). Across from the Lime Inn, this little hole-in-the-wall is very popular with locals, especially when the owner brings in bands for dancing on Wednesday, Friday, and Sunday nights.

✔ **Skinny Legs Bar and Restaurant,** Route 107 (☎ **340-779-4982**). The best sports bar on the island is shack made of tin and wood. The yachting crowd likes to hang out here, though you wouldn't know it at first glance — it often seems that the richer they are, the poorer they dress. The bar has a satellite dish, dartboard, and horseshoe pits. Live music is presented on Saturday nights.

✔ **Woody's,** Cruz Bay (☎ **340-779-4625**). This is the local dive and hangout at Cruz Bay, 50 yards from the ferry dock. It draws both visitors and a cross-section of island life from ex-pats to villa owners. Michigan-born Woody Mann, the bartender, is often compared to the character of the same name on the sitcom *Cheers.* You can come here to eat or drink. The place is particularly popular during happy hour from 3 to 6 p.m. It's about the only place on the island where you can order food at 10 p.m.

Taking a Side Trip

To break the "monotony" of having to go to the beach every day, you can hunt up your passport and take a ferry ride over to the British Virgin Islands such as Tortola (the capital), Virgin Gorda, or the sparsely settled Jost Van Dyke. **Smith's Ferry Service** (☎ **340-775-7592**) offers daily day-trips to Tortola and Virgin Gorda, along with car-rental packages, historic tours, horseback riding, and a two-island day-trip every Saturday.

Part X

The Part of Tens

The 5th Wave   By Rich Tennant

"Did you want to take the Schwinn bicycle dive, the Weber gas grill dive, or the Craftsman riding lawn mower dive?"

In this part . . .

*W*e appeal to the shopper in you by listing our ten
favorite souvenirs to bring home from the
Caribbean. We also reveal the ten dishes that we crave the
most whenever we're away from the islands for too long.
The short chapters in this part will whet your appetite
(and your wallet), and get you ready to hop on the next
Caribbean-bound plane.

Chapter 36

Our Ten Favorite Caribbean Souvenirs

By Echo and Kevin Garrett

● ●

In This Chapter

▶ Shopping with smarts

▶ Finding the best products and deals

● ●

Y ou'll want to bring back memories of your Caribbean vacation, and what better way to preserve the moment than by toting home some souvenirs from the islands? The problem we have with this practice is that many visitors' good taste evaporates as quickly as their cares in the Caribbean. How else can we explain the voluminous number of items with the name of the island emblazoned, stitched, or painted on virtually every hunk of cloth, wood, or plastic you could possibly imagine?

Truly annoying is the fact that hordes of people buy only duty-free items made elsewhere in the world when they're in the Caribbean. These folks are so busy snapping up Irish linens and French perfume that they ignore some of the nifty island items. Making the situation worse is that so-called duty-free has lost its luster and savings in the last several years, meaning it's more of an illusion than reality. Combine that observation with the airlines' crackdown on carryons, and the hassle of transporting items home really isn't worth it, unless you've done your homework and are absolutely sure you're getting a bargain or a unique find. The one that really gets us are these gaggles of tourists lugging home enormous boxes of liquor when the savings are often minimal. Unless you're buying a really unique wine or a hard-to-come-by rum, we don't think the wear-and-tear on your back merits schlepping that stuff back to Cincinnati.

Every island has its own artists and craftspeople. We urge you to take a look. You're almost guaranteed a better buy in the markets than in the gift shops or from authorized vendors at resorts and at the airports. However, if you're the kind of person who can't say no, you won't enjoy the markets. In the markets, you're expected to haggle, but in shops with marked prices generally not. In the markets, expect to pick up items for about 30% less than the first offer you hear or see. Bring lots of small bills with you, because haggling down a vendor and then pulling out a $100 bill and expecting change is bad form.

We like to scope out what's available, and then come back to do business. What are our favorite items to shop for on the islands? Read on.

Aloe Products

The aloe plant grows extensively on Aruba, and you can find wonderful skin-care products and soaps manufactured from this natural plant. Aloe is also the key ingredient in several soothing sunburn remedies, handy items to have on hand when you're this close to the equator.

Coffee Beans

We learned a lot about coffee production by visiting a Blue Mountain coffee plantation. One important tip that we picked up: If you can smell the coffee through the bag, it's losing freshness. Coffee beans should be tightly sealed from air. Ever since James Bond declared Blue Mountain coffee the world's finest, Jamaica's coffee has become synonymous with good quality. However, we also discovered that much like wine producers, different coffee plantations produce different tasting beans depending on an array of factors — the soil, rainfall, mountain temperatures, and the handling and roasting of the beans after they've been plucked. The hot thing among coffee connoisseurs is aged coffees that are marked similarly to wine vintages.

Blue Mountain coffee is extremely expensive, unless, of course, you're on Jamaica. We always buy a few pounds of the pride and joy. The coffee is one of the few items sold at the airport at about the same price you can get it for on the island. Or you can order it on JamaicaThings (www.jamaicathings.com), a cool Web site that offers an incredible selection of reggae as well as our favorite tart island soft drink: Ting.

Another island with coffees worth buying is Puerto Rico. Puerto Rico produces a strong, aromatic coffee that was originally imported from the Dominican Republic. The best brand names from Puerto Rico are Café Crema, Café Rico, and Rioja. We must confess that we're lightweights and usually order ours *con leche* (with milk).

Gouda Cheese and Dutch Chocolates

The direct connection to the Netherlands that Aruba enjoys makes its buys on gouda cheeses and luscious Dutch chocolates too good to pass up. Enjoy the duty-free prospects.

Island Art

Serious collectors of art head to Puerto Rico and Jamaica for fine selections. Old San Juan is ground zero for a vibrant art scene, which highlights internationally known sculptors and painters. At Round Hill Hotel & Villas in Montego Bay, you'll find a small but excellent gallery that features Jamaican and Haitian artists.

Though the selection was out of our price range, we recommend **Galeria Botello,** 208 Cristo St., Old San Juan (☎ **787-723-9987;** Fax: 787-723-2879), where the works of Angel Botello Barros are displayed.

In Charlotte Amalie on St. Thomas, **MAPes MONDe,** Reese's Alley (☎ **340-776-2886;** also at Mongoose Junction on St. John, ☎ **340-779-4545**) is owned by the son of St. Thomas's former governor. The shop features antique prints (some newly discovered) by native son Pissarro. We once watched a German couple consider plunking down the $38,000 asking price for one of them, recognizing its rarity. The famed Impressionist recorded colonial life on the island before departing for France. The small shop also features several fine art prints of contemporary island artists as well as antique maps and books of the region.

Pottery

Several years ago, after a visit to New Mexico where Echo bought four large pieces of pottery (including a particularly beautiful but unwieldy and fragile raku piece), our family established a new rule: You buy it, you carry it. In the Caribbean, you'll find some artisans whose work is too tempting to pass up. The good news is that these places all gladly ship your picks.

Our favorite artisan is **Donald Schnell,** whose St. John studio is at Mongoose Junction (P.O. Box 349, Cruz Bay, St. John 00831; ☎ **800-253-7107** or 340-776-6420; Fax: 340-776-6920; E-mail: DonaldSchnell¢i.com; Internet: www.DonaldSchnell.com.). The Michigan-born Schnell creates handcrafted ceramics imprinted with natural objects such as shells and ferns that give them a fossilized look. His works include water fountains, lights, planters, and windchimes. His unique designs decorate Richard Branson's Necker Island digs, Caneel Bay, and Biras Creek, and some of our favorite Caribbean resorts.

Another great spot is the **Earthworks** studio and shop at Edgehill Heights 2, St. Thomas, Barbados (☎ **246-425-0223;** Fax: 246-425-3224; E-mail: `earthworks@caribsurf.com;` Internet: `www.earthworkpottery.com`). The studio started as a teaching project in the 1970s to revive the tradition of pottery-making on the island. The pieces most commonly associated with Earthworks feature the blue and green hues of the Caribbean Sea. Mosaics decorate the walls and floors of the shop, and guests are left to mill about the studio where you can get a discount by buying at the source. Next door, several artisans display their works at **The Potter's House** (☎ **246-425-2890**), where you can also grab lunch.

In Negril, some of the craftspeople from the Rastafarian communes bring their handsome clay pots past The Caves, hoping to attract buyers' attention. Echo wound up buying a waist-high one with tropical designs etched into the sides for $18. A sympathetic flight attendant on Air Jamaica Express let her stow it, and it made it all the way home to Marietta, Georgia, where it shows off its freshly potted plants in front of our house. Obviously, we don't recommend trying to haul something that large and fragile on a plane in the current environment.

Rum

If you're into spirits, the rums of the Caribbean allow you to bring a taste of the islands home. Several islands produce their own rums, including Barbados, St. Croix, Jamaica, and Puerto Rico. And rum-based drinks are everywhere as well: Puerto Rico claims ownership of the Piña Colada; the BVIs invented the Painkiller; and Barbados's Planter's Punch is famous. The oldest rum distillery still in operation is Mount Gay on Barbados, which has been in continual production since 1703. Of course, each island claims that it has the best rum. Puerto Rico alone produces more than two dozen different rums. If you visit a distillery, you'll often find a rum-tasting counter in the gift shop, much like a wine tasting if you were visiting a vineyard. Our recommendation is to sample a few and make your own pick.

Sarongs

You can purchase sarongs, or parreos, colorful pieces of cloth that you can use as beach cover-ups or evening wraps for overly air-conditioned Caribbean restaurants, at a good price on many islands. Some have batik designs; others display beautiful tropical scenes with birds, flowers, and fish. The best buys and most creative designs that we've found are on Aruba at a shop on **De Palm Island** (☎ **297-85-4799**) and in St. John at a shop called **Flashbacks** (☎ **340-779-4277**) in Coral Bay, next to Skinny Legs, a local watering hole. We think Aruba offers such fabulous ones because it imports them from Indonesia, which was also once a Dutch colony, so its ties to that region are still strong. At the shop on St. John, handpainted sarongs could be had for $12. Some also came tucked into a matching handbag for $16 and $18.

Sarongs also make fantastic gifts. Similar ones in the U.S. are at least double the price, plus you don't find the breadth of choices.

Spices

You can't bring home the fresh fruits or vegetables from your vacation, but you can liven up your meals with fresh spices from the islands. At the open-air market in Castries, ladies sell tidy little baskets packed with carefully labeled spices like mace, saffron, bay leaf, and cinnamon. Just walking through the place is a heady experience. Expect to pay $5 to $15 depending on the size. If you don't want to lug spice baskets home, try Sunny Caribbee (www.sunnycaribbee.com) and order on the Internet.

Straw Hats

Don't doubt the fry-power of the Caribbean sun; you'll need a hat to protect you from the sizzle. Hats are inexpensive, and you can actually use them at home when you're gardening, watching your kids play soccer, or lounging by the pool reflecting on your Caribbean adventure. You can find decent woven hats at most any of the markets. You'll notice a variation of techniques from island to island. Or if you want to spend more and get a good quality hat, you can spring for a spiffy Panama straw hat in Old San Juan. We also found a wide-brimmed, finely woven hat that Echo loves in Oranjestad's main shopping area in Aruba.

Wood Carvings

We've seen incredible works on Jamaica and St. Croix. Most of the carvings are the creations of self-taught artists.

On Jamaica, you can find great buys in the markets. We prefer shopping in the craft markets in **Negril,** or if you're near Ocho Rios, about a hundred craftspeople live and work in **Fern Gully.** We really like the hummingbirds carved into birdfeeders from coconut shells.

In the middle of **St. Croix** near Frederiksted, you'll find an open-air shop called **St. Croix Life and Environmental Arts Project (LEAP)** on Mahogany Road (☎ **340-772-0421**), which features wonderful furniture and decorative objects fashioned from naturally fallen island wood. The artisan will personalize your pick by carving the date or your name in a discreet spot. If you're interested in one of the pieces, we suggest going early in your trip and putting in your order.

Before you but any wood carving, inspect it carefully for problems with worms or bugs. Also, think about how the island art is going to look back home. That cool Rastafarian walking stick looks fine in Negril, but we can't think of too many houses in Atlanta where it would coordinate with the interior design.

Chapter 37

Our Ten (Or So) Favorite Caribbean Dishes

By Echo and Kevin Garrett

- -

In This Chapter

▶ Finding local taste treats

▶ Revisiting recipes back home

- -

Food can be a big expense in the Caribbean, especially if you stick with familiar dishes that you recognize from home (because much of what you eat has to be imported). To us, one of the great pleasures of traveling is experimenting by trying foods with names that we've never even heard before. One great advantage of sampling local cuisine is that it's almost always the cheapest choice. Another is that your sense of adventure will be rewarded by delicious food and drink.

Although you aren't allowed to bring fresh fruit and vegetables from the islands through customs, you can bring spices and alcoholic beverages used in many recipes. Islanders are incredibly warm and generous people, so if you love a particular recipe, the chef generally will be quite flattered and glad to pass the secrets on if you ask.

If you fall in love with a particular type of cooking, pick up a recipe book while you're on the island. We've sometimes thought we'd wait and get the same book back home. Big mistake. Too many times, that terrific little cookbook isn't available in the U.S. Of the Caribbean cookbooks we've surveyed, we especially like *The Essential Caribbean Cookbook: 50 Classic Recipes, with Step-by-Step Photographs,* edited by Heather Thomas (published by Courage Books), and *Culinaria: The Caribbean,* edited by Rosemary Parkinson (published by Konemann).

Ackee and Saltfish (Jamaica)

The first time we saw this dish, a favorite of Jamaicans for breakfast, we thought it looked a lot like scrambled eggs. Being from the U.S., we aren't used to eating fish for breakfast, so we were a little uneasy about the combination. But having the adventurous palates that we do, we decided to give ackee and saltfish a try — especially after we found out it's the national dish.

Ackee was a hit with both of us. It is actually a fruit, but Jamaicans tend to use it like a vegetable. When prepared, it does resemble scrambled eggs and tastes a lot like them, too, with a hint of nuttiness. We found out that it's not commonly shipped to other parts of the world, because the fruit must be eaten when it turns ripe. If you eat ackee at the wrong time, its seeds are poisonous.

Saltfish is a cod cured in salt, and it gives the dish just the right flavor. Over the years, we've been thrilled to find that Air Jamaica occasionally serves ackee and saltfish on its flights. Probably the best saltfish and ackee that we've ever had was prepared by a Jamaican chef at Jake's (see Chapter 26). You'll sometimes see this dish on the morning buffet at all-inclusive resorts, but you may need to request it a day ahead. It's also fairly commonly served on Grand Cayman.

Caribbean Lobster (Anegada, British Virgin Islands)

This small coral atoll is famous for the spiny Caribbean lobsters caught in its waters. You'll find lobster on every menu of every restaurant on the island. Our favorite place to sup on lobster in Anegada is the Cow Wreck Beach Bar & Grill (see Chapter 18). If you want to try a Caribbean cholesterol jamboree diet — Kevin's invention — with lobster and butter at every meal, the British Virgin Islands are the place to do it. Don't try this at home.

Conch Fritters (Grand Cayman)

Pronounced conk, this edible mollusk resides in a beautiful shell with a pink interior that lines the yards of many houses on Grand Cayman. The meat is pounded out to tenderize it, or it's often served chopped up and made into tasty fritters. Conch has become so popular that it now suffers from overcollection. Therefore, on some islands, conch fritters, chowder, marinated, and stewed are no longer so common.

Our first meal in the Caribbean was conch. We'd come on our honeymoon to a small island on a Sunday where there were no restaurants. A few private homes served meals, and you were supposed to make reservations the day before you wanted to dine. We hadn't done that, and we were starving. Finally, the fellow who'd met us at the boat convinced one lady to take pity on us. She served us conch and cabbage floating in vinegar — our first official dinner as a married couple. We much prefer conch in fritters.

Flying Fish (Barbados)

These small, silvery fish, which look like they have wings when they leap out of the sea, are the national fish of Barbados and the main ingredient in several Bajan specialties. One memorable morning, we had flying fish for breakfast. Delicious!

Grouper Sandwich (Anywhere in the Caribbean)

You'll see grouper listed on almost every Caribbean menu that carries a catch-of-the-day selection. Grouper inhabit shallow to mid-range reefs. The meat is a white, sweet, mild-tasting fish. When fried in a nice batter, it's the main ingredient of Kevin's favorite sandwich.

Jerk Chicken (Jamaica)

Spicy jerk chicken has probably become the most widely known Caribbean dish. It originated in Jamaica and is a method of barbecuing using well-seasoned meat. It supposedly originated with the Maroons, escaped slaves who lived in the mountains. They would roast pork seasoned with scotch bonnet pepper, pimento seeds, thyme, and nutmeg over sizzling hot coals covered with the branches of pimento or allspice wood. Although pork was the original meat used, jerk chicken has become more popular, and it's what we prefer.

Besides jerk pork, grill men operating pits around Jamaica have added chicken, sausage, and fish to their repertoire. Port Antonio's Boston Beach is best known, but we'd skip it. Only a few pits remain open, and the quality has suffered for lack of competition. Instead, get a good taste at The Pork Pit in Montego Bay, the Ocho Rios Jerk Center, or the stalls by the beach in Negril (see Chapter 26).

Callaloo and Fungi (U.S. Virgin Islands)

In the South, we'd call this down-home cooking "greens and grits," but the names are certainly more fun in the U.S. Virgin Islands (see Chapter 34). In the USVIs, several dishes are reminiscent of our grandma's cooking. Kallaloo reminds us of spinach, but island cooks add crabs and hot pepper sauce to spice up the popular dish. Funghi (far from mushrooms) is a cornmeal concoction that falls somewhere in between the consistency of cornbread and grits. It's one of those things you just have to try — you'll either love it or hate it.

Keshi Yena (Aruba)

This Dutch treat tastes better than it sounds. You take a wheel of gouda cheese, pack the hollowed out center with a spicy meat mixture of either chicken or beef, and then bake the whole concoction. This dish is especially popular at Christmastime. It's served at restaurants that serve traditional Aruban fare, like Brisas del Mar and Papiamento (see Chapter 10).

Rice and Beans/Peas (Puerto Rico and Jamaica)

The Spanish influence on Puerto Rico is evident in the simple local fare. You can get a steamy plate of rice with either black or red beans for a few dollars. We like to order it with a side of sweet plantains, which are kin to the banana, but you can't eat them raw. (Try plantains baked or fried with a little brown sugar.)

On Jamaica, you'll often find a variation of this cheap but good dish. In that country, rice and peas (red kidney beans) are cooked with coconut milk, a ham bone or bacon, and spices. Rice and peas are served as a side dish to almost every traditional Jamaican meal.

Making Dollars and Sense of It

Expense	Daily cost	x	Number of days	=	Total
Airfare					
Local transportation					
Car rental					
Lodging (with tax)					
Parking					
Breakfast					
Lunch					
Dinner					
Snacks					
Entertainment					
Babysitting					
Attractions					
Gifts & souvenirs					
Tips					
Other					
Grand Total					

Fare Game: Choosing an Airline

When looking for the best airfare, you should cover all your bases — 1) consult a trusted travel agent; 2) contact the airline directly, via the airline's toll-free number and/or Web site; 3) check out one of the travel-planning Web sites, such as www.frommers.com.

Travel Agency_____ Phone_____

    Agent's Name_____ Quoted fare_____

Airline 1_____ Quoted fare_____

    Toll-free number/Internet_____

Airline 2_____ Quoted fare_____

    Toll-free number/Internet_____

Web site 1_____ Quoted fare_____

Web site 2_____ Quoted fare_____

Departure Schedule & Flight Information

Airline_____ Flight #_____ Confirmation #_____

Departs_____ Date_____ Time_____ a.m./p.m.

Arrives_____ Date_____ Time_____ a.m./p.m.

Connecting Flight (if any)

Amount of time between flights_____ hours/mins

Airline_____ Flight #_____ Confirmation #_____

Departs_____ Date_____ Time_____ a.m./p.m.

Arrives_____ Date_____ Time_____ a.m./p.m.

Return Trip Schedule & Flight Information

Airline_____ Flight #_____ Confirmation #_____

Departs_____ Date_____ Time_____ a.m./p.m.

Arrives_____ Date_____ Time_____ a.m./p.m.

Connecting Flight (if any)

Amount of time between flights_____ hours/mins

Airline_____ Flight #_____ Confirmation #_____

Departs_____ Date_____ Time_____ a.m./p.m.

Arrives_____ Date_____ Time_____ a.m./p.m.

Sweet Dreams: Choosing Your Hotel

Make a list of all the hotels where you'd like to stay and then check online and call the local and toll-free numbers to get the best price. You should also check with a travel agent, who may be able to get you a better rate.

Hotel & page	Location	Internet	Tel. (local)	Tel. (Toll-free)	Quoted rate

Hotel Checklist

Here's a checklist of things to inquire about when booking your room, depending on your needs and preferences.

- ❏ Smoking/smoke-free room
- ❏ Noise (if you prefer a quiet room, ask about proximity to elevator, bar/restaurant, pool, meeting facilities, renovations, and street)
- ❏ View
- ❏ Facilities for children (crib, roll-away cot, babysitting services)
- ❏ Facilities for travelers with disabilities
- ❏ Number and size of bed(s) (king, queen, double/full-size)
- ❏ Is breakfast included? (buffet, continental, or sit-down?)
- ❏ In-room amenities (hair dryer, iron/board, minibar, etc.)
- ❏ Other _____

Places to Go, People to See, Things to Do

Enter the attractions you would most like to see and decide how they'll fit into your schedule. Next, use the "Going 'My' Way" worksheets that follow to sketch out your itinerary.

Attraction/activity	Page	Amount of time you expect to spend there	Best day and time to go

Going "My" Way

Day 1

Hotel_____ Tel._____

Morning_____

_____

Lunch_____ Tel._____

Afternoon_____

_____

Dinner_____ Tel._____

Evening_____

_____

Day 2

Hotel_____ Tel._____

Morning_____

_____

Lunch_____ Tel._____

Afternoon_____

_____

Dinner_____ Tel._____

Evening_____

_____

Day 3

Hotel_____ Tel._____

Morning_____

_____

Lunch_____ Tel._____

Afternoon_____

_____

Dinner_____ Tel._____

Evening_____

_____

Going "My" Way

Day 4

Hotel_____ Tel._____

Morning_____

_____

Lunch_____ Tel._____

Afternoon_____

_____

Dinner_____ Tel._____

Evening_____

_____

Day 5

Hotel_____ Tel._____

Morning_____

_____

Lunch_____ Tel._____

Afternoon_____

_____

Dinner_____ Tel._____

Evening_____

_____

Day 6

Hotel_____ Tel._____

Morning_____

_____

Lunch_____ Tel._____

Afternoon_____

_____

Dinner_____ Tel._____

Evening_____

_____

Going "My" Way

Day 7

Hotel _____ Tel. _____

Morning _____

_____

Lunch _____ Tel. _____

Afternoon _____

_____

Dinner _____ Tel. _____

Evening _____

_____

Day 8

Hotel _____ Tel. _____

Morning _____

_____

Lunch _____ Tel. _____

Afternoon _____

_____

Dinner _____ Tel. _____

Evening _____

_____

Day 9

Hotel _____ Tel. _____

Morning _____

_____

Lunch _____ Tel. _____

Afternoon _____

_____

Dinner _____ Tel. _____

Evening _____

_____

Notes

Index

• E •

• *H* •

• J •

• N •

• O •

• *T* •

Accommodations Index

FOR DUMMIES®

A world of resources to help you grow

TRAVEL

0-7645-5453-0   **0-7645-5438-7**   **0-7645-5444-1**

Also available:

America's National Parks
For Dummies
(0-7645-6204-5)

Caribbean For Dummies
(0-7645-5445-X)

Cruise Vacations For
Dummies 2003
(0-7645-5459-X)

Europe For Dummies
(0-7645-5456-5)

Ireland For Dummies
(0-7645-6199-5)

France For Dummies
(0-7645-6292-4)

Las Vegas For Dummies
(0-7645-5448-4)

London For Dummies
(0-7645-5416-6)

Mexico's Beach Resorts
For Dummies
(0-7645-6262-2)

Paris For Dummies
(0-7645-5494-8)

RV Vacations For
Dummies
(0-7645-5443-3)

EDUCATION & TEST PREPARATION

0-7645-5194-9   **0-7645-5325-9**   **0-7645-5249-X**

Also available:

The ACT For Dummies
(0-7645-5210-4)

Chemistry For Dummies
(0-7645-5430-1)

English Grammar For
Dummies
(0-7645-5322-4)

French For Dummies
(0-7645-5193-0)

GMAT For Dummies
(0-7645-5251-1)

Inglés Para Dummies
(0-7645-5427-1)

Italian For Dummies
(0-7645-5196-5)

Research Papers For
Dummies
(0-7645-5426-3)

SAT I For Dummies
(0-7645-5472-7)

U.S. History For Dummies
(0-7645-5249-X)

World History For
Dummies
(0-7645-5242-2)

HEALTH, SELF-HELP & SPIRITUALITY

0-7645-5154-X   **0-7645-5302-X**   **0-7645-5418-2**

Also available:

The Bible For Dummies
(0-7645-5296-1)

Controlling Cholesterol
For Dummies
(0-7645-5440-9)

Dating For Dummies
(0-7645-5072-1)

Dieting For Dummies
(0-7645-5126-4)

High Blood Pressure For
Dummies
(0-7645-5424-7)

Judaism For Dummies
(0-7645-5299-6)

Menopause For Dummies
(0-7645-5458-1)

Nutrition For Dummies
(0-7645-5180-9)

Potty Training For
Dummies
(0-7645-5417-4)

Pregnancy For Dummies
(0-7645-5074-8)

Rekindling Romance For
Dummies
(0-7645-5303-8)

Religion For Dummies
(0-7645-5264-3)

FOR DUMMIES®

A world of resources to help you grow

HOME & BUSINESS COMPUTER BASICS

PCs
FOR DUMMIES

0-7645-0838-5

The Flat-Screen iMac
FOR DUMMIES

0-7645-1663-9

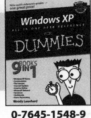

Windows XP
FOR DUMMIES

0-7645-1548-9

Also available:

Excel 2002 All-in-One Desk Reference For Dummies
(0-7645-1794-5)

Office XP 9-in-1 Desk Reference For Dummies
(0-7645-0819-9)

PCs All-in-One Desk Reference For Dummies
(0-7645-0791-5)

Troubleshooting Your PC For Dummies
(0-7645-1669-8)

Upgrading & Fixing PCs For Dummies
(0-7645-1665-5)

Windows XP For Dummies
(0-7645-0893-8)

Windows XP For Dummies Quick Reference
(0-7645-0897-0)

Word 2002 For Dummies
(0-7645-0839-3)

INTERNET & DIGITAL MEDIA

The Internet
FOR DUMMIES

0-7645-0894-6

eBay
FOR DUMMIES

0-7645-1642-6

Digital Photography
FOR DUMMIES

0-7645-1664-7

Also available:

CD and DVD Recording For Dummies
(0-7645-1627-2)

Digital Photography All-in-One Desk Reference For Dummies
(0-7645-1800-3)

eBay For Dummies
(0-7645-1642-6)

Genealogy Online For Dummies
(0-7645-0807-5)

Internet All-in-One Desk Reference For Dummies
(0-7645-1659-0)

Internet For Dummies Quick Reference
(0-7645-1645-0)

Internet Privacy For Dummies
(0-7645-0846-6)

Paint Shop Pro For Dummies
(0-7645-2440-2)

Photo Retouching & Restoration For Dummies
(0-7645-1662-0)

Photoshop Elements For Dummies
(0-7645-1675-2)

Scanners For Dummies
(0-7645-0783-4)

Get smart! Visit www.dummies.com

- **Find listings of even more Dummies titles**

- **Browse online articles, excerpts, and how-to's**

- **Sign up for daily or weekly e-mail tips**

- **Check out Dummies fitness videos and other products**

- **Order from our online bookstore**

Available wherever books are sold. Go to www.dummies.com or call 1-877-762-2974 to order direct